Library and Book Trade Almanac™

formerly **The Bowker Annual**

2017 | 62nd Edition

Library and Book Trade Almanac™

formerly **The Bowker Annual**

2017 | 62nd Edition

Editor Catherine Barr
Consulting Editor Rebecca L. Thomas

 **Information Today, Inc.**

Published by Information Today, Inc.
Copyright © 2017 Information Today, Inc.
All rights reserved

International Standard Book Number 978-1-57387-536-3
International Standard Serial Number 2150-5446
Library of Congress Catalog Card Number 55-12434

Information Today, Inc.
143 Old Marlton Pike
Medford, NJ   08055-8750
Phone: 800-300-9868 (customer service)
         800-409-4929 (editorial queries)
Fax: 609-654-4309
E-mail (orders): custserv@infotoday.com
Web Site: http://www.infotoday.com

Printed and bound in the United States of America

US $299.00
ISBN 13: 978-1-57387-536-3
29900>

9 781573 875363

Contents

Part 1
Reports from the Field

Part 2
Funding and Grants

Part 3
Library/Information Science Education, Placement, and Salaries

Part 4
Research and Statistics

Part 5
Reference Information

Ready Reference

Distinguished Books

Part 6
Directory of Organizations

Directory of Library and Related Organizations

Directory of Book Trade and Related Organizations

Preface

This 62nd edition of the *Library and Book Trade Almanac* (formerly the *Bowker Annual Library and Book Trade Almanac*) once again incorporates practical information and informed analysis of interest to librarians, publishers, and others in the rapidly evolving information world. The past year has seen a degree of turmoil and a new administration in Washington that may lead to changes in federal information agencies. Readers may want to visit the agencies' websites to stay abreast of developments.

In Part 1 of this edition you will find a special report that looks at the importance of collections of translated literature in libraries and the opportunities they offer to both English speakers and non-English speakers alike. Part 1 continues with reports on the activities of federal libraries, federal agencies, and national and international library and publishing organizations.

Part 2 covers the programs and activities of major grant-making agencies.

Part 3 offers a wealth of professional information for librarians, including salary studies, job-seeking advice, and sources of library-related scholarships.

Part 4 contains statistics (tables of book and periodicals prices, library acquisition expenditures, details of numbers of libraries and book outlets) as well as an article on library buildings. Reference information fills Part 5, including a roster of major literary prize winners and lists of notable books and other resources for all ages.

Part 6 is our directory of library and publishing organizations at the state, national, and international levels, and also includes a calendar of major upcoming events.

The Library and Book Trade Almanac is the result of many hands. We are grateful to everyone who responded to our many requests for information. Special gratitude is due to Consultant Editor Rebecca L. Thomas and to Christine McNaull, Jane Higgins, and Nancy Leff Bucenec for their invaluable assistance in making it all come together. We believe you will find this new edition a valuable resource to which you will often turn, and, as always, we welcome your comments and suggestions for future editions.

Catherine Barr
Editor

Part 1
Reports from the Field

Special Report

The Importance of Translated Literature in Libraries

Treasa Bane

Introduction

Translated literature allows U.S. libraries to expand both their collections and their readership. Translated literature also has unique cultural value, which libraries can use to solicit patrons seeking to expand their literary horizons. English speakers and non-English speakers alike can benefit from the opportunity to connect with other cultures. Whether it's going beyond one's educational experience, learning about the human condition in another context, or discovering what resulted in a book being banned in a different sociolinguistic milieu, there is something for every user.

The recent refugee crisis has sparked interest among librarians, translators, and publishers. Translated literature can be a route for communities to connect with new members, and vice versa, and an inability to access translated literature can have a negative impact on the way individuals respond to other cultures.

Making translated works available in libraries is challenging because of problems associated with acquisition and distribution, and various organizations are actively seeking to address these problems. Most of the drawbacks are connected to visibility: distribution problems prevent translated literature from being read, and poor education and awareness affect demand.

This report mostly focuses on the conditions of translated literature in print in the U.S. market.

Background

Translated literature opens doors of opportunity for publishers. Evidence of this market potential is shown by several non-anglophone titles and authors being recognized as possible bestsellers and prizewinners in English. Examples include *The Elegance of the Hedgehog, Please Look After Mom*, and *The Girl with the Dragon Tattoo* as well as titles by Jonas Jonasson and Jo Nesbø.

Bestsellers influence the market, particularly for those who read fiction. The Cultural Transfer's 2016 Diversity Report finds that only one third of the top ranks in bestseller charts were written in English.[1] This report identifies several success stories in which top-ranking titles were never picked up by an English-language publishing house. The distribution of languages in literature diversified and the impact of English-writing authors decreased between 2011 and 2014 compared with 2008 and 2010.

In Germany, HarperCollins' move to rebrand as HarperGermany is an attempt to replicate Harlequin's success with a global presence. Amazon has also implemented AmazonCrossing, which is considered a top producer of translations, introducing award-winning and best-selling translations. The 2016 Diversity Report shows that Amazon published 15,822 Afrikaans titles, 8,726 Yiddish titles, 166,843 Chinese titles, 25.2 million German titles, 2.2 million French titles, 3,079 Bulgarian titles, 48,175 Danish titles, and 7,054 Hindi titles.[1]

Historical perceptions of translated literature have ebbed and flowed. According to Bowker's article cited in *BusinessWire* in 2004, there were only 14,440 new translations that year, which was a little more than 3 percent of all books available for sale.[2] The same article pointed to a statement by Michael Cairns (then president of R. R. Bowker) that the increase in soft literature and the decline of science and technology books creates an environment in which English-speaking countries will find it difficult to compete in the future book trade.

It could be said that the translation trend in the United States started in 2005 when the PEN American Center organized "World Voices" (the first major international literature festival in New York since 1986) and May became World in Translation Month. Outside the United States, the German Book Office created its largest children's book program to date. *Publishers Weekly* launched the weekly "Global Rights Report," and *Publishing Perspectives* started the monthly "International Rights Edition." In 2004 *Publishers Weekly* reviewed 132 translated titles out of a total of 5,588 reviews (a little over 2 percent), but in 2005 they reviewed 197 out of 5,521 titles (3.6 percent).[3]

Although recognition for translated literature has improved, there is much room for improvement, particularly when comparing the United States with European countries. Dalkey Archive Press conducted a study in 2011 focused on booksellers acquiring translated literary texts, revealing that readers' lack of awareness, rather than active bias, is the reason there aren't more translated works. Review coverage and interest from booksellers in translated works are the two main factors that inspire readers' interest in translated works.[4] The study highlights that the translation problem is connected to reviewers' beliefs about readers' lack of familiarity with the languages and literatures of other cultures and the lack of funding and general support for the effort that goes into the translation process.

Distribution

International publishers can be more resourceful by producing English versions themselves rather than pitching to English-language editors. This is a great opportunity for international publishers because self-publishing is on the rise—take Macmillan's self-publishing platform, Pronoun, for instance. As another example, Qissa, Pakistan's first self-publishing platform, published approximately 100 authors in its first six months.

However, getting translated literature into the U.S. market and saving money in the process are not the only challenges; the problem is distributing these texts and raising awareness of them. While stakeholders should look beyond Europe and North America to identify new reading audiences in many regions around the world, some new initiatives hold promise for non-bestsellers to successfully break into the U.S. market and thrive. The Global Literature in Libraries Initiative (GLLI) and BiblioBoard are in the beginning stages of implementing a platform for publication and distribution, as discussed at the end of this report.

Education

One problem with poor visibility for translated literature is insufficient education. Many students have read translated literature, but they do not realize it; therefore, it might be difficult for them to realize the prevalence and importance of translated literature and seek it out for themselves.

Another problem is that school and public libraries have difficulty identifying and finding translated literature that is culturally relevant to their user groups. When librarians seek literature translated from an unfamiliar language, they have little to no support in decision making. And then, after books have been purchased, the only way to gauge use is to evaluate circulation statistics.

Several initiatives to bring translated literature into libraries emphasize the importance of engaging children at an early age, usually in an educational context, not just to retain interest but also to nurture their empathy for different cultures. The International Children's Digital Library, funded by the Institute of Museum and Library Services, has a collection of more than 10,000 books in more than 100 languages freely available to children, teachers, librarians, and scholars, and also supports a number of research projects. The University of Arizona established Worlds of Words (WOW) to support teaching, learning, and sociocultural studies. WOW comprises a database of more than 35,000 items of global literature, with an emphasis on indigenous literature on the website wowlit.org and WorldCat.

Literacy

According to the American Community Survey conducted by the U.S. Census Bureau from 2009 to 2013, approximately 350 languages are spoken in the United States.[5] Asian languages account for the majority of languages spoken in immigrant communities: Korean; varieties of Chinese; Indian and South Asian languages such as Punjabi, Hindi, and Tamil; Arabic; Vietnamese; Persian; and others.[6] While libraries attempt to offer literature in a variety of world languages, many languages are not represented in library collections. This means there is a lot of room for growth in the field of translation and in building library collections to fill this gap. If users see their culture or language represented, they will hopefully be encouraged to read in different languages and will feel more comfortable in their communities. Similarly, if users see a culture or language represented that is not their own, hopefully they will be encouraged to read and they will feel more comfortable with members of their communities.

In 2017 a German market research company, Gesellschaft für Konsumforschung (GfK), or Association for Consumer Research, released a 17-country report that surveys the frequency of reading of participants ages 15 and older. In

China, 36 percent of the population reads every day or most days. Spain and the United Kingdom follow at 32 percent each.[7] In the United States, 30 percent of the population reads every day—the U.S. age groups that read most often are 15 to 19 years and 30 to 39 years (31 percent of respondents), while 13 percent of those over age 50 never read.[8]

According to another U.S. Census Survey, English-speaking ability varies by citizenship status among Spanish speakers in particular.[9] Forty-five percent of non-U.S.-born, naturalized citizens speak English very well, compared with 23 percent of noncitizens. For those whose native language is not Spanish, the discrepancy in ability to speak English between non-U.S.-born naturalized citizens and noncitizens is less pronounced. Small linguistic areas benefit from sharing their language with larger markets through educational publishing, which can represent between one- and two-thirds of the whole publishers' turnover.[10] In some instances, there is fear that entire languages will be lost. The vice president and prime minister of the United Arab Emirates (UAE), HH Sheikh Mohammed bin Rashid al Maktoum reported that 42 percent of students in the UAE read once a week or less, and 64 percent of those students do so in standard Arabic. The publishing industry, in collaboration with teachers and libraries, can potentially save a language and prevent a nation's cultural identity from being sacrificed.[11]

Collections

There are very few studies on collection development issues for translated literature, despite their significant educational value. The OhioLINK OCLC Collection Analysis Project is the first comprehensive study on research collections in all institutions in the state of Ohio. The goal was to investigate whether there was a shift in patterns of use of collections in libraries that have instituted patron-initiated borrowing. This research would also reveal which books were being used in academic libraries, which were not being used, how many copies were needed, and the ideal size of subject collections. The study was limited to books and manuscripts.[12] The study included 17 public universities, 23 community and technical colleges, 47 independent colleges, and the State Library of Ohio—a total of 87 institutions. Additionally, two public libraries participated in online borrowing.[13]

The libraries of Ohio institutions do not represent the academic library collections of all institutions, but the prevalence of older books and the low number and low circulation rates of non-English books is a noticeable issue that is likely not isolated to Ohio institutions.

The non-circulating rates of various non-English literature collections are as follows:

- Spanish: 6.2 percent
- Chinese: 3.3 percent
- German: 12.7 percent
- Japanese: 16.6 percent
- Italian: 11.7 percent
- French: 13.7 percent

The average age of titles within these collections is as follows:

- French: 80 years old
- German: 68.6 years old
- Italian: 58.9 years old
- Spanish: 34 years old
- Japanese: 29 years old
- Chinese: 28.8 years old

English-language books dominated collections with the highest circulation rate, doubling Spanish (the second-most-used language collection).[14] The overall circulation rate for non-English items is less than one third that of English-language items, and that rate has been dropping. While non-English-language material published in the early 1900s composed more than 15 percent of the collection, it now composes less than 5 percent of recently published material.

UNESCO's Transuranium Index

According to UNESCO's Transuranium Index, which indexes translated publishing information from 2011 to 2017, the top countries for producing translated literature are as follows:

- Germany: 269,724 titles
- Spain: 232,852 titles
- France: 198,574 titles
- Japan: 130,496 titles
- Russia: 92,734 titles

The United States ranks at number fifteen with 52,515 titles. The top target languages are German, French, Spanish, English, and Japanese, and the top original languages are English, French, German, Russian, and Italian. But in the United States, the top languages translated are French, German, English, Spanish, and Russian, and the top publishers producing these translations are Dover, University of Chicago, Barron's, Princeton University Press, and Farrar, Straus & Giroux.

English Language Dominance

According to the Diversity Report, UNESCO's Transuranium Index has never been an absolute measure because it depends on contributions of data from national sources—usually a country's national library. Despite the limitations, the index allows for an understanding of fundamental trends.[1] The index reflects a common critique of the translation environment in the United States: there is more export, and more English books are being translated into other languages. In 2013 more than $1.5 billion worth of printed books were exported and nearly $1 billion worth were imported.[15]

The English-language share of the market as a whole has fallen, but its dominance in translations has risen in the last three to four decades.[16] Many problems can and do arise out of English dominance in literature, narrowing the existing pool of talent producing literature due to low investment and visibility for those outside the dominant language.

Advances in technology increase this dominance. For example, in 2009 Google aimed to expand its presence in mobile technology as well as obtain a bigger Arab audience by using programming to translate Arabic content.[17] Ahmed Nassef, general manager of the Arabic web portal Maktoob.com, said cultural tweaking is just as important as translation when launching regional products.

Germany has also expressed discomfort with digitization projects. When Google Editions wanted to launch in 2010, the German government announced its own German Digital Library project for German citizens.[18]

Current Market

The majority of the world's top publishing groups are European-owned, according to the annual Global Ranking of the Publishing Industry. The European Book Sector Report explains that print books, not e-books, seem to account for most of the current recovery from the decrease in sales between 2009 and 2014, but it is difficult to be certain because the emergence of self-publishing and the lack of data from some large retailers do not present reliable information about the e-book market.[19]

In the third quarter of 2016, the United States had a -12.3 consumer confidence rating.[20] However, according to Jonathan Stolper, global managing director for Nielsen Book, this same period saw a 3.3 percent gain in the sale of books, but overall book sales for the entire year fell by 1.3 percent.[21] In particular, e-book sales dropped 16 percent. This is due mostly to e-book pricing and a decline in use.

While translated literature can be expensive, it is not always. U.S. editors are not familiar with the international market. If editors or librarians use an intermediary who knows how the American market works, they will ask for a lot of money. If editors and librarians knew the international market better, they would know how to navigate it and how to take advantage of grants.[22]

Censorship

Increased popularity in translated literature has also resulted from global and political events that have created cultural changes that draw readers to international literature.[23] Publishing translations of literature from authors residing in highly censored countries is often the only means of gaining recognition. Translators have a political stake in their process of interpretation to make the text convey what it couldn't under censorship. Translators always navigate between "domesticating the foreign" and being innovative.[23] One of several problems with censorship is financial loss to all involved.

While the Banned Books Week initiative of the American Library Association (ALA) began in 1982 as a response to local censorship challenges, translated texts also appear on the annual list. Approximately 275 books were challenged in

2015, and ALA estimates that 70 percent to 80 percent of banned titles are never reported. Non-reporting happens in a number of ways. For example, Syria and Lebanon do not report problems with production. Syria's political system isolates the country economically and limits the development of cultural industries.[24] Censorship, as well as religious and educational factors, creates limited supply and demand overall.

Awards and Book Fairs

Authors, publishers, and translators gain much-needed visibility with reviews and awards, and by attendance at book fairs. Translation prizes include:

- Global Humanities Translation Prize: This $5,000 prize was awarded for the first time on April 1, 2017. A Hindi and an Arabic title will be translated by scholars at the University of Chicago and the University of North Carolina, Chapel Hill, and both titles will be published by Northwestern University Press in spring 2018.[25]
- Mildred L. Batchelder Award: This award, given by the Association of Library Services to Children (ALSC) to American publishers of English translations, is a high-quality selection resource for librarians choosing global literature for their collections.
- Warwick Prize for Women in Translation: The University of Warwick's Department of English and Comparative Literary Studies awards the best eligible work of fiction, poetry, literary nonfiction, or children's or young adult fiction written by a woman and translated into English by a female or male translator.
- Marsh Award for Children's Literature in Translation: This literary prize is awarded in the United Kingdom to a translator of fiction for young readers translated into English.

While there are dozens of awards and book fairs, some international book fairs have gained more prominence than others. In 2015 the Frankfurt Book Fair's Literary Agents and Scouts Center sold out its 460 tables by early spring for the October fair, which indicates a strong level of interest in the translation rights markets.[26]

In the United States, BookExpo enables emerging authors to engage with the world's most influential publishers. Only 10,832 people attended BookExpo America in 2016, compared with more than one million attendees at the Cairo International Book Fair, 180,000 at Livre Paris, and 25,000 at the London Book Fair.[27] BookExpo America did not report how many countries were represented, but the Cairo International Book Fair had 47 participating countries; Livre Paris involved 50 countries, London Book Fair 125, and LIBER International Book Fair in Barcelona, Spain 25.

Immigrants, Refugees, and Asylum Seekers

Translated texts potentially serve as a window into another culture—enabling readers to become more informed, empathetic citizens. Because public libraries aim for greater communication among diverse groups of people, they are an excellent space for translated literature. Identifying with literature of other linguistic cultures is an excellent first step to identifying with other members of a community.

A vital element in integrating new community members, particularly for refugee populations, is trust, which is established in a number of ways. From localized programs to border-crossing initiatives, libraries are rapidly responding to the refugee crisis. Project Bright Future partners with publishers to buy books to build collections in under-equipped schools in and around Istanbul. In the United States, the REFORMA Children in Crisis Project has built a task force of Spanish-speaking and bilingual/bicultural librarians to help other library staff and community members more effectively assist unaccompanied refugee children.

Many libraries are translating their entire websites; the Queens Borough Library is perhaps one of the most comprehensive examples. The Opportunity Agenda is a community center based in New York that aims to support greater opportunity in populations and locations where this is often denied.[28] This initiative provides workshops, media training, and advocacy tools. It also synthesizes and translates social science research.

GLLI

Initiatives such as the Global Literature in Libraries Initiative (GLLI) are putting pressure on publishers to produce more international texts; if there's more demand, there will be more need for translated texts in the United States. The visibility of international literature is one step to building cultural bridges, fostering values of diversity, and maintaining truly welcoming communities. GLLI became a limited liability company (LLC) in March 2017; it is an ambitious organization with several goals in progress.

GLLI and similar organizations help libraries by providing insights about vendors for international works. Because translated literature in print and e-book formats can be expensive, libraries can be equalizers. By creating translated literature collections in libraries, these efforts enhance their visibility and therefore the diversity of their materials. Other goals of GLLI include creating programming ideas for various library user groups and creating pan-publisher catalogs and publisher and journal lists to help acquisition librarians identify new works in translation.

Diversity is an asset in every part of GLLI's growing structure. GLLI is in cooperation with members of various organizations, including:

- American Literary Translators Association (ALTA)
- American Library Association (ALA)
- ALA Office of Intellectual Freedom (OIF)
- PLA (Public Library Association)

- ACRL (Association of College and Research Libraries)
- ALSC (Association of Library Services for Children)
- YALSA (Young Adult Library Services Association)

Additionally, GLLI collaborates with several publishers, including the following:

- Archipelago Books
- Asymptote Journal
- Dalkey Archive Press
- Europa Editions
- Open Letter Books
- Words Without Borders

The following are projects that GLLI is currently implementing or planning to implement in the near future:

- Creation of a GLLI module on BiblioBoard (part of BiblioLabs). BiblioBoard is a multimedia digital library where librarians, patrons, organizations, and community members can self-publish.
- Creation of a single website where librarians will find publishers and journals in one place and can browse within such categories as specific language, genre, and time period.
- Creation of lists for prison and juvenile detention center libraries.
- Production of a column in a review publication.
- Creation of programming for libraries centered on translated literature.

Future Considerations

Libraries have a lot of opportunities in the realm of translated literature. While acquisition and distribution may present hurdles, recognizing and representing non-English speakers, immigrants, refugees, and asylum seekers as members of the community by developing translated literature collections are steps toward truly welcoming communities and patron-centered librarianship. This social impact is a meaningful outcome for publishers, authors, translators, patrons, and librarians.

As librarians always have diverse user groups to consider, the intersection of technological, political, and publishing trends will be interesting and important to follow. It is vital to consider translated literature in which the target language is not only English when building collections. Additionally, while new and exciting forms of publication will continue to be generated, it is important to consider the needs of one's community first. Self-publishing platforms, such as the collaboration between GLLI and BiblioBoard, might serve as examples to follow.

Endnotes

1. Rüdiger Wischenbart and Miha Kovac, "Diversity Report 2016: Trends and References in Literary Translations Across Europe," *Cultural Transfers*, 2016.

2. Daryn Teague, "English-Speaking Countries Published 375,000 New Books Worldwide in 2004; Global Books in Print Database Reports Fiction Titles Up Last Year, but Computer Titles Plummeted," *BusinessWire*, October 12, 2005. http://www.businesswire.com/news/home/20051012005663/en/English-Speaking-Countries-Published-375000-Books-Worldwide-2004.

3. Michelle Maczka and Riky Stock, "Literary Translation in the United States: An Analysis of Translated Titles Reviewed by *Publishers Weekly*," *Publishing Research Quarterly* 22, no. 2 (2006): 49–54.

4. Dalkey Archive Press, "Research into Barriers to Translation and Best Practices: A Study for the Global Translation Initiative," March 2011. http://www.dalkeyarchive.com/wp-content/uploads/pdf/Global_Translation_Initiative_Study.pdf.

5. U.S. Census Bureau, "Census Bureau Reports at Least 350 Languages Spoken in U.S. Homes," November 3, 2016. https://www.census.gov/newsroom/press-releases/2015/cb15-185.html.

6. American Community Survey, "Selected Social Characteristics in the United States: 2007," U.S. Census Bureau. https://web.archive.org/web/20090425163238/http://factfinder.census.gov/servlet/ADPTable?_bm=y&-geo_id=01000US&-qr_name=ACS_2007_1YR_G00_DP2&-context=adp&-ds_name=ACS_2007_1YR_G00_&-tree_id=306&-_lang=en&-redoLog=false&-format=.

7. Dennis Abrams, "Reading Habits of International Internet Users: Survey from GfK in Germany," *Publishing Perspectives*, April 3, 2017. https://publishingperspectives.com/2017/04/germany-gfk-survey-reading-17-countries/.

8. "Frequency of Reading Books: Global GfK Survey," GfK, March 2017. https://cdn2.hubspot.net/hubfs/2405078/Landing_Pages_PDF/Global%20Studies%20Roper/Global-GfK-survey_Frequency-reading-books_2017.pdf.

9. Camille Ryan, "Language Use in the United States: 2011," American Community Survey Reports, August 2013. https://www.census.gov/prod/2013pubs/acs-22.pdf.

10. Porter Anderson, "A Big Market Report: 'Largest Cultural Industry in Europe,'" *Publishing Perspectives*, March 31, 2017. https://publishingperspectives.com/2017/03/europe-book-sector-report-fep/.

11. "Educational Publishing: Safeguarding the Future of the Arabic Language," *Publishers Weekly*, November 2013.

12. Edward T. O'Neill and Julia A. Gammon, "Building Collections Cooperatively: Analysis of Collection Use in the OhioLINK Library Consortium," ACRL Fourteenth National Conference, March 2009. http://www.ala.org/acrl/sites/ala.org.acrl/files/content/conferences/confsandpreconfs/national/seattle/papers/36.pdf.

13. Anne T. Gilliland, "The OhioLINK OCLC Collection Analysis Project: A Preliminary Report," *Collection Management* 33 (January 2008): 161–172.

14. Edward T. O'Neill and Julia Gammon, "Consortial Book Circulation Patterns: The OCLC-OhioLINK Study," *College and Research Libraries* 75, no. 6 (November 2014): 791–807.

15. Dave Bogart and Alan Inouye, eds., *Library and Book Trade Almanac*. (Medford, N.J.: Information Today, 2015).

16. Jacques Melitz, "The Impact of English Dominance on Literature and Welfare," *Journal of Economic Behavior and Organization* 64, no. 2 (October 2007).

17. Simeon Kerr, "Google Aims for Bigger Arab Audience," *Financial Times*, April 27, 2009. https://www.ft.com/content/32053fac-3342-11de-8f1b-00144feabdc0.

18. Siobhan O'Leary, "Germany Challenges Google Books at Its Own Game," *Publishing Perspectives*, January 6, 2010. http://publishingperspectives.com/2010/01/germany-challenges-google-books-at-its-own-game/.

19. Porter Anderson, "DBW 2017 Opening Themes: The Trade, Its Resilience, and Its Data," *Publishing Perspectives*, January 18, 2017.

20. Jim Milliot, "The Bad News About E-Books," *Publishers Weekly*, January 20, 2017. http://www.publishersweekly.com/pw/by-topic/digital/retailing/article/72563-the-bad-news-about-e-books.html.

21. Leonard Marcus, "The Global/Local Book Publishing (R)evolution," *Publishing Research Quarterly* 32, no. 1 (March 2016): 64–69.

22. Dalya Alberge, "British Readers Lost in Translations as Foreign Literature Sales Boom," *The Guardian*, August 23, 2014. https://www.theguardian.com/books/2014/aug/24/british-readers-translations-foreign-literature-sales-boom-stieg-larsson-jo-nesbo.

23. Jean Boase-Beier and Michael Holman. *The Practices of Literary Translation: Constraints and Creativity*. Language Arts and Disciplines, 1998.

24. Najib Harabi, "Economic Performance of the Arabic Book Translation Industry in Arab Countries," Gulf Research Center, 2008.

25. M.A. Orthofer, "Global Humanities Translation Prize," April 1, 2017. http://www.complete-review.com/saloon/archive/201704a.htm#zn9.

26. Porter Anderson, "Frankfurt Book Fair's LitAg Sells Out: Publishers Rights Corner Is Open," *Publishing Perspectives*, March 8, 2017. https://publishingperspectives.com/2017/03/frankfurt-book-fairs-litag-publishers-rights-corner/.

27. Joanna Bazan Babczonek and Ben Steward, "IPA World Book Fair Report 2016," February 24, 2016. https://www.internationalpublishers.org/images/data-statistics/IPAWorldBookFairReport2016.pdf.

28. Eric Schadt, "Extended Racial Equity Resource Guide for Libraries," WebJunction, February 9, 2016. https://www.webjunction.org/content/dam/WebJunction/Documents/webJunction/2016-02/RacialEquityGuideforLibraries.pdf.

Federal Agency and Federal Library Reports

Library of Congress

10 First Street S.E., Washington, DC 20540
202-707-5000
http://www.loc.gov

Carla Hayden
Librarian of Congress

Founded in 1800, the Library of Congress is the largest library in the world, with more than 164 million items in various languages, disciplines, and formats. As the world's largest repository of knowledge and creativity, the library's mission is to support the U.S. Congress in fulfilling its constitutional duties and to further the progress of knowledge and creativity for the benefit of the American people.

The library's collections are housed in its three buildings on Capitol Hill and in climate-controlled facilities for books at Fort Meade, Maryland. Its audiovisual materials are held at the Packard Campus for Audio-Visual Conservation in Culpeper, Virginia. The library also provides global access to its resources through its popular website, http://www.loc.gov.

Highlights of 2016

In fiscal year 2016 (October 2015 to September 2016), the Library of Congress:

Responded to more than 1 million reference requests from Congress, the public and other federal agencies and delivered approximately 18,380 volumes from the library's collections to congressional offices

Registered 414,269 claims to copyright through its U.S. Copyright Office

Circulated nearly 22 million copies of Braille and recorded books and magazines to more than 800,000 blind and physically handicapped reader accounts

Circulated more than 997,000 items for use inside and outside the Library

Preserved more than 10.5 million items from the library's collections

Recorded a total of 164,403,119 items in the collections:

- 24,189,688 cataloged books in the Library of Congress classification system

- 14,660,079 items in the non-classified print collections, including books in large type and raised characters, incunabula (books printed before 1501), monographs and serials, bound newspapers, pamphlets, technical reports, and other printed material
- 125,553,352 items in the non-classified (special) collections, including:
  - 3,670,573 audio materials, (discs, tapes, talking books, other recorded formats)
  - 70,685,319 manuscripts
  - 5,581,756 maps
  - 17,153,167 microforms
  - 1,809,351 moving images
  - 8,189,340 items of sheet music
  - 15,071,355 visual materials including:
    - 14,290,385 photographs
    - 107,825 posters
    - 673,145 prints and drawings
  - 3,392,491 other items, (including machine-readable items)

Welcomed nearly 1.8 million onsite visitors and recorded 92.8 million visits and more than 454 million page views on the library's web properties

Employed 3,149 permanent staff members

Operated with a total fiscal 2016 appropriation of $642.04 million, including the authority to spend $42.13 million in receipts

***

Carla D. Hayden, longtime chief executive of the Enoch Pratt Free Library system in Baltimore and a former president of the American Library Association, was sworn in as the 14th Librarian of Congress, for a renewable 10-year term, by Chief Justice of the United States John G. Roberts, Jr.

Hayden is the first woman, and the first African American, to serve as chief executive of the largest library in the world.

She succeeded Acting Librarian David S. Mao, who had served since the 2015 retirement of former Librarian James H. Billington.

Roberta I. Shaffer was named Law Librarian of Congress effective Feb. 21, 2016. Shaffer had been serving in the position in an acting capacity since October 5, 2015, and had served previously as the Law Librarian of Congress from August 2009 through November 2011.

Legislative Transparency

To support transparency in government, the Library of Congress, in collaboration with the U.S. Congress and the Government Printing Office, provides online access to the nation's legislative information on the mobile-friendly website Congress.gov. Congress.gov provides members of Congress, legislative agencies, and the public with accurate, timely, and complete legislative information. The site is presented by the Library of Congress using data from the U.S. House of Representatives, the Senate, the Government Publishing Office, the Congressional Budget Office, and the Congressional Research Service (CRS).

As a result of a series of system updates in 2015, more than 1 million items pertaining to the legislative process are accessible on stationary computers or mobile devices. The site contains metadata for legislation starting with 1973 (the 93rd Congress), full text of the legislation beginning in 1993 (the 103rd Congress), and both the *Congressional Record* and committee reports dating back to 1995 (the 104th Congress). New content includes treaty documents, nominations, executive communications, and the Federalist Papers.

Along with the growth in the volume of data on the site, additional features have been added. Users can now sign up to receive e-mail alerts any time a member of Congress introduces a bill, there is an action on a particular bill, or a new issue of the *Congressional Record* is available on the site.

To make Congress.gov more accessible to people with disabilities, a new feature, "Listen to This Page," reads the legislative summaries aloud. A new video series, "Two-Minute Tips," provides tutorials such as "Creating and Using Congress.gov Email Alerts," "Search Terms and Facets," and "Navigating a Bill." These short videos join a nine-part series on the legislative process, written by CRS experts.

Security

In recent years the library's Office of Security and Emergency Preparedness has focused on strengthening protective services, personnel security, and emergency preparedness programs. Collections security was also enhanced through expansion of the Site Assistance Visit Program, which partnered physical security with preservation elements. The office also implemented additional access controls and electronic security measures for the library's highest-level collections and financial assets. Lastly, the office continued to upgrade its emergency communications systems, including mass alert notifications, mobile radio equipment, and the emergency public address system.

In collaboration with the Office of Security and Emergency Preparedness, the Information Technology Services Office (ITS) worked to ensure the continuity of operation at an Alternate Computing Facility in the event of a pandemic or other emergency. The ITS Security Group was involved in assessing a governance, risk, and compliance system to better manage the library's continuous monitoring activities. ITS ensured that the library's mission-critical systems are reliable and secure and that the technology infrastructure that supports these systems was uncompromised. ITS also ensured that the library's information technology infrastructure and the services it provides continued to adapt to new technology and respond to other changes and requirements. The library's current IT infrastructure includes five data centers in four building locations.

Library Realignment and Strategic Planning

The strategic plan for 2016 to 2020 can be downloaded at https://www.loc.gov/portals/static/about/documents/library_congress_stratplan_2016-2020.pdf.

The realignment was initiated to strengthen the information technology and other support functions, elevate the outreach function, consolidate digital and analog collection management, provide a better support structure for staff, improve overall management, and ultimately result in even better service to the library's customers.

It involves three main elements: the reassignment of Office of Strategic Initiatives functions to the newly created Office of the Chief Information Officer; the establishment of a new National and International Outreach service unit to encompass many of the offices and functions previously performed by Library Services; and the alignment of support services in a new Office of the Chief Operating Officer.

Educational Outreach

The library's outreach to teachers focuses on the use of primary sources in the classroom. Over the past two decades, digital technology has allowed the Library of Congress to make many of its collections accessible in K–12 classrooms in the United States and around the world. Access to these resources assists educators in meeting curriculum goals and creating lifelong learners. The Teachers Page, the library's Web-based resource for teachers, includes lesson plans that meet curriculum standards.

The Educational Outreach Team has expanded the Interactive Student Discovery Series for Apple iPads, which can be downloaded free of charge on iBooks. The series brings together historical artifacts and one-of-a-kind documents on a wide range of topics, from history to science to literature.

Through its Teaching with Primary Sources Program (TPS) the library is providing educators with methods and materials that build student literacy skills, content knowledge, and critical-thinking abilities.

From print journals to social media, the library has sought to connect with educators around the nation. The Educational Outreach Team hosts webinars for educators and reaches more than 10,000 followers on its @TeachingLC, a Twitter feed for K–12 educators offering primary sources, inspiration, and ideas. The team also publishes posts on its "Teaching with the Library of Congress" blog, to showcase the library's collections and strategies for using them in the classroom, and to encourage readers to share their teaching strategies.

Literacy Promotion

The Library of Congress promotes reading and literacy through the Center for the Book, the National Book Festival, the appointment of a National Ambassador for Young People's Literature, and through its popular literacy-promotion website, http://www.Read.gov.

Center for the Book

The Center for the Book, established by Congress in 1977 to "stimulate public interest in books and reading," is a national force for reading and literacy promotion. A public-private partnership, it sponsors educational programs that reach readers of all ages through its affiliated state centers, collaborations with nonprofit reading promotion partners and through the Young Readers Center and the Poetry and Literature Center at the Library of Congress. The center also maintains and updates the library's http://www.Read.gov.

In collaboration with the Children's Book Council (CBC) and the CBC Foundation, and with support from publishers, the center sponsors the National Ambassador for Young People's Literature. Gene Luen Yang, author of the acclaimed graphic novel *American Born Chinese* was named the Fifth National Ambassador for Young People's Literature.

Yang succeeds beloved and esteemed authors Jon Scieszka (2008–2009), Katherine Paterson (2010–2011), Walter Dean Myers (2012–2013) and Kate DiCamillo (2014–2015) in the position.

The Center for the Book also plays a major role in presentation of the National Book Festival, participating in planning the festival, inviting and scheduling authors and illustrators, and organizing the Pavilion of the States.

The Young Readers Center in the Thomas Jefferson Building continues to grow in popularity, with new programs and activities for children that attract nearly 30,000 visitors a year.

The Center for the Book administers the Library of Congress Literacy Awards, an initiative supported and originated by philanthropist David M. Rubenstein.

The awards recognize and support organizations and institutions in the United States and abroad that have made significant contributions to combating illiteracy. Visit https://blogs.loc.gov/loc/2016/09/library-announces-literacy-award-winners/ for details of recent winners.

Online Resources

The library continued to add high-quality digital content to its website.

The library's website at http://www.loc.gov, consistently recognized as one of the top federal sites, gives users access to the institution's vast resources, such as its online catalogs; selected collections in various formats; copyright, legal, and legislative information; library exhibitions; and videos and podcasts of library events.

The library launched a new home page for loc.gov in 2016.

A second annual online conference for educators was titled "Discover and Explore with Library of Congress Primary Sources."

The diaries, notebooks and address books of John J. Pershing, commander-in-chief of the American Expeditionary Forces in World War I, and the diaries of George S. Patton, a tank commander in World War I and a U.S. Army general in World War II, were put online in 2016.

These items join thousands of original materials from the World War I era that the Library of Congress digitized and made accessible for use ahead of the centennial of America's entry into the Great War in April 2017.

Social Media

The library continues to participate in media-sharing and social networking sites to promote its collections, programs, and events. Library of Congress events, booktalks, and concerts reach extensive audiences through the library's YouTube and iTunesU channels.

Thousands of photo enthusiasts continue to not only access but also help identify library photos from the early 1900s through the photo-sharing project on Flickr.

In addition to its main Facebook site—with more than 364,019 "friends"— the library offers Facebook pages for the Law Library, the American Folklife Center, Performing Arts, the National Digital Information Infrastructure and Preservation Program, and the National Library Service for the Blind and Physically Handicapped.

The library's Twitter presence includes feeds for the World Digital Library, the digital preservation program, the Congressional Research Service, teacher resources, the Law Library, legislative resources, map collections, the John W. Kluge Center, library events, and the Register of Copyrights. The library's Pinterest account includes content on boards featuring the library's collections, exhibitions, publications, and events such as the National Book Festival.

The library's main blog—among the first federal blogs at the time of its launch on April 24, 2007—has since been joined by other blogs generated by the Copyright Office; the Law Library; the National Digital Preservation and Information Infrastructure Program; the Music, Prints and Photographs, and Science, Technology and Business Divisions; the Poetry and Literature Center; the Educational Outreach Office; the American Folklife Center; the National Library Service for the Blind and Physically Handicapped; the Packard Campus for Audio-Visual Conservation; the National Book Festival; and the John W. Kluge Center.

Images from current events, concerts, and exhibitions are shared on Instagram.

Global Access

The Library of Congress acquires global resources through cooperative agreements and exchanges with other nations, through its overseas offices, and the World Digital Library initiative. The overseas offices collect and catalog materials from more than 80 countries in some 150 languages and 25 scripts, from Africa, Asia, Latin America, and the Middle East. These items are accessible in the library's area studies reading rooms. Selected items have been digitized—many through cooperative digitizing projects—and are accessible on the library's website.

Overseas Offices

The library's six overseas offices (located in Cairo, Islamabad, Jakarta, Nairobi, New Delhi, and Rio de Janeiro) acquire, catalog, and preserve materials from parts of the world where the book and information industries are not well developed.

World Digital Library

The World Digital Library (WDL) is a website, accessible from anywhere in the world, that presents in digital form, free of charge, documents and images of historical significance about numerous countries and cultures. Participation has grown to 190 partners in 81 countries. A new interface better accommodates use on mobile devices.

A key objective of the WDL project is to build digital library capabilities in the developing world. To that end, the WDL continues to maintain and process content from digital conversion centers at the Egyptian National Library and Archives in Cairo, the National Library of Uganda in Kampala, and the Iraq National Library and Archive in Baghdad.

Preservation

Preserving its unparalleled collections—from cuneiform tablets to born-digital items—is one of the library's major activities in support of its vision to further human understanding and wisdom.

The library's preservation research program conducts analyses and assessments of factors that endanger the library's collections, investigates ways to reduce inherent risks and the effects of the use of collection items, and helps reduce environmental risks to the collections.

The congressionally mandated National Digital Information Infrastructure and Preservation Project (NDIIPP), administered by the library's Office of Strategic Initiatives, continues to collect and preserve at-risk digital content of cultural and historical importance.

Library of Congress, Britain's Royal Library to Collaborate on Papers of King George III

The Library of Congress, the Royal Collection Trust and King's College London in 2016 signed a memorandum of understanding in which they agree to share resources to aid in the digitization of the papers of King George III (1738–1820), the English monarch in power when the American colonies declared independence, creating a new nation.

Some 85 percent of the items in the archive, based at England's Windsor Castle, have never before been examined by scholars. They include correspondence, maps, and royal household ledgers.

The Library of Congress is supporting a National Digital Stewardship Residency Program fellow who will analyze the existing and proposed metadata for historical materials from this era, including the King George papers at Windsor Castle.

Books

A large number of volumes are housed in offsite storage facilities but most can be retrieved and sent to Capitol Hill within 24 hours. To address overcrowding in the bookstacks of the Thomas Jefferson and John Adams Buildings on Capitol Hill, a temporary collection storage facility was leased in Cabin Branch, Maryland, to house 3.1 million books in Fort Meade-compatible containers. Library staff began planning for the construction and transfer of collections to Fort Meade Module 5.

Newspapers

In partnership with the National Endowment for the Humanities, the library sponsors the National Digital Newspaper Program, a project to digitize and provide free and public access to American newspapers that are in the public domain. The scanned newspapers are accessible on the library's Chronicling America website, a free searchable database of nearly 1,900 historic American newspapers published in 38 states, Puerto Rico, and the District of Columbia between 1836 and 1922.

Audiovisual Collections

The Packard Campus for Audio-Visual Conservation in Culpeper, Virginia, houses the library's recorded sound and moving image collections—the world's largest and most comprehensive. In 2015 the Packard Campus digitally preserved nearly 54,000 moving image and recorded sound collection items. Highlights include the digitization of 3,000 hours of content from the Studs Terkel Collection (in collaboration with the Chicago History Museum) and the processing of 2,000 lacquer discs from the Les Paul Collection.

At year's end the Packard Campus Data Center held 6.2 petabytes of collection content comprising nearly 1.5 million digital files. This includes more than 205,000 files from 18,200 public broadcasting programs acquired from the American Archive of Public Broadcasting and ingested into the Digital Archive.

Selected Speech Recordings

The Library of Congress unveiled a new curated web presentation—"Food for Thought: Presidents, Prime Ministers, and other National Press Club Luncheon Speakers, 1954–1989"—that features speeches by 25 of the world's most important newsmakers, including presidents, international leaders and other political and cultural icons of the period.

Most of these select speeches from the library's National Press Club Collection have not been heard in their entirety since they were initially delivered. The online presentation spans 35 years and accompanying essays put relevant historical context around the topics discussed by the speakers.

The selections to the online presentation are part of a trove of nearly 2,000 historic sound recordings in the National Press Club Collection. The 25 selected speakers include:

Muhammad Ali and Ken Norton, Aug. 27, 1976

James Baldwin, Dec. 10, 1986

Menachem Begin, March 23, 1978

Leonard Bernstein, Oct. 13, 1959

James H. Billington, Jan. 12, 1989

George H. W. Bush, March 20, 1981

Jimmy Carter, Oct. 14, 1980

Fidel Castro, April 20, 1959

Charles de Gaulle, April 23, 1960

Dwight D. Eisenhower, Jan. 14, 1959

Gerald R. Ford, June 6, 1988

Audrey Hepburn, April 7, 1989

Alfred Hitchcock, March 14, 1963

Herbert Hoover, March 10, 1954

Bob Hope, July 8, 1980

Nikita Khrushchev, Sept. 16, 1959

Edward R. Murrow, May 24, 1961

Richard M. Nixon, May 21, 1958

A. Philip Randolph, Aug. 26, 1963

Ronald Reagan, June 16, 1966

Anwar Sadat, Feb. 6, 1978

Jonas Salk, April 12, 1965

Adlai E. Stevenson, June 26, 1961

Margaret Thatcher, Sept. 19, 1975

Harry S. Truman, May 10, 1954, April 12, 1958, Dec. 8, 1958, Nov. 2, 1961

Films

It is estimated that half the films produced before 1950 and 80 percent to 90 percent of those made before 1920 are gone forever. The library is working with many organizations to prevent further losses. Under the terms of the National Film Preservation Act of 1988, the Librarian of Congress—with advice from the National Film Preservation Board—began selecting 25 films annually for the National Film Registry to be preserved for all time. The films are chosen on the basis of whether they are "culturally, historically, or aesthetically significant."

On December 14, 2016, the library announced the following additions to the National Film Registry, which brought the total of films on the list to 700.

Atomic Cafe (1982)

Ball of Fire (1941)

The Beau Brummels (1928)

The Birds (1963)

Blackboard Jungle (1955)

The Breakfast Club (1985)

The Decline of Western Civilization (1981)

East of Eden (1955)

Funny Girl (1968)

Life of an American Fireman (1903)

The Lion King (1994)

Lost Horizon (1937)

The Musketeers of Pig Alley (1912)

Paris Is Burning (1990)
Point Blank (1967)
The Princess Bride (1987)
Putney Swope (1969)
Rushmore (1998)
Solomon Sir Jones films (1924–28)
Steamboat Bill, Jr. (1928)
Suzanne, Suzanne (1982)
Thelma & Louise (1991)
20,000 Leagues Under the Sea (1916)
Walk in the Sun, A (1945)
Who Framed Roger Rabbit (1988)

The legislation also directs the library to support archival research projects that would investigate the survival rates of American movies produced in all major categories during the 19th and 20th centuries. With funding from the National Film Preservation Board, the library initiated the Silent Film Project, the goal of which is to borrow, catalog, digitally preserve, and ensure the availability of silent films for public viewing and research. Private collectors may engage in the project by lending their small-gauge silent films that do not otherwise survive or only survive in a less complete form. All borrowed films are scanned for preservation and access purposes.

Sound Recordings

The National Recording Preservation Act of 2000 mandates the preservation of the nation's historic sound recordings, many of which are at risk of deterioration. It directs the Librarian of Congress to name sound recordings of aesthetic, histori- cal, or cultural value to the National Recording Registry, to establish an advisory National Recording Preservation Board, and to create and implement a national plan to assure the long-term preservation and accessibility of the nation's audio heritage.

On March 29, 2017, the Librarian of Congress announced the addition of the following 25 sound recordings to the National Recording Registry, bringing the total to 475.

The 1888 London cylinder recordings of Col. George Gouraud (1888)

"All Things Considered," first broadcast (May 3, 1971)

"Amazing Grace" (single), Judy Collins (1970)

"American Pie" (single), Don McLean (1971)

The Brooklyn Dodgers and the New York Giants at the Polo Grounds, announced by Vin Scully (September 8, 1957)

"Gunfighter Ballads and Trail Songs," Marty Robbins (1959)

"Hound Dog" (single), Big Mama Thornton (1953)

"I'll Fly Away" (single), The Chuck Wagon Gang (1948)

"In the Midnight Hour" (single), Wilson Pickett (1965)

The Incredible Jazz Guitar of Wes Montgomery, Wes Montgomery (1960)

"Lift Every Voice and Sing" (singles), Manhattan Harmony Four (1923); Melba Moore and Friends (1990)

"Over the Rainbow" (single), Judy Garland (1939)

"People" (single), Barbra Streisand (1964)

"Puttin' on the Ritz" (single), Harry Richman (1929)

"Rachmaninoff's Vespers (All-Night Vigil)," Robert Shaw Festival Singers (1990)

Remain in Light, Talking Heads (1980)

The Rise and Fall of Ziggy Stardust and the Spiders from Mars, David Bowie (1972)

Saxophone Colossus, Sonny Rollins (1956)

"Scott Joplin's Treemonisha," Gunter Schuller, arr. (1976)

Signatures, Renée Fleming (1997)

Straight Outta Compton, N.W.A (1988)

Their Greatest Hits (1971–1975), Eagles (1976)

Wanted: Live in Concert, Richard Pryor (1978)

"We Are Family" (single), Sister Sledge (1979)

The Wiz, original cast album (1975)

Oral History

The Library of Congress has been collecting and preserving the nation's oral history since the 1930s, when the Works Progress Administration's (WPA) Federal Writers' Project documented the experiences of former slaves and of Americans living through the Great Depression. The American Folklife Center became the repository for these oral histories and others, such as the man-on-the-street interviews after the attack on Pearl Harbor on December 7, 1941, and similar interviews following the terrorist attacks of September 11, 2001.

Launched in 2000 at the behest of Congress, the Veterans History Project in the American Folklife Center is preserving and making available the recollections of those in the armed services dating to World War I. The Veterans History Project marked its 15th anniversary with the launch of a new Web presentation featuring 15 collections from the project's permanent archive. In recognition of the 70th anniversary of VJ-Day in 2015, the project launched a major campaign to preserve the stories of World War II veterans residing in and around the nation's capital. During the year more than 5,000 personal recollections were deposited in the library, bringing the total to more than 100,000 since the project's inception. Many of these stories are accessible on the project's website.

Veterans History Project Recognizes LGBT Veterans

The Veterans History Project (VHP) has launched the next installment of its ongoing "Experiencing War" website feature. The new installment recognizes lesbian, gay, bisexual and transgender (LGBT) veterans who served in conflicts from WWII to the recent conflicts in Afghanistan and Iraq.

"Speaking Out: LGBT Veterans" not only illustrates these veterans' experiences during their military service, but in the case of some—such as Frank Kameny, Brenda Vosbein and Miriam Ben-Shalom—their post-service advocacy on behalf of LGBT veterans and individuals.

Spotlighted is U.S. Army Reserve Brig. Gen. Tammy Smith, the first openly gay flag officer. Smith describes the atmosphere in the Army in the 1990s, when Don't Ask Don't Tell (DADT) was policy, and what it was like to be a woman in a company command position among men who mistook her for being a "personnel officer" because she was female.

Smith previously participated in a VHP Panel Discussion, "Breaking the Silence: Our Military Stories" in June 2014 that focused on such topics as pre- and post-DADT repeal and experiences, the current status of LGBT equality in the U.S. military, the Defense of Marriage Act (DOMA) and Proposition 8 as it relates to military families and the current ban on transgender service members.

According to the U.S. Department of Veterans Affairs, an estimated 1 million veterans identify as LGBT. As with all participating veterans, VHP encourages LGBT veterans to self-identify when contributing their narrative. By doing so, historic evidence of their personal experiences will not be lost, and a fuller picture of American service during conflict can be reflected.

In 2003 documentary producer Dave Isay was inspired by the library's WPA collections to launch StoryCorps, an innovative oral history project in which ordinary Americans record one another's stories. The thousands of audio interviews that compose the StoryCorps project reside in the Library of Congress, where they can be accessed onsite. In addition to weekly broadcasts on National Public Radio's *Morning Edition*, selected interviews are available as downloadable podcasts from NPR and as animated shorts on the StoryCorps website. The project recently introduced technology that makes it possible for anyone to participate via a new app or through the StoryCorps.me site. The ability to conduct and share interviews independent of a StoryCorps recording booth provides a global platform whereby anyone in the world can record and upload an oral history. The library will regularly gather copies of these uploaded interviews from the StoryCorps.me site for long-term preservation.

Under the Civil Rights History Project Act of 2009, Congress directed the Library of Congress and the Smithsonian Institution's National Museum of African American History and Culture to conduct a survey of existing oral history collections with relevance to the civil rights movement, and to record new interviews with people who participated in the movement, over a five-year period beginning in 2010. The library has since completed the survey and launched the Civil Rights History Project website, which provides information about civil rights collections housed in more than 1,500 archives, libraries, museums, and other repositories around the country, including the Library of Congress.

American Folklife Center Launches "My Tradition" Photo Campaign

In celebration of its 40th anniversary, the American Folklife Center launched a year-long campaign asking Americans to share photos of their folk traditions. The campaign kicked off a year of events to commemorate AFC's four decades as the institution of record for American folk traditions and ensure that it remains the country's most vibrant folklife archive and research center well into the future.

The photo campaign asked people all over the United States and beyond to submit photos of a folk tradition in which they themselves participate, creating a collective snapshot of folklife in 2016.

Digital Preservation and Management

More than three decades of PBS NewsHour broadcasts from 1975 to 2007 will be preserved and available online as part of the American Archive of Public Broadcasting (AAPB). Public media producer WGBH, the Library of Congress, and WETA, Washington, D.C., will digitize, preserve and allow the public online access to PBS NewsHour's predecessor programs from 1975 to 2007, made possible with funding from the Council on Library and Information Resources (CLIR). The project will digitize nearly 10,000 programs comprising more than 8,000 recorded hours that chronicle American and foreign affairs, providing access to original source material, including interviews with presidents and other world leaders and reports on major issues and events. The content will be presented as a part of the American Archive of Public Broadcasting, a collaboration between WGBH and the Library of Congress.

Noting the value of preserving the PBS NewsHour material, Steven Roberts, renowned journalist and the Shapiro Professor of Media and Public Affairs at George Washington University, said "No other broadcast on television has upheld the highest standards of the profession with such consistent devotion."

The digitized PBS NewsHour collection will provide valuable primary-source material not available elsewhere for historians to consider in their explorations into the recent past, especially in the areas of politics, policymaking and international affairs. It will give scholars a previously unavailable source from which to study ideas and rhetoric to illuminate what intellectual historian Daniel Rodgers recently characterized as "a multi-sided contest of arguments and social visions that ranged across the late 20th century."

The programs feature interviews with leading newsmakers including presidents, Supreme Court justices, members of Congress, every secretary of state since 1976 and with world leaders including the Shah of Iran, Ayatollah Khomeini, Fidel Castro, Muammar Khadafy, Yasser Arafat, Menachem Begin, Boris Yeltsin, Vaclav Havel, Nelson Mandela, and Margaret Thatcher. The collection includes extensive coverage of election campaigns, African American history, global and domestic health care, poverty, technology, immigration debates, the end of the Cold War, terrorism, the economy, climate change, energy issues, religion, education issues, rural life, scientific exploration, poetry, and the media.

The PBS NewsHour collection will be made available on the AAPB website, growing the online collection to more than 20,000 programs. The AAPB will ensure that this rich source of American political, social, and cultural history and creativity will be saved and made available once again to future generations.

U.S. Copyright Office

Congress enacted the first copyright law in May 1790; in 1870 it centralized the national copyright function in the Library of Congress. The U.S. Copyright Office in the Library of Congress administers certain major provisions of the U.S. copyright law and provides expert and impartial advice about copyright law and policy to Congress, federal agencies, the courts, and the public. The collections of the Library of Congress have been created largely through the copyright deposit system.

The Copyright Office registers hundreds of thousands of copyright claims, most of which 94 percent are filed online, and records thousands of copyright transfer documents. Additionally, the office processes hundreds of notices terminating transfers of copyrights made in the 1970s, most of which pertained to musical works.

National Library Service for the Blind and Physically Handicapped

The National Library Service for the Blind and Physically Handicapped (NLS) was established in 1931 when President Herbert Hoover signed the Pratt-Smoot Act into law. Through its digital talking-book program, NLS continues to distribute digital players and audiobooks on flash-memory cartridges in specially designed mailing containers to libraries nationwide.

NLS has contracted for the production of thousands of audio books and also selected audio recordings of books from recordings provided free of charge by commercial publishers including Audible, Inc.; Hachette; Penguin; Random House; and Scholastic. NLS also adds materials to its Braille Audio Reading Download (BARD) offerings with those produced by network libraries, thus expanding the scope and quantity of available titles.

The John W. Kluge Center

The John W. Kluge Center was established in 2000 with a gift of $60 million from the late John W. Kluge, Metromedia president and founding chair of the James Madison Council (the library's private-sector advisory group). The center's goal is to bring the world's scholars to the Library of Congress to use the institution's vast resources and interact with policymakers in Washington.

The Kluge Center brings scholars and interns in the humanities and social sciences to Washington. Senior scholars, pre- and post-doctoral fellows, and interns research topics of historical and contemporary significance in the fields of humanities, social sciences, foreign policy, and law.

Honors and Awards

Gershwin Prize for Popular Song

The Library of Congress celebrated Smokey Robinson's career and his selection as the 2016 recipient of the Library of Congress Gershwin Prize for Popular Song in Washington, D.C., with a series of events, culminating in a star-studded concert at DAR Constitution Hall on November 16. Named for George and Ira Gershwin, the prize honors a living music artist's lifetime achievement in promoting song to enhance cultural understanding; entertaining and informing audiences; and inspiring new generations. Previous recipients are Paul Simon, Stevie Wonder, Sir Paul McCartney, songwriting duo Burt Bacharach and the late Hal David, Carole King, Billy Joel and Willie Nelson. The two-day celebration began Robinson took his first tour of the Library of Congress' historic Thomas Jefferson Building and viewed some rare and surprising items in the Library's vast collections. Among them was Robinson's first song ever submitted for copyright, "I Cry." Registered in 1958, the song was co-written by Berry Gordy, who joined Robinson on a tour of the nation's largest library.

Library of Congress Prize for American Fiction

Marilynne Robinson received the Library of Congress Prize for American Fiction during the 2016 Library of Congress National Book Festival on September 24. The prize honors an American literary writer whose body of work is distinguished not only for its mastery of the art but for its originality of thought and imagination. Robinson is the author of such critically acclaimed novels as *Gilead* (2004), *Home* (2008), and *Housekeeping* (1980).

Literacy Awards

Created and sponsored by philanthropist David M. Rubenstein, the Library of Congress Literacy Awards seek to reward those organizations that have been doing exemplary, innovative and easily replicable work over a sustained period of time and to encourage new groups, organizations, and individuals to become involved. Recipients of the 2016 annual awards were announced on September 23.

The winners were WETA Reading Rockets (David M. Rubenstein Prize, $150,000, for groundbreaking or sustained record of advancement of literacy by an individual or entity); Parent-Child Home Program (American Prize, $50,000, for a project developed and implemented successfully during the past decade for combating illiteracy and/or aliteracy); and Libraries Without Borders (International Prize, $50,000, for the work of an individual or nation or nongovernmental organization working in a specific country or region).

Living Legend Award

The Library of Congress Living Legend Award honors those who have made significant contributions to America's diverse cultural, scientific, and social heritage. First presented in 2000, during the library's bicentennial celebration, the award has been given to artists, writers, filmmakers, physicians, entertainers, sports figures, public servants, and musicians who have enriched the nation through their professional accomplishments and personal excellence. In 2016 the award was presented to Mario Vargas Llosa, an internationally known award-winning author.

Poet Laureate

Acting Librarian of Congress David Mao appointed Juan Felipe Herrera to serve a second term as the 21st Poet Laureate Consultant in Poetry.

"We look forward to seeing what Herrera will accomplish in his second term, and we know he will continue to inspire and educate with his warmth, enthusiasm, and creative genius."

Library to Host 2016 Américas Award for Children's and Young Adult Literature

Authors Pam Muñoz Ryan and Ashley Hope-Perez received the Américas Award for Children's and Young Adult Literature.

The Américas Award is administered by the Consortium of Latin American Studies Programs (CLASP) at Vanderbilt University and jointly sponsored by Tulane University's Stone Center for Latin American Studies.

Koussevitzky Foundation Announces Winners

The Serge Koussevitzky Music Foundation in the Library of Congress has awarded commissions for new musical works to five composers. The commissions are granted jointly by the foundation and the organizations that will present performances of the newly composed works.

Award winners and the groups co-sponsoring their commissions are Zosha Di Castri and International Contemporary Ensemble (ICE); David Fulmer and Spektral Quartet; Felipe Lara and Ensemble Modern (Germany); Alexandre Lunsqui and New York New Music Ensemble; and Amy Williams and JACK Quartet.

Serge Koussevitzky, conductor of the Boston Symphony Orchestra from 1924 to 1949, was a champion of contemporary music. Throughout his distinguished career, he played a vital role in the creation of new works by commissioning such composers as Béla Bartók, Leonard Bernstein and Igor Stravinsky. He established the Koussevitzky Foundation in the Library of Congress to continue his lifelong commitment to composers and new music. Applications for commissions are accepted annually.

Additional Sources of Information

Library of Congress website	www.loc.gov
Main phone number	202-707-5000
Reading room hours and locations	www.loc.gov/rr/
	202-707-6400
General reference	www.loc.gov/rr/askalib/
	202-707-3399
	TTY 202-707-4210
Visitor information	www.loc.gov/visit/
	202-707-8000
	TTY 202-707-6200
Exhibitions	ww.loc.gov/exhibits/
	202-707-4604
Copyright information	www.copyright.gov
	202-707-3000
Copyright hotline (to order forms)	202-707-9100

Library catalogs	www.catalog.loc.gov/
Cataloging Information	www.loc.gov/aba/
Services for the Blind and Physically Handicapped	www.loc.gov/nls/
	202-707-5100
	TDD 202-707-0744
Literacy promotion	www.read.gov
Teachers Page	www.loc.gov/teachers/
Legislative information	www.Congress.gov
Library of Congress Shop (credit card orders)	888-682-3557
	www.loc.gov/shop

Federal Library and Information Network (FEDLINK)

Blane K. Dessy
Interim Executive Director

Summary

During fiscal year (FY) 2015 the Federal Library Information Network (FEDLINK) continued its mission to achieve better utilization of federal library and information resources; provide the most cost-effective and efficient administrative mechanism for providing necessary services and materials to federal libraries and information centers; and serve as a forum for discussion of federal library and information policies, programs, and procedures, to help inform Congress, federal agencies, and others concerned with libraries and information centers.

FEDLINK's Advisory Board (FAB) focused its bimonthly meetings on a variety of broad federal information issues including FEDLINK's status as the commodity manager of Information Retrieval for the Federal Strategic Sourcing Initiative (FSSI), the Library of the United States Project (LOTUS), interlibrary loan groups among federal libraries, new technologies for federal librarians, FEDLINK's research agenda, and the Federal Library Census.

The governing body structure of FEDLINK includes a number of committees, working groups, and ad hoc committees that all completed an ambitious agenda in fiscal 2015. Notably, the American Indian Library Initiative participated in the ATALM (Association of Tribal Archives, Libraries and Museums) annual conference, the Education Working Group featured agency options for internship programs and began work on a federal library mentoring project, and the FEDGrey Working Group hosted GreyNet 16, GreyNet International's annual conference.

The Awards Committee announced the following awards:

- 2014 Federal Library/Information Center of the Year in the Large Library/Information Center Category (with a staff of 11 or more employees): Barr Memorial Library, Fort Knox U.S. Army Garrison, Kentucky
- 2014 award in the Small Library/Information Center Category (with a staff of 10 or fewer employees): Darnall Medical Library, Walter Reed National Military Medical Center
- 2014 Federal Librarian of the Year: Richard James King, Branch Chief and Information Architect, National Institutes of Health Library, Bethesda, Maryland
- 2014 Federal Library Technician of the Year: Maria Walls, Library Technician, U.S. Department of Justice

The Human Resources Working Group (HRWG) completed revising the 1410 series and sent out the revision to the FEDLINK Federal Advisory Board and to more than 40 federal librarians who volunteered to review the draft revision from a variety of federal agencies. Following the review, the HRWG addressed and adjudicated the comments and completed additional revisions.

In FY 2014 FEDLINK continued its publication program as a digital communication provider and used the FEDLIB listserv to communicate critical advocacy and program information to more than 2,000 electronic subscribers. New resources for FY 2015 include revisions to the member handbook, adding award-winning exemplars to the website, and a number of research documents on federal information purchasing and strategic sourcing.

FEDLINK continued to enhance its fiscal operations while providing its members with $75.7 million in transfer-pay services, $5.9 million in direct-pay services, and an estimated $106.5 million in the Direct Express service. In total, approximately $188 million of information resource purchasing was done on FEDLINK contracts. This saved federal agencies more than $36.7 million in vendor volume discounts and approximately $49.9 million in cost avoidance.

FEDLINK staff highlighted services at national conferences such as the American Library Association (ALA), Computers in Libraries, National Contracts Management Association World Congress, and the Government Contracts Management Symposium. Staff also represented FEDLINK at regional events such as the House of Representatives Subscription Fair. They also assisted the ALA Federal and Armed Forces Librarians Round Table (FAFLRT) track activities affecting federal libraries and host programs at the annual conference on working in a federal library and best practices for library internships. Staff members also participated in additional national conferences, workshops, and meetings, including CENDI and Computers in Libraries.

FEDLINK continued to provide federal agencies cost-effective access to an array of automated information resources for online research and support for federal library functions. FEDLINK members procured an array of publications in various formats: print and electronic journals, print and electronic books, sound recordings, audiovisual materials, items via document delivery and interlibrary loan, and access to databases of full text, indexes, abstracts, and a variety of other data. Federal libraries obtained support for many functions such as acquisitions, cataloging and related technical processing services, staffing support, information management, resource sharing, information industry market research and library services benchmarking, integrated library systems, digitization, digital archiving, and preservation and conservation services via Library of Congress/FEDLINK contracts with more than 125 vendors.

FEDLINK issued many Requests for Proposals (RFPs) and Requests for Quotes (RFQs). An RFP "open season" established new agreements for preservation and conservation services with six companies, bringing the total to 27 vendors, and expanding the range of services available. Two other "open season" RFPs added a serials subscription agent and several information retrieval vendors. FEDLINK awarded a contract for Interlibrary Loan Fee Management and renewed option years for staffing support and bibliographic resources. In total, FEDLINK issued 40 RFQs for agencies' requirements for these services.

FEDLINK Executive Report

The Advisory Board focused its bimonthly meetings on a variety of broad federal information issues including FEDLINK's status as the commodity manager of Information Retrieval for the Federal Strategic Sourcing Initiative (FSSI), the Library of the United States Project (LOTUS), interlibrary loan groups among federal libraries, new technologies for federal librarians, FEDLINK's research agenda, and the Federal Library Census.

The American Indian Libraries Working Group's first year was filled with outreach and educational initiatives. After building an infrastructure for the group itself and identifying program objectives, the group heard from an archivist with the state of New Mexico (Department of Cultural Affairs) who is developing an online access project with the Museum of Indian Arts and Culture. The group then presented a workshop at the annual Association of Tribal Libraries and Museums (ATALM) and developed programming for a later event on connecting American Indian and federal libraries.

FEDLINK held two expositions in FY 2015. The 2014 Fall Expo featured "The Global Synergy of Federal Information" with discussions of international collections, acquisitions, parallel universes of information, and the latest on programs engaging and participating in the worldwide-networked community. In the spring of 2015 the FEDLINK Expo "Innovation in Federal Libraries" explored the methods and the tools that make federal libraries the center of innovation for both the missions of their agencies and for the benefit of all their users.

The Strategic Sourcing Initiative continued throughout the fiscal year with research reports on federal spending on information and efforts to develop further strategic sourcing of information resources for federal agencies.

FEDLINK Fees

The final budget for FY 2015 held membership fees steady for transfer-pay customers to 6 percent on amounts exceeding $100,000; 6.75 percent below $100,000 and 4 percent on amounts equal to or exceeding $1,000,000. Direct-pay fees remained at FY 2009 levels, as did Direct Express fees of 0.75 percent for all participating commercial online information services vendors.

Accounts Receivable and Member Services

FEDLINK processed registrations from federal libraries, information centers, and other federal offices for a total of 327 signed Interagency agreements (IAAs) and more than 844 IAA amendments for agencies that added, adjusted, or ended service funding. FEDLINK executed service requests by generating 3,132 delivery orders that LC/Contracts and Grants issued to vendors.

Transfer-Pay Accounts Payable Services

Staff members efficiently processed vendor invoices and earned approximately $13,000 in discounts for prompt payment of FEDLINK customer invoices. FEDLINK continued to maintain open accounts for five prior years to pay invoices for members. FEDLINK completed the closing of FY 2010. Statements are issued to members for the current year and prior years.

Direct Express Services

The FEDLINK Direct Express Program now includes 94 vendors offering database retrieval services. The program is set up to provide customers procurement and payment options similar to GSA in which the vendors pay a quarterly service fee to FEDLINK based on customer billings for usage.

Budget, Revenue, and Risks Reserves

In FY 2015, FEDLINK Fee Revenue from signed IAAs was approximately $285,000 lower than FY 2014. The expenditures for FY 2015 were approximately $133,000 lower than FY 2014 due to not filling positions, delayed projects, and a reduced research program. FEDLINK's Reserve requirement for FY 2015 continues to be solvent. The program holds reserves for: 1) mandatory requirements for shutdown and bankruptcy risks; 2) continuity of operations requirements for mission essential systems; and 3) compliance risk mitigation initiatives.

National Agricultural Library

U.S. Department of Agriculture, Abraham Lincoln Bldg.,
10301 Baltimore Ave., Beltsville, MD 20705-2351
E-mail agref@nal.usda.gov
World Wide Web http://www.nal.usda.gov

Jennifer Gilbert
Special Assistant to the Director

The U.S. Department of Agriculture's National Agricultural Library (NAL) is one of the world's largest and most accessible agricultural research libraries, offering service directly to the public via its website, http://www.nal.usda.gov.

The library was instituted in 1862 at the same time as the U.S. Department of Agriculture (USDA). It became a national library in 1962 when Congress established it as the primary agricultural information resource of the United States (7 USCS § 3125a). Congress assigned to the library the responsibilities to

- Acquire, preserve, and manage information resources relating to agriculture and allied sciences
- Organize agricultural information products and services and provide them within the United States and internationally
- Plan, coordinate, and evaluate information and library needs relating to agricultural research and education
- Cooperate with and coordinate efforts toward development of a comprehensive agricultural library and information network
- Coordinate the development of specialized subject information services among the agricultural and library information communities

NAL is located in Beltsville, Maryland, near Washington, D.C., on the grounds of USDA's Henry A. Wallace Beltsville Agricultural Research Center. Its 15-story Abraham Lincoln Building is named in honor of the president who created the Department of Agriculture and signed several of the major U.S. laws affecting agriculture.

The library employs about 100 librarians, information specialists, computer specialists, administrators, and clerical personnel, supplemented by about 50 volunteers, contract staff, and cooperators from NAL partnering organizations.

NAL's reputation as one of the world's foremost agricultural libraries is supported and burnished by its expert staff, ongoing leadership in delivering information services, expanding collaborations with other U.S. and international agricultural research and information organizations, and its extensive collection of agricultural information, searchable through AGRICOLA (AGRICultural On-Line Access), the library's bibliographic database.

In 2012 NAL reorganized to better align its functions with its overall strategic plan, which includes simplified access to all NAL content, expansion of digital content, and the integration of scientific data sets and discovery tools.

The Collection

The NAL collection dates to the congressionally approved 1839 purchase of books for the Agricultural Division of the Patent Office, predating the 1862 establishment of USDA itself. Today NAL provides access to billions of pages of agricultural information—an immense collection of scientific books, journals, audiovisuals, reports, theses, artifacts, and images—and to a widening array of digital media, as well as databases and other information resources germane to the broad reach of agriculture-related sciences.

The library's collection contains more than 8 million items, dating from the 16th century to the present, including the most complete repository of USDA publications and the world's most extensive set of materials on the history of U.S. agriculture.

Building the Collection

NAL has primary responsibility for collecting and retaining publications of USDA and its agencies, and it is the only U.S. national library with a legislated mandate to collect in the following disciplines: plant and animal health, welfare, and production; agricultural economics, products, and education; aquaculture; forestry; rural sociology and rural life; family and consumer science; and food science, safety, and nutrition. In addition to collecting as comprehensively as possible in these core subject areas, NAL collects extensively in many related subjects, such as biology, bioinformatics, biochemistry, chemistry, entomology, environmental science, genetics, invasive species, meteorology, natural resources, physics, soil science, sustainability, water quality, and zoology.

Rare and Special Collections

The NAL Rare and Special Collections program emphasizes access to and preservation of rare and unique materials documenting the history of agriculture and related sciences. Items in the library's special collections include rare books, manuscripts, nursery and seed trade catalogs, posters, objects, photographs, and other rare materials documenting agricultural subjects. Materials date from the 1500s to the present and include many international sources. Detailed information about these special collections is available on the NAL website at https://special collections.nal.usda.gov.

Special collections of note include the following:

- The U.S. Department of Agriculture History Collection (https://special collections.nal.usda.gov/usda-history-collection-introductionindex), assembled over 80 years by USDA historians, includes letters, memoranda, reports, and papers of USDA officials, as well as photographs, oral histories, and clippings covering the activities of the department from its founding through the early 1990s.

- The U.S. Department of Agriculture Pomological Watercolor Collection (http://usdawatercolors.nal.usda.gov) includes more than 7,000 detailed, botanically accurate watercolor illustrations of fruit and nut varieties developed by growers or introduced by USDA plant explorers. Created between 1886 and the 1940s, the watercolors served as official documentation of the work of the Office of the Pomologist and were used to create chromolithographs in publications distributed widely by the department. Although created for scientific accuracy, the works are artistic treasures in their own right. The full collection has been digitized and is now available online.

- The Henry G. Gilbert Nursery and Seed Trade Catalog Collection (https://specialcollections.nal.usda.gov/guide-collections/henry-g-gilbert-nursery-and-seed-trade-catalog-collection), begun in 1904 by USDA economic botanist Percy L. Ricker, has grown to comprise more than 200,000 U.S. and foreign catalogs. The earliest items date from the late 1700s, but the collection is strongest from the 1890s to the present. Researchers commonly use the collection to document the introduction of plants to the United States, study economic trends, and illustrate early developments in American landscape design.

- The Rare Book Collection (https://specialcollections.nal.usda.gov/guide-collections/rare-book-collection) highlights agriculture's printed historical record. It covers a wide variety of subjects but is particularly strong in botany, natural history, zoology, and entomology. International in scope, the collection documents early agricultural practices in Britain and Europe, as well as the Americas. Of particular note are the more than 300 books by or about Carl Linnaeus, the "father of taxonomy," including a rare first edition of his 1735 work *Systema Naturae*.

- Manuscript collections (https://specialcollections.nal.usda.gov/guide-collections/index-manuscript-collections), now numbering more than 400, document the story of American agriculture and its influence on the world.

NAL continues to digitize these and other unique materials to share them broadly via its website and has published detailed indexes to the content of many manuscript collections to improve discovery. AGRICOLA, NAL's catalog, includes bibliographic entries for special collection items, manuscripts, and rare books. The library provides in-house research and reference services for its special collections and offers fee-based duplication services.

Preservation/Digitization

NAL is committed to the preservation of its print and non-print collections. It continues to monitor and improve the environmental quality of its stacks to extend the longevity of all materials in the collection. The library has instituted a long-term strategy to ensure the growing body of agricultural information is systematically identified, preserved, and archived.

NAL's digital conversion program has resulted in a growing digital collection of USDA publications and many non-USDA historical materials not restricted by copyright. NAL is in the midst of a large-scale project to digitize agricultural literature and provide online access to the general public. Important and distinctive items were selected from the NAL collection, with an initial focus on USDA-issued publications and nursery and seed trade catalogs. In 2014 NAL digitized and created citation information for 38,698 items. Publications are accessible at https://archive.org/details/usdanationalagriculturallibrary.

NAL Digital Collections

NAL has undertaken several projects to digitize, store, and provide online access to more than 1.5 million pages of historic print documents and images, primarily from USDA. In an effort to unify all digital content, the library launched an interface for the NAL Digital Collections (http://naldc.nal.usda.gov) accompanied by policies for collecting, storing, and making publicly available federally funded research outcomes published by USDA scientists and researchers. Long-range plans include collecting, maintaining, and providing access to a broad range of agricultural information in a wide variety of digital formats. The result will be a perpetual, reliable, publicly accessible collection of digital documents, data sets, images, and other items relating to agriculture. As of the end of 2014 NAL's digital repository of full-text content comprised nine collections, including nearly 50,000 peer-reviewed journal articles authored by USDA researchers, and more than 30,000 historical documents and reports. The public downloads approximately 3 million full-text items each year.

AGRICOLA

AGRICOLA comprises an online catalog and citation database of NAL collections and delivers worldwide access to agricultural information through its searchable Web interface (http://agricola.nal.usda.gov). Alternatively, users can access AGRICOLA on a fee basis through several commercial vendors, or they can subscribe to the complete AGRICOLA file, also on a fee basis, from the National Technical Information Service within the U.S. Department of Commerce.

The AGRICOLA database covers materials in all formats, including printed works from the 16th century onward. The records describe publications and resources encompassing all aspects of agriculture and allied disciplines. AGRICOLA, updated daily, includes the following two components:

- NAL Public Access Catalog, containing more than 1 million citations to books, audiovisual materials, serial titles, and other materials in the NAL collection. (The catalog also contains some bibliographic records for items cataloged by other libraries but not held in the NAL collection.)
- NAL Article Citation Database, consisting of more than 3 million citations to serial articles, book chapters, reports, and reprints. NAL has chosen and is implementing automated indexing/text analytics software to produce its Article Citation Database. This application combines semantic analysis, machine learning, and human rules to automatically assign subject terms to journal articles.

LCA Digital Commons

NAL launched the LCA Digital Commons, a life cycle inventory database, to address the lack of information resources regarding the life cycle of agricultural products. The LCA Digital Commons provides, through a fully searchable Web interface (http://www.lcacommons.gov), peer-reviewed crop production data sets for commodity crops measuring the material and energy flows to and from the environment.

Information Management and Information Technology

Over the past quarter century, NAL has applied increasingly sophisticated information technology to support the ever more complex and demanding information needs of researchers, practitioners, policymakers, and the general public. Technological developments spearheaded by the library date back to the 1940s and 1950s, when NAL Director Ralph Shaw invented "electronic machines" such as the photo charger, rapid selector, and photo clerk. Over the years NAL has made numerous technological improvements, from automating collections information to delivering full-text and image collections digitally on the Internet.

NAL has fully implemented the Voyager integrated library management system from Ex Libris, Ltd. The system supports ordering, receiving, and invoice processing for purchases; creating and maintaining indexing and cataloging records for AGRICOLA; circulating print holdings; and providing a Web-based online catalog for public searching and browsing of the collection. In addition, the system is fully integrated with an automated interlibrary loan and document delivery system by Relais International that streamlines services and provides desktop delivery of needed materials.

English-Spanish Agricultural Thesaurus and Glossary

NAL is known for its expertise in developing and using a thesaurus, or controlled vocabulary, a critical component of effective digital information systems. The NAL Agricultural Thesaurus (NALT) (http://agclass.nal.usda.gov/agt.shtml) is a hierarchical vocabulary of agricultural and biological terms, organized according to 17 subject categories. It comprises primarily biological nomenclature, with additional terminology supporting the physical and social sciences.

The 15th edition of NALT, issued in 2016, contains more than 120,600 terms and nearly 4,950 definitions. Taxonomic terms from every biological kingdom were expanded in this edition, along with common names of species. Plant species were added following taxonomic verification by the Germplasm Resources Information Network (GRIN). Terminology for genetic soil types was modified according to *USDA Keys to Soil Taxonomy, Twelfth Edition,* 2014. Fish taxonomy was expanded following taxonomic verification from Fishbase. Other subject areas expanded include terms in chromatography, receptors, bacteria, fungi, breeds of animals, endangered species, insects, chemicals, enzymes, economics, food, wood, and forestry.

NALT continues to be available as Linked Open Data. NAL can now connect its vocabulary to other linked data vocabularies, which, in turn, will connect NALT to the larger semantic Web. Such interconnections will help programmers create meaningful relationships that will make it easier to locate related content.

Associated with NALT, the NAL Glossary provides definitions of agricultural terms. The 2015 edition contains 4,488 definitions, ranging across agriculture and its many ancillary subjects, an increase of 667 definitions from last year. Most definitions are composed by NALT staff. (Suggestions for new terms or definitions can be sent by e-mail to agref@ars.usda.gov.)

NAL publishes Spanish-language versions of the thesaurus and glossary, which carry the names *Tesauro Agrícola* and *Glosario,* respectively. Both are updated concurrently with the annual release of the English-language version. The 2016 edition of the Spanish-language version of NALT contains more than 96,700 terms and 4,880 definitions.

The thesaurus and glossary are primarily used for indexing and for improving the retrieval of agricultural information, but they can also be used by students (from fifth grade up), teachers, writers, translators, and others who are seeking precise definitions of words from the agricultural sciences. Users can download all four publications—English and Spanish thesaurus and glossary—in both machine-readable (MARC 21, RDF-SKOS, and XML) and human-readable (doc, pdf) formats at http://agclass.nal.usda.gov/download.shtml.

Library Services

NAL serves the agricultural information needs of customers through a combination of Web-based and traditional library services, including reference, document delivery, and information center services. The NAL website offers access to a wide variety of full-text resources, as well as online access to reference and document delivery services. In 2014 the library provided nearly 8,000 reference transactions, fulfilled more than 1.2 million full-text article requests, and satisfied more than 5,000 requests for interlibrary loans.

The main reading room in the library's Beltsville facility features a walk-up service desk, access to an array of digital information resources (including full-text scientific journals), current periodicals, and an on-site request service for materials from NAL's collection. Services are available 8:30 to 4:30 Monday through Friday, except federal holidays.

NAL's reference services are accessible online using the Ask a Question form on the NAL Web pages; by use of e-mail addressed to agref@ars.usda.gov; by telephone at 301-504-5755; or by mail to Research Services, National Agricultural Library ARS/USDA, 10301 Baltimore Avenue, Beltsville, MD 20705. Requesters receive assistance from Research Services staff in all areas and aspects of agriculture, but staff particularly answer questions, provide research guidance, and make presentations on topics not addressed by the seven subject-focused information centers of the library.

NAL's seven information centers are reliable sources of comprehensive, science-based information on key aspects of U.S. agriculture, providing timely, accurate, and in-depth coverage of their specialized subject areas. Their expert staff offer extensive Web-based information resources and advanced reference services. Each NAL information center has its own website and is a partner in AgNIC.

- The Alternative Farming Systems Information Center (AFSIC) (http:// afsic.nal.usda.gov) specializes in identifying and accessing information relating to farming methods that maintain the health and productivity of the entire farming enterprise, including the world's natural resources. This focus includes sustainable and alternative agricultural systems, crops, and livestock.

- The Animal Welfare Information Center (AWIC) (http://awic.nal.usda. gov) provides scientific information and referrals to help ensure the proper care and treatment of animals used in biomedical research, testing, teaching, and exhibitions, and by animal dealers. Among its varied outreach activities, the center conducts workshops for researchers on meeting the information requirements of the Animal Welfare Act.

- The Food and Nutrition Information Center (FNIC) (http://fnic.nal.usda. gov) provides credible, accurate, and practical resources for nutrition and health professionals, educators, government personnel, and consumers. FNIC maintains a staff of registered dietitians who can answer questions on food and human nutrition.

- The Food Safety Research Information Office (FSRIO) (http://fsrio.nal. usda.gov) delivers information on publicly funded—and, to the extent possible, privately funded—food safety research initiatives. Its Research Projects Database, with more than 8,500 projects cited, provides ready access to the largest searchable collection of food safety research being conducted within U.S. and international governmental agencies.

- The National Invasive Species Information Center (NISIC) (http://www. invasivespeciesinfo.gov) delivers accessible, accurate, referenced, up-to-date, and comprehensive information on invasive species drawn from federal, state, local, and international sources.

- The Rural Information Center (RIC) (http://ric.nal.usda.gov) assists local officials, organizations, businesses, and rural residents working to maintain the vitality of rural areas. It collects and disseminates information on such diverse topics as community economic development, small business development, health care, finance, housing, environment, quality of life, community leadership, and education.

- The Water Quality Information Center (WQIC) (http://wqic.nal.usda.gov) collects, organizes, and communicates scientific findings, educational methodologies, and public policy issues relating to water quality and agriculture.

In addition to these information centers, NAL manages the popular Nutrition. gov website (http://www.nutrition.gov) in collaboration with other USDA agencies and the Department of Health and Human Services. This site provides vetted, science-based nutrition information for the general consumer and highlights the latest in nutrition news and tools from across federal government agencies. The site is an important tool for disseminating the work of multiple federal agencies in a national obesity prevention effort. A team of registered dietitians at NAL's Food and Nutrition Information Center maintains Nutrition.gov and answers questions on food and nutrition issues.

Web-Based Products and Services

The NAL websites, which encompass nearly all the content and services described here, collectively receive millions of pageviews per month from people seeking agricultural information.

DigiTop

DigiTop, USDA's Digital Desktop Library, delivers the full text of thousands of journals and hundreds of newspapers worldwide, provides 17 agriculturally significant citation databases, supplies a range of digital reference resources, and offers focused, personalized services. Navigator is a component of DigiTop that allows cross-searching of multiple bibliographic databases. This system includes AGRICOLA; AGRIS; BIOSIS; CAB Abstracts; Fish, Fisheries, and Aquatic Biodiversity Worldwide; Food Science and Technology Abstracts; GEOBASE; GeoRef; MEDLINE; Wildlife and Ecology Studies Worldwide; Scopus; and Zoological Record. The Navigator service allows researchers to access nearly 79 million records at once and is updated weekly. DigiTop is available to the entire USDA workforce worldwide—more than 100,000 people—around the clock. NAL staff provide help desk and reference services, continuous user education, and training for DigiTop users.

Document Delivery Services

NAL's document delivery operation responds to thousands of requests each year from USDA employees and from libraries and organizations around the world. NAL uses the Relais Enterprise document request and delivery system to support document delivery. With Relais fully integrated with the Voyager library system, with DigiTop, and with other Open-URL and ISO ILL compliant systems, NAL customers can request materials or check on the status of their requests via the Web, and the needed materials can easily be delivered electronically. Document requests can also be submitted via OCLC (NAL's symbol is AGL) and DOCLINE (NAL's libid is MDUNAL). Visit http://www.nal.usda.gov/services/request.shtml for details.

Networks of Cooperation

The NAL collection and information resources are supplemented by networks of cooperation with other institutions, including arrangements with agricultural libraries at U.S. land-grant universities, other U.S. national libraries, agricultural libraries in other countries, and libraries of the United Nations and other international organizations.

AgNIC

The library serves as secretariat for the Agriculture Network Information Center (AgNIC) Alliance, a voluntary, collaborative partnership that hosts a distributed network of discipline-specific agricultural information websites at http://www.agnic.org. AgNIC provides access to high-quality agricultural information selected by its 53 partner members, which include land-grant universities, NAL, and other institutions globally. Together they offer more than 80 information and subject specialists, more than 60 topics covered comprehensively, and links to more than 5 million full-text and bibliographic items.

AGLINET

Through the Agricultural Libraries Network (AGLINET), NAL serves as the U.S. node of an international agricultural information system that brings together agricultural libraries with strong regional or country coverage and other specialized collections. NAL functions as a gateway to U.S. agricultural libraries and resources, fulfilling requests for information via reciprocal agreements with several other libraries, information centers, and consortia. As an AGLINET member, NAL agrees to provide low-cost interlibrary loan and photocopy service to other AGLINET libraries. Most materials requested through AGLINET are delivered digitally, although reproductions via fiche or photocopy are used when appropriate. AGLINET is administered by the Food and Agriculture Organization of the United Nations.

National Library of Medicine

8600 Rockville Pike, Bethesda, MD 20894
301-496-6308, 888-346-3656, fax 301-496-4450
E-mail publicinfo@nlm.nih.gov
World Wide Web http://www.nlm.nih.gov

Kathleen Cravedi
Director, Office of Communications and Public Liaison

Melanie Modlin
Deputy Director, Office of Communications and Public Liaison

The National Library of Medicine (NLM) is one of the 27 Institutes and Centers of the National Institutes of Health (NIH). Founded in 1836 as the Library of the Surgeon General of the Army, NLM has evolved into the world's largest biomedical library.

In today's increasingly digital world, NLM carries out its mission of enabling biomedical research, supporting health care and public health, and promoting healthy behavior by

- Building and providing electronic information resources used billions of times each year by millions of scientists, health professionals, and members of the public
- Creating and maintaining information systems that provide free public access to results of biomedical research supported by NIH and by other government and private funders
- Supporting and conducting research, development, and training in biomedical informatics, computational biology, data science, and health information technology
- Coordinating a 6,000-member National Network of Libraries of Medicine that promotes and provides access to health information in communities across the United States

Through its information systems, a cutting-edge informatics research portfolio, and extensive partnerships, NLM plays an essential role in catalyzing and supporting the translation of basic science into new treatments, new products, improved practice, useful decision support for health professionals and patients, and effective disaster and emergency preparedness and response.

The range of information that NLM organizes and disseminates is enormous, including genetic, genomic, biochemical, and toxicological data; images; published and unpublished research results; decision support resources; scientific and health data standards; informatics tools for system developers; and health information for the public. Scientists, health professionals, and the public can search or download information directly from an NLM website, find it via an Internet search engine, or use an app that provides value-added access to NLM data. Thousands of commercial and nonprofit system developers regularly use the applications programming interfaces (APIs) that NLM provides to fuel private sector innovation.

Delivering High-Quality Information Services

Central to NLM services is the world's largest, continually expanding collection of biomedical literature in all media and a broad array of authoritative digital databases encompassing information for scientists, health professionals, the public, and the librarians and information specialists who serve them. NLM develops and uses sophisticated information systems to support the complex operations necessary to acquire, describe, index, archive, and provide rapid access to physical and digital materials. Special attention is given to developing systems to build and refine electronic databases and services and to responding to changes in user needs and behaviors.

In 2014 NLM greatly expanded the quantity and range of high-quality information readily available to scientists, health professionals, and the general public. Advances included:

- The indexing of more than 765,000 new journal articles for PubMed/MED-LINE, NLM's most heavily used database, which contains more than 24 million references to articles in the biomedical and life sciences journals and delivers information to about 2 million users a day
- Growth in the PubMed Central (PMC) digital archive, which now provides public access to the full-text versions of more than 3.3 million research articles, including those produced by NIH-funded researchers
- Expansion of ClinicalTrials.gov, which now includes more than 181,000 registered studies and summary results for more than 15,700 trials, including many not available elsewhere
- A doubling of the number of tests in the Genetic Testing Registry, where users can find detailed information on more than 33,000 genetic tests
- More than 20 percent growth in the database of Genotypes and Phenotypes (dbGaP), which connects individual-level genomic data with individual-level clinical information and now contains nearly 600 studies involving more than 840,000 people
- Improved dissemination methods and new tools to aid the use of the U.S. clinical terminology standards required for interoperability of electronic health records

NLM also continued to expand access to its rare and unique historical collections by digitizing rare books, manuscripts, pictures, and historical films. In 2014 a total of 2,460 printed historic books, 4,319 historic images, and 895 manuscripts were digitized and added to NLM's Digital Collections, a free online archive of biomedical books and videos. These collections are heavily used by scholars, the media, and the general public.

As the percentage of users accessing NLM databases with mobile phones and tablets continues to rise, NLM is redesigning many of its Web interfaces so that the information display adjusts automatically to the size of the device. In 2014 the library released new "responsive design" versions of AIDS*info,* the Department of Health and Human Services (HHS) authoritative source of HIV/AIDS treatment and prevention information, and of DailyMed, which includes Food and

Drug Administration (FDA)-approved structured label information for medications marketed in the United States. NLM continued to be a leading player in social media among HHS agencies with active Facebook, Twitter, Flickr, Pinterest, and YouTube accounts (including the very popular @medlineplus Twitter feed and a Spanish-language counterpart), several online newsletters, and its National Network of Libraries of Medicine, which covers the United States and hosts 8 Facebook pages, 10 Twitter feeds, and 12 blogs. NLM is consistently ranked among the most liked, most followed, and most mentioned organizations among small government agencies with social media accounts.

Promoting Public Access to Information

NLM has extensive outreach programs to enhance awareness of its diverse information services among biomedical researchers, health professionals, librarians, patients, and the public. To improve access to high-quality health information, NLM works with the National Network of Libraries of Medicine and has formal partnerships such as Partners in Information Access for the Public Health Workforce and the Environmental Health Information Outreach Partnership with Historically Black Colleges and Universities, tribal colleges, and other minority serving institutions.

The member institutions of the National Network of Libraries of Medicine are valued partners in ensuring that health information, including NLM's many services, is available to scientists, health professionals, and the public. The network is coordinated by eight regional medical libraries and is composed of academic health sciences libraries, hospital libraries, public libraries, and community-based organizations.

In 2014 dozens of community-based projects were funded nationwide to enhance awareness of and access to health information, including in disaster and emergency situations, and to address health literacy issues. As part of its outreach efforts, NLM continually solicits feedback from users on how existing resources can be improved.

NLM also fosters more informal community partnerships and uses exhibitions, the media, and new technologies in its efforts to reach underserved populations and to promote interest among young people in careers in science, medicine, and technology. The library continues to expand its successful traveling exhibitions program as another means to enhance access to its services and promote interest in careers in science and medicine. Examples of these exhibitions include "Every Necessary Care and Attention: George Washington and Medicine" and "Surviving and Thriving: AIDS, Politics, and Culture."

With assistance from other NIH components and outside partners, NLM continues to increase the distribution of *NIH MedlinePlus* magazine, and its Spanish-language counterpart, *NIH Salud*. The magazine, which is also available online in Spanish and English, is distributed to doctors' offices, health science libraries, Congress, the media, federally supported community health centers, select hospital emergency and waiting rooms, and other locations where the public receives health services.

Information Systems, Standards, Research Tools

NLM's advanced information services have long benefitted from its intramural research and development (R&D) programs. The library has two organizations that conduct advanced R&D on different aspects of biomedical informatics: the Lister Hill National Center for Biomedical Communications (LHC) and the National Center for Biotechnology Information (NCBI). Both apply their research results to the development of new information services and tools for scientists, informatics researchers, and software developers.

LHC, established in 1968, conducts and supports research in such areas as the development and dissemination of health information technology standards; the capture, processing, dissemination, and use of high-quality imaging data; medical language processing; high-speed access to biomedical information; and advanced technology for emergency and disaster management.

NCBI, created in 1988, conducts R&D on the representation, integration, and retrieval of molecular biology data and biomedical literature, in addition to providing an integrated, genomic information resource consisting of more than 40 databases for biomedical researchers at NIH and around the world. NCBI's development of large-scale data integration techniques with advanced information systems is key to its expanding ability to support the accelerated pace of research made possible by new technologies such as next-generation DNA sequencing, microarrays, and small molecule screening. GenBank at NCBI, in collaboration with partners in Britain and Japan, is the world's largest annotated collection of publicly available DNA sequences. GenBank contains 175 million sequences from more than 310,000 different species. NCBI's Web services for access to these data provide the information and analytic tools for researchers to accelerate the rate of genomic discovery and facilitate the translation of basic science advances into new diagnostics and treatments.

NLM was also a pioneer in developing and sharing novel medical language resources and innovative algorithms and tools, including the UMLS (Unified Medical Language System), MetaMap, Medical Text Indexer (MTI), and SemRep, to advance research in natural language understanding and biomedical text mining. This research has been applied to indexing, information retrieval, question answering, and literature-based discovery to assist NLM's high-volume data creation and service operations, to help other NIH components to identify and summarize new knowledge useful in updating clinical guidelines, and to add standard terminology and codes to clinical and clinical research data to enhance their research value. NLM has many joint research activities with other NIH components and other federal agencies, including collaborations with FDA to use natural language processing and NLM terminology resources to extract adverse event data from publications indexed for PubMed/MEDLINE and drug-drug interactions from product labels submitted by manufacturers.

NLM has also made advances that will facilitate health information exchange and meaningful use of electronic health records (EHRs). NLM researchers have developed advanced and heavily used APIs for medication data, nomenclature, and high-quality pill images, including information submitted to FDA; produced novel algorithms for validating vocabulary components of electronic clinical quality measure specifications in cooperation with the Centers for Medicare and

Medicaid Services; and analyzed frequency data from multiple private healthcare organizations and the Veterans Health Administration to produce manageable subsets of large standard clinical vocabularies. They have also developed effective techniques for mapping clinical vocabularies to administrative code sets and have established partnerships to test the use and impact of personal health records.

NLM's Personal Health Record (PHR) project has developed open source software components that can be used by PHR and EHR developers to provide capabilities that help individuals to manage health and health care for themselves and their families. The strong use of vocabulary standards in the NLM PHR software components enables many computer-generated features such as personalized reminders, automatic calculation of health measures, and direct links to such information sources as MedlinePlus. The use of standards in these components will also enable the direct importing of the consumer's own data from clinical sources.

Administration

The director of the Library, Donald A. B. Lindberg, M.D., is guided in matters of policy by a board of regents consisting of 10 appointed and 11 ex officio members.

Table 1 / Selected NLM Statistics*

Library Operations	Volume
Collection (book and non-book)	26,648,261
Items cataloged	18,755
Serial titles received	17,439
Articles indexed for MEDLINE	765,850
Circulation requests processed	259,285
For interlibrary loan	188,912
For on-site users	70,373
MEDLINE/PubMed Searches	2,650,894,898
Budget Authority	$328,000,000
Staff	830

*For fiscal year ending September 30, 2014

National Technical Information Service

U.S. Department of Commerce, Alexandria, VA 22312
800-553-NTIS (6847) or 703-605-6000
World Wide Web http://www.ntis.gov

The National Technical Information Service (NTIS) is the nation's largest and most comprehensive source of government-funded scientific, technical, engineering, and business information produced or sponsored by U.S. and international government sources. NTIS is a federal agency within the U.S. Department of Commerce.

Since 1945 the NTIS mission has been to operate a central U.S. government access point for scientific and technical information useful to American industry and government. NTIS maintains a permanent archive of this declassified information for researchers, businesses, and the public to access quickly and easily. Release of the information is intended to promote U.S. economic growth and development and to increase U.S. competitiveness in the world market.

The NTIS collection of approximately 3 million titles covers more than 350 subject areas and contains products available in various formats. Such information includes reports describing research conducted or sponsored by federal agencies and their contractors; statistical and business information; multimedia training programs; databases developed by federal agencies; and technical reports prepared by research organizations worldwide. NTIS maintains a permanent repository of its information products.

More than 200 U.S. government agencies contribute to the NTIS collection, including the National Aeronautics and Space Administration; the Environmental Protection Agency; the departments of Agriculture, Commerce, Defense, Energy, Health and Human Services, Homeland Security, Interior, Labor, Treasury, Veterans Affairs, Housing and Urban Development, Education, and Transportation; and numerous other agencies. International contributors include Canada, Japan, Britain, and several European countries.

NTIS on the Web

NTIS offers Web-based access to information on government scientific and technical research products. Visitors to http://www.ntis.gov can search the entire collection dating back to 1964 free of charge. NTIS provides many of the technical reports for purchase on CD, paper copies, or downloaded pdf files. RSS feeds of recently catalogued materials are available in major subject categories.

NTIS Database

The NTIS Database offers unparalleled bibliographic coverage of U.S. government and worldwide government-sponsored research information products acquired by NTIS since 1964. Its contents represent hundreds of billions of research dollars and cover a range of important topics including agriculture, biotechnology, business, communication, energy, engineering, the environment, health and safety, medicine, research and development, science, space, technology, and transportation.

The NTIS Database can be leased directly from NTIS and can also be accessed through several commercial services. To lease the NTIS Database directly from NTIS, contact the NTIS Office of Product Management at 703-605-6515.

NTIS National Technical Reports Library

The National Technical Reports Library (NTRL) enhances accessibility to the NTIS technical reports collection. Subscription rates are based on institutional FTE levels. NTRL operates on a system interface that allows users to do queries on the large NTIS bibliographic database. The intent is to broadly expand and improve access to more than 2.5 million bibliographic records (pre-1960 to the present) and more than 700,000 full-text documents in pdf format that are directly linked to that bibliographic database.

NTIS offers several valuable research-oriented database products. To find out more about accessing the databases, visit http://www.ntis.gov/products/ntrl.

AGRICOLA

As one of the most comprehensive sources of U.S. agricultural and life sciences information, the AGRICOLA (Agricultural Online Access) Database contains bibliographic records for documents acquired by the U.S. Department of Agriculture's National Agricultural Library. It is available at http://www.ntis.gov/products/databases/agricola.

Energy Science and Technology

The Energy Science and Technology Database (EDB) is a multidisciplinary file containing worldwide references to basic and applied scientific and technical research literature. The information is collected for use by government managers, researchers at the national laboratories, and other research efforts sponsored by the U.S. Department of Energy, and the results of this research are transferred to the public. The database is available at http://www.ntis.gov/products/databases/energy-science-technology.

FEDRIP

The Federal Research in Progress Database (FEDRIP) provides access to information about ongoing federally funded projects in such fields as the physical sciences, engineering, and life sciences. To access FEDRIP, go to http://www.ntis.gov/products/databases/federal-research-in-progress.

Online Subscriptions

NTIS offers quick, convenient online access, on a subscription basis, to the following resources:

U.S. Export Administration Regulations

U.S. Export Administration Regulations (EAR) provides the latest rules controlling the export of U.S. dual-use commodities, technology, and software. Step by step, EAR explains when an export license is necessary and when it is not, how to obtain an export license, policy changes as they are issued, new restrictions on exports to certain countries and of certain types of items, and where to obtain further help.

This information is available through NTIS in loose-leaf form, on CD-ROM, and online. An e-mail update notification service is also available.

World News Connection

World News Connection (WNC) was an NTIS online news service accessible via the World Wide Web. It made available English-language translations of time-sensitive news and information culled from non-U.S. media in more than 100 countries. WNC was provided by the Open Source Center (OSC), operated by the Central Intelligence Agency (CIA), and its content was updated throughout every government business day. It was made available by NTIS through the Dialog Corporation. The service ceased operation at the end of 2013.

Special Subscription Services

NTIS eAlerts

More than 1,000 new titles are added to the NTIS collection every week. NTIS prepares a list of search criteria that is run against all new studies and research and development reports in 16 subject areas. An NTIS eAlert provides a twice-monthly information briefing service, by e-mail, covering a wide range of technology topics. For more information, call the NTIS Subscriptions Department at 703-605-6060.

NTIS Selected Research Service

NTIS Selected Research Service (SRS) is a tailored information service that delivers complete electronic copies of government publications based on customers' needs, automatically, within a few weeks of announcement by NTIS. SRS includes the full bibliographic information in XML and HTML formats. Users choose between Standard SRS (selecting one or more of the 320 existing subject areas) or Custom SRS, which creates a new subject area to meet their particular needs. Custom SRS requires a one-time fee to cover the cost of strategy development and computer programming to set up a profile. Except for this fee, the cost of Custom SRS is the same as the Standard SRS. Through this ongoing subscription service, customers download copies of new reports pertaining to their field(s) of interest as NTIS obtains the reports. To place an order, call 800-363-2068 or 703-605-6060.

This service is also available in CD-ROM format as Science and Technology on CD, which delivers the documents digitized and stored in pdf format.

Federal Science Repository Service

Collections of scientific and technical documents, images, videos, and other content represent the mission and work of an agency or other institution. To help preserve these collections, NTIS formed a joint venture with Information International Associates, Inc. of Oak Ridge, Tennessee, to develop for federal agencies a searchable, digital Federal Science Repository Service (FSRS). FSRS provides a supporting infrastructure, long-term storage, security, interface design, and content management and operational expertise. An agency can utilize this entire service or select components, resulting in the design of an agency-specific repository that serves as a distinct gateway to its content. For more information, visit http://www.ntis.gov/products/fsrs.

NTIS Customer Service

NTIS's automated systems make shopping online at NTIS safe and secure. Electronic document storage is fully integrated with NTIS's order-taking process, allowing it to provide rapid reproduction for the most recent additions to the NTIS document collection. Most orders for shipment are filled and delivered anywhere in the United States in five to seven business days. Rush service is available for an additional fee.

Key NTIS Contacts for Ordering

Order by Phone

Sales Desk   800-553-6847 or 703-605-6000
8:00 A.M.–6:00 P.M. Eastern time, Monday–Friday

Subscriptions   800-363-2068 or 703-605-6060
8:30 A.M.–5:00 P.M. Eastern time, Monday–Friday
TDD (hearing impaired only)   703-487-4639
8:30 A.M.–5:00 P.M. Eastern time, Monday–Friday

Order by Fax

24 hours a day, seven days a week   703-605-6900

Order by Mail

National Technical Information Service
5301 Shawnee Rd.
Alexandria, VA 22312

RUSH Service (available for an additional fee)   800-553-6847 or 703-605-6000
Note: If requesting RUSH Service, please do not mail your order

Order Online

Direct and secure online ordering   http://www.ntis.gov

United States Government Publishing Office

732 North Capitol St. N.W., Washington, DC 20401
World Wide Web http://www.gpo.gov

Gary Somerset

Media and Public Relations Manager
202-512-1957, e-mail gsomerset@gpo.gov

The U.S. Government Printing Office (GPO) was created when President James Buchanan signed Joint Resolution 25 on June 23, 1860. GPO opened its doors for business nine months later on March 4, 1861, the same day Abraham Lincoln took the oath of office to become the 16th president of the United States. On that day GPO began operation in buildings purchased by Congress, at the same address it occupies today.

A historic moment occurred for GPO in December 2014 when President Barack Obama signed into law a bill changing the agency's name to the U.S. Government *Publishing* Office. The new name reflects the increasingly prominent role that GPO plays in providing access to government information in digital formats through GPO's Federal Digital System (FDsys), apps, e-books, and related technologies. The information needs of Congress, federal agencies, and the public have evolved beyond only print, and GPO has transformed itself to meet its customers' needs.

Under Title 44 of the United States Code, GPO is responsible for the production and distribution of information products for all three branches of the federal government. These include the official publications of Congress, federal agencies, and the courts. Today GPO provides products in print and a variety of digital forms, all of which are born digital. In addition GPO produces passports for the Department of State and secure credentials for many government agencies.

As the federal government's official, digital, secure resource for gathering, producing, cataloging, providing access to, and preserving published information in all forms, GPO has disseminated millions of publications to the public.

GPO's Superintendent of Documents and its Library Services and Content Management (LSCM) organizations administer and manage the four programs required by Title 44:

- The Federal Depository Library Program (FDLP)
- Cataloging and indexing (C&I)
- Distributing government publications to the International Exchange Service
- The By-Law Program, under which certain government publications are distributed to members of Congress and to other government agencies as mandated by law

FDLP dates back to 1813 when Congress first authorized legislation to ensure the provision of certain congressional documents to selected universities, historical societies, and state libraries. At that time, the secretary of state was responsible for distributing publications. In 1857 the secretary of the interior assumed oversight of printing and the designation of depositories. In the Printing Act of 1895 the governance of the depository program was transferred to the Office of the Superintendent of Documents at GPO. Duties remained largely unchanged until 1993, when Public Law 103-40, the Government Printing Office Electronic Information Access Enhancement Act, amended GPO's duties to not only provide public access to printed publications but to Internet-accessible publications as well. Two centuries after the start of FDLP, the program continues to serve a vital need of the public through the partnership with federal depository libraries located in nearly every congressional district.

GPO is obviously a much different agency in the digital age than it was years ago. While its name has changed, its mission—"Keeping America Informed" is as important and relevant as ever. FDLP and GPO's information dissemination programs are examples of the agency's longstanding commitment to permanent public access to U.S. government information.

Collaboration

Digital Partnerships with Federal Depository Libraries

Since 1997 GPO has developed strategic partnerships with federal depository libraries and other federal agencies to increase access to electronic federal information. All branches of federal government are transitioning away from print, and federal materials are coming to GPO for publishing. This is due to budgetary pressures, open government initiatives, and increasing access to electronic solutions.

One avenue to address this has been to develop strategic partnerships to ensure permanent public access to electronic content, assist depositories in providing access to electronic material, and help libraries better manage their depository collections. Partnerships also allow GPO to take advantage of the expertise and services of federal depository librarians and federal agencies.

Partnership Updates

GPO currently maintains partnerships with sixteen depository libraries, eight federal agencies, and two institutions. During fiscal year (FY) 2014 LSCM signed three new partnership agreements:

- University of North Texas (UNT)—This partnership ensures permanent public access to the university's large current and future digital collections of U.S. government content that are within scope of FDLP. These collections now contain approximately 50,000 federal government information products on a wide range of interesting topics. Notable examples are World War II newsmaps; documents on early aircraft, engines, and more from the National Advisory Committee for Aeronautics; and annual reports from the U.S. Department of Agriculture's experiment stations from 1901 to 1954. Under the agreement, GPO guarantees public access to these materials in perpetuity.
- University of Colorado, Boulder—This is a cooperative cataloging partnership. The university is creating bibliographic records for historic publications from the U.S. Geological Survey Bulletins series and the Bureau of Mines Reports of Investigations series. GPO will enhance the records by

verifying the Superintendent of Documents Classification System (SuDoc) number and performing needed authority work to the subject headings and corporate names. The records will then be available through GPO's Catalog of U.S. Government Publications (CGP) and OCLC.

- Boston Public Library (BPL)—In commemoration of the 50th anniversary of the release of the Warren Commission report on the assassination of President John F. Kennedy, GPO made the complete report and the 26 volumes of hearings testimony available on FDsys through a partnership with BPL. The hearing transcripts were digitized by BPL. This partnership ensures permanent public access to Warren Commission resources.

During FY 2014 LSCM renewed one partnership:

- University of Illinois at Chicago—This partnership ensures permanent public access to the content in DOSFAN, a digital library of electronically archived information produced by the U.S. Department of State from 1990 to 1997 that includes the archived websites of the U.S. Arms Control and Disarmament Agency and the U.S. Information Agency.

Work continued on several cooperative cataloging partnerships:

- University of Florida—LSCM's partnership with the University of Florida combines cooperative cataloging and permanent public access to digitized content. As material is digitized, the university will share bibliographic records with GPO. Records will be added to CGP, and records for the digitized versions will be created with persistent URLs (PURLs). During FY 2014 work was completed on more than 1,600 bibliographic records for titles from the National Recovery Administration.

- University of Iowa—LSCM completed work to convert the University of Iowa's Dublin Core records for their digitized poster collection to 1,454 MARC records. Each poster was also assigned a PURL, and these records are available through CGP.

- University of Montana—LSCM began working with the university's Mansfield Library in 2011 to add bibliographic records to CGP for historic U.S. Forest Service publications. Mansfield Library staff members create bibliographic records for Forest Service publications and submit them to LSCM. Cataloging and classification staff at LSCM verify the SuDoc class and item number and add subject and corporate name headings to the records. As a result of this partnership, more than 1,900 Forest Service records have been added to CGP.

- University of North Texas—LSCM's partnership with the university combines cooperative cataloging and permanent public access to digitized content. During FY 2014 LSCM staff created or updated bibliographic records for titles in the following university digital collections: Federal Register, Congressional Record, World War I, Government Documents General, World War II Newsmaps, and U.S. Experiment Station Reports.

GPO and DPLA

GPO also developed a new partnership with the Digital Public Library of America (DPLA), a repository of digitized content from U.S. libraries, archives, and museums, all available to the public free of charge. In September 2014 GPO and DPLA partnered to increase public access to government information made available through CGP. More than 150,000 records from CGP are available to the public via the DPLA website (http://dp.la). Examples of records include the federal budget; federal laws, such as the Patient Protection and Affordable Care Act; federal regulations; transcripts of congressional hearings; and reports and other documents. GPO continuously adds records to CGP, which will also be available through DPLA, increasing public discoverability of and access to federal government information. GPO adds approximately 1,000 new records to DPLA each month.

During the year LSCM staff participated in and collaborated with a number of outside groups in support of FDLP and the Cataloging and Indexing Program, including CENDI and the CENDI Policy Working Group (CENDI is an interagency working group of senior scientific and technical information managers representing 14 U.S. federal agencies): the CENDI Digitization Specifications Working Group, Ex Libris Users of North America, the Federal Agencies Digitization Guidelines Initiative (FADGI) Preservation Working Group, the FADGI Audio-Visual Working Group, the FADGI Still Image Digitization Working Group, the FADGI Still Image File Format Working Group, the Federal Library and Information Network (FEDLINK), the American Indian Libraries Initiative, the Federal Web Archiving Coordination Group (National Archives and Records Administration, Library of Congress, and GPO), the International Internet Preservation Consortium, the National Digital Strategy Advisory Board, OCLC, the Program for Cooperative Cataloging (Library of Congress), the Science.gov Alliance, the Society of American Archivists, and the Society for Imaging Science and Technology.

Key GPO Tools

Federal Digital System (FDsys)

GPO's Federal Digital System (FDsys) (http://www.fdsys.gov) provides free online access to official publications from the three branches of the federal government. The content in FDsys is available in multiple formats including pdf, XML, audio, and photographs. FDsys provides access to digitized historical content and serial publications that are updated daily.

GPO adds content to FDsys regularly and continuously implements enhancements to system functionality. FDsys offers the public access to approximately 50 collections of government information, and more than 10 million documents are indexed by the FDsys search engine. As of September 2014 FDsys provided access to more than 856,000 searchable online titles and received an average of 34 million retrievals a month.

Catalog of U.S. Government Publications (CGP)

Under the requirements of sections 1710 and 1711 of Title 44, GPO is charged with cataloging a comprehensive index of public documents issued or published by the federal government that are not confidential in character. The goals of the Cataloging and Indexing Program are to:

- Develop a comprehensive and authoritative national bibliography of U.S. government publications
- Increase the visibility and use of government information products
- Create a premier destination for information searchers

This undertaking serves libraries and the public nationwide and enables people to locate desired government publications in all formats. The main public interface for the access of cataloging records is CGP.

The identification and creation of online bibliographic catalog records for new U.S. federal government publications, in all published formats, is accomplished through daily operations. A separate retrospective effort is necessary to build online bibliographic records for historical and fugitive (uncataloged but relevant) materials. This effort is known as the National Bibliographic Records Inventory Initiative (NBRII).

NBRII endeavors to provide an online bibliographic record or serial holding record for historical records not currently captured in CGP. These records include:

- Fugitive materials, with a focus on publications issued prior to 1976
- Older publications where bibliographic records exist only in a non-electronically available resource, such as a catalog card or other paper bibliographic record.
- Materials that were previously cataloged with such minimal information that they require critical record enhancement to reach a full-level bibliographic record

Enhancement/Progression/Innovation

Notable additions to FDsys during FY 2014 included the following:

Warren Commission Report and Hearings

GPO made available the official, digital version of the Warren Commission hearings on FDsys in FY 2014. Georgetown University's Lauinger Library provided a copy of the report to GPO for digitizing, and the Boston Public Library digitized the 26 hearing volumes. The commission was created by President Lyndon Johnson and chaired by Chief Justice Earl Warren and presented its findings on September 24, 1964. The commission also released 26 volumes of hearing transcripts, produced by GPO, composed of testimony from 550 witnesses and other evidence.

U.S. Courts Opinions Collection

GPO enhanced the U.S. Courts Opinions Collection by providing public access to the opinions of the U.S. Court of International Trade, along with the opinions of 31 additional courts (appellate courts, bankruptcy courts, and district courts). The number of courts available on FDsys was expanded from the initial 29 courts in FY 2012 to 95 by the end of FY 2014. The collection saw almost 51 million content retrievals on FDsys for FY 2014.

U.S. House of Representatives Bill Summaries

In February 2014 GPO partnered with the Library of Congress to make House of Representatives bill summaries available in XML format for bulk data download from FDsys. Bill summaries are prepared by the Library of Congress's Congressional Research Service and describe the most significant provisions of a piece of legislation. They also detail the effects the legislative text may have on current law and federal programs. The bill summaries are part of the FDsys bulk data repository starting with the 113th Congress. Making House bill summaries available in XML permits data to be reused and repurposed for mobile Web applications, data mashups, and other analytical tools by third party providers, which contributes to openness and transparency in government. This project commenced at the direction of the House Appropriations Committee and is in support of the task force on bulk data established by the House.

CIA Audiobook

GPO made an audiobook available for the first time on FDsys in FY 2014. Published by the Central Intelligence Agency (CIA), the audiobook, "Getting to Know the President: Intelligence Briefings of Presidential Candidates, 1952–2004," is a historical account of the information-sharing process between the intelligence community and presidential candidates and presidents-elect during campaigns and administration transitions. The audiobook is available in an MP3 format on FDsys.

Historic Bound Congressional Record

GPO has been collaborating with the Library of Congress to digitize volumes of the Bound Congressional Record dating from 1873 to 1998 and to provide access through FDsys. The entire Digitized Bound Congressional Record (DBCR) project, covering the period 1873 to 1998, contains approximately 2,085 parts and a total of 2.6 million pages. The digitized content must be reviewed and descriptive content metadata must be identified and recorded prior to providing access on FDsys. As of the end of FY 2014 nearly all volumes of the Bound Congressional Record had been digitized.

Cataloging and CGP Accomplishments

GPO Among Top Ten Original Catalogers

GPO was again named one of the world's top ten original catalogers in OCLC's annual report for FY 2013 (released in FY 2014). During FY 2013 GPO added 13,793 new records for U.S. government information products to WorldCat, a database of bibliographic information built by libraries around the world and OCLC.

GPO was a founding member of the OCLC network in 1976, and has reached several important milestones as an active contributor to WorldCat. In 1992 a GPO cataloger contributed the 100,000th record to the OCLC Bibliographic Database, and in 1999 another GPO cataloger contributed the 43,000,000th record.

National Bibliographic Records Inventory

Projects associated with the National Bibliographic Records Inventory in FY 2014 included the following:

- Historic Shelflist Transcription—LSCM continued transcribing all non-OCLC cards in its historic shelflist. Contract staff transcribe the shelflist cards, check in serial issues, and add Library of Congress subject headings and corporate name authority to records. By the end of FY 2014 there were 157,623 shelflist records available through CGP.
- Monthly Catalog Transcription—Beginning in January 2013 LSCM initiated an effort to transcribe entries from volumes of the *Monthly Catalog of U.S. Government Publications*. In FY 2014 transcription of entries from the 1895 and 1898 volumes was completed. More than 9,600 Monthly Catalog records are available through CGP.
- Serials Management Plan—In FY 2014 more than 54,770 serial issues were checked into CGP, and 559 publication patterns were created for serial titles. In addition, 785 previously uncataloged serial titles were identified, and new bibliographic records for those titles were created and added to CGP.
- LSCM Internal Manual Records Conversion—Beginning in June 2013 GPO staff have been adding information for historic and current serial issues of government publications from internal GPO sources of CGP. In FY 2014 information for 41,500 historic serial issues of U.S. government publications from internal GPO sources were added to CGP.

E-Books Added to FDLP

In February 2014 GPO introduced more than 100 titles in new e-book formats to FDLP. The new formats, MOBI and EPUB, are available to the public free of charge using CGP. All e-book titles available through CGP are federal publications of public interest or educational value within the scope of Title 44, sections 1902–1903. The titles made available through this program were previously self-distributed on federal websites and available to the public at no cost; they join the growing number of online resources that have been a vital part of FDLP for more than 20 years.

By the end of FY 2014 more than 150 e-book titles were available through CGP through this program. More information is available at FDLP.gov's e-books page.

Resource Description and Access

After the successful implementation of Resource Description and Access (RDA) in early 2013 Library Technical Services librarians engaged in training and outreach to the FDLP community in 2014 to assist in RDA application. GPO librarians presented three webinars in GPO's Library Technical Services Webinar and Webcast Series, all of which cover the interpretation of RDA for government documents—Congressional Publications: An Overview; Name Authority Records in RDA; and Archiving and Cataloging Federal Agency Websites.

Cataloging Record Distribution Program

The Cataloging Record Distribution Program (CRDP) continued in FY 2014 through a contract with MARCIVE, Inc. Through this program, 82 libraries receive free bibliographic records that correspond to their item number selection profile. The annual survey of participants validated the success of the program, with nearly all of the libraries indicating that the CRDP meets expectations and increases access to government information or has made it easier for the libraries to provide it.

FDLP Academy

FDLP Academy was launched by LSCM in FY 2014 as a new resource for educational tools on government information. This educational program was created to support the FDLP community and to advance federal government information literacy. The mission of FDLP Academy is to create and deliver enhanced educational opportunities to the FDLP community by fostering collaboration, by facilitating knowledge sharing, and through the application of new methods and use of multiple media.

FDLP Academy enhances federal government information knowledge through events and conferences coordinated by GPO and webinars and webcasts on a wide variety of government information topics. Many sessions are presented by GPO staff, while others are presented by staff from other federal agencies and from members of the FDLP community, as recruited and hosted by GPO.

Through this program, 51 live webinars were presented to 3,803 attendees, eight recorded webcasts had more than 900 views, and four live classroom sessions attracted 41 attendees during the fiscal year. Collaborators with GPO through this program have included representatives of the U.S. Department of Energy, the U.S. Census Bureau, the National Institutes of Health, the U.S. Department of Health and Human Services, the National Oceanic and Atmospheric Administration, and many more.

FDLP Academy resources include

- An FDLP Events Calendar with information on upcoming events and related registration information
- A Webinars and Webcasts Archive with links to recordings and handouts of all past webinars and webcasts, categorized by learning track (FDsys, GPO, Agency, or FDLP Community)
- An Events and Conferences page with information about GPO's annual FDLP events
- An Events and Conferences Archive with links to recordings and handouts of all past FDLP events and conferences that have been broadcast virtually
- A collection of FDsys training videos
- A form to request specialized training or to volunteer to share expertise through a webinar hosted by GPO

Web Archiving Initiative

GPO continues to be an Archive-It partner for website-level harvesting and has made a number of advances in collection development. LSCM staff members have completed archiving the websites of the Y3 SuDoc classification scheme, which encompasses the committees, commissions, and independent agencies, and have begun to develop a concept for special collections of online content. The first effort began as a request from the Superintendent of Documents to archive federal Web resources that would be beneficial to the Native American community. LSCM envisions similar special collections in the future.

Since the beginning of this program, LSCM staff have focused on increasing the number and types of agencies being archived. LSCM also wants to focus on maintenance of existing collections by completing regular crawls. A workflow has been developed for improving the frequency of crawls on existing collections, and implementation began in FY 2014.

LSCM continues to welcome nominations for Web archiving. The FDLP community can nominate websites through a number of avenues, including Document Discovery, askGPO, or through a direct e-mail to LSCM's Web Archiving team.

The current size of GPO's collection in Archive-It is 3.5 terabytes with more than 24 million documents crawled. There are 57 agencies represented on GPO's Archive-It site and 65 records in CGP.

To avoid duplication of effort, GPO has worked with other federal agencies that are Web archiving in order to foster better communication and cooperation relating to long-term preservation and access initiatives.

In fall 2014 GPO joined with the Library of Congress and the National Archives and Records Administration in forming a Federal Web Archiving Working Group. The group meets monthly to discuss Web archiving strategies and coordinated efforts. Members plan to expand outreach and communication efforts in 2015.

There is an extensive project page on FDLP.gov that provides more information and FAQs on the Web archiving program.

Recognizing Depository Libraries

On April 30, 2014, during the Depository Library Council Meeting and Federal Depository Library Conference, GPO recognized four libraries for their achievements and initiatives in 2013 and 2014. These "libraries of the year" were selected for their leadership, educational outreach, and commitment to providing free public access to federal government information.

These were the honorees:

The University of Iowa Libraries, the state's regional depository library, was honored for its successful blending of partnerships and projects within the institution, the local community, GPO, and the nation. The libraries were found to be exemplary in their cataloging and preservation initiatives. One project included the identification, cataloging, and digitization of nearly 1,500 large-format posters issued by the federal government.

The Ottenheimer Library at the University of Arkansas, Little Rock, was honored for its leadership in scholarship activities that promote government information and depository libraries nationwide. The library is a leader in coordinating federal documents activities at the state level. It was instrumental in acquiring support and financing for the online U.S. Congressional Serial Set while continuing to preserve and maintain the tangible volumes on campus under a cooperative agreement with other institutions in the area.

The State Library of Arizona was honored for its active participation in the electronic distribution of online cataloging records project, creation of the state master plan for depository libraries, and collaboration in the development of a biennial multi-state virtual depository library conference.

Brooklyn College Library was honored for its leadership and mentoring activities for library staff in the greater New York City area. The library provides access and staff with expertise for a wide range of tangible and electronic resources for the public, providing a basis for transitioning from a traditional to a modern library.

Depository Library Spotlight

GPO Depository Library Spotlight highlights a federal depository library and describes the unique services it offers. This feature appears on the GPO website, gpo.gov, and in the *FDLP Connection* newsletter.

The following depositories were highlighted in FY 2014: Hesburgh Libraries, University of Notre Dame; San Diego Public Library; Las Vegas Library of the Las Vegas-Clark County Library District; and Arizona State University Libraries.

LSCM Metrics

Notable LSCM Metrics for FY 2014:

- New titles acquired (online and tangible): 13,384
- Number of serial issues checked in: 64,779
- Searches of CGP: 25,605,364
- Total titles cataloged: 13,697
- Total PURLs created: 11,345
- Total titles distributed: 6,193
- Total copies distributed: 1,363,635
- Number of federal depository libraries: 1,174
- Total titles available through GPO: 1,286,466

Public Access Assessment

Regular communication and consultation between individual depository libraries and GPO staff strengthen and benefit FDLP. A Public Access Assessment (PAA) is a review by a GPO librarian of an individual federal depository library's operation and services; it is one of the significant ways in which GPO communicates and shares information with individual libraries in FDLP. PAAs are intended to support each library through sharing of best practices, recognition of notable achievements, and recommendations so the library can continue enhancing its operation and services. The assessment involves a review of library documentation and a conference call with depository library personnel.

GPO also performs PAAs, pursuant to 44 U.S.C. §19, to ensure that resources distributed to federal depository libraries are readily accessible to all library users, including the general public, and that libraries are complying with requirements and regulations outlined in "Legal Requirements and Program Regulations of the Federal Depository Library Program." If necessary, GPO advises libraries on how to reach greater compliance and requests related follow-up action. Information about PAAs is available to depository library personnel in featured newsletter articles, a webcast, and an FDLP.gov guidance article. In FY 2014 GPO completed 107 PAAs in Colorado, Indiana, Louisiana, Montana, Nevada, New York, Oklahoma, Pennsylvania, Tennessee, and Wisconsin.

National Archives and Records Administration

700 Pennsylvania Ave. N.W., Washington, DC 20408
202-357-5000
World Wide Web http://www.archives.gov

The National Archives and Records Administration (NARA), an independent federal agency, is the nation's record keeper. NARA safeguards and preserves the important records of all three branches of the federal government so that the people can discover, use, and learn from this documentary heritage. NARA ensures continuing access to records that document the rights of American citizens, the actions of government officials, and the history of the nation.

NARA carries out its mission through a national network of archives and records centers stretching from Boston to San Francisco and Atlanta to Seattle, in addition to 13 presidential libraries that document administrations back to that of Herbert Hoover—a total of 46 facilities nationwide.

The agency includes the National Historical Publications and Records Commission (NHPRC), the grant-making arm of NARA; the Office of the Federal Register, which publishes the official records of the actions of the government; the Information Security Oversight Office (ISOO), which oversees the government's classification programs; the National Declassification Center (NDC), which is streamlining the declassification process; and the Office of Government Information Services (OGIS), which reviews agencies' Freedom of Information Act (FOIA) administration and practices.

NARA also assists federal agencies, the courts, and Congress in documenting their activities by providing records storage, offering reference service, administering records management programs, scheduling records, and retiring non-current records to federal records centers. NARA also provides training, advice, and guidance on many issues relating to records management.

NARA's constituents and stakeholders include educators and their students at all levels, a history-minded public, family historians, the media, the archival community, and a broad spectrum of professional associations and researchers in such fields as history, political science, law, library and information services, and genealogy.

The size and breadth of NARA's holdings are staggering. NARA's electronic records holdings amount to nearly 700 terabytes of data, which includes the 2010 census. This consists of records that were "born digital" and managed in a digital form throughout their life cycle.

In addition, NARA maintains traditional holdings that will be converted to digital form for preservation purposes and to ensure access to them far into the future. This, along with the ever-growing quantity of "born digital" records, creates a big data challenge for NARA and the federal government.

NARA's current traditional holdings include more than 11 billion pages, 18 million maps, 50 million photographs, 600,000 artifacts, and 360,000 motion picture films. In addition, 18 Federal Records Centers (FRCs), located around the country, provide storage for about 69 billion pages of non-current records for 400 federal agencies.

NARA is currently operating under a Strategic Plan for fiscal years 2014 to 2018, which sets its long-term objectives. It has four strategic goals: Make Access

Happen, Connect with Customers, Maximize NARA's Value to the Nation, and Build Our Future Through Our People. Specific initiatives are under way at NARA to reach each goal.

Records and Access

Information Security Oversight Office

The Information Security Oversight Office (ISOO) is responsible to the president for policy and oversight of the government-wide security classification system, the National Industrial Security Program, and the emerging federal policy on "controlled unclassified" information. ISOO receives policy and program guidance from the assistant to the president for national security affairs and National Security Council staff in the Executive Office of the President.

ISOO oversees the security classification programs (classification, safeguarding, and declassification) in both government and industry. It is also responsible for exercising NARA's authorities and responsibilities as the executive agent for controlled unclassified information. ISOO contributes materially to the effective implementation of the government-wide security classification program and has a direct impact on the performance of thousands of government employees and contract personnel who work with classified national security information. For more information on ISOO, visit http://www.archives.gov/isoo.

National Declassification Center

In December 2009 President Barack Obama directed an overhaul of how documents created by the federal government are classified and declassified. This initiative aims at promoting transparency and accountability of government. The president also directed the creation of the National Declassification Center (NDC), located within NARA.

NDC is leading the streamlining of the declassification process throughout the federal government. In particular, it is accelerating the processing of historically valuable classified records in which more than one federal agency has an interest. NDC met the president's initial December 31, 2013, goal for the center by successfully addressing referrals and quality assurance problems within the backlog of 352 million pages of accessioned federal records at NARA that were previously subject to automatic declassification. NDC maintained that momentum by meeting its 2014 and 2015 quality assurance goals as well.

NDC also oversees the development of common declassification processes among agencies, and it is prioritizing declassification based on public interest and the likelihood of declassification. For more information about NDC, go to http://www.archives.gov/declassification.

Office of Government Information Services

OGIS's role as the FOIA Ombudsman encompasses a full range of activities, including daily interaction with customers, strategic outreach, and communications and training programs. OGIS also provides dispute resolution training for the

FOIA staff of federal agencies, and it works closely with key FOIA stakeholders, including the requester community and open-government advocates.

The Open Government Act of 2007 created OGIS with three statutorily defined functions. OGIS offers mediation services to help resolve FOIA disputes. It reviews agency FOIA policies, procedures, and compliance. And it makes recommendations to Congress and the president to improve the administration of FOIA as necessary.

As part of the second Open Government National Action Plan, the OGIS director chairs the FOIA Federal Advisory Committee. There are ten members from within government and ten nongovernmental members who have considerable FOIA expertise. The FOIA Advisory Committee works to improve focus on three key issues: oversight and accountability of agency FOIA programs, FOIA fees, and proactive disclosures.

For more information about OGIS, visit http://ogis.archives.gov or follow OGIS on Twitter @FOIA_Ombuds.

Electronic Records Archives

The Electronic Records Archives (ERA) system captures electronic records and information, regardless of format, saves them permanently, and provides access to them. ERA development was completed at the end of fiscal year (FY) 2011, and ERA moved to an operations and maintenance phase at the beginning of FY 2012.

The focus then shifted to increasing the use of ERA by federal departments and agencies in anticipation of ERA becoming mandatory by the end of 2012 for federal agency use in scheduling and transferring permanent electronic records to NARA. The adoption of ERA by federal agencies has led to the transfer of increasing volumes of electronic records to NARA for preservation and eventual access through its public access portal, the National Archives Catalog (NAC).

From 2013 through 2015 NARA made several improvements to better meet the needs of all stakeholders that rely on the ERA system to schedule, transfer, preserve, and provide access to the permanently valuable digital heritage of the federal government.

In early 2016 ERA held 670 terabytes of information in electronic form. For 2016 NARA will continue to evolve the ERA system to improve its capabilities and performance to meet the growing challenges in preserving and providing access to electronic records. For more information about ERA, see http://www.archives.gov/era.

Applied Research Division

NARA's Applied Research Division serves as the agency's center for advanced and applied research capabilities in the fields of computer science, engineering, and archival science. The division's staff conducts research on new technologies, both to be aware of new types of electronic record formats that will need to be preserved and to evaluate new technologies that might be incorporated into electronic records management and preservation systems at NARA to increase their effectiveness. The staff also helps NARA managers and employees acquire the knowledge and skills they need to function effectively in e-government through presentations on new technologies. For more information, visit http://www.archives.gov/applied-research.

National Archives Catalog

Today anyone with a computer connected to the Internet can search descriptions of more than 86 percent of NARA's nationwide holdings and view digital copies of some of its most popular documents through NARA's updated National Archives Catalog. By the end of 2016 NARA will have 95 percent of its vast holdings described in the catalog. Currently the catalog contains more than 8 million descriptions of archival holdings. Included are more than 2,186,000 digital copies of high-interest documents, representing many of the holdings highlighted on NARA's numerous social media platforms and in the Public Vaults, NARA's permanent interactive exhibition. The catalog is available on the Internet at http://www.archives.gov/research/catalog.

NARA's Website

The online entrance to the National Archives is its award-winning website, http://www.archives.gov, which provides the most widely available means of electronic access to information about and services available from NARA. Links to various sections provide help to the particular needs of researchers, including veterans and their families, educators and students, and the general public—as well as records managers, journalists, historians, information security specialists, members of Congress, and federal employees.

The NARA website provides

- Directions on how to contact NARA and do research at its facilities around the country
- Direct access to certain archived electronic records at http://www.archives.gov/aad
- Digital copies of selected archived documents
- An Internet Web form, at http://www.archives.gov/contact/inquire-form.html, for customer questions, reference requests, comments, and complaints
- Electronic versions of *Federal Register* publications
- Online exhibits
- Selected articles about U.S. history from *Prologue* (http://www.archives.gov/publications/prologue), the agency's quarterly magazine
- Classroom resources for students and teachers
- Online tools such as eVetRecs (http://www.archives.gov/veterans/military-service-records), which allows veterans and their next-of-kin to complete and print, for mail-in submission, requests for their military service records

Copies of military pension records from the American Revolution through World War I, census pages, land files, court records, and microfilm publications can be ordered online at http://www.archives.gov/shop. Researchers can also submit reference questions about various research topics online. In FY 2015 NARA welcomed 24 million Web visitors and received more than 80 million page views on its websites.

Digitization Projects

Within its Office of Innovation, NARA is working to digitize its traditional (paper) holdings to preserve them and provide greater access to them. The Office of Innovation will accelerate NARA's innovation activities and culture, support innovation in public access delivery, and demonstrate leadership in the archival and information access field.

As a result of these efforts, the National Archives digitized and added more than 5 million digital objects to the National Archives Catalog (https://catalog. archives.gov/) in FY 2015.

While the National Archives Catalog gives users the ability to view digitized records, the amount of material digitized and fully made available online is limited compared with the total holdings of the National Archives.

To better facilitate access of records, the online catalog has also recently been upgraded and now features more participatory elements, including new tagging and transcription tools to further engage citizen archivists and help make holdings more discoverable to researchers. At the end of FY 2015 citizen archivists had contributed more than 91,000 tags and 35,000 transcriptions to the catalog, with the latter growing at 5 percent each week.

Most of NARA's holdings currently are available only from the archival facility in which they are stored. Through a series of digitization projects, NARA is working to vastly increase online public access to more of its holdings. In 2014 the agency updated the digitization strategy (http://www.archives.gov/digitization/strategy.html) to deal with digitization efforts, which include working with partners in the private sector. In 2016 NARA will be adding millions of images to the catalog. These images were created by its private industry digitization partners. More information about the digitization partnerships is available at http://www.archives.gov/digitization/index.html.

Social Media

NARA uses multiple social media platforms to increase access to the records in its holdings, which is at the heart of its mission. The main goals of social media at NARA are to increase awareness about archival holdings and programs and to enrich the agency's relationship with the public through conversations about its services and holdings. In addition to expanding access, use of social media creates a more collaborative work environment and increases communication and knowledge sharing both within NARA and externally with other federal agencies.

The National Archives has more than a dozen blogs, including one by the Archivist of the United States. NARA also offers historical videos from its holdings and videos of recent public events on the agency's YouTube channel. The agency shares photographs and documents from its collections through Flickr Commons. Across the country, more than 200 NARA staff contribute actively to the agency's 130 social media (http://www.archives.gov/social-media/) accounts (including Facebook, Twitter, Tumblr, Instagram, and others). In FY 2015 almost 250 million people viewed content posted to those social media platforms, up significantly over the previous fiscal year's total of 141 million.

Followers can also use Really Simple Syndication (RSS) feeds of the "Document for Today" feature, NARA news, and press releases. Several mobile apps and e-books have been developed and are available free of charge in the iTunes store and Android Market for Today's Document, DocsTeach, and recent exhibits.

Social media also allow NARA's researchers, friends, and the public to become "citizen archivists" by tagging, sharing, and transcribing documents. For more information, go to http://www.archives.gov/citizen-archivist.

Additional information about NARA's social media projects is available at http://www.archives.gov/social-media.

National Archives Museum

The National Archives Museum, a set of interconnected resources made possible by a public-private partnership between NARA and the National Archives Foundation, provides a variety of ways to explore the power and importance of the nation's records.

The Rotunda for the Charters of Freedom at the National Archives Building in Washington, D.C., is the centerpiece of the National Archives Museum. On display are the Declaration of Independence, the Constitution, and the Bill of Rights—known collectively as the Charters of Freedom. The Public Vaults is a 9,000-square-foot permanent exhibition that conveys the feeling of going beyond the walls of the Rotunda and into the stacks and vaults of the working archives. Dozens of individual exhibits, many of them interactive, reveal the breadth and variety of NARA's holdings.

Complementing the Public Vaults, the Lawrence F. O'Brien Gallery hosts a changing array of topical exhibits based on National Archives records. The 290-seat William G. McGowan Theater is a showplace for NARA's extensive audio-visual holdings and serves as a forum for lectures and discussions. It also is home to the Charles Guggenheim Center for the Documentary Film at the National Archives.

An expanded museum shop opened in 2012, and a new exhibition gallery and visitor orientation plaza opened in 2013. The David M. Rubenstein Gallery houses a permanent interactive exhibit, "Records of Rights," which documents the struggles and debates over civil rights and liberties throughout American history. The Rubenstein Gallery is also the new home for a 1297 copy of the Magna Carta, owned by Rubenstein.

Inside the Boeing Learning Center, the ReSource Room is an access point for teachers and parents to explore documents found in the exhibits and to use NARA records as teaching tools. The center's Constitution-in-Action Learning Lab is designed to provide an intense field trip adventure for middle and high school students that links to curriculum in the classroom.

DocsTeach (http://www.docsteach.org) is an education website designed to provide instruction to teachers in the best practices of teaching with primary sources. Using documents in NARA's holdings as teachable resources, DocsTeach strongly supports civic literacy. This tool gives all teachers access to primary sources, instruction in best practices, and opportunities to interact with their counterparts across the nation.

When developing the DocsTeach site, the agency established an online community that served as a virtual meeting place for NARA's education team and colleagues from schools, institutions, and organizations nationwide to collaborate and share innovative ideas and best practices for this online resource.

The National Archives Museum has expanded to the National Archives in New York City, which is located in the Alexander Hamilton U.S. Custom House at the southern tip of Manhattan. There NARA has not only a new research area but also a learning center for education and public programs and a welcome center with exhibit space. The new Learning Center incorporates many of the resources and activities found in the Washington, D.C., building.

At its Kansas City, Missouri, field office at 400 West Pershing Road, NARA also has a welcome center, changing exhibitions, workshops, and other public programs.

A set of Web pages now makes the National Archives Museum available anywhere. An illustrated history of the Charters of Freedom can be found there, as well as information on educational programs, special events, and current exhibits at the National Archives.

Those traveling to Washington can bypass the public line during peak tourist season by making online reservations at http://www.recreation.gov. For more information, see "The National Archives Museum" at http://www.archives.gov/nae. An online version of the "Records of Rights" exhibition is available at http://recordsofrights.org.

NARA facilities hosted about 4.5 million physical visitors in FY 2015, of which about 3.5 million were headed to exhibits, 887,000 to public programs, and 85,000 to research rooms. More than a million visited the National Archives Museum in Washington, and exhibits in the 13 presidential library museums were visited by about 2.2 million.

Research Services

Few records repositories serve as many customers as NARA. In FY 2015 there were nearly 85,000 researcher visits to NARA facilities nationwide, including archives, presidential libraries, and federal records centers. More than a million people requested information in writing.

National Archives Research Centers

At the Robert M. Warner Research Center in the National Archives Building in Washington, D.C., and the Steny Hoyer Research Center at the National Archives at College Park, Maryland, researchers can consult with staff experts on federal records held in each building and submit requests to examine original documents.

The Warner Research Center holds approximately 275,000 rolls of microfilmed records, documenting military service prior to World War I, immigration into the United States, the federal census, the U.S. Congress, federal courts in the District of Columbia, the Bureau of Indian Affairs, and the Freedmen's Bureau. The center also contains an extensive, ever-expanding system of reference reports, helping researchers conduct research in federal documents.

Executive branch records housed in the National Archives Building include those of the Bureau of Indian Affairs and of civilian agencies responsible for maritime affairs. Military records in this building include records of the Army before World War I and the Navy and Marine Corps before World War II. In addition, the National Archives Building holds many records relating to the federal government's interaction with individuals; these are often consulted for genealogical research.

The Hoyer Research Center in College Park holds textual records of civilian agencies from 1789, investigative records and military holdings that include records from the Army and Army Air Forces dating from World War I and Navy, Marine Corps, intelligence, defense-related, and seized enemy records dating from World War II. In addition to textual records, special media records include motion pictures, still photographs and posters, sound recordings, maps, architectural drawings, aerial photographs, and electronic records. A research room for accessioned microfilm holds records of the Department of State's Berlin Document Center and other World War II-era captured documents.

Regional Archives

NARA has 12 regional archives where the public can do research. They are located in or near Boston, New York, Philadelphia, Atlanta, Chicago, St. Louis, Kansas City, Fort Worth, Denver, Riverside (California), San Francisco, and Seattle. Archived records of regional significance, as well as, in some locations, immigration records, are available for use by the public in these regional archives.

Presidential Libraries

NARA operates the libraries and museums of the 13 most recent U.S. presidents, beginning with Herbert Hoover, whose library is in West Branch, Iowa. The others are Franklin D. Roosevelt, Hyde Park, New York; Harry S. Truman, Independence, Missouri; Dwight D. Eisenhower, Abilene, Kansas; John F. Kennedy, Boston; Lyndon Baines Johnson, Austin; Richard Nixon, Yorba Linda, California; Gerald R. Ford, Ann Arbor (library) and Grand Rapids (museum), Michigan; Jimmy Carter, Atlanta; Ronald Reagan, Simi Valley, California; George Bush, College Station, Texas; William J. Clinton, Little Rock; and George W. Bush, Dallas.

In FY 2015 more than 2.1 million people visited exhibits in the presidential library museums; the libraries had more than 10,000 researcher visits. At http://www.archives.gov/presidential-libraries, visitors can learn about the presidential library system as a whole and link to individual library websites to learn about the lives of the presidents and the times in which they served.

Federal Records Centers

NARA also serves federal agencies, the courts, and Congress by providing records storage, reference service, training, advice, and guidance on many issues relating to records management.

A network of 18 Federal Records Centers (FRCs) stores 30 million cubic feet (about 75 billion pages) of non-current records for 400 agencies. In FY 2015 these records centers replied to more than 9 million requests for information and records, including more than 1 million requests for information regarding military and civilian service records provided by the National Personnel Records Center in St. Louis.

In addition, NARA has records centers in or near Atlanta; Boston; Chicago; Dayton; Denver; Fort Worth; Kansas City; Kingsridge (near Dayton), Ohio; Lee's Summit, Missouri; Lenexa, Kansas; Philadelphia; Pittsfield, Massachusetts; Riverside, California; San Francisco; Seattle; and Suitland, Maryland.

Genealogy Research

Genealogy research brings hundreds of thousands of people to NARA facilities every year. In its holdings NARA has census records dating back to 1790, records dealing with immigration, land and pension records, and passenger lists from ships arriving from all over the world.

NARA is often considered the first stop in searching for one's ancestry, at its facilities in the Washington, D.C., area or one of its 12 regional archives around the country. At these locations, NARA staff offers genealogy workshops to show the public how to look through documents dating back to the Revolutionary period.

NARA also offers an annual Genealogy Fair, which is now a "virtual" event at which NARA staff provides tips and techniques for researching genealogy records at the National Archives. Lectures are designed for experienced genealogy professionals and novices alike.

NARA also maintains close relationships with genealogical associations as well as organizations such as Ancestry.com, which can be accessed without charge at any NARA location.

The National Archives has the census schedules on microfilm available from 1790 to 1940. (Most of the 1890 Census was destroyed in a Department of Commerce fire, although partial records are available for some states.)

Archives Library Information Center

The Archives Library Information Center (ALIC) provides access to information on American history and government, archival administration, information management, and government documents. ALIC is located in the National Archives at College Park. Customers also can visit ALIC on the Internet at http://www.archives.gov/research/alic, where they will find "Reference at Your Desk" Internet links, staff-compiled bibliographies and publications, and an online library catalog. ALIC can be reached by telephone at 301-837-3415.

Government Documents

Government publications are generally available to researchers at many of the 1,250 congressionally designated federal depository libraries throughout the nation. A record set of these publications also is part of NARA's archival holdings. Publications of the U.S. Government (Record Group 287) is a collection of selected publications of government agencies, arranged by the SuDoc classification system devised by the Office of the Superintendent of Documents, U.S. Government Publishing Office (GPO).

The core of the collection is a library established in 1895 by GPO's Public Documents Division. By 1972, when NARA acquired the library, it included official publications dating from the early years of the federal government and selected publications produced for and by federal government agencies. Since 1972 the 25,000-cubic-foot collection has been augmented periodically with accessions of government publications selected by the Office of the Superintendent of Documents as a byproduct of its cataloging activity. As with the federal depository library collections, the holdings in NARA's Record Group 287 comprise only a portion of all U.S. government publications.

NARA Publications

Historically NARA has published guides and indexes to various portions of its archival holdings. Many of these are still in print, though the most up-to-date information about NARA holdings now is available almost exclusively through online searches at http://www.archives.gov. The agency also publishes informational leaflets and brochures and NARA's flagship publication, *Prologue,* a scholarly magazine published quarterly.

Some publications appear on NARA's website, at http://www.archives.gov/publications/online.html, and many are available from NARA's Customer Service Center in College Park, by calling 800-234-8861 or 866-272-6272 (in the Washington, D.C., area, 301-837-2000) or faxing 301-837-0483. The NARA website's publications homepage, http://www.archives.gov/publications, provides more detailed information about available publications and ordering.

General-interest books about NARA and its holdings that will appeal to anyone with an interest in U.S. history, exhibition catalogs, and facsimiles of certain documents are published by the National Archives Foundation. They are for sale at the foundation's myArchives Store in NARA's downtown Washington building and via the NARA website's eStore page at http://www.myarchivesstore.org.

Federal Register

The *Federal Register* is the daily gazette of the U.S. government, containing presidential documents, proposed and final federal regulations, and public notices of federal agencies. It is published by the Office of the Federal Register and printed and distributed by GPO. The two agencies collaborate in the same way to produce the annual revisions of the *Code of Federal Regulations (CFR).* Free access to the full text of the electronic version of the *Federal Register* and *CFR,* and to an unofficial, daily-updated electronic *CFR* (the *e-CFR*), is available via http://www.fdsys.gov. Federal Register documents scheduled for future publication are available for public inspection at the Office of the Federal Register (800 North Capitol St. N.W., Washington, DC 20002) or online at the electronic Public Inspection Desk (http://www.federalregister.gov/public-inspection). Federalregister.gov provides access to proposed rules and rules published in the *Federal Register* and open for public comment (the website https://www.federalregister.gov and the multiagency website http://www.regulations.gov also provide means to comment on these documents).

The full catalog of other Federal Register publications is posted at http://www.ofr.gov and includes the *Compilation of Presidential Documents, Public Papers of the Presidents,* slip laws, *United States Statutes at Large,* and the *United*

States Government Manual. Printed or microfiche editions of Federal Register publications also are maintained at federal depository libraries (http://www.gpo.gov/libraries).

The Public Law Electronic Notification Service (PENS) is a free subscription e-mail service for notification of recently enacted public laws. Varied subscriptions to the daily *Federal Register* are available from http://www.federalregister.gov. Additional information about Federal Register programs appears on Facebook (http://www.facebook.com/federalregister) and Twitter (@FedRegister).

The Office of the Federal Register also publishes information about its ministerial responsibilities associated with the operation of the Electoral College and ratification of constitutional amendments and provides access to related records. Publication information concerning laws, regulations, and presidential documents and services is available from the Office of the Federal Register (telephone 202-741-6070). Information on Federal Register finding aids, the Electoral College, and constitutional amendments is available through http://www.archives.gov/federal-register.

Publications can be ordered by contacting GPO at http://bookstore.gpo.gov, or by toll-free telephone at 866-512-1800. To submit orders by fax or by mail, see http://bookstore.gpo.gov/help/index.jsp.

Grants

The National Historical Publications and Records Commission (NHPRC) is the national grants program of the National Archives. The Archivist of the United States chairs the commission and makes grants on its recommendation. NHPRC's 14 other members represent the president (two appointees), the Supreme Court, the Senate and House of Representatives, the departments of State and Defense, the Librarian of Congress, the American Association for State and Local History, the American Historical Association, the Association for Documentary Editing, the National Association of Government Archives and Records Administrators, the Organization of American Historians, and the Society of American Archivists.

The commission's mission is to provide opportunities for the American people to discover and use records that increase understanding of the nation's democracy, history, and culture. Through leadership initiatives, grants, and fostering the creation of new tools and methods, the commission connects the work of the National Archives to the work of the nation's archives. NHPRC grants help archives, universities, historical societies, professional organizations, and other nonprofit organizations to establish or strengthen archival programs, improve training and techniques, preserve and process records collections, and provide access to them through finding aids, digitization of collections, and documentary editions of the papers of significant historical figures and movements in American history. The commission works in partnership with a national network of state archives and state historical records advisory boards to develop a national archival infrastructure. For more information about the Commission, visit http://www.archives.gov/nhprc. For more information about the projects it supports, go to http://www.facebook.com/nhprc.

Customer Service

Few records repositories serve as many customers as NARA. In FY 2015 there were about 85,000 researcher visits to NARA facilities nationwide, including archives, presidential libraries, and federal records centers. At the same time, more than a million customers submitted written requests for information.

NARA also maintains an Internet form (http://www.archives.gov/contact/inquire-form.html) to facilitate continuous feedback from customers about what is most important to them and what NARA might do better to meet their needs.

Administration

The head of NARA is David S. Ferriero, who was appointed Archivist of the United States in 2009 by President Obama. As of March 1, 2016, the agency employed 2,928 people, of whom 2,855 were full-time permanent staff members working at NARA locations around the country.

National Center for Education Statistics

U.S. Department of Education, Institute of Education Sciences
Potomac Center Plaza, 550 12th St. S.W., 4th fl., Washington, DC 20202

Christopher A. Cody
Academic Libraries, Integrated Postsecondary Education Data System

Chelsea Owens
School Library Media Centers, Schools and Staffing Survey

In an effort to collect and disseminate more complete statistical information about libraries, the National Center for Education Statistics (NCES) initiated a formal library statistics program in 1989 that included surveys on academic libraries, school library media centers, public libraries, and state libraries.* At the end of December 2006, the Public Libraries Survey and the State Library Agencies Survey were officially transferred to the Institute of Museum and Library Services (IMLS). The Academic Libraries Survey and the School Library Media Centers Survey continued to be administered and funded by NCES. However, the School Library Media Centers Survey was incorporated into the School and Staffing Survey (SASS), and the Academic Libraries Survey was incorporated into the Integrated Postsecondary Education Data System (IPEDS). [For detailed information on the surveys now being handled by IMLS, see "Institute of Museum and Library Services Library Programs" in Part 2 and "Highlights of IMLS and NCES Surveys" in Part 4—Ed.]

The library surveys conducted by NCES are designed to provide comprehensive nationwide data on the status of libraries. Federal, state, and local officials, professional associations, and local practitioners use these surveys for planning, evaluating, and making policy. These data are also available to researchers and educators.

Past information about elementary and secondary public school library media centers is available on the School and Staffing Survey website, http://nces.ed.gov/surveys/sass/. The Library Statistics Program's website, http://nces.ed.gov/surveys/libraries, provides links to data search tools, data files, survey definitions, and survey designs for the Academic Libraries Survey from 1996 to 2012. The IPEDS Academic Libraries Information Center, http://nces.ed.gov/ipeds/Section/AIscenter, contains current survey definitions and designs, and the IPEDS Data Center at http://nces.ed.gov/ipeds/datacenter/ contains data files for the Academic Libraries component beginning in 2014. The two library surveys conducted by NCES are described below.

Academic Libraries

The IPEDS Academic Libraries (AL) component provides descriptive statistics from academic libraries in the 50 states, the District of Columbia, and, if appli-

---

*The authorization for the National Center for Education Statistics (NCES) to collect library statistics is included in the Education Sciences Reform Act of 2002 (PL 107-279), under Title I, Part C.

cable, the outlying areas of the United States (Guam, the Commonwealth of the Northern Mariana Islands, Puerto Rico, and the U.S. Virgin Islands).

NCES surveyed academic libraries on a three-year cycle between 1966 and 1988. From 1988 to 1998, AL was a component of IPEDS collected on a two-year cycle. From 2000 to 2012, the Academic Libraries Survey separated from IPEDS but remained on a two-year cycle as part of the Library Statistics Program. IPEDS and ALS data were still linked by the identification codes of the postsecondary education institutions. In aggregate, these data provide an overview of the status of academic libraries nationally and by state. Beginning with the 2014–2015 collection cycle, AL was reintegrated back into IPEDS.

AL collects data on libraries in the entire universe of degree-granting postsecondary institutions using a Web-based data collection system. The survey component collects counts of library books, e-books, media, and databases, both in the physical and electronic formats. Academic libraries are also asked to report salaries, wages, and fringe benefits, if paid from the library budget; materials and services expenditures; operations and maintenance expenditures; and total expenditures. Libraries with reported total expenditures over zero but less than $100,000 were required to report collections data, while those with expenditures equal to or greater than $100,000 were required to report collections and detailed expenditures data.

A First Look report, "Academic Libraries: 2012" (NCES 2014-038), was released on the NCES website in February 2014, as were the final data file and documentation for the 2012 ALS (NCES 2014-039). NCES has developed a Web-based peer analysis tool for AL called "Compare Academic Libraries" (https:// nces.ed.gov/surveys/libraries/compare/). This tool currently uses AL 2012 data. A First Look report, "Enrollment and Employees in Postsecondary Institutions, Fall 2014; and Financial Statistics and Academic Libraries, Fiscal Year 2014" (NCES 2016-005), was released in November 2015. AL 2014 data and all future library data collected will be available via the IPEDS Data Center tool. Academic library statistics information can be obtained from Christopher A. Cody, Integrated Postsecondary Education Data System, e-mail IPEDS@ed.gov.

School Library Media Centers

National surveys of school library media centers in elementary and secondary schools in the United States were conducted in 1958, 1962, 1974, 1978, and 1986, 1993–1994, 1999–2000, 2003–2004, 2007–2008, and 2011–2012.

NCES, with the assistance of the U.S. Bureau of the Census, conducted the School Library Media Center Survey as part of the Schools and Staffing Survey (SASS). SASS is the nation's largest sample survey of teachers, schools, and principals in K–12 public and private schools. Data from the school library media center questionnaire provide a national picture of public school library staffing, collections, expenditures, technology, and services. Results from the 2011–2012 survey can be found in "Characteristics of Public Elementary and Secondary School Library Media Centers in the United States: Results from the 2011–12 Schools and Staffing Survey" (NCES 2013–315).

NCES also published a historical report about school libraries titled *Fifty Years of Supporting Children's Learning: A History of Public School Libraries and Federal Legislation from 1953–2000* (NCES 2005-311). Drawn from more than 50 sources, this report gives descriptive data about public school libraries since 1953. Along with key characteristics of school libraries, the report also presents national and regional standards, and federal legislation affecting school library media centers. Data from sample surveys are provided at the national, regional, and school levels, and by state.

NCES has recently redesigned the Schools and Staffing Survey into the National Teacher and Principal Survey (NTPS). NTPS will focus on teachers, principals, and the schools in which they work. The redesigned study collects counts of the number of school library media centers. The first NTPS (2015–2016) is currently in the field for data collection. Results will be available in summer of 2017.

Additional information on school library media center statistics can be obtained from Chelsea Owens, e-mail chelsea.owens@ed.gov.

NCES has included some library-oriented questions relevant to the library usage and skills of the parent and the teacher instruments of the new Early Childhood Longitudinal Study (ECLS). For additional information, visit http://nces.ed.gov/ecls. Library items also appear in National Household Education Survey (NHES) instruments. For more information about that survey, visit http://nces.ed.gov/nhes.

NCES included a questionnaire about high school library media centers in the Education Longitudinal Study of 2002 (ELS: 2002). This survey collected data from tenth graders about their schools, their school library media centers, their communities, and their home life. The report, "School Library Media Centers: Selected Results from the Education Longitudinal Study of 2002" (ELS: 2002) (NCES 2005-302), is available on the NCES website. For more information about this survey, visit http://nces.ed.gov/surveys/els2002.

How to Obtain Printed and Electronic Products

Reports are currently published in the First Look format. First Look reports consist of a short collection of tables presenting state and national totals, a survey description, and data highlights. NCES also publishes separate, more in-depth studies analyzing these data.

Internet Access

Many NCES publications (including out-of-print publications) and edited raw data files from the library surveys are available for viewing or downloading at no charge through the Electronic Catalog on the NCES website at http://nces.ed.gov/pubsearch.

Ordering Printed Products

Many NCES publications are also available in printed format. To order one free copy of recent NCES reports, contact the Education Publications Center (ED Pubs) at http://www.edpubs.org, by e-mail at edpubs@edpubs.ed.gov, by toll-free telephone at 877-4-ED-PUBS (1-877-433-7827) or TTY/TDD 877-576-7734, by fax at 703-605-6794, or by mail at ED Pubs, P.O. Box 22207, Alexandria, VA 22304.

Many publications are available through the Education Resources Information Clearinghouse (ERIC) system. For more information on services and products, visit the EDRS website at http://www.eric.ed.gov.

Out-of-print publications and data files may be available through the NCES Electronic Catalog on the NCES website at http://nces.ed.gov/pubsearch or through one of the 1,250 federal depository libraries throughout the United States (see http://catalog.gpo.gov/fdlpdir/FDLPdir.jsp). Use the NCES publication number included in the citations for publications and data files to quickly locate items in the NCES Electronic Catalog. Use the GPO number to locate items in a federal depository library.

Defense Technical Information Center

Fort Belvoir, VA 22060
World Wide Web http://www.dtic.mil

Michele Finley
Public Affairs Officer

The Defense Technical Information Center (DTIC) is responsible for developing, coordinating, and enabling a strong scientific and technical information (STINFO) program for the Assistant Secretary of Defense for Research and Engineering, and the Department of Defense (DoD) scientific and technical (S&T) enterprise. In this role, DTIC sets policy for scientific and technical information exchanges for the research and engineering community. DTIC's aim is to maximize the availability, use, and collaboration of technical information resulting from DoD-funded technical activities while ensuring restrictions to safeguard national security, export control, and intellectual property rights.

Since its inception in 1945 DTIC has served as a vital link in the transfer of defense-related information. The center offers access to more than 4 million research records to engineers, researchers, scientists, and information professionals in laboratories, universities, and the acquisition field. DTIC's mission is to collect and deliver rapid, accurate, and reliable technical research, development, test, and evaluation information to DoD customers. As a DoD field activity, DTIC is under the office of the Under Secretary of Defense for Acquisition, Technology, and Logistics and reports to the Assistant Secretary of Defense, Research and Engineering (ASD[R&E]).

In 2013 DTIC marked nine years as a DoD field activity and saw the renewal of its field activity charter. Signed by Deputy Secretary of Defense Ashton B. Carter, the charter, in force until 2018, reaffirmed DTIC's position as DoD's central scientific, research, and engineering information support activity for ASD(R&E). In 2013 DTIC also saw the approval of DoD Instruction 3200.12, "DoD Scientific and Technical Information Program (STIP)." Now an instruction, this issuance establishes policy and responsibilities and proposes procedures for DTIC to carry out STIP. The instruction outlines the vital role played by DTIC in collecting, indexing, cataloging, and providing storage for scientific and technical information obtained from DoD components and their contractors, non-DoD organizations, and foreign sources.

The instruction reiterates that DoD should sustain a coordinated program to manage scientific and technical information, which will maximize resources while eliminating duplication of efforts by the reuse of DoD research, development, test, and evaluation investments and assets. DoDI 3200.12 can be found on the DoD Issuances website, http://www.dtic.mil/whs/directives/corres/pdf/320012p.pdf.

In 2014 DoD Manual 3200.14, Volume 2, "Principles and Operational Parameters of the DoD Scientific and Technical Information Program (STIP): Information Analysis Centers (IACs)," was updated. The DoD establishes IACs to acquire, digest, analyze, evaluate, synthesize, store, publish, and distribute STI and engineering data in a clearly defined specialized field or subject area of significant DoD interest or concern. Additionally IACs provide advisory and other user services to their authorized user community. This volume describes the DoD IAC Program and implements its policy, principles, and concepts for procedural functions and is available at http://www.dtic.mil/whs/directives/corres/pdf/320014vol2.pdf.

Early in 2015 the Defense Acquisition Regulation Supplement clause on Electronic Submission of Technical Reports was updated to require electronic submissions instead of paper copies of approved final scientific or technical reports of research funded by DoD. This reaffirms the requirement for all final scientific and technical reports on DoD-funded research to be submitted to DTIC.

Reaching Customers

DTIC offers its suite of services to a diverse population of the defense community. Because of the nature of the information it handles, some of DTIC's products are only accessible to the federal government and its contractors. While DTIC also has a public website and search, there are advantages to accessing the secured sites. These value-added services include having research assistance from trained information professionals and having access to limited (not publicly available) information. More information about who is eligible to access DTIC's suite of products can be found at http://www.dtic.mil/dtic/registration.

Who uses DTIC information? Some of its more than 25,000 users are:

- Acquisition community
- Active duty military personnel
- Congressional staff
- DoD and federal contractors
- Engineers
- Faculty and students at military schools
- Historians
- Information professionals/librarians
- Intelligence community
- Logistics management specialists
- Researchers
- Scientists
- Security managers
- Software engineers and developers

Resources

DTIC's holdings include technical reports on completed research; research summaries of planned, ongoing, and completed work; independent research and development summaries; defense technology transfer agreements; DoD planning documents; budget data; DoD directives and instructions; international agreements; conference proceedings; security classification guides; command histories; and special research collections that date back to World War II. DoD-funded researchers are required to search DTIC's collections to ensure that they do not undertake unnecessary or redundant research. The general public can access "unclassified, unlimited" information, including many full-text downloadable documents, through the public DTIC website at http://www.dtic.mil. The information on the site is free of charge, and no registration is required.

Information Sources

DTIC information is derived from many sources, including DoD organizations (civilian and military) and DoD contractors; the Information Analysis Centers, U.S. government organizations and their contractors; nonprofit organizations working on DoD scientific, research, and engineering activities; academia; and foreign governments. DTIC accepts information in print, nonprint (CDs and DVDs), and electronically over the Web. DTIC gets information from the defense community, for the defense community, on defense topics and more. Having a full range of science and technology and research and development information within the DTIC collection ensures that technological innovations are linked to defense development and acquisition efforts. New research projects can begin with the highest level of information available. This avoids duplication of effort, maximizing the use of DoD project dollars and saving taxpayer dollars.

Creating Tools for DoD

DTIC continues to play a key role in DoD by producing collaboration tools (often not available to the public) to help the defense research and engineering community work in a secure environment. In order to utilize many of these websites, individuals must be eligible to access DTIC's products.

In a more networked world, the defense workforce needs the tools to create, share, and reuse knowledge developed both within DoD and by its external partners (industry and academia, for example). DTIC has made strides in creating and hosting sites aimed at enhancing the ability of DoD to connect internally and externally. In addition, DTIC is working to map relationships to enable users to access the life cycle of research projects from planning to final results. DTIC employs technology to verify and validate information submitted and improve user confidence in DoD research documentation.

The Research and Engineering (R&E) Gateway provides the means to connect the acquisition enterprise (DoD Labs); Federally Funded Research and Development Centers (FFRDCs); Program Executive Offices; Acquisition, Technology, and Logistics (AT&L) commands; and Combatant commands (CCMDs). In an access-controlled environment, all of DTIC's unclassified assets, tools, and community interaction capabilities foster innovation, competition, and identification of solutions. DoD conducts research at its 60-plus labs, in the FFRDCs, in DTIC's IACs, through contracts and grants, and across 17 distinct priority area communities of interest. This work is available through the R&E Gateway. In addition, the R&E Gateway offers access to official defense scientific and technical information, collaborative tools, and subject matter experts. The gateway helps the defense S&T community build on past work, collaborate on current projects, and avoid duplication of effort. With better connections within DoD, the development and delivery of technologies to the armed forces can be accelerated.

The R&E Gateway is the entry point to DTIC's suite of tools. Some of the tools within the gateway are:

- DTIC Collection Search—This tool aids in the quick discovery of public and access-controlled DoD research projects and documents, as well as people (subject matter experts), places (organizations), and content (past and current research) from DoDTechSpace. DTIC continually works to enable additional features within its search capabilities and from commercial partners to improve information discovery and relevance.

- DoDTechipedia—Designed by DTIC in 2008, DoDTechipedia was one of the first DoD scientific and technical wikis. A secure online system, it facilitates transparency and communication among DoD scientists, engineers, program managers, and the armed forces. It helps members of the DoD S&T community collaborate and identify solutions for technology challenges. Among its numerous features are interest area pages for DoD personnel and DoD contractors to work together on challenges and solutions.

- DoDTechSpace—A social business tool, DoDTechSpace is a place for DTIC's customers to collaborate, share, find, and post information. It connects the defense research and engineering community, DoD laboratories, and other DoD agencies, while providing current and next-generation researchers with advanced Web 2.0 tools. Offering real-time discussions on capability needs and solutions, events, and people, this collaborative environment can support community activities, social networking, lessons learned, and discussions.

- DoD Budget Tools—DTIC publishes searchable congressional budget data shortly after its release and offers both public and access-controlled sites to review and analyze DoD research and engineering funding data. The center posts reports from the House and Senate committees that oversee the DoD budget information, all of which can be found on the public site http://www.dtic.mil/congressional_budget. DTIC posts this reformatted budget data within days of its release on the Congress.gov legislative information website operated by the Library of Congress. The budget data is thoroughly checked prior to posting, ensuring its accuracy and reliability.

- Defense Innovation Marketplace—The Defense Innovation Marketplace was launched in late 2011 and continues to be used as an online resource (both public and access-controlled) for the purpose of "connecting industry with government customers." Creation of this site was a direct result of the "Better Buying Power" initiative within DoD, which called for the department to deliver better value by improving the way it was doing business. In short, industry submits information about DoD-related ideas and projects, which helps DoD to see what industry is developing. The site helps the department plan acquisitions and identify potential research gaps.

These tools are available through the R&E Gateway at https://www.dtic.mil. Links to these sites are also available through DTIC's public website at http://www.dtic.mil.

DoD Information Analysis Centers (IACs)

DoD Information Analysis Centers (IACs), established under DoD Manual 3200.14, Vol. 2, serve as a vital resource in providing timely, relevant information directly to users when and where it is needed. IACs serve as a bridge between the armed forces and the acquisition/research community, providing essential technical analysis and data support to a diverse customer base, to include the Combatant Commands (CCMDs), Program Executive Offices, the Office of the Secretary of Defense, Defense Agencies, and the military services. IACs actively partner and collaborate with Defense R&E focus groups and communities of interest in specialized fields or specific technologies. IACs create and maintain comprehensive knowledge analysis centers that include historical, technical, scientific, and other data and information collected worldwide. They are staffed with scientists, engineers, and information specialists to provide research and analysis to customers with diverse, complex, and challenging requirements. IAC operations directly support the fighting forces, and play an ongoing and critical role in solving key CCMD operational issues such as cybersecurity, unmanned aerial vehicles, human–machine teaming, and improvements to the ballistic resistance of body armor. More information on IACs is available at http://iac.dtic.mil.

Expanding Free Training Opportunities

Webinars have been mainstays of the opportunities offered to DTIC registered users to learn about DTIC's products and services. Three webinars, on DoDTechSpace, DoDTechipedia, and DTIC Search, are offered on a monthly basis.

"DTIC Boot Camp: S&T Resources for the DoD Community" offers hands-on training (at DTIC headquarters), including sessions about the center's numerous resources as well as instruction about submitting documents. This interactive one-day workshop is held monthly for users. DTIC users can request additional training sessions at DTIC headquarters or at their own locations.

DoD Scientific and Technical Information (STINFO) training is offered in one- and three-day classes that review the management and conduct of an organizational STINFO program. It can be held at DTIC or requested off-site.

Public Access to Federally Funded Research

DTIC is in a leading role for the department's efforts to implement public access to published journal articles and digital data from research funded by taxpayers. In this role, DTIC is actively working with partners across the services, other federal agencies, and publishers.

Summary

DTIC protects and preserves DoD's multibillion-dollar investment in research, which empowers the acquisition enterprise through innovative tools, information systems, and decision support capabilities. DTIC is uniquely positioned to support and unleash the value of DoD's R&D portfolio.

Education Resources

National Library of Education

Knowledge Utilization Division
National Center for Education Evaluation and Regional Assistance
Institute of Education Sciences, U.S. Department of Education
400 Maryland Ave. S.W., Washington, DC 20202
World Wide Web http://ies.ed.gov/ncee/projects/nle

Pamela Tripp-Melby
Director
202-453-6536, e-mail pamela.tripp-melby@ed.gov

The U.S. Department of Education's National Library of Education (NLE), created in 1994, is the primary resource center for education information in the federal government, serving the research needs of the Department of Education, the education community, and the public. NLE resides in the National Center for Education Evaluation and Regional Assistance, Institute of Education Sciences.

NLE was created by Public Law 103-227, the Educational Research, Development, Dissemination, and Improvement Act of 1994, and reauthorized under Public Law 107-279, the Education Sciences Reform Act of 2002. The act outlines four primary functions of NLE:

- Collect and archive information, including products and publications developed through, or supported by, the Institute of Education Sciences; and other relevant and useful education-related research, statistics, and evaluation materials and other information, projects, and publications that are consistent with scientifically valid research or the priorities and mission of the institute, and developed by the department, other federal agencies, or entities
- Provide a central location within the federal government for information about education
- Provide comprehensive reference services on matters relating to education to employees of the Department of Education and its contractors and grantees, other federal employees, and the public
- Promote greater cooperation and resource sharing among providers and repositories of education information in the United States

NLE works closely with the Education Resources Information Center (ERIC). ERIC collects and archives information and provides a central location within the federal government for information about education. Because ERIC serves as the major public program, it is covered separately. [See "Education Resources Information Center" below.—*Ed.*]

The primary responsibility of NLE is to provide information services to agency staff and contractors, the general public, other government agencies, and other libraries. Located in the agency's headquarters building in Washington, D.C., the library houses current and historical collections and archives of information on education issues, research, statistics, and policy; there is a special emphasis on agency publications and contractor reports, as well as current and historical federal education legislation.

NLE has a staff of 12 as of 2015, four full-time federal staff and eight contract librarians. Staffing and organizational structure are kept flexible to support changing needs and to allow for fast, competent response to customer requests, institutional initiatives, and advances in technology. NLE's primary customer base includes about 5,000 department staff nationwide; department contractors performing research; education organizations and media; and academic, special, and government libraries. All services are supported by NLE's budget, which in fiscal year 2015 is approximately $2 million.

Collections

The focus of NLE's collection is on education issues, with an emphasis on research and policy, with some materials on related topics including law, public policy, economics, urban affairs, sociology, history, philosophy, psychology, and cognitive development. In addition to current materials, the collection has books dating from the early 19th century, including approximately 800 books on education research in the United States and more than 25,000 historical textbooks. Some of these books were donated to the library by Henry Barnard, the first U.S. Commissioner of Education.

NLE maintains collections of historical documents associated with its parent agency, the U.S. Department of Education, having a complete collection of ERIC microfiche; research reports reviewed by the What Works Clearinghouse and special panels; and publications of or relating to the department's predecessor agencies, including the National Institute of Education and the U.S. Office of Education in the Department of Health, Education, and Welfare. These collections include reports, studies, manuals, statistical publications, speeches, and policy papers. NLE also serves as a selective federal depository library under the U.S. Government Publishing Office program.

Services

NLE provides reference and other information services, including legislative reference and statistical information services, to department staff, to the education community at large, and to the general public, as well as offering document delivery services to department staff and interlibrary loan services to other libraries and government agencies.

Contact Information

The U.S. Department of Education Research Library can be contacted by e-mail at askalibrarian@ed.gov. The library's reference desk is available by telephone from 9 A.M. to 5 P.M. weekdays, except federal holidays, at 800-424-1616 (toll free) or 202-205-5015, and by fax at 202-401-0547. For the hearing-impaired, the toll-free number for the Federal Relay Service is 800-877-8339.

Located in the department's headquarters building at 400 Maryland Ave. S.W., the library is open to researchers by appointment from 9 A.M. to 5 P.M. weekdays, except federal holidays.

Education Resources Information Center

Knowledge Utilization Division
National Center for Education Evaluation and Regional Assistance
Institute of Education Sciences, U.S. Department of Education
555 New Jersey Ave. N.W., Washington, DC 20208
World Wide Web http://eric.ed.gov

Erin Pollard
Program Officer, ERIC
202-219-3400, e-mail erin.pollard@ed.gov

The Education Resources Information Center (ERIC) is the world's largest and most frequently used digital library of education resources. It is composed of more than 1.5 million bibliographic records and more than 340,000 full-text materials indexed from 1966 to the present. Each ERIC bibliographic record contains an abstract of a journal article or non-journal document (for example, a technical report or conference paper), along with such indexed information as author, title, and publication date.

Background

ERIC has served the information needs of schools, institutions of higher education, educators, parents, administrators, policymakers, researchers, and public and private entities for decades, through a variety of library services and formats—first in paper copy, then in microfiche, and today exclusively in electronic format. ERIC provides service directly to the public via its website, http://eric.ed.gov.

With more than 50 years of service to the public, ERIC is one of the oldest programs in the U.S. Department of Education. As the world's largest education resource, it is distinguished by two hallmarks: free dissemination of bibliographic records and the collection of gray literature such as research conference papers and government contractor reports.

The authorizing legislation for ERIC is part of the Education Sciences Reform Act of 2002, Public Law 107-279. This legislation envisioned ERIC subject areas or topics (previously covered by the ERIC Clearinghouses) as part of the totality of enhanced information dissemination to be conducted by the Institute of Education Sciences. In addition, information dissemination includes material on closing the achievement gap and on educational practices that improve academic achievement and promote learning.

ERIC Mission

ERIC's mission is to provide a comprehensive, easy-to-use, searchable, Internet-based bibliographic and full-text database of education research and information for educators, researchers, and the general public. Terms defining the ERIC mission are as follows:

- *Comprehensive:* The ERIC digital library consists of journal articles and non-journal materials, including materials not published by commercial publishers that are directly related to education and education research.
- *Easy-to-use and searchable:* ERIC users will be able to find the education information they need quickly and efficiently.
- *Electronic:* ERIC is an entirely electronic system comprising the ERIC website and the digital library. It links to libraries, publishers, and commercial sources of journal articles, and is made available to commercial database vendors through authorization agreements.
- *Bibliographic and full-text:* Bibliographic records convey the information that users need in a simple and straightforward manner, and, whenever possible, full-text journal articles and non-journal materials are included free of charge in the digital library. Other full-text articles and materials, whenever possible, will be immediately available for purchase through an online link to the publisher's website.

Selection Standards

The selection policy provides that all materials added to the ERIC database are rigorous and relevant sources of research directly related to the field of education. The majority of the journals indexed in ERIC are peer-reviewed, and peer-reviewed status is indicated for all journals indexed since 2004 when this data began to be documented by the ERIC system. The collection scope includes early childhood education through higher education, vocational education, and special education; it includes teacher education, education administration, assessment and evaluation, counseling, information technology, and the academic areas of reading, mathematics, science, environmental education, languages, and social studies.

To be considered for selection, all submissions must be in digital format and accompanied by author permission for dissemination. For individual document submissions, authors (copyright holders) can upload materials through a link on the ERIC website. Journal publishers, associations, and other entities with multiple documents also submit electronic content following guidance and instructions consistent with provider agreements from ERIC.

ERIC Collection

In addition to being the largest education library, ERIC is one of the few collections to index non-journal materials as well as journal literature. The largest share of the collection consists of citations to journal articles (more than 825,000 records), and a smaller portion consists of non-journal materials (more than 725,000 records). The non-journal materials are frequently called gray literature, materials that are not easy to find and are not produced by commercial publishers. In ERIC, the gray literature consists of research syntheses, dissertations, conference proceedings, and such selected papers as keynote speeches, technical reports, policy papers, literature reviews, bibliographies, congressional hearings and reports, reports on federal and state standards, testing and regulations, U.S. Department of Education reports (such as those produced by the department's What Works Clearinghouse and the National Center for Education Statistics), and working papers for established research and policy organizations.

The ERIC selection policy was recently revised and can be found at http://eric.ed.gov/?selection. The list of journals approved for indexing can be found at http://eric.ed.gov/?journals, and the list of non-journals approved for indexing can be found at http://eric.ed.gov/?nonjournals.

To facilitate electronic access to more archived materials, ERIC launched a microfiche digitization project in 2006; this project was concluded in 2009. The project scope was to digitize and archive microfiche full-text documents containing an estimated 43 million pages and to provide copyright due diligence by seeking permission from the copyright holders to make the electronic version available to users.

Approximately 340,000 full-text documents, indexed 1966–1992, were converted from microfiche to digital image files, and more than 65 percent of these documents were added to the ERIC digital library.

In 2010 ERIC established a partnership with ProQuest to begin indexing education-related doctoral dissertations from 700 academic institutions worldwide. More than 17,900 recent records from the ProQuest Dissertations and Thesis Database have been added to the ERIC collection.

ERIC Website

In August 2013 ERIC released a new website to provide an improved level of service to the community at a reduced cost to taxpayers. The new home page has a light visual design that emphasizes ERIC's most crucial features—Search and Thesaurus. The search feature is fast, robust, and fully comparable to widely used commercial search products. Additionally, the ERIC Thesaurus is integrated with ERIC Search, increasing its ease of use. Easy-to-find limiters allow searchers to retrieve only records with full text in ERIC and/or only peer-reviewed materials. The goal of the website is to make its use easier and more productive for novice users and skilled searchers alike. New functionality is being added on an ongoing basis, and there are plans for new support tools designed especially for practitioners and new ERIC users.

Automated systems for acquisition and processing help to reduce the total time required to produce a database record, and most records are processed in fewer than 30 days. New content is added to the ERIC database every day, and ERIC publishes approximately 4,000 new records to the ERIC digital library each month. New updates to the database will be available to download at eric.ed.gov/download.

The website also provides links to find ERIC on Facebook and Twitter. This feature provides frequent news updates, links, and downloadable materials, with the goal of broadening ERIC outreach.

ERIC Access

Use of ERIC continues to grow. In addition to the government-sponsored website at http://www.eric.ed.gov, ERIC is carried by search engines including Google and Google Scholar, MSN, and Yahoo!, as well as by commercial database providers including EBSCO, OCLC, OVID, ProQuest, SilverPlatter, and Dialog. ERIC is also available through statewide networks in Ohio, Texas, Kentucky, and North Carolina.

The ERIC digital library can be reached toll-free by telephone in the United States, Canada, and Puerto Rico at 800-LET-ERIC (800-538-3742), Monday through Friday, 9 A.M. to 7 P.M. eastern time. Questions can also be transmitted via the message box on the "Contact Us" page on the ERIC website.

National Association and Organization Reports

American Library Association

50 E. Huron St., Chicago, IL 60611
800-545-2433
World Wide Web http://www.ala.org

Sari Feldman
President

The American Library Association (ALA)—the oldest, largest, and most influential library association in the world—was founded in 1876 in Philadelphia and later chartered in the Commonwealth of Massachusetts. ALA has approximately 58,000 members, including librarians, library trustees, and other interested people from every state and many nations. The association serves public, state, school, and academic libraries, as well as special libraries for people working in government, commerce and industry, the arts, and the armed services or in hospitals, prisons, and other institutions.

ALA's mission is "to provide leadership for the development, promotion, and improvement of library and information services and the profession of librarianship in order to enhance learning and ensure access to information for all."

ALA is governed by an elected council, which is its policy making body, and an executive board, which acts for the council in the administration of established policies and programs. In this context, the executive board is the body that manages the affairs of the association, delegating management of its day-to-day operation to the executive director. ALA also has 37 standing committees, designated as committees of the association or of the council. ALA operations are directed by the executive director and implemented by staff through a structure of programmatic offices and support units.

ALA is home to 11 membership divisions, each focused on a type of library or library function. They are the American Association of School Librarians (AASL), the Association for Library Collections and Technical Services (ALCTS), the Association for Library Service to Children (ALSC), the Association of College and Research Libraries (ACRL), the Association of Specialized and Cooperative Library Agencies (ASCLA), the Library and Information Technology Association (LITA), the Library Leadership and Management Association (LLAMA), the Public Library Association (PLA), the Reference and User Services Association (RUSA), United for Libraries, and the Young Adult Library Services Association (YALSA).

ALA also hosts 20 round tables for members who share interests that lie outside the scope of any of the divisions. A network of affiliates, chapters, and other organizations enables ALA to reach a broad audience.

Key action areas include diversity, equitable access to information and library services, education and lifelong learning, intellectual freedom, advocacy for libraries and the profession, literacy, transforming libraries, and organizational excellence.

ALA offices address the broad interests and issues of concern to ALA members; they track issues and provide information, services, and products for members and the general public. Current ALA offices are the Chapter Relations Office (CRO), the Development Office, the Governance Office, the International Relations Office (IRO), the Office for Accreditation, the Office of Government Relations (OGR), the Office for Human Resource Development and Recruitment (HRDR), the Office for Information Technology Policy (OITP), the Office for Intellectual Freedom (OIF), the Office for Library Advocacy (OLA), the Office for Diversity, Literacy and Outreach Services (ODLOS), the Office for Research and Statistics (ORS), the Public Awareness Office (PAO), the Public Programs Office (PPO), and the Washington Office.

ALA's headquarters is in Chicago. OGR and OITP are located at ALA's Washington Office, and United for Libraries is located in Philadelphia. ALA also has an editorial office for *Choice*, a review journal for academic libraries, in Middletown, Connecticut.

ALA is a 501(c)(3) charitable and educational organization.

Leadership and Strategic Planning

Sari Feldman, executive director of the Cuyahoga County Public Library, Parma, Ohio, was inaugurated as ALA president at the 2015 Annual Conference in San Francisco.

Feldman's presidency focused on the Libraries Transform™ Campaign, an effort to increase public awareness of the value, impact, and services provided by libraries and library professionals. The campaign showcases the transformative nature of today's libraries and elevates the critical role libraries play in the digital age. The purpose of the campaign is to amplify the message that libraries today are less about what they have for people, and more about what they do for and with people. The goal of the campaign is to increase funding support for libraries and advance information policy issues in alignment with ALA's advocacy priorities.

Julie Todaro, dean of library services at Austin (Tex.) Community College, will be inaugurated as ALA president at the 2016 Annual Conference in Orlando.

Three new ALA Executive Board members were elected by the ALA Council in a vote taken at the 2015 ALA Midwinter Meeting. Loida Garcia-Febo, Julius C. Jefferson, Jr., and Mike L. Marlin are each serving three-year terms that will conclude in June 2018.

In a planning retreat at the 2014 Midwinter Meeting, the ALA Executive Board identified three areas of strategic direction to guide the association into the future: Advocacy, Information Policy, and Professional and Leadership Development. Throughout 2014 and 2015, in-person and virtual forums provided the broadest possible opportunity for member groups to contribute to the vision, assumptions, goals, strategies, and objectives in each of the three areas. ALA Council approved the new ALA strategic plan at the 2015 Annual Conference in San Francisco.

Highlights of the Year

For details of ALA's Highlights and Accomplishments in 2016 go to http://www.ala.org/aboutala/sites/ala.org.aboutala/files/content/ala-annual-report-2016-for-web-accessible.pdf.

Programs and Partners

Public Library Initiatives

PLA's advocacy training curriculum "Turning the Page: Supporting Libraries, Strengthening Communities" is available for free download. The package includes an Advocacy Training Implementation Guide and a set of 15 training sessions that each include a trainer script, PowerPoint presentation, and handouts. An Advocacy Action Plan Workbook accompanies the training so that participants can develop an advocacy plan for their libraries in real-time.

Since launching in June PLA's "Project Outcome" has quickly met public library demand and desire for standardized performance measures. "Project Outcome" is dedicated to helping public libraries understand and share the true impact of essential library services and programs with simple survey instruments and an easy-to-use process for measuring and analyzing outcomes. The surveys were designed and developed by the Performance Measurement Task Force comprising library leaders, researchers, and data analysts.

Libraries Transforming Communities

ALA and the Harwood Institute for Public Innovation partnered on "Libraries Transforming Communities (LTC)," an ALA initiative that sought to strengthen libraries' roles as core community leaders and change-agents. In 2015 ALA released a free, six-part online course designed to help libraries strengthen their role as core community leaders and work with residents to bring about positive change. The LTC initiative was funded by the Bill and Melinda Gates Foundation, and the ten public libraries participating in the initiative concluded their 18-month projects in December.

Building STEAM with Día Toolkit

ALSC launched a free downloadable "Building STEAM with Día Toolkit." The toolkit provides a research-based overview of the importance of intentionally planning for the inclusion of diverse content and community partners in programming centered on science, technology, engineering, arts, and math. The toolkit was made possible by the Dollar General Literacy Foundation.

Beyond Words Disaster Relief Grants

Old Dock Elementary School in Whiteville, North Carolina, and James Monroe Elementary in Edison, New Jersey, were the recipients of the 2015 catastrophic disaster relief grants offered as a part of the AASL Beyond Words Grant funded by the Dollar General Literacy Foundation. Since 2012 two catastrophic grants are awarded yearly to schools that suffered a 90 percent or greater loss to the school library program due to a natural disaster, fire, or an act recognized by the federal government as terrorism.

Conferences and Workshops

ACRL 2015 National Conference

More than 5,000 library staff, exhibitors, speakers, and guests from all 50 states and 24 countries attended the ACRL 2015 Conference, held March 25–28 in Portland, Oregon. Themed "Creating Sustainable Community," the conference offered more than 500 programs that explored a host of pressing issues affecting higher education. Key topics included the changing nature and role of academic and research librarians, libraries as partners in higher education, scholarly communication, libraries and social justice, assessment, and trends in information literacy instruction, along with a variety of technology-related subjects such as e-textbooks, mobile services, and social media.

2015 Annual Conference

The 2015 ALA Annual Conference & Exhibition, June 25–30 in San Francisco, brought 22,696 attendees and exhibitors from all over the world.

The Opening General Session kicked off with cheers for that morning's announcement of the historic Supreme Court decision on marriage equality. As the litigator responsible for invalidating a key section of the Defense of Marriage Act (DOMA) two years to the day earlier, Roberta A. Kaplan was an especially timely and inspiring speaker, and surprise guest Nancy Pelosi, minority leader of the House of Representatives, added to the celebration. Pelosi attended to honor managers who kept the Enoch Pratt Free Library and its branches open and engaged with the Baltimore community during the civil unrest in April 2015.

"Show Your Pride" was a consistent conference theme, with special events and programs, and the wrap-up of ALA's first time sponsoring the nationwide GLBT Book Month. Around 100 conference attendees marched with staff from the San Francisco Public Library in Sunday's exuberant Pride Parade that passed just blocks from the conference site, while others cheered them on. Many other areas of equality, diversity, and inclusion provided a focus at the conference. Dozens of attendees suggested possible actions relating to diversity and inclusion by completing the sentence on the Networking Uncommons wall: "In order to improve the climate of diversity and inclusion within ALA, I plan to_____."

Some content was organized around ALA's three strategic directions: advocacy, information policy, and professional and leadership development. Rooms were packed for sessions on digital content, community engagement, the impact and potential of the newest technologies, digital literacy, the state of the school library, privacy and surveillance, services for makers, accessible gaming, innovative services for English Language Learners and immigrants, services for veterans, financial education, intellectual property and 3D printing, sustainable libraries, and many more.

Standing-room-only Auditorium Speaker sessions included writers, activists, thought-leaders, actors, and artists Gloria Steinem, Haifaa al-Mansour, Sarah Vowell, Nick Offerman, Joshua Davis with Rick Jacobs and David Thomson, Edwidge Danticat, and Sonia Manzano. At the President's Program, Courtney Young presented Sarah Lewis, whose "Embrace the Near Win" was selected as one of TED Talks' 2014 Collection of the Most Powerful Talks.

ALA at IFLA Congress in Cape Town

More than 3,000 delegates from 120 countries attended the IFLA Congress held in Cape Town, South Africa, August 15–21. ALA President Sari Feldman and Past-President Courtney Young led a delegation of 275 U.S. library professionals. President Feldman represented ALA at numerous high-level meetings and discussed ALA accreditation as a panelist at the "Quality Assurance of Library and Information Science" program. ALA member Donna Scheeder was inaugurated as the new IFLA President on August 21, and will serve a two-year term. ALA Executive Board Member Loida Garcia-Febo was re-elected to another two-year term on the IFLA Governing Board.

ALSC National Institute

The ALSC National Institute with the theme of "Believe. Build. Become" was held September 15–17, 2015, in Charlotte, North Carolina. The institute featured educational programming and inspirational speakers. A number of award-winning authors and illustrators were present and a special reception, held at ImaginOn, was a highlight event.

Sharjah International Book Fair/ALA Library Conference

Approximately 300 librarians gathered at the Sharjah International Book Fair (SIBF) in the United Arab Emirates, November 10–12, for the second SIBF/ALA Library Conference, ALA's most ambitious international professional development event. Librarians participated in the three days of programs, training, and networking, in both Arabic and English, with translation provided. ALA President Sari Feldman's opening keynote on Libraries Transform was followed by 17 concurrent sessions and poster sessions on a wide range of topics for all types of libraries.

LITA Forum

More than 270 attendees participated in the 2015 LITA Forum, November 12–15 in Minneapolis. Attendees participated in more than 55 sessions and heard three keynote speakers. LITA partnered with LLAMA to provide content specifically for administrators and managers at the forum.

2016 Midwinter Meeting

More than 11,700 attendees and exhibitors shared the latest library-related trends, updates, innovations, products, titles, and services at the 2016 ALA Midwinter Meeting and Exhibits in Boston, January 8–12, 2016.

With an emphasis on ALA's new national public awareness campaign, Libraries Transform, dozens of updates, discussion groups, workshops, and several high-profile speakers addressed in different ways how libraries are less about what they *have* and more about what they do *for* and *with* people. The "Because of You" branding at Midwinter honored library workers for their role in transforming libraries.

Several future-forward sessions were sponsored by ALA's Center for the Future of Libraries, the Office for Diversity, Literacy, and Outreach Services, and the Task Force on Equity, Diversity and Inclusion. They included the well-attended "Libraries Transform: Understanding Change," a three-hour interactive exploration with trainers from Kotter International, experts in the process and leadership of change, around libraries' current context and the question, "What do I need to be doing now to move my library into the future?" "Libraries Transform: Civic and Social Innovation" offered drop-in sessions with Boston-based civic and social innovators for two outward-looking forums exploring the changes happening in our communities, leading to engaged discussion about how those changes relate to libraries.

In "Creativity, Innovation and Change: Libraries Transform in the Digital Age," Harvard Law School's Jonathan Zittrain, ALA President Sari Feldman, ALA President-Elect Julie Todaro, and Director of ALA Office for Information Technology Policy Alan Inouye examined innovative library environments and how we can leverage them to illustrate our value to decision-makers and influencers at both national and local levels.

An interactive workshop, "If I Hadn't Believed It, I Wouldn't Have Seen It: Exploring Systemic Racism and Its Implications for Our Lives and Work," sponsored by the Office for Diversity, Literacy, and Outreach Services with the Task Force on Equity, Diversity, and Inclusion, engaged attendees at two sessions in an exploration of how race, systemic racism, and racial privilege have implications for our personal and professional lives.

Senator Cory Booker, featured speaker on the President's Program, addressed a standing-room-only crowd. In his impassioned talk, he focused on seeing opportunity and hope rather than just challenges. The senator talked about libraries as "treasures for all," and great equalizers in advancing digital inclusion.

ALA kicked off its 140th Anniversary at Midwinter with a "Because of You: Libraries Transform" cake celebration in front of the timeline in the ALA Lounge that offered a glimpse of how ALA has been engaged in supporting library transformation since 1876, and invited people to add their own highlights to the record.

Grants and Contributions

Research on Student Achievement

AASL was awarded a grant from the Institute of Museum and Library Services to discover what works at that intersection of formal and informal learning in the school library learning space, in order to provide reliable information to assess the impact of specific actions in library programs and by certified school library staffing.

Curiosity Grants

ALSC awarded 79 Curiosity Create grants of up to $7,500 each, made possible through a $800,000 donation from Disney. The grants spanned a broad range of geographic regions and service populations to support libraries in promoting exploration and discovery programming for children ages 6 to 14.

Google Grants to Boost Federal Advocacy

OGR received $25,000 through Google's Washington-based policy office to underwrite two initiatives: a series of advocacy videos to be jointly written and produced with the Harry Potter Alliance; and a series of events to be held at libraries around the country.

Public Programming

Grants from PPO enable libraries of all types, sizes, and budgets to boost their offerings and infuse their communities with new ideas. In 2015 the National Endowment for the Humanities (NEH) provided funding for the following programs: "Latino Americans: 500 Years of History" was awarded to 203 libraries to facilitate informed discussion in their communities about the long and fascinating history of Latinos in the United States; 50 sites received grants for the Great Stories Club, a reading and discussion program that gives at-risk youth the chance to read, reflect, and share ideas on topics that resonate with them; 50 sites were selected for a nationwide tour of Shakespeare's First Folio.

The U.S. National Library of Medicine provided funding for 104 libraries to host the traveling exhibition "Native Voices: Native Peoples' Concepts of Health and Illness."

The Institute of Museum and Library Services provided funding for ten libraries to offer "StoryCorps @ your library," allowing them to collect oral histories at their libraries.

The AARP Foundation provided funding to develop the AARP Integrated Services for Older Adults model for public libraries. Four public libraries were chosen as pilot sites for the new program, becoming a one-stop location for vulnerable older adults to receive assistance in their communities in AARP's four priority areas: hunger, income, housing, and isolation.

In collaboration with the Smithsonian's National Museum of Natural History Human Origins Program, PPO selected 19 public libraries to host the traveling exhibition "Exploring Human Origins: What Does It Mean to Be Human?"

Twenty-four public libraries from across the country will host interactive science- and technology-focused traveling exhibitions, bringing learning about the stars and planets, earth science and climate change, and technology to audiences of all ages. The exhibitions are offered by PPO in collaboration with the Space Science Institute National Center for Interactive Learning, the Lunar and Planetary Institute, and the Afterschool Alliance.

The Financial Industry Regulatory Authority (FINRA) Investor Education Foundation gave ALA more than $1.6 million to support financial literacy education in U.S. public libraries. The funding will support the development of a traveling exhibition on personal finance topics, which will tour public libraries nationwide over a two-year period. The FINRA Foundation support will also fund a research study of financial literacy resources and services available in U.S. public libraries.

Publishing

ALA Editions/ALA Neal-Schuman

The ALA Editions publishing strategy focuses on professional development titles whereas the Neal-Schuman publishing strategy focuses on library education. Together the two imprints published 50 titles in fiscal year (FY) 2015. Lead titles on the professional development side included Rebecca Vnuk's *The Weeding Handbook*, Ben Bizzle's *Start a Revolution: Stop Acting Like a Library*, and Paige Andrews's *RDA and Cartographic Resources*. Lead titles on the library education side included *Preserving Our Heritage* by Michelle Valerie Cloonan and *Introduction to Reference Sources in the Health Sciences, 6th edition,* by Jeffrey Huber and Susan Swogger. ALA Editions authors have played a substantial role in online continuing education for the profession and Neal-Schuman's rich content and author-experts allow ALA to expand the range and number of its growing list of e-books.

ALA TechSource

ALA TechSource, which continues to be the source for two enduring periodicals, *Library Technology Reports* and *Smart Libraries Newsletter*, also develops and presents online content for professional development through webinars and e-courses. It produces both original and re-purposed content (from ALA Editions and Neal-Schuman authors) for its growing list of programs. It also produces the ground-breaking AL Live series for *American Libraries* magazine. AL Live streams live interviews and panel discussions that are underwritten by industry sponsors and are free to participants. They can be viewed in real time from home, library, or a favorite wifi spot, and allow viewers to interact with hosts and expert panelists via active live chat. Notable webinars included "Building Great Programs for Patrons in the 20s and 30s" by Katie LaMantia and Emily Vinci, "How to Respond to a Security Incident in Your Library" by Steve Albrecht, and "Copyright, Licensing and the Law of eBooks" by Mary Minow. Notable e-courses included "Music Cataloging with RDA" by Sonia Archer-Capuzzo and "Basic Reference Skills for Non-Reference Librarians" by Francisca Goldsmith.

RDA: Resource Description and Access

Total users now number 8,500, a 10 percent increase over FY 2014, and the renewal rate is increasing. International sales are strong and growing. The RDA Toolkit now includes German, Spanish, and Finnish translation with Italian scheduled for release in the spring of 2016. Germany has adopted RDA as its national cataloging standard. Development is moving strongly into linked data. Training in RDA and RDA-related issues is offered from a number of sources, including regular, well-attended, free "RDA Toolkit Essentials" webinars and a number of "Janeathons" that offer live hackathon-like seminars to practice applying RDA principles to cataloging exercises.

ALA Graphics

Celebrities, beloved book characters, tie-ins with movies adapted from books, and event-related themes all continued to inspire ALA Graphics products and customers. Collaborating with units across ALA to create new posters, bookmarks, and other products for library-related celebrations is a hallmark of ALA Graphics' success every year: National Library Week (April) and Library Card Sign-up Month (September) with PAO; Banned Books Week (September) and Choose Privacy Week (May) with OIF; Teen Read Week (October) and Teen Tech Week (March) with YALSA; School Library Month (April) with AASL; Día (April) with ALSC; and National Friends of Libraries Week (October) with United for Libraries. Four catalogs mailed and distributed during the fiscal year introduce a host of new products, and FY 2015 included a range of posters featuring popular book characters, READ celebrities, TV series, and book-to-movie-inspired images, many with accompanying bookmarks, included the following: character posters featuring Olaf from the Disney movie *Frozen*, Pizzoli's Pals, another version of Bad Kitty to coincide with the publication of a new book in the popular series, Kate DiCamillo's Flora and Ulysses, Cece Bell's El Deafo, and the adoption of Snoopy as the Honorary Chair of Library Card Sign-up month. A Super Heroes series featured Wonder Woman, Bat Girl, Superman, and The Flash. Celebrity posters included Jane Lynch, Tim Howard, and Octavia Spencer.

Booklist Publications

The multi-platform suite of 13 products includes a new digital version of the magazine, The Booklist Reader, which aggregates all its e-newsletters, *Booklist* webinars (sponsor-supported online programs, free to registrants); Booklist Delivers (an e-blast service delivering sponsors' HTML promotions to the *Booklist* audience), *Booklist Online* (now serving more than 1.75 million pages per month), 22 print issues of *Booklist* and four issues of *Book Links*. *Booklist* webinars have continued to be a high-profile success, with well over 60,000 registrants (averaging 400 for each program) for the 40 to 50 programs moderated by *Booklist* editors and special guests. Registrants who are unable to attend can access archived recordings. In post-webinar surveys, 91.2 percent of attendees said the programs are useful. All past webinars can be accessed through the *Booklist* webinar archive. In conjunction with RUSA, *Booklist* co-sponsors the Andrew Carnegie Medal for Excellence in Fiction and Nonfiction. Awards in 2015 went to Anthony Doerr for *All the Light We Cannot See* and *Just Mercy: A Story of Justice and Redemption* by Bryan Stevenson. Both authors spoke in acceptance of the awards at the standing-room-only presentation at Annual Conference. *Booklist* programs at Annual Conference and Midwinter include the ERT/Booklist Author Forum and a popular new program called "Read and Rave," which brings together a panel of young adult and middle grade collection development librarians who roam the exhibit aisles in search of galleys to rave about.

American Libraries

American Libraries' new website, americanlibrariesmagazine.org, now includes responsive design and generated a 45 percent increase in sessions. On the home-page, *AL* introduced a Twitter-like feed called Latest Library Links, which pro-vides up-to-date content about the industry and ALA. An increase in online-only content also boosted views, thanks in part to the hiring of a senior editor dedicated to generating and posting digital content. The magazine published many high-pro-file interviews featuring big names such as musician Pharrell Williams, bestselling author James Patterson, and National Book Award winners Jacqueline Woodson and Ursula K. Le Guin. Social media engagement includes more than 46,000 Twit-ter followers, nearly 9,000 Facebook fans, and 32 Pinterest boards with almost 5,000 pins. *AL*'s Twitter post about speaker Sonia Manzano's (a.k.a. "Maria") re-tirement from *Sesame Street* went viral, getting picked up by major news outlets such as *The New York Times*, the Associated Press, NPR, and *The Washington Post*. The publishing calendar included six print issues, one digital issue, and several digital supplements that covered ALA Online Learning, the State of America's Libraries Report, E-Content, American Dream Starts @ your library (with ALA's Office for Diversity, Literacy, and Outreach Services), and the IFLA edition—a print issue of which was distributed at the IFLA conference in Cape Town, South Africa. A final wrap-up piece appeared in a digital version of the supplement, accessible to all ALA members. AL Live, a live, interactive, sponsored stream-ing webinar produced in conjunction with ALA TechSource, continued to garner nearly 2,000 viewers per episode. AL Direct, the twice-a-week digital newsletter, will be approaching its 10th anniversary in 2016.

American Booksellers Association

333 Westchester Ave., Suite 202, White Plains, NY 10604
914-406-7500
World Wide Web http://www.bookweb.org

Founded in 1900, the American Booksellers Association (ABA) is a national not-for-profit trade organization that works to help independently owned bookstores grow and succeed.

ABA's core members are key participants in their communities' local economies and culture, and to assist them ABA creates relevant programs; provides education, information, business products, and services; and engages in public policy and industry advocacy. The association actively supports and defends free speech and the First Amendment rights of all Americans. A volunteer board of booksellers governs the association.

At the end of 2015 independent bookstore members of ABA reported another year of growth both in numbers and overall business, as well as strong holiday sales. The national resurgence in independent stores continued, with new stores opening, established stores finding new owners, and a new generation coming into the business as owner/managers and frontline booksellers.

In 2015 ABA welcomed 60 independent bookstores that opened in 31 states and the District of Columbia. In another sign of the health of independent bookstores, 16 established ABA member businesses were bought by new owners.

Following the final rush of holiday shoppers, booksellers reported healthy sales in 2015 and an equally encouraging start to 2016. A strong kickoff on Small Business Saturday, November 28, launched a successful holiday season for independent bookstores, boosted by "buy local" campaigns and widespread media coverage that trumpeted local booksellers and the unique draw of neighborhood stores.

Nationally, ABA reported that, based on the more than 500 stores reporting to the weekly Indie Bestsellers List, unit sales of books maintained the growth seen over the past few years, with an increase over 2014 of a little more than 10 percent.

ABA member bookstores and other independent businesses experienced strong sales growth in 2015, buoyed by their strong community ties and growing public awareness of the benefits of locally owned businesses, according to the results of the 2016 Independent Business Survey. Released in February 2016, the ninth annual survey conducted by the Institute for Local Self-Reliance in partnership with Advocates for Independent Business gathered data from more than 3,200 locally owned businesses, including members of ABA.

Survey respondents reported brisk sales in 2015, with revenue growing 6.6 percent on average in 2015, up from 5.3 percent the previous year. Independent retailers, who made up just under half the sample, saw revenue increase 4.7 percent in 2015. Holiday sales at local stores also grew by an average of 3.1 percent, beating the performance of many national chains and coming in ahead of the 1.6 percent rise in December retail sales reported by the U.S. Department of Commerce.

The survey results suggest that the strength of the independent sector is owed partly to an improving economy and partly to the spread of the "buy local" movement. Two-thirds of respondents in cities with an active Local First, or "buy local," campaign said that the initiative is having a noticeable positive impact on their business, including attracting new customers and fostering increased loyalty among existing customers. Survey respondents cited a wide range of direct benefits from "buy local" campaigns, with about one-third of businesses in Local First cities reporting that the initiative had led them to become more engaged in advocating on public policy issues and 45 percent saying they had resulted in more awareness and support among city officials.

However, the survey found that independent businesses are facing a number of challenges, including a lack of credit for businesses seeking to grow. One in three independent businesses applying for a bank loan in the last two years reported being unable to secure one. That figure was 54 percent among minority-owned businesses, and 41 percent among young firms, whose expansion has historically been a key source of net job growth.

Other challenges included public policy issues, competition from large Internet companies and large competitors that can use their market power to secure better pricing and terms from suppliers, the rising cost of commercial rent, and steep swipe fees set by credit card companies.

For the third year in a row, Indies First, a national campaign of activities and events in support of independent bookstores, marked another successful kickoff to the holiday shopping season on Small Business Saturday. Nearly 500 independent bookstores participated, inviting hundreds of authors into their stores to serve as honorary booksellers for the day.

Unit sales of books were up slightly over 2014 for the week including Indies First on Small Business Saturday. According to the Small Business Saturday Consumer Insights Survey, released on November 30, 2015, by American Express and the National Federation of Independent Business, total spending among U.S. consumers who were aware of Small Business Saturday increased by 14 percent in 2015, reaching $16.2 billion spent at independent retailers and restaurants on the day, up from $14.3 billion in 2014.

In December 2015 author James Patterson awarded $250,000 in holiday bonuses to independent bookstore employees to thank them for their dedication to spreading the joy of reading. Anyone was allowed to nominate a bookseller by answering the question, "Why does this bookseller deserve a holiday bonus?" Bonuses of $2,500 and $5,000 were awarded to 87 independent booksellers out of 2,848 nominations received.

"These grants and bonuses are my humble acknowledgment of some of the terrific work taking place in libraries and bookstores," Patterson said. ABA CEO Oren Teicher said "Once again, we are enormously grateful for James Patterson's wonderful generosity. Nobody puts their money where their mouth is more than Jim. Providing extra financial support to individuals who spend their entire day putting books into the hands of customers and spreading the joy of reading is an extraordinary gesture."

Also in 2015 booksellers celebrated the inaugural Independent Bookstore Day on May 2 with author events, discounts and giveaways, tasty treats, and special literary-themed merchandise available exclusively at 400 bookstores across the country. Results from a survey of the participating stores showed solid sales gains, with 80 percent of the responding stores reporting a sales increase over the first Saturday of May 2014. ABA created an interactive Independent Bookstore

Day map on its IndieBound.org website that allowed users to find bookstores that would be hosting events and selling the special literary-themed merchandise.

In July 2015 independent bookstores and other locally owned businesses across the nation took part in the fourth annual Find Waldo Local community-building event. Co-sponsored by the American Booksellers Association and Where's Waldo? publisher Candlewick Press, the campaign invited shoppers to pick up passports at any of 250 participating bookstores throughout July and to visit nearby businesses to hunt for the famous children's book character, earning stamps to be redeemed for prizes along the way.

In October ABA launched the Revisit and Rediscover program, a new feature on the Indie Next Lists that provides the independent bookstore channel opportunities to showcase and support favorite backlist titles. The initiative was developed in response to requests from booksellers and publishers to find new ways of highlighting the strong backlist works that provide a foundation for both bookstores and publishing houses. Two panels of booksellers compiled lists of enduring backlist titles they consider critical for bookstores to have on their shelves at all times. The first round of featured titles debuted on the December Indie Next List and the Winter Kids' Indie Next List fliers.

Also in October ABA launched a test designed to increase traffic to member stores—and to their e-commerce websites—by improving the online shopping experience for an initial purchase on IndieBound.org. ABA will evaluate the test results and report back to members in 2016.

Association and Governance

The results of balloting by the bookstore members of ABA to elect three directors to serve three-year terms on the ABA Board (2015–2018) were announced in May 2015.

In keeping with the 2011 amendment to ABA's Bylaws, which established two-year terms for board officers, Betsy Burton of The King's English Bookshop in Salt Lake City, Utah, was elected to a two-year term (2015–2017) as ABA president, and Robert Sindelar of Third Place Books in Lake Forest Park, Washington, was elected to serve a two-year term as vice president/secretary.

Elected to three-year terms (2015–2018) as directors were Valerie Koehler of Blue Willow Bookshop in Houston, Texas; Pete Mulvihill of Green Apple Books in San Francisco, California; and Jonathon Welch of Talking Leaves . . . Books in Buffalo, New York. This marked the second three-year term for Koehler and Welch, and the first for Mulvihill.

Continuing on the 10-member board were Sarah Bagby of Watermark Books and Café in Wichita, Kansas; John Evans of DIESEL, A Bookstore in Oakland, Larkspur, and Brentwood, California; Jamie Fiocco of Flyleaf Books in Chapel Hill, North Carolina; Matthew Norcross of McLean & Eakin Booksellers in Petoskey, Michigan; and Annie Philbrick of Bank Square Books in Mystic, Connecticut.

Leaving the board was Steve Bercu of BookPeople in Austin, Texas, who finished his second year as ABA president at the end of May.

At its July meeting, the ABA board unanimously approved a proposal to amend the association's bylaws in order to increase the number of booksellers serving on the board from 10 to 11. In explaining the reasoning behind this decision, ABA President Betsy Burton said that, "one more place at the board table will encourage the opportunity for diversity," and that the proposed change would also improve the association's governance by avoiding tie votes.

The change was approved by the membership in a vote that concluded on October 26. With more than 10 percent of ABA membership participating in the balloting—which the association's bylaws require for the voting process to be valid—the amendment passed with 299 in favor and 1 opposed.

Book Awards

The winners of the 2015 Indies Choice Book Awards and the E. B. White Read-Aloud Awards, as voted by independent booksellers nationwide, were announced in April 2015.

The **2015 Indies Choice Book Award winners** "reflecting the spirit of independent bookstores nationwide" were:

- Adult Fiction: *All the Light We Cannot See: A Novel* by Anthony Doerr (Scribner)
- Adult Nonfiction: *Being Mortal: Medicine and What Matters in the End* by Atul Gawande (Metropolitan Books)
- Adult Debut Book: *The Martian: A Novel* by Andy Weir (Crown)
- Young Adult: *The Darkest Part of the Forest* by Holly Black (Little, Brown)

E. B. White Read-Aloud Awards "reflecting the playful, well-paced language, the engaging themes, and the universal appeal embodied by E. B. White's collection of beloved books":

- Middle Reader: *Brown Girl Dreaming* by Jacqueline Woodson (Nancy Paulsen Books)
- Picture Book: *Sam and Dave Dig a Hole* by Mac Barnett, illus. by Jon Klassen (Candlewick)

Indie Champion Award "presented to the author or illustrator who booksellers feel has the best sense of the importance of independent bookstores to their communities at large and the strongest personal commitment to foster and support the mission and passion of independent booksellers":

- Neil Gaiman and Amanda Palmer (HarperCollins/Hachette)

Indie booksellers choose three classic picture books each year for induction into the **Picture Book Hall of Fame**. The 2015 inductees were:

- *Blueberries for Sal* by Robert McCloskey (Viking)
- *Frog and Toad* by Arnold Lobel (HarperCollins)

- *If You Give a Mouse a Cookie* by Laura Numeroff, illus. by Felicia Bond (HarperCollins)

The **2015 Honor Award** recipients were:

- Adult Fiction: *The Bone Clocks: A Novel* by David Mitchell (Random House); *The Magician's Land: A Novel* by Lev Grossman (Viking); *The Museum of Extraordinary Things: A Novel* by Alice Hoffman (Scribner); *Natchez Burning: A Novel* by Greg Iles (William Morrow); *Station Eleven: A Novel* by Emily St. John Mandel (Knopf).
- Adult Nonfiction: *Can't We Talk About Something More Pleasant? A Memoir* by Roz Chast (Bloomsbury); *The Empathy Exams: Essays* by Leslie Jamison (Graywolf); *In the Kingdom of Ice: The Grand and Terrible Polar Voyage of the USS Jeannette* by Hampton Sides (Doubleday); *Just Mercy: A Story of Justice and Redemption* by Bryan Stevenson (Spiegel & Grau); *On Immunity: An Inoculation* by Eula Biss (Graywolf).
- Adult Debut: *Fourth of July Creek: A Novel* by Smith Henderson (Ecco); *I Am Pilgrim: A Thriller* by Terry Hayes (Emily Bestler Books/Atria); *Painted Horses: A Novel* by Malcolm Brooks (Grove Press); *The Queen of the Tearling: A Novel* by Erika Johansen (Harper); *Shotgun Lovesongs: A Novel* by Nickolas Butler (Thomas Dunne).
- Young Adult: *Glory O'Brien's History of the Future* by A. S. King (Little, Brown); *Noggin* by John Corey Whaley (Atheneum); *The Shadow Hero* by Gene Luen Yang, illus. by Sonny Liew (First Second); *Tell Me Again How a Crush Should Feel: A Novel* by Sara Farizan (Algonquin); *This One Summer* by Jillian Tamaki and Mariko Tamaki (First Second).

E. B. White Read-Aloud:

- Middle Reader: *The Boundless*, by Kenneth Oppel, illus. by Jim Tierney (Simon & Schuster); *The Fourteenth Goldfish* by Jennifer L. Holm (Random House); *A Snicker of Magic* by Natalie Lloyd (Scholastic); *The Terrible Two* by Mac Barnett and Jory John, illus. by Kevin Cornell (Amulet); *The War That Saved My Life* by Kimberly Brubaker Bradley (Dial).
- Picture Book: *Goodnight Already!* by Jory John, illus. by Benji Davies (HarperCollins); *Kid Sheriff and the Terrible Toads* by Bob Shea, illus. by Lane Smith (Roaring Brook); *Last Stop on Market Street* by Matt de la Peña, illus. by Christian Robinson (Putnam); *The Smallest Girl in the Smallest Grade* by Justin Roberts, illus. by Christian Robinson (Putnam); *This Is a Moose* by Richard T. Morris, illus. by Tom Lichtenheld (Little, Brown).

Indie Champion:

- Authors United, represented by Douglas Preston (Hachette); Jeff Kinney (Abrams); Dav Pilkey (Scholastic); Richard Russo (Knopf/Vintage); Garth Stein (Simon & Schuster, HarperCollins).

Personnel

ABA experienced personnel changes during 2015. In March Robyn DesHotel was appointed chief financial officer to replace long-time ABA CFO Eleanor Chang. A graduate of Rice University and the Stanford Graduate School of Business with more than 20 years of finance-related experience, DesHotel came to ABA from PEN American Center, Inc., where she had served as the organization's director of finance and administration since 2010.

At the end of June Neil Strandberg left his position as ABA's director of technology to join the staff of Shelf Awareness as director of technology and operations. Following the restructuring of the organization's technology department, ABA CEO Oren Teicher announced the promotion of Marketing and Content Technology Manager Greg Galloway to ABA technology director; with this promotion, Galloway joined ABA's senior staff. Geetha Nathan, lead developer for IndieCommerce, was promoted to manager of IndieCommerce. After further reorganization, Phil Davies joined ABA's IndieCommerce Department in January 2016, stepping into the newly minted position of IndieCommerce director.

On June 27 former CEO Avin Mark Domnitz, who served from 1997 to 2009, died of cancer at the age of 71. Domnitz was the owner of Dickens Books and then co-owner of the Harry W. Schwartz Bookshops in Milwaukee, Wisconsin, when his many years of service to independent booksellers began. He served on the ABA board for two terms and was president of the association from 1994 to 1996. Domnitz was honored by his ABA colleagues at BookExpo America 2015.

Member Education

The 11th Winter Institute (Wi11), held in Denver, Colorado, January 23–26, 2016, brought close to 600 ABA member booksellers, 100-plus authors, and 40 international guests from Australia, New Zealand, the Netherlands, and France to the Sheraton Downtown Denver Hotel.

Wi11 featured three days of keynote addresses and featured speakers, education sessions, rep picks presentations, publisher/bookseller focus groups, and breakout sessions. The event was made possible by the generous support of lead sponsor Ingram Content Group and 72 publisher sponsors. Booksellers and international guests had the opportunity to take tours of bookstores in the Denver area.

In celebration of ABA's new Revisit and Rediscover backlist initiative, the opening reception was followed by the first annual Backlist Book Swap, where hundreds of booksellers and publishers shared their favorite backlist books. Those who participated were encouraged to bring a copy of their favorite "under-read" book, a title at least five years old and still in print.

ABA CEO Oren Teicher welcomed booksellers on January 25 and shared new evidence that the resurgence of independent bookstores is continuing apace:

Overall sales across the network of independent bookstores were up 10 percent in 2015, almost 8 percent on a per store basis, Teicher said, and total book sales at indie bookstores exceeded $500 million last year, which does not count non-book or other store revenues.

"In a year that saw bricks-and-mortar retailers pressured by lots of things, independent bookstores once again fulfilled their mission of putting the right books in the hands of readers and book buyers while growing their businesses in what obviously remains a challenging environment," said Teicher. "At ABA, we appreciate these challenges and we know that not every store in every community is seeing this growth, but the important fact is that nationally you are succeeding, and we will continue to work hard to see that growth across the country."

On the same day representatives from the economics consulting group Civic Economics released "Amazon and Empty Storefronts: The Fiscal and Land Use Impact of Online Retail," a groundbreaking new study commissioned by ABA that details the overall negative impact that Amazon has had on Main Street retailers and jobs. The study revealed that the real costs and ramifications of Amazon's expansion have been even more pronounced than many people had thought.

The study found that in 2014 Amazon sold $44.1 billion worth of retail goods nationwide, and that this growth and retail displacement resulted in a total of more than $1 billion in revenue lost to state and local governments. In addition, the study estimates that the shift to online sales has resulted in a national reduction in demand for retail space totaling over 100 million square feet, the equivalent of more than 30,000 traditional storefronts employing 136,000 workers

ABA awarded 67 scholarships to the Winter Institute, including several aimed at fostering diversity. Fifty-eight scholarships were supported by the event's publisher sponsors; five were sponsored by the Book Industry Charitable Foundation (Binc), a nonprofit dedicated to providing financial assistance to booksellers; and three were awarded in honor of former ABA CEO Avin Mark Domnitz, including one awarded by ABA to a bookseller at a store participating in this year's ABA-CUS survey, and two supported by memorial contributions to ABA following his death. Candlewick Press again awarded a scholarship to a bookseller active in the Candlewick Handselling Indie Recognition Program (CHIRP).

In 2015 ABA staff traveled around the country during the regional spring forums, meeting with approximately 350 member booksellers during the months of March and April. Held in conjunction with the regional bookseller associations, the annual forums are designed to provide an opportunity to share ideas, discuss industry issues, and receive updates on various association projects. At this year's forums, ABA presented a new education session, "Exploring New Markets," which examined opportunities provided by customer demographics and proven sales and marketing initiatives, as well as the practical steps necessary for booksellers to implement appropriate programs in their bookstores.

In May 2015 the annual BookExpo America conference and trade show was held at the Javits Convention Center in New York City. ABA hosted two networking events for editors and publicists—"Meet the Editor" and "Publicists Speed Dating"—open exclusively to ABA bookseller members. "Publicists Speed Dating" provided stores with the opportunity to meet one-on-one with publicists for approximately 12 minutes each to learn what publicists look for when planning an author tour, while "Meet the Editor" allowed booksellers to meet in a small group with book editors at a publisher's New York City offices for a behind-the-scenes peek at the editing process.

In fall 2015 ABA presented the all-new education session "The Economics of Publishing and How They Impact Booksellers" at each of the eight fall regional trade shows. Leading publishing executives provided booksellers with important insights into the financial realities they face every day.

A special bookseller workshop focused on human resources in conjunction with the Pacific Northwest Booksellers Association and New England Independent Booksellers Association trade shows. The new, in-depth education event, presented by Dr. John Sherlock, director of the Master of Science in Human Resources Program at Western Carolina University, covered essential aspects of HR for small businesses.

ABA's programming regarding children's bookselling also continued to grow in 2015.

The ABC Children's Group at ABA welcomed 190 booksellers to Pasadena, California, in April 2015 for an upbeat and energetic ABC Children's Institute, ABA's third standalone event for children's booksellers.

ABA published its annual financial survey of participating independent bookstores, the ABACUS report, once again in 2015. Stores participating in the ABACUS project receive a customized report that analyzes their financial results, including comparisons with other businesses based on multiple criteria (such as sales level, store size, and community type) in addition to year-to-year trending information.

ABACUS helps participating stores benchmark key economic indicators and create a roadmap for growth and profitability. In addition, ABACUS is used in aggregate by ABA to create timely education for all members.

The IndieCommerce team completed its execution of the migration of several hundred stores' e-commerce websites to the Drupal 7 platform. Throughout the process, IndieCommerce staff communicated and worked with bookstores in a number of ways, including through dedicated e-mail updates, conference calls, a series of webinars, and sessions and one-on-one meetings at BookExpo America.

Advocacy

ABA's vigorous advocacy efforts on behalf of member bookstores continued during 2015.

Among other activities, ABA focused much of its advocacy resources on the growing minimum wage issue, in addition to the ongoing sales tax fairness campaign and health care reform.

As a growing number of cities tackle the question of raising the minimum wage, ABA called on mayors across the country to include indie retailers, such as booksellers, in any discussions on increasing the minimum wage in their cities.

To assist booksellers in advocating for minimum wage policies that take into account the economic realities of independent retailing, ABA also created the Minimum Wage Legislative Tool Kit, which provides a number of items to help booksellers work with lawmakers, town officials, and the media to develop good minimum wage policy. Included is an interactive spreadsheet and a "Minimum

Wage Impact Calculator," a powerful visual tool that booksellers can use when meeting with key decision-makers.

ABA continued to work with the Marketplace Fairness Coalition, which includes a diverse array of trade associations and businesses of all sizes, in order to more effectively advocate for its members in the nation's capital.

In addition, Advocates for independent Business (AIB), a coalition of independent trade associations and businesses that ABA co-founded in late 2013, continued to advocate on behalf of independent business. In response to the subsidies and tax incentives that Amazon has been receiving from a growing number of municipalities to entice the online giant to open distribution centers, AIB and the Institute for Local Self-Reliance (ILSR) created and released a one-page fact sheet, "5 Things Local Officials Need to Know Before Welcoming an Amazon Warehouse," which provides data that reveal how these deals actually do more harm than good to local economies. Between 2012 and 2014, Amazon received $431 million in local tax incentives and other subsidies from local and state governments to finance its warehouse expansion. But Amazon has a long history of shirking its obligation to collect and remit sales tax, and still does not collect in 19 of the 45 states that collect and remit sales tax.

In addition, ABA, as part of a broad coalition of booksellers and authors, asked the U.S. Supreme Court to review a decision by the Second Circuit Court of Appeals in the case *U.S.* v. *Apple*, which found that Apple violated antitrust law by coordinating with major U.S. book publishers to influence the price of e-books.

The friend-of-the-court brief created by the Authors Guild, Authors United, the American Booksellers Association, and Barnes & Noble was filed in December in the interest of competitive e-book pricing, and was a continuation of the efforts of authors and booksellers to ensure that the nation's book markets aren't controlled by a single dominant player.

The brief highlights the benefits of a competitive e-book economy and argues that Apple's entry into the e-book market enhanced competition by decreasing the average price of e-books and increasing the number of e-book titles and of e-book distributors. This, the brief notes, has led to technological improvements in the e-book market and enhanced freedom of expression and access to e-books.

On the health reform front, ABA continued to provide its members with key information about the Affordable Care Act, such as how to claim health care tax credits and how to purchase insurance through exchanges.

After merging in late 2014 with the American Booksellers Association, the American Booksellers for Free Expression, or ABFE (formerly known as the American Booksellers Foundation for Free Expression, or ABFFE), dove right into its free speech advocacy efforts as the year started. Joining with the National Coalition Against Censorship (NCAC), ABA and ABFE condemned the January 7, 2015, terrorist attack on French satirical magazine *Charlie Hebdo*, in which ten staffers were killed by gunmen who stormed the publication's Parisian headquarters.

Later in the year ABFE served as a sponsor of Banned Books Week along with such organizations as the American Library Association, the Association of American Publishers, and PEN American Center. Nationwide, bookstores put their own unique spins on Banned Books Week with creative events, social media posts, and eye-catching displays that celebrate the freedom to read. The 2015 event focused on YA books that have been challenged or banned.

Association of Research Libraries

21 Dupont Circle N.W., Washington, DC 20036
202-296-2296, e-mail arlhq@arl.org
World Wide Web http://www.arl.org

Kaylyn Groves
Senior Writer and Editor

The Association of Research Libraries (ARL) is a nonprofit organization of 124 research libraries in the United States and Canada. ARL's mission is to influence the changing environment of scholarly communication and the public policies that affect research libraries and the diverse communities they serve. ARL pursues this mission by advancing the goals of its member research libraries, providing leadership in public and information policy to the scholarly and higher education communities, fostering the exchange of ideas and expertise, facilitating the emergence of new roles for research libraries, and shaping a future environment that leverages its interests with those of allied organizations.

The year 2015 saw transformation for the association. ARL and its member libraries began implementing the Strategic Framework and System of Action that were developed in 2014. The System of Action fosters efforts in five areas: the ARL Academy, Collective Collections, Innovation Lab, Libraries That Learn, and Scholarly Dissemination Engine. Four enabling capacities address advocacy and public policy, assessment, diversity and inclusion, and member engagement and outreach across all initiatives within the System of Action.

Below are highlights of the association's achievements in 2015, many of which were undertaken in partnership with member libraries or other organizations. For links to additional information about these accomplishments and an infographic of ARL's 2015 transformations and impact in higher education and society, visit http://www.arl.org/about/arl-key-accomplishments-in-2015.

Advocacy and Public Policy

ARL's Advocacy and Public Policy capacity includes analysis of legal and legislative public policy issues and encompasses advocacy for issues of timely importance to the research library and higher education community.

In February the association published *Research Library Issues* (*RLI*) no. 285, a special issue focusing on recent developments in U.S. copyright law as well as international copyright agreements. Many of these developments have significant implications for research libraries and higher education, such as affirming the right to provide access to digitized text for people with print disabilities.

In late February 64 organizations and institutions participated in Fair Use Week, an annual celebration of the doctrines of fair use and fair dealing, which allow the use of copyrighted materials without permission from the copyright holder under certain circumstances. Fair Use Week 2015 was organized by ARL, and participants included universities, libraries, library associations, and a number of other organizations. Over the course of the week, more than 90 blog posts, 13 videos, 2 podcasts, a comic book, ARL's "Fair Use Fundamentals" infographic, and several other resources were released. See "Fair Use Week 2015 Highlights" on the ARL website for an overview and links to many of the week's resources.

Also in February the U.S. Federal Communications Commission (FCC) voted in favor of adopting rules to protect and promote the open Internet, also known as net neutrality. The Open Internet Order ensures that Internet providers do not create "fast lanes" for those willing and able to pay a premium and "slow lanes" for everyone else—and that the Internet remains open and available to all. ARL participated actively with partner organizations in FCC's Open Internet proceeding that led to the adoption of the Open Internet Order, which incorporated many of the joint principles filed by library and higher education organizations in 2014. In September ARL joined the American Library Association, Association of College and Research Libraries, and Chief Officers of State Library Agencies in submitting an amicus brief in the DC Court of Appeals case *United States Telecom Association, et al.*, v. *Federal Communications Commission (FCC) and the United States of America.* The brief expresses these organizations' support of FCC's Open Internet Order establishing rules protecting net neutrality.

In March and October ARL presented two free webinars about the accessibility of electronic resources. The March webinar, "Working Together: Research Libraries and Publishers on the Value of Inclusive Learning Resources," raised awareness about the value of producing or procuring accessible born-digital resources to support library users of all abilities. The October webinar, "Library and Publisher Roles in Making E-Resources Accessible to Users of All Abilities," looked at recent successes and challenges to spur an active dialogue about the future of the digital book and the roles of research libraries and publishers in facilitating improved access to information.

In June the U.S. Senate voted in favor of the USA Freedom Act—legislation that bans the bulk collection of phone records that has been practiced by the National Security Agency since 2006—and President Obama signed the bill into law. ARL supported this bill as the first step forward in meaningful surveillance reform.

Also in June ARL's Accessibility and Universal Design Working Group launched a new blog devoted to facilitating web accessibility in research libraries, as an enhancement of ARL's Web Accessibility Toolkit. The working group hopes the blog will stimulate discussion of accessibility issues in the research library community, and encourages individuals to share their ideas and knowledge by contributing posts to the blog.

In October the U.S. Court of Appeals for the Second Circuit unanimously ruled in *Authors Guild* v. *Google*—also known as the "Google Books" case—that Google's mass scanning and digital indexing of books for use in creating a searchable online library constituted a legal "fair use" of copyrighted material rather than an infringement. ARL supported Google in this ten-year case. For an in-depth analysis of the Second Circuit's decision, see the ARL issue brief on the Google Books case. The Library Copyright Alliance—consisting of the American Library Association, Association of Research Libraries, and Association of College and Research Libraries—updated its one-page "Google Books Litigation Family Tree," summarizing the case's chronology in a graphical format.

Also in October the Library of Congress released its final rules for the current three-year cycle of the Digital Millennium Copyright Act's (DMCA) Section

1201 rulemaking. The updated rules continue to support access for people who are print disabled by allowing them to circumvent technological protection measures on literary works distributed electronically. The rules also expand a copyright exemption for motion picture excerpts for educational purposes. ARL, as part of the Library Copyright Alliance, submitted five filings in the rulemaking process in February.

The 12 negotiating parties for the Trans-Pacific Partnership Agreement (TPP)—a large regional trade agreement that had been under negotiation since 2010—announced the conclusion of the agreement in October. ARL had been actively involved over the course of the negotiations, and the release of the final text revealed mixed results. While there are some areas of text that are disappointing, overall the final language of the copyright provisions improved significantly from the initial proposals made by the United States. The final text includes more flexibility for the TPP parties and also includes language supporting limitations and exceptions, including for those with print disabilities. ARL published an issue brief on the final TPP text regarding intellectual property.

Over the course of the year, ARL worked closely with the Obama administration and members of Congress to support ratification of the World Intellectual Property Organization (WIPO) Marrakesh Treaty to Facilitate Access to Published Works for Persons Who Are Blind, Visually Impaired, or Otherwise Print Disabled. The Marrakesh Treaty is a significant achievement as the first WIPO treaty dedicated to limitations and exceptions, focusing on the rights of users rather than increasing the rights of rightholders. The United States has signed but not yet ratified the treaty; it was expected that the treaty would be sent to the Senate in early 2016 for ratification. ARL published an issue brief on the Marrakesh Treaty background and ratification status in December.

ARL Academy

With the ARL Academy initiative, the association is fostering the development of an agile, diverse workforce and the inspiring leadership necessary to meet present and future challenges. (See the "Diversity and Inclusion" section below for accomplishments specific to that area.)

In 2015 ARL published three *Workforce Transformation Stories* in which library leaders describe new workplace developments and promote organizational change: "Communities of Practice to Deepen Leadership Practice" and "Creating an Aboriginal Internship" by Jill Mierke, director of human resources for the University of Saskatchewan Library, and "Changes in Hiring Accelerate and Enhance Culture Change" by Joyce E. B. Backus, associate director for library operations, and Kathel Dunn, program coordinator of the Associate Fellowship Program, at the U.S. National Library of Medicine.

ARL, Columbia University Libraries, Cornell University Libraries, and the University of Toronto Libraries held a pilot Library Liaison Institute in June. Nearly 50 liaison librarians from the three institutions convened at Cornell for two days to examine—through a mix of presentations and active learning experiences—future models for structuring liaison work, and to discuss ways to measure the impact of liaison work on fulfilling the mission of the university. In December ARL published the final report of the event, which summarizes the institute and provides critical reflections and recommendations for reorganizing liaison work as well as guidance for offering future Library Liaison Institutes.

Also in June the association created the Julia C. Blixrud Memorial Fund to honor the memory and extend the legacy of long-time ARL staff member Julia Blixrud. The fund supports a scholarship for one master of library and information science (MLIS) student or recent graduate to attend the ARL Fall Forum each year. The forum is a one-day conference on a topic of interest to the research library community, held immediately after ARL's Fall Meeting in Washington, D.C., each October. Generous contributions from the community have established the memorial fund for the scholarship, to which organizations and individuals are welcome to contribute. In addition to the scholarship, ARL founded an annual keynote lecture at the Fall Forum in memory of Julia.

In November ARL selected 28 individuals to participate in the 2016–2017 Leadership Fellows program. This executive leadership program facilitates the development of future senior-level leaders in large research libraries and archives. Three sponsor libraries—University of Alberta, Colorado State University, and Duke University—and the Leadership Fellows Advisory Group are helping to design and support the 2016–2017 offering of this program.

ARL in November released *Evolution of Library Liaisons*, SPEC Kit 349, an exploration of the changing role of library liaison, the shifting goals and strategies of liaison programs at ARL member libraries, and the factors that influence these changes on an institutional level. A December webcast presented the SPEC survey findings and enabled webcast participants to discuss trends with the survey authors.

Assessment

ARL's Assessment capacity collects data that offer information and support decision making. This capacity also creates processes for collecting and disseminating analytics and metrics.

A series of four webinars in March and April focused on data visualization for library stories. Using Tableau software, libraries can better harness, analyze, and report their data to internal and external stakeholders. Video recordings of the series are freely available on ARL's YouTube channel.

In June the association published the *ARL Annual Salary Survey 2014–2015*, which analyzes salary data for all professional staff working in the 125 ARL member libraries in fiscal 2014–2015. The data show that Canadian ARL librarians' salaries kept pace with inflation, but U.S. ARL librarians' salaries did not.

In August Quinn Galbraith was appointed a visiting program officer (VPO) for 2015–2016 to research salary trends using the ARL Annual Salary Survey data. Galbraith, a social science librarian and former human resources manager for the Harold B. Lee Library at Brigham Young University (BYU), is examining whether minority- and gender-based differences in salaries can be explained by such factors as family size, family-related leaves, attitudes toward promotion, and years of experience, among other variables. The ARL Assessment Committee is serving in an advisory capacity on the project. In an effort to examine these additional variables, Galbraith distributed a survey to 44 ARL libraries; more than 1,250 librarians responded. He will use this data in conjunction with 35 years of ARL

Annual Salary Survey data to conduct his analysis. Galbraith recently published the results of a separate survey of 719 librarians at ARL institutions, examining academic librarians' job satisfaction and work/life balance: "The Impact of Faculty Status and Gender on Employee Well-being in Academic Libraries" by Quinn Galbraith, Leanna Fry, and Melissa Garrison, in *College & Research Libraries* 77, no. 1 (January 2016): 71–86.

In October ARL published *ARL Statistics 2013–2014, ARL Academic Health Sciences Library Statistics 2013–2014*, and *ARL Academic Law Library Statistics 2013–2014*. These are the latest in a series of annual publications that describe the collections, staffing, expenditures, and service activities of member libraries.

Also in October the Integrated Postsecondary Education Data System (IPEDS) Academic Libraries Component adopted revised definitions for fiscal year (FY) 2015 as a result of recommendations made by a joint ARL, ACRL, and ALA task force. The task force offered a free webinar to inform academic libraries of the changes and help the community prepare to complete the FY 2015 IPEDS Academic Libraries Component survey.

Collective Collections

With the Collective Collections initiative ARL is motivating the creation of deep and wide platforms for ensuring that knowledge resources are accessible and sustained through federated networks of print, digital, data, and artifactual repositories, created and managed by collectives of institutions in North America and beyond. SHARE is a key part of this strategy, operating at the network level and unifying distributed resources.

ARL—in partnership with the Association of American Universities, Association of Public and Land-grant Universities, and Center for Open Science—in 2015 further developed the SHARE initiative, higher education's venture to promote accessibility of research:

> In April the project launched the public beta of SHARE Notify, which generates a feed of research release events—such as posting a preprint to a disciplinary repository, depositing a data set into a data repository, publishing a peer-reviewed article—from diverse sources. By the end of the year the SHARE Notify database included more than 3 million research releases contributed by 77 data providers.
>
> In June 60 individuals from universities, corporations, nonprofit organizations, and government agencies gathered in Washington, D.C., for the second SHARE Community Meeting. Participants included SHARE Working Group members, SHARE Notify beta participants, technical partners, and other stakeholders. Most of the meeting was devoted to a small number of breakout task groups to explore specific issues, helping to define SHARE's opportunities, scope out limitations and boundaries, and identify what successful execution will look like and who it will benefit.
>
> In September ARL appointed two visiting program officers to work on SHARE from September 2015 to March 2017. Cynthia Hudson-Vitale, digital data librarian in research data and GIS services at Washington University in St.

Louis Libraries, is providing outreach and engagement support for SHARE. Rick Johnson, program co-director for the Digital Initiatives and Scholarship Program and head of data curation and digital library solutions at University of Notre Dame's Hesburgh Libraries, is fostering SHARE metadata enhancements and strengthening partnerships between SHARE and other research data stewards and providers.

In October the Institute of Museum and Library Services (IMLS) and the Alfred P. Sloan Foundation awarded ARL a joint $1.2 million grant to expand and enhance SHARE's open data set of research and scholarly activities across their life cycle. The grant will help support SHARE's investigations with several research universities about the value and challenges of tracking and reporting their research activities. The grant will also help the team increase the quantity of sources coming into the SHARE data set, and add or impute missing elements to improve the quality of the data set.

In July ARL released *Community-Based Collections*, SPEC Kit 347, an exploration of collections that have been amassed not by one individual but by a collective, which may take the form of a museum, ethnic or cultural organization, or other diaspora group active in the documentation of its past. In August the association offered a webcast that presented the SPEC survey findings and enabled webcast participants to discuss trends with the survey authors.

Diversity and Inclusion

ARL's diversity programs recruit people from underrepresented racial and ethnic groups into careers in research libraries, into the field of music and performing arts librarianship, and into the archives and special collections professional workforce.

At ALA Midwinter in January ARL hosted the 11th Annual Leadership Symposium for MLIS students participating in ARL diversity recruitment programs. The symposium focuses on topics relating to major strategic areas, as well as transitioning into, and building career networks in, research libraries and archives. Thirty-six students participated in the three-day event.

Research Library Issues (RLI) no. 286 was published in April, a special issue focusing on fostering diversity and inclusion in research library operations and culture. The three articles in this issue cover recruitment and retention of staff from traditionally underrepresented groups, organizational climate and health, and library services to people with disabilities.

In May ARL and the Society of American Archivists (SAA) selected six MLIS students specializing in archival studies to participate in the 2015–2017 ARL/SAA Mosaic Program. Funded by IMLS, this program strives to promote much-needed diversification of the archives and special collections professional workforce.

Seven ARL partner institutions hosted internships for the 2015 ARL Career Enhancement Program fellows. Fourteen MLIS students from underrepresented racial and ethnic minority groups participated in a six- to twelve-week practical field experience as a major component of this diversity recruitment fellowship. The Career Enhancement Program is funded by IMLS and ARL member libraries.

In July a selection committee chose four recipients for the 2015 ARL/Digital Library Federation (DLF) Forum Fellowships for Underrepresented Groups. Each fellow received financial support to attend the DLF Forum in Vancouver in October. The fellows wrote blog posts reflecting on their experiences at the forum.

The July 2015 issue of *Synergy: News from ARL Diversity Programs* features three essays by former ARL diversity and leadership program participants on advancement for library and information professionals at various stages in their careers, from library school students to mid-career librarians.

In August ARL chose 18 MLIS students to participate in the 2015–2017 Initiative to Recruit a Diverse Workforce (IRDW) as ARL Diversity Scholars. Underwritten by ARL member libraries, the IRDW offers financial benefits and leadership development to participants.

Also in August, ARL and the Music Library Association (MLA) selected four MLIS students to participate in the 2015–2017 ARL/MLA Diversity and Inclusion Initiative. This initiative—funded by IMLS, ARL, and MLA—seeks to address the growing need for professional staff in music and performing arts libraries to better reflect the changing demographics of students and faculty in those fields.

In December ARL and five partner institutions recruited a 2016 cohort of six Career Enhancement Program fellows. The new fellows participated in the 12th ARL Annual Leadership Symposium in Boston in early January 2016 and will complete internships in ARL member libraries throughout the winter/spring term. The ARL Career Enhancement Program is funded by IMLS and the partner institutions.

Scholarly Dissemination Engine

With the Scholarly Dissemination Engine initiative ARL is promoting wide-reaching and sustainable publication of research and scholarship to ensure that such publications retain and enhance rigor and quality, embed a culture of rights sympathetic to the scholarly enterprise, and use financial models that are sustainable.

In March the ARL/ACRL Institute on Scholarly Communication held its first unconference, ScholCommCamp, in Portland, Oregon. During this community-driven experience, participants shared skills, learned what has worked at other campuses, and built plans to improve their libraries' scholarly communication programs.

In May ARL released *Scholarly Output Assessment Activities*, SPEC Kit 346, which explores current ARL member library activities that help scholars manage and measure their output and impact. A June webcast presented the SPEC survey findings and enabled webcast participants to discuss trends with the survey authors.

Published in September, *Research Library Issues (RLI)* no. 287 offers an overview of the history of scholarly communication from its beginnings in the 17th century to recent innovations in digital and hybrid publishing.

Also in September, ARL released *Rapid Fabrication/Makerspace Services*, SPEC Kit 348, an exploration of current ARL member library engagement with 3D printing, rapid fabrication and digitization technologies, and makerspaces. An

October webcast presented the SPEC survey findings and enabled webcast participants to discuss trends with the survey authors.

The Fall Forum 2015, "Research Partnerships in Digital Scholarship for the
Humanities and Social Sciences," took place in Washington, D.C., in October.
This year's forum launched the Julia C. Blixrud Memorial Lecture along with the
Julia C. Blixrud Scholarship, which supports the attendance of one master of li-
brary and information science (MLIS) student or recent graduate at the Fall Forum
each year. The 2015 lecturer was Tara McPherson of the University of Southern
California, and the scholarship recipient was Liz Hamilton of Northwestern Uni-
versity Press.

In December representatives from Asia, Europe, and North America—including ARL's Elliott Shore and Kathleen Shearer, Rick Luce (Oklahoma), and Leslie
Weir (Ottawa)—gathered at the invitation-only Berlin 12 Open Access Conference
to discuss a proposal to flip subscription-based journals to open access models. For
a summary of the key points of the proposal and a description of the discussions
and concerns raised at the conference, read the Association of Research Libraries
report on the Berlin 12 Open Access Conference, available on the ARL website.

Spring and Fall Association Meetings

ARL holds two meetings of all member representatives each year. The Spring
Meeting is hosted by a member library or libraries; the Fall Meeting is hosted by
ARL in Washington, D.C.

President Deborah Jakubs (Duke University) convened the Spring 2015
Meeting in Berkeley, California. The theme was "Global Connections of Research
Libraries" and program sessions explored international copyright issues, shared
print repositories, and tools and services for open science. Member representatives, ARL Leadership Fellows, and ARL staff discussed the transition to ARL's
new Strategic Framework and System of Action. This meeting also marked the
completion of the 2013–2015 ARL Leadership Fellows program with recognition
of the fellows for their achievements. All available presentation slides are linked
from the speakers' names or session titles in the summary of the program sessions
on the ARL website.

Jakubs convened the Fall 2015 Meeting on October 6–7. The Strategic Thinking and Design Transition Team presented its final report, and System of Action
groups presented their interim reports. The meeting schedule on the ARL website
provides an annotated outline of the program sessions.

During the October 7 Business Meeting, the ARL membership ratified the
board's election of Mary Case (Illinois at Chicago) as ARL vice president/pres-
ident-elect. Three new board members were elected by the membership to serve
three-year terms: Lorraine Haricombe (Texas at Austin), Steven Smith (Tennessee, Knoxville), and Ann Thornton (Columbia). At the end of the meeting, Jakubs
transferred the president's gavel to Larry Alford (Toronto), who then started his
one-year term as ARL president. View a photo roster of the ARL Board of Directors on the association's website.

Strategic Thinking and Design

ARL embarked upon an intensive and extensive Strategic Thinking and Design process in the fall of 2013 to reimagine the future of the research library and re-shape ARL to help bring that future into being.

In February 2015 the association released the final report on the Strategic Thinking and Design work that ARL conducted from the fall of 2013 through the spring of 2014. The report includes a detailed description of the innovative process as well as the Strategic Framework and the System of Action that emerged from the process.

In early 2015 a Strategic Thinking and Design Transition Team worked with the ARL board, committees, and senior staff to develop recommendations for implementing the new framework. The Transition Team reported its recommendations at the Spring Meeting. Five design teams composed of ARL library directors and ARL staff/visiting program officer liaisons were appointed to further develop the scope and contextual framework of each System of Action initiative in order to define the breadth, focus, and type of projects that could be undertaken. The five initiatives are the ARL Academy, Collective Collections, Innovation Lab, Libraries That Learn, and Scholarly Dissemination Engine. Four enabling capacity committees composed of ARL library directors and ARL staff liaisons were appointed to address their respective issues—advocacy and policy, assessment, diversity and inclusion, and member engagement and outreach—across all initiatives and projects within the System of Action.

To support the new design teams and the Coordinating Committee, two visiting program officers were appointed to serve from June 2015 to May 2016; a part-time program director was hired in October. Melissa Just, associate university librarian for research and instructional services at Rutgers University, is a visiting program officer for the Libraries That Learn Design Team. Mark Robertson, associate university librarian for information services at York University, is a visiting program officer for the Innovation Lab Design Team. As program director for research and strategic initiatives, Elizabeth Waraksa is working closely with the Coordinating Committee to foster the development of project activities brought forward by member directors, staff, or partners in response to the System of Action.

The Scholarly Publishing and Academic Resources Coalition

Heather Joseph

Executive Director

21 Dupont Circle N.W., Suite 800, Washington, DC 20036
202-296-2296, e-mail sparc@sparcopen.org
World Wide Web http://www.sparcopen.org

Background and Mission

SPARC (the Scholarly Publishing and Academic Resources Coalition) works to enable the open sharing of research outputs and educational materials in order to democratize access to knowledge, accelerate discovery, and increase the return on our investment in research and education. As a catalyst for action, SPARC focuses on collaborating with other stakeholders—including authors, publishers, libraries, students, funders, policymakers, and the public—to build on the opportunities created by the Internet, promoting changes to both infrastructure and culture needed to make "open" the default for research and education.

SPARC counts more than 600 members globally, including 210 members in North America—representing seven Canadian provinces, 45 states, and the District of Columbia. The membership includes several institutions from outside North America and affiliate memberships of four major library associations. In addition to SPARC's three global affiliates (SPARC Europe, SPARC Japan, and SPARC Africa), this broad and comprehensive representation helps reinforce the coalition's international focus.

Its members are primarily academic and research libraries that use the resources and support provided by SPARC to actively promote open access to scholarly articles, the open sharing of research data, and the creation and adoption of open educational resources (OER) on their campuses.

Strategy

SPARC works internationally to make the open agenda the default mode for research and education through the adoption of open access, open data, and open education policies and practices. SPARC's strategy focuses on four strategic pillars critical to ensuring the open sharing and broad use of knowledge:

- Advocacy—raising the public policy profile of the open agenda
- Education—increasing the understanding of the benefits of the open agenda
- Collaboration—working with stakeholders to encourage the emergence of new norms that support the open agenda
- Incubation—advancing new demonstrations of scalable business models that sustainably support open sharing of these materials

Priorities

SPARC's strategy focuses on reducing barriers to the access, sharing, and use of knowledge. The highest priority is advancing the understanding and implementation of policies and practices that make openness the default for research outputs and educational materials—including journal articles, digital data, and educational resources.

The following were among key priorities in 2015:

Advocacy/Policy Strategy. The top priority for SPARC was to raise the public policy profile of open access to the outputs of research—including journal articles, data, and educational resources. SPARC advanced this priority by:

- Leading efforts to advocate for policies that open up access to journal articles, data, and educational resources on the institutional, state, national, and international levels
- Identifying and capitalizing on opportunities to open new advocacy fronts
- Supporting research on social/economic benefits of open access to research outputs
- Leading the U.S. National Open Access Working Group, and establishing a new Working Group on Open Data
- Working with media outlets to promote public awareness of open access
- Working with public and private research funders to create and implement open access policies
- Expanding communications and outreach efforts to maximize reach of campaigns
- Actively participating in coalitions working on target "open" issue areas
- Participating in and promoting productive collective efforts to build scalable capacity to support effective implementations of open access policies
- Hosting (or co-hosting) annual meeting on issues relating to open access to journal articles, data, and educational resources

Communications Reset. A key priority for SPARC was to retool communications efforts to better reflect the breadth of its expanded program portfolio by:

- Conducting a comprehensive review of current communications assets and priorities
- Analyzing recommended changes to the communications portfolio and creating a new strategic communications plan that emphasizes SPARC's role in the wider "open" movement
- Creating a new communications plan in concert with technical/IT platform changes required by SPARC's recent move to the New Venture Fund

Member Outreach. SPARC worked to articulate how SPARC's programs specifically support its members' campus education and advocacy activities by:

- Creating and refining members-only services (i.e., a monthly digest of key developments along with suggested campus-based responses; a new web area containing "talking points" documents, slide decks, and other communications tools for campus use, etc.)
- Expanding a successful OA/OER education "roadshow" for member campuses
- Creating OA and OER toolkits and other resources for campus use
- Building out resources for promoting/supporting the adoption of campus-based, faculty-driven open access policies and funds
- Sponsoring Open Access Week and its growing related activities
- Updating the "Author Rights" educational campaign
- Continuing the production and promotion of targeted educational materials

Continuing Priorities

Globalization. SPARC continued to expand its presence and programs to reflect and support the global nature of scholarly communications by:

- Actively promoting the updated SPARC brand as a reflection of global presence and activity
- Co-sponsoring biennial meetings outside the United States with partner organizations
- Developing SPARC brand-based MOU templates for use by prospective international partners
- Establishing SPARC-branded activities in South Africa
- Identifying new opportunities and establishing partnerships with key stakeholders in other global regions

Student Campaign. SPARC promoted the inclusion of students and student organizations in all areas of open access by:

- Providing financial and managerial resources to support the operations of this rapidly growing program;
- Co-funding an additional staff person for the Right to Research Coalition (R2RC)
- Strengthening joint advocacy efforts with R2RC and member organizations to leverage community presence on open access, open data, OER, and related issues
- Developing and presenting regular joint SPARC/student educational programs
- Supporting R2RC in organizing OpenCon for Students and Early Stage Researchers
- Seeking additional support/partnerships to help strengthen ongoing R2RC activities

Open Access Infrastructure Support. SPARC continued its leadership role in promoting digital repositories and open access publishing outlets by:

- Supporting academy-based publishing initiatives
- Actively partnering with OA publishers to promote awareness and adoption of open access journal publishing options
- Collaborating with university presses, scholarly societies, and other non-profit publishing initiatives to develop educational materials highlighting successful alternative publishing models for journals, monographs, and other scholarly communication genres
- Providing expert consulting services exploring and supporting transition strategies for subscription-based publishers to move to open-access models;
- Contributing to evaluations of potential business models supporting community-wide open access infrastructure
- Partnering with key digital repository organizations to promote educational programs of interest to the community
- Participating in workshops and symposia on access issues

Ensuring Organizational Stability and Strength. SPARC continued to place a premium on ensuring that its organizational structure is designed to achieve its mission by:

- Expanding representation on the SPARC Steering Committee to include experts in key issues areas and constituencies (i.e. data, OER, students)
- Deploying flexible employment arrangements to ensure high-level talent can be strategically deployed to meet changing resource needs
- Identifying and capitalizing on opportunities to build internal capacity, via ongoing monitoring of dues structure, grant funding for program support, expanded partnership arrangements, etc.
- Promoting and expanding member retention and recruitment efforts

Program Activities and Outcomes

Advocacy and Policy

- SPARC continued to achieve significant success with its high-profile policy advocacy program. As a direct result of its work in securing the 2013 White House Directive on Public Access, 13 U.S. federal agencies released plans in 2015 for policies ensuring that articles and data resulting from their funded research be made freely available.
- SPARC and its member organizations actively contributed to the ongoing consultations that resulted in the three major Canadian Research Councils issuing a new, harmonized Tri-Agency Open Access Policy in early 2015.

- The SPARC-supported "Fair Access to Science and Technology Research (FASTR) Act," a bill that would codify the White House Directive into law, successfully advanced through the U.S. Senate Homeland Security and Governmental Affairs Committee.
- SPARC introduced a new campaign to educate declared 2016 U.S. presidential candidates on the importance of open access, open data, and OER, and to advocate for the inclusion of these issues in campaign events and platforms.
- SPARC staff worked with the White House and U.S. federal agencies to raise the profile of OER as a policy issue, co-organizing a government-wide workshop on open licenses and OER, and leading coalition efforts to advocate for Executive Branch actions in support of OER.
- SPARC also worked to generate support for "open" practices within the foundation community. With support from the Robert Wood Johnson Foundation, SPARC convened leading research foundations (including the Gates Foundation, the Arnold Foundation, and the Soros Foundation) to explore the adoption of open access funder policies, and the establishment of an ongoing open access "community of practice" of research foundations in North America.
- To generate direct input on its programming from its members, SPARC established three new members-only advisory groups to help develop new programs and services, and to refine efforts to best serve members.
- To keep members ahead of the curve in understanding the latest developments in the scholarly communication environment, SPARC hosted regular webcasts (free to members) on important topics ranging from the Elsevier article "sharing" policy, to complying with new public access mandates, to developing campus rights-retention-based open access policies.
- SPARC continued to provide a full suite of educational tools and opportunities, ranging from "directors only" calls connecting SPARC members to thought leaders in scholarly communication to regular webcasts.

Communication and Media

SPARC was regularly consulted and quoted as an expert source on topics relating to scholarly communication. SPARC and SPARC-sponsored programs were featured in both the national and trade press, in outlets including the *New York Times, Times Higher Education, Science, Inside Higher Ed, Chronicle of Higher Education, Boston Herald, Library Journal,* NBC News, and Salon. SPARC staff also authored articles for various publications.

Through its website, SPARC highlighted the work of open access champions. SPARC honored the Bill and Melinda Gates Foundation and the Open Access Button developers David Carroll and Joseph McArthur with its 2015 Innovator Awards.

Campus Education

SPARC actively supported members' local, campus efforts by providing SPARC-sponsored speakers for campus events, practical guides, talking points, templates, and expert counsel on campus open access and OER issues.

With continued support from the Hewlett Foundation, SPARC expanded its OER program to provide regular campus-based opportunities for education and advocacy in support of the creation and adoption of OER. In partnership with ACRL, SPARC co-hosted the first Scholarly Communications Institute devoted to OER.

SPARC supported campus-based policy action in conjunction with a panel of experts to promote resources that support data-driven, community-engaging, and successful open access policy development. SPARC provides Web and administrative support for the Coalition of Open Access Policy Institutions (COAPI), a group of U.S. and Canadian institutions that have implemented or are in the process of implementing campus-based open access policies. SPARC also serves as a platform for the work of COAPI.

In keeping with its commitment to partner with the next generation of leaders, SPARC and the Right to Research Coalition (R2RC) co-hosted OpenCon 2015 on November 14–16 in Brussels, Belgium. In its second year, OpenCon brought together more than 100 students and early career academic professionals from approximately 40 countries to advance open access, OER, and open data. Since the inaugural event in 2014, more than 5,000 individuals from 150 countries have applied to attend OpenCon.

Through the R2RC, SPARC partnered with Texas A&M University to secure a grant to develop programming for the first ever "SECU Academic Collaboration Award" Workshop. The program brought teams of library directors and leaders together with student government leaders with the aim of identifying and developing ongoing campus open access and OER collaborations.

SPARC provided incubation support for the student-led "Open Access Button" project, a browser-based app that lets readers register when they've hit an article behind a paywall, maps those instances, and ultimately, will provide access to an open version of the article where possible.

SPARC's annual International Open Access Week continues. The 2015 kickoff event reflected the theme of "Open for Collaboration," with SPARC and the Wikimedia Library co-sponsoring a global, virtual edit-a-thon for open access-related content on Wikipedia.

SPARC-ACRL Forums

A major component of SPARC's community outreach occurs at meetings of the American Library Association (ALA) when SPARC works with the Association of College and Research Libraries (ACRL) and its scholarly communication committee to bring current issues to the attention of the community.

In January 2015 the SPARC-ACRL Midwinter forum, "The Integration of Open Education Resources into Your Library," was held in Chicago. In June a second forum, "Advancing 'Open' Through Library Partnerships with Students and Early Career Researchers," was held in San Francisco at ALA's Annual Meeting.

Governance

SPARC is guided by a steering committee. The 2015 committee members were Jun Adachi (Japanese National Institute of Informatics; for SPARC Japan), Prudence Adler (Association of Research Libraries), Juan Pablo Alperin (Simon Fraser University), Theresa Byrd (University of San Diego), Ada Emmett (University of Kansas), Lorraine Haricombe (University of Texas Austin), Loubna Ghaouti (Universite Laval), Vivian Lewis (McMaster University), Virginia Steel (UCLA), John Ulmschneider (Virginia Commonwealth University), Mary Marlino (University Corporation for Atmospheric Research), Barbara Dewey (Pennsylvania State University), Deborah Jakubs (Duke University), Mary Case (University of Illinois Chicago).

Council on Library and Information Resources

1707 L St. N.W., Suite 650, Washington, DC 20036
202-939-4754
World Wide Web http://www.clir.org
Twitter @CLIRNews

Kathlin Smith
Director of Communications

The Council on Library and Information Resources (CLIR) is an independent, nonprofit organization that forges strategies to enhance research, teaching, and learning environments in collaboration with libraries, cultural institutions, and communities of higher learning. CLIR President Charles Henry leads the 13-member staff.

CLIR is supported by fees from sponsoring institutions, grants from public and private foundations, contracts with federal agencies, and donations from individuals. A list of current sponsors, members, and funders is available at http://www.clir.org/about/current-sponsors-and-funders.

CLIR's board establishes policy, oversees the investment of funds, sets goals, and approves strategies for their achievement. A full listing of CLIR board members is available at http://www.clir.org/about/governance.

In 2015 CLIR had five Distinguished Presidential Fellows: Michael Edson, of the Smithsonian Institution; Stephen G. Nichols, of Johns Hopkins University; Elliott Shore, of the Association for Research Libraries; Michael F. Suarez, of the University of Virginia; and John Unsworth, of Brandeis University.

CLIR's activities in 2015 are described in the following sections.

Digital Libraries

Digital Library Federation

Strategy meets practice at the Digital Library Federation (DLF). DLF is a robust and diverse community of practitioners who advance research, learning, and the public good through the creative design and wise application of digital library technologies. Through its programs, working groups, and initiatives, DLF connects CLIR's vision and research agenda to a network of practitioners working in digital libraries, archives, labs, and museums. The organization promotes work on standards and best practices; research and data management across disciplines; aggregation and preservation services for digital collections; digital library assessment; and services that expand access to resources for research, teaching, and learning.

In April 2015 Bethany Nowviskie became director of DLF, succeeding Rachel Frick, who left the organization in September 2014. Nowviskie had been a distinguished presidential fellow at CLIR, president of the Association for Computers and the Humanities, and director of the internationally known Scholars' Lab at the University of Virginia Library.

In 2015 DLF partnered with the Samuel H. Kress Foundation to initiate a museums cohort within DLF. The initial group of new-member museums and museum libraries includes the Dallas Museum of Art, the Philadelphia Museum of Art, and the New York Art Resources Consortium (NYARC), which represents the libraries and archives of the Brooklyn Museum, the Frick Collection, and MoMA, the Museum of Modern Art. Representatives of these organizations will join the Smithsonian Institution Libraries, a longtime DLF member, in engaging in a series of continuing conversations over the coming year on how DLF and the broader digital library community might better engage and support museums and museum libraries.

DLF members post regular updates on their work in the blog series DLF Contribute, available at https://www.diglib.org/topics/contribute/.

The following paragraphs describe current initiatives at DLF. Additional information can be found on DLF's website, https://www.diglib.org.

DLF Forum. The DLF Forum is convened annually and is open to digital library practitioners from member institutions and the broader community. The forum serves as a meeting place, marketplace, and congress. As a meeting place it provides an opportunity for DLF working groups, affiliated organizations, and community members to conduct business and present their work. As a marketplace of ideas, the forum provides an opportunity to disseminate experiences and develop best practices, and to support a broader level of information sharing among digital library professionals. As a congress, the forum provides an opportunity for DLF to continually review and assess its programs with input from the community at large.

The 2015 DLF Forum, in Vancouver, British Columbia, was the first to take place outside the United States. The largest to date, it drew some 600 attendees, including those attending DLF's affiliated events. A Liberal Arts Preconference was held in conjunction with the forum. The one-day meeting was designed to foster conversation and build community among those who work with digital libraries or digital scholarships at liberal arts colleges. A fuller report on the forum, and links to live-streamed sessions, is available at http://www.clir.org/pubs/issues/issues108/issues108#forum.

Digital Library Assessment. The DLF Digital Library Assessment group, formed in 2014, met during the 2015 Forum to share problems, ideas, and solutions. The group continues its work year-round through a dedicated e-mail list and a DLF-supported wiki. Membership is open to anyone interested in learning about or collaborating on the improvement of digital library assessment measures. Current subcommittees are focusing on tools and best-practices documents to support cost assessment, to measure digital library analytics, to standardize digital library content citations, and to assess user needs and usability. Links to the group's recent draft and finalized white papers are available at https://www.diglib.org/groups/assessment/.

Digitizing Special Formats Wiki. DLF is curating a list of resources for professionals planning projects involving the digitization of rare and unique materials. The list, available at https://wiki.diglib.org/Digitizing_Special_Formats, includes introductory and reference materials relevant to digitizing cultural heritage.

National Digital Stewardship Alliance. In October 2015 the National Digital Stewardship Alliance (NDSA) announced that it had selected DLF to serve as NDSA's home starting in January 2016. Launched in 2010 by the Library of Congress as a part of the National Digital Information Infrastructure and Preservation Program, NDSA works to establish, maintain, and advance the capacity to preserve the nation's digital resources for the benefit of present and future generations. For an inaugural four-year term, the Library of Congress provided secretariat and membership management support to NDSA, contributing working group leadership, expertise, and administrative support. Today, NDSA has 165 members, including universities, government and nonprofit organizations, commercial businesses, and professional associations. The mission and structure of NDSA will remain largely unchanged. It is a distinct organization within CLIR and DLF, with all organizations benefiting from the pursuit of common goals while leveraging shared resources. More information on NDSA is available at https://ndsa.diglib.org.

DLF eResearch Network. The DLF eResearch Network (eRN) is a cohort-based learning and networking experience designed to help academic and research libraries devise collaborative strategies for data management support. eResearch Network members develop plans appropriate for their institutions through collaboration, resource sharing, webinars, and custom consultations by eRN faculty. Network members come from colleges and universities of varying size. To date, 13 institutions from across the United States and Canada have participated in the eRN, and the 2016 cohort will be the largest yet.

The 2015 DLF eRN cohort kicked off with an in-person meeting in April, co-located with the Research Data Access and Preservation (RDAP) summit in Minneapolis. Work concluded with a meeting at the 2015 DLF Forum in Vancouver. Over the course of the program, participants from five institutions learned more about data management surveys; some identified and filled needs for repository software, conducted outreach with local scholars and administrators, and piloted educational workshops.

Openlab Workshop. In December 2015 CLIR co-hosted a series of meetings to assess the feasibility of a new venture, Openlab, to accelerate change in the GLAM (gallery, library, archive, and museum) sector. Openlab is envisioned as a solutions lab, convener, and consultancy. The idea for Openlab, spearheaded by CLIR Distinguished Presidential Fellow Michael Edson, grew from an observation that GLAMs are not leveraging their use of technology to address the grand challenges of our time, and are not at the forefront of debates that affect the public good.

A workshop held on December 2 at the offices of the American Alliance of Museums was preceded by a day of ignite talks and an unconference that generated ideas and participation from a larger community than could be accommodated in a workshop setting. More than 100 professionals from 80 institutions attended the unconference and ignite talks, and 36 individuals participated. The meetings were supported with funding from the National Endowment for the Humanities Office of Digital Humanities and Division of Public Programs. Information and materials from Openlab events are available at the project's wiki, at http://openlabworkshop. wikispaces.com/. The site includes videos of the ignite talks, unconference session notes, and workshop information.

Assessment of National Digital Stewardship Residency Programs

With funding from the Institute of Museum and Library Services (IMLS), CLIR is assessing the impact of five National Digital Stewardship Residency (NDSR) initiatives. Between 2012 and 2015 the IMLS Laura Bush 21st Century Librarian Program funded a series of five projects designed to build capacity in the information services and cultural heritage professions for the collection, management, preservation, and distribution of digital assets to the American public. By the summer of 2016, 35 recent graduates of master's programs in library and information science and related fields will have completed working residencies at leading U.S. institutions in the field of digital stewardship.

In fall 2015 a research team led by former CLIR Postdoctoral Fellow Meridith Beck Sayre began gathering data through interviews, site visits, and a survey in order to evaluate the significance of the residency experience for the residents and their host institutions, to identify the differences among the five projects and the perceived effects of those differences on the residents, and to articulate the factors common to successful and productive residencies. In late 2016 the team will produce a report with recommendations for future initiatives that build on the work of the residents and their mentors. CLIR will publish the report at the conclusion of the project.

International Image Interoperability Framework Consortium

In fall 2015 CLIR became administrative host to the International Image Interoperability Framework Consortium (IIIF-C). Formed in June 2015, the consortium aims to standardize and improve sharing and display of image-based scholarly resources on the Web.

Founding members of the consortium are the British Library, Oxford University, Stanford University, Bayerisches Staatsbibliothek (Bavarian State Library), Bibliothèque nationale de France (National Library of France), Cornell University, Nasjonalbibliotek (National Library of Norway), Princeton University, Wellcome Trust, and Yale University.

IIIF-C aims to reduce the inefficiency and redundancy that result from incompatibility in how images are delivered, and to collaboratively produce an interoperable technology and community framework for image delivery. The framework includes two application programming interfaces (APIs). The Image API provides access to the image content and technical descriptions. The Preservation API gives structural and descriptive information about the image's context so that it can be appropriately rendered for a Web-based viewing environment.

Study on Needs in Continuing Education for Managing Cultural Heritage Data

In September 2013 IMLS awarded CLIR a grant to examine federally mandated plans for open access and their implications for continuing education needs for libraries, museums, and other cultural heritage institutions. Under this grant, CLIR is conducting research in three areas. Part 1 is a highly structured content analysis of select federal agency plans for supporting open access to data and publications, identifying the commonalities and differences among the plans with emphasis on access to data. Part 2 takes the results of the content analysis and traces its implications for IMLS program areas and the cultural heritage institutions they serve. Part 3 identifies gaps in continuing education opportunities for cultural heritage professionals, assessing the readiness of the current professional workforce and identifying how best to address the needs and close the gaps in the immediate and longer term. Final results will be released by summer 2016.

Committee on Coherence at Scale

CLIR established the Committee on Coherence at Scale for Higher Education in October 2012, in partnership with Vanderbilt University. The committee's charge is to examine emerging national-scale digital projects and their potential to help transform higher education in terms of scholarly productivity, teaching, cost-efficiency, and sustainability. The committee currently comprises 24 members, representing university and college presidents and provosts, heads of national education associations and other organizations, and library and information science deans. The committee meets twice yearly.

In spring 2015 the University of Pittsburgh's iSchool announced the first two iFellows under the new doctoral fellowship program for information science students that support research for the Committee on Coherence at Scale. Timothy Schultz, Ph.D. student at Drexel University's iSchool, and Wei Jeng, Ph.D. student at the University of Pittsburgh's iSchool, were selected from a competitive pool of applicants. Timothy Schultz's research will dive into the world of "big data" as it pertains to collaborating, visualizing, and sharing information in the medical industry. Wei Jeng's research will focus on her interest in information sharing, with an emphasis on investigating how scholars communicate and share research data with one another. The program, funded by an award from the Andrew W. Mellon Foundation, will ultimately support ten iFellows in total.

Scholarship and Research

Postdoctoral Fellowship Program

CLIR's Postdoctoral Fellowship Program offers recent Ph.D. graduates an opportunity to work on projects that forge and strengthen connections among library collections, educational technologies, and current research. Launched in 2004, the program has supported 130 fellows at 60 host institutions across the United States and Canada. Since 2012, in response to a growing recognition within the professional community that research data management poses particular challenges to libraries and other departments serving today's researchers, CLIR expanded the program's focus to data curation. With grant support from the Alfred P. Sloan and Andrew W. Mellon foundations, CLIR seeks to help host institutions establish staffing models, policies, resources, and services relating to research data curation through matching those institutions with Ph.D.'s with expertise relevant to their needs.

In May 2015 CLIR announced the award of 14 postdoctoral fellowships: five Postdoctoral Fellowships in Academic Libraries, five CLIR/DLF Postdoctoral Fellowships in Data Curation for Visual Studies, and four CLIR/DLF Postdoctoral Fellowships in Data Curation for the Sciences and Social Sciences. The Fellowships in Data Curation for Visual Studies were launched with funding from the Andrew W. Mellon Foundation. In June CLIR received additional funding from the Mellon Foundation to support five two-year Fellowships in Data Curation for Medieval Studies, starting in July 2016. An animated overview of the data curation program, produced in fall 2015, is available at http://www.clir.org/fellowships/postdoc/info. A list of current and previous fellows is available at http://www.clir.org/fellowships/postdoc/fellowsupdate.

All new fellows attended a summer seminar, hosted at Bryn Mawr College, addressing issues faced by 21st-century libraries, including data curation and management. The seminar provided an opportunity for fellows to participate in cohort-building activities. Fellows' supervisors joined the seminar for one day to discuss expectations and establish effective communication strategies.

In September 2015 CLIR published a volume of essays written by 20 previous and present CLIR postdoctoral fellows, in which they reflect on their experiences and, more broadly, on the direction of academia. The essays focus on working conditions associated with creating a new profession of expertise and responsibilities in light of emerging forms of scholarly communication and pedagogy. The volume, titled *The Process of Discovery: The CLIR Postdoctoral Fellowship Program and the Future of the Academy*, is available at http://www.clir.org/pubs/reports/pub167.

Cataloging Hidden Special Collections and Archives

Launched in 2008 with the support of the Andrew W. Mellon Foundation, CLIR's Cataloging Hidden Special Collections and Archives Program announced its final round of 19 grants in December 2014. The program, which had supported efforts to expose unknown or underused cultural materials, has been succeeded by a new program to digitize hidden collections, described below.

A capstone event for the Cataloging Hidden Special Collections and Archives program was held in March 2015 at the Kislak Center for Special Collections, Rare Books and Manuscripts at the University of Pennsylvania Libraries. The symposium, titled "Innovation, Collaboration, and Models," and the unconference that preceded the symposium drew 172 participants, including representatives from 62 Hidden Collections projects. More than 75 presenters and discussion leaders contributed to the program, vividly illustrating the impact that the Hidden Collections initiative has had over its seven-year history. Grant recipients addressed problems that today's library and cultural heritage professionals face as they organize collections and make them accessible to scholars and other users. In October CLIR published the symposium proceedings, which are available at http://www.clir.org/pubs/reports/pub169.

Since its inception, the program has awarded 129 grants amounting to $27.5 million. Grants have gone to academic libraries, museums, public libraries, archives, and historical societies, among other types of cultural institutions. Through the grant program, one quarter of the funded projects were collaborative partnerships. By June 2015 grant recipients reported the archival processing of at least 2,952 collections, comprising a reported 53,608 linear feet, an additional 4,229 cubic feet, plus 960 boxes of mixed materials. Recipients have created item-level descriptions for a reported 273,728 items, including 50,551 books and manuscripts; 46,702 audio and audiovisual recordings; 29,393 items of ephemera; 27,125 pamphlets; 15,600 pamphlet plays; 8,560 maps and map series; 6,956 artifacts; 5,537 artworks; and 2,978 architectural drawings.

Digitizing Hidden Special Collections and Archives

In January 2015 CLIR announced a major new program to fund the digitization of rare and unique content in cultural memory institutions, thanks to a grant from the Andrew W. Mellon Foundation. The national competition is built on the model of CLIR's Cataloging Hidden Special Collections and Archives program. Developed through consultation with digital library practitioners and funders, and with input from the broader community, the program is designed to:

- encourage approaches to digitization that make possible new kinds of scholarship in the digital research environment
- support the digitization of entire collections, rather than selected items
- promote strategic partnerships, as few institutions have the capacity to handle and scan the wide array of objects in their collections
- promote best practices for ensuring the long-term availability and discoverability of digital files
- ensure that digitized content is made available to the public as easily and completely as possible

The two-stage application process was completed by late July 2015, and the first round of 18 awards, totaling $4 million, was announced January 4, 2016. A list and description of the projects is available at http://www.clir.org/hiddencollections/awards/for-2015.

Mellon Dissertation Fellowships

In 2015, 15 graduate students were selected to receive Mellon Dissertation Fellowships. The fellowship program, initiated in 2002, is intended to help graduate students in the humanities and related social science fields pursue doctoral research using original sources and gain skill and creativity in using original source materials in libraries, archives, museums, and related repositories. To date, the program has supported 194 graduate students who have carried out their dissertation research in public and private libraries and archives worldwide. A list of current and past fellowship recipients is available at http://www.clir.org/fellowships/mellon/fellrecipients.html. A brief video, in which Mellon Dissertation Fellows talk about the impact of the fellowship on their work, is available at https://vimeo.com/138078078. An assessment of the program's reach and impact will be available in 2016.

Leadership Education and Cultivation

Leading Change Institute

CLIR and EDUCAUSE hosted the second Leading Change Institute (LCI) May 31–June 5, 2015. Thirty-six participants joined deans Elliott Shore, executive director of the Association of Research Libraries, and Joanne Kossuth, vice president for operations and CIO at the Olin College of Engineering. In the months since LCI, participants have joined deans Shore and Kossuth for regular, hour-long online chats, allowing them to continue exchanges beyond the institute and to provide ongoing support and advice for one another.

LCI aims to prepare and develop the next generation of leaders in libraries, information services, and higher education by engaging those who seek to further develop their skills for the benefit of higher education. A list of participants from 2015 and previous years is available at http://www.clir.org/initiatives-partnerships/leading-change-institute.

Chief Information Officers Group

CLIR's Chief Information Officers Group is composed of 30 directors of organizations that have merged their library and technology units on liberal arts college and university campuses. A list of members is available at http://www.clir.org/initiatives-partnerships/cios. At their meetings and via a listserv, members discuss library and computing issues as an integrated whole. They have explored such topics as recent changes in merged organizations, strategic and tactical issues concerning cloud computing, trends in the uses of technology in teaching, and effective ways to provide faculty support.

Rovelstad Scholarship in International Librarianship

Kelly Grogg, a library and information sciences student at the University of Iowa, was selected to receive the 2015 Rovelstad Scholarship in International Librarianship. Grogg spent two years teaching at a rural high school in Cambodia through the U.S. Peace Corps. Grogg has a B.A. in English Literature from the University of Iowa and works as a graduate research assistant in Special Collections and University Archives. The Rovelstad Scholarship provides travel funds for a student of library and information science to attend the annual meeting of the World Library and Information Congress, which took place in Cape Town, South Africa, in August 2015.

National Institute for Technology in Liberal Education (NITLE)

In April 2015 it was announced that the National Institute for Technology in Liberal Education (NITLE) would migrate from its home at Southwestern University to CLIR on July 1, 2015. The decision to move NITLE to CLIR stemmed from a recognition that the two organizations' programmatic interests are closely aligned and that CLIR could help expand NITLE's audience and potential collaborators.

In addition, the environment for liberal arts colleges has changed fundamentally in 15 years, and the transition provides an opportunity to re-evaluate NITLE's focus and activities.

Shortly after the migration, W. Joseph King was appointed NITLE interim director to oversee planning, member relations, and outreach. Since the migration, CLIR has been managing a rigorous analysis and assessment of the organization. The assessment, based on surveys and interviews, will identify the opportunities and challenges facing NITLE and will be completed in spring 2016.

Publications

The Center of Excellence Model for Information Services, by Joy Kirchner, José Diaz, Geneva Henry, Susan Fliss, John Culshaw, Heather Gendron, and Jon E. Cawthorne. February 2015. Available at http://www.clir.org/pubs/reports/pub163. Used in a variety of industries, the center of excellence (CoE) model is designed to attract the most talented researchers in a particular field, enhance collaboration, and improve access to the resources needed for their research. This report examines the feasibility of using the CoE model to provide the new services required for the effective use of digital information.

ARSC Guide to Audio Preservation, Sam Brylawski, Maya Lerman, Robin Pike, Kathlin Smith, eds. May 2015. Available at http://www.clir.org/pubs/reports/pub164. A practical introduction to caring for and preserving audio collections, the guide is aimed at individuals and institutions that have recorded sound collections but lack the expertise in one or more areas to preserve them. Nine chapters, contributed by a range of experts, cover audio conservation and preservation, recorded sound formats and their associated risks, appraisal, related copyright issues, and disaster preparedness. The guide offers advice on making informed decisions about digitization, as well as strategies for managing digital content. An appendix to the guide focuses on fair use and sound recordings.

Getting Found: SEO Cookbook, by Patrick O'Brien and Kenning Arlitsch. May 2015. Available at http://www.clir.org/pubs/reports/pub165. *Getting Found* provides a step-by-step video guide to help libraries measure and monitor the search engine optimization (SEO) performance of their digital repositories. It includes everything necessary to implement a preconfigured Google Analytics dashboard that continuously monitors SEO performance metrics relevant to digital repositories.

The Once and Future Publishing Library, by Anne Okerson and Alex Holzman. July 2015. Available at http://www.clir.org/pubs/reports/pub166. This report explores the revitalization of library publishing and its possible future, and examines elements that influence the success and sustainability of library publishing initiatives. Authors include results of a survey they conducted to better understand how current library publishing initiatives are supported financially.

The Process of Discovery: The CLIR Postdoctoral Fellowship Program and the Future of the Academy, by John C. Maclachlan, Elizabeth A. Waraksa, and Christa Williford, eds. September 2015. Available at http://www.clir.org/pubs/reports/pub167. This volume celebrates the first decade of CLIR's Postdoctoral Fellowship Program by bringing together 20 previous and current CLIR postdoctoral fellows to reflect on their experiences and, more broadly, on the direction of academia. Each essay is a look into the working conditions associated with creating a new profession of expertise and responsibilities in response to emerging forms of scholarly communication and pedagogy.

Building Expertise to Support Digital Scholarship: A Global Perspective, by Vivian Lewis, Lisa Spiro, Xuemao Wang, and Jon E. Cawthorne. October 2015. Available at http://www.clir.org/pubs/reports/pub168. This report explores the expertise required to support a robust and sustainable digital scholarship program. It focuses first on defining and describing the key domain knowledge, skills, competencies, and mindsets at prominent digital scholarship programs. It then identifies the main strategies used to build this expertise, both formally and informally. The work examines leading digital scholarship organizations in China, India, Taiwan, the United Kingdom, Germany, Mexico, Canada, and the United States, and provides recommendations to help those currently involved in or considering embarking on a digital scholarship program.

Innovation, Collaboration and Models: Proceedings of the CLIR Cataloging Hidden Special Collections and Archives Symposium, March 2015, Cheryl Oestreicher, ed. November 2015. Available at http://www.clir.org/pubs/reports/pub169. This volume documents the capstone event to the seven-year Cataloging Hidden Special Collections and Archives program, funded by the Andrew W. Mellon Foundation. In the proceedings, more than 20 symposium presenters examine inter-institutional collaboration, student and faculty involvement, cataloging, arrangement and description, audiovisual collections, science collections, and outreach.

CLIR Annual Report, 2014–2015. December 2015.

CLIR Issues 103–108.

Re:Thinking blog series, http://connect.clir.org/blogs/allrethinkingblogs.

Association for Library and Information Science Education

ALISE Headquarters, 2150 N. 107th St., Suite 205, Seattle, WA 98133
206-209-5267, fax 206-367-8777, e-mail office@alise.org
World Wide Web http://www.alise.org

Samantha Hastings
President 2015–2016

The Association for Library and Information Science Education (ALISE) is an independent, nonprofit professional association, founded in 1915 as the Association of American Library Schools (AALS). It changed to its current name in 1983 to reflect more accurately the mission, goals, and membership of the association. Its mission is to promote innovation and excellence in research, teaching, and service for educators and scholars in library and information science and cognate disciplines internationally through leadership, collaboration, advocacy, and knowledge creation.

Membership

Membership is open to individuals and institutions. Personal members can include anyone interested in the objectives of the association, with categories including full-time (faculty member, administrator, librarian, researcher, or other interested individual); new professional (doctoral students as they transition to faculty member status, maximum of three years); part-time/retired (part-time or adjunct faculty, or retired professionals); and student (doctoral or other students, maximum of six years). Institutional members include schools with programs accredited by the American Library Association (ALA) and other U.S. and Canadian schools that offer a graduate degree in library and information science or a cognate field. International affiliate institutional membership is open to any school outside the United States or Canada that offers an educational program in library and information science at the professional level as defined or accepted by the country in which the school is located. Associate institutional membership status is accorded to libraries and organizations other than schools of library and information science.

Structure and Governance

ALISE is constituted of operational groups including the board of directors; committees; the council of deans, directors, and program chairs; school representatives; and special interest groups (SIGs). The association was managed from 2006 to July 2014 by the Medical Library Association, with Kathleen Combs as executive director. After a national search, SBI Association Management in Seattle was selected to manage ALISE starting in August 2014, with Andrew Estep as executive director. The board of directors is composed of seven elected officers serving three-year terms. Officers for 2015–2016 were Samantha K. Hastings (University of South Carolina), president; Louise Spiteri (Dalhousie University), vice-president/president-elect; Clara M. Chu (University of Illinois at Urbana-Champaign), past president; Denice Adkins (University of Alabama), secretary/treasurer; Laurie Bonnici (University of Alabama), director for membership services; Carol Tilley (University of Illinois at Urbana-Champaign), director for external relations; and Leanne Bowler (University of Pittsburgh), director for special interest groups. At the end of the January 2016 Annual Conference, Bonnici and Chu concluded their terms of service and two newly elected officers joined the board: Dietmar Wolfram (University of Wisconsin–Milwaukee), vice-president/president-elect, and Cecilia Salvatore (Dominican University), director for membership services.

The board establishes policy, sets goals and strategic directions, and provides oversight for the management of the association. Face-to-face meetings are held in January in conjunction with the Annual Conference and in spring and fall to focus on policy, planning, programmatic, and other matters. For the remainder of the year, business is conducted through teleconferences and e-mail.

Committees play a vital role in carrying out the work of the association. Since fall 2008 an open call for volunteers to serve on committees has been used to ensure broader participation in committee service, with members for the coming year appointed by the vice-president/president-elect for most committees. Principal areas of activity include awards, budget and finance, conference program planning, governance, nominations, research competitions, and tellers. (See http://www.alise.org/mc/page.do?sitePageId=86452 for a full list.) Each committee is given an ongoing term of reference to guide its work as well as the specific charges for the year. Task forces can be charged to carry out tasks outside the scope of the existing standing committees. For example, the board established the ALISE Committee on Accreditation Reform in Education (CARE), chaired by Tula Giannini, to address concerns regarding the quality and process of accreditation of LIS professional education. It is working with the American Library Association (ALA) Subcommittee on Accreditation to enhance the quality of LIS education and the accreditation process. The board is also working with ALA in providing statistics in searchable formats.

The ALISE Council of Deans, Directors, and Program Chairs consists of the chief executive officers of each ALISE institutional member school. The group convenes at the Annual Conference and discusses issues via e-mail in the interim. Tula Giannini (Pratt University) and Seamus Ross (University of Toronto) serve as 2014–2016 co-chairs.

Within each institutional member school, a school representative is named to serve as a direct link between the membership and the ALISE board. These individuals communicate to the faculty of their school about ALISE and the association's events and initiatives and provide input on membership issues to the ALISE board.

Special interest groups (SIGs) enable members with shared interests to communicate and collaborate, with a particular emphasis on programs at the Annual Conference. New SIGs are established as areas of interest emerge. Ongoing SIGs, grouped by thematic clusters, are:

- *Roles and Responsibilities*: Assistant/Associate Deans and Directors, Doctoral Students, New Faculty, Part-time and Adjunct Faculty, Student Services

- *Teaching and Learning*: Curriculum, Distance Education, Innovative Pedagogies
- *Topics and Courses*: Archival/Preservation Education; Development and Fundraising; Gender Issues; Historical Perspectives; Information Ethics; Information Policy; International Library Education; Multicultural, Ethnic, and Humanistic Concerns; Research; School Library Media; Technical Services Education, Youth Services

Communication

ALISE communication channels are mainly electronic. The organization's presence on social media including Facebook, LinkedIn, and Twitter has grown. LinkedIn continues to be ALISE's most popular social media tool with 1,786 members in January 2016.

Publications

The ALISE publications program has four components:

- The *Journal of Education for Library and Information Science* (*JELIS*) is a peer-reviewed quarterly journal edited by Peta Wellstead. The journal is a scholarly forum for discussion and presentation of research and issues within the field of library and information science (LIS) education. Dr. Wellstead transitioned *JELIS* to an online journal, with its first electronic issue published in January 2015. The journal is open access at a green level.
- The *ALISE Directory of LIS Programs and Faculty in the United States and Canada* is published annually in electronic format and is freely available to members. Listings of faculty for each school include teaching and research areas, using codes from the LIS Research Areas Classification Scheme that ALISE maintains. The classification is currently under revision.
- The *ALISE Library and Information Science Education Statistical Report* publishes data collected annually from its institutional members on their curriculum, faculty, students, income and expenditures, and continuing professional education. In 2015 the report moved to an Excel format, which allows users to further analyze the data. Members can gain free access to existing reports by logging in on the members-only area of the website.
- The ALISE website is the public face of the association and provides information about the association and news of activities and opportunities of interest to members. It provides login access to the MemberClicks system, where members can access members-only benefits (reports, member directory, etc.), renew membership, register for the conference and webinars, and access other services.

Annual Conference

The ALISE Annual Conference is held immediately before the ALA Midwinter Meeting. The 2016 conference, also the centennial conference, drew almost 400 attendees to Boston, January 5th–8th, to explore the theme "Radical Change: Inclusion and Innovation," celebrating the far-reaching impact of Eliza T. Dresang's work. Program Co-Chairs Kathleen McDowell (University of Illinois) and Lisa Hussey (Simmons College), with President Hastings, planned ALISE traditional conference offerings (presentations, poster sessions, and networking and placement opportunities); and continued some new programs: the ALISE President's Program, an unConference, and the unCommons—a gathering place to share, debate, brainstorm, and network. The Pre-Conference Workshop on innovative education for the future and the ALISE Academy on radical change led off the conference.

Professional Development

Starting in Spring 2014 ALISE launched the ALISE Xchange Forums, a webinar series offered free to members to facilitate virtual engagement with research and other membership interests during the year between conferences. The webinars have been successful, and ALISE plans to continue to offer them, creating a Professional Development Committee to review opportunities.

ALISE is also contributing to the future direction of professional development nationally. It is a founding member of the Coalition to Advance Learning in Archives, Libraries and Museums (coalitiontoadvancelearning.org). The coalition is supported by grants from the Institute of Museum and Library Services, and the Bill and Melinda Gates Foundation, with administration provided by OCLC. The goal of the group is to work in deliberate coordination across organizational boundaries to devise and strengthen sustainable continuing education and professional development programs that will transform the library, archives, and museum workforce in ways that lead to measurable impact on the nation's communities.

Grants and Awards

ALISE supports research and recognizes accomplishments through its grants and awards programs. Research competitions include the ALISE Research Grant Competition, the ALISE/Bohdan S. Wynar Research Paper Competition, the ALISE/Dialog Methodology Paper Competition, the ALISE/Eugene Garfield Doctoral Dissertation Competition, the ALISE/Linworth Youth Services Paper Award, and the OCLC/ALISE Library and Information Science Research Grant Competition. Support for conference participation is provided by the University of Washington Information School Youth Services Graduate Student Travel Award, the Doctoral Student to ALISE Award, and the ALISE Diversity Travel Award to the ALISE Annual Conference. This last award was created in collaboration with the ALA Office for Diversity Spectrum Scholarship Program, which created a parallel award, the ALA/ALISE Spectrum Travel Award to ALISE, partially funded by ALISE.

Awards recognizing outstanding accomplishments include the ALISE/Norman Horrocks Leadership Award (for early-career leadership), the ALISE/Pratt-Severn Faculty Innovation Award, the ALISE Service Award, the ALISE Award for Professional Contribution, the ALISE/Connie Van Fleet Award for Research Excellence in Public Library Services to Adults, and the LJ/ALISE Excellence in Teaching Award, sponsored by Rowman & Littlefield, a collaboration with *Library Journal*, which also had its own teaching award. Winners are recognized at an awards luncheon at the Annual Conference. [For a list of award winners, see http://www.alise.org/awards-grants.]

Collaboration with Other Organizations

ALISE seeks to collaborate with other organizations on activities of mutual interest. A critical collaboration with ALA is joint work on revising accreditation of professional LIS education. ALISE members are serving as representatives to national organizations, including the FEDLINK Network, the 2016 IFLA Conference National Committee, the ALA Committee on Education, the ALA Library Services and Technology Act Committee, the ACRL Committee on Education, and the Coalition to Advance Learning in Archives, Libraries and Museums.

ALISE continues to build its international connections, with members serving on IFLA Standing Committees that address education and research, and support of initiatives to address access to information, including the Lyon Declaration that calls on the United Nations to incorporate information in advancing equity and sustainability in the development of the UN post-2015 millennium goals, which will shape policies worldwide.

Conclusion

ALISE is guided by its strategic plan, "Setting in Motion a New Century of Leadership Strategic Directions, 2014–2017," and looks forward to new developments led by President Sam Hastings.

International Reports

International Federation of Library Associations and Institutions

Mailing Address: P.O. Box 95312, 2509 CH The Hague, Netherlands
Physical Address: Prins Willem-Alexanderhof 5, 2595 BE The Hague, Netherlands
Tel. 31-70-3140884, fax 31-70-3834827, e-mail ifla@ifla.org
World Wide Web www.ifla.org

Beacher Wiggins
Director for Acquisitions and Bibliographic Access, Library of Congress
Corresponding Member, IFLA Standing Committee on Government Libraries, 2015–2017

The International Federation of Library Associations and Institutions (IFLA) is the preeminent international organization representing librarians, other information professionals, and library users. Despite budgetary pressures, throughout 2015 IFLA promoted its four core values: freedom of access to information and expression, as stated in Article 19 of the Universal Declaration of Human Rights; the belief that such access must be universal and equitable to support human well-being; delivery of high-quality library and information services in support of that access; and the commitment to enabling all members of IFLA to participate without regard to citizenship, disability, ethnic origin, gender, geographical location, political philosophy, race, or religion.

Throughout the year, IFLA promoted an understanding of libraries as cultural heritage resources that are the patrimony of every nation.

World Library and Information Congress

The World Library and Information Congress (WLIC)/81st IFLA General Conference and Council attracted 3,188 registered, paying attendees from 112 countries to Cape Town, South Africa, August 15–21, 2015. The number of attendees was nearly identical to the 3,222 from 132 countries who attended the 2014 WLIC in Lyon, France, and far exceeded the number of registrations at the 2013 WLIC in Singapore (2,704) and the 2012 WLIC in Helsinki, Finland (2,486). Ms. Ujala Satgoor, president of the Library and Information Association of South Africa (LIASA) for 2012–2015, chaired the National Committee that planned the Cape Town conference, with incoming LIASA president Ms. Segametsi Molawa as co-chair.

The conference theme, "Dynamic Libraries: Access, Development, and Transformation," was highlighted by the keynote address by Dr. Rob Adam, director-designate of the Square Kilometer Array South Africa Project and a political prisoner during South Africa's apartheid era. The Square Kilometer Array is the largest radio telescope system on Earth, with components in nine African countries and in Australia. The keynote address by this distinguished theoretical nuclear physicist indicates libraries' growing emphasis on supporting research in the sciences and on compiling, preserving, and accessing "big data" resources. The Cape Town conference offered delegates opportunities for service, including "Gift a Book, Change a Life" with the American Library Association International Relations Committee, which collected approximately 430 new books and 41 DVDs for Cape Town schoolchildren, and the Knitting Librarians project that created 67 blankets for Nelson Mandela Day to aid Cape Town's neediest citizens.

Seventeen satellite meetings, organized by IFLA sections, afforded more-detailed discussions on specific topics such as the role of libraries in the United Nations Sustainable Development Goals; personal career management; digital preservation; and online newspapers. The satellite meetings were held in Botswana, Namibia, and in South Africa's major centers in Cape Town, Durban, Pretoria, and Stellenbosch.

The next World Library and Information Congress will take place in Columbus, Ohio, United States, in August 2016. The 2017 meeting will be held in Wrocław, Poland (formerly called Breslau). Under the current IFLA WLIC conference planning guidelines, the conference cities are selected three years in advance, and at each WLIC the IFLA Governing Board announces the specific location of the conference that will take place two years later. The 2017 conference in Poland will be followed by conferences in Latin America or the Caribbean region (2018), and again in Europe (2019). The IFLA Governing Board is committed to continuously improving both the conference experience for participants and the financial security of the organization. Although the exhibitor fees and registration are higher than for most conferences in the library community, WLIC historically has not made money for IFLA, and the custom of convening all registered participants in opening and closing ceremonies limits the number of cities that can host the conference to those with conference halls seating at least 3,000 people. Furthermore, member organizations have commented that it is difficult to send representatives to both the general conference and the numerous specialized satellite meetings that occur at a distance from the general conference site. The current seven-year planning cycle and conference model were adopted after a consultation in early 2010 that Pleiade Management and Consultancy of Amsterdam conducted for IFLA. Through its Governing Board, IFLA retains overall ownership of each conference, and the Governing Board, IFLA Headquarters, and the conference National Committee (the local organizing committee) are responsible for each conference overall. Program content is guided by the IFLA Professional Committee. Actual conference planning and services are contracted to a "congress secretariat" or event management company. The Helsinki, Singapore, Lyon, and Cape Town conferences were managed by the K.I.T. Group of Berlin, Germany. A more extensive review of conference governance, the host city selection process, the planning cycle, and financial management is planned after the site of the 2018 conference is announced and all of IFLA's regions have hosted at least one recent conference.

Five Key Initiatives

In 2010 IFLA's Governing Board adopted a new Strategic Plan for the years 2010–2015. The plan, grounded in the four core values, set forth four strategic directions: empowering libraries to enable their user communities to have equitable access to information; building the strategic capacity of IFLA and that of its members; transforming the profile and standing of the library profession; and representing the interests of IFLA's members and their users throughout the world. The five key initiatives for 2010–2015 were the digital content program, international leadership development for librarianship, outreach for advocacy and advancement of the profession, cultural heritage disaster reconstruction, and the multilingualism program. The Governing Board determined priority activities every two years under the strategic plan. The Governing Board developed a new Strategic Plan in 2015 to take effect in 2016.

Digital Content Program

In its digital content program, IFLA advocates vigorously for open access to digital content and for the right of libraries to benefit from fair use and exemptions from copyright restrictions. The federation's position is that the current framework of copyright exceptions is not adequate for the digital era. Through participation in the World Intellectual Property Organization's Standing Committee on Copyright and Related Rights (SCCR), IFLA has worked toward a binding international instrument on copyright limitations and exceptions that will enable the world's libraries to continue their historic mission of providing universal access to knowledge and information. With the International Council on Archives (ICA), Electronic Information for Libraries (EIFL), and Corporación Innovarte, IFLA's Committee on Copyright and Other Legal Matters drafted the Treaty Proposal on Copyright Limitations and Exceptions for Libraries and Archives (TLIB). It would protect libraries in the areas of preservation, right of reproduction and supply of copies, legal deposit, library lending, parallel importation, cross-border uses, orphan works, retracted and withdrawn works, liability of libraries and archives, technological measures of protection, contracts, and the right to translate works. Following intensive efforts by IFLA and its partners throughout 2013 and 2014 to gain the support of WIPO member states for the proposed TLIB, the SSCR in 2015 reviewed a study by American copyright lawyer Kenneth Crews of existing copyright exceptions for libraries and museums in 188 countries.

IFLA continues to be an active participant in follow-up to the World Summit of the Information Society (WSIS), which held two summits in Geneva, Switzerland (2003) and Tunis, Tunisia (2005). IFLA sends representatives to the Internet Governance Forum, a series of annual follow-up meetings to the WSIS; in 2015 the Governance Forum took place in João Pessoa, Brazil. IFLA is responsible for reporting to UNESCO on two of the eleven WSIS action lines, Action Line C3: Access to Information and Action Line C8: Cultural Diversity and Identity, Linguistic Diversity, and Local Content. The follow-up activities have become part of the "WSIS+10" review that commenced in 2013, ten years after the Geneva summit. In January 2013 the IFLA Governing Board issued a revised Position on Internet Governance that states clearly the issues IFLA believes should be addressed in any post-WSIS framework, especially the right of equitable public access to the

Internet, and advocates a multi-stakeholder model of Internet governance. IFLA's membership and officers worked tirelessly in 2014 and 2015 to ensure that the review would acknowledge the place of libraries in the WSIS vision of a people-centered, inclusive and development-oriented information society. The WSIS+10 review was presented at the United Nations General Assembly High-Level Meeting, December 15–16, 2015, and the General Assembly adopted the review's outcome document that calls for bridging the digital divide and welcoming participation by all stakeholders.

In January 2015 IFLA released its Sustainable Development Toolkit, to assist libraries in promoting the role of information in sustainable development from 2015 through 2030. At the Lyon WLIC in August 2014 IFLA had promulgated the Lyon Declaration on Access to Information and Development and publicly invited other stakeholders in the information society to co-sign. The declaration states that access to information has a central role in sustainable development for all of the world's people, and it calls on member states of the United Nations to acknowledge the necessity of access to information and the skills to use information effectively, and to ensure that this necessity is recognized in the United Nations' post-2015 development agenda. The declaration attracted more than 500 co-signers. Most are libraries, library associations, or institutions of higher education, but the co-signers also include the Wellcome Foundation, Wikipedia Foundation, and Engineers for Social Responsibility.

The officers of IFLA, particularly incoming president Donna Scheeder, achieved a milestone when the United Nations included, as Target 16.10 of its 2030 Agenda for Sustainable Development, the aim to "ensure public access to information and protect fundamental freedoms, in accordance with national legislation and international agreements."

International Leadership and Advocacy Program

Planning for this key initiative essentially began at the 2012 WLIC in Helsinki, Finland, and is being carried out through IFLA's existing Action for Development Through Libraries (ALP) program. The Building Strong Library Associations initiative provides training materials and mentoring to help library associations build capacity. The ALP International Leaders program sponsors in-person sessions for emerging library leaders at each WLIC. The ALP program also contributed to the federation's goals for sustainable development.

Cultural Heritage Disaster Reconstruction Program

Since 1996 IFLA has been a founding member of the International Committee of the Blue Shield (ICBS) to protect cultural property in the event of natural and human disasters. Its current partners in ICBS are the International Council on Archives, the International Council on Monuments and Sites, the International Council of Museums, and the Coordinating Council of Audiovisual Archives Associations. In 2015 the IFLA North American regional center for preservation and conservation, hosted at the Library of Congress, continued to develop a network of colleague institutions to provide a safety net for library collections during emergencies. An additional focus in 2015 was IFLA's work to help libraries recover from the earthquake that struck Nepal on April 25. Also in 2015 IFLA began building a Risk Register for Documentary Cultural Heritage, to be launched the following year.

Multilingualism Program

Recognizing that the Internet is now a prevalent means of communication and resource sharing, IFLA continues efforts to make its website at http://www.ifla.org multilingual. The website is available now in English, French, and Spanish versions. To assist libraries in China, francophone Africa, the Arab world, and Russia, IFLA maintains four language centers at the National Library of China in Beijing; the Central Library of Cheikh Anta Diop University in Dakar, Senegal; the Bibliotheca Alexandrina in Alexandria, Egypt; and the Russian State Library in Moscow.

Grants and Awards

IFLA continues to work with corporate partners and national libraries to maintain programs and opportunities that would otherwise not be possible, especially for librarians and libraries in developing countries. The Jay Jordan IFLA/OCLC Early Career Development Fellowships provide four weeks of intensive experience, based in OCLC headquarters in Dublin, Ohio, for library and information science professionals from countries with developing economies who are in the early stages of their careers. The fellows for 2015 were from Pakistan, the Philippines, Serbia, Swaziland, and Zimbabwe. At the Cape Town WLIC in August 2015 OCLC and IFLA announced the fellows for 2016, from Bangladesh, Kenya, Nigeria, the Philippines, and Serbia. (The American Theological Library Association ended its co-sponsor role in 2013.) Since its inception in 2001, the program has supported 75 librarians from 38 countries with developing economies.

The Frederic Thorpe Awards, established in 2003, are administered by the IFLA Libraries Serving Persons with Print Disabilities Section and the Ulverscroft Foundation of Leicester, England, which Thorpe founded to support visually impaired people. The Ulverscroft Foundation renewed the program as the Ulverscroft/IFLA Best Practice Awards (Frederic Thorpe Awards) in 2006, 2007, 2008, 2010, and 2011, with no award in 2009 or 2012. In 2013 the Ulverscroft Foundation again began funding the award. The 2013 award supported a Serbian librarian to visit the Royal National Institute of Blind People (RNIB) National Library for the Blind in the United Kingdom. In 2014 and 2015 the Frederic Thorpe Award program was revamped in order to resume the awards in 2016 in the form of travel grants for three librarians from countries with developing economies to attend the two-day satellite meeting of the IFLA Libraries Serving Persons with Print Disabilities Section planned in conjunction with the 2016 WLIC in Columbus, Ohio.

The Bill and Melinda Gates Foundation Access to Learning Award was presented annually from 2000 to 2014 to a library, library agency, or comparable organization outside the United States that was innovative in providing free public access to information. To IFLA's regret, the Gates Foundation announced in 2014 that it would conclude its Global Libraries program within the next three to five years. The final Access to Learning Award was presented at the 2014 WLIC in Lyon, France, to Sri Lanka's e-Library Nenasala Program.

Numerous awards and grants encourage travel to the annual IFLA conferences. The IFLA International Marketing Award includes a stipend and travel to
the conference for representatives of the winning libraries. The Emerald Group
sponsored the award from 2008 through 2014. After a hiatus in 2015, it became
the IFLA/BibLibre International Marketing Award in 2016. BibLibre, a library
systems and services vendor in Marseille, France, made a commitment to award
three stipends in 2016 and to continue its sponsorship through 2018.

The Council on Library and Information Resources (CLIR) sponsors the
Rovelstad Scholarship in International Librarianship that brings one international
library science student to the WLIC each year. In 2015 the awardee was Kelly
Grogg, Olson Graduate Research Assistant in Special Collections and University
Archives, University of Iowa Libraries. The Dr. Shawky Salem Conference Grant,
the Kwarim Ltd. Conference Grant, and the Naseej (Arabian Advanced Systems
Co.) Conference Grant support conference attendance from Arab countries. Many
national library professional associations subsidize travel to the IFLA conference
for their members; the Comité Français IFLA supports travelers from any franco-
phone country. The Aspire Award supports travel to conferences of IFLA and of
CILIP, the Chartered Institute of Library and Information Professionals (United
Kingdom), in memory of Dr. Bob McKee (1950–2010), chief executive of CILIP.

The IFLA Academic and Research Libraries Section sponsors an annual competition awarding conference registration and travel support for three contestants
from Africa, Latin America, and the Asia/Pacific region. Formerly the De Gruyter/
Saur Research Paper Award, this competition was co-sponsored by Ex Libris and
Sage in 2015. The Section on Education and Training sponsors a Student Paper
Award, funded by the library services vendor ekz (ekz.bibliotheksservice GmbH),
for library science students.

With IFLA, the large commercial publisher Brill sponsors the Open Access
Award for initiatives in the area of open access monograph publishing. The first
award, in 2013, recognized Open Book Publishers, Cambridge (United Kingdom).
In 2014 the award was presented to Knowledge Unlatched, a United Kingdom
project to ensure that scholarly publications are open accessible once the costs of
publication have been met. The 2015 recipient was the Directory of Open Access
Books (DOAB), a discovery service for open-access books that is operated by the
OAPEN Foundation, headquartered at the Koninklijke Bibliotheek, The Hague.
The award includes funding to attend the WLIC and a cash award of 1,000 euros.

The IFLA Honorary Fellowships, the IFLA Medal, and the IFLA Scroll of
Appreciation recognize service to IFLA by individuals. The IFLA Scroll of Appreciation was presented to the National Committee for the Cape Town WLIC in
2015, in keeping with the customary award to each National Committee for the
WLIC. In addition, Susan Schnuer, associate director of the Mortenson Center for
International Library Programs, University of Illinois, received the Scroll of Appreciation in Cape Town in recognition of her distinguished service to the international library community. An IFLA Medal was not awarded in 2015. Ingrid Parent,
university librarian of the University of British Columbia and a former president
of IFLA (2011–2013), was named an IFLA Honorary Fellow in 2015.

Membership and Finances

IFLA has more than 1,500 members in 150 countries. Initially established at a conference in Edinburgh, Scotland, in 1927, it has been registered in the Netherlands since 1971 and has headquarters facilities at the Koninklijke Bibliotheek (Royal Library) in The Hague. Although IFLA did not hold a General Conference outside Europe and North America until 1980, there has since been steadily increasing participation from Asia, Africa, South America, and Australia. The federation now maintains regional offices for Africa (in Pretoria, South Africa); Asia and Oceania (in Singapore); and Latin America and the Caribbean (in Mexico City since 2011; formerly in Rio de Janeiro, Brazil). The organization has seven official working languages: Arabic, Chinese, English, French, German, Russian, and Spanish. It maintains four language centers: for Arabic, in Alexandria, Egypt; for Chinese, in Beijing, China; for the French-speaking communities of Africa, in Dakar, Senegal; and for Russian, in Moscow, Russia. The language centers contribute to more effective communication with their respective language communities by providing translations of IFLA publications and becoming involved in local or regional professional events.

IFLA offers a range of membership categories: international library associations, national library associations, other associations (generally regional or special library associations), institutions, institutional sub-units, one-person libraries, school libraries, association affiliates (limited to three consecutive years and open only to national associations with operating budgets of 10,000 euros or less, to encourage membership in countries with developing economies), personal affiliates, student affiliates, new graduate members, and non-salaried personal members. Association and institution members have voting rights in the IFLA General Council and IFLA elections and may nominate candidates for IFLA offices. Institutional sub-units, one-person libraries, and school libraries have limited voting rights for section elections; association affiliates and personal members do not have voting rights but may submit nominations for any IFLA office, and individuals may run for office themselves. Except for affiliates, membership fees are keyed to the UNESCO Scale of Assessment and the United Nations List of Least Developed Countries, to encourage participation regardless of economic circumstances.

UNESCO has given IFLA formal associate relations status, the highest level of relationship accorded to nongovernmental organizations by UNESCO. In addition, IFLA has observer status with the United Nations, WIPO, the International Organization for Standardization, and the World Trade Organization, and associate status with the International Council of Scientific Unions.

IFLA has extended consultative status to many organizations in the information field, including the Arab League Educational, Cultural and Scientific Organization; Conference of Directors of National Libraries; European Dyslexia Association; International Council on Archives; International Standard Serial Number (ISSN) International Centre; International Board on Books for Young People; International Organization for Standardization (ISO); International Publishers Association; World Blind Union; and World Federation of the Deaf.

More than a dozen corporations in the information industry have formed working relationships with IFLA as corporate partners. The corporate partners provide financial and in-kind support and in turn gain the opportunity to convey information about their products and services to IFLA members and others who pay attention to IFLA's publications and activities. Several levels of corporate partnership are available. Most prominently, in 2014 OCLC became IFLA's first and sole Platinum Partner, providing support at an extraordinary level. Most corporate partners choose to support IFLA at one of three levels: gold (annual support equaling 3,500 euros), silver (annual support equaling 2,000 euros), or bronze (annual support equaling 1,000 euros). Gold Corporate Partners in 2015 were Emerald and Sage Publications. De Gruyter Saur was a Silver Partner, and Bronze Partners were Brill, Elsevier, Gale Cengage Learning, Innovative Interfaces Inc., Rockefeller University Press, and Sabinet. IFLA's Associate Partners were Annual Reviews, Axiell, Harrassowitz, and nbd/biblion. A review of the current corporate partnership program began in 2012 and is ongoing, in recognition that corporate sponsors need the benefits of IFLA institutional membership as well as opportunities to expose their products and services to the IFLA community.

In addition, a number of national libraries provide financial support to IFLA either directly or in-kind. In 2014 the Bill and Melinda Gates Foundation announced that it would donate approximately $4.9 million to IFLA over the next five years.

The IFLA Foundation (Stichting IFLA) was established in 2007. The foundation accepts private donations and bequests and also is funded by other IFLA income. It gives funding priority to proposals and projects that promise to have a long-term impact in developing and strengthening IFLA; are clearly related to at least one of IFLA's strategic priorities; and are not likely to be funded by other bodies. The foundation also occasionally makes grants for attendance at the World Library and Information Conference; the grants are administered by the IFLA headquarters and governance structure rather than directly by the foundation. The foundation's board of trustees consists of IFLA's president, president-elect, treasurer, secretary general, and an appointed expert in foundation law and management.

Personnel, Structure, and Governance

The secretary general of IFLA is Jennefer Nicholson, former executive director of the Australian Library and Information Association. Ms. Nicholson planned to retire on May 31, 2016, and the IFLA Governing Board has announced that her successor will be Gerald Leitner, currently secretary general of the Austrian Library Association.

At IFLA Headquarters, Fiona Bradley manages development programs; Joanne Yeomans is professional support officer; Julia Brungs and Asha Uche-Roosberg are both policy and projects officers. Stuart Hamilton was named deputy secretary general in 2014 and also continues as director for policy and advocacy, with Christina de Castell as manager for policy and advocacy. The editor of the quarterly *IFLA Journal* is Stephen W. Witt, succeeding J. Stephen Parker. Esther Doria is the voucher program administrator. Louis Takács is content editor for the IFLA website. The IFLA manager for conference and business relations is Josche Ouwerkerk. Christine Zuidwijk is IFLA's financial officer, and Ina Dijkstra is the human resources adviser while the federation seeks to hire a human resources officer. Tatjana Hoeink is the membership officer and Helen Mandl is the manager for member services.

New officers and board members took office at the close of the 2015 conference in Cape Town. Donna Scheeder, retired from the Congressional Research Service, Library of Congress, and currently president of Library Strategies International, is the new president of IFLA, succeeding Sinikka Sipilä, secretary-general of the Finnish Library Association. The new president-elect is Glòria Pérez-Salmerón of FESABID (Federación Española de Sociedades de Archivística, Biblioteconomía, Documentación y Museística). The treasurer is Christine Mackenzie, chief executive officer of Yarra Plenty Regional Libraries, Victoria, Australia.

Under the revised 2008 IFLA Statutes, the 19 members of IFLA's Governing Board (plus the secretary general, ex officio) are responsible for the federation's general policies, management and finance. Additionally, the board represents the federation in legal and other formal proceedings. The board is composed of the president, president-elect, secretary general (ex officio), ten directly elected members, the chair of the Professional Committee, the chairs of each IFLA division, and the chair of the Standing Committee of the Management of Library Associations Section, currently Barbara Schleihagen, executive director, Deutsche Bibliotheksverband. Current members, in addition to Scheeder, Pérez-Salmerón, Nicholson, and Schleihagen, are Margaret Allen (Australia), Kirsten Boelt (Denmark), Loida Garcia-Febo (United States), Ágnes Hajdu Barát (Hungary), Ngian Lek Choh (Singapore), Andrew McDonald (United Kingdom), Ellen Ndeshi Namhila (Namibia), Victoria Owen (Canada), and Christine Wellems (Germany), plus the chairs of the Professional Committee and divisions, named below.

The Governing Board delegates responsibility for overseeing the direction of IFLA between board meetings, within the policies established by the board, to the IFLA Executive Committee, which includes the president, president-elect, treasurer, chair of the Professional Committee, two members of the Governing Board (elected every two years by members of the board from among its elected members), and IFLA's secretary general, ex officio. The current elected Governing Board members of the Executive Committee are Ngian and McDonald.

The IFLA Professional Committee monitors the planning and programming of professional activities carried out by IFLA's two types of bodies: professional groups—five divisions, forty-four sections, and special interest groups—and strategic programs (formerly called core programs or core activities). The Professional Committee is composed of one elected officer from each division, plus a chair elected by the outgoing committee; the president, the president-elect, and the professional support officer, who serves as secretary; the chairs of the CLM and FAIFE committees, and two elected members of the Governing Board, currently Boelt and Wellems. Maria Carme Torras i Calvo, library director, Universitetsbiblioteket i Bergen, Norway, chairs the Professional Committee.

The five divisions of IFLA and their representatives on the Professional Committee are I: Library Types (Raissa Teodori, Italy); II: Library Collections (Frederick Zarndt, United States); III: Library Services (Viviana Quiñones, France); IV: Support of the Profession (Perry Moree, Netherlands); and V: Regions (Victoria Okojie, Nigeria). The chair of the Copyright and Legal Matters Committee is Evelyn Woodberry (Australia). The chair of the Freedom of Access to Information and Freedom of Expression Committee is Martyn Wade, national librarian of

Scotland. A total of forty-four sections focus on topical interests, such as statistics and evaluation, library theory and research, and management and marketing, or on particular types of libraries or parts of the world.

The six strategic programs, which replace the former five core activities, are Action for Development Through Libraries (ALP, originally Advancement of Librarianship); Preservation and Conservation (PAC); IFLA UNIMARC Strategic Programme, which maintains and develops the Universal MARC Format, UNIMARC; Committee on Standards; Free Access to Information and Freedom of Expression (FAIFE); and Copyright and Other Legal Matters (CLM). The UNIMARC Strategic Programme has a separate office headed by Maria-Inês Cordeiro at the National Library of Portugal in Lisbon. Two other longstanding IFLA projects are the IFLA website and the IFLA Voucher Scheme, which replaced the IFLA Office for International Lending. The voucher scheme enables libraries to pay for international interlibrary loan requests using vouchers purchased from IFLA rather than actual currency or credit accounts. By eliminating bank charges and invoices for each transaction, the voucher scheme reduces the administrative costs of international library loans and allows libraries to plan budgets with less regard to short-term fluctuations in the value of different national currencies. The voucher scheme has also encouraged participating libraries to voluntarily standardize their charges for loans.

To ensure an arena within IFLA for discussion of new social, professional, or cultural issues, the Professional Committee approves the formation of special interest groups for a limited time period. There currently are discussion groups for Access to Information Network/Africa (ATINA); Agricultural Libraries; Big Data; E-Metrics; Environmental Sustainability and Libraries; LGBTQ (Lesbian, Gay, Bisexual, Transgender, Queer/Questioning) Users; Library and Information Science Education in Developing Countries; Library History; National Information and Library Policy; National Organizations and International Relations; New Professionals; Radio Frequency Identification (RFID); Religious Libraries in Dialogue; Semantic Web; and Women, Information, and Libraries. Special interest groups operate for a maximum period of three years. If there is sufficient interest, a special interest group may then become a permanent IFLA section. The Indigenous Matters Section was established from a special interest group in 2015.

Library and Archives Canada: 2015—The Year of Possibilities

Guy Berthiaume
Librarian and Archivist of Canada

The year 2015 opened up many possibilities for Library and Archives Canada (LAC), and allowed the organization to translate a broad vision of access into a working reality. There were four main priorities identified at the beginning of the year: increasing access to Canada's documentary heritage, developing a coherent approach to stakeholders, establishing LAC as a client-driven organization and making sure that LAC has the necessary infrastructure to fulfill its mandate.

One of the key factors in achieving these priorities was giving LAC staff the chance to contribute their ideas and their expertise, leveraging their individual and collective strengths to put LAC at the leading edge of archival and library science and new technologies. Harnessing the views of staff is part of LAC's overall commitment to consultation.

From June to December 2015 LAC gathered the views of its users, its main stakeholders, and its employees. It conducted four focus groups, five employee consultation sessions, a public opinion survey, a town hall, and a formal discussion with its Stakeholder's Forum, the twelve Canadian professional associations with which staff deal frequently. The ideas generated by these consultations helped to develop a road map, a three-year plan for 2016 to 2019, so that the work of LAC will meet the needs of its clients. LAC also get to know its clients better, allowing it to stay relevant, optimize its content and services, and demonstrate its value to Canadians as a whole.

LAC is one of many organizations that represent the interests of Canada's archival and library communities abroad. As a combined library and archives, and as a departmental agency within Canada's federal government, LAC has a unique opportunity, at home and abroad, to connect communities, facilitate discussions, compare standards, and share professional perspectives. LAC is committed to engaging with international networks in an open and inclusive way, and in this spirit it completed an International Engagement Strategy in 2015. The goal of this strategy is to promote coherence among LAC's various international activities, and to better position LAC to play an active role internationally—with other national memory institutions and alongside other Canadian experts.

Increasing Access

A digital strategy for LAC was an important focus of 2015, one that will ensure a long-term, secure system for preserving digital content and making it available. The work of creating this strategy has been undertaken in consultation with the government of Canada, and the provincial and territorial governments. LAC is now looking into commercially available solutions for a secure digital platform, which other archives could then benefit from.

Report prepared by Sandra Nicholls, Senior Writer, Library and Archives Canada

The digital strategy will mean that LAC can:

* Build the right technology platform to achieve its goals
* Ensure its collections include new forms of born-digital content
* Digitize those portions of its analog collections in greatest demand
* Ensure high-quality metadata is provided
* Facilitate the use of its holdings by anyone, anywhere, anytime
* Promote its holdings and engage with clients
* Play a leadership role among the network of memory institutions
* Be aware of client needs
* Inform decisions with the best use of data
* Build a digital culture

Documentary heritage is a cornerstone of all democratic societies, and, throughout the world, memory institutions such as LAC are creating targeted approaches to digitizing their national heritage. Canada's National Heritage Digitization Strategy (NHDS) has been developed in collaboration with the Stakeholder's Forum, and draws from international best practices, such as the Digital Public Library of America and the Swedish Digisam initiative. The official launch of the strategy is scheduled for June 2016.

LAC has already been actively digitizing materials together with some of its partners. For example, with Canadiana.org, LAC digitized 35 million pages of archival material on microfilm, and with Ancestry.ca, LAC digitized and indexed 11 archival collections representing 3 million pages online. New partnerships with these two partners are underway, for newspaper reels and certificates of military instruction.

LAC in the Community

Canada's national library and archives has always been involved at the community, grassroots level. It's part of LAC's mandate. But in 2015 LAC took this commitment even further through new kinds of partnerships and collaborative arrangements.

The Documentary Heritage Communities Program (DHCP) was introduced in June 2015. It provides financial help directly to community organizations across Canada so they can preserve, promote, and provide access to their collections. Archives, library associations, historical societies, and other heritage groups can all apply for this funding, which totals $1.5 million per year over five years.

The program funded 65 projects in its first year. Recipients included the Inuit Broadcasting Corporation, the Dr. James Naismith Basketball Foundation, Les Amis des Jardins de Métis, the Canadian Association of Research Libraries, the Prairie Tractor and Engine Museum Society, the Vancouver Holocaust Education Centre, and the Fédérations des associations de familles du Québec.

LAC is also bringing researchers and specialists from across Canada together to discuss how LAC works, and as a way to find solutions to common problems. For example, the Acquisitions Advisory Committee invites art experts and historians to look at the best ways of adding to its collections. The Services Consultation Committee looks at the kinds of services it offers, and how they can be improved.

The TD Summer Reading Club is a national program that gets children to read—in 2015 participants enjoyed some 1.2 million books. The program is offered by LAC in partnership with TD Bank, the Toronto Public Library, and libraries across the country. During the summer of 2015 more than 2,000 libraries hosted the program, and more than 650,000 children discovered the fun of reading.

Since 1965 LAC has collected theses and dissertations working together with Canadian universities; in 2015 LAC consulted more than 75 universities to design a new approach. As a result, universities can now manage licenses for this intellectual property directly with their students. The theses portal continues to grow in popularity, with more than 43,000 new titles submitted in 2014–2015, and more than 600,000 downloads.

LAC and Bibliothèque et Archives nationales du Québec (BAnQ) signed a partnership in 2015 that will allow BAnQ to provide digital publications directly to LAC, with the publisher's permission. This means that up to 10,000 digital publications from Quebec publishing houses could be added to LAC's collection over the next two years.

The Continuing Record of Government

There is a new trend in government: making it more open. More than 68 countries have joined the Open Government Partnership, including Canada. LAC has a key role to play by opening up government information and making it more available to the public.

LAC has all kinds of government records, including documents about Canada's military history, trade relations, residential schools, and even how Canada celebrates its birthdays. Taking one "block" of records at a time, and seeing if it can remove any restrictions, LAC has opened 18 million pages of records since 2010. From April 1, 2015, to December 31, 2015 alone, LAC made 5,802,398 pages of government records openly available to the public.

LAC also continues to create historical data sets, everything from census data to records of land grants, and then puts them on Canada's open data portal. In 2015 LAC created new data sets, covering topics ranging from environmental observations to Canadian airmen of the First World War, studies of immigrants, and the results of Canadian elections.

LAC's Public Identity

LAC is an active player in Canada's cultural life. Through public programs and special events, exhibitions and joint displays, an active loans program, and the creative use of its public spaces, LAC engages clients with the cultural heritage of an entire nation.

Visitors from around the world toured LAC's Preservation Centre in 2015, from Serbia's ambassador to architectural students from Carleton University to representatives of the National Archives of the United Arab Emirates. LAC's flagship building at 395 Wellington Street, in the heart of Canada's capital city, Ottawa, was extensively renovated in 2015, offering a much-needed focal point for the public programming. With its marbled stairways and engraved glass windows, 395 Wellington speaks to the noble and enduring purpose of a national archives and library.

A major exhibition was held in its sunken floor lobby in 2015. "Hockey Marching as to War" explored the impact of the First World War on hockey players, and the way it transformed organized hockey during and after the war. Items featured included reproductions of photographs, posters and documents from the collections of LAC and the Hockey Hall of Fame (HHOF), and digital copies of Canadian Expeditionary Force files and the attestation papers of more than 25 HHOF inductees.

The second floor reading room is now the go-to site for public events and cultural activities, as well as a place of quiet beauty for people to read. The room is flanked by two murals created by famous Quebec artist Alfred Pellan. Among the public program highlights in 2015:

- David Fricker, the director general of the National Archives of Australia, gave a public talk on e-Government and Policy Responses from the National Archives of Australia.
- Dr. Robert Darnton, university librarian emeritus at Harvard, gave a talk on the digital public library of America and where he sees the future of books, libraries, and information.
- Sherry Simon from the French Department at Concordia University brought literary Montreal in the 1940s to life with her talk on Yiddish Language Modernism in "Montreal: A Tale of Three Cities."
- Pierre Anctil, professor of history at the University of Ottawa, gave a talk on the modernist Yiddish poetry of Jacob-Isaac Segal.

Whether a national treasure or a hidden gem, LAC is also proud to contribute items for public display at museums, archives, libraries, and other memory institutions large and small. Here are a few that LAC helped put on display in 2015.

- The 1982 Proclamation of the Constitution Act was loaned to the Canadian Museum for Human Rights for its grand opening in Winnipeg.
- The earliest known oil portrait of former Prime Minister Sir John A. Macdonald was displayed at Macdonald's former residence, historic Bellevue House in Kingston, Ontario.
- The *Red River Expedition at Kakabeka Falls*, Ontario, an 1877 painting by Frances Anne Hopkins, traveled to the Art Gallery of Ontario in Toronto, the Crystal Bridges Museum of American Art in Arizona, and the Pinacoteca do Estado de São Paulo in Brazil.

LAC also contributed to exhibitions at the Canadian Museum of Immigration at Pier 21, the Library of Parliament, the Museum of Canadian History, Canada's Hockey Hall of Fame, the National Gallery of Canada, the Musée des beaux-arts de Montréal, the Canadian Centre for Architecture in Montreal, and the Galt Museum and Archives in Lethbridge, Alberta, among others.

Also in 2015, the groundwork was set for an innovative new series known as *Signatures*. *Signatures* is both a magazine and a public program featuring lively and informal discussions between the Librarian and Archivist of Canada and individual donors to LAC. Both the journal and the conversations interpret the living cultural, civic, historical, and literary record of Canada as reflected in its documentary heritage.

LAC in the World

As Librarian and Archivist of Canada, Guy Berthiaume was elected in 2015 as the chair of the Standing Committee on National Libraries at the International Federation of Libraries and Library Associations (IFLA). This global organization represents the voice of the library and information community around the world. The National Libraries section supports national libraries as guardians of the world's intellectual heritage.

Organizations from more than 45 countries make up the International Internet Preservation Consortium, which is dedicated to collecting and preserving the knowledge found on the global web, and then making it available. LAC's chief information officer was voted in as the chair of its steering committee for 2015.

Conclusion

In 2015 LAC continued its journey to self-definition by opening up numerous possibilities for growth and change, and re-imagining the future for an organization which is, at once, a government agency, an archives, and a library. By consistently demonstrating its value to Canadians, providing an accessible link between the past, present, and future, and staying open to new kinds of collaborations and partnerships, LAC has ensured that it will be around for the future, whatever that future holds.

Part 2
Funding and Grants

Funding Programs and Grant-Making Agencies

National Endowment for the Humanities

400 7th St. S.W., Washington, DC 20506
202-606-8400, 800-634-1121
TDD (hearing impaired) 202-606-8282 or 866-372-2930 (toll free)
E-mail info@neh.gov, World Wide Web http://neh.gov

The National Endowment for the Humanities (NEH) is an independent federal agency created in 1965. It is one of the largest funders of humanities programs in the United States.

Because democracy demands wisdom, NEH promotes excellence in the humanities and conveys the lessons of history to all Americans, seeking to develop educated and thoughtful citizens. It accomplishes this mission by providing grants for high-quality humanities projects in six funding areas: education, preservation and access, public programs, research, challenge grants, and digital humanities.

Grants from NEH enrich classroom learning, create and preserve knowledge, and bring ideas to life through public television, radio, new technologies, museum exhibitions, and programs in libraries and other community places. Recipients typically are cultural institutions, such as museums, archives, libraries, colleges and universities, and public television and radio stations, as well as individual scholars. The grants

- Strengthen teaching and learning in the humanities in schools and colleges
- Preserve and provide access to cultural and educational resources
- Provide opportunities for lifelong learning
- Facilitate research and original scholarship
- Strengthen the institutional base of the humanities

Over nearly half a century, NEH has reached millions of people with projects and programs that preserve and study the nation's culture and history while providing a foundation for the future.

The endowment's mission is to enrich cultural life by promoting the study of the humanities. According to the National Foundation on the Arts and the Humanities Act, "The term 'humanities' includes, but is not limited to, the study of the following: language, both modern and classical; linguistics; literature; history; jurisprudence; philosophy; archaeology; comparative religion; ethics; the history, criticism, and theory of the arts; those aspects of social sciences which have humanistic content and employ humanistic methods; and the study and application of the humanities to the human environment with particular attention to reflecting our diverse heritage, traditions, and history and to the relevance of the humanities to the current conditions of national life."

The act, adopted by Congress in 1965, provided for the establishment of the National Foundation on the Arts and the Humanities in order to promote progress and scholarship in the humanities and the arts in the United States. The act included the following findings:

- The arts and the humanities belong to all the people of the United States.
- The encouragement and support of national progress and scholarship in the humanities and the arts, while primarily matters for private and local initiative, are also appropriate matters of concern to the federal government.
- An advanced civilization must not limit its efforts to science and technology alone, but must give full value and support to the other great branches of scholarly and cultural activity in order to achieve a better understanding of the past, a better analysis of the present, and a better view of the future.
- Democracy demands wisdom and vision in its citizens. It must therefore foster and support a form of education, and access to the arts and the humanities, designed to make people of all backgrounds and locations masters of technology and not its unthinking servants.
- It is necessary and appropriate for the federal government to complement, assist, and add to programs for the advancement of the humanities and the arts by local, state, regional, and private agencies and their organizations. In doing so, the government must be sensitive to the nature of public sponsorship. Public funding of the arts and humanities is subject to the conditions that traditionally govern the use of public money. Such funding should contribute to public support and confidence in the use of taxpayer funds. Public funds provided by the federal government ultimately must serve public purposes the Congress defines.
- The arts and the humanities reflect the high place accorded by the American people to the nation's rich culture and history and to the fostering of mutual respect for the diverse beliefs and values of all persons and groups.

What NEH Grants Accomplish

Since its founding, NEH has awarded more than 69,300 competitive grants.

Interpretive Exhibitions

Interpretive exhibitions provide opportunities for lifelong learning in the humanities for millions of Americans. Since 1967 NEH has awarded approximately $300 million in grants for interpretive exhibitions, catalogs, and public programs, which are among the most highly visible activities supported by the endowment. NEH support finances exhibitions; reading, viewing, and discussion programs; Web-based programs; and other public education programs at venues across the country.

Renewing Teaching

Over NEH's history, more than 100,000 high school and college teachers have deepened their knowledge of the humanities through intensive summer study supported by the endowment; tens of thousands of students benefit from these better-educated teachers every year.

Reading and Discussion Programs

Since 1982 NEH has supported reading and discussion programs in the nation's libraries, bringing people together to discuss works of literature and history. Scholars in the humanities provide thematic direction for the discussion programs. Using selected texts and such themes as "Work," "Family," "Diversity," and "Not for Children Only," these programs have attracted more than 2 million Americans to read and talk about what they've read.

Chronicling America

NEH's National Digital Newspaper Program is supporting projects to convert microfilm of historically important U.S. newspapers into fully searchable digital files. Developed in partnership with the Library of Congress, this long-term project ultimately will make more than 30 million pages of newspapers accessible online. For more on this project, visit http://chroniclingamerica.loc.gov.

Stimulating Private Support

About $2 billion in humanities support has been generated by NEH's Challenge Grants program, which requires most grant recipients to raise $3 in nonfederal funds for every dollar they receive.

Presidential Papers

Ten presidential papers projects, from Washington to Eisenhower, have received support from NEH. Matching grants for the ten projects have leveraged millions of dollars in nonfederal contributions.

New Scholarship

NEH grants enable scholars to do in-depth study. Jack Rakove explored the making of the Constitution in his *Original Meanings* and James McPherson chronicled the Civil War in his *Battle Cry of Freedom*. Projects supported by NEH grants have earned nearly 20 Pulitzer Prizes.

History on Screen

Since 1967 NEH has awarded approximately $300 million to support the production of films for broad public distribution, including the Emmy Award-winning series *The Civil War*, the Oscar-nominated films *Brooklyn Bridge, The Restless*

Conscience, and *Freedom on My Mind,* and film biographies of John and Abigail Adams, Eugene O'Neill, and Ernest Hemingway. More than 20 million people have watched Ken Burns's critically acclaimed *The War* (2007), which chronicles the United States in World War II. More than 8 million saw the April 2010 debut of *The Buddha,* a documentary made for PBS by filmmaker David Grubin, and it has been streamed into hundreds of classrooms nationwide.

American Voices

NEH support for scholarly editions makes the writings of prominent and influential Americans accessible. Ten presidents are included, along with such key figures as Martin Luther King, Jr., George C. Marshall, and Eleanor Roosevelt. Papers of prominent writers—among them Emily Dickinson, Walt Whitman, Mark Twain, and Robert Frost—are also available.

Library of America

Millions of books have been sold as part of the Library of America series, a collection of the riches of the nation's literature. Begun with NEH seed money, the nearly 200 published volumes include the works of such figures as Henry Adams, Edith Wharton, William James, Eudora Welty, and W. E. B. Du Bois.

The Library of America also received a $150,000 grant for the publication of *American Poetry: The Seventeenth and Eighteenth Centuries* (two volumes) and an expanded volume of selected works by Captain John Smith—a key figure in the establishment of the first permanent English settlement in North America, at Jamestown, Virginia—and other early exploration narratives.

Technical Innovation

NEH support for the digital humanities is fueling innovation and new tools for research in the humanities. Modern 3D technology allows students to visit things ranging from ancient Egypt to the 1964–1965 New York World's Fair. Spectral imaging was used to create an online critical edition of explorer David Livingstone's previously unreadable field diary of 1871.

Science and the Humanities

The scientific past is being preserved with NEH-supported editions of the letters of Charles Darwin, the works of Albert Einstein, and the 14-volume papers of Thomas Edison. Additionally, NEH and the National Science Foundation have joined forces in Documenting Endangered Languages (DEL), a multiyear effort to preserve records of key languages that are in danger of becoming extinct.

EDSITEment

EDSITEment (http://edsitement.neh.gov) assembles the best humanities resources on the Web, drawing more than 400,000 visitors each month. Incorporating these Internet resources, particularly primary documents, from more than 350 peer-reviewed websites, EDSITEment features more than 500 online lesson plans in all areas of the humanities. Teachers use EDSITEment's resources to enhance lessons and to engage students through interactive technology tools that hone critical-thinking skills.

Federal-State Partnership

The Office of Federal-State Partnership links NEH with the nationwide network of 56 humanities councils, which are located in each state, the District of Columbia, Puerto Rico, the U.S. Virgin Islands, the Northern Mariana Islands, American Samoa, and Guam. Each council funds humanities programs in its own jurisdiction.

Directory of State Humanities Councils

Alabama

Alabama Humanities Foundation
1100 Ireland Way, Suite 202
Birmingham, AL 35205-7001
205-558-3980, fax 205-558-3981
http://www.alabamahumanities.org

Alaska

Alaska Humanities Forum
161 E. First Ave., Door 15
Anchorage, AK 99501
907-272-5341, fax 907-272-3979
http://www.akhf.org

Arizona

Arizona Humanities Council
Ellis-Shackelford House
1242 N. Central Ave.
Phoenix, AZ 85004-1887
602-257-0335, fax 602-257-0392
http://www.azhumanities.org

Arkansas

Arkansas Humanities Council
407 President Clinton Ave., Suite 201
Little Rock, AR 72201
501-320-5761, fax 501-537-4550
http://www.arkhums.org

California

Cal Humanities
312 Sutter St., Suite 601
San Francisco, CA 94108
415-391-1474, fax 415-391-1312
http://www.calhum.org

Colorado

Colorado Humanities
7935 E. Prentice Ave., Suite 450
Greenwood Village, CO 80111
303-894-7951, fax 303-864-9361
http://www.coloradohumanities.org

Connecticut

Connecticut Humanities Council
37 Broad St.
Middletown, CT 06457
860-685-2260, fax 860-685-7597
http://cthumanities.org

Delaware

Delaware Humanities Forum
100 W. Tenth St., Suite 1009
Wilmington, DE 19801
302-657-0650, fax 302-657-0655
http://dehumanities.org

District of Columbia

Humanities Council of Washington, D.C.
925 U St. N.W.
Washington, DC 20001
202-387-8393, fax 202-387-8149
http://wdchumanities.org

Florida

Florida Humanities Council
599 Second St. S.
St. Petersburg, FL 33701-5005
727-873-2000, fax 727-873-2014
http://www.flahum.org

Georgia

Georgia Humanities Council
50 Hurt Plaza S.E., Suite 595
Atlanta, GA 30303-2915
404-523-6220, fax 404-523-5702
http://www.georgiahumanities.org

Hawaii

Hawai'i Council for the Humanities
First Hawaiian Bank Bldg.
3599 Waialae Ave., Room 25
Honolulu, HI 96816
808-732-5402, fax 808-732-5432
http://www.hihumanities.org

Idaho

Idaho Humanities Council
217 W. State St.
Boise, ID 83702
208-345-5346, fax 208-345-5347
http://www.idahohumanities.org

Illinois

Illinois Humanities Council
17 N. State St., No. 1400
Chicago, IL 60602-3296
312-422-5580, fax 312-422-5588
http://www.prairie.org

Indiana

Indiana Humanities
1500 N. Delaware St.
Indianapolis, IN 46202
317-638-1500, fax 317-634-9503
http://www.indianahumanities.org

Iowa

Humanities Iowa
100 Library, Room 4039
Iowa City, IA 52242-4038
319-335-4153, fax 319-335-4154
http://humanitiesiowa.org

Kansas

Kansas Humanities Council
112 S.W. Sixth Ave., Suite 210
Topeka, KS 66603

785-357-0359, fax 785-357-1723
http://www.kansashumanities.org

Kentucky

Kentucky Humanities Council
206 E. Maxwell St.
Lexington, KY 40508
859-257-5932, fax 859-257-5933
http://www.kyhumanities.org

Louisiana

Louisiana Endowment for the Humanities
938 Lafayette St., Suite 300
New Orleans, LA 70113-1782
504-523-4352, fax 504-529-2358
http://www.leh.org

Maine

Maine Humanities Council
674 Brighton Ave.
Portland, ME 04102-1012
207-773-5051, fax 207-773-2416
http://www.mainehumanities.org

Maryland

Maryland Humanities Council
108 W. Centre St.
Baltimore, MD 21201-4565
410-685-0095, fax 410-685-0795
http://www.mdhc.org

Massachusetts

Mass Humanities
66 Bridge St.
Northampton, MA 01060
413-584-8440, fax 413-584-8454
http://www.masshumanities.org

Michigan

Michigan Humanities Council
119 Pere Marquette Drive, Suite 3B
Lansing, MI 48912-1270
517-372-7770, fax 517-372-0027
http://michiganhumanities.org

Minnesota

Minnesota Humanities Center
987 E. Ivy Ave.
St. Paul, MN 55106-2046
651-774-0105, fax 651-774-0205
http://www.minnesotahumanities.org

Mississippi

Mississippi Humanities Council
3825 Ridgewood Rd., Room 311
Jackson, MS 39211
601-432-6752, fax 601-432-6750
http://www.mshumanities.org

Missouri

Missouri Humanities Council
543 Hanley Industrial Court, Suite 201
St. Louis, MO 63144-1905
314-781-9660, fax 314-781-9681
http://www.mohumanities.org

Montana

Humanities Montana
311 Brantly
Missoula, MT 59812-7848
406-243-6022, fax 406-243-4836
http://www.humanitiesmontana.org

Nebraska

Nebraska Humanities Council
215 Centennial Mall South, Suite 330
Lincoln, NE 68508
402-474-2131, fax 402-474-4852
http://www.humanitiesnebraska.org

Nevada

Nevada Humanities
1670-200 N. Virginia St.
P.O. Box 8029
Reno, NV 89507
775-784-6587, fax 775-784-6527
http://www.nevadahumanities.org

New Hampshire

New Hampshire Humanities Council
117 Pleasant St.
Concord, NH 03301-3852
603-224-4071, fax 603-224-4072
http://www.nhhc.org

New Jersey

New Jersey Council for the Humanities
28 W. State St., 6th floor
Trenton, NJ 08608
609-695-4838, fax 609-695-4929
http://www.njch.org

New Mexico

New Mexico Humanities Council
4115 Silver Ave. S.E.
Albuquerque, NM 87108
505-633-7370, fax 505-633-7377
http://www.nmhum.org

New York

New York Council for the Humanities
150 Broadway, Suite 1700
New York, NY 10038
212-233-1131, fax 212-233-4607
http://www.nyhumanities.org

North Carolina

North Carolina Humanities Council
320 East 9th St., Suite 414
Charlotte, NC 28202
704-687-1520, fax 704-687-1525
http://www.nchumanities.org

North Dakota

North Dakota Humanities Council
418 E. Broadway, Suite 8
P.O. Box 2191
Bismarck, ND 58502
701-255-3360, fax 701-223-8724
http://www.ndhumanities.org

Ohio

Ohio Humanities Council
471 E. Broad St., Suite 1620
Columbus, OH 43215-3857
614-461-7802, fax 614-461-4651
http://www.ohiohumanities.org

Oklahoma

Oklahoma Humanities Council
Festival Plaza
428 W. California, Suite 270
Oklahoma City, OK 73102
405-235-0280, fax 405-235-0289
http://www.okhumanities.org

Oregon

Oregon Council for the Humanities
921 S.W. Washington St., #150
Portland, OR 97205
503-241-0543, fax 503-241-0024
http://www.oregonhumanities.org

Pennsylvania

Pennsylvania Humanities Council
325 Chestnut St., Suite 715
Philadelphia, PA 19106-2607
215-925-1005, fax 215-925-3054
http://www.pahumanities.org

Rhode Island

Rhode Island Council for the Humanities
131 Washington St., Suite 210
Providence, RI 02903
401-273-2250, fax 401-454-4872
http://www.rihumanities.org

South Carolina

Humanities Council of South Carolina
2711 Middleburg Drive, Suite 203
P.O. Box 5287
Columbia, SC 29254
803-771-2477, fax 803-771-2487
http://www.schumanities.org

South Dakota

South Dakota Humanities Council
1215 Trail Ridge Rd., Suite A
Brookings, SD 57006
605-688-6113, fax 605-688-4531
http://sdhumanities.org

Tennessee

Humanities Tennessee
306 Gay St., Suite 306
Nashville, TN 37201
615-770-0006, fax 615-770-0007
http://www.humanitiestennessee.org

Texas

Humanities Texas
1410 Rio Grande St.
Austin, TX 78701
512-440-1991, fax 512-440-0115
http://www.humanitiestexas.org

Utah

Utah Humanities Council
202 W. 300 North
Salt Lake City, UT 84103
801-359-9670, fax 801-531-7869
http://www.utahhumanities.org

Vermont

Vermont Humanities Council
11 Loomis St.
Montpelier, VT 05602
802-262-2626, fax 802-262-2620
http://www.vermonthumanities.org

Virginia

Virginia Foundation for the Humanities and
    Public Policy
145 Ednam Drive
Charlottesville, VA 22903-4629
434-924-3296, fax 434-296-4714
http://www.virginiafoundation.org

Washington

Humanities Washington
1015 Eighth Ave. North, Suite B
Seattle, WA 98109
206-682-1770, fax 206-682-4158
http://www.humanities.org

West Virginia

West Virginia Humanities Council
1310 Kanawha Blvd. East
Charleston, WV 25301
304-346-8500, fax 304-346-8504
http://www.wvhumanities.org

Wisconsin

Wisconsin Humanities Council
222 S. Bedford St., Suite F
Madison, WI 53703-3688
608-262-0706, fax 608-263-7970
http://www.wisconsinhumanities.org

Wyoming

Wyoming Humanities Council
1315 E. Lewis St.
Laramie, WY 82072-3459
307-721-9243, fax 307-742-4914
http://www.thinkwy.org

American Samoa

Amerika Samoa Humanities Council
P.O. Box 5800
Pago Pago, AS 96799
684-633-4870, fax 684-633-4873
http://ashcouncil.org

Guam

Guam Humanities Council
222 Chalan Santo Papa
Reflection Center, Suite 106

Hagatna, Guam 96910
671-472-4460, fax 671-472-4465
http://www.guamhumanitiescouncil.org

Northern Marianas Islands

Northern Marianas Humanities Council
P.O. Box 506437
Saipan, MP 96950
670-235-4785, fax 670-235-4786
http://northernmarianashumanities.org

Puerto Rico

Fundación Puertorriqueña de las Humanidades
109 San José St., 3rd floor
Box 9023920
San Juan, PR 00902-3920
787-721-2087, fax 787-721-2684
http://www.fphpr.org

Virgin Islands

Virgin Islands Humanities Council
1829 Kongens Gade
St. Thomas, VI 00802-6746
340-776-4044, fax 340-774-3972
http://www.vihumanities.org

NEH Overview

Common Good: Humanities in the Public Square

The Common Good is a new initiative of the National Endowment for the Humanities designed to demonstrate the critical role humanities scholarship can play in our public life.

The launch of this initiative coincided with NEH's celebration of its 50th anniversary beginning in 2015. NEH's enabling legislation speaks eloquently of the need to attend to "the relevance of the humanities to the current conditions of national life." Today, as our country grapples with both remarkable opportunities and extraordinary challenges, the "conditions of national life" suggest that this need is greater than ever.

Through NEH's traditional grant-making programs and several special initiatives, The Common Good will encourage humanities scholars to turn their attention to topics that have widespread resonance with the American people and that lend themselves to the methods and concerns of the humanities. For more information, visit www.neh.gov/commongood/about.

Contact: 202-606-8446, e-mail commongood@neh.gov.

Division of Education Programs

Through grants to educational institutions and professional development programs for scholars and teachers, this division is designed to support study of the humanities at all levels of education.

Grants support the development of curriculum and materials, faculty study programs among educational institutions, and conferences and networks of institutions.

Contact: 202-606-8500, e-mail education@neh.gov.

Seminars and Institutes

Grants support summer seminars and institutes in the humanities for college and school teachers. These faculty-development activities are conducted at colleges and universities in the United States and abroad. Those wishing to participate in seminars should submit their seminar applications to the seminar director.

Contact: 202-606-8471, e-mail sem-inst@neh.gov.

Landmarks of American History and Culture

Grants for Landmarks workshops provide support to school teachers and community college faculty. These professional development workshops are conducted at or near sites important to American history and culture (such as presidential residences or libraries, colonial era settlements, major battlefields, historic districts, and sites associated with major writers or artists) to address central themes and issues in American history, government, literature, art history, and related subjects in the humanities.

Contact: 202-606-8463, e-mail landmarks@neh.gov.

Division of Preservation and Access

Grants are made for projects that will create, preserve, and increase the availability of resources important for research, education, and public programming in the humanities.

Support may be sought to preserve the intellectual content and aid bibliographic control of collections; to compile bibliographies, descriptive catalogs, and guides to cultural holdings; and to create dictionaries, encyclopedias, databases, and electronic archives. Applications also may be submitted for education and training projects dealing with issues of preservation or access; for research and development leading to improved preservation and access standards, practices, and tools; and for projects to digitize historic U.S. newspapers and to document endangered languages. Grants are also made to help smaller cultural repositories preserve and care for their humanities collections. Proposals may combine preservation and access activities within a single project.

Contact: 202-606-8570, e-mail preservation@neh.gov.

Division of Public Programs

Public humanities programs promote lifelong learning in American and world history, literature, comparative religion, philosophy, and other fields of the humanities. They offer new insights into familiar subjects and invite conversation about important humanities ideas and questions.

The Division of Public Programs supports a wide range of public humanities programs that reach large and diverse public audiences through a variety of program formats, including interpretive exhibitions, radio and television broadcasts, lectures, symposia, interpretive multimedia projects, printed materials, and reading and discussion programs.

Grants support the development and production of television, radio, and digital media programs; the planning and implementation of museum exhibitions, the interpretation of historic sites, the production of related publications, multimedia components, and educational programs; and the planning and implementation of reading and discussion programs, lectures, symposia, and interpretive exhibitions of books, manuscripts, and other library resources.

Contact: 202-606-8269, e-mail publicpgms@neh.gov.

Division of Research Programs

Through fellowships to individual scholars and grants to support complex, frequently collaborative research, the Division of Research Programs contributes to the creation of knowledge in the humanities.

Fellowships and Stipends

Grants provide support for scholars to undertake full-time independent research and writing in the humanities. Grants are available for a maximum of one year and a minimum of two months of summer study.

Contact: 202-606-8200, e-mail (fellowships) fellowships@neh.gov, (summer stipends) stipends@neh.gov.

Research

Grants provide up to three years of support for collaborative research in the preparation for publication of editions, translations, and other important works in the humanities, and in the conduct of large or complex interpretive studies, including archaeology projects and humanities studies of science and technology. Grants also support research opportunities offered through independent research centers and international research organizations.

Contact: 202-606-8200, e-mail research@neh.gov.

Office of Challenge Grants

Nonprofit institutions interested in developing new sources of long-term support for educational, scholarly, preservation, and public programs in the humanities can be assisted in these efforts by an NEH Challenge Grant. Grantees are required to raise $3 in nonfederal donations for every federal dollar offered. Both federal and nonfederal funds may be used to establish or increase institutional endowments and therefore guarantee long-term support for a variety of humanities needs. Funds also can be used for limited direct capital expenditures where such needs are compelling and clearly related to improvements in the humanities.

Contact: 202-606-8309, e-mail challenge@neh.gov.

Office of Digital Humanities

The Office of Digital Humanities encourages and supports projects that utilize or study the impact of digital technology on research, education, preservation, and public programming in the humanities. Launched as an initiative in 2006, Digital Humanities was made permanent as an office within NEH in 2008.

NEH is interested in fostering the growth of digital humanities and lending support to a wide variety of projects, including those that deploy digital technologies and methods to enhance understanding of a topic or issue; those that study the impact of digital technology on the humanities; and those that digitize important materials, thereby increasing the public's ability to search and access humanities information.

The office coordinates the endowment's efforts in the area of digital scholarship. Currently NEH has numerous programs throughout the agency that are actively funding digital scholarship, including Humanities Collections and Resources, Institutes for Advanced Topics in the Digital Humanities, Digital Humanities Challenge Grants, Digital Humanities Start-Up Grants, and many others. NEH is also actively working with other funding partners in the United States and abroad in order to better coordinate spending on digital infrastructure for the humanities.

Contact: 202-606-8401, e-mail odh@neh.gov.

A full list of NEH grants programs and deadlines is available on the endowment's website at http://www.neh.gov/grants.

Institute of Museum and Library Services Office of Library Services

955 L'Enfant Plaza North, S.W., Suite 4000, Washington, DC 20024-2135
202-653-4657, fax 202-653-4600
World Wide Web http://www.imls.gov

Kathryn K. Matthew
Director

Vision and Mission

The vision of the Institute of Museum and Library Services (IMLS) is a democratic society where communities and individuals thrive with broad public access to knowledge, cultural heritage, and lifelong learning.

Its mission is to inspire libraries and museums to advance innovation, lifelong learning, and cultural and civic engagement. It provides leadership through research, policy development, and grant making.

Strategic Goals

- IMLS places the learner at the center and supports engaging experiences in libraries and museums that prepare people to be full participants in their local communities and our global society.
- IMLS promotes museums and libraries as strong community anchors that enhance civic engagement, cultural opportunities, and economic vitality.
- IMLS supports exemplary stewardship of museum and library collections and promotes the use of technology to facilitate discovery of knowledge and cultural heritage.
- IMLS advises the president and Congress on plans, policies, and activities to sustain and increase public access to information and ideas.
- IMLS achieves excellence in public management and performs as a model organization through strategic alignment of resources and prioritization of programmatic activities, maximizing value for the American public.

There are 123,000 libraries and 35,000 museums in the United States. IMLS supports the full range of libraries, including public, academic, research, special, and tribal, and the full range of museums including art, history, science and technology, children's museums, historical societies, tribal museums, planetariums, botanic gardens, and zoos. Nearly 170 million people in the United States over the age of 14 (69 percent of the population) are library users, and every year 148 million over the age of 18 visit a museum.

Overview

U.S. museums and libraries are at the forefront of the movement to create a nation of learners. As stewards of cultural heritage with rich, authentic content, they provide learning experiences for everyone. With built infrastructure in nearly every community in the nation, robust online networks, and dedicated and knowledgeable staff, they connect people to one another and to the full spectrum of human experience.

The role of IMLS is to provide leadership and funding for the nation's museums and libraries—resources these institutions need to fulfill their mission of becoming centers of learning for life, crucial to achieving personal fulfillment, a productive workforce, and an engaged citizenry.

The Museum and Library Services Act, which includes the Library Services and Technology Act (LSTA) and the Museum Services Act (MSA), authorizes IMLS to support the following activities:

LSTA

- Enhance coordination among federal programs that relate to library and information services
- Promote continuous improvement in library services in all types of libraries in order to better serve the people of the United States
- Facilitate access to resources in all types of libraries for the purpose of cultivating an educated and informed citizenry
- Encourage resource sharing among all types of libraries for the purpose of achieving economical and efficient delivery of library services to the public
- Promote literacy, education, and lifelong learning and enhance and expand the services and resources provided by libraries, including those services and resources relating to workforce development, 21st century skills, and digital literacy skills
- Enhance the skills of the current library workforce and recruit future professionals to the field of library and information services
- Ensure the preservation of knowledge and library collections in all formats and enable libraries to serve their communities during disasters
- Enhance the role of libraries within the information infrastructure of the United States in order to support research, education, and innovation
- Promote library services that provide users with access to information through national, state, local, regional, and international collaborations and networks

MSA

- Encourage and support museums in carrying out their public service role of connecting the whole of society to the cultural, artistic, historical, natural, and scientific understandings that constitute our heritage

- Encourage and support museums in carrying out their educational role as core providers of learning and in conjunction with schools, families, and communities
- Encourage leadership, innovation, and applications of the most current technologies and practices to enhance museum services through international, national, regional, state, and local networks and partnerships
- Assist, encourage, and support museums in carrying out their stewardship responsibilities to achieve the highest standards in conservation and care of the cultural, historic, natural, and scientific heritage of the United States to benefit future generations
- Assist, encourage, and support museums in achieving the highest standards of management and service to the public, and ease the financial burden borne by museums as a result of their increasing use by the public
- Support resource sharing and partnerships among museums, libraries, schools, and other community organizations
- Encourage and support museums as a part of economic development and revitalization in communities
- Ensure museums of various types and sizes in diverse geographic regions of the United States are afforded attention and support
- Support efforts at the state level to leverage museum resources and maximize museum services

A general provision of the Museum and Library Services Act calls for IMLS to develop and implement policy to ensure the availability of museum, library, and information services throughout the U.S. Specific duties include the following: advising the president, Congress, and other federal agencies and offices on museum, library, and information services in order to ensure the creation, preservation, organization, and dissemination of knowledge; engaging federal, state, and local governmental agencies and private entities in assessing the needs of museum, library, and information services, and coordinating the development of plans, policies, and activities to meet such needs effectively; carrying out programs of research and development, data collection, and financial assistance to extend and improve the nation's museum, library, and information services; ensuring that museum, library, and information services are fully integrated into the information and education infrastructures.

Funding

In fiscal year (FY) 2015, Congress appropriated $180,909,000 for the programs authorized by LSTA. The Office of Library Services within IMLS, under the policy direction of the IMLS director and deputy director, administers LSTA programs. The office comprises the Division of State Programs—which administers the Grants to States program—and the Division of Discretionary Programs, which administers the National Leadership Grants for Libraries program, the Laura Bush 21st Century Librarian Program, the Native American Library Services program, and the Native Hawaiian Library Services program. IMLS presents annual awards to libraries through the National Medal for Museum and Library Service program. Additionally, IMLS supports two award programs administered by the President's Committee on the Arts and the Humanities: the National Arts and Humanities Youth Program Awards and the National Student Poets Program.

Library Statistics

The president's budget request for FY 2015 included funds for IMLS to continue administering the Public Libraries Survey (PLS) and the State Library Administrative Agencies Survey. In addition to reporting on the survey data, IMLS provides shorter research products to highlight report findings. These brief reports leverage the survey data to address a wide range of public policy priorities, including education, employment, community and economic development, and telecommunications policy.

In the Data Collection section of the IMLS website (www.imls.gov/research-tools/data-collection), visitors can link to data search tools, the latest available data for each survey, other publications, and survey definitions.

Public Libraries Survey

Descriptive statistics for more than 9,000 public libraries are collected and disseminated annually through a voluntary census, the Public Libraries Survey (PLS). The survey is conducted through the Public Library Statistics Cooperative (PLSC, formerly the Federal-State Cooperative System [FSCS]). In FY 2015 IMLS completed the 27th collection of this data. In 2015, final imputed data files for the FY 2013 Public Libraries Survey (PLS) were made available in the PLS Data Files section of the IMLS website. The PLS is designed as a universal survey whose FY 2013 frame consisted of 9,290 public libraries as identified by state library agencies (9,228 public libraries in the 50 states and the District of Columbia and 62 public libraries in the outlying areas of American Samoa, Guam, the Northern Mariana Islands, Puerto Rico, and the U.S. Virgin Islands). The Compare Public Libraries Tool and the Public Library Locator Tool on the IMLS website were updated with FY 2013 data, along with the new IMLS Data Catalog (data.imls.gov), which allows users to access and analyze IMLS data and create charts, graphs and maps without the need of technical statistical or GIS mapping software.

The survey collects identifying information about public libraries and each of their service outlets, including street address, city, county, zip code, and telephone number. The survey collects data on staffing; type of legal basis; type of geographic boundary; type of administrative structure; type of interlibrary relationship; type and number of public service outlets; operating revenue and expenditures; capital revenue and expenditures; size of collection (including number of electronic books, audio and video resources, and databases); and such service measures as number of reference transactions, interlibrary loans, circulation, public service hours, library visits, circulation of children's materials, number of programs (including programs for children and for young adults), program attendance, number of Internet terminals used by the general public, and number of users of electronic resources. This survey also collects several data items about outlets, including geo-location information (such as latitude and longitude), number of books-by-mail-only outlets, number of bookmobiles by bookmobile outlet, and square footage of the outlet.

The 50 states and the District of Columbia have participated in data collection from the survey's inception in 1989. In 1993 Guam, the Commonwealth of the Northern Mariana Islands, Puerto Rico, and the U.S. Virgin Islands joined in the survey, and American Samoa provided data for FY 2013 for the first time. The first release of Public Libraries Survey data occurred with the launch of the updated Compare Public Libraries Tool on the IMLS website. The data used in this Web tool are final but do not include imputations for missing data. (Imputation is a statistical means for providing an estimate for each missing data item.)

An important feature of the public library data tools is the availability of locale codes for all administrative entities and outlets. These locale codes allow users to quickly identify which library outlets and administrative entities are located in cities, suburbs, towns, or rural areas. The locale codes are based on an address's proximity to an urbanized area (a densely settled core with densely settled surrounding areas). The locale code system classifies territory into four major types: city, suburban, town, and rural. Each type has three subcategories. For city and suburb, these gradations are based on population size: large, midsize, and small. Towns and rural areas are further distinguished by their distance from an urbanized area. They can be characterized as fringe, distant, or remote. The coding methodology was developed by the U.S. Census Bureau as a way to identify the location of public schools in the National Center for Education Statistics' (NCES's) Common Core of Data. Each library outlet and administrative entity survey has one of the twelve locale codes assigned to it.

Locale codes provide a new way to analyze library services in the U.S. By incorporating objective measures of rurality and urbanicity into the data files, researchers and practitioners can benchmark services in a fundamentally different way by basing comparisons on community attributes as well as the attributes of the libraries themselves. In other words, library services in rural remote areas can now be compared with library services in other rural remote areas of the state or country using a standardized urbanicity/rurality metric that is applied consistently to each library. Once communities of interest have been selected, comparisons can be made to any data that are available in the survey whether financial, operational, or service output related.

State Library Administrative Agencies Survey

The State Library Administrative Agencies Survey collects and disseminates information about the state library administrative agencies in the 50 states and the District of Columbia. A State Library Administrative Agency (SLAA) is the official unit of state government charged with statewide library development and the administration of federal funds under the IMLS Grants to States program. SLAAs' administrative and developmental responsibilities affect the operation of thousands of public, academic, school, and special libraries. SLAAs provide important reference and information services to state governments and sometimes also provide service to the general public. SLAAs often administer state library and special operations such as state archives and libraries for the blind and physically handicapped and the state Center for the Book.

The SLAA Survey began in 1994 and was administered by NCES until 2007. Beginning with FY 1999 data, the survey used a Web-based data collection system and included imputations for missing data. IMLS has shifted to a biannual data collection of the survey. In FY 2015 the FY 2014 data file was released.

National Medal for Museum and Library Service

The National Medal for Museum and Library Service honors outstanding institutions that make significant and exceptional contributions to their communities. Selected institutions demonstrate extraordinary and innovative approaches to public service, exceeding the expected levels of community outreach and core programs generally associated with its services. The medal includes a prize of $5,000 to each recipient, an awards ceremony held in Washington, D.C., and a visit from StoryCorps to interview community members about how the library or museum affected their lives. The 2015 ceremony was held at the White House on May 18.

Winners of the medal in 2015 were Amazement Square, Lynchburg, Virginia; Cecil County Public Library, Elkton, Maryland; Craig Public Library, Craig, Alaska; Embudo Valley Library and Community Center, Dixon, New Mexico; Los Angeles Public Library, Los Angeles, California; Louisiana Children's Museum, New Orleans, Louisiana; Museum of Northern Arizona, Flagstaff, Arizona; New York Hall of Science, Queens, New York; the Schomburg Center for Research in Black Culture, New York, New York; and the Tech Museum of Innovation, San Jose, California.

State-Administered Programs

In FY 2015 approximately 85 percent ($154,848,000) of the annual federal appropriation under LSTA was distributed through the Grants to States program to SLAAs according to a formula set by the law. The formula consists of a base amount for each SLAA—the 50 states, Puerto Rico, and the District of Columbia receive $680,000 each; other U.S. territories receive $60,000 each—plus a supplemental amount based on population (Table 1).

SLAAs may use the appropriation for statewide initiatives and services. They may also distribute the funds through competitive subawards to, or cooperative agreements with, public, academic, research, school, or special libraries. For-profit and federal libraries are not eligible applicants. Grants to States funds have been used to meet the special needs of children, parents, teenagers, the unemployed, senior citizens, and the business community, as well as adult learners. Many libraries have partnered with community organizations to provide a variety of services and programs, including access to electronic databases, computer instruction, homework centers, summer reading programs, digitization of special collections, access to e-books and adaptive technology, bookmobile service, and development of outreach programs to the underserved. States are required by law to match the IMLS

Table 1 / Library Services and Technology Act, State Allotments
FY 2015 (H.J. Res 83; Public Law 113-235)
Total Distributed to States: $154,848,000

State	Federal Funds from IMLS (66%)[1,2]	State Matching Funds (34%)	Total Federal and State Funds
Alabama	$2,476,238	$1,275,638	$3,751,876
Alaska	952,890	490,883	1,443,773
Arizona	3,173,382	1,634,773	4,808,155
Arkansas	1,778,761	916,331	2,695,092
California	15,052,678	7,754,410	22,807,088
Colorado	2,663,845	1,372,284	4,036,129
Connecticut	2,012,231	1,036,604	3,048,835
Delaware	1,026,557	528,832	1,555,389
Florida	8,048,596	4,146,246	12,194,842
Georgia	4,420,116	2,277,029	6,697,145
Hawaii	1,205,813	621,176	1,826,989
Idaho	1,285,415	662,183	1,947,598
Illinois	5,451,043	2,808,113	8,259,156
Indiana	3,123,514	1,609,083	4,732,597
Iowa	1,830,898	943,190	2,774,088
Kansas	1,755,667	904,435	2,660,102
Kentucky	2,314,771	1,192,458	3,507,229
Louisiana	2,117,896	1,091,037	3,208,933
Maine	1,172,672	604,104	1,776,776
Maryland	2,893,697	1,490,692	4,384,389
Massachusetts	3,178,539	1,637,429	4,815,968
Michigan	4,350,678	2,241,258	6,591,936
Minnesota	2,701,369	1,391,614	4,092,983
Mississippi	1,789,025	921,619	2,710,644
Missouri	2,925,990	1,507,328	4,433,318
Montana	1,059,140	545,618	1,604,758
Nebraska	1,376,920	709,322	2,086,242
Nevada	1,731,619	892,046	2,623,665
New Hampshire	1,171,459	603,479	1,774,938
New Jersey	3,990,753	2,055,842	6,046,595
New Mexico	1,452,508	748,262	2,200,770
New York	7,929,546	4,084,918	12,014,464
North Carolina	4,363,304	2,247,763	6,611,067
North Dakota	953,909	491,408	1,445,317
Ohio	4,974,547	2,562,645	7,537,192
Oklahoma	2,116,453	1,090,294	3,206,747
Oregon	2,150,600	1,107,885	3,258,485
Pennsylvania	5,416,459	2,790,297	8,206,756
Rhode Island	1,070,842	551,646	1,622,488
South Carolina	2,469,980	1,272,414	3,742,394
South Dakota	996,021	513,102	1,509,123
Tennessee	3,105,919	1,600,019	4,705,938
Texas	10,665,018	5,494,100	16,159,118
Utah	1,770,068	911,853	2,681,921
Vermont	912,082	469,860	1,381,942
Virginia	3,764,107	1,939,085	5,703,192

Table 1 / Library Services and Technology Act, State Allotments
FY 2015 (H.J. Res 83; Public Law 113-235)
Total Distributed to States: $154,848,000

State	Federal Funds from IMLS (66%)[1,2]	State Matching Funds (34%)	Total Federal and State Funds
Washington	3,295,633	1,697,750	4,993,383
West Virginia	1,365,372	703,373	2,068,745
Wisconsin	2,663,262	1,371,983	4,035,245
Wyoming	896,374	461,768	1,358,142
District of Columbia	924,058	476,030	1,400,088
Puerto Rico	1,928,368	993,402	2,921,770
American Samoa[4]	80,129	0	80,129
Northern Marianas[4]	79,389	0	79,389
Guam[4]	119,926	0	119,926
Virgin Islands[4]	98,364	0	98,364
Pacific Territories[3,5]	253,590	130,637	384,227
Total	$154,848,000	$79,575,553	$234,423,553

1 The IMLS Federal funds (allotments) are calculated using the current minimum base set into law (P.L. 108-81) and population figures from the Bureau of the Census (BOC) published in December 2014.
Population data is pulled from the BOC. Data used in the state allotment table are calculated based on the most recent Census data available at the time of the grant award notification. Therefore, the population data used in the FY2015 table is what was available on the BOC website http://www.census.gov/popest/ as of December, 2014.
Population data for American Samoa, Northern Marianas, Guam, Virgin Islands, Marshall Islands, Federated States of Micronesia, and Palau is used from the Census International Programs International Database. http://www.census.gov/population/international/data/idb/informationGateway.php This table reflects what was available as of December, 2014.

2 The agency is required to reduce the FY2015 allotment of any State that did not meet their FY2012 Maintenance of Effort (MOE) requirement and did not apply for, or receive, a waiver of the requirement. Those funds deducted from states not meeting the MOE requirement have been distributed across the remaining states in accordance with (1).

3 Aggregate allotments (including administrative costs) for Palau, Marshall Islands, and Federated States of Micronesia are awarded on a competitive basis to eligible applicants after taking into consideration recommendations from the Regional Educational Laboratory—Pacific (REL-P).

4 Waived pursuant to 48 U.S.C. § 1469a(d).

5 Subject to the provisions of U.S.C. § 1469a(d).

grant with non-federal funds at a 1-to-2 (non-federal to federal) ratio. No more than 4 percent of a state's program funds may be used for administrative costs.

A Special Rule, 20 USCA 9131(b)(3)(C), authorizes a small competitive grants program for four U.S. territories (American Samoa, the Commonwealth of Northern Mariana Islands, Guam, and the U.S. Virgin Islands) and three Freely Associated States (the Federated States of Micronesia, the Republic of the Marshall Islands, and the Republic of Palau). The funds for this grant program are taken from the total allotment for the Freely Associated States. In FY 2015 a total of $253,590 was available for the seven entities. This amount included a set-aside of 5 percent for the contractor for the Regional Educational Laboratory—Pacific, Mid-continent Research for Education and Learning (McREL) to facilitate the grants review process, in accordance with IMLS legislation. The total amount awarded in FY 2015, therefore, was $240,000.

The IMLS-funded programs and services delivered by each SLAA support the purposes and priorities set forth in LSTA. The SLAAs determine goals and objectives for the Grants to States funds through a planning process that includes statewide needs assessments. These goals and objectives are included in each state's statutorily required five-year plan on file with IMLS.

On a rotating basis, IMLS Grants to States program staff members conduct site visits to SLAAs to provide technical support and to monitor the states' success in administering the program. In 2015 program officers visited eight SLAAs in Alabama, Delaware, Florida, Iowa, Massachusetts, South Carolina, South Dakota, and Vermont. Each site visit includes a critical review of the administration of the LSTA program at the SLAA as well as trips into the field to visit libraries that are recipients of subawards or beneficiaries of statewide IMLS-funded projects. For more information about state priorities and projects, see www.imls.gov/programs.

Discretionary Grants Programs

In FY 2015 IMLS's four library discretionary programs awarded the following total amounts: National Leadership Grants: $12,039,953; Laura Bush 21st Century Librarian Program: $9,609,274; Native American Library Services: $ 3,311,000; and Native Hawaiian Library Services: $550,000.

National Leadership Grants for Libraries

The National Leadership Grants for Libraries program provides funding for research and innovative model programs to enhance the quality of library services nationwide. National Leadership Grants are competitive and intended to produce results useful for the broader library community.

For FY 2015 there were four categories of National Leadership Grants for Libraries:

Project Grants ($10,000 to $2,000,000)

This category supports fully developed projects for which needs assessments, partnership development, feasibility analyses, prototyping, and other planning activities have been completed.

Research Grants ($10,000 to $2,000,000)

These grants support the investigation of key questions important to library or archival practice. The term "research" includes systematic study directed toward fuller scientific knowledge or understanding of the subject studied. It also includes activities involving the training of individuals in research techniques where such activities utilize the same facilities as other research and development activities and where such activities are not included in the instruction function.

Planning Grants (up to $50,000)

This category allows project teams to perform preliminary planning activities, such as analyzing needs and feasibility, solidifying partnerships, developing project work plans, or developing prototypes or proofs of concept. These activities should have the potential to lead to a full project, such as those described in Project Grants above.

National Forum Grants (up to $100,000)

These grants provide the opportunity to convene qualified groups of experts and key stakeholders to consider issues or challenges that are important to libraries or archives across the nation. Grant-supported meetings are expected to produce reports for wide dissemination with expert recommendations for action or research that address a key challenge identified in the proposal. The expert recommendations resulting from these meetings are intended to guide future applications to the NLG-Libraries program. National Forum Grant recipients are required at the end of the project to submit to us a brief white paper for public distribution summarizing those expert recommendations, which we will post online.

The program received 267 complete and eligible proposals in FY 2015. Collectively, these proposals requested over $98 million. In March 2015 the program announced 6 awards to libraries and archives, totaling $4.1 million, and in August 2015 the program announced 17 awards to libraries and archives, totaling $6.4 million (for details, see www.imls.gov/grants/awarded-grants).

In addition to these awards to libraries and archives, remaining program funds were used to sponsor special initiatives, out-of-cycle special opportunities, and other projects, including 21 Sparks! Ignition Grants and multiple other small awards in support of efforts such as the National Medal for Museum and Library Service and the interagency Performance Partnership Pilots for Disconnected Youth (P3).

Laura Bush 21st Century Librarian Program

The Laura Bush 21st Century Librarian Program provides competitive grants to support projects to recruit and educate the next generation of librarians and library leaders; build institutional capacity in graduate schools of library and information science and develop faculty who will help in this endeavor; and support programs of continuing education and training in library and information science for librarians and library staff. In FY 2015 the program offered three funding categories for Project Grants up to $500,000, Planning Grants up to $50,000 and National Forum Grants up to $100,000 in the following project categories:

Doctoral Programs

- Develop faculty to educate the next generation of library and archives professionals. In particular, increase the number of students enrolled in doctoral programs that will prepare faculty to teach master's students who will work in school, public, academic, research, and special libraries and archives.
- Develop the next generation of library and archives leaders to assume positions as managers and administrators.

Master's Programs

- Educate the next generation of librarians and archivists in nationally accredited graduate library programs to meet the evolving needs of the profession and society.

Early Career Development

- Support the early career development of new faculty members in library and information science by supporting innovative research by untenured, tenure-track faculty.

Research

- Investigate issues and trends affecting library and archival practices.
- For all research projects, except Early Career Development Projects, all eligible library entities may apply, either individually or collaboratively.

Programs to Build Institutional Capacity

- Develop or enhance curricula within graduate schools of library and information science to better meet the needs of cultural heritage and information professionals.
- Broaden the library and information science curriculum by incorporating perspectives from other disciplines and fields of scholarship.
- Develop projects or programs of study to increase the abilities of future library and archives professionals in developing the 21st century skills of their users, including information and digital literacy skills.

Continuing Education

- Improve the knowledge, skills, and abilities of library and archives staff through programs of continuing education, both formal and informal, including post-master's programs such as certificates of advanced study, residencies, enhanced work experiences, and other training programs for professional staff.

IMLS received a total of 121 applications in the Laura Bush 21st Century Librarian Program in FY 2015. In March 2015 the program announced 16 awards to libraries and archives, totaling $5.15 million, and in August 2015 the program announced 11 awards to libraries and archives, totaling $3.4 million (for details, see www.imls.gov/grants/awarded-grants).

Native American/Native Hawaiian Library Services Grants

The Native American and Native Hawaiian Library Services program provides opportunities for improved library services to an important part of the nation's community of library users. The program offers three types of support:

1 Basic library services grants in the amount of $6,000, which support core library operations on a noncompetitive basis for all eligible Indian tribes and Alaska Native villages and corporations that apply for such support
2 Basic library services grants with a supplemental education/assessment option of $1,000 to provide funding for library staff to attend continuing education courses and/or training workshops on- or off-site, for library

staff to attend or give presentations at conferences related to library services, or to hire a consultant for an on-site professional library assessment

3 Enhancement grants, which support new levels of library service for activities specifically identified under the LSTA

Collectively, these programs received 256 applications in FY 2015. IMLS funded 227 of these proposals, totaling $3,313,000. This included basic grants and basic grants with the education/assessment option to 214 tribes, and 13 enhancement grants (for details, see www.imls.gov/grants/awarded-grants).

The Native Hawaiian Library Services program provides opportunities for improved library services through grants to nonprofit organizations that primarily serve and represent Native Hawaiians, as the term "Native Hawaiian" is defined in section 7207 of the Native Hawaiian Education Act (20 U.S.C. 7517). In FY 2015 IMLS awarded four grants in this program, totaling $550,000 (for details, see www.imls.gov/grants/awarded-grants).

Museum and Library Cooperative and Interagency Agreements

IMLS has numerous cooperative and interagency agreements to support and enhance agency priorities and services to the library and museum community:

Sundance Film Forward
Sundance Institute—Park City, Utah

- Film Forward is an international touring program designed to enhance greater cultural understanding and dialogue in both the U.S. and abroad by engaging underserved audiences, particularly 18–24 year olds, through the exhibition of films, workshops, and conversations with filmmakers. It is an initiative of the President's Committee on the Arts and Humanities and the Sundance Institute, supported by IMLS, the National Endowment for the Arts (NEA), and the National Endowment for the Humanities (NEH).

Integrating Early Learning Activities with State Systems
The BUILD Initiative—Boston, Massachusetts

- The BUILD Initiative was launched in May 2002 by a consortium of private foundations. Its aim is to stimulate public investments in early learning and help coordinate programs, policies, and services for young children. BUILD and IMLS have a year-long effort to integrate museums and libraries into statewide early childhood systems.

Learning Labs Community of Practice
National Writing Project—Berkeley, California

- The National Writing Project (NWP) is a professional development network that reaches more than 100,000 teachers across the country. With IMLS support, NWP has partnered with the Association of Science-Technology Centers (ASTC) to build an open online Community of Practice (CoP) to expand access to peer-driven professional learning for educators both in and beyond the current network of Learning Labs, originally fund-ed by IMLS and the MacArthur Foundation. Launched in January 2015, the YOUmedia Network CoP connects educators in libraries, museums, community organizations, and schools, and is free and open to share, learn, engage in discussions, and contribute resources and materials. More than 170 members have engaged in ongoing webinars, resource development activities, and cross-site support discussions. The NWP plans to expand the community in the next year and offer targeted resources and learning op-portunities that support the creation and development of learning labs sites.

Clinic Networks and Early Learning
Reach Out and Read, Inc.—Boston, Massachusetts

- IMLS funded Reach Out and Read to develop Prescription for Success, a year-long project aimed at helping more families benefit from museum and library services that foster literacy development in young children. As a national nonprofit organization comprised of doctors and nurses who en-courage family reading habits, Reach Out and Read will explore new ways doctors and their staff can collaborate with museums and libraries. It will also survey and document current partnerships between its network and li-braries and museums, create an online toolkit of best literacy practices, and further develop statewide library and museum collaborations in Colorado, Connecticut, and South Carolina.

Open Source eBook Platform
New York Public Library—New York, New York

- The New York Public Library (NYPL), in close collaboration with the Digital Public Library of America (DPLA), and 19 partner libraries and library consortia from across the country will use IMLS funds to expand and provide outreach for the Library Simplified open source eBook plat-form. Through this work, the partners aim to unify and improve the eBook borrowing and reading experience for library users across the country. The project directly supports technology development and implementation of the Open eBooks initiative, an effort to make eBooks available to children and youth from low-income families. The project also supports a broader strategy to enhance open source software tools for public library systems across the country to provide access to eBooks.

One Card Convening
Urban Libraries Council—Washington, D.C.

- The Urban Libraries Council (ULC) will identify strategies and define models for barrier-free access to learning for kids, from Universal Library Card adoption to fully integrated municipal One Card systems. On April 30, 2015, President Obama issued the ConnectED Library Challenge call-ing upon library leaders to work with their mayors, school leaders and librarians to create or strengthen partnerships so that every child enrolled in school can receive a library card. In response, ULC successfully rallied over 30 public libraries and their communities to answer the challenge. To ensure success, the cooperative agreement will identify and share leading practices for adoption of universal or one card systems. ULC will also describe and document successful programs and models so that other cities and counties across the United States can successfully implement a program that ensures a library card in every student's hand.

Sustaining and Advancing Indigenous Cultures
Association of Tribal Archives, Libraries, and Museums—Oklahoma City, Oklahoma

- The Association of Tribal Archives, Libraries, and Museums (ATALM) will provide two annual conferences with continuing education programs targeted to the needs of tribal archivists, librarians, and museum staff; and will conduct a survey of tribal archives, libraries, and museums, followed by a report documenting activities, challenges, and needs. Funded activities will contribute to improving the informational, educational, and cultural programs and services available to the nation's 4.5 million indigenous peoples, and $150,000 of award funds will be used to support conference scholarships.

Digital Skills for Digital Librarians
Mozilla Foundation—Mountain View, California

- The Mozilla Foundation, in collaboration with the Technology and Social Change Group (TASCHA) at the University of Washington Information School, will refine and launch an open source curriculum, training, tools, and credentials for a library audience to learn web literacy skills and develop digital competencies. The project intends to empower library staff to provide patrons with opportunities to develop the digital skills they need for better success in such areas as education, workforce development, and civic engagement. The project will first identify core digital literacy badges for library professionals that include technical and 21st century skills aligned with Mozilla's Web Literacy Map. The team will pilot the resources in five public library systems representing geographic, demographic, and experiential diversity. Emphasis will be placed on underserved communities, and populations will be selected for testing. In addition, one school of library information studies will also be selected to test curriculum, training, and credentials.

Performance Partnership Pilots for Disconnected Youth
U.S. Department of Education—Washington, D.C.

- IMLS is one of six federal agencies contributing to Performance Partnership Pilots for Disconnected Youth (P3), a newly authorized federal program. Other participating agencies include the U.S. Departments of Education, Labor, Health and Human Services, and Justice, as well as the Corporation for National and Community Service. From the first year's applicant pool, agencies announced nine pilots from states, localities, tribal governments, and their partners to test strategies for reaching "disconnected youth." The initiative allows awarded pilots to blend funds that they already receive from participating agencies, request waivers around those federal funds, and receive supplemental start-up grants of up to $700,000. The P3 program is intended to break down silos and improve educational and workforce outcomes for disconnected youth, and it has been authorized for an additional two years of pilots.

Museum Assessment Program
American Alliance of Museums—Washington, D.C.

- The Museum Assessment Program (MAP) helps museums assess their strengths and weaknesses, and plan for the future. A MAP assessment requires the museum staff and governing authority to complete a self-study. Following the study, a site visit is conducted by one or more museum professionals, who tour the museum and meet with staff, governing officials, and volunteers and produce a report evaluating the museum's operations, making recommendations, and suggesting resources. Three types of MAP assessments are offered: Organizational; Collections Stewardship; and Community Engagement. In FY 2015 the Museum Assessment Program received 123 applications and funded 111 museums in 40 states.

Museums for All
Association of Children's Museums—Arlington, Virginia

- The Association of Children's Museums is working with IMLS to establish a nationwide museum access program that encourages visitation at all types of museums. Piloted with children's museums and, if successful, eventually expanding to include all types of museums, Museums for All will invite low-income families to visit participating museums for a nominal fee. By promoting affordable museum experiences, ACM and IMLS can encourage families of all backgrounds to visit museums regularly, building lifelong museum habits that bolster museums' role as community anchors.

National Arts and Humanities Youth Program Awards
President's Committee on the Arts and the Humanities—Washington, D.C.

- The National Arts and Humanities Youth Program Award is the Nation's highest honor for out-of-school arts and humanities programs in museums, libraries and other youth-serving organizations. The awards recognize and support excellence in programs that open new pathways to learning, self-discovery, and achievement for young people.

National Book Festival
The Library of Congress—Washington, D.C.

- This effort supports the Library of Congress National Book Festival's "Pavilion of the States," which highlights the work of state library agencies and regional library services. Representatives from state libraries and Centers for the Book across the country interact with festival attendees (adults and children) and provide information on their state's literary heritage and its local libraries, book festivals, activities dedicated to promoting local authors and reading, and careers and opportunities in library and information science. The "Pavilion of the States" is one of the most highly attended activities at the National Book Festival with a diverse audience of families, teachers and students.

Chief Officers of State Library Agencies (COSLA)—Lexington, Kentucky

- IMLS funding supports the participation of representatives from throughout the U.S. and the territories in the National Book Festival. Representatives use this opportunity to talk about the enormous variety of reading programs around the country and the critical role of libraries in the community.

National Digital Stewardship Residency Program
The Library of Congress—Washington, D.C.

- The program, administered by the Library of Congress and supported by IMLS, allows ten recent master's program graduates in relevant fields to complete a nine-month residency at various institutions in the Washington, D.C. area. Accepted residents attend an intensive two-week digital stewardship workshop at the Library of Congress. Thereafter, residents move to a host institution to work on significant digital stewardship projects. All ten members of the first NDSR cohort received jobs in the field by the end of the residency. IMLS and the Library of Congress renewed the project in 2014 for two more cohorts. IMLS also funded similar NDSR programs in Boston and New York. These efforts will increase the capacity of the library and archives professions to manage, preserve and provide access to the nation's cultural heritage in digital formats.

National Medal for Museum and Library Service: StoryCorps Recordings
StoryCorps—Brooklyn, New York

- This Cooperative Agreement highlights the contributions that IMLS National Medal for Museum and Library Service award winners have made to their communities. A team from StoryCorps visits each award winner and conducts interviews with community members about how the library or museum affected their lives.

National Student Poets Program
Alliance for Young Artists and Writers—New York, New York

- Along with the NEA on behalf of the President's Committee on the Arts and Humanities, this agreement supports the National Student Poets Program, a national initiative that highlights the work of young poets for a national audience. The program also tries to inspire other young people to excellence in their creative endeavors and showcase the role of writing and the arts in academic and personal success.

Maker/STEM Education Support for 21st Century Community Learning Centers
Exploratorium—San Francisco, California

- The Exploratorium worked with IMLS and the Department of Education to develop and deliver STEM-rich making and tinkering programs for elementary school-aged children in a select set of 21st Century Community Learning Centers (CCLC). Professional development, activities, tools, and other resources were provided to support programming in 25 sites in five states.

STEM Video Game Challenge
Joan Ganz Cooney Center at Sesame Workshop—New York, New York

- This award helps museums and libraries in the STEM Video Game Challenge, sponsored by the Joan Ganz Cooney Center and other funders, by holding workshops at 20 institutions for youth to develop students' ability to participate in the Challenge.

Supporting Making in Museums and Libraries
Children's Museum of Pittsburgh—Pittsburgh, Pennsylvania

- Supporting Making in Museums and Libraries is designed to build the capacity of libraries and museums to develop effective maker spaces and related programs for learning. Working with the Exploratorium, Maker Education Initiative, Chicago Public Library and North Carolina State University Library, the Children's Museum is developing a framework to guide the development of effective maker spaces, supported by a website, downloadable publication, and additional tools and resources.

Federal Partnerships

Americans depend upon libraries and museums to deliver a wide range of public services. As more and more government services are only available online, museums and libraries have an increased role in the delivery of federal information and services. In the past three years, federal agencies are increasingly seeking partnerships with IMLS, as they recognize the power that libraries and museums have in reaching the American public.

IMLS was one of three federal agencies in 2015 (along with NASA and the National Park Service) that collaborated with the U.S. Department of Education around its 21st Century Community Learning Center (CCLC) program, the largest out-of-school program in the nation. The initiative will expand programs and benefit more underserved students in sites nationwide. Specifically, IMLS partnered with the Exploratorium, the San Francisco-based science museum with a history of innovation in maker education, to increase Science, Technology, Engineering, and Mathematics (STEM) programming for underserved students in sites nationwide. Beginning in spring 2015, the Exploratorium introduced students at 25 21st CCLC sites in communities in California, Florida, New York, Pennsylvania, and Texas to STEM-rich making and tinkering activities, building on the growing maker movement. It also supported local networks of science museums and youth serving programs so they can work directly with the 21st CCLC sites.

IMLS is one of six federal agencies contributing to Performance Partnership Pilots (P3), a newly authorized federal program. Other participating agencies include the U.S. Departments of Education, Labor, Health and Human Services, and Justice, as well as the Corporation for National and Community Service. The P3 program is intended to break down silos and improve educational and workforce outcomes for disconnected youth through programs offered by states, localities, tribal governments, and their partners.

In 2013 the U.S. Citizenship and Immigration Services (USCIS) signed a memorandum of understanding with IMLS pledging to support local libraries' services to new immigrants. More than 55 percent of people who immigrated to the U.S. within the last 15 years use the public library at least once a week and more mock naturalization interviews take place at public libraries than at any other community institution. In FY 2014 and FY 2015 IMLS worked with USCIS to conduct a webinar series to help librarians meet the needs of new immigrants and to provide libraries with resources on citizenship and immigration. By the end of FY 2015 ten webinars had been held with over 900 total attendees, covering a range of USCIS products and services of interest to libraries.

IMLS is working with the Consumer Financial Protection Bureau (CFPB) to help libraries access and use financial education tools. In 2015 CFPB continued its financial literacy webinars for libraries, established partnerships at the individual library and statewide level, and worked with IMLS on plans for future dissemination of financial education information to libraries.

In 2015 IMLS continued working with the Office of Career, Technical, and Adult Education (OCTAE) at the U.S. Department of Education to encourage effective collaborations between libraries and federally funded adult education programs. The goal of this joint effort is to enhance the skills, employability, and quality of life of youths and adults with low skills. In 2015 IMLS and OCTAE conducted a series of webinars. IMLS also works with the Employment and Training Administration (ETA) of the U.S. Department of Labor, to address workforce development challenges. In October 2014, IMLS, ETA, and OCTAE presented a webinar to libraries around the new Workforce Innovation and Opportunity Act (WIOA) and discussed ways that public and community college libraries could receive funding for employment skills training and job search.

In June 2015 representatives from USCIS, CFPB, OCTAE, and ETA participated in an IMLS Focus convening for library leaders and professionals entitled, "Engaging Communities." One purpose of the meeting was to highlight federal partners, and a white paper summarizing the meeting and its takeaways was published in September.

IMLS worked with the Federal Communications Commission (FCC) in 2015 to disseminate new information about its programs to libraries. Following the FCC's First E-rate Modernization Order in July 2014, which began the reform of this critical program for broadband access, the FCC adopted a Second Order in December 2014, which ensures that all libraries and schools have access to high-speed broadband connectivity. In addition to raising funding levels, the order revises language defining what constitutes "rural," a very positive change for the many libraries and schools whose discount rates had been in question.

IMLS participates in the International Visitor Leadership Program (IVLP) run by the U.S. Department of State, Bureau of Educational and Cultural Affairs, which brings international visitors to the U.S. to learn about cultural organizations. As part of the program, IMLS met with visitors from a number of countries in 2015, including Uzbekistan and Brazil.

As part of an ongoing partnership with NEA, IMLS participated in the May 2015 Summit on Creative Aging in America: A Pre-Conference to the 2015 White House Conference on Aging. This preconference addressed needs related to life-long learning and the arts and viable federal government solutions.

IMLS works with federal agencies through the Partners in Tourism initiative—advancing the nation's National Tourism Strategy and spotlighting the role of cultural heritage organizations in supporting economic development through tourism.

IMLS participates in the multi-agency Informal Science Education Forum, which brings together Federal agency representatives to share information and resources on STEM-focused programming.

IMLS administers a sub-initiative of the Let's Move! program called Let's Move! Museums and Gardens to help millions of museum and garden visitors learn about healthy food choices and promote physical activity through interactive exhibits and programs. Over 650 museums participate in the Let's Move! Museums and Gardens program.

IMLS has an ongoing partnership with the President's Committee on the Arts and the Humanities, and the Alliance for Young Artists & Writers to present the National Student Poets Program, the nation's highest honor for young poets (grades 9–11) presenting original work.

In 2015 IMLS partnered with the Congressional Maker Caucus to organize the first Capitol Hill Maker Faire on June 11, 2015, a celebration of making in the nation's capital, which was held in conjunction with the National Week of Making. It was an entertaining and interactive event for attendees, including members of Congress and their staff. Preceding the faire, there was a series of panel discussions with leaders of the Maker movement discussing its impact on the economy, education, and community development. Additionally, IMLS program staff actively participate in an interagency working group focused on advancing making that is organized by the White House Office of Science and Technology Policy.

IMLS worked with the White House on several new initiatives in 2015, including the Open eBooks initiative and ConnectED Library Challenge, which strengthen student learning by improving access to public libraries and reading materials, particularly for children from low-income families. IMLS was represented in the president's new interagency Broadband Opportunity Council (BOC) charged with developing a framework of recommendations to support broadband deployment and adoption.

Evaluation of IMLS Programs

IMLS's evaluation strategy during FY 2015 continued to address the diverse needs of the Grants to States formula grant program and its discretionary grant programs. The work balanced capacity-building efforts to improve program and performance data with summative evaluations of completed grant projects. The following section highlights achievements during the year.

Measuring Success

The Measuring Success initiative is a long-term strategic planning effort begun in FY 2011 to improve performance reporting for the Grants to States program. The aim of the initiative is to increase the comparability of program data within and across the participating states. Standardization of program data will also increase the utility of the data for monitoring project accomplishments over time and comparing library service initiatives with other educational and social programming at the local level.

In FY 2015 IMLS worked collaboratively with 16 state partners to test the new State Program Reporting tool and roll it out to 37 additional states. Continued build-out of the new reporting tool in FY 2015 was enabled through a contract with the private firm Information International Associates.

IMLS Conferences and Activities

IMLS Focus Convenings

In FY 2015 IMLS hosted a series of three strategic priority meetings, each focused on a different priority. The sessions were designed to help inform future strategies, particularly for the agency's National Leadership Grant program and Laura Bush 21st Century Librarian Program. The first convening, held at the District of Columbia Public Library on April 28, examined national digital initiatives. The second, held at the Kansas City (MO) Public Library on May 14, addressed learning in libraries, and the third, held at the Los Angeles Public Library on June 2, focused on engaging communities. More information, including convening videos and white papers, is available at www.imls.gov/news-events/events-archive.

Measuring Success

In April 2015 the Grants to States program held a two-day conference in Herndon, Virginia, for representatives from the State Library Administrative Agencies (SLAAs). Following a series of lead-up webinars, the conference officially rolled out the new State Program Report framework to all the states, along with a sandbox system for testing it. Representatives from 16 pilot states were paired with other states at the conference to serve as mentors throughout the year.

In July 2015 IMLS staff also held a special half day training session for SLAA attendees of the Research Institute for Public Libraries in Colorado to address the next phase of the Measuring Success initiative.

Library Statistics State Data Coordinators Conference

The seventh IMLS-sponsored Library Statistics State Data Coordinators Conference was held in Louisville in December 2014. The conference included training for the state representatives on data collection and input, a review of existing data elements included in the Public Libraries Survey, workshops on data presentation and analysis, and a comprehensive review of survey data elements for the FY 2015 survey and beyond.

Data Catalog

In February 2015 IMLS hosted an Open Data Open House for a small group of stakeholders to discuss ideas for the agency's new online data catalog (data.imls. gov). The site allows users to access and analyze IMLS data and create charts, graphs and maps without the need of technical statistical or GIS mapping software.

Continuing Education

To develop a consensus around continuing education and professional development (CE/PD) priorities, IMLS continued to support the work of the Coalition to Advance Learning in Archives, Libraries and Museums, a collaboration of associations from all three professions. As part of this work, IMLS staff led two webinars in February 2015 focused on the key elements of a project plan. The coalition held its third in-person convening in March 2015, where planning for the deployment of other cross-cutting topics continued.

Crowdsourcing

Funding from IMLS and NEH supported a May 2015 convening to explore the potential for crowdsourcing to broaden the reach of a diverse array of institutions. Lead organizers included Dartmouth College and the University of Maryland–College Park, with additional support from the Alfred P. Sloan Foundation. The meeting, "Engaging the Public: Best Practices in Crowdsourcing Across the Disciplines," brought together more than 60 stakeholders from the humanities, sciences, and cultural heritage domains to share their experiences managing digital projects that invite contributions from virtual volunteers.

IMLS Website and Publications

The IMLS website (www.imls.gov) provides information on the various grant programs, including funded projects and application forms, as well as special agency initiatives and staff contacts. The website highlights model projects developed by libraries and museums throughout the country and provides information about IMLS-sponsored conferences, webinars, and publications. A grant search tool, detailing awarded IMLS grants is at www.imls.gov/grants/awarded-grants.

In September 2015 IMLS launched a website redesign to address the agency's growing number of audiences and expanding role. The new website enhanced the agency's mission, increased accessibility, and simplified content management.

In early 2015 IMLS released an annual report for FY 2014, which highlighted how the agency furthered learning, community, and content goals through its grant making and other activities. The report is available online at www.imls.gov/publications/2014-annual-report.

Through an electronic newsletter, *Primary Source*, and the *UpNext* blog, IMLS provides information on grant deadlines, success stories, and opportunities. Information on subscribing to the IMLS newsletter is also located on the website, along with guidelines for each of the grant programs and other publications.

IMLS is on twitter @US_IMLS and Facebook (www.facebook.com/USIMLS).

Part 3
Library/Information Science Education, Placement, and Salaries

Library Employment Sources on the Internet

Catherine Barr

Library Journal's article "Placements and Salaries 2016: Bouncing Back" [see pp. 206–220 for the full report.—*Ed.*] provides a snapshot of a healthy job market characterized by rising salary levels and work that calls for both traditional and nontraditional skills and roles.

Librarians and information professionals have many options to consider when seeking employment both within and outside the library field. The following is not a comprehensive list of the hundreds of relevant job-related sites on the Internet. These are, however, some of the best starting places for a general job search in this ever-widening field. Many offer additional information that will be helpful to those considering a career in librarianship or a change in position, including advice on conducting a successful search, writing résumés, preparing for interviews, and negotiating salaries.

Before spending a lot of time on any website, users should check that the site has been updated recently and that out-of-date job listings no longer appear.

The Directory of Organizations in Part 6 of this volume may also prove useful, and many large libraries and library associations maintain Facebook pages that may give details of vacancies.

Background Information

The Bureau of Labor Statistics of the Department of Labor provides an overview of the work librarians do and average salaries in various sectors (schools, academia, government, and "other information services") at this page: http://www.bls.gov/oes/current/oes254021.htm. Maps show where the most jobs are located and where the salaries are highest. A useful companion page (http://www.bls.gov/ooh/Education-Training-and-Library/Librarians.htm#tab-1) looks at work environments, necessary qualifications, and similar occupations (with information on archivists, curators, museum technicians, and conservators; library technicians and assistants; and teachers).

The American Library Association (ALA) has a user-friendly introduction to librarianship at all levels—from pages and library assistants to managers and directors—at LibraryCareers.org (http://www.ala.org/educationcareers/careers/librarycareerssite/home). There are also links to discussions of career paths, education choices, and core competencies. This site will be particularly useful for young people considering a possible career in librarianship. A companion page is "ALA Overview of Library Support Staff" (http://www.ala.org/offices/hrdr/librarysupportstaff/library_support_staff_resource_center).

San José State University's School of Library and Information Science has created a "Career Development" page (http://slisweb.sjsu.edu/resources/career_development/index.htm) that aims to "help our students, alumni, and prospective students navigate a myriad of career opportunities, learn about emerging trends in the field, and develop an effective job search strategy." "Emerging Career Trends for Information Professionals: A Snapshot of Job Titles in Summer 2014" provides an interesting analysis of job listings and their requirements. A lively career blog at http://slisapps.sjsu.edu/blogs/career/ and links to career webinars are also useful.

The focus on alternatives to traditional librarianship is echoed in the many print and online publications about the profession, among them:

- *The Atlas of New Librarianship* by R. David Lankes (MIT, 2011)
- *Career Q&A: A Librarian's Real-Life, Practical Guide to Managing a Successful Career* by Susanne Markgren and Tiffany Eatman Allen (Information Today, 2013)
- "Getting the Library Job You Want" by Joseph Thompson, *Reference and User Services Quarterly* (Winter 2014)
- *The Librarian's Skillbook: 51 Essential Career Skills for Information Professionals* by Deborah Hunt and David Grossman (Information Edge, 2013)
- *LIS Career Sourcebook: Managing and Maximizing Every Stop of Your Career* by G. Kim Dority (Libraries Unlimited, 2012)
- *Making the Most of Your Library Career* ed. by Lois Stickell and Bridgette Sanders (ALA Editions, 2014)
- *The New Information Professional: Your Guide to Careers in the Digital Age* by Judy Lawson and Joanna Kroll (Neal-Schuman, 2010)
- *What Do Employers Want? A Guide for Library Science Students* by Priscilla K. Shontz and Richard A. Murray (Libraries Unlimited, 2012)

There are also many resources that address the challenges facing jobseekers and suggest strategies for success. A number of chats and webinars can be found on the ALA JobLIST site at http://www.ala.org/educationcareers/employment/career-resources. The April 2010 issue of *College and Research Library News* includes an article—"Making the Best of the Worst of Times: Global Turmoil and Landing Your First Library Job"—that looks at job listings and how to prepare for an interview. And https://opencoverletters.com/ provides actual examples of cover letters with details of names and institutions redacted.

Those who have succeeded in getting an interview will find these resources helpful:

- "Congratulations! You've Landed an Interview: What Do Hiring Committees Really Want?" by Megan Hodge and Nicole Spoor. *New Library World* Vol. 113 Iss: 3/4, pp. 139–161 (2012). This article gives the results of a survey of members of library hiring committees, offering insight for jobseekers in the public and academic library fields.

- The Library Interview Question "Database," a spreadsheet on Google Drive available at http://tinyurl.com/InterviewQuestionsRepository, gives fascinating insight into the kinds of questions job applicants may encounter. Participants describe the level of interview, the kind of position involved, the questions they were asked, and the questions they themselves asked in return.
- Finally, should you be agonizing over what to wear to an interview, visit http://librarianhirefashion.tumblr.com/ for photographs of suitable and unsuitable attire, with comments by librarians who hire.

General Sites/Portals

How to Apply for a Library Job

http://liswiki.org/wiki/HOWTO:Apply_for_a_library_job

A general guide with advice on phone, video, and in-person interviews.

ALA JobLIST

http://joblist.ala.org

Sponsored by the American Library Association and the Association of College and Research Libraries, this site is free for jobseekers, who can post their résumés and browse recent job postings or search jobs by library type, date, state, institution name, salary range, and other parameters offered in the advanced search function. Employers can choose from a menu of print and electronic posting combinations.

ALA JobLIST: Career Development Resources

http://www.ala.org/educationcareers/employment/career-resources

This ALA site lists job placement opportunities at forthcoming conferences, along with details of workshops and tips on various aspects of the job search. At the top of the page, you can do a quick search for job openings by state. Also available on this page are links to career assessment resources, advice on creating effective resumes and cover letters, general career information, and tips on job hunting, interviews, negotiating salaries, and so forth. A multimedia section includes webinars and podcasts on various aspects of job searches.

San José State University Job Listing Sites and Resources

http://slisweb.sjsu.edu/career-development/job-search/job-listing-sites-and-resources

This page provides an extensive list of library employment sites as well as tips on conducting an effective job search, with webcasts and advice on creating an e-portfolio. A related page, Professional Associations (http://slisweb.sjsu.edu/resources/orgs.htm), is a comprehensive listing of organizations in the United States and abroad that will be helpful to jobseekers with specific interests.

INALJ

http://inalj.com/

This community of information professionals working to help find and share jobs and job hunting advice is also present on Facebook, Twitter, and LinkedIn. Along with regularly updated, well-organized job listings (domestic and international), this site offers interesting articles and interviews, inspiring success stories, plus an extensive list of keywords for job searches that reveals the breadth of opportunities in the field. Check individual states for openings; the "last updated" date on splash pages may not apply.

Metropolitan New York Library Council

http://metro.org/career-resources/

A job board for library and related organizations in the NYC area, plus a calendar of events.

The Riley Guide

http://www.rileyguide.com

In addition to job listings (try http://www.rileyguide.com/info.html#lib to access positions suitable for librarians), the Riley Guide allows users to explore all aspects of job hunting, from proper preparation to résumés and cover letters, researching and targeting employers, and networking, interviewing, and negotiating salaries and job conditions.

Sites by Sector

Public Libraries

Public library openings can be found at all the general sites/portals listed above.

Careers in Public Librarianship

http://www.ala.org/pla/tools/careers

The Public Library Association offers information on public librarianship, with a webcast on finding and keeping public library jobs

Competencies for Librarians Serving Children in Public Libraries

http://www.ala.org/ala/mgrps/divs/alsc/edcareeers/alsccorecomps/

A detailed listing of skills and knowledge required to be a children's librarian in a public library.

School Libraries

School library openings can be found at many of the sites listed above and general education sites, and comprehensive employment sites such as Monster.com often include school library openings.

AASL: Recruitment to School Librarianship

http://www.ala.org/ala/mgrps/divs/aasl/aasleducation/recruitmentlib/
aaslrecruitment.cfm

The American Association of School Librarians hosts this site, which describes the role of school librarians, salary and job outlooks, and mentoring programs; provides testimonials from working library media specialists; and offers state-by-state information on licensure, scholarships, library education, job hunting, mentoring, and recruitment efforts.

Special and Academic Libraries

AALL Career Center

http://www.aallnet.org/main-menu/Careers/career-center

Maintained by the American Association of Law Libraries, this site has an online job board and useful tips for job seekers (in academic libraries, court libraries, and law firms).

Careers in Law Librarianship

http://www.lawlibrarycareers.org/

This excellent site answers the question "Is a career as a law librarian right for you?" and provides broad information on the profession, educational require-ments, and available financial assistance.

Association of College and Research Libraries

http://www.ala.org/acrl/

Under the heading Professional Tools, there are useful descriptions of various po-sitions and information on recruitment and retention. Job listings are found at ALA JobLIST (see above).

ASIS&T: Careers

https://www.asist.org/about/careers/

The Careers page maintained by the Association for Information Science and Technology offers access to a Jobline, profiles of selected members, and continu-ing education information.

Association of Research Libraries: Leadership & Recruitment

http://www.arl.org/leadership-recruitment

In addition to user-friendly listings of openings at ARL member institutions and at other organizations, there is information on ARL's diversity programs plus a database of research library residency and internship programs.

Chronicle of Higher Education: Vitae

https://chroniclevitae.com/

Listings can be browsed, with geographical options, using keywords. Articles and advice on job searching are also available.

EDUCAUSE Job Posting Service

http://www.educause.edu/Jobs

EDUCAUSE member organizations post positions "in the broad field of information technology in higher education."

HigherEdJobs.com

http://www.higheredjobs.com

The category "Libraries" is found under Administrative Positions.

Medical Library Association: Career Center

http://www.mlanet.org/p/cm/ld/fid=352

The Medical Library Association offers much more than job listings here, with brochures on medical librarianship, a video, career tips, and a mentor program.

Music Library Association Job Openings

http://www.musiclibraryassoc.org/?page=JobsAndCareers

Along with job postings and a résumé review service, this site features useful career resources.

SLA: Career Center

http://www.sla.org/career-center/

The Career Center is the place to apply for jobs, post résumés, and find information on career enhancement.

Government

Library of Congress

http://www.loc.gov/hr/employment

An extensive survey of what it's like to work at the library, the kinds of employees the library is seeking, the organizational structure, benefits, current job openings, internships, fellowships, and volunteering.

National Archives and Records Administration

http://www.archives.gov/careers/

In addition to information on employment opportunities, internships, and volunteering, NARA provides profiles of employees and interns, describing the kinds of work they do.

Serials

NASIG Jobs

http://nasigjobs.wordpress.com/

Managed by the North American Serials Interest Group. Accepts serials-related job postings.

Library Periodicals

American Libraries

See ALA JobLIST above.

Library Journal

http://www.libraryjournal.com

Job listings are found under the Job Zone tab found under the Careers heading, which also leads to archived articles relating to employment.

School Library Journal

http://www.schoollibraryjournal.com

Click on the Job Zone tab for access to a general list of job openings (jointly maintained with *Library Journal*).

Employment Agencies/Commercial Services

A number of employment agencies and commercial services in the United States and abroad specialize in library-related jobs. Among those that keep up-to-date listings on their Web sites are:

Advanced Information Management

http://www.aimusa.com

Specializes in librarians and support staff in a variety of types of libraries across the country.

LAC Group

http://careers.lac-group.com/

An easy-to-use list of openings that can be sorted by function, location, and key-word. The LibGig site (http://www.libgig.com/) was created by the LAC Group and offers news, career profiles, and résumé consultation.

Listservs and Networking Sites

Many listservs allow members to post job openings on a casual basis.

ALA Think Tank

https://www.facebook.com/groups/ALAthinkTANK/

A lively Facebook group with nearly 12,000 members who post and comment on all aspects of librarianship.

LIBJOBS

http://www.ifla.org/en/mailing-lists

LIBJOBS is a mailing list for librarians and information professionals seeking em-ployment. It is managed by the International Federation of Library Associations and Institutions (IFLA). Subscribers to this list receive posted job opportunities by e-mail.

LIS New Prof Network

https://twitter.com/lisnpn

A Twitter forum with news, blogs, and postings of general and specific (job open-ings, grants, etc.) interest.

PUBLIB

http://www.webjunction.org/documents/webjunction/PubLib_Overview.html

Public library job openings often appear on this list.

Blogs

hls: How Would You Hack Library School?

http://hacklibschool.wordpress.com/

A blog that looks at various aspects of librarianship and its evolution.

Library Career People

http://librarycareerpeople.com/

This attractive and user-friendly blog is maintained by librarians Tiffany Allen, Susanne Markgren, and Carrie Netzer Wajda and is intended to "create an enlightening discussion forum, and career development archive, of professional guidance and advice for librarians, library staff, and those thinking of entering the profession."

Placements and Salaries 2016: Bouncing Back

Suzie Allard

The first placements and salaries after completing library and information science (LIS) programs reported this year provide a snapshot of a healthy job market characterized by rising salary levels and work that calls for both traditional and nontraditional skills and roles.

This year, 39 of the 52 U.S. LIS schools reported 4,002 graduates in 2015, with 29 percent participating in the *LJ* survey. Overall, 2015 graduates were successful in finding jobs, with 82 percent of those responding to the employment status question reporting that they had full-time employment. About 74 percent of these full-time professionals work in a library setting and an additional 13 percent use their library skills in a different environment. Full-time employment declined slightly from last year, when 2014 graduates reported 83 percent full-time employment, however it is still well ahead of 2013, when only 69.6 percent reported having full-time employment. The average starting salary is $48,371, up 2.9 percent from last year.

Members of the 2015 class tended to be younger and beginning a career for the first time. More than two-thirds were under 36 and more than half said that library and information sciences is the first career they pursued. About 46 percent of the graduates were working in a library before beginning the degree program.

While these graduates found full-time employment, it required hard work and patience. More than half of the graduates remained with an employer they were with during their program, and those who did not began their job search almost six months before graduation. A little over a third found jobs before graduation; those who did not took nearly five months after graduation to find full-time employment.

Respondents' satisfaction with their placement is closely tied to full-time status and salary level. More than three-quarters of graduates who found full-time placements were satisfied with these appointments, as opposed to only 30 percent of those with part-time placements. One part-timer from the East Coast cited many reasons for dissatisfaction, among them scheduling issues and a lack of benefits. Among full-timers, a key to satisfaction may be salary, with graduates who are satisfied earning a salary 15 percent higher than those who were not.

LIS schools also reported an active market for LIS graduates, with an average of 634 employment postings, which translated into an average of 32.6 more positions posted than the previous year. About half of the schools didn't have data to compare salaries to last year, but about 13 percent said salaries were higher, which is supported by the findings from the graduates.

Salary Levels

In 2015, the salary level for full-time placements grew overall, and the story was much better for women than for men. The average salary was $48,371 among

Suzie Allard is a Professor of Information Sciences and Associate Dean of Research, University of Tennessee College of Communication and Information, Knoxville.

Adapted from *Library Journal*, October 17, 2016.

Table 1 / Status of 2015 Graduates

School Region	Number of Schools Reporting	Number of Graduates Responding	Employed in LIS Field	Employed Outside United States	Currently Unemployed or Continuing Education	Total Answering	Percentage Employed Full-Time
Northeast	11	245	208	27	8	243	80
Midwest	9	318	174	32	22	228	78
Southeast	8	214	111	21	12	144	92
South Central	8	169	138	22	7	167	87
West	3	234	184	9	18	211	78
Total	39	1,180	815	111	67	993	82

*Table based on survey responses from schools and individual graduates. Figures will not necessarily be fully consistent with some of the other data reported. Tables do not always add up, individually or collectively, since both schools and individuals omitted data in some cases.

Table 2 / Placements and Full-Time Salaries of 2015 Graduates/Summary by Region*

Region	Number of Placements	Number Responding			Low Salary		High Salary		Average Salary			Median Salary		
		Women	Men	All**	Women	Men	Women	Men	Women	Men	All**	Women	Men	All**
Northeast	167	115	19	134	24,000	39,000	106,000	165,000	49,724	59,087	51,052	47,000	53,500	47,650
Southeast	200	114	26	141	20,000	19,200	97,850	85,000	46,075	44,899	45,876	44,750	43,700	44,500
Midwest	141	102	12	114	19,500	26,250	150,000	76,000	46,385	50,313	46,798	45,500	50,500	46,000
South Central	102	75	12	88	19,000	32,000	87,500	82,500	40,797	46,125	41,515	40,000	43,000	40,175
Mountain	40	23	9	32	25,000	32,000	75,000	51,500	45,374	42,667	44,612	45,000	45,000	45,000
Pacific	114	79	21	100	28,800	45,000	150,000	100,000	55,858	59,145	56,548	55,000	55,000	55,000
Canada/Intl.	16	10	1	11	24,000	38,513	95,000	38,513	59,105	38,513	57,233	60,790	38,513	60,800
Total	900	583	113	698	19,000	19,200	150,000	165,000	47,759	51,602	48,371	45,000	49,225	45,000

*This table represents only salaries reported as full-time. Some data were reported as aggregate without breakdown by gender or region. Comparison with other tables will show different numbers of placements.

**All includes transgender, other, and no answer.

the 698 graduates who shared their salary information, an increase of 2.9 percent over last year, on top of a similar increase recorded for 2014. While the low and high salaries are far apart (ranging from $19,000 to $165,000), the average and the median are quite close ($3,371 apart), suggesting that the salaries are highly concentrated near this average. In addition, the substantial differences between the lowest and highest salary levels reflect that more than half of these graduates are entering their first professional position, while other graduates may be adding the master's degree as further certification to an already accomplished career, or may be switching careers using prior experience as a springboard.

Women's average salary showed a healthy 5.3 percent increase over last year, at $47,759. However, the situation for men was not as rosy, with their average salary declining by 3.2 percent to $51,602. This year, the 2015 graduates who responded to this question were 83.8 percent women and 16.2 percent men. Less than 1 percent of respondents identified as genderqueer. The ratio is similar to 2013 but quite different from last year, when men represented 22.2 percent of respondents.

Salary by Region

Similar to last year, there was considerable difference in salary level when viewed by region.

Graduates sharing salary information were identified as working in seven regions, with the largest proportion of respondents coming from the Southeast (20.2 percent) and Northeast (19.3 percent). Other regions were the Midwest (16.3 percent), Pacific (14.3 percent), South Central (12.6 percent), Mountain (4.6 percent), and international (1.6 percent). The Midwest, South Central, and Northeast regions had a higher proportion of women than the average, as did Canada or other international locations.

Graduates holding jobs outside the United States reported the highest average salary ($57,233), but this group represents only a small proportion (1.6 percent) of those who answered this question.

Within the United States, the pattern of salary levels by region was similar to last year. Graduates with jobs in the Pacific states reported the highest average salary of $56,548, 16.9 percent higher than the overall average salary. This difference is not as great as last year, when Pacific state salaries were 36.2 percent higher than the overall average. The Northeast is the only other region that reports a salary level above the overall average (+5.5 percent). Salaries in the other four regions fall below the overall average: Midwest (-3.3 percent), Southeast (-5.2 percent), Mountain (-7.8 percent), and South Central (-14.2 percent).

There is a substantial difference between the Pacific region, which reported the highest average salary, and South Central, which reported the lowest average salary. The gap between these two salary levels likely reflects more than the difference in cost of living for these two regions (25 percent difference between Portland, OR, and Louisville, KY), however it is much closer than last year ($15,033 vs. $22,914).

(text continues on page 212)

Table 3 / 2015 Total Graduates and Placements by School*

Schools	Graduates			Employed			Response Rate	
	Women	Men	All	Women	Men	All**	No. Rec'd.	Rate
Alabama	79	17	96	15	6	21	27	28.1%
Albany	27	25	52	7	3	10	14	26.9
Buffalo	49	13	62	9	1	11	12	19.4
Catholic	52	17	69	9	2	12	15	21.7
Clarion				16	1	17	23	
Dominican	89	26	116	37	6	43	60	51.7
Drexel	103	17	120	4	1	5	8	6.7
Florida State	88	6	94	9	2	11	19	20.2
Hawaii	15	3	18	7	0	7	13	72.2
Illinois Urbana-Champaign*	181	43	224	60	12	72	103	46.0
Indiana–Bloomington	61	30	91	18	8	26	28	30.8
Iowa	25	3	28	18	1	19	20	71.4
Kentucky	63	12	75	18	5	23	31	41.3
Long Island	93	16	109	3	4	7	10	9.2
Louisiana State				7	1	8	9	
Maryland	81	35	116	36	9	45	48	41.4
Michigan	129	58	187	1	0	1	1	0.5
Missouri	50	6	56	14	0	14	16	28.6
NC Chapel Hill*	51	22	74	46	17	64	69	93.2
NC Greensboro	62	15	77	6	2	8	15	19.5
North Texas	206	49	255	25	5	30	33	12.9
Oklahoma	37	7	44	4	3	7	9	20.5
Pittsburgh	59	17	76	3	0	3	5	6.6
Pratt	92	13	105	14	3	17	25	23.8
Rutgers	88	20	108	31	1	32	41	38.0
San Jose*	392	93	485	89	18	108	138	28.5
Simmons*	222	45	267	62	6	69	82	30.7
South Carolina	93	15	108	5	1	6	7	6.5
South Florida	49	10	59	6	0	6	9	15.3
So. Mississippi	23	3	26	12	2	14	16	61.5
St. Catherine	50	10	60	9	2	11	19	31.7
St. John's	24	2	26	4	1	5	6	23.1
Syracuse	47	18	65	12	1	13	19	29.2
Tennessee	53	20	73	16	6	23	24	32.9
Texas Woman's	142	6	148	14	0	15	20	13.5
Valdosta State	38	6	44	22	6	28	32	72.7
Washington*	103	23	126	41	7	48	83	65.9
Wayne State	136	30	166	21	5	26	50	30.1
Wisconsin–Madison*	78	19	97	10	5	15	21	21.6
Total Answering	3,230	770	4,002	740	153	900	1,180	29.5

Tables do not always add up, individually or collectively, OWING to omitted data from schools and/ or individuals.

*Some schools conducted their own survey and provided raw data. Comparison with other tables MAY show different numbers of placements.

**All includes nonbinary gender, other, and no answer.

Table 4 / Placements by Average Full-Time Salary of Reporting 2015 Graduates*

Schools	Average Salary			Median Salary		Low Salary		High Salary		Placements		Total Placements
	Women	Men	All	Women	Men	Women	Men	Women	Men	Women	Men	
Alabama	$43,128	$41,117	$42,525	$39,500	$38,500	$23,296	$19,200	$94,000	$76,000	14	6	20
Albany	39,716	62,167	48,135	42,000	62,000	26,500	49,500	48,800	75,000	5	3	8
Buffalo	44,517	39,000	43,827	43,000	39,000	34,750	39,000	53,369	39,000	7	1	8
Catholic	61,012	45,500	57,910	55,000	45,500	41,000	38,000	97,850	53,000	8	2	10
Clarion	52,583	44,500	52,044	48,368	44,500	38,000	44,500	89,000	44,500	14	1	15
Dominican	43,321	38,050	42,609	42,922	32,000	19,500	26,250	70,000	55,000	32	5	37
Drexel	40,000	45,000	41,000	38,500	45,000	35,000	45,000	48,000	45,000	4	1	5
Florida State	38,000	30,000	37,111	33,500	30,000	22,000	30,000	62,000	30,000	8	1	9
Hawaii	48,320	–	48,320	45,000	–	38,000	–	65,000	–	5	–	5
Illinois Urbana-Champaign**	46,019	55,955	47,727	43,000	50,000	25,000	36,000	84,000	100,000	53	11	64
Indiana-Bloomington	51,486	49,500	50,968	45,000	45,000	29,000	40,000	150,000	62,000	17	6	23
Iowa	50,934	–	50,934	54,000	–	29,000	–	67,000	–	15	–	15
Kentucky	48,833	42,000	47,627	45,000	40,000	29,300	34,000	105,000	52,000	14	3	17
Long Island	45,500	80,125	68,583	45,500	54,250	39,000	47,000	52,000	165,000	2	4	6
Louisiana State	42,467	45,000	42,829	43,500	45,000	37,500	45,000	45,700	45,000	6	1	7
Maryland	49,133	50,200	49,325	47,250	52,000	35,000	41,000	90,000	60,000	32	7	39
Michigan	42,000	–	42,000	42,000	–	42,000	–	42,000	–	1	–	1
Missouri	48,921	–	48,921	51,000	–	24,000	–	68,000	–	9	–	9
NC Greensboro	47,740	44,250	46,868	48,500	44,250	37,440	37,000	57,000	51,500	6	2	8

School											
North Texas	43,697	46,134	44,205	42,000	45,000	21,827	36,670	65,000	62,000	19	5	24
Oklahoma	45,000	58,750	51,875	45,000	58,750	43,000	35,000	47,000	82,500	2	2	4
Pittsburgh	39,770	39,770	39,770	40,000	–	39,311	40,000	40,000	–	3	–	3
Pratt	58,578	48,000	57,697	56,109	48,000	340,00	48,000	85,000	48,000	11	1	12
Rutgers	57,136	60,000	57,261	50,500	60,000	37,000	60,000	106,000	60,000	22	1	23
San Jose**	52,902	58,395	53,889	50,000	52,300	26,000	43,000	110,000	100,000	73	16	89
Simmons**	45,159	43,912	45,055	44,000	45,000	24,000	38,513	70,000	50,000	55	5	60
South Carolina	33,167	–	33,167	37,500	–	21,000	–	41,000	–	3	–	3
South Florida	41,356	–	41,356	42,000	–	30,000	–	50,000	–	5	–	5
Southern Mississippi	39,396	32,000	38,780	40,000	32,000	28,000	32,000	55,000	32,000	11	1	12
St. Catherine	51,062	51,000	51,046	50,500	51,000	41,371	48,000	64,000	54,000	6	2	8
St. John's	49,925	39,850	47,910	50,850	39,850	42,000	39,850	56,000	39,850	4	1	5
Syracuse	50,237	53,000	50,488	46,500	53,000	33,000	53,000	100,000	53,000	10	1	11
Tennessee	40,253	54,094	44,016	41,000	53,000	24,190	35,000	67,300	69,215	15	6	22
Texas Woman's	42,708	–	43,154	40,500	–	19,000	–	71,000	–	12	–	13
Valdosta State	39,050	38,651	38,970	38,750	38,755	20,000	31,000	54,000	44,000	20	5	25
Washington**	54,103	57,857	54,674	55,000	55,000	25,000	45,000	150,000	65,000	39	7	46
Wayne State	42,153	61,125	45,767	37,000	57,500	25,000	44,500	80,000	85,000	17	4	21
Wisconsin–Madison**	51,500	55,000	52,667	50,000	55,000	45,000	55,000	61,000	55,000	4	2	6
Total	47,759	51,602	48,371	45,000	49,225	19,000	19,200	150,000	165,000	583	113	698

*This table represents only placements and salaries reported as full-time. Some individuals or schools omitted information, rendering information unusable.
**Some schools conducted their own survey and provided raw data.

Table 5 / Average Salary for Starting Library Positions, 2011–2015

Year	Library Schools Represented	Average Starting Salary	Difference in Average Salary	Percentage Change
2011	41	$44,565	$2,009	4.72
2012	41	44,503	($62)	-0.14
2013	40	45,650	1,147	2.58
2014	39	46,987	1,337	2.93
2015	39	48,371	1,384	2.95

(continued from page 208)

Women's salaries are higher than men's in the Mountain (+6.3 percent) and Southeast (+2.6 percent) regions. Men see much higher salaries than women in the Northeast (+18.8 percent) and South Central (13.1 percent) regions. This pattern is somewhat less pronounced in the Midwest (+8.5 percent) and Pacific (+5.9 percent) regions.

Salary by Library Type

Salary levels vary by library type, with several below the overall salary average, with all but private industry salaries recording an increase in pay over last year. In addition, several types of libraries have very strong regional performance. Given the variable cost of living for different parts of the country, this is an important consideration.

The gender ratio varies across library types. School libraries (93 percent female), nonprofit organizations (88.9 percent), archives/special collections (87.9 percent), and public libraries (87.8 percent) demonstrate a higher proportion of female placements than the average. Government libraries (20.8 percent male), private industry (20.8 percent), college/university libraries (21.6 percent), and special libraries (26.8 percent) demonstrate a higher proportion of male placements than the average.

While more than half of the graduates are finding jobs in either public libraries (29.9 percent of graduate placements) or college/university libraries (23.7 percent), these libraries have salary levels that fall below the overall average (-7.9 percent for public libraries; -3.1 percent for college/university libraries). This suggests that graduates are finding jobs but at lower salaries.

Public Libraries

Similar to last year, public libraries have the lowest salary level ($44,565), but this represents the second year of an upward trend with a substantial increase (+9.7 percent) over last year and was nearly tied with the salary level of archives/special collections. The Southeast region public libraries' salary was 14 percent below the region's average. The Pacific was the only region that was marginally above the average (+.9 percent). Salary levels for public libraries continue to suggest a range of responsibilities with salaries reported from $19,000 to $100,000.

There are marked differences in public library salaries for men and women. Men account for only 11.8 percent of the public library placements, yet they report

Table 6 / Full-Time Salaries of Reporting Professionals
by Primary Job Assignment

Assignment	No. Rec'd.	Percent of Total	Low Salary	High Salary	Average Salary	Median Salary
Access Services	9	1.7	$21,000	$52,000	$38,259	$42,000
Administration	32	6.1	19,000	100,000	50,636	45,500
Adult Services	35	6.6	22,300	70,000	44,225	45,000
Archival and Preservation	32	6.1	19,200	165,000	48,066	42,450
Children's Services	42	8.0	29,000	68,000	44,179	41,880
Circulation	11	2.1	23,296	53,000	37,174	34,200
Collection Development/ Acquisitions	12	2.3	21,827	65,000	40,236	39,500
Communications, PR, and Social Media	3	0.6	30,000	55,000	42,333	42,000
Data Analytics	5	0.9	40,000	75,000	56,793	55,000
Data Curation & Management	5	0.9	39,600	87,500	58,227	53,000
Digital Content Management	15	2.8	28,000	76,000	45,920	46,300
Emerging Technologies	5	0.9	42,000	62,000	51,800	51,000
Government Documents	9	1.7	26,250	54,000	42,396	39,311
Information Technology	13	2.5	37,000	82,500	58,438	55,000
Knowledge Management	4	0.8	47,000	65,000	54,000	52,000
Market Intelligence/Business Research	3	0.6	35,000	55,000	43,000	39,000
Metadata, Cataloging, and Taxonomy	30	5.7	24,500	65,000	45,041	45,000
Outreach	7	1.3	34,000	61,500	49,214	50,000
Patron Programming	2	0.4	39,000	42,000	40,500	40,500
Public Services	11	2.1	34,000	55,000	44,917	45,000
Records Management	14	2.7	26,500	90,500	45,780	43,092
Reference/Information Services	55	10.4	22,000	80,000	48,593	48,000
Rights and Permissions	2	0.4	50,000	58,000	54,000	54,000
School Librarian/School Library Media Specialist	39	7.4	24,000	106,000	53,478	50,000
Solo Librarian	15	2.8	29,000	52,520	43,805	45,000
Systems Technology	10	1.9	34,000	70,000	48,900	42,750
Teacher Librarian	20	3.8	34,000	110,000	58,148	51,750
Technical Services	9	1.7	30,000	53,000	39,053	33,512
Training, Teaching, and Instruction	29	5.5	24,000	85,000	48,992	49,500
User Experience/Usability Analysis	3	0.6	50,000	58,000	55,167	57,500
Website Design	2	0.4	34,000	52,000	43,000	43,000
YA/Teen Services	15	2.8	32,000	58,000	45,439	46,300
Other	29	5.5	26,000	85,000	51,703	53,000
Total Answering	528	100.0	19,000	165,000	47,814	45,065

This table represents full-time placements reported by primary job assignment. Some individuals omitted placement information,therefore comparison with other tables may show different numbers of placements and average and median salaries.

an average salary that is 8.45 percent higher than what women report. The range of salaries for women is also much greater (from a low of $19,000 to a high of $100,000) than for men ($32,000–$69,215), and the median suggests that many of the salaries fall on the lower side of this range.

Academic Libraries

Salaries for college and university libraries averaged $46,850, up 9.4 percent over last year. Regionally, salaries in the Mountain states were 17.9 percent above the average. Unlike last year, the salary level in the Pacific region was well below the average for the region (-11.7 percent). The range of salaries reported is nearly as broad as those for public libraries, suggesting that there is a wide array of responsibilities.

(text continues on page 216)

Table 7 / Comparison of Full-Time Salaries by Type of Organization and Region

	Total Placements	Low Salary	High Salary	Average Salary	Median Salary
Public Libraries					
Northeast	42	32,000	100,000	46,631	45,352
Southeast	36	22,000	54,300	39,418	38,050
South Central	26	19,000	55,000	37,767	39,000
Midwest	35	19,500	80,000	44,036	45,000
Mountain	10	25,000	50,000	41,876	44,000
Pacific	30	34,000	85,000	57,048	56,500
Canada/Intl.	3	46,216	68,250	60,822	68,000
All Public	204	19,000	100,000	44,565	43,533
College/University Libraries					
Northeast	23	24,000	75,000	51,191	51,500
Southeast	29	21,000	67,300	41,830	42,000
South Central	32	21,827	82,500	41,869	42,250
Midwest	30	25,480	65,000	45,459	47,750
Mountain	8	45,000	65,000	52,598	51,140
Pacific	24	28,800	72,000	49,935	48,613
Canada/Intl.	2	58,000	60,080	59,040	59,040
All Academic	162	21,000	100,000	46,850	45,000
Northeast	25	37,000	106,000	56,993	50,000
Southeast	14	30,000	56,911	43,459	43,065
South Central	11	31,000	60,000	44,609	44,000
Midwest	18	24,000	68,000	52,054	54,000
Mountain	0	–	–	–	–
Pacific	9	40,000	110,000	67,556	58,000
Canada/Intl.	2	24,000	80,000	52,000	52,000
All School Government Libraries	86	24,000	110,000	52,848	50,000
Northeast	6	35,000	42,500	39,105	39,315
Southeast	24	31,065	90,000	53,669	53,025
South Central	5	33,930	87,500	48,009	39,600
Midwest	3	30,500	76,000	48,300	38,400

Mountain	6	32,000	45,000	39,256	40,769
Pacific	5	35,000	90,500	58,100	55,000
Canada/Intl.	0	–	–	–	–
All Government Private Industry	53	29,000	90,500	49,012	44,000
Northeast	11	26,500	60,000	45,136	43,000
Southeast	8	19,200	94,000	54,213	54,250
South Central	1	52,000	52,000	52,000	52,000
Midwest	9	30,000	105,000	50,829	48,965
Mountain	1	39,520	39,520	39,520	39,520
Pacific	16	30,000	150,000	62,813	55,000
Canada/Intl.	0	–	–	–	–
All Private Industry	53	19,200	150,000	53,473	51,000
Special Libraries					
Northeast	8	37,500	165,000	66,563	49,750
Southeast	7	40,400	60,000	50,560	52,520
South Central	2	55,000	75,000	65,000	65,000
Midwest	7	25,000	51,000	39,571	40,000
Mountain	4	25,000	75,000	48,250	46,500
Pacific	8	40,000	65,000	50,550	48,950
Canada/Intl.	1	38,513	38,513	38,513	38,513
All Special Archives/ Special Collections	41	25,000	165,000	51,606	46,500
Northeast	8	32,000	60,000	47,825	47,000
Southeast	8	25,000	97,850	46,700	38,874
South Central	6	28,000	46,300	36,133	36,750
Midwest	5	28,800	47,258	37,712	34,000
Mountain	2	36,000	58,000	47,000	47,000
Pacific	2	55,000	60,000	57,500	57,500
Canada/Intl.	1	61,500	61,500	61,500	61,500
All Archives/Special Collections	33	25,000	97,850	44,570	40,600
Nonprofit Organizations					
Northeast	3	55,000	85,000	66,000	58,000
Southeast	8	41,000	76,000	51,327	47,250
South Central	1	26,500	26,500	26,500	26,500
Midwest	1	64,000	64,000	64,000	64,000
Mountain	0	–	–	–	–
Pacific	4	42,000	65,000	50,500	47,500
Canada/Intl.	0	–	–	–	–
All Nonprofit	18	26,500	85,000	52,562	48,750
Other Organizations					
Northeast	7	28,000	80,000	54,000	50,000
Southeast	7	43,000	62,000	52,571	55,000
South Central	4	38,000	49,500	43,875	44,000
Midwest	6	22,300	150,000	60,183	44,400
Mountain	1	26,000	26,000	26,000	26,000
Pacific	2	55,000	65,000	60,000	60,000
Canada/Intl.	2	30,000	95,000	62,500	62,500
All Other	33	22,300	150,000	53,291	48,800

This table represents only full-time salaries and all placements reported by type. Some individuals omitted placement information, rendering some information unusable.

(continued from page 214)

College and university libraries employ the second highest proportion of men, and men report salaries that are 8.4 percent higher than women's salaries. Low salaries for women and men are fairly close ($21,000/$24,500), suggesting that entry-level positions are similar.

Salaries in archives/special collections ($44,570) are also below the overall average (-7.9 percent), however they experienced a small increase over last year (+2.6 percent). About 4.8 percent of the graduate respondents are employed in this type of library. There were only a small number of these placements, making comparisons across regions difficult. However, comparing salary levels to regional averages does provide some interesting insights. Archival salaries in the South Central (-13 percent) and Midwestern (-19.4 percent) areas fell considerably below the regional average. Similar to other library types, salaries range from $25,000 to $97,850, which may reflect responsibilities or available resources.

School Libraries

The story for school libraries is heartening. The reported average salary of $52,848 is 9.3 percent higher than the overall average and up 8.8 percent over last year. School library positions in the Pacific (+19.5 percent), Northeast (+11.6), and Midwest (+11.2 percent) were compensated at levels well above their regional averages. No placements were reported in the Mountain states.

While this year school librarian/school media specialist showed a salary above the average at $53,478, note that last year the school librarian and school media specialist titles were separated and school librarians were paid below the overall average.

School libraries employ the highest percentage of women (93 percent), yet salaries for men exceed those for women by 2.7 percent. The differences fall at the low salary levels, while the highest salaries are at a similar level.

Other Libraries

Government library salary levels are substantially higher than last year (+14.7 percent) but only slightly above this year's overall average (+1.3 percent). The number of placements more than doubled over last year (53 to 26) and, interestingly, 45 percent of these placements were in the Southeast, where salary levels were 17 percent above the regional average. The five positions in the South Central region are at 15.6 percent above the regional average. Government libraries are tied for third in terms of the proportion of men employed (20.8 percent), yet salaries for women are 5 percent higher.

Private industry reported the highest salary level among the library types at $53,437, which was 21.9 percent down from last year but 10.5 percent above the overall average salary. Similar to last year, private industry salaries were strong in the Pacific (+11.1 percent over regional average). However, when examining regions with at least two placements, average salary levels against regional average were even stronger in the Southeast (+18.2). Private industry is tied for third in terms of the proportion of men employed (20.8 percent); salaries for men are 2.4 percent higher than for women.

Table 8 / Full-Time Salaries by Type of Organization and Gender

	Total Placements			Low Salary		High Salary		Average Salary			Median Salary		
	Women	Men	All**	Women	Men	Women	Men	Women	Men	All**	Women	Men	All
Public Libraries	179	24	204	$19,000	$32,000	$100,000	$69,215	$44,146	$47,876	$44,565	$42,843	$45,675	$43,533
College/University Libraries	127	35	162	21,000	24,500	72,000	100,000	46,020	49,864	46,850	45,000	47,000	45,000
School Libraries	80	6	86	24,000	30,000	110,000	100,000	52,749	54,167	52,848	50,000	49,000	50,000
Government Libraries	42	11	53	29,000	32,000	90,500	76,000	49,543	46,986	49,012	43,361	45,000	44,000
Private Industry	41	11	53	20,000	19,200	150,000	85,000	53,302	54,564	53,473	48,000	55,000	51,000
Special Libraries	30	11	41	25,000	38,513	80,000	165,000	47,777	62,047	51,606	46,000	51,500	46,500
Archives/Special Collections	29	4	33	25,000	38,000	97,850	56,000	44,605	44,312	44,570	40,600	41,624	40,600
Nonprofit Organizations	16	2	18	26,500	45,000	85,000	55,000	52,882	50,000	52,562	48,750	50,000	48,750
Other Organizations	27	6	33	22,300	45,000	150,000	65,000	52,096	58,667	53,291	47,000	61,000	48,800

This table represents only full-time salaries and all placements reported by type. Some individuals omitted placement information, rendering some information unusable.
**All includes nonbinary gender, other, and no answer.

Special library salaries ($51,606) increased over last year by 6.3 percent and are 6.7 percent higher than this year's average. Special librarians in the South Central region are seeing pay that is 56.6 percent above the regional average, while Northeast special libraries are also paying well above their region's average (+30.4 percent). Special libraries employ the highest proportion of men (26.8 percent) and also pay men at a rate that is 29.9 percent higher than it is for women. This disparity is clear at the lowest level and highest levels alike.

Nonprofit organizations were added as a library type last year and only represented 2.6 percent of the placements reported. However, the average salary ($52,562) is up 18.2 percent over last year. Nonprofit organization placements are held mostly by women (88.9 percent), with salaries for women 5.8 percent higher than for men. Interestingly, the low salary for women is markedly less than for men, but the high salary for women is higher than for men.

Graduates could also specify if they were employed by other organizations. This category accounted for the same level of graduates (4.8 percent) as archives/special collections and reported a 10.1 percent hike in salary level over last year.

Working in the Field

The LIS profession is expanding into unexpected venues. As we did last year, we focused on whether graduates were employed in the LIS field or outside of it. Most graduates (71 percent) are employed in a library or information science institution, 11 percent are employed in a library or information science capacity but are working outside a traditional institution, and another 11 percent are employed outside the LIS field entirely. About 6.7 percent claimed to be still unemployed.

We also asked graduates to tell us about their assignments since job titles do not tell the whole tale. We found that salary levels varied markedly based on the primary job assignment. The top three average salaries are more than 20 percent over the overall average and included two that focus on technical components, information technology ($58,438), and data curation and management ($58,227), and one that is a foundation to the profession, teacher librarian ($58,148). The other assignments in the top five were also relative newcomers—data analytics ($56,793) and user experience (UX)/usability analysis ($55,167).

Other assignments that have salaries more than 10 percent higher than the average also reflect this mix of the traditional and the nontraditional—knowledge management and rights and permissions (both at $54,000) and school librarian/school media specialist ($53,478). There are six other assignments that fall above the average. One of them, emerging technologies ($51,800), reflects the nontraditional focus as well.

Emerging Services

We asked graduates to tell us more about emerging library services. These included areas employing digital platforms such as scholarly communication, digital archives, data curation, digital humanities, visualization, and born digital objects. Graduates also referenced areas such as bibliometrics/altmetrics, business librarianship, early childhood learning, e-learning, custom information solutions, adult technology programming, and research management/research data management.

Core activities round out the list of items garnering above average compensation: administration ($50,636), outreach ($49,214), training, teaching, and instruction ($48,992), systems technology ($48,900), and reference/information services ($48,593).

Interestingly, among the assignments earning these top 14 salaries, only four represent more than 5 percent of graduates (reference/information services, school librarian/school library media specialist, administration, and training, teaching, and instruction). Other assignments with more than 5 percent of the graduates, but with salary levels below the overall average salary, are archival and preservation ($48,066), children's services ($44,179), adult services ($44,255), and metadata, cataloging, and taxonomy ($45,041).

Charting the Job Course

The job search was not easy for those who were looking for a first position, or who did not stay with the organization they were working in while in school. Those who were looking for a position began the hunt about 5.5 months before graduation, and it took an average of 4.7 months after graduation to find a placement.

LIS schools are active in helping students with the job search, with most posting opportunities on Listservs (87 percent) or through social media (65 percent). Other common approaches include sending information through student groups (58 percent) or posting announcements on bulletin boards or in student areas (55 percent). Less than half offer formal placement services, but this has increased compared to last year.

A third of schools (34 percent) offer formal mentoring programs, a slight increase over last year. Schools have different approaches to these programs including involving alumni in ongoing programs or one-day mentoring events, having faculty advisors guide students, and using the services of a dedicated mentoring coordinator or a career services office. One school noted that its program includes workshops and internship fairs as well as coordinated posts on a career-focused blog.

Graduates also told us about the resources they used to help them during their search. Many used the school resources mentioned above. They augmented these with other resources including the American Library Association (ALA) job placement website, Archives Gig, Higher Ed jobs, online communities such as the federal libraries Google group, LinkedIn, job websites (i.e., indeed.com, glassdoor.com, monster), INALJ (formerly I Need a Library Job), regional job listing sites (i.e., usajob.gov, KDLA [Kentucky Department for Libraries and Archives]), professional society resources, and personal or professional networks.

Graduates said that searching was exhausting at times but that finding ways to maintain a positive attitude and to be open-minded was important. A recurring theme for success was gaining practical experience to augment coursework and to help develop professional networks. Students used a variety of strategies including gaining experience by completing practicums and internships, developing professional networks through tools such as LinkedIn, creating a portfolio/e-portfolio, and attending colloquiums. Some complained that online applications do not provide an opportunity for job seekers to demonstrate how they can fit a position, while some graduates noted that internships or practica provided an opportunity to become known within an organization that may have an open position in the future. Another suggestion was to find someone to practice interviewing skills with and to get feedback on résumés. Graduates also noted that it helped to look at job skill requirements rather than job titles, since titles can be misleading. A willingness to relocate can be helpful, too, although they acknowledged that this is not a possibility for everyone.

The basic tenets and skills of librarianship are the foundation of library work and a focus of LIS education, and they are being extended into different job titles in libraries and outside the traditional library organization. Finding the right place in this environment means graduates should prepare for their professional position during their education. This includes taking challenging courses that help students acquire the most up-to-date knowledge and skills, working to build professional networks well before they are in the job market, and gaining practical experience that will help with skills and networking.

It is important to take time to prepare for the search by acquiring skills that may not be part of formal professional preparation such as learning how to write cover letters and résumés and how to ace an interview. Even those students who are already working in the libraries that will be their home after graduation benefit from following this path. One key message emerged: stepping outside their comfort zone can help LIS graduates find their best fit in the evolving library landscape.

Accredited Master's Programs in Library and Information Studies

This list of graduate programs accredited by the American Library Association is issued by the ALA Office for Accreditation. Regular updates and additional details appear on the Office for Accreditation's website at http://www.ala.org/CFApps/lisdir/index.cfm. A total of 145 U.S. and Canadian institutions offering both accredited and nonaccredited programs in librarianship are included in the 68th edition (2015–2016) of *American Library Directory* (Information Today, Inc.)

Northeast: D.C., Md., Mass., N.J., N.Y., Pa., R.I.

Catholic University of America, School of Arts and Sciences, Dept. of Lib. and Info. Science, 620 Michigan Ave. N.E., Washington, DC 20064. Bill Kules, chair. Tel. 202-319-5085, fax 319-5574, e-mail cua-slis@cua. edu, World Wide Web http://slis.cua.edu. Admissions contact: Louise Gray. Tel. 202-319-5085, fax 319-5574, e-mail grayl@cua. edu.

Clarion University of Pennsylvania, College of Business Admin. and Info. Sciences, Dept. of Lib. Science, 210 Carlson Lib. Bldg., Clarion, PA 16214. Linda L. Lillard, chair. Tel. 866-272-5612, fax 814-393-2150, World Wide Web http://www.clarion.edu/ libsci. Admissions contact: Lois Dulavitch. Tel. 866-272-5612, e-mail ldulavitch@ clarion.edu.

Drexel University, College of Computing and Informatics, 3141 Chestnut St., Philadelphia, PA 19104-2875. David E. Fenske, dean. Tel. 215-895-2474, fax 215-895-2494, e-mail istinfo@drexel.edu, World Wide Web http://www.cci.drexel.edu. Admissions contact: Matthew Lechtenburg. Tel. 215-895-1951, e-mail ml333@ischool.drexel.edu.

Long Island University, Palmer School of Lib. and Info. Science, C. W. Post Campus, 720 Northern Blvd., Brookville, NY 11548-1300. Valeda Dent, interim dir. Tel. 516-299-4109, fax 516-299-4168, e-mail palmer @cwpost.liu.edu, World Wide Web http:// www.liu.edu/palmer. Admissions contact: Christine Prete. Tel. 516-299-2857, e-mail christine.prete@liu.edu.

Pratt Institute, School of Info. and Lib. Science, 144 W. 14 St., New York, NY 10011. Tula Giannini, dean. Tel. 212-647-7682, fax 202-367-2492, e-mail infosils@pratt.edu, World Wide Web http://www.pratt.edu/academics/ information_and_library_sciences. Admissions contact: Quinn Lai. Tel. 212-647-7682, e-mail infosils@pratt.edu.

Queens College, City Univ. of New York, Grad. School of Lib. and Info. Studies, Rm. 254, Rosenthal Lib., 65-30 Kissena Blvd., Flushing, NY 11367-1597. Colleen Cool, chair. Tel. 718-997-3790, fax 718-997-3797, e-mail gc_gslis@qc.cuny.edu, World Wide Web http://www.qc.cuny.edu/academics/ degrees/dss/gslis/Pages/default.aspx. Admissions contact: Roberta Brody. Tel. 718-997-3790, e-mail roberta_brody@qc.edu.

Rutgers University, School of Communication and Info., Dept. of Lib. and Info. Science, New Brunswick, NJ 08901-1071. Marie L. Radford, chair. Tel. 848-932-8797, fax 732-932-6916, e-mail mlis@comminfo.rutgers. edu, World Wide Web http://comminfo. rutgers.edu. Admissions contact: Kay Cassell. Tel. 732-932-7500 ext. 8264.

Saint John's University, College of Liberal Arts and Sciences, Div. of Lib. and Info. Science, 8000 Utopia Pkwy., Queens, NY 11439. Jeffery E. Olson, dir. Tel. 718-990-6200, fax 718-990-2071, e-mail dlis@stjohns. edu, World Wide Web http://www.stjohns. edu/dlis. Admissions contact: Deborah Martinez. Tel. 718-990-6200, e-mail dlis@ stjohns.edu.

Simmons College, Grad. School of Lib. and Info. Science, 300 The Fenway, Boston, MA 02115. Eileen Abels, dean. Tel. 617-521-2800, fax 617-521-3192, e-mail gslis@ simmons.edu, World Wide Web http://www. simmons.edu/gslis. Admissions contact:

Sarah Petrakos. Tel. 617-521-2868, e-mail gslisadm@simmons.edu.

Syracuse University, School of Info. Studies, 343 Hinds Hall, Syracuse, NY 13244. Elizabeth D. Liddy, dean. Tel. 315-443-2911, fax 315-443-6886, e-mail ischool@syr.edu, World Wide Web http://www.ischool.syr.edu. Admissions contact: Jill Hurst-Wahl. Tel. 315-443-2911, e-mail mslis@syr.edu.

University at Albany, State Univ. of New York, College of Computing and Info., Dept. of Info. Studies, Draper 113, 135 Western Ave., Albany, NY 12222. Philip B. Eppard, chair. Tel. 518-442-5110, fax 518-442-5367, e-mail infostudies@albany.edu, World Wide Web http://www.albany.edu/information studies/index.php. Admissions contact: Daphne Jorgensen. Tel. 518-442-5110, e-mail djorgensen@albany.edu.

University at Buffalo, State Univ. of New York, Graduate School of Educ., Lib. and Info. Studies, 534 Baldy Hall, Buffalo, NY 14260-1020. Heidi Julien, chair. Tel. 716-645-2412, fax 716-645-3775, e-mail ublis@buffalo.edu, World Wide Web http://gse.buffalo.edu/lis. Admissions contact: Radhika Suresh. Tel. 716-645-2110, e-mail gse-info@buffalo.edu.

University of Maryland, College of Info. Studies, 4105 Hornbake Bldg., College Park, MD 20742. John Carlo Bertot, MLIS Program Dir. Tel. 301-405-2033, fax 301-314-9145, e-mail ischooladmission@umd.edu, World Wide Web http://ischool.umd.edu. Admissions contact: Joanne Briscoe. Tel. 301-405-2038, e-mail ischooladmission@umd.edu.

University of Pittsburgh, School of Info. Sciences, 135 N. Bellefield Ave., Pittsburgh, PA 15260. Sheila Corrall, chair. Tel. 412-624-9420, fax 412-648-7001, e-mail lisinq@mail.sis.pitt.edu, World Wide Web http://www.ischool.pitt.edu. Admissions contact: Debbie Day. Tel. 412-624-9420, e-mail dday@sis.pitt.edu.

University of Rhode Island, Grad. School of Lib. and Info. Studies, Rodman Hall, 94 W. Alumni Ave., Kingston, RI 02881. Valerie Karno, interim dir. Tel. 401-874-2878, fax 401-874-4964, e-mail gslis@etal.uri.edu, World Wide Web http://www.uri.edu/artsci/lsc.

Southeast: Ala., Fla., Ga., Ky., La., Miss., N.C., S.C., Tenn., P.R.

East Carolina University, College of Educ., Lib. Science Degree Program, Mailstop 172, ECU, Greenville, NC 27858. John B. Harer, program coord. Tel. 252-328-4389, fax 252-328-4368, e-mail harerj@ecu.edu, World Wide Web http://www.ecu.edu/cs-educ/idp/lsed/index.cfm. Admissions contact: Camilla King. Tel. 252-328-6012, e-mail grad school@ecu.edu.

Florida State University, College of Communication and Info., School of Lib. and Info. Studies, 142 Collegiate Loop, P.O. Box 3062100, Tallahassee, FL 32306-2100. Kathleen Burnett, dir. Tel. 850-644-5775, fax 850-644-9763, World Wide Web http://slis.fsu.edu. Admissions e-mail slisgrad admissions@admin.fsu.edu, tel. 850-644-8121.

Louisiana State University, School of Lib. and Info. Science, 267 Coates Hall, Baton Rouge, LA 70803. Ed Holton, interim dir. Tel. 225-578-3158, fax 225-578-4581, e-mail slis@lsu.edu, World Wide Web http://slis.lsu.edu. Admissions contact: LaToya Coleman Joseph. E-mail lcjoseph@lsu.edu.

North Carolina Central University, School of Lib. and Info. Sciences, P.O. Box 19586, Durham, NC 27707. Irene Owens, dean. Tel. 919-530-6485, fax 919-530-6402, e-mail slisadmissions@nccu.edu, World Wide Web http://www.nccuslis.org. Admissions contact: Sofia Harrison.

University of Alabama, College of Communication and Info. Sciences, School of Lib. and Info. Studies, Box 870252, Tuscaloosa, AL 35487-0252. Ann E. Prentice, interim dir. Tel. 205-348-4610, fax 205-348-3746, e-mail info@slis.ua.edu, World Wide Web http://www.slis.ua.edu. Admissions contact: Beth Riggs. Tel. 205-348-1527, e-mail briggs@slis.ua.edu.

University of Kentucky, School of Lib. and Info. Science, 320 Little Lib., Lexington, KY 40506-0224. Jeffrey T. Huber, dir. Tel. 859-257-8876, fax 859-257-4205, e-mail ukslis@uky.edu, World Wide Web http://www.uky.edu/cis/slis. Admissions contact: Will Buntin. Tel. 859-257-3317, e-mail wjbunt0@uky.edu.

University of North Carolina at Chapel Hill, School of Info. and Lib. Science, CB 3360, 100 Manning Hall, Chapel Hill, NC 27599-3360. Gary Marchionini, dean. Tel. 919-962-8366, fax 919-962-8071, e-mail info@ils.unc.edu, World Wide Web http://www.sils.unc.edu. Admissions contact: Lara Bailey.

University of North Carolina at Greensboro, School of Educ., Dept. of Lib. and Info. Studies, 446 School of Educ. Bldg., Greensboro, NC 27402-6170. O. Lee Shiflett, interim chair. Tel. 336-334-3477, fax 336-334-4120, World Wide Web http://lis.uncg.edu. Admissions contact: Touger Vang. E-mail t_vang@uncg.edu.

University of Puerto Rico, Info. Sciences and Technologies, P.O. Box 21906, San Juan, PR 00931-1906. Mariano A. Maura, acting dir. Tel. 787-763-6199, fax 787-764-2311, e-mail egcti@uprrp.edu, World Wide Web http://egcti.upr.edu. Admissions contact: Migdalia Dávila-Perez. Tel. 787-764-0000 ext. 3530, e-mail migdalia.davila@upr.edu.

University of South Carolina, College of Mass Communications and Info. Studies, School of Lib. and Info. Science, 1501 Greene St., Columbia, SC 29208. Samantha K. Hastings, dir. Tel. 803-777-3858, fax 803-777-7938, e-mail hastings@sc.edu, World Wide Web http://www.libsci.sc.edu. Admissions contact: Tilda Reeder. Tel. 800-304-3153, e-mail tildareeder@sc.edu.

University of South Florida, College of Arts and Sciences, School of Lib. and Info. Science, 4202 E. Fowler Ave., CIS 1040, Tampa, FL 33620. James Andrews, dir. Tel. 813-974-3520, fax 813-974-6840, e-mail lisinfo@usf.edu, World Wide Web http://si.usf.edu. Admissions contact: Daniel Kahl. Tel. 813-974-8022, e-mail djkahl@usf.edu.

University of Southern Mississippi, College of Educ. and Psychology, School of Lib. and Info. Science, 118 College Drive, No. 5146, Hattiesburg, MS 39406-0001. Dorothy Elizabeth Haynes, dir. Tel. 601-266-4228, fax 601-266-5774, e-mail slis@usm.edu, World Wide Web http://www.usm.edu/slis. Admissions tel. 601-266-5137, e-mail graduatestudies@usm.edu.

University of Tennessee, College of Communication and Info., School of Info. Sciences, 451 Communication Bldg., Knoxville, TN 37996. Edwin M. Cortez, dir. Tel. 865-974-2148, fax 865-974-4967, World Wide Web http://www.sis.utk.edu. Admissions contact: Tanya Arnold. Tel. 865-974-2858, e-mail tnarnold@utk.edu.

Valdosta State Univ., Dept. of Info. Studies, 1500 N. Patterson St., Valdosta, GA 31698-0133. Linda R. Most, interim dept. head. Tel. 229-333-5966, fax 229-259-5055, e-mail mlis@valdosta.edu, World Wide Web http://www.valdosta.edu/mlis. Admissions contact: Sheila Peacock.

Midwest: Ill., Ind., Iowa, Kan., Mich., Minn., Mo., Ohio, Wis.

Dominican Univ., Grad. School of Lib. and Info. Science, 7900 W. Division St., River Forest, IL 60305. Kate Marek, dean. Tel. 708-524-6845, fax 708-524-6657, e-mail gslis@dom.edu, World Wide Web http://www.dom.edu/gslis. Admissions contact: Meagan Sather Tel. 708-524-6983, e-mail msather@dom.edu.

Emporia State University, School of Lib. and Info. Management, Campus Box 4025, 1 Kellogg Circle, Emporia, KS 66801-5415. Gwen Alexander, dean. Tel. 620-341-5203, fax 620-341-5233, e-mail sliminfo@emporia.edu, World Wide Web http://slim.emporia.edu. Admissions contact: Kathie Buckman. Tel. 620-341-5065, e-mail sliminfo@emporia.edu.

Indiana University, School of Informatics and Computing, Lib. and Info. Science, 1320 E. 10 St., LI 011, Bloomington, IN 47405-3907. Robert Schnabel, dean. Tel. 812-855-2018, fax 812-855-6166, e-mail ilsmain@indiana.edu, World Wide Web http://soic.iu.edu. Admissions contact: Rhonda Spencer.

Kent State University, School of Lib. and Info. Science, P.O. Box 5190, Kent, OH 44242-0001. Jeffrey Fruit, interim dir. Tel. 330-672-2782, fax 330-672-7965, e-mail slisinform@kent.edu, World Wide Web http://www.kent.edu/slis. Admissions contact: Cheryl Tennant.

Saint Catherine University, School of Business and Leadership, Educ. and LIS, MLIS Program/Information Management Department, 2004 Randolph Ave. No. 4125, St.

Paul, MN 55105. Deborah S. Grealy, assoc. dean/dir. Tel. 651-690-6802, fax 651-690-8724, e-mail imdept@stkate.edu, World Wide Web https:// www2.stkate.edu/mlis. Admissions contact: Kristina Sande. Tel. 651-690-6507, e-mail kmsande@stkate.edu.

University of Illinois at Urbana-Champaign, Grad. School of Lib. and Info. Science, 501 E. Daniel St., Champaign, IL 61820-6211. Allen Renear, interim dean. Tel. 217-333-3280, fax 217-244-3302, e-mail gslis@illinois.edu, World Wide Web http://www.lis.illinois.edu. Admissions contact: Penny Ames. Tel. 217-333-7197, e-mail pames@illinois.edu.

University of Iowa, Graduate College, School of Lib. and Info. Science, 3087 Main Lib., Iowa City, IA 52242-1420. David Eichmann, dir. Tel. 319-335-5707, fax 319-335-5374, e-mail slis@uiowa.edu, World Wide Web http://slis.grad.uiowa.edu. Admissions contact: Carol Ives. Tel. 319-335-5709, e-mail carol-ives@uiowa.edu.

University of Michigan, School of Info., 4322 North Quad, 105 S. State St., Ann Arbor, MI 48109-1285. Jeffrey Makie-Mason, dean. Tel. 734-763-2285, fax 734-764-2475, e-mail umsi.admissions@umich.edu, World Wide Web http://www.si.umich.edu. Admissions contact: Laura Elgas.

University of Missouri, College of Educ., School of Info. Science and Learning Technologies, 303 Townsend Hall, Columbia, MO 65211. Joi Moore, dir. Tel. 877-747-5868, fax 573-884-0122, e-mail sislt@missouri.edu, World Wide Web http://lis.missouri.edu. Admissions tel. 573-882-4546.

University of Wisconsin–Madison, College of Letters and Sciences, School of Lib. and Info. Studies, 600 N. Park St., Madison, WI 53706. Kristin Eschenfelder, dir. Tel. 608-263-2900, fax 608-263-4849, e-mail uw-slis@slis.wisc.edu, World Wide Web http://www.slis.wisc.edu. Admissions contact: Tanya Cobb. Tel. 608-263-2909, e-mail student-services@slis.wisc.edu.

University of Wisconsin–Milwaukee, School of Info. Studies, P.O. Box 413, Milwaukee, WI 53211. Char Zahrt, assistant dean. Tel. 414-229-4707, fax 414-229-6699, e-mail soisinfo@uwm.edu, World Wide Web http://www4.uwm.edu/sois.

Wayne State University, School of Lib. and Info. Science, 106 Kresge Lib., Detroit, MI 48202. Stephen T. Bajjaly, assoc. dean. Tel. 313-577-1825, fax 313-577-7563, e-mail asklis@wayne.edu, World Wide Web http://www.slis.wayne.edu. Admissions contact: Matthew Fredericks. Tel. 313-577-2446, e-mail mfredericks@wayne.edu.

Southwest: Ariz., Okla., Texas

Texas Woman's University, School of Lib. and Info. Studies, P.O. Box 425438, Denton, TX 76204-5438. Ling Hwey Jeng, dir. Tel. 940-898-2602, fax 940-898-2611, e-mail slis@twu.edu, World Wide Web http://www.twu.edu/slis. Admissions contact: Brenda Mallory. E-mail bmallory@mail.twu.edu.

University of Arizona, College of Social and Behavioral Sciences, School of Info. Resources and Lib. Science, 1515 E. 1 St., Tucson, AZ 85719. P. Bryan Heidorn, dir. Tel. 520-621-3565, fax 520-621-3279, e-mail sirls@email.arizona.edu, World Wide Web http://www.sirls.arizona.edu. Admissions contact: Geraldine Fragoso. Tel. 520-621-5230, e-mail gfragoso@u.arizona.edu.

University of North Texas, College of Info., Dept. of Lib. and Info. Sciences, 1155 Union Circle, No. 311068, Denton, TX 76203-5017. Suliman Hawamdeh, chair. Tel. 940-565-2445, fax 940-369-7600, e-mail lis-chair@unt.edu, World Wide Web http://lis.unt.edu. Admissions contact: Toby Faber. Tel. 940-565-2445, e-mail ci-advising@unt.edu.

University of Oklahoma, School of Lib. and Info. Studies, College of Arts and Sciences, 401 W. Brooks, Norman, OK 73019-6032. Cecelia Brown, dir. Tel. 405-325-3921, fax 405-325-7648, e-mail slisinfo@ou.edu, World Wide Web http://www.ou.edu/cas/slis. Admissions contact: Sarah Connelly.

University of Texas at Austin, School of Info., Suite 5.202, 1616 Guadalupe St., Austin, TX 78701-1213. Andrew Dillon, dean. Tel. 512-471-3821, fax 512-471-3971, e-mail info@ischool.utexas.edu, World Wide Web http://www.ischool.utexas.edu. Admissions contact: Carla Criner. Tel. 512-471-5654, e-mail criner@ischool.utexas.edu.

West: Calif., Colo., Hawaii, Wash.

San José State University, School of Lib. and Info. Science, 1 Washington Sq., San José, CA 95192-0029. Sandy Hirsh, dir. Tel. 408-924-2490, fax 408-924-2476, e-mail sjsu ischool@gmail.com, World Wide Web http://ischool.sjsu.edu. Admissions contact: Linda Main. Tel. 408-924-2494, e-mail lindxain@sjsu.edu.

University of California, Los Angeles, Graduate School of Educ. and Info. Studies, Dept. of Info. Studies, Box 951520, Los Angeles, CA 90095-1520. Jonathan Furner, chair. Tel. 310-825-8799, fax 310-206-3076, e-mail info@gseis.ucla.edu, World Wide Web http://is.gseis.ucla.edu. Admissions contact: Susan Abler. Tel. 310-825-5269, e-mail abler@gseis.ucla.edu.

University of Denver, Morgridge College of Educ., Lib. and Info. Science Program, 1999 E. Evans Ave., Denver, CO 80208-1700. Mary Stansbury, chair. Tel. 303-871-3587, fax 303-871-4456, e-mail mary.stansbury@du.edu, World Wide Web http://www.du.edu/education. Admissions contact: Kristina Coccia. E-mail kristina.coccia@du.edu.

University of Hawaii, College of Natural Sciences, Lib. and Info. Science Program, 2550 McCarthy Mall, Honolulu, HI 96822. Andrew Wertheimer, chair. Tel. 808-956-7321, fax 808-956-5835, e-mail slis@hawaii.edu, World Wide Web http://www.hawaii.edu/lis.

University of Washington, The Information School, 370 Mary Gates Hall, Seattle, WA 98195-2840. Harry Bruce, dean. Tel. 206-685-9937, fax 206-616-3152, e-mail ischool@uw.edu, World Wide Web http://ischool.uw.edu. Admissions contact: Tel. 206-543-1794, e-mail mlis@uw.edu.

Canada

Dalhousie University, School of Info. Management, Kenneth C. Rowe Management Bldg., Halifax, NS B3H 3J5. Louise Spiteri, dir. Tel. 902-494-3656, fax 902-494-2451, e-mail sim@dal.ca, World Wide Web http://www.sim.management.dal.ca. Admissions contact: JoAnn Watson. Tel. 902-494-2471, e-mail joann.watson@dal.ca.

McGill University, School of Info. Studies, 3661 Peel St., Montreal, QC H3A 1X1. France Bouthillier, dir. Tel. 514-398-4204, fax 514-398-7193, e-mail sis@mcgill.ca, World Wide Web http://www.mcgill.ca/sis. Admissions contact: Kathryn Hubbard. Tel. 514-398-4204 ext. 0742, e-mail sis@mcgill.ca.

University of Alberta, School of Lib. and Info. Studies, 3-20 Rutherford S., Edmonton, AB T6G 2J4. Anna Altmann, interim dir. Tel. 780-492-4578, fax 780-492-2430, e-mail slis@ualberta.ca, World Wide Web http://www.slis.ualberta.ca. Admissions contact: Lauren Romaniuk. Tel. 780-492-4140, e-mail slisadmissions@ualberta.ca.

University of British Columbia, School of Lib., Archival, and Info. Studies, Irving K. Barber Learning Centre, Suite 470, 1961 East Mall, Vancouver, BC V6T 1Z1. Caroline Haythornthwaite, dir. Tel. 604-822-2404, fax 604-822-6006, e-mail ischool.info@ubc.ca, World Wide Web http://www.slais.ubc.ca. Admissions contact: Dan Slessor. Tel. 604-822-2461, e-mail slais.ssc@ubc.ca.

Université de Montréal, École de Bibliothéconomie et des Sciences de l'Information, C.P. 6128, Succursale Centre-Ville, Montreal, QC H3C 3J7. Clément Arsenault, dir. Tel. 514-343-6044, fax 514-343-5753, e-mail ebsiinfo@ebsi.umontreal.ca, World Wide Web http://www.ebsi.umontreal.ca. Admissions contact: Alain Tremblay. Tel. 514-343-6044, e-mail alain.tremblay.1@umontreal.ca.

University of Ottawa, School of Info. Studies, Desmarais Bldg., Ottawa, ON K1N 6N5. Tel. 613-562-5130, fax 613-562-5854, e-mail esis@uOttawa.ca, World Wide Web http://www.sis.uottawa.ca. Daniel Paré, interim dir. Admissions contact: Marisa Simard Swangha. Tel. 613-562-5800 ext. 3392, e-mail gradsi@uottawa.ca.

University of Toronto, Faculty of Info., 140 George St., Toronto, ON M5S 3G6. Seamus Ross, dean. Tel. 416-978-3202, fax 416-978-5762, e-mail inquire.ischool@utoronto.ca, World Wide Web http://www.ischool.

utoronto.ca. Admissions contact: Adriana Rossini. Tel. 416-978-8589, e-mail adriana. rossini@utoronto.ca.
University of Western Ontario, Grad. Programs in Lib. and Info. Science, Faculty of Info. and Media Studies, Room 240, North Campus Bldg., London, ON N6A 5B7. Nick Dyer-Whitheford, acting dean; Pam McKenzie, assoc. dean. Tel. 519-661-4017, fax 519-661-3506, e-mail mlisinfo@uwo.ca, World Wide Web http://www.fims.uwo.ca. Admissions contact: Shelley Long.

Library Scholarship Sources

For a more complete list of scholarships, fellowships, and assistantships offered for library study, see *Financial Assistance for Library and Information Studies,* published annually by the American Library Association (ALA). The document is also available on the ALA website at http://www.ala.org/educationcareers/scholarships.

American Association of Law Libraries. (1) A varying number of scholarships of varying amounts for graduates of an accredited law school who are degree candidates in an ALA-accredited library school; (2) a varying number of scholarships of varying amounts for library school graduates working on a law degree and non-law graduates enrolled in an ALA-accredited library school; (3) the George A. Strait Minority Stipend for varying numbers of minority librarians working toward a library or law degree; and (4) a varying number of $200 scholarships for law librarians taking courses relating to law librarianship. For information, write to: AALL Scholarship Committee, 105 W. Adams, Suite 3300, Chicago, IL 60603.

American Library Association. (1) The David H. Clift Scholarship of $3,000 for a student who has been admitted to an ALA-accredited library school; (2) the Tom and Roberta Drewes Scholarship of $3,000 for library support staff; (3) the Mary V. Gaver Scholarship of $3,000 for an individual specializing in youth services; (4) the Miriam L. Hornback Scholarship of $3,000 for an ALA or library support staff member; (5) the Christopher J. Hoy/ERT Scholarship of $5,000 for a student who has been admitted to an ALA-accredited library school; (6) the Tony B. Leisner Scholarship of $3,000 for a library support staff member; (7) the Peter Lyman Memorial/Sage Scholarship in New Media of $2,500 for a student admitted to an ALA-accredited library school who will specialize in new media; (8) the Cicely Phippen Marks Scholarship of $1,500 for a student admitted to an ALA-accredited program who will specialize in federal librarianship; and (9) Spectrum Initiative Scholarships of $6,500 for a varying number of minority students admitted to a master's degree program at an ALA-accredited library school. For information, write to: ALA Scholarship Clearinghouse, 50 E. Huron St., Chicago, IL 60611, or see http://www.ala.org/scholarships.

ALA/Association for Library Service to Children. (1) The Bound to Stay Bound Books Scholarship of $7,500 each for four U.S. or Canadian citizens who have been admitted to an ALA-accredited master's or doctoral program, and who will work with children in a library for one year after graduation; and (2) the Frederic G. Melcher Scholarship of $6,000 each for two U.S. or Canadian citizens admitted to an ALA-accredited library school who will work with children in school or public libraries for one year after graduation. For information, write to: ALA Scholarship Clearinghouse, 50 E. Huron St., Chicago, IL 60611, or see http://www.ala.org/scholarships.

ALA/Association of College and Research Libraries Thomson Reuters. The WESS-SEES De Gruyter European Librarianship Study Grant of €2,500 for up to 30 consecutive days of study in Europe. Application is electronic only. For information, e-mail Chase Ollis at collis@ala.org.

ALA/Association of Specialized and Cooperative Library Agencies. Century Scholarship of up to $2,500 for a varying number of disabled U.S. or Canadian citizens admitted to an ALA-accredited library school. For information, write to: ALA Scholarship Clearinghouse, 50 E. Huron St., Chicago, IL 60611, or see http://www.ala.org/scholarships.

ALA/International Relations Committee. The Bogle Pratt International Library Travel Fund grant of $1,000 for a varying number of ALA members to attend a first international conference. For information, write to:

Michael Dowling, ALA/IRC, 50 E. Huron St., Chicago, IL 60611.

ALA/Library and Information Technology Association. (1) The LITA/Christian Larew Memorial Scholarship of $3,000 for a U.S. or Canadian citizen admitted to an ALA-accredited library school; (2) the LITA/OCLC Minority Scholarship in Library and Information Technology of $3,000 and (3) the LITA/LSSI Minority Scholarship of $2,500, each for a minority student admitted to an ALA-accredited program. For information, write to: ALA Scholarship Clearinghouse, 50 E. Huron St., Chicago, IL 60611, or see http://www.ala.org/scholarships.

ALA/Public Library Association. The Demco New Leaders Travel Grant Study Award of up to $1,500 for a varying number of PLA members with MLS degrees and five years or less experience. For information, write to: PLA Awards Program, ALA/PLA, 50 E. Huron St., Chicago, IL 60611.

American-Scandinavian Foundation. Fellowships and grants for 25 to 30 students, in amounts from $5,000 to $23,000, for advanced study in Denmark, Finland, Iceland, Norway, or Sweden. For information, write to: Fellowships and Grants, American-Scandinavian Foundation, 58 Park Ave., New York, NY 10026, or see http://www.amscan.org/fellowships_grants.html.

Association for Library and Information Science Education (ALISE). A varying number of research grants of up to $2,500 each for members of ALISE. For information, write to: ALISE, 2150 N.W. 107th St., Suite 205, Seattle, WA 98133.

Association of Bookmobile and Outreach Services (ABOS). (1) The Bernard Vavrek Scholarship of $1,000 for a student with a grade-point average of 3.0 or better admitted to an ALA-accredited program and interested in becoming an outreach/bookmobile librarian; (2) the John Philip Award of $300 to recognize outstanding contributions and leadership by an individual in bookmobile and outreach services; (3) the Carol Hole Conference Attendance Travel Grant of $500 for a public librarian working in outreach or bookmobile services. For information, write to President, ABOS, c/o AMIGOS Library Services, 3610 Barrett Office Drive, Suite 216, Ballwin, MO 63021.

Association of Jewish Libraries. The AJL Scholarship Fund offers up to two scholarships of $1,000 for MLS students who plan to work as Judaica librarians. For information, write to: Tina Weiss, AJL Scholarship Committee, Hebrew Union College, 1 W. 4th St., New York, NY 10012.

Association of Seventh-Day Adventist Librarians. The D. Glenn Hilts Scholarship of $1,200 for a member of the Seventh-Day Adventist Church in a graduate library program. For information, write to: Lori Curtis, Association of Seventh-Day Adventist Librarians, Loma Linda University, 11072 Anderson St., Loma Linda, CA 92350.

Beta Phi Mu. (1) The Sarah Rebecca Reed Scholarship of $2,000 for a person accepted in an ALA-accredited library program; (2) the Frank B. Sessa Scholarship of $1,500 for a Beta Phi Mu member for continuing education; (3) the Harold Lancour Scholarship of $1,750 for study in a foreign country relating to the applicant's work or schooling; (4) the Blanche E. Woolls Scholarship for School Library Media Service of $2,250 for a person accepted in an ALA-accredited library program; and (5) the Eugene Garfield Doctoral Dissertation Scholarship of $3,000 for a person who has approval of a dissertation topic. For information, write to Isabel Gray, Program Director, Beta Phi Mu, c/o Drexel University College of Computing and Informatics (CCI), 3141 Chestnut St., Philadelphia, PA 19104.

Canadian Association of Law Libraries. The Diana M. Priestly Scholarship of $2,500 for a student enrolled in an approved Canadian law school or accredited Canadian library school. For information, write to: Ann Marie Melvie, Librarian, Saskatchewan Court of Appeal, 2425 Victoria Ave., Regina, SK S4P 4W6.

Canadian Federation of University Women. (1) The Alice E. Wilson Award of $6,000 for five mature students returning to graduate studies in any field, with special consideration given to those returning to study after at least three years; (2) the Margaret McWilliams Pre-Doctoral Fellowship of $13,000 for a female student who has completed at least one full year as a full-time student in doctoral-level studies; (3) the Marion Elder Grant Fellowship of $11,000 for a full-time student at any level of a doctoral program; (4) the CFUW Memorial Fellowship of $10,000 for a student who is currently enrolled in a master's program in science, mathematics, or engineering in Canada or abroad; (5) the Beverly Jackson Fellowship of $2,000 for a student over the age of 35 at the time of application who is enrolled in graduate studies at an Ontario university; (6) the 1989 Ecole Polytechnique Commemorative Award of $7,000 for graduate studies in any field; (7) the Bourse Georgette LeMoyne award of $7,000 for graduate study in any field at a Canadian university (the candidate must be studying in French); (8) the Margaret Dale Philp Biennial Award of $3,000 for studies in the humanities or social sciences; and (9) the Canadian Home Economics Association Fellowship of $6,000 for a student enrolled in a postgraduate program in Canada. For information, write to: Fellowships Program Manager, Canadian Federation of University Women, 251 Bank St., Suite 305, Ottawa, ON K2P 1X3, Canada, or visit http://www.cfuw.org/en-ca/fellowships/fellowshipsandawards.aspx.

Canadian Library Association. (1) The CLA Dafoe Scholarship of $5,000 and (2) the H. W. Wilson Scholarship of $2,000, each given to a Canadian citizen or landed immigrant to attend an accredited Canadian library school; and (3) the Library Research and Development Grant of $1,000 for a member of the Canadian Library Association, in support of theoretical and applied research in library and information science. For information, write to: CLA Membership Services Department, Scholarship Committee, 1150 Morrison Drive, Suite 400, Ottawa, ON K2H 8S9, Canada.

Chinese American Librarians Association. (1) The Sheila Suen Lai Scholarship and the CALA Scholarship of Library and Information Science, each $500, to a Chinese descendant who has been accepted in an ALA-accredited program. For information, write to: MengXiong Liu, Clark Library, San José State University, 1 Washington Sq., San José, CA 95192-0028.

Church and Synagogue Library Association. The Muriel Fuller Memorial Scholarship of $200 (including texts) for a correspondence course offered by the association. For information, write to: CSLA, 10157 S.W. Barbur Blvd., No. 102C, Portland, OR 97219-5957.

Council on Library and Information Resources. The Rovelstad Scholarship in International Librarianship, to enable a student enrolled in an accredited LIS program to attend the IFLA Annual Conference. For more information, write to: Rovelstad Scholarship, Council on Library and Information Resources, 1707 L St. N.W., Suite 650, Washington, DC 20036.

Massachusetts Black Librarians' Network. Two scholarships of at least $500 and $1,000 for minority students entering an ALA-accredited master's program in library science with no more than 12 semester hours completed toward a degree. For information, write to: Pearl Mosley, Chair, Massachusetts Black Librarians' Network, 17 Beech Glen St., Roxbury, MA 02119.

Medical Library Association. (1) The Cunningham Memorial International Fellowship of $3,500 for each of two health sciences librarians from countries other than the United States and Canada; (2) a scholarship of $5,000 for a person entering an ALA-accredited library program, with no more than one-half of the program yet to be completed; (3) a scholarship of $5,000 for a minority student studying health sciences librarianship; (4) a varying number of Research, Development, and Demonstration Project Grants of $100 to $1,000 for U.S. or Canadian citizens, preferably MLA members; (5) the Thomson Reuters/MLA Doctoral Fellowship of $2,000 for doctoral work in medical librarianship or information science; (6) the Rittenhouse Award of $500 for a student enrolled in an ALA-accredited library program or a recent graduate working as a trainee in a library internship program; and (7) the Librarians without Borders Ursula Poland International Scholarship of $5,000 for a librarian working in a U.S. or Canadian health sciences library. For information, write to: MLA Grants and Scholarships, Medical Library Association, 65 E. Wacker Place, Suite 1900, Chicago, IL 60601-7298.

Mountain Plains Library Association. A varying number of grants of up to $600 for applicants who are members of the association and have been for the preceding two years.

For information, write to: Judy Zelenski, Interim Executive Secretary, MPLA, 14293 W. Center Drive, Lakewood, SD 80228.

Society of American Archivists. (1) The F. Gerald Ham Scholarship of $7,500 for up to two graduate students in archival education at a U.S. university that meets the society's criteria for graduate education; (2) the Mosaic Scholarship of $5,000 for up to two U.S. or Canadian minority students enrolled in a graduate program in archival administration; (3) the Josephine Foreman Scholarship of $10,000 for a U.S. citizen or permanent resident who is a minority graduate student enrolled in a program in archival administration; (4) the Oliver Wendell Holmes Travel Award to enable foreign students involved in archival training in the United States or Canada to attend the SAA Annual Meeting; (5) the Donald Peterson Student Travel Award of up to $1,000 to enable graduate students or recent graduates to attend the meeting; and (6) the Harold T. Pinkett Minority Student Awards to enable minority students or graduate students to attend the meeting. For details, write to: Teresa Brinati, Society of American Archivists, 17 N. State St., Suite 1425, Chicago, IL 60607, or see http://www2.archivists.org/governance/handbook/section12.

Special Libraries Association. (1) Three $6,000 scholarships for students interested in special-library work; (2) the Plenum Scholarship of $1,000 and (3) the ISI Scholarship of $1,000, each also for students interested in special-library work; (4) the Affirmative Action Scholarship of $6,000 for a minority student interested in special-library work; and (5) the Pharmaceutical Division Stipend Award of $1,200 for a student with an undergraduate degree in chemistry, life sciences, or pharmacy entering or enrolled in an ALA-accredited program. For information on the first four scholarships, write to: Scholarship Committee, Special Libraries Association, 331 S. Patrick St., Alexandria, VA 22314-3501. For information on the Pharmaceutical Division Stipend, write to: Susan E. Katz, Awards Chair, Knoll Pharmaceuticals Science Information Center, 30 N. Jefferson St., Whippany, NJ 07981.

Part 4
Research and Statistics

Library Research and Statistics

Number of Libraries in the United States and Canada

Statistics are from *American Library Directory (ALD) 2017–2018* (Information Today, Inc., 2017). Data are exclusive of elementary and secondary school libraries.

Libraries in the United States

Public Libraries	16,874*
Public libraries, excluding branches	9,649
Main public libraries that have branches	1,418
Public library branches	7,209
Academic Libraries	3,606*
Community college	1,098
Departmental	206
Medical	5
Religious	6
University and college	2,508
Departmental	1,191
Law	191
Medical	231
Religious	251
Armed Forces Libraries	237*
Air Force	64
Medical	3
Army	112
Medical	22
Marine Corps	12
Navy	48
Law	1
Medical	9
Government Libraries	864*
Law	351
Medical	125
Special Libraries (excluding public, academic, armed forces, and government)	5,145*
Law	710
Medical	989
Religious	404

Total Special Libraries (including public, academic, armed forces, and government)	6,340
Total law	1,253
Total medical	1,384
Total religious	853
Total Libraries Counted(*)	26,726

Libraries in Regions Administered by the United States

Public Libraries	27*
Public libraries, excluding branches	9
Main public libraries that have branches	3
Public library branches	18
Academic Libraries	38*
Community college	3
Departmental	1
University and college	35
Departmental	19
Law	3
Medical	3
Religious	1
Armed Forces Libraries	2*
Air Force	1
Army	1
Navy	0
Government Libraries	3*
Law	1
Medical	1
Special Libraries (excluding public, academic, armed forces, and government)	5*
Law	3
Religious	1
Total Special Libraries (including public, academic, armed forces, and government)	14
Total law	7
Total medical	4
Total religious	2
Total Libraries Counted(*)	75

Libraries in Canada

Public Libraries	2,160*
Public libraries, excluding branches	813
Main public libraries that have branches	146
Public library branches	1,347

Academic Libraries	324*
Community college	74
Departmental	13
Religious	1
University and college	250
Departmental	172
Law	16
Medical	18
Religious	32
Government Libraries	186*
Law	27
Medical	4
Special Libraries (excluding public, academic, armed forces, and government)	607*
Law	88
Medical	142
Religious	21
Total Special Libraries (including public, academic, armed forces, and government)	705
Total law	131
Total medical	164
Total religious	72
Total Libraries Counted(*)	3,277

Summary

Total U.S. Libraries	27,726
Total Libraries Administered by the United States	75
Total Canadian Libraries	3,277
Grand Total of Libraries Listed	30,078

Note: Numbers followed by an asterisk are added to find "Total libraries counted" for each of the three geographic areas (United States, U.S.-administered regions, and Canada). The sum of the three totals is the "Grand total of libraries listed" in *ALD*. For details on the count of libraries, see the preface to the 69th edition of *ALD—Ed.*

Highlights of IMLS and NCES Surveys

The Institute of Museum and Library Services (IMLS) and the National Center for Education Statistics (NCES) collect and disseminate statistical information about libraries in the United States and its outlying areas. Two major surveys are conducted by NCES, the Academic Libraries Survey and the School Library Media Centers Survey; two others, the Public Libraries Survey and the State Library Agencies Survey, were formerly conducted by NCES, but are now handled by IMLS.

This article presents highlights from three of the most recently conducted surveys. For more information, see "National Center for Education Statistics" in Part 1 and "Institute of Museum and Library Services, Office of Library Services" in Part 2 of this volume.

Public Libraries

The following are highlights from the IMLS report *Public Libraries in the United States, Fiscal Year 2013.*

Library Use

- In FY 2013 there were 1.5 billion in-person visits to public libraries across the United States, the equivalent of more than 4.0 million visits each day. Although this reflects an increase of 17.6 percent over 10 years, libraries have experienced a decrease in physical visitation of 8.2 percent since a peak in FY 2009.
- Public libraries circulated 2.4 billion materials in FY 2013, a 10-year increase of 25.4 percent. There has been a slowing in overall circulation in recent years, with a decrease of 3.6 percent since a peak in FY 2010. However, circulation has not declined at the same rate as in-person visitation, which may be explained by the increase in access to digital materials that can be accessed remotely.
- Circulation of children's materials has seen long-term increases that may be related to increases in library programming aimed at early childhood learning and summer reading. Libraries lent 835.6 million children's books and materials in FY 2013. This is a 10-year increase of 22.7 percent, remaining stable over recent years.

Program Attendance

- There were 96.5 million attendees at public library programs in FY 2013. In support of the role of public libraries as gathering places, attendance at public library programs has continued to increase over prior years, with an increase of 28.6 percent for all programs since FY 2006.
- Children under 18 years comprised 23.1 percent of the total U.S. population in FY 2013. To meet the needs of this segment of the population, public libraries provide programming targeted to children and young adults.

Children's programming at libraries has long been a popular community resource. In addition to story hour, children's librarians have continued to meet the needs of their communities through scientifically-based programs to foster early learning and school readiness. There were 67.4 million attendees at children's programs, a 10-year increase of 29.7 percent.

- Libraries have had programs and services developed for young adults for many years, but over the past decade there has been a reconceptualization of these programs.

Public Access Computer Use

- There were 333.9 million user sessions on public access computer terminals in public libraries in FY 2013. This is a decrease of 9.2 percent from FY 2010. Many public libraries offer broadband, which can be accessed not only through the library-provided computers, but also through patrons' personal devices that they bring to the library.
- Although the uses of public access Internet computers may be decreasing, we will be exploring how to capture the many different ways that people use and access public library wireless and broadband services in future surveys.

Public Library Investments

- Public investments allow libraries to provide access to many popular services and resources. Financial investments are made by the public at the local, state, and federal levels. Public libraries direct these revenues to be spent in ways that support their local communities through services and resources. Although services may vary from place to place, most library expenditures are used to provide public resources such as the collection of materials for loan, varied programming, digital access, and knowledgeable staff.
- The PLS collects key measures of investment in public libraries: the financial investments of revenue and operating expenditures, collection size, the number of programs, the number of public access Internet computers, and levels of staffing.

Revenue

- In FY 2013 the public invested more than $11.5 billion in revenue for public libraries. After adjusting for inflation, this reflects no change from the prior year and a 10-year increase of 7.5 percent. Over $9.9 billion of public libraries' revenues (85.7 percent) came from local governments, reflecting a 10-year increase of 16.5 percent, a continuation of the increased share of library budgets. Revenue from state governments was $805.4 million, 7.0 percent of the total revenue in FY 2013.
- Although state contributions to library revenues have been steadily declining, with a 10-year decrease of 35.9 percent, there was no change in rev-

enues from states from FY 2012. The federal government provided 0.5 percent of total public library revenues.

- The remaining 6.8 percent of public library revenues came from other sources.

Operating Expenditures

- Total operating expenditures for public libraries were $10.9 billion in FY 2013, unchanged from expenditures from FY 2012 after adjusting for inflation. This is an increase of 9.1 percent over 10 years.
- The highest operating expenditures were for staffing expenses, which accounted for $7.4 billion of the total operating expenditures (67.2 percent). Although most of the expenditures for staffing are apportioned for salaries (73.7 percent), changes in the cost of health care have had a stronger impact on expenditures. Within staffing expenditures, $1.9 billion was spent on benefits. Although flat from the prior year, this budget item has increased by 54.0 percent over 10 years.
- More than $1.2 billion was spent on collections in FY 2013, unchanged from the prior year. Overall, expenditures on collections have been decreasing by 14.5 percent over 10 years. Although most public library collections expenditures still go to print materials (60.5 percent), changes in the composition of collection expenditures illustrate the ways in which public libraries are adjusting to the new models of service delivery, particularly regarding digital materials. Expenditures on electronic materials, such as e-books, were $239.3 million in FY 2013. More importantly, expenditures on electronic materials have increased by 186.8 percent over 10 years.

Collections

- Public librarians curate their collections to meet the needs of the communities they serve. Collections comprise both physical and digital materials, which may include print books, e-books, DVDs, and downloadable audio files. The average collection size across all public libraries was 116,481.6 items (median = 46,948.0), including printed materials, e-books, audio and video in all formats.
- Collections ranged from the smallest, with 399 materials, to the largest at 24,119,329.
- Print materials still make up most of public libraries' collections. There were 774.7 million print materials available at public libraries in FY 2013. This is a decrease of 4.7 percent since FY 2008, the highest volume over the prior 10 years. Public libraries also provide access to audio and video materials, including audio books and DVDs of popular movies. These collections have continued to grow. Public libraries had 46.6 million audio materials, a 10-year increase of 30.8 percent, and 59.2 million video materials, a 10-year increase of 107.0 percent.
- In FY 2013, 6,569 public libraries reported having e-books, an increase of 14.6 percent from FY 2012. For libraries that reported having e-books, their

e-book holdings ranged from 1 to 398,013 books. The average number of e-books at U.S. public libraries in FY 2013 was 20,170.0 (median = 8,770).

- In addition to e-books, public libraries provide access to digital audio and video materials. Like e-books, these materials can be downloaded and used either on devices loaned by the library or on patrons' personal devices. Most public libraries (67.3 percent) offered downloadable audio materials in FY 2013. Those libraries that offered this service ranged from 1 to 147,925 audio downloads, an average of 7,056.5 (median = 4,229.0). There were 2,725 public libraries to offer video downloads in FY 2013. Holdings ranged from 1 to 14,676 files, with an average of 1,016.1 (median = 321.0).

Public Library Programs

- Public libraries are committed to providing opportunities for learning experiences that educate and inspire people throughout their lifetime. Programs vary from digital learning and job training for adults, makerspaces for young adults, and summer reading programs and storytime for children. Public libraries have been increasing their program offerings over the previous decade.
- Public libraries offered 4.3 million programs in FY 2013, a one-year increase of 6.6 percent.

Public Access Internet Computers

- A core function of public libraries is to facilitate open access to information and ideas. In the 21st century, public libraries accomplish this by providing public access to computers and the Internet, serving as technology access points for communities.
- There were 278,733 public access Internet computers available at public libraries across the nation. This reflects a one-year increase of 2.8 percent and 10-year increase of 98.5 percent.

Public Library Staff

- One of the most important assets found in public libraries is the knowledgeable library workforce.
- Public library services were supported by 137,183 total full-time equivalent (FTE) staff. Staffing levels had fluctuated over the 10-year period prior to FY 2013. Staffing levels at public libraries declined during the recession, decreasing by 5.4 percent from a high of 145,070 in FY 2008, but stabilizing by FY 2013. Librarians composed 34.6 percent of total staff, with 47,441 librarian FTEs. This was a 10-year increase of 6.1 percent.
- There were 3.9 librarian FTEs per 25,000 people, a 3.9 percent decrease since FY 2002.
- Two-thirds (67.1 percent) of librarians had a master's of library science from an American Library Association-accredited graduate program. Half

of public libraries (52.5 percent) had at least one librarian on staff with an ALA-MLS degree.

State Library Administrative Agencies

The following are highlights from the IMLS report *State Library Administrative Agencies Survey, Fiscal Year 2012,* released in May 2014.

Revenue and Expenditures

- State Library Administrative Agency (SLAA) revenues totaled nearly $1 billion in fiscal year (FY) 2012, which represented a 27 percent decrease from FY 2003 and a 12 percent decrease from FY 2010.
- Revenues from the federal government for all SLAAs totaled $181.6 million in FY 2012. State revenues totaled $766.2 million, which included $265.8 million received from the states to support SLAA operation, $455.6 million in state aid to libraries, and $40.9 million received from the states for any other purposes (such as interagency transfers).
- Total expenditures for FY 2012 across all SLAAs were $995.5 million, which represented a 26 percent decrease from FY 2003 and an 11 percent decrease from FY 2010. When looking across the types of expenditures, $640.6 million went toward financial assistance to libraries, $335.4 million went toward operating expenditures, $14.8 million was allocated to other services, and $2.5 million was spent on capital outlay.
- More than $89 million of LSTA (Library Services and Technology Act) funds was used to support access to technology and information resources for libraries in 2012, and $36 million went toward programs and services for lifelong learning.

Workforce and Staff Development

- In FY 2012 SLAAs employed 2,814 full-time equivalent (FTE) staff, which was a decrease of 5 percent from 2010.
- In FY 2012 a total of 360 staff (13 percent of all budgeted FTEs) was reported within the service of administration, more than 600 budgeted FTEs (22 percent) were reported within library development, and 1,354 budgeted FTEs (48 percent) were reported within library services.

Services

- A total of 40 SLAAs funded or facilitated digitization programs and services in 2012, and 15 SLAAs provided preservation and conservation services to public libraries and library cooperatives.
- During FY 2012 the number of library service transactions that served the general public and state government employees reported by SLAAs included library visits (29,051), circulation transactions (45,971), reference

transactions (15,992), and interlibrary loan services provided to another library (6,222) and received from another library (2,368).

* Fifty SLAAs funded summer reading programs and continuing education programs for public libraries in FY 2012.

Identification and Governance

* Of the 50 states and the District of Columbia, three SLAAs (Michigan, New York, and Tennessee) were located within the legislative branch in state government, and 48 were located within the executive branch.
* Thirty-seven of the 51 SLAAs reported having allied operations in addition to their SLAA functions, ten reported state archives and state records management services, and eight reported some other type of allied operation.

School Libraries

The following are highlights from the NCES publication *Characteristics of Public Elementary and Secondary School Library Media Centers in the United States: Results from the 2011–2012 Schools and Staffing Survey* (NCES 2013-315).

* During the 2011–2012 school year, 79,000 of the 85,500 traditional public schools in the United States reported having a library media center, while 2,200 of the 4,500 public charter schools reported having one.
* About two-thirds (67 percent) of library media centers in traditional public schools had full-time, paid, state-certified library media center specialists, while one-third (33 percent) of those in public charter schools had this type of staff. In traditional public schools, 20 percent of library media centers did not have any paid, state-certified library media center specialists (full or part time), and 56 percent of those in public charter schools did not have this type of staff.
* The percentage of paid, professional library media center staff with a master's degree in a library-related major field was 52 percent for all public schools, 52 percent in traditional public schools, and 27 percent in public charter schools.
* During the 2010–2011 school year, public school library media centers spent an average of $9,340 for all information resources. This included an average of $6,010 for the purchase of books and $490 for the purchase of audio/video materials.
* The number of holdings in public library media centers per 100 students was 2,188 for book titles and 81 for audio/video materials at the end of the 2010–2011 school year.
* Public school library media centers provided technological services, including automated catalog(s) for student and/or staff use (88 percent), laptops for staff use outside the library media center (54 percent), laptops for

student use outside the library media center (40 percent), and technology to assist students and/or staff with disabilities (31 percent).

- The percentage of library media centers with computer workstations for student and/or staff use was 97 percent in traditional public schools and 88 percent in public charter schools. Of the library media center computer workstations, 95 percent had Internet access. Among all public school library media centers, 86 percent provided student access to online, licensed databases.

- For classes and other activities, 61 percent of public school library media centers had both flexible scheduling (available as needed) and regular scheduling (previously specified times), while 19 percent had only flexible scheduling, and 19 percent had only regular scheduling. The percentage of public school library media centers that were available for independent student use was 89 percent during regular school hours, 57 percent before school, and 54 percent after school.

- About one-fourth (24 percent) of public school library media centers were open to community members who do not attend the school and do not have children who attend the school. Of these, 61 percent had workstations that community members could use to access the Internet.

- Public school library media centers supported programs that encourage students to read (65 percent) and family literacy activities (36 percent). Per 100 students in the school, there was an average of 100 student visits to the library media center and 110 books or other materials checked out during a full week of school.

Library Acquisition Expenditures, 2016–2017: U.S. Public, Academic, Special, and Government Libraries

The information in these tables is taken from the 2016–2017 edition of *American Library Directory* (*ALD*) (Information Today, Inc.). The tables report acquisition expenditures by public, academic, special, and government libraries.

Understanding the Tables

Number of libraries includes only those U.S. libraries in *ALD* that reported annual acquisition expenditures. Libraries that reported annual income but not expenditures are not included in the count. Academic libraries include university, college, and junior college libraries. Special academic libraries, such as law and medical libraries, that reported acquisition expenditures separately from the institution's main library are counted as independent libraries.

The amount in the *total acquisition expenditures* column for a given state is generally greater than the sum of the categories of expenditures. This is because the total acquisition expenditures amount also includes the expenditures of libraries that did not itemize by category.

Figures in *categories of expenditure* columns represent only those libraries that itemized expenditures. Libraries that reported a total acquisition expenditure amount but did not itemize are only represented in the total acquisition expenditures column.

Table 1 / Public Library Acquisition Expenditures

State	Number of Libraries	Total Acquisition Expenditures	Books	Other Print Materials	Periodicals/ Serials	Manuscripts & Archives	AV Equipment	AV Materials	Microforms	Electronic Reference	Preservation
										Category of Expenditures (in U.S. dollars)	
Alabama	16	18,543,670	1,128,080	3,252	15,329	2,000	4,700	171,519	2,013	24,866	20,400
Alaska	10	1,860,486	896,775	17,876	86,635	43,021	—	293,211	500	228,457	6,871
Arizona	20	18,047,150	3,151,446	138,319	158,227	575	—	1,102,856	—	621,632	—
Arkansas	9	3,231,299	1,606,976	20,564	45,702	500	22,000	682,515	—	523,862	—
California	61	80,057,296	31,234,172	1,401,433	2,424,816	9,000	43,417	7,952,112	67,472	8,901,734	72,861
Colorado	26	15,505,150	4,531,436	448,462	397,669	—	15,000	2,117,246	500	2,475,299	—
Connecticut	49	19,520,678	2,921,320	99,513	688,298	1,605	8,000	652,350	1,080	982,576	39,562
Delaware	4	303,475	40,000	—	5,000	—	—	—	—	—	—
District of Columbia	0	—	—	—	—	—	—	—	—	—	—
Florida	32	30,668,342	12,074,121	825,706	799,014	—	176,480	4,678,047	10,305	4,299,087	—
Georgia	14	2,884,373	929,233	42,253	76,568	—	2,026	253,970	2,350	234,628	198
Hawaii	1	4,178,963	2,521,002	69,009	134,607	—	—	—	25,221	1,347,359	—
Idaho	7	544,371	118,637	500	82	—	—	6,611	—	11,360	—
Illinois	96	36,173,546	13,022,355	82,495	642,369	3,000	73,789	3,807,741	21,629	4,802,731	26,369
Indiana	60	26,659,848	10,820,015	12,000	1,041,810	—	105,168	4,395,935	152,653	4,542,046	75,647
Iowa	55	7,288,648	2,107,234	66,914	156,705	4,000	7,853	664,815	6,333	366,347	—
Kansas	25	4,833,636	1,195,495	105,110	159,795	—	4,600	310,425	8,554	165,908	700
Kentucky	21	10,806,099	3,203,505	107,345	183,241	—	30,224	1,166,912	14,806	1,868,797	64,276
Louisiana	7	7,161,803	3,326,968	5,000	427,174	—	109,597	1,076,461	54,882	2,037,185	—
Maine	30	1,063,338	453,857	1,000	81,654	2,000	5,000	108,794	800	238,350	1,000
Maryland	3	10,501,681	1,600,410	—	70,634	—	—	864,124	—	175,455	—
Massachusetts	60	17,896,214	2,964,349	85,653	373,557	—	6,014	872,069	17,190	440,859	700
Michigan	60	24,253,463	5,321,440	176,030	365,444	—	30,000	1,784,698	10,186	1,359,673	1,500
Minnesota	23	79,032,752	1,937,952	1,403	52,514	—	83	413,558	—	173,204	516
Mississippi	7	991,086	572,478	—	88,964	—	—	89,621	26,000	151,496	2,162
Missouri	31	747,502,160	303,751,388	122,513,065	21,581,555	—	25,796	181,917,266	1,916,226	101,035,377	150

Montana	15	971,589	399,383	73,040	76,892	200	5,500	116,763	1,000	98,766	2,500
Nebraska	20	1,863,082	942,397	304,138	21,417	—	47	47,892	—	405,239	46
Nevada	5	414,283	129,932	—	9,896	—	—	32,808	—	21,203	1,406
New Hampshire	39	1,180,490	563,607	1,031	48,048	—	7,428	161,837	4,400	67,247	2,650
New Jersey	58	22,497,344	11,190,266	117,614	1,053,688	500	21,500	2,322,421	101,249	1,674,416	7,306
New Mexico	13	3,428,860	1,962,329	215,399	57,242	—	6,000	403,794	10,213	506,130	—
New York	100	40,833,928	15,509,345	80,311	1,307,856	3,000	271,369	3,416,090	46,103	2,392,938	8,133
North Carolina	14	12,185,805	4,948,254	1,306,038	175,001	—	7,000	473,133	1,040	326,019	—
North Dakota	12	1,735,525	490,409	300	70,879	—	—	92,969	2,000	523,660	1,000
Ohio	57	62,598,860	18,734,193	324,735	2,750,184	6,921	48,301	9,216,429	262,529	9,778,733	213,293
Oklahoma	13	13,033,538	4,840,186	18,002	860,958	—	—	2,225,908	3,610	1,951,314	—
Oregon	29	6,411,910	3,189,234	14,862	334,189	—	3,500	1,086,916	23,699	307,311	3,000
Pennsylvania	48	19,279,835	3,810,875	846,770	794,805	156,260	2,226	2,281,105	170,236	1,237,755	243,610
Rhode Island	7	9,778,939	636,378	71,214	46,943	—	—	104,686	70	821,999	950
South Carolina	11	10,890,369	4,793,099	31,426	114,500	—	—	1,973,010	—	1,071,527	—
South Dakota	10	1,308,258	773,581	15,756	71,199	—	16,846	301,386	—	120,031	—
Tennessee	19	58,462,535	24,134,049	270,414	759,001	1,000	2,438,770	8,761,978	—	18,597,479	12,107
Texas	92	53,526,353	9,291,576	316,614	763,163	—	272,843	1,611,563	49,773	2,123,844	34,700
Utah	8	2,285,120	1,167,709	—	10,200	—	—	653,930	—	311,205	—
Vermont	33	832,578	457,887	311	23,009	—	—	114,882	—	32,250	500
Virginia	24	10,335,712	4,154,718	151,005	427,604	44,810	6,071	1,312,392	39,329	1,349,050	1,339,701
Washington	19	5,105,087	1,042,627	56,771	111,597	—	1,975	323,145	622	337,704	400
West Virginia	10	3,746,902	1,243,508	3,000	58,055	—	—	219,634	13,500	908,542	1,500
Wisconsin	49	7,024,105	2,742,811	142,087	176,514	—	15,952	895,258	13,150	276,134	—
Wyoming	8	3,725,990	161,233	500	13,360	—	—	58,923	40	13,388	—
Puerto Rico	0	—	—	—	—	—	—	—	—	—	—
Total	1,440	1,522,966,524	528,740,230	130,584,240	40,193,563	278,392	3,795,075	253,591,708	3,081,263	182,262,172	2,185,714
Estimated % of Acquisition Expenditures			34.72	8.57	2.64	0.02	0.25	16.65	0.20	11.97	0.14

Table 2 / Academic Library Acquisition Expenditures

State	Number of Libraries	Total Acquisition Expenditures	Books	Other Print Materials	Periodicals/ Serials	Manuscripts & Archives	AV Equipment	AV Materials	Microforms	Electronic Reference	Preservation
Alabama	10	7,125,700	1,097,509	6,031	3,073,914	—	5,000	95,554	73,811	1,622,598	52,319
Alaska	4	6,770,113	556,433	20,000	2,444,608	—	300	77,137	16,807	938,392	18,827
Arizona	3	2,515,647	13,985	—	30,022	—	6,955	3,074	—	132,289	—
Arkansas	6	9,741,450	1,287,164	419,834	6,459,342	34,264	1,000	28,972	431,418	1,028,027	9,187
California	43	68,236,162	4,025,984	548,107	6,008,720	4,199	47,081	246,906	27,338	11,134,789	148,919
Colorado	13	22,194,484	1,368,662	24,882	1,432,217	—	—	128,202	—	5,352,637	41,747
Connecticut	8	10,556,657	1,032,774	250	2,612,933	—	80,000	29,832	8,518	1,062,189	25,311
Delaware	3	12,420,225	40,000	—	8,419	—	—	—	—	—	—
District of Columbia	4	16,518,550	1,435,677	110,000	5,900,251	—	—	3,267	34,380	1,825,723	47,000
Florida	19	32,377,804	4,626,804	830,328	14,261,899	—	—	371,172	107,698	11,508,079	189,793
Georgia	17	22,183,976	849,810	2,000	1,968,301	—	3,098	96,378	42,731	1,973,149	25,946
Hawaii	—	—	—	—	—	—	—	—	—	—	—
Idaho	3	8,855,854	368,331	54,040	1,886,540	—	—	11,776	—	597,018	24,910
Illinois	26	52,467,962	1,810,128	7,648	3,901,881	—	20,000	146,274	27,582	2,970,195	92,729
Indiana	19	22,955,091	3,165,633	39,211	12,078,218	—	18	97,749	9,719	3,620,016	71,460
Iowa	15	23,743,615	2,065,937	391,576	6,021,086	—	6,000	87,076	38,687	2,161,111	78,787
Kansas	13	8,270,959	794,698	22,300	6,086,100	3,000	5,000	49,943	27,314	735,349	40,089
Kentucky	9	17,395,771	527,121	19,245	2,407,088	—	2,886	89,465	38,443	305,428	8,170
Louisiana	8	4,789,841	326,824	2,935	2,531,820	500	—	4,935	36,508	1,243,435	41,421
Maine	3	10,402,740	1,264,860	177,656	7,564,612	—	—	—	53,849	475,000	32,730
Maryland	13	11,960,194	1,475,784	8,912	8,229,168	12,434	—	43,256	18,247	1,725,816	48,324
Massachusetts	17	28,215,237	1,270,951	35,056	2,711,988	36,000	19,011	84,359	3,234	7,762,443	125,962
Michigan	24	23,546,347	2,285,550	139,140	9,371,644	25,203	1,000	151,664	1,400,837	6,858,710	47,766
Minnesota	13	7,566,871	1,346,500	10,000	2,579,887	280	53,955	104,826	38,367	1,208,817	70,905
Mississippi	2	246,040	10,000	—	2,700	—	—	—	—	83,340	—

Missouri	16	12,502,085	531,012	—	2,021,172	8,767	4,120	102,294	115,045	1,103,221	30,576
Montana	2	257,080	101,825	—	91,192	—	—	7,000	—	15,000	—
Nebraska	7	15,426,591	453,643	86,211	2,652,464	15,000	—	67,021	66,665	1,299,572	14,160
Nevada	—	—	—	—	—	—	—	—	—	—	—
New Hampshire	3	7,148,753	942,175	—	4,049,060	—	—	700	700	984,990	76,271
New Jersey	11	60,756,841	1,194,450	—	2,604,873	1,000	—	68,764	—	2,168,634	7,603
New Mexico	4	3,330,114	137,311	—	2,685,913	11,802	—	19,878	16,450	112,334	28,574
New York	44	77,212,577	5,976,314	242,079	15,621,643	84,772	132,269	389,851	138,672	16,287,497	287,118
North Carolina	22	77,184,882	2,259,922	38,088	6,782,069	—	1,140,846	284,199	287,139	2,014,201	54,273
North Dakota	2	2,965,537	365,806	—	2,011,935	—	—	30,752	684	539,766	16,594
Ohio	27	31,809,291	2,706,300	14,193	4,434,596	3,798	17,088	172,057	126,584	2,207,298	146,282
Oklahoma	9	6,316,847	597,001	—	2,293,418	2,000	—	125,951	—	2,254,401	8,491
Oregon	10	23,250,076	957,824	—	2,825,033	—	32,779	92,700	—	891,920	25,447
Pennsylvania	23	15,456,274	2,372,702	8,585	5,783,923	1,485	2,000	191,870	27,486	2,924,486	90,008
Rhode Island	3	1,681,147	477,893	—	751,097	8,000	—	38,270	8,000	391,213	6,674
South Carolina	12	9,209,520	1,087,114	304,035	1,089,337	20,000	48,951	74,449	64,255	2,227,532	60,034
South Dakota	3	3,123,018	295,311	—	2,296,269	—	3,255	16,418	8,284	390,276	36,646
Tennessee	12	18,598,201	812,742	—	1,386,668	—	—	38,858	58,900	2,736,364	6,613
Texas	35	56,825,792	4,584,973	58,935	13,690,619	5,050	109,474	195,124	107,924	5,458,472	134,268
Utah	5	8,371,446	1,236,920	—	4,986,138	—	5,000	79,715	3,500	221,588	10,196
Vermont	2	1,270,095	222,300	5,330	915,981	1,644	—	27,766	2,194	89,600	5,280
Virginia	16	36,701,901	4,724,541	615,565	12,769,349	—	1,970	302,016	16,799	5,763,981	100,785
Washington	11	14,372,381	1,703,911	—	7,482,834	2,000	46,000	235,372	7,900	1,814,577	18,098
West Virginia	9	3,048,850	182,839	975	329,380	6,750	14,300	16,675	51,837	496,352	10,778
Wisconsin	12	11,299,224	533,277	1,964	1,403,169	1,879	21,000	130,716	43,945	1,706,514	17,429
Wyoming	2	7,344,506	3,458,937	—	2,201,321	—	—	13,200	—	863,481	—
Puerto Rico	8	6,698,035	740,673	7,205	4,646,621	5,000	14,490	50,440	—	939,148	9,800
Total	605	943,218,354	71,704,835	4,252,316	217,379,432	294,827	1,844,846	4,723,873	3,588,451	122,226,968	2,444,300
Estimated % of Acquisition Expenditures			7.60	0.45	23.05	0.03	0.20	0.50	0.38	12.96	0.26

Table 3 / Special Library Acquisition Expenditures

State	Number of Libraries	Total Acquisition Expenditures	Books	Other Print Materials	Periodicals/ Serials	Manuscripts & Archives	AV Equipment	AV Materials	Microforms	Electronic Reference	Preservation
						Category of Expenditures (in U.S. dollars)					
Alabama	—	—	—	—	—	—	—	—	—	—	—
Alaska	—	—	—	—	—	—	—	—	—	—	—
Arizona	2	5,324	3,500	—	324	—	—	—	—	—	1,000
Arkansas	—	—	—	—	—	—	—	—	—	—	—
California	9	164,093	22,635	1,000	35,958	—	1,000	500	—	10,000	3,000
Colorado	—	—	—	—	—	—	—	—	—	—	—
Connecticut	1	1,000	—	—	—	—	—	—	—	—	—
Delaware	—	—	—	—	—	—	—	—	—	—	—
District of Columbia	3	309,000	61,000	—	100,000	—	—	—	2,000	145,000	1,000
Florida	1	5,250	2,250	—	3,000	—	—	—	—	—	—
Georgia	—	—	—	—	—	—	—	—	—	—	—
Hawaii	—	—	—	—	—	—	—	—	—	—	—
Idaho	—	—	—	—	—	—	—	—	—	—	—
Illinois	8	3,319,500	58,600	30,500	110,200	4,000	1,500	2,000	1,500	67,500	6,700
Indiana	1	87,400	—	—	—	—	—	—	—	—	—
Iowa	2	111,529	17,681	—	6,204	—	—	—	77,644	—	—
Kansas	1	6,000	3,000	—	3,000	—	—	—	—	—	—
Kentucky	—	—	—	—	—	—	—	—	—	—	—
Louisiana	1	18,000	5,000	—	13,000	—	—	—	—	—	—
Maine	1	200	—	—	—	—	—	—	—	—	—
Maryland	3	166,500	22,650	—	130,450	100	—	—	—	12,000	100
Massachusetts	—	—	—	—	—	—	—	—	—	—	—
Michigan	1	12,000	3,000	500	3,600	—	—	400	—	—	—
Minnesota	1	50,000	20,000	5,000	9,000	—	—	—	—	16,000	—
Mississippi	—	—	—	—	—	—	—	—	—	—	—

State	Count										
Missouri	1	67,500	24,000	—	29,500	—	—	—	—	14,000	—
Montana	1	17,348	15,848	—	—	—	—	—	—	1,500	—
Nebraska	1	800	300	—	500	—	—	—	—	—	—
Nevada	—	—	—	—	—	—	—	—	—	—	—
New Hampshire	2	92,000	16,000	10,000	5,000	20,000	—	—	—	32,000	9,000
New Jersey	4	40,500	15,000	—	3,000	3,000	—	6,000	—	8,800	4,700
New Mexico	2	11,500	1,000	—	1,000	—	—	—	—	—	500
New York	10	560,537	297,284	—	53,278	—	500	—	—	38,475	151,000
North Carolina	—	—	—	—	—	—	—	—	—	—	—
North Dakota	1	8,098	2,660	—	3,975	—	—	—	—	—	1,463
Ohio	6	692,043	78,824	550	73,362	1,679	—	850	—	32,107	5,047
Oklahoma	1	4,500	3,000	—	1,500	—	—	—	—	—	—
Oregon	1	600	200	—	—	—	—	—	—	400	—
Pennsylvania	1	106,357	7,108	47,812	5,059	18,351	—	4,671	—	3,322	20,034
Rhode Island	1	75,313	44,726	—	5,000	15,387	—	—	—	—	10,200
South Carolina	—	—	—	—	—	—	—	—	—	—	—
South Dakota	—	—	—	—	—	—	—	—	—	—	—
Tennessee	—	—	—	—	—	—	—	—	—	—	—
Texas	3	1,584,500	2,256	12,000	2,393	—	670	625	—	805,000	1,556
Utah	1	75,000	5,000	5,000	10,000	—	5,000	—	—	50,000	—
Vermont	—	—	—	—	—	—	—	—	—	—	—
Virginia	4	185,724	86,442	—	49,560	4,026	—	—	—	44,000	1,696
Washington	—	—	—	—	—	—	—	—	—	—	—
West Virginia	—	—	—	—	—	—	—	—	—	—	—
Wisconsin	2	85,500	4,000	—	20,000	—	—	—	—	60,000	—
Wyoming	—	—	—	—	—	—	—	—	—	—	—
Puerto Rico	—	—	—	—	—	—	—	—	—	—	—
Total	77	7,863,616	822,964	112,362	677,863	66,543	8,670	15,046	81,144	1,340,104	216,996
Estimated % of Acquisition Expenditures			10.47	1.43	8.62	0.85	0.11	0.19	1.03	17.04	2.76

Table 4 / Government Library Acquisition Expenditures

State	Number of Libraries	Total Acquisition Expenditures	Books	Other Print Materials	Periodicals/ Serials	Manuscripts & Archives	AV Equipment	AV Materials	Microforms	Electronic Reference	Preservation
Alabama	2	626,295	243,777	—	575	—	—	—	—	381,472	471
Alaska	—	—	—	—	—	—	—	—	—	—	—
Arizona	1	2,012	2,000	—	12	—	—	—	—	—	—
Arkansas	—	—	—	—	—	—	—	—	—	—	—
California	7	1,523,931	556,948	—	1,442	—	—	555	—	302,966	—
Colorado	—	—	—	—	—	—	—	—	—	—	—
Connecticut	—	—	—	—	—	—	—	—	—	—	—
Delaware	—	—	—	—	—	—	—	—	—	—	—
District of Columbia	—	—	—	—	—	—	—	—	—	—	—
Florida	—	—	—	—	—	—	—	—	—	—	—
Georgia	—	—	—	—	—	—	—	—	—	—	—
Hawaii	—	—	—	—	—	—	—	—	—	—	—
Idaho	—	—	—	—	—	—	—	—	—	—	—
Illinois	—	—	—	—	—	—	—	—	—	—	—
Indiana	—	—	—	—	—	—	—	—	—	—	—
Iowa	—	—	—	—	—	—	—	—	—	—	—
Kansas	2	789,260	296,852	—	400,491	—	—	—	—	85,690	6,227
Kentucky	—	—	—	—	—	—	—	—	—	—	—
Louisiana	2	1,050,279	91,080	—	42,318	—	—	1,000	—	41,663	—
Maine	1	380,116	—	—	—	—	—	—	—	—	—
Maryland	2	214,000	93,000	11,800	98,000	—	—	7,700	—	—	3,500
Massachusetts	—	—	—	—	—	—	—	—	—	—	—
Michigan	1	35,000	—	—	—	—	—	—	—	—	—
Minnesota	1	74,500	10,000	—	45,500	—	—	—	—	19,000	—
Mississippi	—	—	—	—	—	—	—	—	—	—	—

Category of Expenditures (in U.S. dollars)

Missouri	—	—	—	—	—	—	—	—	—	—	—
Montana	1	425,961	328,391	—	—	—	—	—	—	97,570	—
Nebraska	—	—	—	—	—	—	—	—	—	—	—
Nevada	1	768,769	562,656	—	10,803	—	—	—	3,151	186,357	5,802
New Hampshire	—	—	—	—	—	—	—	—	—	—	—
New Jersey	—	—	—	—	—	—	—	—	—	—	—
New Mexico	—	—	—	—	—	—	—	—	—	—	—
New York	—	—	—	—	—	—	—	—	—	—	—
North Carolina	—	—	—	—	—	—	—	—	—	—	—
North Dakota	—	—	—	—	—	—	—	—	—	—	—
Ohio	—	—	—	—	—	—	—	—	—	—	—
Oklahoma	—	—	—	—	—	—	—	—	—	—	—
Oregon	—	—	—	—	—	—	—	—	—	—	—
Pennsylvania	4	618,000	—	—	—	—	—	—	—	—	—
Rhode Island	—	—	—	—	—	—	—	—	—	—	—
South Carolina	—	—	—	—	—	—	—	—	—	—	—
South Dakota	—	—	—	—	—	—	—	—	—	—	—
Tennessee	—	—	—	—	—	—	—	—	—	—	—
Texas	—	—	—	—	—	—	—	—	—	—	—
Utah	—	—	—	—	—	—	—	—	—	—	—
Vermont	—	—	—	—	—	—	—	—	—	—	—
Virginia	—	—	—	—	—	—	—	—	—	—	—
Washington	—	—	—	—	—	—	—	—	—	—	—
West Virginia	1	650,000	50,000	—	400,000	—	—	—	—	200,000	—
Wisconsin	2	91,000	45,000	—	—	—	—	—	—	36,000	—
Wyoming	—	—	—	—	—	—	—	—	—	—	—
Puerto Rico	—	—	—	—	—	—	—	—	—	—	—
Total	28	7,249,123	2,279,704	11,800	999,141	0	0	9,255	3,151	1,350,718	16,000
Estimated % of Acquisition Expenditures			31.45	0.16	13.78	0	0	0.13	0.04	18.63	0.22

Public Library State Rankings, 2014

State	Library Visits per Capita[1]	Registered Users per Capita[1]	Circulation Transactions per Capita[1]	Interlibrary Loans Received per 1,000 Population[1]	Average Number Public-use Internet Computers per Stationary Outlet
Alabama	42	23	47	22	23
Alaska	23	28	27	34	44
Arizona	37	45	33	30	4
Arkansas	35	16	41	46	40
California	34	24	38	21	15
Colorado	7	5	5	18	5
Connecticut	11	46	18	14	22
Delaware	36	50	32	6	6
District of Columbia[2]	5	29	37	50	1
Florida	39	30	36	49	2
Georgia	51	51	49	24	10
Hawaii[3]	45	9	45	51	42
Idaho	3	15	7	20	36
Illinois	9	43	13	7	12
Indiana	15	17	4	27	11
Iowa	14	8	16	19	46
Kansas	19	3	10	11	45
Kentucky	32	18	28	43	7
Louisiana	41	33	46	38	27
Maine	13	11	22	8	48
Maryland	27	22	11	31	3
Massachusetts	6	37	14	3	32
Michigan	26	36	20	12	19
Minnesota	30	2	12	17	26
Mississippi	48	27	51	48	37
Missouri	22	20	9	25	33
Montana	28	42	35	15	39
Nebraska	21	4	19	41	43
Nevada	40	44	25	33	28
New Hampshire	2	6	17	16	51
New Jersey	24	39	31	13	18
New Mexico	31	13	39	45	31
New York	20	25	26	9	21
North Carolina	44	38	42	40	14
North Dakota	46	48	34	28	41
Ohio	1	1	1	5	20
Oklahoma	33	10	29	44	29
Oregon	16	35	2	2	30
Pennsylvania	43	49	43	10	35
Rhode Island	18	47	30	4	13
South Carolina	38	26	40	36	9
South Dakota	25	40	24	35	49

State	Library Visits per Capita[1]	Registered Users per Capita[1]	Circulation Transactions per Capita[1]	Interlibrary Loans Received per 1,000 Population[1]	Average Number Public-use Internet Computers per Stationary Outlet
Tennessee	47	34	48	42	24
Texas	49	32	44	37	8
Utah	10	14	3	47	25
Vermont	4	31	23	23	50
Virginia	29	21	15	39	16
Washington	12	12	6	32	17
West Virginia	50	41	50	26	47
Wisconsin	17	19	8	1	34
Wyoming	8	7	21	29	38

State	Public-use Internet Computers per 5,000 Population[1]	Print Materials per Capita[1]	Current Print Serial Subscriptions per 1,000 Population[1]	Audio Physical Units per 1,000 Population[1]	Video Physical Units per 1,000 Population[1]
Alabama	21	38	48	43	43
Alaska	6	15	7	21	2
Arizona	38	51	47	40	37
Arkansas	27	30	33	47	40
California	49	45	41	46	44
Colorado	17	39	23	20	15
Connecticut	18	6	18	7	9
Delaware	40	44	26	36	30
District of Columbia[2]	5	23	37	33	25
Florida	36	48	44	42	36
Georgia	42	49	51	51	50
Hawaii[3]	51	31	49	25	49
Idaho	13	21	28	23	19
Illinois	11	11	10	8	12
Indiana	10	8	9	3	4
Iowa	4	9	4	10	10
Kansas	7	13	16	16	7
Kentucky	23	37	31	37	32
Louisiana	20	29	22	41	20
Maine	3	1	8	15	11
Maryland	41	34	32	17	29
Massachusetts	29	4	13	9	13
Michigan	19	18	21	13	16
Minnesota	25	25	25	27	35
Mississippi	32	42	46	50	48
Missouri	35	22	14	19	27
Montana	14	27	30	38	31
Nebraska	1	10	6	26	23
Nevada	50	50	42	30	26
New Hampshire	16	2	3	5	3

State	Public-use Internet Computers per 5,000 Population[1]	Print Materials per Capita[1]	Current Print Serial Subscriptions per 1,000 Population[1]	Audio Physical Units per 1,000 Population[1]	Video Physical Units per 1,000 Population[1]
New Jersey	33	20	19	14	18
New Mexico	28	28	34	34	33
New York	26	16	5	18	14
North Carolina	46	46	43	49	51
North Dakota	15	17	20	32	34
Ohio	22	12	1	1	1
Oklahoma	30	33	40	28	45
Oregon	39	26	27	12	17
Pennsylvania	48	36	35	24	41
Rhode Island	12	7	24	31	24
South Carolina	34	40	38	45	39
South Dakota	9	14	15	29	28
Tennessee	43	43	50	44	46
Texas	45	47	45	48	47
Utah	47	32	29	11	21
Vermont	2	3	2	6	8
Virginia	37	35	39	35	42
Washington	31	41	17	22	22
West Virginia	44	24	36	39	38
Wisconsin	24	19	12	4	5
Wyoming	8	5	11	2	6

State	Total Paid FTE Staff per 25,000 Population[1]	Paid FTE Librarians per 25,000 Population[1]	Paid FTE Librarians with "ALA-MLs" per 25,000 Population[1]	Other Paid FTE Staff per 25,000 Population[1]
Alabama	36	31	38	34
Alaska	29	28	29	23
Arizona	45	48	40	40
Arkansas	34	43	47	24
California	46	47	32	42
Colorado	10	27	12	6
Connecticut	9	5	2	17
Delaware	41	36	42	39
District of Columbia[2]	1	18	1	1
Florida	44	45	30	44
Georgia	51	51	46	45
Hawaii[3]	37	39	14	29
Idaho	17	32	39	10
Illinois	4	10	6	5
Indiana	5	13	9	4
Iowa	13	3	25	30
Kansas	7	7	17	11
Kentucky	24	9	31	41
Louisiana	16	16	24	15
Maine	12	6	10	22

State	Total Paid FTE Staff per 25,000 Population[1]	Paid FTE Librarians per 25,000 Population[1]	Paid FTE Librarians with "ALA-MLs" per 25,000 Population[1]	Other Paid FTE Staff per 25,000 Population[1]
Maryland	15	15	18	16
Massachusetts	18	8	4	25
Michigan	25	26	13	20
Minnesota	35	34	26	31
Mississippi	43	20	50	51
Missouri	14	33	49	8
Montana	38	25	36	47
Nebraska	23	14	35	27
Nevada	47	50	44	38
New Hampshire	6	1	5	26
New Jersey	21	30	11	12
New Mexico	33	29	33	36
New York	8	21	7	7
North Carolina	48	49	37	43
North Dakota	39	22	43	49
Ohio	3	17	8	2
Oklahoma	30	19	28	32
Oregon	26	35	20	14
Pennsylvania	40	42	27	33
Rhode Island	19	12	3	19
South Carolina	32	37	22	28
South Dakota	28	11	45	37
Tennessee	49	46	51	46
Texas	50	44	41	48
Utah	31	38	34	21
Vermont	11	2	19	35
Virginia	27	41	21	13
Washington	20	40	16	9
West Virginia	42	24	48	50
Wisconsin	22	23	15	18
Wyoming	2	4	23	3

	Total Operating Revenue per Capita[1]	State Operating Revenue per Capita[1]	Local Operating Revenue per Capita[1]	Other Operating Revenue per Capita[1]
Alabama	45	29	44	33
Alaska	6	17	9	10
Arizona	43	42	40	47
Arkansas	36	15	37	35
California	31	39	27	32
Colorado	9	43	7	17
Connecticut	8	36	12	3
Delaware	39	8	42	27
District of Columbia[3]	1	49	1	51
Florida	42	25	39	48
Georgia	49	13	48	42

	Total Operating Revenue per Capita[1]	State Operating Revenue per Capita[1]	Local Operating Revenue per Capita[1]	Other Operating Revenue per Capita[1]
Hawaii[3]	44	2	51	36
Idaho	25	28	23	18
Illinois	3	9	2	15
Indiana	10	10	11	20
Iowa	22	30	21	14
Kansas	16	20	14	9
Kentucky	21	24	18	29
Louisiana	14	23	10	44
Maine	26	41	33	2
Maryland	13	3	16	7
Massachusetts	19	27	17	11
Michigan	20	26	20	22
Minnesota	24	18	24	12
Mississippi	51	12	50	25
Missouri	18	32	15	21
Montana	41	34	36	28
Nebraska	29	38	25	26
Nevada	34	4	41	43
New Hampshire	15	45	13	13
New Jersey	11	35	6	24
New Mexico	35	19	34	37
New York	2	11	4	1
North Carolina	46	22	45	40
North Dakota	37	14	38	31
Ohio	4	1	32	4
Oklahoma	30	33	26	34
Oregon	12	40	8	19
Pennsylvania	40	7	46	8
Rhode Island	17	5	30	6
South Carolina	38	21	35	46
South Dakota	33	50	28	45
Tennessee	50	44	47	49
Texas	48	47	43	50
Utah	28	37	22	41
Vermont	27	51	31	5
Virginia	32	16	29	39
Washington	5	46	3	30
West Virginia	47	6	49	38
Wisconsin	23	31	19	23
Wyoming	7	48	5	16

	Total Operating Expenditures per Capita[1]	Total Collection Expenditures per Capita[1]	Total Staff Expenditures per Capita[1]	Salaries and Wages Expenditures per Capita[1]
Alabama	45	47	45	45
Alaska	6	15	10	17
Arizona	41	31	43	44
Arkansas	36	36	41	41
California	31	40	30	33
Colorado	11	5	14	11
Connecticut	5	10	3	2
Delaware	38	43	35	36
District of Columbia[2]	1	8	1	1
Florida	42	39	44	43
Georgia	49	50	48	49
Hawaii[3]	44	46	42	31
Idaho	26	25	29	28
Illinois	3	4	5	3
Indiana	10	3	16	14
Iowa	22	18	19	21
Kansas	14	9	17	15
Kentucky	33	23	33	34
Louisiana	18	14	22	22
Maine	25	34	20	19
Maryland	15	7	12	13
Massachusetts	16	11	15	9
Michigan	24	28	25	25
Minnesota	23	24	24	24
Mississippi	51	51	51	51
Missouri	19	6	23	23
Montana	43	42	37	38
Nebraska	29	19	28	27
Nevada	34	33	34	35
New Hampshire	13	13	9	7
New Jersey	9	21	8	10
New Mexico	35	30	39	42
New York	2	12	2	4
North Carolina	46	49	46	46
North Dakota	40	32	40	39
Ohio	4	1	6	5
Oklahoma	27	20	27	29
Oregon	12	16	11	16
Pennsylvania	39	41	38	40
Rhode Island	17	37	13	12
South Carolina	37	35	36	37
South Dakota	32	27	32	30
Tennessee	50	48	50	50
Texas	47	45	47	47
Utah	28	17	31	32
Vermont	20	29	21	18
Virginia	30	38	26	26

	Total Operating Expenditures per Capita[1]	Total Collection Expenditures per Capita[1]	Total Staff Expenditures per Capita[1]	Salaries and Wages Expenditures per Capita[1]
Washington	7	2	7	8
West Virginia	48	44	49	48
Wisconsin	21	26	18	20
Wyoming	8	22	4	6

[1]Per 5,000 population is based on the total unduplicated population of legal service areas.

[2]The District of Columbia, although not a state, is included in the state rankings. Special care should be used in comparing its data to state data.

[3]Caution should be used in making comparisons with the state of Hawaii, as Hawaii reports only one public library for the entire state.

Source: Institute of Museum and Library Services, Public Libraries Survey, Fiscal Year 2014. Data users who create their own estimates using data from this report should cite the Institute of Museum and Library Services as the source of the original data only. Although the data in this table come from a census of all public libraries and are not subject to sampling error, the census results may contain nonsampling error. Additional information on nonsampling error, response rates, and definitions may be found in Appendix B of the report for the Public Libraries Survey.

Year in Architecture 2016: Open for Business

Bette-Lee Fox

Managing Editor, *Library Journal*

This year's selection of library construction efforts are each unique in their own way, but most share a significant guiding principle: keep it open. The 105 capital projects completed between July 1, 2015, and June 30, 2016, exemplify a dedication to the totality of users' experience with regard to sight lines, maneuverability, accessibility, and natural light but also in consideration of others' ideas, needs, and potential. With atria, lots of glass, and coworking and group study spaces, libraries are indeed open for business.

Education and Growth

Among our baker's dozen of academic projects, a large portion of the first floor of the new Bibliothèque Desjardins, the first building on the new campus of the Université du Québec à Trois-Rivières, Drummondville, consists entirely of windows, flooding the space with natural light. The site was home to a former missionary congregation. The transformation of the brutalist Mendel Gottesman Library at New York's Yeshiva University improved the visual relation of the suspended stack levels at the center of a four-level space.

At Maine's Bowdoin College, the Media Commons in the Hawthorne-Longfellow Library features studios for audio and video recording, editing, and production. The Fenwick Library at George Mason University, Washington, D.C., features multiuse instructional spaces designed with movable partitions to accommodate a range of seating capacities.

The Castle Pines Branch of Douglas County Libraries, Colorado, went from a 2,300-square-foot storefront to a two-story, 15,000-square-foot structure. The second-story terrace has an outdoor fireplace and a green roof. Not to be outdone, the system's Lone Tree Branch has three terraces and interactive alcoves. A metal screen solar veil regulates the temperature.

Designed to be reflective of the local seaside vernacular, the Lewes Public Library, Delaware, took its cues from old lifesaving stations. The interior features natural light provided by a central spine of clerestory windows. The two-level Alpharetta Library, part of the Atlanta-Fulton Public Library System, creates a defining front porch to the city center. Atlanta's Metropolitan Branch consists of simple geometric volumes knit together, with the glass box reading room representing a totally open floor plan.

The design of the Christa McAuliffe Branch Library, Framingham, Massachusetts, was inspired by the life of teacher McAuliffe, the first lay astronaut (and a Framingham native), who died in the *Challenger* space shuttle disaster in 1986.

Adapted from *Library Journal,* November 15, 2016.
For the Year in Architecture 2016, *Library Journal* solicited information from public libraries nationwide that had undergone new builds and renovation/addition projects completed between July 1, 2015, and June 30, 2016. The tables below comprise complete financial and construction statistics for the 92 public library buildings submitted, including Canadian projects.

Referencing flight and a nod to the stars, the building features an expansive children's space that flows into the adult reading area underneath a soaring roof.

The Hennepin County Library–Brooklyn Park, Minnesota, houses a wind-tunnel learning installation, a giant microscope, and engineering challenge cubes, all developed in conjunction with the Minnesota Children's Museum. An expanded children's area with discovery-themed details, a new business center, and an enlarged teen zone enhance the Lewis & Clark Branch of the St. Louis County Library. The Parsons Branch, Columbus Metropolitan Library, Ohio, targets service to customers of all ages, with a Ready for Kindergarten area, a brightly lit children's area with a sunken story time space, a mother's room, and a fireplace.

The distinctive arched roof of the Hewitt Public Library, Texas, beckons visitors, while its teen area features a 3-D printer that "one teenager uses to design and create buttons for her own business."

The Weber County Library HQ and Southwest Branch, Roy, Utah, includes a 255-seat black box theater, a public gallery, a catering kitchen, and a cyber café. Both the east and west wings frame views of the adjacent George Wahlen North Park.

Award-Winning Design

The Dayton Metro Library's Northwest Library is organized around an atrium marketplace, an idea that struck a chord as the branch was awarded an Honorable Mention by the American Institute of Architects (AIA) Dayton Chapter for Newly Completed Buildings. The second floor of the Marmalade Branch of the Salt Lake City Public Library features a wraparound terrace. The entire building was named a 2016 Best Small Project in the *Engineering News-Record*, Mountain States special regional coverage.

The Varina Area Library, Henrico County Public Library, Virginia, has a demonstration kitchen and large glass windows with views of the nearby wetlands and woods. With a nod to the Puget Sound community, Kitsap Regional Library's Kingston Branch, Washington, incorporates sea and shore elements throughout.

A vacated grocery store conversion, the Betty Rodriguez Regional Library, Fresno, California, now has "light shafts" clad in perforated metal panels to define the main circulation path. The major remodel to the Scoville Memorial Library, Salisbury, Connecticut, which opened in 1895, encompassed a new staircase, a new children's area with a garden, and flexible reading and study areas.

Water Damage

The Hereford Branch, Baltimore County Public Library, was completely redesigned and renovated after flooding forced the building to close. The facility features a flexible design with open spaces, an expanded children's area, and the Hive, a collaborative art-maker space. The Waterbury Public Library commissioners had been trying to replace the overcrowded, historic building housing the library since 1916 when tropical storm Irene flooded much of the business district. Now, the library hosts everything from tai chi classes to an adult coloring club to book discussions. The Lake City Public Library, Minnesota, boasts a new fireplace, a vaulted lobby space with a skylight, and a "Color Me Thursdays" program for teens and adults. Minnesota's Marshall-Lyon County Library includes a new children's wing that is entered through replicas of large children's books. The Northfield Public Library, Minnesota, upgraded with a glass atrium/commons to combine a 1910 Carnegie building with a 1982 addition.

Customer Demands

Much of the existing architecture of the original branch of the Jamestown Bluff Branch, Florissant, Missouri, was retained in the remodel, such as the cathedral-like roofline and the tall windows at the "prow" of the building. The Rock Road Branch, St. Ann, Missouri, added a business center and dedicated areas for children and teens. The Wildwood Crest Branch, Cape May County, New Jersey, was inspired by the beach region's iconic Doo Wop style architecture, with a children's area that includes a carpet pool and hot tub and umbrella chairs. The new Hudson Area Library, New York, located in the newly renovated Hudson historic armory, includes a repurposed 12,000 square foot drill shed that serves as the main space.

While the Richland Library, Columbia, South Carolina, encompasses a state-of-the-art Business, Careers and Research Center, the Nashville Public Library includes a reading fort crafted as an homage to the city's skyline encouraging children to "climb, explore, and find the perfect reading nook."

The new wing of the Raleigh Court Branch, Roanoke, Virginia, encompasses large glass curtain walls and an adult reading room as well as a large interactive children's learning center. The Tippecanoe Branch, Milwaukee, has an outdoor garden for children's programming and makes the most of great natural light.

Openness is at the heart of these new buildings and renovations, which, one hopes, will become the pulse of their communities for years to come.

Table 1 / New Academic Buildings, Additions, and Renovations, 2016

Institution	Type	Status	Project Cost	Gross Area (Sq. Ft.)	Sq. Ft. Cost	Constr. Cost	Furniture/ Equip. Cost	Book Capacity	Architect
Bibliothèque Desjardins, Université du Québec à Trois-Rivières, Drummondville	N		$24,000,000	80,730	$185.80	$15,000,000	$180,000	10,000	Daoust Lestage Inc.
Fenwick Library, George Mason University, Fairfax, VA	A		n.a.	157,359	268.81	42,300,000	n.a.	n.a.	Shepley Bulfinch; Lukmire Partnership
De Anza College Library, Cupertino, CA	R		12,200,000	43,527	206.52	8,989,295	n.a.	n.a.	Noll & Tam Architects
Mendel Gottesman Library, Yeshiva University, New York	R		6,000,000	58,000	86.21	5,000,000	$1,000,000	400,000	ROART
Sidney E. Frank Digital Studio, Rockefeller Library, Brown University, Providence, RI	R		2,500,000	3,660	511.47	1,872,000	625,000	n.a.	Höweler & Yoon Architecture
Faculty Research Commons, D.H. Hill Library, North Carolina State University Libraries, Raleigh	R		774,347	4,430	98.68	437,150	251,115	n.a.	RND Architects
Adobe Digital Studio, R.M. Cooper Library, Clemson University, SC	R		525,000	3,750	n.a.	n.a.	n.a.	n.a.	McMillan Pazdan Smith
Digital Scholarship Laboratory, Evans Library, Florida Institute of Technology, Melbourne	R		459,663	4,427	36.41	161,171	298,493	n.a.	Florida Institute of Technology
Hawthorne-Longfellow Library, Bowdoin College, Brunswick, ME	R		247,633	2,400	n.a.	n.a.	35,187	6,800	Bowdoin Coll. Facilities Mgt.

	TYPE								Architect
Information Commons, University of South Florida Sarasota-Manatee (USFSM)	R		217,610	1,300	97.47	126,710	90,900	n.a.	Harvard Jolly Architecture; Willis A. Smith Construction
James Branch Cabell Library, Virginia Commonwealth University, Richmond	A&R	Total	51,000,000	156,097	205	32,000,000	4,897,000	n.a.	Shepley Bulfinch; Moseley Architects
	A&R	New	n.a.	n.a.	n.a.	n.a.	n.a.	n.a.	
	A&R	Renovated	n.a.	n.a.	n.a.	n.a.	n.a.	n.a.	
Mary Couts Burnett Library, Texas Christian University, Fort Worth	A&R	Total	35,520,000	78,671	305.70	24,050,323	1,752,000	51,285	Hahnfeld Hoffer Stanford; CannonDesign
	A&R	New	8,880,000	26,223	305.71	8,016,774	584,000	1,301	
	A&R	Renovated	26,640,000	52,448	305.7	16,033,549	1,168,000	49,984	
Charles E. Shain Library, Connecticut College, London	A&R	Total	9,839,200	71,968	136.72	6,429,000	n.a.	n.a.	Schwartz/Silver Architects
	A&R	New	n.a.	1,328	460.00	610,880	n.a.	n.a.	
	A&R	Renovated	n.a.	70,640	82.36	5,818,120	n.a.	861,000	

TYPE: N = New Building; A = Addition; R = Renovation; A&R = Addition & Renovation

Table 2 / New Public Library Buildings, 2016

Community	Pop. ('000)	Code	Project Cost	Const. Cost	Gross Area (Sq. Ft.)	Sq. Ft. Cost	Equip. Cost	Other Costs	Federal Funds	State Funds	Local Funds	Gift Funds	Architect
California													
Alpine	15	B	$10,200,000	n.a.	12,700	n.a.	$738,216	n.a.	0	0	$9,762,000	$438,000	Ferguson Pape; Manuel Oncina; C.W. Driver
San Jose	28	B	13,560,000	$9,060,000	16,000	$566.25	500,000	$3,000,000	0	0	13,560,000	0	IBI Group
Colorado													
Castle Pines	12	B	7,860,772	5,591,959	15,652	357.27	1,055,364	819,109	0	0	7,466,432	451,840	AndersonMasonDale
Lone Tree	12	B	14,679,448	9,484,426	24,826	382.04	2,702,874	1,092,148	0	0	13,279,448	1,400,000	AndersonMasonDale
Delaware													
Lewes	17	M	12,092,218	8,568,100	28,500	300.64	608,352	1,469,200	50,000	6,057,133	220,066	5,765,019	Becker Morgan Group
Florida													
Clearwater	27	B	6,423,511	5,283,752	22,404	235.84	420,924	718,835	0	0	6,323,511	100,000	Harvard Jolly Architecture
Georgia													
Alpharetta	79	B	16,276,000	9,970,145	25,543	390.33	1,360,000	3,945,855	0	0	15,276,000	1,000,000	Cooper Carry; Vines Architecture
Atlanta	138	B	16,179,000	8,305,549	23,606	351.84	1,105,000	5,265,763	0	0	16,179,000	0	Smith Dalia Architects
Atlanta	61	B	19,755,743	8,298,528	25,570	324.54	1,378,836	8,578,379	0	0	19,755,743	0	Collins Cooper Carusi
Atlanta	152	B	11,982,033	5,549,351	15,200	365.09	1,019,777	4,462,905	0	0	11,982,033	0	Stanley, Love-Stanley
Milton	132	B	17,708,207	8,342,820	25,000	333.71	1,236,580	7,028,807	0	0	17,708,207	0	Stevens & Wilkinson
Massachusetts													
Edgartown	4	M	10,515,739	7,772,638	14,630	531.28	327,105	2,415,996	0	5,002,129	5,200,000	313,600	Tappé Architects
Framingham	68	B	8,731,913	6,414,171	16,882	379.94	447,723	1,161,019	0	3,207,086	4,924,827	600,000	Finegold Alexander Architects
Minnesota													
Brooklyn Park	76	B	19,000,000	14,800,000	39,600	373.74	1,263,400	1,879,600	0	0	19,000,000	0	HGA Architects & Engineers
Columbia Heights	20	M	10,102,486	8,101,850	22,300	363.32	864,548	1,126,088	300,000	600,000	9,231,850	63,509	HGA Architects & Engineers
Missouri													
St. Louis	111	B	16,240,000	9,600,000	35,340	271.65	809,000	2,905,000	0	0	16,240,000	0	Christner, Inc.

Symbol Code: B=Branch Library; BS=Branch & System Headquarters; M=Main Library; MS=Main & System Headquarters; S=System Headquarters; O=combined use space; n.a.=not available

St. Louis	45	B	7,320,000	4,450,000	20,050	221.90	560,000	2,310,000	0	7,320,000	0	KAI
North Carolina												
Durham	73	B	7,238,000	6,400,000	22,000	290.91	278,000	560,000	0	7,238,000	0	Little Diversified Architectural Consulting
Ohio												
Canfield	24	B	5,220,063	4,181,458	18,513	225.86	457,228	581,377	0	5,220,063	732,943	Faniro Architects
Columbus	30	B	9,839,511	5,837,299	19,025	306.83	401,027	2,374,610	0	9,839,511	0	Moody Nolan
Dayton	54	B	12,717,000	8,710,000	30,100	289.37	1,521,000	2,263,000	0	12,717,000	0	Group 4 Architecture w/Levin Porter
Texas												
Hewitt	14	M	5,280,000	4,500,000	26,500	169.80	500,000	280,000	0	5,280,000	0	RBDR
Mont Belvieu	34	O	5,371,965	3,800,000	12,500	304.00	411,965	700,000	0	5,229,123	602,842	PBK Architects
Utah												
Kaysville	35	B	4,694,987	3,905,768	15,000	260.38	139,000	650,219	0	4,394,987	300,000	FFKR Architects
Roy	74	BS	21,220,524	16,690,600	74,614	223.69	1,999,872	1,265,973	0	21,220,524	230,235	Prescott Muir Architects
Salt Lake City	191	B	8,976,000	5,726,000	18,600	307.85	350,000	2,900,000	0	8,976,000	0	Blalock and Partners
Virginia												
Dumfries	60	B	15,335,086	11,953,855	57,815	318.81	2,247,073	1,134,158	0	16,197,020	23,500	Lukmire Partnership
Haymarket	60	B	12,171,492	8,644,409	21,734	397.74	2,282,830	1,244,253	0	13,923,944	119,169	Lukmire Partnership
Henrico	66	B	31,118,664	20,521,542	59,975	342.17	5,645,250	4,495,530	0	30,662,322	456,342	BCWH; Tappé Associates
Henrico	66	B	27,618,923	18,159,813	43,885	413.80	3,815,263	4,916,955	0	27,618,923	0	BCWH; Tappé Associates
Vinton	8	B	9,500,000	7,300,000	21,821	334.54	800,000	1,400,000	0	9,500,000	0	HBM Architects
Washington												
Bremerton	8	B	2,222,897	1,289,839	5,225	246.86	275,906	657,152	158,886	272,720	1,791,313	Rice Fergus Miller
Canada												
Summerland, BC *	15	B	4,775,000	3,000,000	8,000	375.00	175,000	750,000	0	4,700,000	75,000	Urban Arts Architecture

* Figures listed in Canadian dollars

Symbol Code: B=Branch Library; BS=Branch & System Headquarters; M=Main Library; MS=Main & System Headquarters; S=System Headquarters; O=combined use space; n.a.=not available

Table 3 / Public Library Buildings, Additions and Renovations, 2016

Community	Pop. ('000)	Code	Project Cost	Const. Cost	Gross Area (Sq. Ft.)	Sq. Ft. Cost	Equip. Cost	Other Costs	Federal Funds	State Funds	Local Funds	Gift Funds	Architect
California													
Carlsbad	111	M	$6,583,738	$3,919,000	64,000	$61.23	$900,000	$1,764,738	0	0	$6,413,863	$169,875	Group 4 Architecture
Carlsbad	111	B	5,725,000	3,910,000	24,400	160.25	707,000	1,108,000	0	0	5,091,000	634,000	Group 4 Architecture
Chula Vista	260	BS	51,284	35,040	500	70.08	7,244	9,000	0	0	41,284	10,000	Aplomb Studio (Eva Salas)
Fresno	72	B	4,473,603	1,527,406	13,969	109.34	450,000	99,990	0	0	4,473,603	0	Paul Halajian Architects
Los Alamos	2	B	191,232	153,098	1,275	120.08	27,000	11,134	0	0	0	191,232	Sollievo Architecture & Design
Poway	49	B	2,020,000	n.a.	20,000	n.a.	191,584	n.a.	1,895,000	0	0	125,000	Davy Architecture
Sacramento	121	B	653,705	479,570	9,280	51.68	94,135	80,000	0	0	653,705	0	Noll & Tam Architects
San Clemente	66	B	3,623,604	2,231,651	11,400	195.76	349,677	1,041,976	0	0	3,423,304	200,000	OC Public Works
San Lorenzo	60	B	9,425,264	6,000,000	19,500	307.69	790,085	2,635,179	0	0	9,425,264	0	Group 4 Architecture w/ Murakami/Nelson
Santa Monica	107	B	1,117,826	942,348	7,735	121.83	175,478	0	0	0	1,117,826	0	City of Santa Monica Architectural Svcs.
Woodside	6	B	3,621,000	2,800,000	4,800	583.33	321,000	500,000	0	0	3,621,000	0	Group 4 Architecture
Colorado													
Aspen	13	MS	14,333,760	10,727,455	38,774	276.67	882,692	2,723,613	0	0	1,014,716	13,319,044	MSR Design
Boulder	105	M	4,949,373	3,326,484	72,320	46	1,177,976	444,913	0	0	4,949,373	0	studiotrope Design Collective
Connecticut													
Salisbury	4	M	1,522,888	773,788	7,501	103.16	454,008	295,092	0	0	100,000	1,482,000	Poesis Design
Illinois													
Pekin	34	M	6,200,000	5,600,000	37,455	149.51	150,000	450,000	0	0	5,650,000	550,000	Dewberry
Indiana													
Indianapolis	75	B	100,000	36,000	1,800	20	42,000	22,000	0	0	100,000	0	Lohr Design
Mount Vernon	21	M	2,184,884	1,847,119	22,800	81	308,870	28,895	0	0	2,184,884	0	VPA Architecture
Kansas													
Winfield	12	M	1,401,600	1,046,199	16,915	61.85	237,262	118,139	0	0	1,101,600	300,000	Clark Enersen Partners
Kentucky													
Lexington	87	B	8,204,888	3,420,355	32,628	104.84	508,021	281,512	0	0	4,804,888	3,400,000	Pearson & Peters Architects

Symbol Code: B=Branch Library; BS=Branch & System Headquarters; M=Main Library; MS=Main & System Headquarters; S=System Headquarters; O=combined use space; n.a.=not available

Louisiana

Location													
Ball	5	B	1,002,200	785,500	6,800	115.51	50,500	166,200	0	1,002,200	0	0	Alliance Design Group
Maryland													
Hereford	28	B	3,300,000	2,500,000	15,000	166.67	400,000	400,000	0	0	3,300,000	0	Manns Woodward Studios
Minnesota													
Golden Valley	20	B	844,235	844,235	15,455	54.63	325,000	119,700	0	0	1,288,935	0	Paul Gates Architect
Lake City	8	M	2,063,000	1,423,990	6,800	209.41	207,000	432,010	0	0	1,760,000	303,000	MSR Design
Luverne	9	M	225,000	175,000	n.a.	n.a.	50,000	0	0	0	225,000	0	Honken Construction
Marshall	22	M	2,121,008	1,683,542	6,049	278.32	123,026	314,440	0	0	207,415	1,913,593	TSP
Northfield	26	M	3,112,500	2,619,500	15,334	170.83	250,000	243,000	0	0	1,766,603	1,345,897	RoehrSchmitt; Rothholz Architecture
Rogers	11	B	386,500	230,000	4,168	55.18	100,000	56,500	0	0	386,500	0	Paul Gates Architect
Saint Paul	295	MS	1,396,614	932,618	12,074	77.24	301,538	162,458	0	0	0	1,396,614	Lawal Scott Erickson Architects
Wayzata	4	B	363,323	158,000	9,665	16.34	154,000	51,323	0	0	363,323	0	Paul Gates Architect
Missouri													
Florissant	109	B	2,865,000	1,872,400	14,520	128.95	365,000	627,600	0	0	2,865,000	0	Bond Architects
Kansas City	218	BS	481,976	206,899	7,600	27.22	240,619	34,458	0	0	231,976	250,000	Hammer Out Design
St. Ann	29	B	4,195,000	2,784,000	19,740	141.03	408,000	1,003,000	0	0	4,195,000	0	Bond Architects
St. Louis	26	B	3,228,000	2,256,000	15,180	148.62	328,000	644,000	0	0	3,228,000	0	Bond Architects
St. Louis	39	B	3,569,000	2,541,000	14,920	170.31	359,000	669,000	0	0	3,569,000	0	Bond Architects
Montana													
Bigfork	6	B	47,564	11,710	1,440	8.13	17,109	18,745	0	0	23,500	24,064	CTA Architects
New Jersey													
Long Branch	30	M	6,000	0	360	0	6,000	0	0	0	6,000	0	none
Wildwood Crest	83	B	6,510,000	5,000,000	12,000	416.67	300,000	210,000	0	0	6,510,000	0	BKP Architects
New York													
Hudson	11	M	2,790,000	2,220,000	120,000	185	190,000	380,000	0	182,000	200,000	2,408,000	Kimberly Bolan; Vincent Benic
Middle Island	65	M	20,450,175	14,545,870	45,360	320.68	1,446,936	4,457,369	0	602,838	19,847,337	0	Peter Gisolfi Associates
Ohio													
Bellevue	8	M	4,120,133	3,382,445	11,550	292.85	320,634	417,054	0	0	4,120,133	0	HBM Architects
Columbus	873	M	39,715,228	26,780,971	255,400	104.86	1,598,915	10,035,917	0	0	39,715,228	0	Schooley Caldwell
Dayton	n.a.	S	9,345,000	6,345,000	39,400	161.04	747,000	1,381,000	0	0	9,345,000	0	Group 4 Architecture w/Levin Porter Architects

Symbol Code: B=Branch Library; BS=Branch & System Headquarters; M=Main Library; MS=Main & System Headquarters; S=System Headquarters; O=combined use space; n.a.=not available

Table 3 / Public Library Buildings, Additions and Renovations, 2016 *(cont.)*

Community	Pop. ('000)	Code	Project Cost	Const. Cost	Gross Area (Sq. Ft.)	Sq. Ft. Cost	Equip. Cost	Other Costs	Federal Funds	State Funds	Local Funds	Gift Funds	Architect
Miamisburg	25	B	5,945,000	3,781,000	18,200	207.75	858,000	1,157,000	0	0	5,945,000	0	Group 4 Architecture w/ Ruetschle Architects
Oregon	24	B	4,106,831	3,450,000	18,430	187.19	211,831	445,000	0	0	4,106,831	0	HBM Architects
Pennsylvania													
Ardmore	10	B	2,350,994	1,560,883	7,530	207.29	136,472	653,639	0	0	2,168,494	182,500	VITETTA
Pittsburgh	12	B	3,250,000	2,490,000	9,764	255.02	220,000	540,000	0	500,000	100,000	2,650,000	GBBN/EDGE Studio
Scranton	96	M	1,180,112	1,044,865	16,503	63.31	0	135,247	0	500,000	680,112	0	Quad Three Group
Wynnewood	8	B	2,819,980	1,761,073	6,130	287.29	240,902	818,005	0	0	2,790,048	29,932	VITETTA
South Carolina													
Columbia	399	MS	3,820,990	2,727,024	49,349	55.26	624,173	469,793	0	0	3,820,990	0	Boudreaux Group
Tennessee													
Nashville	668	M	1,444,166	1,065,100	18,900	56.35	277,989	101,077	0	0	1,341,733	102,433	EOA Architects
Sevierville	95	MS	579,300	495,500	8,000	61.94	83,800	0	0	0	0	579,300	BarberMcMurry Architects
Texas													
Austin	49	B	1,160,000	550,000	8,266	66.54	185,000	425,000	0	0	1,160,000	0	Stanley Studio
Austin	27	MS	2,149,899	1,810,882	15,821	114.46	162,017	177,000	0	0	2,149,899	0	Studio 8 Architects
Dallas	61	B	5,607,043	4,724,101	19,707	239.72	340,686	542,256	0	0	5,607,043	0	PGAL
Vermont													
Waterbury	5	M	3,064,000	2,089,000	7,656	272.86	424,000	551,000	528,000	0	1,645,000	891,000	Vermont Integrated Architecture
Virginia													
Roanoke	99	B	4,120,133	3,382,445	11,550	292.85	320,634	417,054	0	0	4,070,133	50,000	HBM Architects
Washington													
Camano Island	13	B	2,215,844	1,023,691	4,900	208.92	103,629	461,685	0	0	2,215,844	0	Designs Northwest; Stig Carlson Architecture
Wisconsin													
Kenosha	10	B	83,224	11,790	3,756	3.14	71,434	0	0	0	4,315	78,909	none
Milwaukee	41	B	4,483,700	3,382,700	16,900	200.16	378,800	722,200	0	0	4,433,700	50,000	Engberg Anderson Architects

Symbol Code: B=Branch Library; BS=Branch & System Headquarters; M=Main Library; MS=Main & System Headquarters; S=System Headquarters; O=combined use space; n.a.=not available

Table 4 / Six-Year Cost Summary

	Fiscal 2011	Fiscal 2012	Fiscal 2013	Fiscal 2014	Fiscal 2015	Fiscal 2016
Number of new buildings	62	34	27	29	38	33
Number of ARRs	89	73	47	55	54	59
Sq. ft. new buildings	1,555,598	898,865	470,167	717,973	896,195	831,110
Sq. ft. ARRs	1,672,664	1,375,307	715,380	1,164,535	1,222,795	1,297,229
New Buildings						
Construction cost	$454,425,651	$263,313,088	$139,136,298	$212,257,074	$274,900,907	$257,213,872
Equipment cost	47,836,977	30,533,085	16,184,831	34,002,671	26,895,130	37,522,113
Site cost	35,104,201	14,215,747	28,272,719	18,929,131	12,031,896	19,242,482
Other cost	113,525,121	53,113,752	29,983,512	49,676,815	68,193,630	73,601,931
Total—Project cost	650,871,920	361,175,672	212,079,360	314,866,191	360,746,279	397,152,182
ARRs—Project cost	447,583,852	241,643,154	145,668,398	260,983,928	311,990,635	237,347,021
New & ARR Project cost	$1,098,455,772	$602,818,826	$357,747,758	$575,850,119	$672,736,914	$634,499,203

Symbol Code: ARR—Additions, Renovations, and Remodels

Table 5 / Funding Sources

	Fiscal 2011	Fiscal 2012	Fiscal 2013	Fiscal 2014	Fiscal 2015	Fiscal 2016
Federal, new buildings	$5,854,589	$38,465,599	$1,000,000	$25,617,538	$475,000	$350,000
Federal, ARRs	9,270,750	18,882,075	1,684,211	6,239,463	1,500,000	2,423,000
Federal, total	$15,125,339	$57,347,674	$2,684,211	$31,857,001	$1,975,000	2,773,000
State, new buildings	$43,548,440	$19,558,708	$9,570,111	$64,563,247	$15,169,766	15,025,234
State, ARRs	33,147,756	9,286,208	2,017,590	19,563,872	5,251,244	2,787,038
State, total	$76,696,196	$28,844,916	$11,587,701	$84,127,119	$20,421,010	17,812,272
Local, new buildings	$567,608,480	$284,164,989	$192,466,192	$215,147,978	$331,311,400	371,719,254
Local, ARRs	348,642,090	184,662,609	133,692,708	188,446,449	244,614,937	199,559,402
Local, total	$916,250,570	468,827,598	326,158,900	403,594,427	575,926,337	571,278,656
Gift, new buildings	$37,374,332	$19,573,952	$12,366,431	$13,312,404	$24,430,676	14,388,312
Gift, ARRs	58,733,738	29,367,511	8,996,727	50,361,901	63,353,240	32,636,393
Gift, total	$96,108,070	$48,941,463	$21,363,158	$63,674,305	$87,783,916	47,024,705
Total—Funds Used	$1,104,180,175	$603,961,651	$361,793,970	$583,252,852	$686,106,263	$638,888,633

Symbol Code: ARR—Additions, Renovations, and Remodels

Book Trade Research and Statistics

Prices of U.S. and Foreign Published Materials

Narda Tafuri

Editor, ALA ALCTS Library Materials Price Index Editorial Board

The Library Materials Price Index (LMPI) Editorial Board of the American Library Association's Association for Library Collections and Technical Services' Publications Committee continues to monitor prices for a range of library materials from sources within North America and from other key publishing centers around the world.

The U.S. Consumer Price Index (CPI) increased by 2.1 percent in 2016, the largest increase since 2011. CPI figures are obtained from the Bureau of Labor Statistics Web site at http://www.bls.gov/.

The U.S. Periodical Price Index (USPPI) (Table 1) reestablished by Stephen Bosch in 2014, continues in this year's article using data provided by EBSCO Information Services. Readers are reminded that the new USPPI is based on a mix of both print and online pricing, which is a more accurate representation of an average library's journal collection.

The North American Academic Books Price Indexes (Tables 4, 4A, and 4B) have changed from previous versions due to changes in how the raw data are supplied. Data for these indexes is supplied by ProQuest Books (formerly Coutts) and GOBI Library Solutions (formerly YBP Library Services).

All other indexes continue unchanged in source and format from last year's article.

U.S. Published Materials

Tables 1 through 7B indicate average prices and price indexes for library materials published primarily in the United States. These indexes are U.S. Periodicals (Table 1), Legal Serials Services (Table 2), U.S. Hardcover Books (Table 3), North American Academic Books (Table 4), North American Academic E-Books (Table 4A), North American Academic Textbooks (Table 4B), U.S. College Books (Table 5), U.S. Mass Market Paperback Books (Table 6), U.S. Paperbacks (Excluding Mass Market) (Table 7), U.S. Audiobooks (Table 7A), and U.S. E-Books (Table 7B).

Periodical and Serials Prices

The U.S. Periodical Price Index (USPPI) (Table 1) was reestablished by Stephen Bosch in 2014 and is updated for 2017 using data supplied by EBSCO Information

Index	Percent Change				
	2012	2013	2014	2015	2016
CPI	1.7	1.5	0.8	0.7	2.1
Periodicals	5.9	6.1	6.1	6.0	7.1
Legal serials services	6.1	10.5	11.3	13.9	9.0
*Hardcover books	5.18	-2.57	6.45	0.44	-1.41
+Academic books	n.a.	n.a.	-2.2	1.3	n.a.
+Academic e-books	n.a.	n.a.	-8.3	-4.3	n.a.
+Textbooks	n.a.	n.a.	-7.2	10.5	n.a.
College books	2.15	4.21	-1.41	-0.59	3.39
*Mass market paperbacks	1.00	-0.28	0.57	-0.14	2.12
*Trade paperbacks	31.96	-12.31	5.04	-2.72	8.73
*Audiobooks	-10.96	-4.76	0.18	-15.21	-20.50
*U.S. e-books	-6.37	22.03	-9.12	-17.19	7.21
++Serials	n.a.	7.2	6.7	5.8	6.0
++Online Serials	n.a.	6.0	7.2	6.4	6.2
British academic books	10.81	1.67	1.0	7.1	9.9

n.a. = not available
* = figures revised based on BISAC categories
+Beginning with 2009, new data source
++Data set changes each year.

Services. This report includes 2013–2017 data indexed to the base year of 2010. The title list used in the new Table 1 differs from previous versions, so a new base year is appropriate. Table 1 is derived from a selected set of titles that, as much as possible will remain as the sample base for future comparisons. The data in Table 1 are created from a print preferred data pull, but about half the data in the index ended up being online pricing so that the data provide a strong mix of both print and online pricing, characteristic of a current academic library's serials collection. The subscription prices used are publishers' list prices, excluding publisher discount or vendor service charges. The pricing data for 2010–2014 are based on a single report that pulled pricing information for a static set of titles for the five-year period. The pricing data for 2015–2017 are based on that same sampling of titles, but is not an exact match due to changes that occur with serial titles. Some titles fell off the list due to pricing not being available, while other titles on the list did have pricing available that did not have pricing available in 2014. The situation continues for 2017 as the exact same sample title list was used as the basis for the data pull, but there are small variations in the titles that had pricing available.

The USPPI in 2017 treats a little more than 5,900 titles in comparison with the original title list, which covered only about 3,700 titles. The previous versions of the USPPI treated Russian translations as a separate category. Russian translations are no longer a focus of this index and are not tracked as a category. These were once seen as a major cost factor, but this is no longer the case and therefore their inclusion in or exclusion from the index no longer makes sense. There are Russian translation titles in the index but they are not reported separately.

The main barrier to reestablishing this index was the difficulty of maintaining the title list and obtaining standard retail pricing for titles on the list. Changes in serials titles due to ceased publication, movement to open access, mergers, combining titles in packages, moving to direct orders, and publication delays are a few of the situations that can affect compilers' ability to obtain current pricing information. The new index retained that part of the title list from the previous index that remained viable and added new titles to that list based on data from EBSCO on the most frequently ordered serials in their system. From that list of serials, titles were selected for the new index to ensure that the distribution by subject was similar to the distribution in the original index. There are more titles in the selected title set than the number of titles that produced prices over the past six years. This should allow the current index to be sustainable into the future as titles fall off the list and pricing becomes available for titles that may have been delayed, or are no longer in memberships, etc.

The first five years of data showed consistent price changes across subject areas because the pricing data took a historical look at the prices of the exact same set of journals. The data for 2015, 2016, and 2017 are based on the same sample list but are not the exact same list of titles as the data for 2010–2014, due to the issues mentioned above that can impact pricing availability. Across subject areas, the changes in price were more volatile this year but the overall 6 percent increase mirrors increases seen in other pricing studies, which nearly all show a 6 percent increase. Also at the subject level the sample sizes are smaller so a few changes can cause a large swing in the overall price for that area. A good example of this is food science. Looking at the raw data, 80 percent of the overall costs in food science are from only eight journals and those titles all showed very high increases in prices for 2017. So a small number of titles had a large impact due to the overall small sample size.

Direct comparisons between Table 1 and Table 8 at the subject level should be avoided. While both tables show the overall rate of increase in serial prices to be around 6 percent; there is little else that makes them statistically comparable. Table 8 has slightly higher overall average prices in most areas, and this is due to the survey's largest sets of data coming from the Clarivate Analytics (formerly ISI) Citation Indexes and Scopus which include higher impact—and consequently more expensive—journals. Table 1 is a broader mix of journals that attempts to reflect the journal collections in an average library so the mix of journals contains more trade and popular titles than would be found in the Clarivate Analytics indexes or Scopus. Trade and popular journals tend to be cheaper, with lower average prices. Differences in data sets will yield different results.

The most important trend seen in this data (Table 1) is that increases in prices have remained fairly constant since the economic recovery began in 2010. Price increases have hovered around 6 percent annually during that time. Science does not dominate the list of subjects with the largest price increases. The subject areas that displayed the largest increases were quite varied: food science, geography, anthropology, general science, zoology, political science, and library science. Average prices for journals in the science and technology areas are still far higher than in other areas, and that trend continues, with the average cost of chemistry journals being $4,685 and of physics journals being $3,906.

(text continues on page 276)

Table 1 / U.S. Periodicals: Average Prices and Price Indexes, 2013–2017

Index Base: 2010 = 100

Subject	LC Class	Titles	2010 Average Price	2013 Average Price	2014 Average Price	2015 Average Price	2016 Average Price	2017 Average Price	Price Increase 2016–2017	Price Index (Base = 2010)
Agriculture	S	246	$579.48	$687.22	$726.67	$780.01	$978.61	$956.80	-2.2 %	165.1
Anthropology	GN	50	373.64	430.83	453.36	428.52	426.99	525.98	23.2	140.8
Arts and architecture	N	115	112.39	125.24	130.70	180.35	234.50	195.47	-16.6	173.9
Astronomy	QB	28	1,793.08	2,049.88	2,186.19	2,083.50	2,602.51	2,393.22	-8.0	133.5
Biology	QH	330	2,053.06	2,405.68	2,535.65	2,727.29	2,655.14	3,016.39	13.6	146.9
Botany	QK	55	1,361.09	1,583.36	1,667.34	1,646.31	1,926.69	1,852.98	-3.8	136.1
Business and economics	HA-HJ	492	351.29	410.55	434.12	480.98	546.45	553.47	1.3	157.6
Chemistry	QD	124	3,396.26	4,024.45	4,244.38	4,335.51	4,465.42	4,685.46	4.9	138.0
Education	L	229	354.92	409.63	433.05	499.55	585.29	609.83	4.2	171.8
Engineering	T	542	1,244.39	1,486.54	1,584.81	1,692.44	1,716.47	1,897.32	10.5	152.5
Food science	TX	51	356.17	416.09	439.51	617.45	520.09	767.91	47.6	215.6
General science	Q	97	998.51	1,153.60	1,218.88	1,401.48	1,322.20	1,617.12	22.3	162.0
General works	A	131	85.84	95.41	99.14	106.87	165.98	125.62	-24.3	146.3
Geography	G-GF	84	670.60	783.49	836.61	872.34	806.55	1,000.77	24.1	149.2

Subject	LC class	Titles							%	Index
Geology	QE	74	1,368.79	1,603.07	1,699.34	1,648.20	1,707.46	1,954.00	14.4	142.8
Heath sciences	R	803	1,009.55	1,224.65	1,309.43	1,402.65	1,557.18	1,596.42	2.5	158.1
History	C,D,E,F	312	202.39	231.75	245.88	277.95	330.37	334.47	1.2	165.3
Language and literature	P	277	168.12	194.56	205.49	232.29	258.50	256.95	-0.6	152.8
Law	K	251	214.01	239.11	251.93	297.45	355.43	326.59	-8.1	152.6
Library science	Z	107	290.02	336.34	355.38	376.47	379.89	441.07	16.1	152.1
Math and computer science	QA	329	1,242.13	1,406.66	1,480.16	1,623.12	1,559.12	1,785.80	14.5	143.8
Military and naval science	U,V	28	239.90	301.03	288.80	276.33	458.94	343.57	-25.1	143.2
Music	M	49	82.18	92.24	95.74	151.67	212.73	164.13	-22.8	199.7
Philosophy and religion	B-BD, BH-BX	212	232.37	266.63	281.45	316.77	362.03	359.03	-0.8	154.5
Physics	QC	148	2,845.54	3,282.05	3,499.54	3,538.93	3,537.87	3,905.91	10.4	137.3
Political science	J	103	312.76	362.82	382.91	562.63	563.12	659.97	17.2	211.0
Psychology	BF	111	648.21	767.19	828.57	970.19	1,049.83	1,114.23	6.1	171.9
Recreation	GV	86	69.79	84.44	90.20	122.06	176.76	147.49	-16.6	211.3
Social sciences	H	41	351.40	410.60	435.17	645.60	753.59	709.57	-5.8	201.9
Sociology	HM-HX	240	482.59	567.96	608.13	717.56	760.32	836.08	10.0	173.2
Technology	TA-TT	136	535.73	624.46	679.00	723.65	775.03	843.36	8.8	157.4
Zoology	QL	117	1,454.26	1,675.90	1,762.83	1,816.13	1,655.65	1,947.87	17.7	133.9
Total		5,998	$843.46	$991.39	$1,051.73	$1,114.32	$1,193.10	$1,265.92	6.1 %	150.1

Compiled by Stephen Bosch, University of Arizona, based on subscription information supplied by EBSCO Information Services.

(continued from page 273)
In this price index, like similar price indexes, the data is less accurate at describing price changes the smaller the sample becomes. For that reason, drawing conclusions about price changes in subject areas with a limited number of titles is less accurate than for large areas or the broader price index. Price changes are far more volatile where smaller data sets are used. For example, all of the subjects listed above as having higher than average price increases have a small sample base. To conclude that all journals in the food science area will increase 47 percent this year is incorrect. If a specific inflation figure for food science is needed, it would be better to look at an average over the period or the overall number for the price study (6.1 percent) than to use the actual numbers year-by-year. The variation in pricing is too volatile in smaller sample sizes to be comparable on a year-to-year basis. In a small sample size the change in just one or two titles could easily have a large impact on the overall price for an area.

More extensive reports from the periodical price index have been published annually in the April 15 issue of Library Journal through 1992, in the May issue of American Libraries from 1993 to 2002, and in the October 2003 issue of Library Resources and Technical Services.

The Legal Serials Services Index (Table 2) has been compiled by Ajaye Bloomstone using data collected from a number of different legal serials vendors. The base year for this index is 2009. This index presents price data covering the years 2009 through 2017.

Table 2 / Legal Serials Services: Average Prices and Price Indexes, 2009–2017
Index Base: 2009 = 100

Year	Number of Titles	Average Price	Percent Change	Index
2009	217	$1,658.20	n.a.	100.0
2010	217	1,716.30	3.5%	103.5
2011	217	1,905.20	11.0	114.9
2012	217	2,020.83	6.1	124.1
2013	217	2,233.00	10.5	134.7
2014	217	2,486.04	11.3	149.9
2015	217	2,831.00	13.9	170.7
2016	217	3,085.34	9.0	186.1
2017	217	3,506.20	13.6	210.5

Vendors were asked again to provide cost data on particular titles with the assumption that the title/set has been held by a large academic research law library, and the cost recorded in the index is that for the upkeep of the title in question, not the cost incurred in purchasing a new set. A nuance of legal publishing is that for some of the larger legal publishers, hard prices for a calendar year are not set at the beginning of that year but rather halfway through, so in some cases only price estimates may be available for this article. In addition to titles issued on a regular basis (journals, law reviews, etc.), legal serial services can be updated as regular/irregular updates ("releases") throughout the year, new "editions" made available on an annual or so basis, or as added/revised volumes. If a title is updated irregularly, the price for a title may increase or decrease from one year to the next, depending on the publisher's plans for keeping a title current. It should be noted that although legal serials in print format continue to be produced, titles seem to be migrating, albeit slowly, to an electronic-only format. There seems to be a trend for titles purchased in print format to come with an electronic component for which the purchasing library has no choice but to accept both formats although the print format is the one of primary interest to the purchasing library.

Some prices were provided for several titles with the caveat "no longer available for new sales." This statement would lead one to believe that although the publication may not totally be phased out, either the title might soon no longer be available as a print product, or it may cease publication entirely, in any format.

Book Prices

Tables 3 (hardcover books), 6 (mass market paperbacks), 7 (other—trade—paperbacks), 7A (audiobooks), and table 7B (e-books), prepared by Narda Tafuri, are derived from data provided by book wholesaler Baker & Taylor. Figures for 2015 are revised to reflect late updates to the Baker & Taylor database (publishers were still adding 2015 titles in early 2016); the 2016 figures given here may be similarly revised in next year's tables and should be considered preliminary. These five tables use the Book Industry Study Group's BISAC categories. The BISAC juvenile category (fiction and nonfiction) has been divided into children's and young adult. For more information on the BISAC categories, visit http://www.bisg.org.

Average book prices overall declined slightly in 2016. List prices for hardcovers overall (Table 3) fell by 1.41 percent. Mass market paperback prices (Table 6) showed an increase of 2.12 percent and trade paperbacks (Table 7) showed a healthy increase of 8.73 percent. Audiobook prices (Table 7A) have been falling since 2009, but saw the steepest decline in five years at 20.50 percent. E-book prices showed a modest increase of 7.21 percent.

The North American Academic Books Price Indexes (Tables 4, 4A, and 4B) are prepared by Stephen Bosch. The current version of North American Academic Books: Average Prices and Price Indexes 2013–2015 (Table 4) again has evolved from previous versions due to changes in how the delivery of the raw data. Direct comparisons with earlier published versions will be difficult since the numbers of titles and average prices have changed, especially those versions published prior to 2009. Data for the current indexes is supplied by ProQuest Books (formerly Coutts) and by GOBI Library Solutions (formerly YBP Library Services). Over the course of time, data suppliers and the data they can supply have changed. When compared with earlier versions, the North American Academic Books Price Index (NAABPI) now contains many more titles in the source data, which has affected the index considerably. The reason for this is ProQuest Books (Coutts) treats far more titles in their approval programs than the former Blackwell Book Services. For indexes published prior to 2009, Blackwell was a supplier of data for the index. YBP purchased Blackwell in 2009 and the vendor data used to create the index changed at that time. After 2009 the data came from Ingram (Coutts) and YBP; prior to 2009 the data came from Blackwell and YBP. Recent staffing

(text continues on page 286)

Table 3 / Hardcover Books: Average Prices and Price Indexes, 2013–2016

Index Base: 2005 = 100

BISAC Category	2005 Average Prices	2013 Final Volumes	2013 Final Average Prices	2013 Final Index	2014 Final Volumes	2014 Final Average Prices	2014 Final Index	2015 Final Volumes	2015 Final Average Prices	2015 Final Index	2016 Preliminary Volumes	2016 Preliminary Average Prices	2016 Preliminary Index
Antiques and collectibles	$71.07	137	$70.41	99.1	146	$67.04	94.3	136	$96.65	136.0	138	$80.29	113.0
Architecture	66.99	879	88.92	132.7	799	89.48	133.6	967	99.89	149.1	947	103.84	155.0
Art	62.33	2,042	71.34	114.5	1,896	81.03	130.0	1,971	74.12	118.9	2,088	75.70	121.5
Bibles	48.05	197	37.43	77.9	137	33.71	70.2	168	36.10	75.1	206	41.05	85.4
Biography and autobiography	46.20	1,939	44.12	95.5	1,779	48.33	104.6	1,747	47.39	102.6	1,802	49.68	107.5
Body, mind and spirit	26.76	237	31.99	119.5	158	46.64	174.3	156	30.29	113.2	159	28.26	105.6
Business and economics	120.56	4,386	150.18	124.6	4,370	145.78	120.9	4,775	152.81	126.7	4,948	159.32	132.1
Children	23.14	12,179	23.78	102.8	12,763	23.99	103.7	13,136	24.74	106.9	14,765	25.32	109.4
Comics and graphic novels	32.75	639	37.53	114.6	664	40.31	123.1	685	37.81	115.5	648	39.52	120.7
Computers	113.07	880	139.41	123.3	901	159.86	141.4	990	150.02	132.7	1,084	146.63	129.7
Cooking	28.68	1,215	29.54	103.0	1,244	28.93	100.9	1,256	28.63	99.8	1,200	29.33	102.3
Crafts and hobbies	28.82	195	29.10	101.0	204	28.76	99.8	170	28.90	100.3	154	31.80	110.3
Design	59.41	399	62.97	106.0	394	67.56	113.7	459	66.07	111.2	438	71.74	120.8
Drama	60.81	76	74.53	122.6	81	81.21	133.5	56	84.48	138.9	105	91.90	151.1
Education	95.10	1,747	118.72	124.8	1,930	122.49	128.8	2,235	125.09	131.5	2,624	134.45	141.4
Family and relationships	25.37	265	36.53	144.0	209	45.46	179.2	210	59.13	233.1	189	54.86	216.2
Fiction	28.37	5,155	30.29	106.8	4,625	30.05	105.9	4,455	29.80	105.0	4,642	29.80	105.0
Foreign language study	116.89	270	115.33	98.7	220	115.88	99.1	289	152.19	130.2	225	116.60	99.8
Games	32.07	111	40.05	124.9	95	39.54	123.3	117	38.21	119.2	166	34.94	108.9
Gardening	38.20	115	37.42	98.0	97	30.64	80.2	123	37.83	99.0	102	32.97	86.3
Health and fitness	54.05	378	64.67	119.6	353	58.45	108.1	408	92.58	171.3	350	72.94	134.9
History	88.17	5,030	86.61	98.2	5,489	94.66	107.4	5,792	93.24	105.7	6,279	102.06	115.8
House and home	31.51	108	35.83	113.7	91	33.66	106.8	109	35.71	113.3	90	36.27	115.1
Humor	19.00	246	19.94	104.9	288	23.74	125.0	295	24.26	127.7	286	21.59	113.6

Language arts and disciplines	120.71	1,253	141.23	117.0	1,302	147.81	122.4	1,585	146.32	121.2	1,566	144.44	119.7
Law	155.28	1,966	178.70	115.1	2,105	178.45	114.9	2,248	178.28	114.8	2,453	184.68	118.9
Literary collections	74.92	282	90.16	120.3	271	100.18	133.7	213	113.14	151.0	240	93.22	124.4
Literary criticism	123.84	1,990	121.24	97.9	2,284	126.91	102.5	2,328	123.15	99.4	2,943	123.47	99.7
Mathematics	144.88	910	133.13	91.9	963	141.42	97.6	1,031	158.84	109.6	1,097	137.31	94.8
Medical	156.54	3,443	185.17	118.3	3,488	204.11	130.4	4,119	185.02	118.2	3,247	174.98	111.8
Music	77.63	534	89.37	115.1	540	91.28	117.6	569	95.23	122.7	658	96.93	124.9
Nature	67.75	470	84.27	124.4	420	90.35	133.4	467	90.78	134.0	475	98.65	145.6
Performing arts	71.74	583	94.64	131.9	684	94.85	132.2	813	98.38	137.1	854	99.39	138.5
Pets	25.45	107	25.64	100.7	107	24.44	96.0	88	24.97	98.1	110	22.64	89.0
Philosophy	127.22	1,291	105.67	83.1	1,406	109.89	86.4	1,532	110.15	86.6	1,657	119.98	94.3
Photography	56.77	801	93.22	164.2	841	66.87	117.8	913	68.32	120.3	856	69.87	123.1
Poetry	36.58	420	33.92	92.7	352	34.64	94.7	280	46.85	128.1	432	55.21	150.9
Political science	103.39	2,608	113.25	109.5	3,036	116.68	112.9	3,139	119.01	115.1	3,477	115.17	111.4
Psychology	93.85	1,171	131.91	140.6	1,193	152.10	162.1	1,420	151.62	161.6	1,418	148.16	157.9
Reference	202.23	409	356.07	176.1	400	320.62	158.5	359	393.07	194.4	349	330.24	163.3
Religion	62.29	2,804	77.10	123.8	2,538	80.02	128.5	2,517	87.31	140.2	2,825	81.57	130.9
Science	203.44	3,325	194.94	95.8	3,536	199.58	98.1	4,251	203.05	99.8	4,024	203.51	100.0
Self-help	22.43	377	28.15	125.5	282	25.13	112.0	304	27.73	123.6	280	24.44	109.0
Social science	96.17	3,335	115.72	120.3	3,328	141.10	146.7	3,829	135.13	140.5	4,161	130.29	135.5
Sports and recreation	38.77	690	47.29	122.0	621	60.84	156.9	616	52.99	136.7	605	55.43	143.0
Study aids	105.28	14	116.17	110.3	19	92.75	88.1	15	138.63	131.7	17	98.07	93.2
Technology and engineering	187.80	2,540	172.73	92.0	2,567	189.95	101.1	3,416	168.57	89.8	3,753	177.66	94.6
Transportation	68.68	316	71.76	104.5	248	85.61	124.6	293	86.15	125.4	282	61.48	89.5
Travel	37.11	205	41.30	111.3	181	38.16	102.8	208	34.31	92.4	212	40.36	108.8
True crime	29.28	87	28.20	96.3	78	28.83	98.5	67	42.26	144.3	89	35.51	121.3
Young adult	50.17	1,965	30.98	61.8	2,169	33.93	67.6	2,056	33.47	66.7	2,290	37.83	75.4
Totals	$80.36	72,721	$92.56	115.2	73,892	$98.53	122.6	79,381	$101.62	126.5	84,005	$100.19	124.7

Compiled by Narda Tafuri, University of Scranton, from data supplied by Baker & Taylor.

Table 4 / North American Academic Books: Average Prices and Price Indexes 2013–2015

Index Base: 1989 = 100

Subject Area	LC Class	1989		2013		2014		2015			
		No. of Titles	Average Price	No. of Titles	Average Price	No. of Titles	Average Price	No. of Titles	Average Price	% Change 2014–2015	Index
Agriculture	S	897	$45.13	1,359	$96.55	1,429	$105.24	1,883	$112.73	7.1 %	249.8
Anthropology	GN	406	32.81	580	97.64	626	88.37	855	90.60	2.5	276.1
Botany	QK	251	69.02	308	154.52	384	133.44	475	134.96	1.1	195.5
Business and economics	H	5,979	41.67	11,227	106.47	13,167	103.40	15,128	106.94	3.4	256.6
Chemistry	QD	577	110.61	747	223.64	796	197.77	1,037	228.56	15.6	206.6
Education	L	1,685	29.61	4,568	90.91	5,887	87.12	6,443	94.47	8.5	319.1
Engineering and technology	T	4,569	64.94	8,451	138.39	9,445	144.17	11,503	137.85	-4.4	212.3
Fine and applied arts	M-N	3,040	40.72	7,159	68.24	7,561	66.92	8,592	67.71	1.2	166.3
General works	A	333	134.65	151	109.21	209	82.83	227	90.60	9.4	67.3
Geography	G	396	47.34	1,169	112.45	1,421	112.30	1,772	116.18	3.5	245.4
Geology	QE	303	63.49	320	161.92	337	130.35	426	120.64	-7.4	190.0
History	C-D-E-F	5,549	31.34	10,293	75.82	12,375	70.61	15,412	70.43	-0.3	224.7
Home economics	TX	535	27.10	1,057	54.97	780	61.55	909	62.05	0.8	229.0

Subject	LC								%	Index
Industrial arts	TT	175	23.89	361	42.97	314	66.17	332	65.67	-0.7	274.9
Law	K	1,252	51.10	5,749	129.66	5,844	129.03	6,956	125.55	-2.5	246.1
Library and information science	Z	857	44.51	877	100.59	1,030	101.99	1,131	106.76	4.7	239.8
Literature and language	P	10,812	24.99	23,176	59.32	27,054	57.70	32,304	55.87	-3.2	223.6
Mathematics and computer science	QA	2,707	44.68	4,480	109.37	4,788	104.21	6,195	100.60	-3.5	225.2
Medicine	R	5,028	58.38	8,704	120.76	10,009	124.46	13,079	132.72	6.6	227.3
Military and naval science	U-V	715	33.57	925	80.13	1,108	73.18	1,349	73.34	0.2	218.5
Philosophy and religion	B	3,518	29.06	8,376	88.88	9,390	80.69	12,035	81.53	1.0	280.6
Physical education and recreation	GV	814	20.38	2,170	64.85	2,355	64.96	2,926	64.51	-0.7	316.5
Physics and astronomy	QB	1,219	64.59	1,764	126.46	1,886	130.83	2,413	136.27	4.2	211.0
Political science	J	1,650	36.76	3,712	103.06	4,551	98.76	5,348	105.17	6.5	286.1
Psychology	BF	890	31.97	1,980	89.42	2,098	96.20	2,770	94.97	-1.3	297.1
Science (general)	Q	433	56.10	594	122.19	823	115.18	994	122.46	6.3	218.3
Sociology	HM	2,742	29.36	7,247	94.95	9,009	93.72	10,704	94.13	0.4	320.6
Zoology	QH,L,P,R	1,967	71.28	3,148	142.10	3,219	141.85	4,219	135.38	-4.6	189.9
Average for all subjects		59,299	$41.69	120,652	$94.64	137,895	$92.61	167,417	$93.83	1.3 %	225.0

Compiled by Stephen Bosch, University of Arizona from electronic data provided by ProQuest Books (formerly Coutts), and GOBI Library Solutions (formerly YBP). The data represents all titles (includes hardcover, trade & paperback books, as well as annuals) treated for all approval plan customers serviced by the vendors.years listed. This table covers titles published or distributed in the United States and Canada during the calendar years listed. This index does include paperback editions and electronic books. The inclusion of these items does impact pricing in the index.

Table 4A / North American Academic E-Books: Average Prices and Price Indexes 2013–2015

Index Base: 2007 = 100

| Subject Area | LC Class | 2007 | | 2013 | | 2014 | | 2015 | | | |
		No. of Titles	Average Price	No. of Titles	Average Price	No. of Titles	Average Price	No. of Titles	Average Price	% Change 2014–2015	Index
Agriculture	S	894	$128.59	730	$133.30	779	$139.89	752	$141.61	1.2 %	110.1
Anthropology	GN	382	105.28	317	117.22	329	106.44	344	104.38	-1.9	99.1
Botany	QK	287	168.18	197	167.96	232	173.90	193	153.67	-11.6	91.4
Business and economics	H	9,807	97.25	6,684	122.64	7,839	115.62	6,771	115.18	-0.4	118.4
Chemistry	QD	934	213.76	526	238.79	486	198.34	480	201.45	1.6	94.2
Education	L	2,565	107.62	2,423	115.02	3,202	103.97	2,797	108.98	4.8	101.3
Engineering and technology	T	7,176	133.60	5,069	171.42	5,671	177.18	4,725	154.50	-12.8	115.6
Fine and applied arts	M-N	1,141	84.30	1,749	111.24	2,119	96.12	1,973	98.31	2.3	116.6
General works	A	60	107.85	67	107.59	101	104.42	80	105.01	0.6	97.4
Geography	G	888	132.67	623	151.05	814	131.23	745	134.16	2.2	101.1
Geology	QE	201	136.49	189	218.25	178	149.33	166	133.69	-10.5	97.9
History	C-D-E-F	4,452	93.55	4,804	105.73	6,375	87.98	6,055	84.17	-4.3	90.0

Subject	LC	No.	Avg. price	No.	Avg. price	No.	Avg. price	No.	Avg. price	% change	Index
Home economics	TX	255	104.31	449	82.81	360	88.37	296	83.63	-5.4	80.2
Industrial arts	TT	20	52.73	86	72.30	88	96.18	68	84.57	-12.1	160.4
Law	K	1,743	99.61	2,465	158.66	2,511	151.57	2,363	141.20	-6.8	141.8
Library and information science	Z	308	74.70	439	105.38	524	115.57	438	110.22	-4.6	147.5
Literature and language	P	5,517	90.59	8,953	100.92	10,877	86.18	10,137	82.15	-4.7	90.7
Mathematics and computer science	QA	4,285	102.93	2,376	132.14	2,574	119.58	2,271	107.84	-9.8	104.8
Medicine	R	7,420	123.59	5,466	158.45	6,227	166.07	5,561	159.90	-3.7	129.4
Military and naval science	U-V	684	82.89	509	102.68	615	92.14	556	81.74	-11.3	98.6
Philosophy and religion	B	3,612	93.77	4,147	127.62	5,030	98.35	4,974	99.83	1.5	106.5
Physical education and recreation	GV	610	96.00	923	96.45	1,161	83.85	1,145	77.28	-7.8	80.5
Physics and astronomy	QB	1,965	142.11	1,158	152.64	1,187	144.96	1,005	151.96	4.8	106.9
Political science	J	2,447	102.72	2,177	128.46	2,709	111.84	2,356	118.58	6.0	115.4
Psychology	BF	1,113	83.51	1,033	113.93	1,167	115.32	1,115	113.86	-1.3	136.3
Science (general)	Q	468	117.19	346	145.77	453	136.01	373	143.16	5.3	122.2
Sociology	HM	4,139	98.02	3,966	119.32	5,088	113.47	4,539	109.49	-3.5	111.7
Zoology	QH,L,P,R	3,394	154.01	1,967	175.72	1,904	173.50	1,709	155.12	-10.6	100.7
Average for all subjects		66,767	$110.82	59,838	$130.08	70,604	$119.29	63,987	$114.12	-4.3 %	103.0

Compiled by Stephen Bosch, University of Arizona from electronic data provided by ProQuest Books (formerly Coutts) and GOBI Library Solutions (formerly YBP). The data represents all e-book titles treated for all approval plan customers serviced by the vendors. This table covers titles published or distributed in the United States and Canada during the calendar years listed. It is important to note that e-books that were released in a given year may have been published in print much earlier.

Table 4B / North American Academic Text Books: Average Prices and Price Indexes 2013–2015

Index Base: 2007 = 100

Subject Area	LC Class	2007		2013		2014		2015			
		No. of Titles	Average Price	No. of Titles	Average Price	No. of Titles	Average Price	No. of Titles	Average Price	% Change 2014–2015	Index
Agriculture	S	68	$134.75	62	$131.30	71	$123.05	119	$127.79	3.9 %	94.8
Anthropology	GN	40	89.15	35	114.63	35	112.17	61	105.68	-5.8	118.5
Botany	QK	4	98.00	9	207.69	13	121.02	31	125.78	3.9	128.3
Business and economics	H	666	110.18	849	139.79	1,037	126.85	1,248	134.91	6.4	122.4
Chemistry	QD	80	138.70	99	154.16	119	149.17	127	195.03	30.7	140.6
Education	L	235	79.58	322	99.91	444	89.06	559	96.90	8.8	121.8
Engineering and technology	T	668	106.13	835	136.07	925	124.31	1,120	138.56	11.5	130.6
Fine and applied arts	M-N	82	73.69	104	107.49	112	108.03	163	101.01	-6.5	137.1
General works	A	1	48.00	3	120.33	4	65.08	2	50.01	-23.2	104.2
Geography	G	59	100.42	91	134.77	115	126.88	148	125.22	-1.3	124.7
Geology	QE	26	118.28	30	138.20	43	132.58	38	138.50	4.5	117.1
History	C-D-E-F	72	78.41	106	90.00	155	94.48	220	94.67	0.2	120.7
Home economics	TX	54	68.23	50	105.95	18	116.70	35	126.90	8.7	186.0
Industrial arts	TT	13	73.90	14	87.95	9	104.47	28	91.49	-12.4	123.8

Subject	LC	No.	Price	No.	Price	No.	Price	No.	Price	%	Index
Law	K	163	87.67	316	113.67	442	103.35	529	126.02	21.9	143.7
Library and information science	Z	24	65.54	24	75.73	56	81.40	45	109.29	34.3	166.7
Literature and language	P	269	71.35	382	91.06	522	85.79	687	97.98	14.2	137.3
Mathematics and computer science	QA	732	91.42	783	108.08	895	101.64	1,105	105.41	3.7	115.3
Medicine	R	1210	126.37	1,596	135.40	1,824	131.76	2,310	150.38	14.1	119.0
Military and naval science	U-V	10	104.58	12	75.62	20	108.76	19	87.58	-19.5	83.7
Philosophy and religion	B	85	55.51	122	73.20	162	69.26	229	67.54	-2.5	121.7
Physical education and recreation	GV	47	72.14	62	121.16	60	106.17	147	100.01	-5.8	138.6
Physics and astronomy	QB	237	107.05	258	119.37	278	102.04	360	121.54	19.1	113.5
Political science	J	104	74.21	148	102.16	173	93.56	261	109.06	16.6	147.0
Psychology	BF	120	100.17	174	132.07	183	123.97	199	124.84	0.7	124.6
Science (general)	Q	24	111.30	35	99.37	50	86.29	55	114.08	32.2	102.5
Sociology	HM	330	84.88	489	104.24	575	95.75	645	105.31	10.0	124.1
Zoology	QH,L,P,R	250	116.73	256	137.69	258	126.66	391	153.45	21.1	131.5
Average for all subjects		5,673	$102.52	7,266	$122.07	8,598	$113.25	10,881	$125.18	10.5 %	122.1

Compiled by Stephen Bosch, University of Arizona from electronic data provided by ProQuest Books (formerly Coutts) and GOBI Library Solutions (formerly YPB). The data represents all Textbook titles treated for all approval plan customers serviced by the vendors. This table covers titles published or distributed in the United States and Canada during the calendar years listed.

This index does not include paperback editions. The inclusion of these items does impact pricing in the index.

(continued from page 277)
changes at both Coutts and YBP have affected how the annual price data is pulled for books. Starting this year, the data is supplied by each vendor in separate files for print, e-books and textbooks. Prior to this year, this was not the case and this resulted in some changes in numbers of titles in the tables as well as in the average prices. The data for 2014 and 2013 were redone this year to conform to the current sets of data so the numbers of titles and prices have changed from those published last year and previous years. In the future, this will improve the consistency of the data especially for e-books.

The overall average price for books in the North American Academic Books Price Index (NAABPI) for 2015 increased 1.3 percent, a slight hike from the previous year. The average price increased to $93.83 from $92.61. The number of titles increased significantly from 137,895 to 167,417, so the growth in available titles as opposed to increasing prices will be the pressure point for library budgets. The increase this year was primarily due to rising costs for books that cost more than $120. This was due to the growth in the number of expensive titles available and not because of increases in the prices. Many of these expensive titles are e-books. As e-books are more expensive than print books, the cost of e-books was a driver in the overall price increase for 2015. E-books now make up about 40 percent of the base table.

Since 2008 two additional indexes have been available, one for e-books only (Table 4A) and another for textbooks (Table 4B). Both of these indexes are of high interest to users. Based on that input, the indexes continue to be published with the base index year set to 2007. In the academic market, it has always been assumed that e-books are more expensive than their print counterparts. Users might be surprised to find that the cheaper versions of e-books, available to consumers through such channels as Amazon and the Apple Store, are not available to libraries at similar prices, if they are available at all. The e-book index clearly points out the difference in price: the average price of an e-book in 2015 was $114.12 while the average price for all books was $93.83. The average price of a print book drops to $81.00 if the e-books are removed from the overall index. The high price for e-books is not that surprising as pricing models for academic e-books generally charge a large percentage of the list print price for access to the e-books. Multi-user licenses are an even larger percentage. In most situations, even single-user academic e-book titles are more expensive than their print counterparts. Responding to customer demands, vendors offer e-books on multiple platforms with multiple pricing models; consequently, there can be multiple prices for the same title. Only the first instance of an e-book is included in the data, so if the same book was treated by a vendor from one e-book aggregator and then treated again from another aggregator, only the first instance of the e-book is in the index. If different pricing models are available, the single user price is supplied. Where multiple prices are available for different use models, the lowest price is provided. Because electronic access is where the market is going it is appropriate to have e-books as a separate index. It is important to note that the e-book market is rapidly changing. The availability of additional pricing models could be a factor in the upward shift

Figure 1 / Comparison of Number of Titles in Sample Grouped by Price

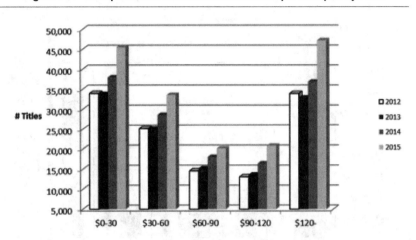

in e-book prices and by using the lowest price available for e-books this approach may be artificially keeping the average price of e-books low.

The cost of textbooks has been a hot topic on many college campuses. The index for textbooks documents price changes in this area. The data shows that textbooks tend to be much more expensive than other types of books, with an average price of $125.18 in 2015. There was a large increase in the average price of 10.5 percent after a 7 percent drop the year before. This is not good news for students, who are essentially hostages of the textbook market. Textbooks are expensive and the prices are not dropping significantly despite pressure on the textbook market from alternative sources like rental services for either print or electronic versions. "E" versions are included in the textbook index, so a migration to "e" format does not seem to be lowering costs. This is not much consolation for cash-strapped students.

The average price of North American academic books in 2015 (Table 4) increased by 1.3 percent as compared with the 2014 average price. This is mainly due to a large increase in the number of titles treated in the higher part of the price bands ($120 and up) as well as a large increase in the top price band. Nearly all price bands showed only modest growth, in the number of titles between 2013 and 2015 except for the price band above $120 and the lowest price band $0–30, and both showed very large increases. This led to a leveling in the average price for all books as increases at both ends of the spectrum evened out the overall increase in prices. The increase in the upper price bands was primarily due to increases in e-books; their prices average well above the $110 threshold. Take e-books out of the sample and the upper price bands shrink considerably. See Figure 1.

One thing that really stands out when looking at the data by price band is that the highest end of the price bands ($120.00 and up) has continued to have a huge impact on the costs for books. The impact on pricing from the titles in the

Figure 2 / Comparison of Total Costs in Sample Grouped by Price

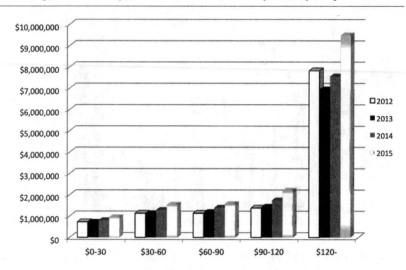

Figure 3 / Comparison of Average Price Grouped by Price Band

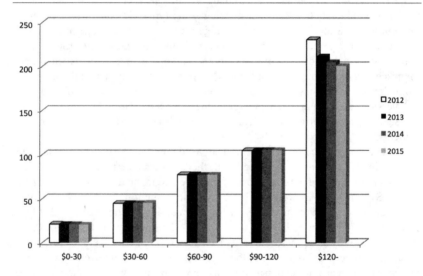

$120-and-up price band is confirmed if you look at the actual dollar values in groups (sum of all prices for titles in the group). It is clear that the increase in the top end of the index was the main component in the overall increase in the index for 2015. Although the $0–$30 price area has the second-largest number of titles, dollar-wise it remains the smallest portion as far as total cost (sum of all prices) goes in the index. The increase in the number of titles available in the upper end of the index was what added to the overall level of increase. Again, growth in the number of titles available was a significant driver in that increase as within the price bands the average price remains fairly constant except for the area with prices over $120, which actually showed a decrease in the overall average price over the past four years. This clearly shows that the growth in the number of titles was the primary driver in escalating costs not increases in price. See Figures 2 and 3.

The data used for this index is derived from all titles treated by ProQuest Books (formerly Coutts Information Services) and GOBI Library Solutions (formerly YBP Library Services) in their approval plans during the calendar years listed. The index includes e-books as well as paperback editions as supplied by these vendors, and this inclusion of paperbacks and e-books as distributed as part of the approval plans has clearly influenced the prices reflected in the index figures. The index is inclusive of the broadest categories of materials as that is the marketplace in which academic libraries operate, and the index attempts to chart price changes that impact that market.

E-books are also now being treated in a separate index (Table 4A), so the differences in the indexes will be interesting to observe. Currently the vast majority of titles are not published in both print and "e" version, so the number of titles in the e-book index should remain smaller than the broader index. It is safe to say that in the future the number of titles in the broader index could decline and at the same time the number of e-books should rise, especially as we see more publishers move to publishing electronic versions of their books. Many e-book pricing models add extra charges of as much as 50 percent to 100 percent to the retail price. This pricing model is reflected in the higher prices for e-books. The overall price for e-books did show a decline from 2014 to 2015. This is due to decreases in the number of titles available in the upper ends of the price bands. As more e-books are released with multiple pricing models, it may be that using the lowest price is a factor in the declining number of titles in the most expensive price bands. Publishers distributing their e-books directly to customers may also be a factor in lower prices. The index does clearly show that for the library market, e-books are much more expensive than print. Many publishers and e-book aggregators are still adding "e" versions of print books from backlists, and these are showing up in the index; this is also the basis for the wide swings in numbers of titles in the index from year to year.

The price index for textbooks (Table 4B) shows a 10.5 percent increase for overall prices between 2014 and 2015. Textbook prices remain much higher than those of regular books. These are indicators that the angst experienced by students as they purchase their texts is well justified as prices appear to be much higher than for regular academic books.

(text continues on page 293)

Table 5 / U.S. College Books: Average Prices and Price Indexes 1989, 2014–2016

Index Base for all years: 1989 = 100

Subject	1989 No. of Titles	1989 Avg. Price per Title	2014 No. of Titles	2014 Avg. Price per Title	2014 Indexed to 1989	2014 Indexed to 2013	2015 No. of Titles	2015 Avg. Price per Title	2015 Indexed to 1989	2015 Indexed to 2014	2016 No. of Titles	2016 Avg. Price per Title	2016 Indexed to 1989	2016 Indexed to 2015	Percent Change 2015–2016
GENERAL*	19	$40.19	n.a.	n.a.	n.a.	n.a.	n.a.	n.a.	n.a.	n.a.	n.a.	n.a.	n.a.	n.a.	n.a.
HUMANITIES	21	$32.33	110	$74.73	231.1	106.8	69	$70.45	217.9	94.3	53	$72.55	224.4	103.0	3.0%
Art and architecture	276	55.56	186	62.00	111.6	95.5	134	66.00	118.8	106.5	143	68.61	123.5	107.1	4.0
Fine Arts**	n.a.	n.a.	87	60.99	n.a.	92.9	105	69.49	n.a.	113.9	83	74.43	n.a.	107.1	7.1
Architecture**	n.a.	n.a.	63	88.46	n.a.	122.7	44	90.81	n.a.	102.7	44	84.94	n.a.	93.5	-6.5
Photography	24	44.11	37	60.00	136.0	106.0	21	56.32	127.7	93.9	18	56.50	128.1	100.3	0.3
Communication	42	32.70	114	65.00	198.8	90.7	84	91.52	279.9	140.8	119	77.65	237.5	84.8	-15.2
Language and literature	110	35.17	115	89.67	255.0	126.6	90	76.81	218.4	85.7	86	80.92	230.1	105.4	5.4
African and Middle Eastern**	n.a.	n.a.	18	59.32	n.a.	112.3	16	75.27	n.a.	126.9	6	49.81	n.a.	66.2	-33.8
Asian and Oceanian**	n.a.	n.a.	21	59.37	n.a.	90.9	23	55.78	n.a.	94.0	18	69.93	n.a.	125.4	25.4
Classical	75	43.07	39	85.24	197.9	97.0	34	67.83	157.5	79.6	26	86.84	201.6	128.0	28.0
English and American	547	30.27	365	69.18	228.5	95.5	326	67.34	222.5	97.3	283	73.29	242.1	108.8	8.8
Germanic	38	32.18	30	66.44	206.5	90.5	35	72.87	226.4	109.7	20	78.94	245.3	108.3	8.3
Romance	97	30.30	66	76.29	251.8	98.6	62	69.34	228.8	90.9	39	64.67	213.4	93.3	-6.7
Slavic	41	27.92	10	85.40	305.9	152.3	13	63.37	227.0	74.2	14	75.25	269.5	118.7	18.7
Other	63	25.09	n.a.	n.a.	n.a.	n.a.	n.a.	n.a.	n.a.	n.a.	n.a.	n.a.	n.a.	n.a.	n.a.
Performing arts	20	29.41	37	70.72	240.5	118.2	28	57.72	196.3	81.6	12	63.10	214.6	109.3	9.3
Film	82	33.00	146	74.68	226.3	96.7	130	71.02	215.2	95.1	96	81.62	247.3	114.9	14.9
Music	156	35.34	141	68.10	192.7	96.7	129	65.32	184.8	95.9	106	74.51	210.8	114.1	14.1
Theater and dance	58	34.18	49	70.75	207.0	105.2	26	79.14	231.5	111.9	38	83.52	244.4	105.5	5.5
Philosophy	185	37.25	241	76.70	205.9	101.9	244	74.60	200.3	97.3	150	70.50	189.3	94.5	-5.5
Religion	174	33.49	271	68.68	205.1	103.6	290	57.51	171.7	83.7	240	61.94	185.0	107.7	7.7
TOTAL HUMANITIES	2,009	$36.09	2,146	$71.35	197.7	101.2	1,903	$69.05	191.3	96.8	1,594	$72.53	201.0	105.0	5.0
SCIENCE AND TECHNOLOGY	99	$46.90	102	$59.53	126.9	86.6	67	$58.57	124.9	98.4	59	$69.30	147.8	118.3	18.3
History of science and technology	74	40.56	85	54.60	134.6	115.0	77	58.08	143.2	106.4	60	53.16	131.1	91.5	-8.5

Astronautics and astronomy	22	50.56	57	57.52	113.8	87.7	66	48.00	94.9	83.4	42	48.65	96.2	101.4	1.4
Biology	97	51.01	154	72.79	142.7	100.5	152	77.01	151.0	105.8	95	81.12	159.0	105.3	5.3
Botany	29	63.91	62	91.94	143.9	111.7	79	95.71	149.8	104.1	47	98.08	153.5	102.5	2.5
Zoology	53	49.21	139	58.54	119.0	80.2	115	69.55	141.3	118.8	88	67.89	138.0	97.6	-2.4
Chemistry	21	70.76	36	86.65	122.5	80.9	30	73.21	103.5	84.5	27	105.31	148.8	143.8	43.8
Earth science	34	79.44	115	84.08	105.8	103.3	119	75.86	95.5	90.2	103	79.97	100.7	105.4	5.4
Engineering	87	66.74	58	91.42	137.0	92.8	57	93.02	139.4	101.8	56	113.67	170.3	122.2	22.2
Health sciences	94	34.91	162	66.98	191.9	113.3	151	70.27	201.3	104.9	121	72.17	206.7	102.7	2.7
Information and computer science	70	40.35	62	72.94	180.8	123.3	51	53.35	132.2	73.1	41	62.78	155.6	117.7	17.7
Mathematics	60	48.53	85	62.64	129.1	95.1	102	67.01	138.1	107.0	93	67.60	139.3	100.9	0.9
Physics	22	43.94	51	58.96	134.2	88.7	44	56.54	128.7	95.9	36	79.75	181.5	141.1	41.1
Sports and physical education	18	27.46	54	69.08	251.6	116.8	52	66.43	241.9	96.2	45	83.86	305.4	126.2	26.2
TOTAL SCIENCE	780	$49.54	1,222	$69.20	139.7	98.5	1,162	$70.11	141.5	101.3	913	$75.90	153.2	108.3	8.3
SOCIAL AND BEHAVIORAL SCIENCES	92	$37.09	126	$81.26	219.1	117.0	144	$81.06	218.5	99.8	134	$79.19	213.5	97.7	-2.3
Anthropology	96	39.94	123	84.95	212.7	103.5	113	82.79	207.3	97.5	102	81.45	203.9	98.4	-1.6
Business management and labor	145	35.72	160	65.21	182.6	105.1	127	54.39	152.3	83.4	120	54.75	153.3	100.7	0.7
Economics	332	40.75	247	60.59	148.7	100.6	238	67.44	165.5	111.3	170	56.26	138.1	83.4	-16.6
Education	71	34.50	138	73.24	212.3	112.1	161	77.82	225.6	106.3	109	74.80	216.8	96.1	-3.9
History, geography and area studies	59	42.10	117	68.10	161.8	89.4	139	70.59	167.7	103.7	95	76.90	182.7	108.9	8.9
Africa	44	34.85	34	71.62	205.5	99.8	34	72.54	208.1	101.3	30	67.02	192.3	92.4	-7.6
*Ancient history***	n.a.	n.a.	41	102.96	n.a.	115.8	45	95.74	n.a.	93.0	45	88.15	n.a.	92.1	-7.9
Asia and Oceania	76	34.75	92	71.77	206.5	103.4	86	78.82	226.8	109.8	63	64.10	184.5	81.3	-18.7
*Central and Eastern Europe***	n.a.	n.a.	59	72.77	n.a.	114.2	63	68.25	n.a.	93.8	48	69.47	n.a.	101.8	1.8
Latin America and Caribbean	42	37.23	67	65.86	176.9	108.4	60	68.61	184.3	104.2	54	68.08	182.9	99.2	-0.8
Middle East and North Africa	30	36.32	35	74.43	204.9	123.6	49	77.79	214.2	104.5	31	75.41	207.6	96.9	-3.1
North America	349	30.56	441	49.60	162.3	78.1	397	50.10	163.9	101.0	386	51.15	167.4	102.1	2.1
*United Kingdom***	n.a.	n.a.	86	72.12	n.a.	92.0	68	74.65	n.a.	103.5	48	83.05	n.a.	111.3	11.3
Western Europe	287	42.08	122	75.99	180.6	101.9	122	69.43	165.0	91.4	108	67.92	161.4	97.8	-2.2
Political science	28	33.56	4	124.99	372.4	312.6	3	48.98	145.9	39.2	67	66.96	199.5	136.7	36.7
Comparative politics	236	37.82	202	69.93	184.9	99.6	190	79.17	209.3	113.2	215	73.22	193.6	92.5	-7.5
International relations	207	35.74	177	73.64	206.0	104.4	187	77.60	217.7	105.6	151	69.69	195.0	89.8	-10.2

Table 5 / U.S. College Books: Average Prices and Price Indexes 1989, 2014–2016 (cont.)

Index Base for all years: 1989 = 100

Subject	1989		2014				2015				2016				Percent Change 2015–2016
	No. of Titles	Avg. Price per Title	No. of Titles	Avg. Price per Title	Indexed to 1989	Indexed to 2013	No. of Titles	Avg. Price per Title	Indexed to 1989	Indexed to 2014	No. of Titles	Avg. Price per Title	Indexed to 1989	Indexed to 2015	
Political theory	59	37.76	85	62.83	166.4	105.0	80	62.88	166.5	100.1	128	72.56	192.2	115.4	15.4
U.S. politics	212	29.37	241	63.49	216.2	116.9	216	63.43	216.0	99.9	201	65.21	222.0	102.8	2.8
Psychology	179	36.36	96	75.08	206.5	92.0	67	85.63	235.2	113.9	61	87.45	240.5	102.1	2.1
Sociology	178	36.36	193	78.79	216.7	110.6	169	79.70	219.2	101.2	162	78.90	217.0	99.0	-1.0
TOTAL BEHAVIORAL SCIENCES	2,722	$36.43	2,886	$68.19	187.2	100.2	2,758	$70.05	192.3	102.7	2,528	$68.12	187.0	97.2	-2.8
TOTAL GENERAL, HUMANITIES, SCIENCE AND SOCIAL SCIENCE (without Reference)	5,511	$38.16	6,254	$69.47	182.0	100.2	5,823	$69.73	182.7	100.4	5,035	$70.92	185.8	101.7	1.7
REFERENCE															
General	636	$61.02	40	$98.18	160.9	83.6	59	$80.62	132.1	82.1	37	$102.52	168.0	127.2	27.2
Humanities**	n.a.	n.a.	136	114.67	n.a.	110.8	90	106.96	n.a.	93.3	72	119.53	n.a.	111.8	11.8
Science and technology**	n.a.	n.a.	43	149.99	n.a.	77.5	39	119.96	n.a.	80.0	35	147.98	n.a.	123.4	23.4
Social and behavioral sciences**	n.a.	n.a.	178	134.98	n.a.	87.9	130	145.39	n.a.	107.7	164	150.84	n.a.	103.7	3.7
TOTAL REFERENCE	636	$61.02	397	$124.29	203.7	86.6	318	$119.38	195.6	96.0	308	$137.39	225.2	115.1	15.1
GRAND TOTAL	6,147	$40.52	6,651	$72.74	179.5	98.6	6,141	$72.31	178.5	99.4	5,343	$74.76	184.5	103.4	3.4 %

Compiled by Frederick Lynden, Brown University and Narda Tafuri, University of Scranton

* General category no longer appears after 1999.

** Began appearing as separate sections after 1989.

(continued from page 289)

Price changes vary, as always, among subject areas. This year there were few double-digit increases in subject areas, and many areas showed price decreases. This is a normal occurrence. The 2015 data indicate that those areas with the largest increases were nearly exclusively in the social sciences and sciences. This increase is most likely due to e-book publishing in these subject areas especially in large expensive online reference works and encyclopedias. STM and social science publishers have tended to be early adopters of e-books and have been publishing e-books for a while. The large price increases in science and the social sciences reflect the availability and higher pricing of e-books in these areas.

It is good to remember that price indexes become less accurate at describing price changes the smaller the sample becomes. Chemistry and general works are small samples and showed very large price changes, but to conclude that all books in those areas increased or decreased at like amounts is not correct. These areas have a small sample size (fewer than 1,500 titles) and the inclusion/exclusion of just a few large expensive items can have a major impact on prices for the category. The increases in chemistry, for example, were due to a few very expensive titles that showed up in the data. Because the sample is very small, these titles caused the overall price to jump dramatically.

The U.S. College Books Price Index (Table 5), prepared by Frederick C. Lynden and Narda Tafuri, contains average price and index number data for the years 2014 through 2016 (index base year of 1989), and also the percentage change in price between 2015 and 2016.

Data for the index was compiled from 5,343 reviews of books published in *Choice* during 2016. Expensive titles ($500 or more) were omitted from the analysis, thus the total number of titles reported is smaller than the actual number of books reviewed in 2016. This index includes some paperback prices; as a result, the average book price is less than if only hardcover books were included.

The average price for humanities titles in 2016 increased by 5.04 percent from the previous year, and the average price for science and technology titles increased at a rate of 8.26 percent. Finally, the average price for social and behavioral sciences decreased slightly at a rate of 2.76 percent. Nevertheless, combined the overall subject area increase was 1.71 percent. This increase is in line with the CPI rise for 2016, which has been around 2.1 percent. For all titles, which include reference, there was an increase of 3.39 percent.

For 2016, the overall price average for books in the four major sections of *Choice*—humanities, science and technology, social and behavioral sciences, and reference—was $74.76, a 3.39 percent increase compared with the average 2015 book price of $72.31. Reference books calculated separately had an average price increase of 15.09 percent over the previous year, with a 2016 average price of $137.39 (after items $500 or over were removed) compared to last year's average price of $119.38. However, excluding reference books, the 2016 average price was $70.92, a 1.71 percent increase over the average 2015 price of $69.73.

Questions regarding this index should be addressed to the authors at their email addresses: (e-mail Frederick Lynden: Flynden@stanfordalumni.org; email Narda Tafuri: narda.tafuri@scranton.edu).

(text continues on page 308)

Table 6 / U.S. Mass Market Paperback Books: Average Prices and Price Indexes, 2013–2016

Index Base: 2005 = 100

BISAC Category	2005 Average Prices	2013 Final Volumes	2013 Final Average Prices	2013 Final Index	2014 Final Volumes	2014 Final Average Prices	2014 Final Index	2015 Final Volumes	2015 Final Average Prices	2015 Final Index	2016 Preliminary Volumes	2016 Preliminary Average Prices	2016 Preliminary Index
Antiques and collectibles	$7.69	5	$8.99	116.9	4	$8.99	116.9	n.a.	n.a.	n.a.	n.a.	n.a.	n.a.
Architecture	n.a.	n.a.	n.a.	n.a.	n.a.	n.a.	n.a.	n.a.	n.a.	n.a.	n.a.	n.a.	n.a.
Art	n.a.	n.a.	n.a.	n.a.	n.a.	n.a.	n.a.	n.a.	n.a.	n.a.	n.a.	n.a.	n.a.
Bibles	n.a.	n.a.	n.a.	n.a.	n.a.	n.a.	n.a.	n.a.	n.a.	n.a.	n.a.	n.a.	n.a.
Biography and autobiography	7.83	3	9.66	123.4	6	8.98	114.7	2	$8.49	108.4	6	$10.66	136.1
Body, mind and spirit	7.11	14	8.13	114.3	2	9.99	140.5	n.a.	n.a.	n.a.	2	8.99	126.4
Business and economics	12.47	n.a.	n.a.	n.a.	n.a.	n.a.	n.a.	1	8.99	72.1	n.a.	n.a.	n.a.
Children	5.29	217	6.70	126.7	272	6.10	115.4	204	6.32	119.5	224	6.89	130.2
Comics and graphic novels	8.47	n.a.	n.a.	n.a.	n.a.	n.a.	n.a.	n.a.	n.a.	n.a.	n.a.	n.a.	n.a.
Computers	n.a.	n.a.	n.a.	n.a.	n.a.	n.a.	n.a.	n.a.	n.a.	n.a.	n.a.	n.a.	n.a.
Cooking	7.50	n.a.	n.a.	n.a.	n.a.	n.a.	n.a.	1	8.99	119.9	n.a.	n.a.	n.a.
Crafts and hobbies	n.a.	n.a.	n.a.	n.a.	n.a.	n.a.	n.a.	n.a.	n.a.	n.a.	n.a.	n.a.	n.a.
Design	n.a.	n.a.	n.a.	n.a.	n.a.	n.a.	n.a.	n.a.	n.a.	n.a.	n.a.	n.a.	n.a.
Drama	6.32	n.a.	n.a.	n.a.	1	9.99	158.1	n.a.	n.a.	n.a.	n.a.	n.a.	n.a.
Education	n.a.	n.a.	n.a.	n.a.	n.a.	n.a.	n.a.	n.a.	n.a.	n.a.	n.a.	n.a.	n.a.
Family and relationships	6.98	n.a.	n.a.	n.a.	n.a.	n.a.	n.a.	1	8.99	128.8	n.a.	n.a.	n.a.
Fiction	6.34	3,524	7.00	110.4	3,603	7.09	111.9	3,234	7.11	112.2	3,016	7.22	113.9
Foreign language study	n.a.	n.a.	n.a.	n.a.	1	6.99	n.a.	n.a.	n.a.	n.a.	n.a.	n.a.	n.a.
Games	7.14	1	9.99	139.9	2	9.25	129.5	1	7.99	111.9	3	8.66	121.2
Gardening	n.a.	n.a.	n.a.	n.a.	n.a.	n.a.	n.a.	n.a.	n.a.	n.a.	n.a.	n.a.	n.a.
Health and fitness	7.43	8	8.24	110.9	3	9.33	125.5	3	8.99	121.0	n.a.	n.a.	n.a.
History	7.90	3	9.99	126.5	2	9.99	126.5	2	9.99	126.5	3	9.32	118.0
House and home	5.99	n.a.	n.a.	n.a.	n.a.	n.a.	n.a.	n.a.	n.a.	n.a.	n.a.	n.a.	n.a.
Humor	6.99	2	8.00	114.4	n.a.	n.a.	n.a.	n.a.	n.a.	n.a.	1	7.99	114.3

Language arts and disciplines	6.99	n.a.	n.a.	n.a.	1	7.99	114.3	n.a.	n.a.	n.a.	n.a.	n.a.	n.a.
Law	n.a.	n.a.	n.a.	n.a.	n.a.	n.a.	n.a.	n.a.	n.a.	n.a.	n.a.	n.a.	n.a.
Literary collections	n.a.	n.a.	n.a.	n.a.	1	4.95	n.a.	n.a.	n.a.	n.a.	n.a.	n.a.	n.a.
Literary criticism	7.95	n.a.	n.a.	n.a.	n.a.	n.a.	n.a.	n.a.	n.a.	n.a.	n.a.	n.a.	n.a.
Mathematics	n.a.	n.a.	n.a.	n.a.	n.a.	n.a.	n.a.	n.a.	n.a.	n.a.	n.a.	n.a.	n.a.
Medical	7.83	n.a.	n.a.	n.a.	1	7.99	102.0	n.a.	n.a.	n.a.	n.a.	n.a.	n.a.
Music	7.95	n.a.	n.a.	n.a.	n.a.	n.a.	n.a.	n.a.	n.a.	n.a.	n.a.	n.a.	n.a.
Nature	n.a.	n.a.	n.a.	n.a.	n.a.	n.a.	n.a.	n.a.	n.a.	n.a.	n.a.	n.a.	n.a.
Performing arts	8.23	1	10.99	133.5	1	10.99	133.5	1	9.99	n.a.	n.a.	n.a.	n.a.
Pets	n.a.	1	7.99	n.a.	n.a.	n.a.	n.a.	1	6.95	92.8	n.a.	n.a.	n.a.
Philosophy	7.49	n.a.	n.a.	n.a.	n.a.	n.a.	n.a.	n.a.	n.a.	n.a.	n.a.	n.a.	n.a.
Photography	n.a.	n.a.	6.62	115.1	n.a.	n.a.	n.a.	2	6.45	112.2	1	3.99	69.4
Poetry	5.75	3	n.a.	n.a.	n.a.	n.a.	n.a.	2	8.47	n.a.	n.a.	n.a.	n.a.
Political science	n.a.	n.a.	n.a.	n.a.	1	9.99	n.a.	n.a.	n.a.	n.a.	n.a.	n.a.	n.a.
Psychology	7.97	n.a.	n.a.	n.a.	n.a.	n.a.	n.a.	1	7.99	116.6	5	15.70	229.2
Reference	6.85	3	6.49	94.7	5	12.89	188.2	n.a.	n.a.	n.a.	n.a.	n.a.	n.a.
Religion	9.96	n.a.	n.a.	n.a.	n.a.	n.a.	n.a.	n.a.	n.a.	n.a.	1	13.99	n.a.
Science	n.a.	n.a.	n.a.	n.a.	n.a.	n.a.	n.a.	n.a.	n.a.	n.a.	n.a.	13.99	n.a.
Self-help	12.45	n.a.	n.a.	n.a.	n.a.	n.a.	n.a.	n.a.	n.a.	n.a.	1	7.99	64.2
Social science	7.08	n.a.	n.a.	n.a.	n.a.	n.a.	n.a.	n.a.	n.a.	n.a.	n.a.	9.99	131.1
Sports and recreation	7.62	n.a.	n.a.	n.a.	n.a.	n.a.	n.a.	1	n.a.	n.a.	1	n.a.	n.a.
Study aids	n.a.	n.a.	n.a.	n.a.	n.a.	n.a.	n.a.	n.a.	n.a.	n.a.	n.a.	n.a.	n.a.
Technology and engineering	n.a.	n.a.	n.a.	n.a.	n.a.	n.a.	n.a.	n.a.	n.a.	n.a.	n.a.	n.a.	n.a.
Transportation	12.95	n.a.	n.a.	n.a.	n.a.	n.a.	n.a.	1	7.99	n.a.	n.a.	n.a.	n.a.
Travel	n.a.	n.a.	n.a.	n.a.	n.a.	n.a.	n.a.	n.a.	n.a.	n.a.	n.a.	n.a.	n.a.
True crime	7.19	26	8.49	118.1	20	8.69	120.9	13	8.30	115.4	13	8.45	117.5
Young adult	6.46	44	9.22	142.7	44	9.42	145.9	22	9.40	145.5	12	9.49	146.9
Totals	$6.34	3,855	$7.04	111.0	3,970	$7.08	111.7	3,492	$7.09	111.9	3,289	$7.24	114.2

Compiled by Narda Tafuri, University of Scranton, from data supplied by Baker & Taylor.
n.a. = not available

Table 7 / U.S. Paperback Books (Excluding Mass Market): Average Prices and Price Indexes, 2013–2016

Index Base: 2005 = 100

BISAC Category	2005 Average Prices	2013 Final Volumes	2013 Final Average Prices	2013 Final Index	2014 Final Volumes	2014 Final Average Prices	2014 Final Index	2015 Final Volumes	2015 Final Average Prices	2015 Final Index	2016 Preliminary Volumes	2016 Preliminary Average Prices	2016 Preliminary Index
Antiques and collectibles	$24.80	134	$34.08	137.4	139	$36.02	145.2	126	$33.55	135.3	146	$34.36	138.5
Architecture	38.90	780	43.74	112.4	689	45.98	118.2	814	44.20	113.6	720	49.34	126.8
Art	31.28	1,697	41.70	133.3	1,679	39.58	126.5	1,680	41.96	134.2	1,659	47.43	151.6
Bibles	36.87	808	41.74	113.2	770	45.41	123.2	966	40.51	109.9	643	44.06	119.5
Biography and autobiography	19.19	3,092	19.80	103.2	2,920	20.41	106.4	2,692	20.40	106.3	2,595	19.73	102.8
Body, mind and spirit	17.48	1,013	18.31	104.7	861	18.11	103.6	677	18.20	104.1	688	17.76	101.6
Business and economics	71.12	7,243	88.39	124.3	7,334	92.17	129.6	8,946	103.95	146.2	6,550	92.73	130.4
Children	11.11	10,360	12.31	110.8	11,493	12.97	116.7	12,215	15.20	136.8	12,287	14.68	132.1
Comics and graphic novels	12.75	1,834	16.73	131.2	2,077	17.56	137.7	2,043	18.03	141.4	2,235	18.42	144.5
Computers	57.01	3,636	85.88	150.6	3,506	83.75	146.9	2,903	84.97	149.0	3,689	120.08	210.6
Cooking	18.30	1,190	20.06	109.6	1,279	19.65	107.4	1,110	20.41	111.5	986	20.74	113.3
Crafts and hobbies	18.49	1,201	18.40	99.5	1,203	18.77	101.5	1,103	19.63	106.2	843	20.27	109.6
Design	32.87	327	38.64	117.6	308	42.13	128.2	258	44.92	136.6	244	37.93	115.4
Drama	16.40	611	20.09	122.5	584	20.75	126.5	542	22.79	139.0	515	21.37	130.3
Education	35.10	4,195	48.89	139.3	4,380	55.91	159.3	3,989	52.38	149.2	4,211	62.64	178.5
Family and relationships	17.10	767	19.42	113.6	756	22.89	133.9	674	20.08	117.4	636	21.09	123.3
Fiction	15.74	13,231	17.00	108.0	13,114	17.28	109.8	11,041	17.18	109.2	10,537	16.89	107.3
Foreign language study	41.90	1,006	52.51	125.3	1,370	44.78	106.9	1,005	49.25	117.5	735	49.49	118.1
Games	16.53	619	15.64	94.6	548	17.56	106.2	766	15.17	91.7	1,843	14.23	86.1
Gardening	20.59	194	22.83	110.9	163	21.94	106.6	158	24.97	121.3	121	22.66	110.0
Health and fitness	22.81	1,095	26.30	115.3	1,108	26.78	117.4	1,080	32.70	143.4	1,023	35.85	157.2
History	33.53	6,513	37.88	113.0	7,750	40.70	121.4	7,044	40.69	121.4	6,144	38.31	114.3
House and home	19.33	145	20.08	103.9	949	95.61	494.6	117	20.35	105.3	87	19.83	102.6
Humor	12.96	353	14.39	111.0	344	14.97	115.5	324	15.15	116.9	285	15.40	118.8
Language arts and disciplines	49.14	1,875	73.94	150.5	2,151	76.56	155.8	1,762	75.20	153.0	2,057	76.36	155.4

Law	60.92	3,154	76.13	125.0	3,690	80.11	131.5	3,793	86.00	141.2	3,549	86.99	142.8
Literary collections	28.07	474	34.38	122.5	673	21.41	76.3	343	36.55	130.2	397	34.72	123.7
Literary criticism	31.99	1,587	40.32	126.0	2,554	50.49	157.8	1,972	43.85	137.1	1,752	40.89	127.8
Mathematics	75.77	1,479	86.74	114.5	1,518	90.43	119.3	1,033	83.11	109.7	1,286	90.77	119.8
Medical	64.27	5,120	96.56	150.2	4,605	96.33	149.9	3,743	106.16	165.2	5,002	112.16	174.5
Music	22.66	2,653	24.31	107.3	2,188	28.87	127.4	2,722	25.61	113.0	2,282	27.80	122.7
Nature	26.90	564	31.58	117.4	593	31.73	118.0	516	31.27	116.3	568	46.79	173.9
Performing arts	27.85	867	35.48	127.4	924	36.71	131.8	955	39.24	140.9	808	38.60	138.6
Pets	18.86	154	18.87	100.1	146	18.67	99.0	150	17.91	95.0	158	20.13	106.7
Philosophy	31.40	1,522	44.41	141.4	1,776	47.91	152.6	1,654	44.03	140.2	1,637	53.94	171.8
Photography	27.74	445	34.43	124.1	420	35.74	128.9	472	38.18	137.6	399	32.61	117.6
Poetry	16.09	2,399	16.62	103.3	2,279	17.64	109.6	1,993	17.82	110.8	2,002	16.92	105.2
Political science	45.65	3,555	47.80	104.7	4,114	55.48	121.5	3,865	55.26	121.1	3,685	48.26	105.7
Psychology	45.74	1,944	67.22	147.0	2,121	58.16	127.2	2,292	52.10	113.9	2,345	56.33	123.2
Reference	52.54	823	100.88	192.0	891	99.54	189.5	720	156.99	298.8	559	153.96	293.0
Religion	20.54	7,968	22.24	108.3	7,585	23.72	115.5	7,410	24.55	119.5	6,845	25.15	122.4
Science	71.05	4,523	90.07	126.8	4,417	88.76	124.9	2,654	100.65	141.7	4,041	123.08	173.2
Self-help	16.36	1,291	17.72	108.3	1,153	18.81	114.9	1,038	17.26	105.5	1,020	17.41	106.4
Social science	36.83	4,502	50.00	135.9	4,673	54.55	148.1	4,779	51.57	140.0	5,265	54.53	148.0
Sports and recreation	21.82	1,111	23.88	109.4	1,185	24.36	111.7	1,091	25.09	115.0	1,050	24.81	113.7
Study aids	30.90	535	47.44	153.5	1,888	44.88	145.2	939	43.64	141.2	698	35.75	115.7
Technology and engineering	85.80	2,805	101.16	117.9	3,688	104.67	122.0	1,914	113.98	132.8	3,225	135.99	158.5
Transportation	40.19	427	39.45	98.2	465	42.34	105.4	385	39.52	98.3	483	36.26	90.2
Travel	19.18	1,736	20.64	107.6	1,716	20.60	107.4	1,617	21.28	110.9	1,594	20.93	109.1
True crime	17.71	169	19.84	112.0	175	19.01	107.3	176	18.97	107.1	144	19.42	109.7
Young adult	14.06	2,169	16.83	119.7	2,929	18.67	132.8	2,336	20.70	147.2	2,580	26.26	186.7
Totals	$33.90	117,895	$43.81	129.2	125,841	$46.02	135.7	114,597	$46.52	137.2	114,853	$50.58	149.2

Compiled by Narda Tafuri, University of Scranton, from data supplied by Baker & Taylor.

Table 7A / U.S. Audiobooks: Average Prices and Price Indexes, 2013–2016

Index Base: 2005 = 100

BISAC Category	2005 Average Prices	2013 Final Volumes	2013 Final Average Prices	2013 Final Index	2014 Final Volumes	2014 Final Average Prices	2014 Final Index	2015 Final Volumes	2015 Final Average Prices	2015 Final Index	2016 Preliminary Volumes	2016 Preliminary Average Prices	2016 Preliminary Index
Antiques and collectibles	n.a.	n.a.	n.a.	n.a.	n.a.	n.a.	n.a.	n.a.	n.a.	n.a.	3	$26.66	n.a.
Architecture	$68.95	7	$42.82	62.1	1	$59.95	86.9	2	$14.97	21.7	7	25.42	36.9
Art	57.51	3	29.95	52.1	9	39.32	68.4	8	30.61	53.2	22	16.95	29.5
Bibles	47.08	20	81.48	173.1	11	70.88	150.6	16	37.35	79.3	7	122.85	260.9
Biography and autobiography	37.68	1,199	41.12	109.1	982	41.60	110.4	1,226	36.61	97.2	1,671	31.52	83.7
Body, mind and spirit	26.74	244	26.93	100.7	181	28.51	106.6	163	23.60	88.3	145	29.38	109.9
Business and economics	42.11	452	34.51	82.0	607	29.96	71.2	701	29.51	70.1	1,300	27.51	65.3
Children	26.57	1,713	40.92	154.0	1,032	35.62	134.0	2,361	39.89	150.1	1,201	33.30	125.3
Comics and graphic novels	n.a.	2	14.99	n.a.	n.a.	n.a.	n.a.	n.a.	n.a.	n.a.	3	9.99	n.a.
Computers	41.39	2	52.47	126.8	18	41.26	99.7	9	29.77	71.9	30	29.05	70.2
Cooking	14.45	20	47.19	326.6	14	49.06	339.5	21	30.56	211.5	40	31.69	219.3
Crafts and hobbies	n.a.	3	24.95	n.a.	5	24.78	n.a.	3	28.63	n.a.	2	27.47	n.a.
Design	n.a.	1	29.95	n.a.	n.a.	n.a.	n.a.	1	29.99	n.a.	1	9.99	n.a.
Drama	23.45	100	32.53	138.7	59	25.91	110.5	52	29.76	126.9	152	14.35	61.2
Education	27.46	33	39.25	142.9	32	36.84	134.1	26	36.09	131.4	52	39.75	144.7
Family and relationships	24.58	119	35.16	143.0	119	32.01	130.2	157	30.76	125.2	247	29.17	118.7
Fiction	41.47	11,434	38.34	92.5	11,447	38.92	93.8	13,094	31.95	77.0	19,068	23.90	57.6
Foreign language study	70.04	114	69.35	99.0	273	64.32	91.8	137	69.30	98.9	46	107.83	154.0
Games	32.68	n.a.	n.a.	n.a.	5	47.18	144.4	1	11.99	36.7	4	32.49	99.4
Gardening	n.a.	n.a.	n.a.	n.a.	n.a.	n.a.	n.a.	1	14.99	n.a.	2	31.49	n.a.
Health and fitness	26.61	131	42.91	161.3	111	41.17	154.7	162	40.47	152.1	288	32.08	120.6
History	41.61	480	47.52	114.2	476	51.94	124.8	550	43.41	104.3	1,195	32.80	78.8
House and home	25.00	4	29.98	119.9	1	9.99	40.0	5	35.79	143.2	27	36.98	147.9
Humor	29.60	70	37.80	127.7	98	32.93	111.3	108	32.83	110.9	101	27.03	91.3
Language arts and disciplines	60.84	14	40.79	67.0	11	38.17	62.7	20	33.29	54.7	40	29.21	48.0

Law	55.32	16	64.24	116.1	12	62.41	112.8	9	55.11	99.6	41	27.94	50.5
Literary collections	24.71	18	37.09	150.1	41	54.10	218.9	58	40.13	162.4	72	34.98	141.6
Literary criticism	26.41	11	48.62	184.1	12	29.98	113.5	20	43.63	165.2	52	27.83	105.4
Mathematics	n.a.	5	38.97	n.a.	5	20.59	n.a.	6	36.81	n.a.	6	24.99	n.a.
Medical	153.72	24	40.98	26.7	12	37.74	24.6	27	32.39	21.1	22	19.13	12.4
Music	29.83	34	41.10	137.8	25	51.25	171.8	21	30.66	102.8	82	28.74	96.3
Nature	28.92	25	42.26	146.1	23	46.63	161.2	35	31.38	108.5	85	21.97	76.0
Performing arts	25.78	45	39.34	152.6	65	39.62	153.7	79	36.53	141.7	180	37.83	146.7
Pets	33.05	30	39.28	118.9	13	37.05	112.1	17	39.33	119.0	50	37.32	112.9
Philosophy	35.30	38	29.62	83.9	25	32.02	90.7	17	29.04	82.3	124	24.75	70.1
Photography	n.a.	n.a.	n.a.	n.a.	n.a.	n.a.	n.a.	n.a.	n.a.	n.a.	2	34.99	n.a.
Poetry	22.87	19	26.39	115.4	38	39.07	170.8	25	37.22	162.7	25	14.98	65.5
Political science	42.66	166	45.06	105.6	130	45.11	105.7	173	36.92	86.6	397	28.91	67.8
Psychology	35.70	73	43.95	123.1	96	32.57	91.2	106	35.49	99.4	188	27.92	78.2
Reference	21.20	5	49.77	234.8	8	25.99	122.6	4	15.49	73.1	13	24.22	114.2
Religion	26.52	675	29.06	109.6	698	28.74	108.4	950	25.86	97.5	1,216	26.04	98.2
Science	39.86	95	41.15	103.2	98	41.78	104.8	122	35.31	88.6	199	27.35	68.6
Self-help	23.58	212	31.10	131.9	231	30.43	129.0	286	30.12	127.7	528	32.85	139.3
Social science	35.73	111	38.11	106.7	103	35.46	99.2	122	31.13	87.1	317	25.49	71.3
Sports and recreation	28.46	48	39.93	140.3	52	38.52	135.4	64	34.30	120.5	221	25.88	91.0
Study aids	41.85	1	24.99	59.7	5	131.00	313.0	3	24.97	59.7	2	52.98	126.6
Technology and engineering	61.47	8	36.61	59.6	11	52.44	85.3	20	43.13	70.2	80	93.97	152.9
Transportation	28.00	10	48.68	173.9	5	52.39	187.1	9	35.98	128.5	17	32.10	114.6
Travel	41.91	37	35.89	85.6	9	47.76	114.0	26	26.37	62.9	145	17.10	40.8
True crime	35.97	136	39.89	110.9	94	34.20	95.1	111	29.19	81.2	172	33.86	94.1
Young adult	35.68	1,271	42.20	118.3	1,285	43.27	121.3	1,714	31.71	88.9	1,711	29.18	81.8
Totals	$40.49	19,278	$38.92	96.1	18,588	$38.99	96.3	22,848	$33.27	82.2	31,599	$26.45	65.3

Compiled by Narda Tafuri, University of Scranton from data supplied by Baker & Taylor.
n.a. = not available

Table 7B / U.S. E-Books: Average Prices and Price Indexes, 2013–2016

Index Base: 2008 = 100

BISAC Category	2008 Average Prices	2013 Final Volumes	2013 Final Average Prices	2013 Final Index	2014 Final Volumes	2014 Final Average Prices	2014 Final Index	2015 Final Volumes	2015 Final Average Prices	2015 Final Index	2016 Preliminary Volumes	2016 Preliminary Average Prices	2016 Preliminary Index
Antiques and collectibles	$55.97	177	$20.96	37.4	132	$17.05	30.5	154	$12.50	22.3	93	$13.83	24.7
Architecture	70.50	823	63.80	90.5	1,083	144.57	205.1	542	60.93	86.4	338	45.55	64.6
Art	45.41	1,812	18.09	39.8	1,884	22.27	49.0	4,913	10.59	23.3	2,020	15.05	33.2
Bibles	25.79	495	8.76	34	247	9.16	35.5	194	8.92	34.6	125	9.65	37.4
Biography and autobiography	14.58	8,156	15.10	103.6	9,542	17.89	122.7	6,770	15.67	107.5	5,543	15.97	109.5
Body, mind and spirit	12.41	1,984	11.94	96.2	1,815	10.52	84.7	1,344	11.14	89.7	1,531	11.20	90.3
Business and economics	57.52	11,760	56.43	98.1	10,599	48.79	84.8	21,656	23.30	40.5	7,332	41.55	72.2
Children	12.01	20,257	11.53	96	21,565	14.62	121.8	19,174	12.37	103.0	19,425	14.15	117.8
Comics and graphic novels	25.04	551	7.31	29.2	1,535	6.13	24.5	3,344	8.13	32.5	3,682	8.77	35.0
Computers	66.87	4,170	54.38	81.3	4,358	66.63	99.6	4,420	64.30	96.2	4,066	70.12	104.9
Cooking	20.20	3,437	12.45	61.6	2,870	12.01	59.5	3,086	12.11	59.9	2,228	13.94	69.0
Crafts and hobbies	14.35	1,388	10.22	71.2	960	11.94	83.2	1,269	9.73	67.8	1,042	11.02	76.8
Design	36.04	193	26.00	72.1	144	28.03	77.8	145	26.25	72.8	112	23.70	65.8
Drama	29.49	1,629	7.91	26.8	1,799	9.90	33.6	1,724	7.58	25.7	861	10.75	36.4
Education	51.98	5,038	51.32	98.7	4,642	38.80	74.6	3,574	38.27	73.6	6,788	38.38	73.8
Family and relationships	19.88	1,927	28.32	142.5	2,200	14.11	71.0	1,767	11.22	56.4	1,931	11.12	55.9
Fiction	8.71	94,876	6.55	75.2	104,416	6.42	73.7	88,146	6.22	71.4	78,523	7.08	81.3
Foreign language study	43.01	1,589	16.08	37.4	1,657	16.19	37.6	1,645	20.18	46.9	1,035	12.64	29.4
Games	17.73	506	9.43	53.2	682	8.20	46.2	1,246	22.64	127.7	782	8.28	46.7
Gardening	20.40	360	13.77	67.5	311	11.59	56.8	307	10.89	53.4	272	12.33	60.4
Health and fitness	18.54	3,562	17.61	95	3,170	11.71	63.2	2,934	13.79	74.4	2,916	12.60	68.0
History	57.53	9,775	39.71	69	12,548	34.26	59.5	10,472	40.49	70.4	7,731	31.49	54.7
House and home	22.89	425	10.39	45.4	310	9.67	42.2	312	10.26	44.8	238	10.96	47.9
Humor	11.27	1,085	8.81	78.2	1,080	9.37	83.1	858	10.64	94.4	893	9.94	88.2

Language arts and disciplines	93.27	2,413	52.09	55.8	2,274	76.99	82.5	1,861	90.30	96.8	1,255	80.33	86.1
Law	81.23	1,745	94.15	115.9	1,840	99.07	122.0	1,747	105.84	130.3	1,207	87.45	107.7
Literary collections	24.50	1,468	13.90	56.7	1,615	23.78	97.1	6,373	5.16	21.1	1,140	10.75	43.9
Literary criticism	86.62	2,336	61.37	70.8	2,354	76.03	87.8	2,926	66.15	76.4	1,630	63.74	73.6
Mathematics	106.16	1,434	84.14	79.3	1,425	94.42	88.9	1,239	84.84	79.9	1,314	89.40	84.2
Medical	135.21	4,242	98.63	72.9	3,737	104.04	77.0	2,992	103.42	76.5	3,018	114.07	84.4
Music	33.83	1,942	30.36	89.7	1,431	47.07	139.1	1,661	21.53	63.6	1,195	18.32	54.2
Nature	59.76	1,017	33.08	55.4	952	35.52	59.4	731	42.19	70.6	685	46.25	77.4
Performing arts	38.06	1,599	39.69	104.3	1,421	32.68	85.9	1,329	31.22	82.0	1,448	36.23	95.2
Pets	15.91	750	8.41	52.9	424	10.75	67.6	292	10.48	65.9	422	9.88	62.1
Philosophy	79.19	2,676	56.26	71	2,362	61.24	77.3	2,188	57.86	73.1	1,635	48.07	60.7
Photography	30.30	535	22.02	72.7	556	19.79	65.3	497	17.76	58.6	400	19.05	62.9
Poetry	13.66	3,047	6.93	50.7	3,813	7.06	51.7	3,783	6.34	46.4	2,770	5.99	43.9
Political science	59.03	5,129	50.02	84.7	3,913	55.78	94.5	4,026	56.26	95.3	3,007	48.24	81.7
Psychology	65.30	4,119	139.89	214.2	3,273	57.59	88.2	2,169	50.16	76.8	1,480	41.89	64.2
Reference	48.33	1,543	82.84	171.4	4,062	25.72	53.2	3,502	24.66	51.0	4,200	12.37	25.6
Religion	27.29	9,800	20.59	75.4	11,208	19.21	70.4	9,383	20.83	76.3	8,715	16.94	62.1
Science	210.57	4,491	105.83	50.3	4,710	118.56	56.3	3,833	98.18	46.6	4,030	101.72	48.3
Self-help	14.15	4,299	29.36	207.5	4,825	8.57	60.6	4,032	9.69	68.5	4,192	9.84	69.5
Social science	69.42	6,941	79.66	114.8	4,888	67.16	96.7	4,269	55.12	79.4	2,855	53.60	77.2
Sports and recreation	22.44	2,727	19.47	86.8	2,344	17.87	79.6	1,844	17.28	77.0	1,796	16.43	73.2
Study aids	21.95	6,142	18.79	85.6	4,721	18.59	84.7	1,155	11.04	50.3	20,200	30.51	139.0
Technology and engineering	153.73	3,886	114.23	74.3	3,859	145.82	94.9	3,175	119.72	77.9	3,417	124.01	80.7
Transportation	35.47	327	26.12	73.6	336	19.36	54.6	324	25.62	72.2	296	21.35	60.2
Travel	15.61	2,546	10.96	70.2	2,320	11.28	72.3	3,291	9.50	60.9	2,271	11.10	71.1
True crime	11.60	616	12.03	103.7	545	12.37	106.7	447	13.57	117.0	457	16.03	138.2
Young adult	8.83	6,502	13.60	154	6,613	13.50	152.9	5,476	12.30	139.3	5,182	16.92	191.6
Totals	$57.38	260,247	$27.97	48.7	271,370	$25.42	44.3	254,541	$22.18	38.7	229,724	$23.78	41.4

Compiled by Narda Tafuri, University of Scranton, from data supplied by Baker & Taylor.

Table 8 / Average Price of Serials, Based on Titles in Select Serial Indices, 2013–2017

Subject	LC Class	Avg. No. of Titles	2013 Avg. Price	2014 Avg. Price	2014–13 % of Price Increase	2015 Avg. Price	2015–14 % of Price Increase	2016 Avg. Price	2016–15 % of Price Increase	2017 Avg. Price	2017–16 % of Price Increase
Agriculture	S	505	$788	$835	6.0 %	$883	5.7 %	$938	6.2 %	$1,001	6.8 %
Anthropology	GN	130	429	469	9.3	494	5.2	521	5.5	552	6.0
Arts and architecture	N	207	331	356	7.5	377	6.0	421	11.6	446	5.9
Astronomy	QB	67	1,529	1,617	5.8	1,731	7.1	1,788	3.3	1,880	5.2
Biology	QH	1,150	1,814	1,918	5.7	2,029	5.8	2,143	5.6	2,267	5.8
Botany	QK	151	1,069	1,158	8.3	1,218	5.1	1,276	4.8	1,353	6.0
Business and economics	HA-HJ	1,275	1,072	1,148	7.1	1,224	6.6	1,305	6.6	1,353	3.7
Chemistry	QD	390	3,439	3,652	6.2	3,808	4.3	3,965	4.1	4,136	4.3
Education	L	473	604	657	8.9	708	7.7	759	7.1	800	5.5
Engineering	T	1,799	1,411	1,510	7.1	1,616	7.0	1,725	6.8	1,818	5.4
Food science	TX	80	1,265	1,376	8.7	1,472	7.0	1,547	5.1	1,623	5.0
General science	Q	245	991	1,051	6.0	1,121	6.7	1,176	5.0	1,241	5.5
General works	A	166	236	264	11.7	268	1.4	300	12.0	310	3.4
Geography	G-GF	292	819	879	7.4	927	5.4	984	6.2	1,056	7.3
Geology	QE	219	1,288	1,371	6.4	1,466	6.9	1,565	6.7	1,664	6.4
Health sciences	R	4,079	895	959	7.2	1,018	6.1	1,088	6.9	1,159	6.5

Subject	LC Class	No. of titles	Price	Price	%	Price	%	Price	%	Price	%
History	C,D,E,F	762	284	307	8.0	324	5.6	340	4.8	362	6.6
Language and literature	P	784	302	323	6.9	339	4.9	358	5.6	378	5.7
Law	K	420	374	392	5.0	420	7.1	433	3.2	457	5.6
Library science	Z	148	768	815	6.1	858	5.4	899	4.8	927	3.1
Math and computer science	QA	940	1,117	1,187	6.3	1,247	5.0	1,302	4.4	1,367	5.0
Military and naval science	U,V	80	441	469	6.4	519	10.8	549	5.7	570	3.8
Music	M	143	180	191	6.3	200	4.6	209	4.3	218	4.6
Philosophy and religion	B-BD, BH-BX	540	264	281	6.6	300	6.6	317	5.6	333	5.3
Physics	QC	447	2,847	3,005	5.5	3,111	3.5	3,217	3.4	3,357	4.3
Political science	J	240	548	581	6.0	609	4.9	664	9.0	703	5.9
Psychology	BF	306	608	664	9.2	709	6.7	757	6.8	802	6.0
Recreation	GV	106	435	484	11.4	515	6.2	560	8.8	604	7.8
Social sciences	H	128	561	635	13.2	666	4.8	754	13.2	790	4.8
Sociology	HM-HX	715	629	675	7.3	724	7.2	769	6.3	813	5.7
Technology	TA-TT	361	1,273	1,350	6.0	1,411	4.5	1,491	5.7	1,550	3.9
Zoology	QL	289	1,090	1,152	5.7	1,220	5.9	1,324	8.6	1,384	4.5
Totals		17,637	$1,013	$1,081	6.7 %	$1,144	5.8 %	$1,213	6.0 %	$1,280	5.6 %

Compiled by Stephen Bosch, University of Arizona. Data on serial pricing supplied by EBSCO and is based on titles indexed in EBSCO Academic Search Premier, EBSCO Masterfile Premier, Clarivate Analytics (fomerly ISI) Arts and Humanities Citation Index, Clarivate Analytics Science Citation Index, Clarivate Analytics Science Citation Index, and Elsevier's Scopus.

Table 8A / Changes in the Average Price of Online Serials 2013–2017, Based on Titles in Select Serial Indices

Subject	LC Class	Avg. No. of Titles	2013 Avg. Price	2014 Avg. Price	2014–13 % of Price Increase	2015 Avg. Price	2015–14 % of Price Increase	2016 Avg. Price	2016–15 % of Price Increase	2017 Avg. Price	2017–16 % of Price Increase
Agriculture	S	258	$767	$804	4.8 %	$846	5.2 %	$893	5.6 %	$949	6.3%
Anthropology	GN	70	573	619	8.0	656	6.0	689	5.1	728	5.7
Arts and architecture	N	92	460	497	7.9	532	7.1	571	7.3	611	7.0
Astronomy	QB	41	1,702	1,786	4.9	1,928	7.9	1,980	2.7	2,094	5.7
Biology	QH	585	1,602	1,707	6.5	1,808	5.9	1,914	5.9	2,026	5.9
Botany	QK	84	1,087	1,187	9.2	1,240	4.5	1,287	3.8	1,360	5.7
Business and economics	HA-HJ	736	1,383	1,472	6.4	1,575	7.0	1,675	6.4	1,717	2.5
Chemistry	QD	211	3,277	3,553	8.4	3,756	5.7	3,947	5.1	4,158	5.3
Education	L	319	751	815	8.4	885	8.6	946	6.9	997	5.4
Engineering	T	943	1,349	1,446	7.2	1,559	7.8	1,671	7.2	1,750	4.7
Food science	TX	55	1,308	1,417	8.3	1,512	6.7	1,573	4.0	1,624	3.3
General science	Q	132	1,229	1,319	7.3	1,396	5.9	1,463	4.8	1,538	5.2
General works	A	36	475	553	16.6	574	3.8	690	20.1	723	4.8
Geography	G-GF	174	782	851	8.9	890	4.5	946	6.4	1,019	7.7
Geology	QE	109	1,215	1,302	7.1	1,378	5.9	1,461	6.0	1,555	6.4
Health sciences	R	1,902	896	961	7.3	1,021	6.2	1,087	6.5	1,158	6.5

Subject	LC Class									
History	C,D,E,F	349	384	417	8.5	445	6.8	467	4.8	504	8.0
Language and literature	P	338	436	465	6.7	491	5.5	523	6.5	558	6.7
Law	K	138	573	607	5.9	655	7.9	656	0.2	701	6.7
Library science	Z	91	982	1,042	6.2	1,100	5.6	1,156	5.0	1,183	2.4
Math and computer science	QA	586	1,107	1,182	6.8	1,251	5.8	1,319	5.4	1,391	5.5
Military and naval science	U,V	48	506	535	5.7	608	13.7	646	6.2	673	4.2
Music	M	52	290	307	6.0	329	7.0	348	5.7	370	6.4
Philosophy and religion	B-BD, BH-BX	195	427	456	6.8	487	6.8	522	7.0	556	6.7
Physics	QC	262	3,011	3,221	6.9	3,388	5.2	3,536	4.4	3,717	5.1
Political science	J	166	610	646	5.8	681	5.5	743	9.1	788	6.0
Psychology	BF	159	669	732	9.4	777	6.2	832	7.0	882	5.9
Recreation	QV	57	628	702	11.6	745	6.2	811	8.7	877	8.2
Social sciences	H	65	677	800	18.0	833	4.2	969	16.3	1,015	4.7
Sociology	HM-HX	470	727	779	7.2	838	7.5	891	6.4	943	5.9
Technology	TA-TT	204	1,511	1,614	6.8	1,699	5.3	1,800	5.9	1,866	3.7
Zoology	QL	134	983	1,032	5.0	1,097	6.3	1,269	15.6	1,325	4.5
Totals		9,061	$1,093	$1,171	7.2%	$1,245	6.4%	$1,323	6.2%	$1,393	5.3%

Compiled by Stephen Bosch, University of Arizona. Data on serial pricing supplied by EBSCO and is based on titles indexed in EBSCO Academic Search Premier, EBSCO Masterfile Premier, Clarivate Analytics (fomerly ISI) Arts and Humanities Citation Index, Clarivate Analytics Science Citation Index, Clarivate Analytics Social Sciences Citation Index, and Elsevier's Scopus.

Table 9 / British Academic Books: Average Prices and Price Indexes 2009–2016

Index Base: 2009 = 100

Subject	LC Class	2009		2013		2014		2015		2016			
		No. of Titles	Average Price (£)	No. of Titles	Average Price (£)	No. of Titles	Average Price (£)	No. of Titles	Average Price (£)	No. of Titles	Average Price (£)	% Average Change 2015–2016	Index
Agriculture	S	140	53.96	163	68.55	134	73.28	131	73.63	142	77.66	5.5%	143.9
Anthropology	GN	109	53.60	124	55.11	109	57.63	92	59.65	148	53.08	-11.0	99.0
Botany	QK	22	145.94	33	81.54	35	74.78	21	95.19	19	84.68	-11.0	58.0
Business and economics	H-HJ	1,634	59.08	1,877	71.29	1,911	71.19	1,866	75.13	1,897	73.35	-2.4	124.2
Chemistry	QD	88	101.14	96	149.82	91	125.67	72	127.89	57	113.66	-11.1	112.4
Education	L	386	49.70	440	64.49	517	64.50	583	68.39	577	179.48	162.4	361.1
Engineering and technology	T-TS	796	60.97	758	78.35	788	76.69	732	85.51	681	78.93	-7.7	129.5
Fine and applied arts	M, N	762	38.43	1,005	43.35	1,009	44.54	991	50.40	908	51.19	1.6	133.2
General works	A	15	76.73	17	91.58	32	72.25	21	83.47	27	106.91	28.1	139.3
Geography	G-GF, GR-GT	233	54.43	268	64.44	245	67.55	457	72.62	447	75.21	3.6	138.2
Geology	QE	41	53.80	34	77.70	33	59.80	34	60.87	28	69.53	14.2	129.2
History	C,D,E,F	1,572	43.41	1,690	44.63	1,725	48.11	1,835	51.22	1,914	55.21	7.8	127.2

Home economics	TX	59	39.02	58	67.22	38	63.79	29	85.98	32	67.49	-21.5	172.9
Industrial arts	TT	21	24.32	37	35.50	27	45.43	33	46.11	27	51.62	12.0	212.3
Law	K	1,117	76.13	1,264	88.46	1,253	88.30	1,184	85.16	1,117	101.35	19.0	133.1
Library and information science	Z	98	60.32	100	59.99	106	69.71	114	71.04	106	69.09	-2.7	114.5
Literature and language	P	2,928	34.77	3,448	37.25	3,553	38.95	3,008	42.33	3,070	46.86	10.7	134.8
Mathematics and computer science	QA	216	49.30	212	61.40	180	54.91	172	57.46	188	61.90	7.7	125.6
Medicine	R	1,110	48.50	1,126	60.74	1,113	63.10	946	67.52	905	69.56	3.0	143.4
Military and naval sciences	U, V	112	48.42	173	48.95	201	50.67	165	53.43	171	59.75	11.8	123.4
Philosophy and religion	B-BD, BH-BX	1,091	45.65	1,074	53.96	1,187	52.78	1,184	56.72	1,098	61.29	8.1	134.2
Physics and astronomy	QB, QC	196	54.73	221	72.08	161	72.29	185	65.07	179	66.85	2.7	122.2
Political Science	J	621	59.74	732	66.67	794	65.82	819	73.18	827	73.83	0.9	123.6
Psychology	BF	195	44.46	266	54.88	295	63.42	278	69.09	304	73.32	6.1	164.9
Science (general)	Q	45	41.65	47	54.85	54	57.89	53	62.95	62	80.73	28.3	193.8
Sociology	HM-HX	958	59.36	1,111	63.65	1,221	64.89	1,281	70.21	1,361	71.40	1.7	120.3
Sports & Recreation	GV	181	30.90	165	54.18	170	61.49	179	68.49	180	71.38	4.2	231.0
Zoology	QH, QL-QR	336	62.59	396	81.41	285	79.00	263	79.76	254	67.99	-14.8	108.6
Total, All Books		15,082	50.42	16,935	58.47	17,267	59.05	16,728	63.22	16,726	69.46	9.9%	137.7

Compiled by George Aulisio, University of Scranton, based on information provided by YBP U.K./Baker & Taylor.

(continued from page 293)

Foreign Prices

During 2016, the dollar slipped slightly against the Canadian dollar and Japanese yen. However, it has continued to gain against the euro and British pound sterling.

Dates	12/31/12*	12/31/13*	12/31/14*	12/31/15*	12/31/16*
Canada	0.9950	1.0640	1.1580	1.3860	1.3460
Euro	0.7590	0.7260	0.8220	0.9190	0.9490
U.K.	0.6180	0.6050	0.6420	0.6750	0.8120
Japan	86.1600	105.0100	119.4500	120.4200	117.0300

* Data from Bureau of Fiscal Services. U.S. Treasury Department (http://www.fiscal.treasury.gov/fsreports/rpt/treasRptRateExch/treasRptRateExch_home.htm).

Serials Prices

Average Price of Serials (Table 8) and Average Price of Online Serials (Table 8A), compiled by Stephen Bosch, provide the average prices and percent increases for serials based on titles in select serials abstracting and indexing products. The serials in this price survey are published in the United States as well as overseas and are indexed in the Clarivate Analytics' (formerly ISI) Arts and Humanities Citation Index, Science Citation Index, and Social Sciences Citation Index, as well as EBSCO's Academic Search Premier and Masterfile Premier and Elsevier's Scopus. This is the second year where titles indexed in Scopus are included in the data. Adding Scopus expands this price survey from about 11,000 titles in 2015 to the current 17,637. The increase in the sample size makes the results more likely to accurately reflect pricing trends.

Tables 8 and 8A cover prices for periodicals and serials for a five-year period, 2013 through 2017. The 2017 pricing is the actual renewal pricing for 2017 for serials that were indexed in the selected products. These tables are derived from pricing data supplied by EBSCO Information Services and reflect broad pricing changes aggregated from titles that are indexed in the six major products mentioned above. The U.S. Periodicals: Average Prices and Price Indexes (USPPI) (Table 1) is based on price changes seen in a static set of approximately 5,900 serial titles. The Average Price of Serials (Table 8) is based on a much broader set of titles, approximately 17,600; however, the titles are not static, so this pricing study does not rise to the level of a price index. This study is still useful in showing price changes for periodicals. The indexes selected for this price survey were deemed representative of serials that are frequently purchased in academic and public libraries. There are some foreign titles in the indexes, so the scope is broader and this may give a better picture of the overall price pressures experienced in libraries. Table 8 contains both print and online serials pricing. Table 8A is a subset of the titles treated in Table 8 and contains only online serials pricing.

The most important trend seen in the data in Table 8 is that increases in prices have remained constant since the economic recovery began. Price increases have hovered around 6 percent annually since 2013. For titles with online availability (Table 8A), the rates of increase for those titles are very similar, averaging around six percent over the past five years. There is a difference between the average prices for print serials and online serials, so, at least for this set of data, print formats do cost less than their online counterparts. Several large publishers have made online pricing only available through custom quotes, so there is not a standard retail price and the pricing data is not available for this survey. Since these titles tend to be more expensive than titles from other publishers, this may affect the overall prices making them lower.

Another interesting trend is that the science areas do not dominate the list of subjects with the largest price increases. The subject areas that displayed large increases were quite varied. Social sciences, general works, arts and architecture, political science, recreation, and zoology saw higher increases than most areas. Some of these same areas showed the highest increases in the online table (Table 8A) as well. Average prices of journals in the science and technology areas are by far higher than in other areas and that trend continues with the average cost of chemistry and physics journals being $4,136 and $3,357 respectively. Although these STM titles are not inflating at high rates, the impact of a 4 percent increase in a $4,000 title is much higher than a 9 percent increase on a $300 title. Online journals (Table 8A) showed similar average prices for chemistry ($4,158) and physics ($3,717).

In this price study, as in similar price surveys, the data become less accurate at describing price changes as the sample becomes smaller. For that reason, drawing conclusions about price changes in subject areas with a limited number of titles will be less accurate than for large areas or the broader price survey. Price changes are far more volatile where smaller data sets are used. For example, military and naval science (about 80 titles) showed price changes of 6.4 percent, 10.8 percent, and 5.7 and 3.8 percent between 2013 and 2017. Librarians are encouraged to look at an average price change over the period (military and naval science averaged 6.7 percent) or the overall number for the price study (5.6 percent) to calculate inflation. Year-to-year price changes in small subject areas are too unstable to be used for this purpose.

Book Prices

British Academic Books (Table 9), compiled by George Aulisio, indicates the average prices and price indexes from 2013 through 2016. The percent of change in titles and average price is calculated for 2015 to 2016, and the index price shows the percent of change between 2016 and the base year of 2009. This index is compiled using data from YBP and utilizes prices from cloth editions except when not available. YBP U.K. also profiles select titles from continental Europe and Africa. The index does not separate out more expensive reference titles. Small numbers of titles that include higher-priced reference sets may not be reliable indicators of price changes. This table does not include e-book prices.

Data on "Total, All Books" production illustrates the sum total of the LC Classes profiled in this table, not the sum total of all books profiled by YBP. In 2016, total British academic books were comparable with last year's numbers with 16,726 titles as against 16,728 titles in 2015.

In 2016 there was a significant overall price increase of 9.9 percent, bringing the average price for all books profiled to £69.46. The 2016 increase is significantly higher than the United Kingdom's Consumer Price Index, which, according to the Office of National Statistics, was at a modest 1.6 percent inflation in December 2016 (http://www.ons.gov.uk).

Table 9 shows how average prices have increased or decreased in comparison with the 2009 base year. For 2016, the overall index price for all LC subjects profiled in this table is at 137.7 percent. All LC classes are currently above their 2009 base prices, except for anthropology, which is now at 99.0 percent of the 2009 base price, and botany, which is now at 58.0 percent of the 2009 base price. The highest increases in comparison with the 2009 base prices are education (361.1 percent), sports and recreation (231.0 percent), industrial arts (212.3 percent), science (general) (193.8 percent), home economics (172.9 percent), and psychology (164.9 percent). The high individual price increase from 2015 to 2016 in general works (28.1 percent), geology (14.2 percent), and industrial arts (12.0 percent) may be due to small sample sizes of less than 30 titles.

The 9.9 percent price increase of 2016 is the second-highest average price increase recorded in this table, with the 10.7 percent price increase of 2012 being the highest recorded. This is the second year in a row with a high price increase. In 2013 and 2014, the years immediately following the largest recorded price increase, there were modest average price increases of 1.7 percent and 1.0 percent, respectively. There are no reliable indicators for a 2016 industry forecast. However, given the health of the industry, the improvement in print book sales, and historical data, cautious optimism suggests the U.K. book publishing industry may return to its recent practice of modest price increases.

Using the Price Indexes

Librarians are encouraged to monitor trends in the publishing industry and changes in economic conditions when preparing budget forecasts and projections. The ALA ALCTS Library Materials Price Index Editorial Board endeavors to make information on publishing trends readily available by sponsoring the annual compilation and publication of price data contained in Tables 1 to 9. The indexes cover newly published library materials and document prices and rates of percent changes at the national and international level. They are useful benchmarks against which local costs can be compared, but because they reflect retail prices in the aggregate, they are not a substitute for cost data that reflect the collecting patterns of individual libraries, and they are not a substitute for specific cost studies.

Differences between local prices and those found in national indexes arise partially because these indexes exclude discounts, service charges, shipping and handling fees, and other costs that the library might incur. Discrepancies may also relate to a library's subject coverage; mix of titles purchased, including both current and backfiles; and the proportion of the library's budget expended on domestic or foreign materials. These variables can affect the average price paid by an individual library, although the individual library's rate of increase may not differ greatly from the national indexes.

LMPI is interested in pursuing studies that would correlate a particular library's costs with the national prices. The group welcomes interested parties to its meetings at ALA Annual and Midwinter conferences.

The Library Materials Price Index Editorial Board consists of compilers George Aulisio, Catherine Barr, Ajaye Bloomstone, Stephen Bosch, Kittie Henderson, Frederick C. Lynden, and editor Narda Tafuri.

Book Title Output and Average Prices: 2012–2016

Catherine Barr

Constance Harbison

Baker & Taylor

Overall American book title output has generally showed growing strength since the economic downturn, but this recovery has been uneven. After reaching a high of 210,772 in 2012 (up from 2009's 178,841), revised figures for 2013 show a dip to 204,402 followed by a rebound to nearly 220,000 in 2014 and a drop back to 200,337 in 2015. Preliminary figures for 2016 indicate a recovery, and these numbers may be revised upward as late-arriving materials are added to the database.

The figures for this edition of the *Library and Book Trade Almanac* were provided by book wholesaler Baker & Taylor and are based on the Book Industry Study Group's BISAC categories. The BISAC juvenile category (fiction and nonfiction) has been divided into children's and young adult. Figures for 2014 and 2015 have been restated, reflecting late updates to the Baker & Taylor database. Figures for 2016 are preliminary.

For more information on the BISAC categories, visit http://www.bisg.org.

Output by Format and by Category

Revised results for 2015 were mixed. Output of hardcover titles has grown steadily apart from a slight dip in 2014; hardcovers priced at less than $81 have moved in a tight range over this period; mass market paperbacks fell 12 percent and trade paperbacks declined also, with output down nearly 9 percent. The rapid increase in audiobook output stalled in 2013 (after soaring more than 43 percent in 2012) recovered in 2014 and 2015 with optimistic indicators for 2016; and e-books, which had scored an impressive gain of 93.28 percent in 2012, found their momentum slowing, with a decline of 13.70 percent in 2013, and a further 3.70 percent in 2014 and 5 percent in 2015.

Output of fiction, a key category, grew 13.07 percent in 2013 after a drop of 8.64 percent in 2012; but output fell again in 2014 and 2015. Output of hardcover fiction priced at less than $81 rebounded a little more than 17 percent in 2013, but dropped just over 10 percent in 2014 and dipped again in 2015; preliminary results for 2016 indicated a rebound. In the paperback sector, both mass market and trade fiction continued to decline. Audiobook fiction is showing robust growth. E-book fiction output, after climbing steadily for several years, has shown uneven results, dropping in 2013 and rising in 2014 only to fall again.

The important juveniles category is broken down into children's (PreK–6) and young adult (YA; grades 7–12) titles. Overall children's books output has been rising steadily as has production of hardcover books priced at less than $81, but mass market paperbacks remain low lost 3.55 percent while trade paperbacks maintain a slow but steady rise. Children's audiobooks and e-books showed inconsistent growth.

Output of YA titles bounces up and down but the decline in mass market paperbacks continues. Trade paperbacks remain stronger. YA audiobook production held fairly steady but e-books have shown more challenges.

Book prices overall fell in 2015, but preliminary results for 2016 showed an increase, back to the level of 2014.

Table 1 / American Book Production, 2012–2016

BISAC Category	2012	2013	2014	2015	2016
Antiques and collectibles	289	283	294	262	284
Architecture	1,402	1,747	1,515	1,782	1,667
Art	3,554	4,029	3,613	3,740	3,783
Bibles	840	995	912	1,134	849
Biography and autobiography	4,365	5,122	4,808	4,441	4,403
Body, mind, and spirit	1,207	1,267	1,041	833	849
Business and economics	13,811	12,335	13,952	14,302	12,092
Children	22,461	23,127	25,829	25,587	27,309
Comics and graphic novels	2,941	2,495	2,742	2,728	2,883
Computers	5,379	4,693	4,624	3,944	5,294
Cooking	2,435	2,473	2,578	2,370	2,193
Crafts and hobbies	1,291	1,446	1,387	1,278	1,008
Design	894	732	704	718	682
Drama	578	703	671	605	627
Education	5,996	6,289	6,852	6,633	7,148
Family and relationships	977	1,046	987	887	828
Fiction	19,379	22,526	21,858	18,732	18,195
Foreign language study	1,483	1,501	1,698	1,360	981
Games	787	747	743	885	2,014
Gardening	370	315	263	281	223
Health and fitness	1,544	1,525	1,557	1,536	1,401
History	12,007	12,199	14,189	12,968	12,505
House and home	236	267	1,041	226	177
Humor	640	605	642	619	573
Language arts and disciplines	3,549	3,383	3,899	3,518	3,839
Law	5,476	5,530	6,122	6,147	6,204
Literary collections	752	797	958	556	637
Literary criticism	3,628	3,889	5,545	4,309	4,721
Mathematics	4,100	2,726	2,828	2,264	2,587
Medical	12,572	9,223	9,000	7,906	8,291
Music	3,222	3,378	2,860	3,320	2,946
Nature	1,045	1,051	1,037	987	1,044
Performing arts	1,502	1,546	1,877	1,790	1,674
Pets	310	268	254	239	268
Philosophy	2,836	3,011	3,603	3,208	3,304
Photography	1,379	1,260	1,321	1,385	1,255
Poetry	2,248	2,859	2,651	2,275	2,435
Political science	6,239	6,480	8,758	7,056	7,189
Psychology	3,327	3,401	3,660	3,834	3,905
Reference	1,537	1,253	1,304	1,081	918
Religion	9,927	11,230	10,402	9,998	9,706
Science	12,575	9,217	9,471	7,296	8,291
Self-help	1,707	1,696	1,478	1,350	1,307
Social science	8,708	8,148	9,411	8,747	9,561
Sports and recreation	1,777	1,813	1,843	1,710	1,658
Study aids	626	628	1,904	959	716
Technology and engineering	7,971	5,935	7,129	5,373	7,013
Transportation	631	759	724	678	765
Travel	2,367	1,960	1,929	1,828	1,809
True crime	277	285	282	256	246
Young adult	5,618	4,209	5,233	4,416	4,882
Totals	210,772	204,402	219,983	200,337	205,139

Table 2 / Hardcover Average Per-Volume Prices, 2013–2016

BISAC Category	2013			2014			2015			2016		
	Vols.	$ Total	Prices	Vols.	$ Total	Prices	Vols.	$ Total	Prices	Vols.	$ Total	Prices
Antiques and collectibles	139	$9,835.83	$70.76	144	$9,487.94	$65.89	136	$13,143.96	$96.65	138	$11,080.50	$80.29
Architecture	926	82,744.31	89.36	807	72,230.36	89.50	967	96,590.03	99.89	947	98,337.51	103.84
Art	2,081	151,950.06	73.02	1,915	155,398.28	81.15	1,971	146,097.54	74.12	2,088	158,065.92	75.70
Bibles	189	7,162.74	37.90	137	4,663.56	34.04	168	6,065.48	36.10	206	8,455.72	41.05
Biography and autobiography	1,946	91,629.44	47.09	1,822	87,930.02	48.26	1,747	82,785.30	47.39	1,802	89,515.74	49.68
Body, mind, and spirit	240	7,910.46	32.96	165	7,619.45	46.18	156	4,724.68	30.29	159	4,493.83	28.26
Business and economics	4,506	696,067.00	154.48	4,408	650,519.08	147.58	4,775	729,663.14	152.81	4,948	788,302.62	159.32
Children	12,266	292,561.26	23.85	12,943	315,470.50	24.37	13,136	325,003.94	24.74	14,765	373,805.46	25.32
Comics and graphic novels	648	24,471.38	37.76	658	26,553.40	40.35	685	25,902.09	37.81	648	25,609.88	39.52
Computers	911	132,799.45	145.77	926	146,255.58	157.94	990	148,515.70	150.02	1,084	158,949.52	146.63
Cooking	1,214	36,161.73	29.79	1,263	36,752.99	29.10	1,256	35,965.48	28.63	1,200	35,195.37	29.33
Crafts and hobbies	201	5,890.82	29.31	207	5,896.27	28.48	170	4,913.07	28.90	154	4,896.56	31.80
Design	401	25,263.24	63.00	395	26,561.36	67.24	459	30,326.56	66.07	438	31,424.28	71.74
Drama	88	7,133.37	81.06	80	6,532.21	81.65	56	4,730.99	84.48	105	9,649.76	91.90
Education	1,794	220,807.27	123.08	1,955	243,927.90	124.77	2,235	279,574.74	125.09	2,624	352,799.13	134.45
Family and relationships	273	10,863.74	39.79	213	9,898.48	46.47	210	12,417.75	59.13	189	10,367.76	54.86
Fiction	5,146	155,859.00	30.29	4,834	145,610.01	30.12	4,455	132,748.86	29.80	4,642	138,313.09	29.80
Foreign language study	303	40,492.06	133.64	229	26,741.97	116.78	289	43,983.92	152.19	225	26,236.01	116.60
Games	114	4,717.26	41.38	95	3,762.39	39.60	117	4,471.14	38.21	166	5,799.46	34.94
Gardening	115	4,404.39	38.30	97	2,964.57	30.56	123	4,652.87	37.83	102	3,363.24	32.97
Health and fitness	382	24,840.64	65.03	366	21,232.03	58.01	408	37,774.32	92.58	350	25,528.35	72.94
History	5,385	487,856.44	90.60	5,540	533,039.86	96.22	5,792	540,021.24	93.24	6,279	640,861.86	102.06
House and home	108	3,971.65	36.77	92	3,090.98	33.60	109	3,892.86	35.71	90	3,264.48	36.27
Humor	246	4,876.22	19.82	292	6,912.30	23.67	295	7,156.79	24.26	286	6,173.42	21.59

	Count	Amount	Avg.	Count	Amount	Avg.	Count	Amount	Avg.	Count	Amount	Avg.
Language arts and disciplines	1,328	195,738.83	147.39	1,292	191,057.94	147.88	1,585	231,916.98	146.32	1,566	226,187.75	144.44
Law	2,109	382,556.42	181.39	2,183	395,750.25	181.29	2,248	400,778.75	178.28	2,453	453,013.88	184.68
Literary collections	305	29,246.50	95.89	279	27,411.27	98.25	213	24,099.70	113.14	240	22,372.00	93.22
Literary criticism	2,210	276,713.60	125.21	2,315	300,861.37	129.96	2,328	286,687.12	123.15	2,943	363,380.05	123.47
Mathematics	961	139,720.81	145.39	973	143,238.05	147.21	1,031	163,761.97	158.84	1,097	150,632.14	137.31
Medical	3,527	672,625.04	190.71	3,511	721,964.87	205.63	4,119	762,092.87	185.02	3,247	568,152.19	174.98
Music	594	56,800.22	95.62	544	50,100.71	92.10	569	54,183.05	95.23	658	63,778.55	96.93
Nature	472	41,465.90	87.85	422	38,401.63	91.00	467	42,392.37	90.78	475	46,856.71	98.65
Performing arts	649	63,392.74	97.68	686	65,867.90	96.02	813	79,980.24	98.38	854	84,881.37	99.39
Pets	109	2,828.59	25.95	110	2,684.58	24.41	88	2,197.23	24.97	110	2,490.51	22.64
Philosophy	1,396	154,299.60	110.53	1,429	161,432.15	112.97	1,532	168,756.13	110.15	1,657	198,811.79	119.98
Photography	812	75,419.59	92.88	848	56,000.21	66.04	913	62,375.50	68.32	856	59,805.96	69.87
Poetry	422	14,567.61	34.52	358	12,471.43	34.84	280	13,117.42	46.85	432	23,849.91	55.21
Political science	2,807	325,881.22	116.10	3,051	359,950.72	117.98	3,139	373,564.26	119.01	3,477	400,430.97	115.17
Psychology	1,209	169,979.17	140.59	1,197	184,097.82	153.80	1,420	215,298.34	151.62	1,418	210,085.22	148.16
Reference	419	155,759.03	371.74	403	129,469.64	321.26	359	141,113.14	393.07	349	115,255.32	330.24
Religion	2,904	228,392.63	78.65	2,579	208,492.49	80.84	2,517	219,751.11	87.31	2,825	230,429.20	81.57
Science	3,486	772,346.52	221.56	3,582	722,421.95	201.68	4,251	863,171.83	203.05	4,024	818,926.05	203.51
Self-help	379	10,716.30	28.28	297	7,579.30	25.52	304	8,430.50	27.73	280	6,843.87	24.44
Social science	3,436	412,577.21	120.07	3,369	478,592.34	142.06	3,829	517,395.12	135.13	4,161	542,145.34	130.29
Sports and recreation	691	33,056.86	47.84	628	38,283.71	60.96	616	32,640.82	52.99	605	33,534.91	55.43
Study aids	14	1,629.34	116.38	19	1,785.30	93.96	15	2,079.40	138.63	17	1,667.24	98.07
Technology and engineering	2,583	465,501.51	180.22	2,616	503,535.97	192.48	3,416	575,825.34	168.57	3,753	666,745.36	177.66
Transportation	326	24,598.44	75.46	249	21,301.14	85.55	293	25,243.31	86.15	282	17,338.62	61.48
Travel	205	8,368.64	40.82	184	7,025.50	38.18	208	7,136.05	34.31	212	8,556.86	40.36
True crime	86	2,383.18	27.71	79	2,278.95	28.85	67	2,831.23	42.26	89	3,160.48	35.51
Young adult	1,975	62,425.67	31.61	2,188	75,441.16	34.48	2,056	68,809.17	33.47	2,290	86,624.06	37.83
Totals	75,036	$7,309,260.93	$97.41	74,974	$7,456,549.84	$99.46	79,381	$8,066,751.40	$101.62	84,005	$8,416,445.78	$100.19

Table 3 / Hardcover Average Per-Volume Prices, Less Than $81, 2013–2016

BISAC Category	2013			2014			2015			2016		
	Vols.	$ Total	Prices	Vols.	$ Total	Prices	Vols.	$ Total	Prices	Vols.	$ Total	Prices
Antiques and collectibles	112	$4,375.41	$39.07	112	$4,573.46	$40.83	89	$4,048.64	$45.49	106	$5,061.57	$47.75
Architecture	578	30,887.66	53.44	493	25,982.33	52.70	551	28,304.74	51.37	485	23,790.34	49.05
Art	1,550	73,837.42	47.64	1,397	66,750.34	47.78	1,471	70,361.27	47.83	1,519	70,478.71	46.40
Bibles	185	6,746.81	36.47	136	4,518.53	33.22	164	5,539.49	33.78	200	7,290.76	36.45
Biography and autobiography	1,794	56,737.95	31.63	1,625	50,630.07	31.16	1,593	49,633.10	31.16	1,612	49,995.89	31.01
Body, mind, and spirit	228	6,272.46	27.51	146	3,252.34	22.28	145	3,150.68	21.73	152	3,444.88	22.66
Business and economics	1,624	71,694.02	44.15	1,601	73,906.53	46.16	1,528	68,664.68	44.94	1,502	67,188.92	44.73
Children	11,965	234,239.70	19.58	12,452	249,944.50	20.07	12,764	256,563.51	20.10	14,342	292,022.65	20.36
Comics and graphic novels	606	19,741.65	32.58	615	19,290.33	31.37	641	20,207.27	31.52	600	19,299.99	32.17
Computers	189	11,487.51	60.78	205	12,824.02	62.56	231	14,892.54	64.47	270	17,033.56	63.09
Cooking	1,187	31,718.02	26.72	1,231	33,582.29	27.28	1,235	33,435.52	27.07	1,179	32,348.77	27.44
Crafts and hobbies	193	4,965.42	25.73	198	5,180.12	26.16	168	4,729.07	28.15	150	4,194.56	27.96
Design	327	15,469.19	47.31	312	15,209.12	48.75	358	16,538.05	46.20	342	16,007.16	46.80
Drama	43	2,093.46	48.69	41	1,858.67	45.33	25	1,316.35	52.65	43	1,871.63	43.53
Education	558	29,608.85	53.06	686	35,079.56	51.14	629	32,587.66	51.81	639	33,901.70	53.05
Family and relationships	240	6,014.54	25.06	166	3,972.21	23.93	156	3,402.43	21.81	149	3,555.09	23.86
Fiction	5,109	149,209.22	29.21	4,593	133,306.73	29.02	4,427	127,232.26	28.74	4,600	131,165.75	28.51
Foreign language study	126	7,058.40	56.02	94	5,454.75	58.03	97	5,794.39	59.74	99	5,731.69	57.90
Games	104	3,364.29	32.35	88	2,811.36	31.95	108	3,385.17	31.34	155	4,509.59	29.09
Gardening	107	3,215.89	30.06	96	2,792.03	29.08	120	4,327.87	36.07	100	3,124.24	31.24
Health and fitness[1]	274	7,612.95	27.78	279	8,077.10	28.95	265	7,700.07	29.06	242	7,180.48	29.67
History	2,948	129,892.36	44.06	2,968	132,724.91	44.72	3,004	135,241.74	45.02	2,977	131,874.68	44.30
House and home	106	3,771.65	35.58	90	2,937.99	32.64	107	3,569.39	33.36	89	3,164.53	35.56
Humor	246	4,876.22	19.82	286	6,588.37	23.04	290	6,251.79	21.56	284	5,953.48	20.96

Category	Count	Amount	Pct	Count	Amount	Pct	Count	Amount	Pct	Count	Amount	Pct
Language arts and disciplines	302	17,219.62	57.02	257	15,376.35	59.83	287	16,453.91	57.33	268	15,164.10	56.58
Law	344	20,088.16	58.40	290	16,935.64	58.40	276	15,286.62	55.39	290	15,935.56	54.95
Literary collections	141	5,698.67	40.42	152	5,695.43	37.47	122	4,645.82	38.08	143	5,331.92	37.29
Literary criticism	781	45,761.32	58.59	781	46,220.44	59.18	714	40,589.60	56.85	840	49,247.20	58.63
Mathematics	190	11,308.44	59.52	208	12,766.88	61.38	156	10,071.06	64.56	217	14,062.80	64.81
Medical	330	17,690.49	53.61	282	15,912.67	56.43	312	18,254.92	58.51	333	19,379.96	58.20
Music	291	12,970.94	44.57	307	13,963.85	45.48	265	11,584.70	43.72	302	13,242.24	43.85
Nature	275	9,185.68	33.40	238	8,563.18	35.98	225	8,126.69	36.12	235	7,886.14	33.56
Performing arts	282	13,979.00	49.57	301	15,167.17	50.39	295	14,388.97	48.78	291	13,922.64	47.84
Pets	109	2,828.59	25.95	106	2,509.65	23.68	86	1,938.23	22.54	109	2,353.01	21.59
Philosophy	523	29,341.82	56.10	501	28,350.42	56.59	506	27,322.09	54.00	465	25,762.70	55.40
Photography	705	33,661.99	47.75	730	34,846.78	47.74	778	37,094.58	47.68	756	35,421.81	46.85
Poetry	408	11,644.16	28.54	329	9,075.10	27.58	258	7,599.52	29.46	337	11,900.46	35.31
Political science	902	44,621.94	49.47	942	48,196.34	51.16	864	43,565.51	50.42	1,025	49,040.34	47.84
Psychology	332	16,197.03	48.79	327	15,931.90	48.72	346	17,854.85	51.60	293	14,956.30	51.05
Reference	172	5,427.63	31.56	159	4,729.06	29.74	150	4,451.57	29.68	147	5,020.23	34.15
Religion	1,871	63,128.53	33.74	1,579	57,535.48	36.44	1,435	51,071.86	35.59	1,667	60,816.28	36.48
Science	539	24,504.29	45.46	515	24,559.16	47.69	543	25,935.20	47.76	596	29,176.41	48.95
Self-help	369	9,382.30	25.43	278	6,523.11	23.46	292	6,839.29	23.42	276	6,372.87	23.09
Social science	1,204	66,309.79	55.07	1,031	57,581.77	55.85	1,034	57,249.80	55.37	1,028	55,414.81	53.91
Sports and recreation	606	19,133.04	31.57	514	16,365.97	31.84	518	16,259.02	31.39	503	15,730.01	31.27
Study aids	9	409.64	45.52	14	648.60	46.33	8	454.70	56.84	9	519.59	57.73
Technology and engineering	217	12,128.75	55.89	210	11,867.72	56.51	196	11,107.74	56.67	190	10,425.72	54.87
Transportation	251	10,255.76	40.86	170	7,134.70	41.97	211	8,739.39	41.42	233	10,223.02	43.88
Travel	187	5,813.74	31.09	169	5,281.70	31.25	201	6,171.15	30.70	192	5,306.06	27.64
True crime	85	2,302.18	27.08	78	2,249.05	28.83	60	1,841.28	30.69	86	2,580.53	30.01
Young adult	1,912	47,749.65	24.97	2,075	55,068.34	26.54	1,971	50,364.08	25.55	2,156	57,028.82	26.45
Totals	43,736	$1,473,634.20	$33.69	42,453	$1,440,304.12	$33.93	42,275	$1,422,139.83	$33.64	44,823	$1,492,412.15	$33.30

Table 4 / Mass Market Paperbacks Average Per-Volume Prices, 2013–2016

BISAC Category	2013 Vols.	2013 $ Total	2013 Prices	2014 Vols.	2014 $ Total	2014 Prices	2015 Vols.	2015 $ Total	2015 Prices	2016 Vols.	2016 $ Total	2016 Prices
Antiques and collectibles	5	$44.95	$8.99	4	$35.96	$8.99	n.a.	n.a.	n.a.	n.a.	n.a.	n.a.
Architecture	n.a.	n.a.	n.a.	n.a.	n.a.	n.a.	n.a.	n.a.	n.a.	n.a.	n.a.	n.a.
Art	n.a.	n.a.	n.a.	n.a.	n.a.	n.a.	n.a.	n.a.	n.a.	n.a.	n.a.	n.a.
Bibles	n.a.	n.a.	n.a.	n.a.	n.a.	n.a.	2	$16.98	$8.49	n.a.	n.a.	n.a.
Biography and autobiography	3	28.98	9.66	6	53.90	8.98	n.a.	n.a.	n.a.	6	$63.95	$10.66
Body, mind and spirit	14	113.86	8.13	2	19.98	9.99	1	8.99	8.99	2	17.98	8.99
Business and economics	n.a.	n.a.	n.a.	n.a.	n.a.	n.a.	n.a.	n.a.	n.a.	n.a.	n.a.	n.a.
Children	282	1,803.65	6.40	272	1,660.26	6.10	204	1,289.96	6.32	224	1,542.63	6.89
Comics and graphic novels	n.a.	n.a.	n.a.	n.a.	n.a.	n.a.	n.a.	n.a.	n.a.	n.a.	n.a.	n.a.
Computers	n.a.	n.a.	n.a.	n.a.	n.a.	n.a.	n.a.	n.a.	n.a.	n.a.	n.a.	n.a.
Cooking	n.a.	n.a.	n.a.	n.a.	n.a.	n.a.	1	8.99	8.99	n.a.	n.a.	n.a.
Crafts and hobbies	n.a.	n.a.	n.a.	n.a.	n.a.	n.a.	n.a.	n.a.	n.a.	n.a.	n.a.	n.a.
Design	n.a.	n.a.	n.a.	n.a.	n.a.	n.a.	n.a.	n.a.	n.a.	n.a.	n.a.	n.a.
Drama	n.a.	n.a.	n.a.	1	9.99	9.99	n.a.	n.a.	n.a.	n.a.	n.a.	n.a.
Education	n.a.	n.a.	n.a.	n.a.	n.a.	n.a.	n.a.	n.a.	n.a.	n.a.	n.a.	n.a.
Family and relationships	n.a.	n.a.	n.a.	n.a.	n.a.	n.a.	1	8.99	8.99	n.a.	n.a.	n.a.
Fiction	3,620	25,413.42	7.02	3,603	25,557.48	7.09	3,234	23,000.85	7.11	3,016	21,780.58	7.22
Foreign language study	n.a.	n.a.	n.a.	1	6.99	6.99	n.a.	n.a.	n.a.	n.a.	n.a.	n.a.
Games	1	9.99	9.99	2	18.49	9.25	1	7.99	7.99	3	25.97	8.66
Gardening	n.a.	n.a.	n.a.	n.a.	n.a.	n.a.	n.a.	n.a.	n.a.	n.a.	n.a.	n.a.
Health and fitness	8	65.92	8.24	3	27.98	9.33	3	26.97	8.99	n.a.	n.a.	n.a.
History	3	29.98	9.99	2	19.98	9.99	2	19.98	9.99	3	27.97	9.32
House and home	n.a.	n.a.	n.a.	n.a.	n.a.	n.a.	n.a.	n.a.	n.a.	n.a.	n.a.	n.a.

Humor	2	15.99	8.00	n.a.	n.a.	n.a.	n.a.	n.a.	n.a.	1	7.99	7.99
Language arts and disciplines	n.a.	n.a.	n.a.	1	7.99	7.99	1	7.99	7.99	n.a.	n.a.	n.a.
Law	n.a.	n.a.	n.a.	n.a.	n.a.	n.a.	n.a.	n.a.	n.a.	n.a.	n.a.	n.a.
Literary collections	n.a.	n.a.	n.a.	1	4.95	4.95	1	4.95	4.95	n.a.	n.a.	n.a.
Literary criticism	n.a.	n.a.	n.a.	n.a.	n.a.	n.a.	n.a.	n.a.	n.a.	n.a.	n.a.	n.a.
Mathematics	n.a.	n.a.	n.a.	n.a.	n.a.	n.a.	n.a.	n.a.	n.a.	n.a.	n.a.	n.a.
Medical	n.a.	n.a.	n.a.	1	7.99	7.99	1	7.99	7.99	n.a.	n.a.	n.a.
Music	n.a.	n.a.	n.a.	n.a.	n.a.	n.a.	n.a.	n.a.	n.a.	n.a.	n.a.	n.a.
Nature	n.a.	n.a.	n.a.	n.a.	n.a.	n.a.	n.a.	n.a.	n.a.	n.a.	n.a.	n.a.
Performing arts	1	10.99	10.99	1	10.99	10.99	1	10.99	10.99	n.a.	n.a.	n.a.
Pets	1	7.99	7.99	n.a.	n.a.	n.a.	1	9.99	9.99	1	9.99	9.99
Philosophy	n.a.	n.a.	n.a.	n.a.	n.a.	n.a.	1	6.95	6.95	1	6.95	6.95
Photography	n.a.	n.a.	n.a.	n.a.	n.a.	n.a.	n.a.	n.a.	n.a.	n.a.	n.a.	n.a.
Poetry	3	19.85	6.62	n.a.	n.a.	n.a.	2	12.90	6.45	1	3.99	3.99
Political science	n.a.	n.a.	n.a.	1	9.99	9.99	2	16.94	8.47	n.a.	n.a.	n.a.
Psychology	n.a.	n.a.	n.a.	n.a.	n.a.	n.a.	n.a.	n.a.	n.a.	n.a.	n.a.	n.a.
Reference	3	19.48	6.49	5	64.46	12.89	1	7.99	7.99	5	78.50	15.70
Religion	n.a.	n.a.	n.a.	n.a.	n.a.	n.a.	n.a.	n.a.	n.a.	n.a.	n.a.	n.a.
Science	n.a.	n.a.	n.a.	n.a.	n.a.	n.a.	n.a.	n.a.	n.a.	1	13.99	13.99
Self-help	n.a.	n.a.	n.a.	n.a.	n.a.	n.a.	n.a.	n.a.	n.a.	1	7.99	7.99
Social science	n.a.	n.a.	n.a.	n.a.	n.a.	n.a.	n.a.	n.a.	n.a.	n.a.	n.a.	n.a.
Sports and recreation	n.a.	n.a.	n.a.	n.a.	n.a.	n.a.	n.a.	n.a.	n.a.	1	9.99	9.99
Study aids	n.a.	n.a.	n.a.	n.a.	n.a.	n.a.	n.a.	n.a.	n.a.	n.a.	n.a.	n.a.
Technology and engineering	n.a.	n.a.	n.a.	n.a.	n.a.	n.a.	n.a.	n.a.	n.a.	n.a.	n.a.	n.a.
Transportation	1	5.99	5.99	n.a.	n.a.	n.a.	n.a.	n.a.	n.a.	n.a.	n.a.	n.a.
Travel	n.a.	n.a.	n.a.	n.a.	n.a.	n.a.	1	7.99	7.99	n.a.	n.a.	n.a.
True crime	26	220.74	8.49	20	173.80	8.69	13	107.87	8.30	13	109.87	8.45
Young adult	61	568.32	9.32	44	414.57	9.42	22	206.78	9.40	12	113.86	9.49
Totals	4,034	$28,380.10	$7.04	3,970	$28,105.75	$7.08	3,492	$24,767.11	$7.09	3,289	$23,805.26	$7.24

n.a. = not available

Table 5 / Trade Paperbacks Average Per-Volume Prices, 2013–2016

BISAC Category	2013			2014			2015			2016		
	Vols.	$ Total	Prices	Vols.	$ Total	Prices	Vols.	$ Total	Prices	Vols.	$ Total	Prices
Antiques and collectibles	139	$4,672.53	$33.62	139	$5,006.33	$36.02	126	$4,227.20	$33.55	146	$5,016.04	$34.36
Architecture	820	36,370.96	44.35	689	31,681.47	45.98	814	35,977.69	44.20	720	35,527.05	49.34
Art	1,942	94,634.29	48.73	1,679	66,455.05	39.58	1,680	70,497.95	41.96	1,659	78,682.54	47.43
Bibles	806	33,713.40	41.83	770	34,963.39	45.41	966	39,128.59	40.51	643	28,332.12	44.06
Biography and autobiography	3,176	63,288.72	19.93	2,920	59,600.10	20.41	2,692	54,930.01	20.40	2,595	51,190.76	19.73
Body, mind, and spirit	1,013	18,498.57	18.26	861	15,589.75	18.11	677	12,323.79	18.20	688	12,219.01	17.76
Business and economics	7,580	681,420.67	89.90	7,334	675,979.24	92.17	8,946	929,938.74	103.95	6,550	607,385.69	92.73
Children	10,461	125,925.45	12.04	11,493	149,042.21	12.97	12,215	185,660.55	15.20	12,287	180,351.41	14.68
Comics and graphic novels	1,847	30,718.11	16.63	2,077	36,463.18	17.56	2,043	36,836.56	18.03	2,235	41,167.92	18.42
Computers	3,814	342,365.27	89.77	3,506	293,638.64	83.75	2,903	246,666.62	84.97	3,689	442,958.69	120.08
Cooking	1,255	24,793.50	19.76	1,279	25,135.87	19.65	1,110	22,654.55	20.41	986	20,452.43	20.74
Crafts and hobbies	1,243	22,872.55	18.40	1,203	22,579.86	18.77	1,103	21,648.75	19.63	843	17,085.72	20.27
Design	331	12,981.36	39.22	308	12,974.68	42.13	258	11,588.27	44.92	244	9,254.57	37.93
Drama	615	12,460.59	20.26	584	12,118.54	20.75	542	12,351.57	22.79	515	11,007.28	21.37
Education	4,334	217,569.08	50.20	4,380	244,900.65	55.91	3,989	208,925.01	52.38	4,211	263,786.13	62.64
Family and relationships	770	15,480.74	20.10	756	17,307.38	22.89	674	13,534.96	20.08	636	13,410.10	21.09
Fiction	13,770	237,057.78	17.22	13,114	226,651.58	17.28	11,041	189,703.37	17.18	10,537	178,015.35	16.89
Foreign language study	1,108	63,542.06	57.35	1,370	61,346.00	44.78	1,005	49,496.52	49.25	735	36,378.44	49.49
Games	630	9,803.72	15.56	548	9,620.37	17.56	766	11,617.20	15.17	1,843	26,228.47	14.23
Gardening	200	4,569.29	22.85	163	3,576.37	21.94	158	3,946.05	24.97	121	2,741.72	22.66
Health and fitness	1,106	29,564.38	26.73	1,108	29,676.90	26.78	1,080	35,317.95	32.70	1,023	36,678.17	35.85
History	6,796	261,567.64	38.49	7,750	315,413.83	40.70	7,044	286,623.08	40.69	6,144	235,368.08	38.31
House and home	158	3,697.48	23.40	949	90,730.38	95.61	117	2,381.32	20.35	87	1,725.44	19.83
Humor	357	5,200.11	14.57	344	5,149.17	14.97	324	4,907.06	15.15	285	4,389.50	15.40

Category	Count	Amount	Avg	Count	Amount	Avg	Count	Amount	Avg	Count	Amount	Avg
Language arts and disciplines	1,967	143,901.20	73.16	2,151	164,675.94	76.56	1,762	132,497.03	75.20	2,057	157,079.62	76.36
Law	3,322	259,091.99	77.99	3,690	295,619.73	80.11	3,793	326,195.89	86.00	3,549	308,735.10	86.99
Literary collections	498	17,486.91	35.11	673	14,412.07	21.41	343	12,536.32	36.55	397	13,784.93	34.72
Literary criticism	1,692	69,515.84	41.09	2,554	128,955.62	50.49	1,972	86,471.08	43.85	1,752	71,631.34	40.89
Mathematics	1,536	140,747.93	91.63	1,518	137,270.79	90.43	1,033	85,847.94	83.11	1,286	116,732.64	90.77
Medical	5,625	634,447.70	112.79	4,605	443,601.59	96.33	3,743	397,360.01	106.16	5,002	561,037.88	112.16
Music	2,782	70,511.07	25.35	2,188	63,168.82	28.87	2,722	69,721.61	25.61	2,282	63,430.91	27.80
Nature	575	18,773.91	32.65	593	18,815.35	31.73	516	16,136.18	31.27	568	26,575.31	46.79
Performing arts	892	32,184.86	36.08	924	33,923.10	36.71	955	37,470.65	39.24	808	31,191.45	38.60
Pets	158	2,950.43	18.67	146	2,726.10	18.67	150	2,686.35	17.91	158	3,179.99	20.13
Philosophy	1,586	77,919.52	49.13	1,776	85,079.41	47.91	1,654	72,818.42	44.03	1,637	88,297.92	53.94
Photography	445	15,421.04	34.65	420	15,012.44	35.74	472	18,022.88	38.18	399	13,011.62	32.61
Poetry	2,434	40,729.81	16.73	2,279	40,202.41	17.64	1,993	35,518.95	17.82	2,002	33,876.89	16.92
Political science	3,659	180,331.55	49.28	4,114	228,228.69	55.48	3,865	213,598.38	55.26	3,685	177,820.86	48.26
Psychology	1,977	138,997.64	70.31	2,121	123,365.31	58.16	2,292	119,421.43	52.10	2,345	132,100.28	56.33
Reference	824	84,308.77	102.32	891	88,689.36	99.54	720	113,031.86	156.99	559	86,063.44	153.96
Religion	8,275	187,160.47	22.62	7,585	179,954.12	23.72	7,410	181,950.37	24.55	6,845	172,124.74	25.15
Science	4,662	448,507.42	96.20	4,417	392,054.12	88.76	2,654	267,114.30	100.65	4,041	497,350.53	123.08
Self-help	1,308	23,213.62	17.75	1,153	21,682.71	18.81	1,038	17,919.41	17.26	1,020	17,756.80	17.41
Social science	4,623	241,344.93	52.21	4,673	254,906.87	54.55	4,779	246,442.59	51.57	5,265	287,079.60	54.53
Sports and recreation	1,119	26,982.96	24.11	1,185	28,869.47	24.36	1,091	27,370.86	25.09	1,050	26,053.40	24.81
Study aids	614	29,275.04	47.68	1,888	84,729.17	44.88	939	40,980.49	43.64	698	24,952.99	35.75
Technology and engineering	2,950	314,880.86	106.74	3,688	386,011.52	104.67	1,914	218,159.40	113.98	3,225	438,556.46	135.99
Transportation	432	17,210.84	39.84	465	19,689.21	42.34	385	15,214.92	39.52	483	17,512.63	36.26
Travel	1,752	36,177.72	20.65	1,716	35,350.68	20.60	1,617	34,409.17	21.28	1,594	33,368.48	20.93
True crime	173	3,446.61	19.92	175	3,326.61	19.01	176	3,337.99	18.97	144	2,796.50	19.42
Young adult	2,173	37,021.97	17.04	2,929	54,681.32	18.67	2,336	48,353.46	20.70	2,580	67,739.99	26.26
Totals	122,324	$5,645,310.86	$46.15	125,841	$5,790,603.47	$46.02	114,597	$5,331,471.30	$46.52	114,853	$5,809,194.92	$50.58

Table 6 / Audiobook Average Per-Volume Prices, 2013–2016

BISAC Category	2013			2014			2015			2016		
	Vols.	$ Total	Prices	Vols.	$ Total	Prices	Vols.	$ Total	Prices	Vols.	$ Total	Prices
Antiques and collectibles	n.a.	n.a.	n.a.	n.a.	n.a.	n.a.	n.a.	n.a.	n.a.	3	$79.97	$26.66
Architecture	7	$299.77	$42.82	1	$59.95	$59.95	2	$29.94	$14.97	7	177.94	25.42
Art	4	149.80	37.45	9	353.91	39.32	8	244.90	30.61	22	372.79	16.95
Bibles	20	1,629.54	81.48	11	779.70	70.88	16	597.64	37.35	7	859.97	122.85
Biography and autobiography	1,215	50,171.75	41.29	982	40,855.38	41.60	1,226	44,889.41	36.61	1,671	52,669.45	31.52
Body, mind, and spirit	245	6,631.36	27.07	181	5,160.21	28.51	163	3,847.32	23.60	145	4,259.97	29.38
Business and economics	452	15,589.57	34.49	607	18,187.51	29.96	701	20,685.85	29.51	1,300	35,761.78	27.51
Children	1,743	71,387.45	40.96	1,032	36,755.87	35.62	2,361	94,172.12	39.89	1,201	39,990.62	33.30
Comics and graphic novels	2	29.98	14.99	n.a.	n.a.	n.a.	n.a.	n.a.	n.a.	1	9.99	9.99
Computers	2	104.94	52.47	18	742.73	41.26	9	267.89	29.77	30	871.63	29.05
Cooking	20	943.75	47.19	14	686.78	49.06	21	641.78	30.56	40	1,267.49	31.69
Crafts and hobbies	2	49.90	24.95	5	123.88	24.78	3	85.89	28.63	2	54.94	27.47
Design	2	74.94	37.47	n.a.	n.a.	n.a.	1	29.99	29.99	1	9.99	9.99
Drama	100	3,250.44	32.50	59	1,528.64	25.91	52	1,547.60	29.76	152	2,181.75	14.35
Education	33	1,296.50	39.29	32	1,178.72	36.84	26	938.26	36.09	52	2,066.77	39.75
Family and relationships	119	4,183.77	35.16	119	3,809.20	32.01	157	4,829.87	30.76	247	7,205.03	29.17
Fiction	11,561	445,335.72	38.52	11,447	445,467.43	38.92	13,094	418,352.36	31.95	19,068	455,661.48	23.90
Foreign language study	141	7,255.85	51.46	273	17,559.20	64.32	137	9,494.72	69.30	46	4,960.10	107.83
Games	n.a.	n.a.	n.a.	5	235.90	47.18	1	11.99	11.99	4	129.96	32.49
Gardening	n.a.	n.a.	n.a.	n.a.	n.a.	n.a.	1	14.99	14.99	2	62.98	31.49
Health and fitness	133	5,761.77	43.32	111	4,569.96	41.17	162	6,555.57	40.47	288	9,238.62	32.08
History	489	23,425.98	47.91	476	24,721.41	51.94	550	23,877.88	43.41	1,195	39,194.58	32.80
House and home	4	119.92	29.98	1	9.99	9.99	5	178.95	35.79	27	998.43	36.98

Humor	79	2,950.80	37.35	98	3,227.52	32.93	108	3,545.20	32.83	101	2,730.20	27.03
Language arts and disciplines	13	495.48	38.11	11	419.85	38.17	20	665.83	33.29	40	1,168.46	29.21
Law	16	1,038.88	64.93	12	748.88	62.41	9	495.96	55.11	41	1,145.69	27.94
Literary collections	18	667.57	37.09	41	2,218.06	54.10	58	2,327.80	40.13	72	2,518.69	34.98
Literary criticism	11	534.78	48.62	12	359.78	29.98	20	872.50	43.63	52	1,447.25	27.83
Mathematics	5	199.87	39.97	5	102.96	20.59	6	220.88	36.81	6	149.95	24.99
Medical	25	1,013.37	40.53	12	452.88	37.74	27	874.65	32.39	22	420.80	19.13
Music	33	1,352.91	41.00	25	1,281.28	51.25	21	643.80	30.66	82	2,356.46	28.74
Nature	27	1,094.38	40.53	23	1,072.54	46.63	35	1,098.42	31.38	85	1,867.04	21.97
Performing arts	58	2,403.87	41.45	65	2,575.33	39.62	79	2,885.58	36.53	180	6,808.82	37.83
Pets	30	1,178.29	39.28	13	481.64	37.05	17	668.67	39.33	50	1,866.14	37.32
Philosophy	38	1,125.56	29.62	25	800.54	32.02	17	493.75	29.04	124	3,069.39	24.75
Photography	n.a.	n.a.	n.a.	n.a.	n.a.	n.a.	0	0.00		2	69.98	34.99
Poetry	19	501.50	26.39	38	1,484.47	39.07	25	930.48	37.22	25	374.61	14.98
Political science	166	7,480.77	45.06	130	5,863.68	45.11	173	6,387.83	36.92	397	11,476.68	28.91
Psychology	74	3,268.54	44.17	96	3,126.47	32.57	106	3,761.74	35.49	188	5,249.56	27.92
Reference	5	248.87	49.77	8	207.91	25.99	4	61.96	15.49	13	314.85	24.22
Religion	677	19,698.58	29.10	698	20,059.46	28.74	950	24,567.44	25.86	1,216	31,659.19	26.04
Science	97	4,024.00	41.48	98	4,094.52	41.78	122	4,307.97	35.31	199	5,442.11	27.35
Self-help	212	6,589.63	31.08	231	7,028.94	30.43	286	8,613.80	30.12	528	17,343.05	32.85
Social science	111	4,229.66	38.11	103	3,652.24	35.46	122	3,797.31	31.13	317	8,080.39	25.49
Sports and recreation	48	1,916.81	39.93	52	2,003.15	38.52	64	2,195.16	34.30	221	5,720.54	25.88
Study aids	1	24.99	24.99	5	654.98	131.00	3	74.90	24.97	2	105.95	52.98
Technology and engineering	9	381.84	42.43	11	576.83	52.44	20	862.61	43.13	80	7,517.32	93.97
Transportation	10	486.78	48.68	5	261.95	52.39	9	323.80	35.98	17	545.69	32.10
Travel	37	1,327.79	35.89	9	429.84	47.76	26	685.59	26.37	145	2,479.56	17.10
True crime	137	5,499.55	40.14	94	3,214.65	34.20	111	3,240.47	29.19	172	5,823.50	33.86
Young adult	1,288	54,938.12	42.65	1,285	55,598.45	43.27	1,714	54,342.95	31.71	1,711	49,925.54	29.18
Totals	19,538	$762,365.89	$39.02	18,588	$724,785.17	$38.99	22,848	$760,241.97	$33.27	31,599	$835,763.64	$26.45

n.a. = not available

Table 7 / E-Book Average Per-Volume Prices, 2013–2016

BISAC Category	2013			2014			2015			2016		
	Vols.	$ Total	Prices	Vols.	$ Total	Prices	Vols.	$ Total	Prices	Vols.	$ Total	Prices
Antiques and collectibles	181	$3,655.88	$20.20	132	$2,251.26	$17.05	153	$1,925.69	$12.59	89	$1,285.93	$14.45
Architecture	926	59,043.35	63.76	1,083	156,573.26	144.57	538	33,025.17	61.39	333	15,395.83	46.23
Art	1,881	37,433.22	19.90	1,884	41,959.39	22.27	4,881	52,010.14	10.66	1,989	30,408.69	15.29
Bibles	516	4,419.77	8.57	247	2,263.10	9.16	187	1,730.31	9.25	115	1,206.70	10.49
Biography and autobiography	8,493	125,801.56	14.81	9,542	170,668.20	17.89	6,644	106,066.18	15.96	5,421	88,508.62	16.33
Body, mind, and spirit	1,997	21,040.54	10.54	1,815	19,086.88	10.52	1,308	14,968.51	11.44	1,492	17,148.34	11.49
Business and economics	12,835	632,939.18	49.31	10,599	517,119.53	48.79	21,438	504,483.65	23.53	7,108	304,634.17	42.86
Children	20,511	293,257.09	14.30	21,565	315,345.81	14.62	18,437	237,250.08	12.87	18,972	274,890.71	14.49
Comics and graphic novels	581	4,197.53	7.22	1,535	9,409.04	6.13	3,279	27,197.01	8.29	3,625	32,293.62	8.91
Computers	5,073	311,796.95	61.46	4,358	290,377.53	66.63	4,348	284,213.84	65.37	4,011	285,125.54	71.09
Cooking	3,554	44,226.31	12.44	2,870	34,481.13	12.01	3,021	37,360.11	12.37	2,113	31,051.25	14.70
Crafts and hobbies	1,437	14,003.52	9.74	960	11,462.67	11.94	1,247	12,342.35	9.90	1,030	11,482.68	11.15
Design	199	5,499.02	27.63	144	4,036.50	28.03	142	3,805.50	26.80	108	2,653.96	24.57
Drama	1,848	14,873.48	8.05	1,799	17,801.62	9.90	1,683	13,073.02	7.77	832	9,253.84	11.12
Education	5,305	265,959.51	50.13	4,642	180,118.87	38.80	3,485	136,778.69	39.25	6,720	260,500.23	38.76
Family and relationships	2,099	29,409.79	14.01	2,200	31,040.77	14.11	1,676	19,824.49	11.83	1,826	21,469.69	11.76
Fiction	100,029	674,571.51	6.74	104,416	670,233.30	6.42	81,091	548,410.72	6.76	72,487	556,116.60	7.67
Foreign language study	1,738	26,902.95	15.48	1,657	26,826.69	16.19	1,613	33,189.44	20.58	1,005	13,078.59	13.01
Games	529	4,811.65	9.10	682	5,591.37	8.20	1,232	28,205.84	22.89	747	6,473.18	8.67
Gardening	373	4,838.56	12.97	311	3,603.95	11.59	298	3,342.91	11.22	270	3,352.99	12.42
Health and fitness	3,765	46,743.20	12.42	3,170	37,128.71	11.71	2,735	40,450.20	14.79	2,758	36,749.96	13.32
History	11,010	467,959.52	42.50	12,548	429,850.67	34.26	10,373	423,964.21	40.87	7,665	243,418.55	31.76
House and home	442	4,344.72	9.83	310	2,996.65	9.67	307	3,201.27	10.43	230	2,607.97	11.34

Humor	1,125	9,936.70	8.83	1,080	10,117.32	9.37	808	9,130.32	11.30	852	8,876.32	10.42
Language arts and disciplines	2,900	193,052.28	66.57	2,274	175,067.42	76.99	1,813	168,043.10	92.69	1,197	100,813.45	84.22
Law	2,641	272,375.07	103.13	1,840	182,295.48	99.07	1,724	184,910.29	107.26	1,185	105,548.59	89.07
Literary collections	1,538	20,026.52	13.02	1,615	38,412.77	23.78	6,174	32,899.64	5.33	885	12,257.06	13.85
Literary criticism	2,730	214,535.08	78.58	2,354	178,963.40	76.03	2,895	193,546.13	66.86	1,612	103,896.95	64.45
Mathematics	1,572	135,922.36	86.46	1,425	134,546.94	94.42	1,235	105,120.38	85.12	1,310	117,476.48	89.68
Medical	9,492	700,007.81	73.75	3,737	388,814.98	104.04	2,959	309,440.10	104.58	2,982	344,276.94	115.45
Music	2,053	62,911.50	30.64	1,431	67,350.95	47.07	1,617	35,761.70	22.12	1,167	21,897.86	18.76
Nature	1,168	40,239.30	34.45	952	33,812.53	35.52	710	30,840.33	43.44	674	31,681.31	47.00
Performing arts	1,665	65,563.23	39.38	1,421	46,442.24	32.68	1,251	41,492.05	33.17	1,421	52,458.53	36.92
Pets	817	6,498.27	7.95	424	4,557.65	10.75	283	3,060.39	10.81	417	4,169.64	10.00
Philosophy	3,067	162,069.50	52.84	2,362	144,651.49	61.24	2,102	126,604.66	60.23	1,597	78,601.03	49.22
Photography	566	12,730.32	22.49	556	11,001.83	19.79	483	8,824.13	18.27	369	7,621.50	20.65
Poetry	3,272	22,040.23	6.74	3,813	26,903.93	7.06	3,211	23,985.10	7.47	2,266	16,588.00	7.32
Political science	5,274	259,462.37	49.20	3,913	218,284.16	55.78	3,895	226,511.19	58.15	2,900	145,053.56	50.02
Psychology	4,757	299,923.60	63.05	3,273	188,481.82	57.59	2,123	108,804.17	51.25	1,440	61,999.62	43.06
Reference	1,702	85,807.18	50.42	4,062	104,480.29	25.72	3,457	86,349.78	24.98	4,156	51,962.78	12.50
Religion	10,626	219,959.34	20.70	11,208	215,279.54	19.21	8,639	195,442.06	22.62	7,877	147,629.28	18.74
Science	4,823	514,561.79	106.69	4,710	558,419.82	118.56	3,760	376,338.69	100.09	3,948	409,938.70	103.83
Self-help	4,497	42,203.50	9.38	4,825	41,353.84	8.57	3,755	39,065.69	10.40	3,888	41,227.34	10.60
Social science	7,081	487,756.60	68.88	4,888	328,282.53	67.16	4,024	235,317.65	58.48	2,776	153,023.88	55.12
Sports and recreation	2,837	51,932.80	18.31	2,344	41,894.22	17.87	1,799	31,859.87	17.71	1,758	29,513.47	16.79
Study aids	6,165	115,936.64	18.81	4,721	87,747.44	18.59	1,145	12,751.04	11.14	20,192	616,401.95	30.53
Technology and engineering	4,106	476,087.09	115.95	3,859	562,712.67	145.82	3,137	380,124.24	121.17	3,388	423,734.30	125.07
Transportation	319	8,073.13	25.31	336	6,506.60	19.36	319	8,299.94	26.02	294	6,319.75	21.50
Travel	2,586	28,211.42	10.91	2,320	26,165.78	11.28	3,232	31,260.21	9.67	2,202	25,215.37	11.45
True crime	631	7,559.42	11.98	545	6,744.22	12.37	438	6,067.02	13.85	446	7,325.22	16.42
Young adult	6,485	88,563.26	13.66	6,613	89,272.68	13.50	5,147	67,336.62	13.08	4,970	87,658.78	17.64
Totals	281,817	$7,701,675.12	$27.33	271,370	$6,898,791.44	$25.42	242,251	$5,646,005.79	$23.31	219,115	$5,462,275.30	$24.93

Number of Book Outlets
in the United States and Canada

The *American Book Trade Directory* (Information Today, Inc.) has been published since 1915. Revised annually, it features lists of booksellers, wholesalers, periodicals, reference tools, and other information about the U.S. and Canadian book markets. The data shown in Table 1, the most current available, are from the 2017–2018 edition of the directory.

The 13,628 stores of various types shown are located throughout the United States, Canada, and regions administered by the United States. "General" bookstores stock trade books and children's books in a general variety of subjects. "College" stores carry college-level textbooks. "Educational" outlets handle school textbooks up to and including the high school level. "Mail order" outlets sell general trade books by mail and are not book clubs; all others operating by mail are classified according to the kinds of books carried. "Antiquarian" dealers sell old and rare books. Stores handling secondhand books are classified as "used." "Paperback" stores have more than 80 percent of their stock in paperbound books. Stores with paperback departments are listed under the appropriate major classification ("general," "department store," "stationer," and so forth). Bookstores with at least 50 percent of their stock on a particular subject are classified by subject.

Table 1 / Bookstores in the United States and Canada, 2016

Category	United States	Canada
Antiquarian General	483	46
Antiquarian Mail Order	182	5
Antiquarian Specialized	98	2
Art Supply Store	45	1
College General	2,716	136
College Specialized	99	4
Comics	177	24
Computer Software	2	0
Cooking	237	11
Department Store	1,287	17
Educational*	144	24
Federal Sites†	298	1
Foreign Language*	14	2
General	2,181	455
Gift Shop	93	5
Juvenile*	62	11
Mail Order General	49	6
Mail Order Specialized	218	9
Metaphysics, New Age, and Occult	108	17
Museum Store and Art Gallery	399	26
Nature and Natural History	31	5
Newsdealer	18	2
Office Supply	7	1
Other‡	1,747	310
Paperback§	30	1

Religious*	1,186	101
Self Help/Development	13	4
Stationer	3	3
Toy Store	33	48
Used*	387	54
Totals	12,297	1,331

* Includes Mail Order Shops for this topic, which are not counted elsewhere in this survey.

† National Historic Sites, National Monuments, and National Parks.

‡ Stores specializing in subjects or services other than those covered in this survey.

§ Includes Mail Order. Excludes used paperback bookstores, stationers, drugstores, or wholesalers handling paperbacks.

Part 5
Reference Information

Bibliographies

The Librarian's Bookshelf

Staff of the American Library Association Library:
Karen Muller, Librarian; Rebecca Gerber, Electronic Resources Librarian; and
David Sievers, Library Assistant.

Most of the books on this selective bibliography have been published since 2014; a few earlier titles are retained because of their continuing importance. Many are also available as ebooks, though that has not been noted.

General

ALA Glossary of Library and Information Science. 4th ed. By Michael Levine-Clark and Toni M. Carter. ALA Editions, 2013.

American Library Directory, 2017–2018. Information Today, Inc., 2017. 2v. Print and online.

Annual Review of Information Science and Technology (ARIST). Ed. by Blaise Cronin. Information Today, Inc., 2010.

Encyclopedia of Library and Information Science. 3rd ed. Ed. by Miriam A. Drake. CRC, 2009. Print and online.

Exploring Digital Libraries: Foundations, Practice, Prospects. By Karen Calhoun. Neal-Schuman, 2014.

Foundations of Library and Information Science. 4th ed. By Richard E. Rubin. Neal-Schuman, 2016.

Information Services Today: An Introduction. By Sandra Hirsh. Rowman & Littlefield, 2015.

Introduction to the Library and Information Professions. 2nd ed. By Roger C. Greer, Robert J. Grover, and Susan G. Fowler. Libraries Unlimited, 2013.

Library and Book Trade Almanac, 2016. Ed. by Catherine Barr. Information Today, Inc., 2016.

Library and Information Science Source. EBSCO Publishing Online database.

Library and Information Science: A Guide to Key Literature and Sources. By Michael F. Bemis. ALA Editions, 2014.

Library Programs and Services: The Fundamentals. 8th ed. By G. Edward Evans, [and others]. Libraries Unlimited, 2015.

Library World Records. 2nd ed. By Godfrey Oswald. McFarland, 2009.

Academic Libraries

Becoming an Embedded Librarian: Making Connections in the Classroom. By Michelle Reale. ALA Editions, 2016.

Digital Humanities in the Library: Challenges and Opportunities for Subject Specialists. By Arianne Hartsell-Gundy, Laura Braunstein, and Liorah Golomb. Association of College and Research Libraries, 2015.

Library Assessment in Higher Education. By Joseph R. Matthews. Libraries Unlimited, 2015.

Twenty-First Century Access Services: On the Front Line of Academic Librarianship. Ed. by Michael J. and Trevor A. Dawes. Association of College and Research Libraries, 2013.

Administration

Assessing Service Quality: Satisfying the Expectations of Library Customers. By Peter Hernon, Ellen Altman, and Robert E. Dugan. ALA Editions, 2015.

The Complete Library Trustee Handbook. By Sally Gardner Reed and Jillian Kolonick. Neal-Schuman, 2010.

Digital Literacy and Digital Inclusion: Information Policy and the Public Library. By Kim M. Thompson … [et al.]. Rowman & Littlefield, 2014.

Exploring Digital Libraries: Foundations, Practice, Prospects. By Karen Calhoun. Neal-Schuman, 2014.

Financial Management of Libraries and Information Centers. By Robert H. Burger. Libraries Unlimited, 2017.

Five Steps of Outcome-Based Planning and Evaluation for Public Libraries. By Melissa Gross, Cindy Mediavilla, and Virginia A. Walter. ALA Editions, 2016.

The Good, the Great, and the Unfriendly: A Librarian's Guide to Working with Friends Groups. By Sally Gardner Reed. ALA Editions, 2017.

Letting Go of Legacy Services: Library Case Studies. By Mary Evangeliste and Katherine Furlong. ALA Editions, 2014.

Library and Information Center Management. 8th ed. By Barbara B. Moran, Robert D. Stueart, and Claudia J. Morner. Libraries Unlimited, 2013.

Library Consortia: Models for Collaboration and Sustainability. By Valerie Horton and Greg Pronevitz. ALA Editions, 2015.

Moving Materials: Physical Delivery in Libraries. Ed. by Valerie Horton and Bruce Smith. American Library Association, 2010.

Neal-Schuman Library Technology Companion: A Basic Guide for Library Staff. 5th ed. By John J. Burke. Neal-Schuman, 2016.

Running A Small Library: A How-to-do-it Manual for Librarians. 2nd ed. By John A. Moorman. Neal-Schuman, 2015.

Stellar Customer Service: Training Library Staff to Exceed Expectations. By Mou Chakraborty. Libraries Unlimited, 2016.

Useful, Usable, Desirable: Applying User Experience Design to Your Library. By Aaron Schmidt and Amanda Etches. American Library Association, 2014.

What Every Library Director Should Know. By Susan Carol Curzon. Rowman & Littlefield, 2014.

Advocacy and Public Awareness

Activism and the School Librarian: Tools for Advocacy and Survival. Ed. by Deborah D. Levitov. Libraries Unlimited, 2012.

ALA Book of Library Grant Money. 9th ed. Ed. by Nancy Kalikow Maxwell. American Library Association, 2014.

Beyond Book Sales: the Complete Guide to Raising Real Money for Your Library. Ed. by Susan Dowd for Library Strategies, a consulting group of The Friends of the Saint Paul Public Library. Neal-Schuman, 2014.

A Book Sale How-to Guide: More Money, Less Stress. By Pat Ditzler and JoAnn Dumas. American Library Association, 2012.

Crash Course in Dealing with Difficult Library Customers. By Shelley Mosley, Dennis C. Tucker, and Sandra Van Winkle. Libraries Unlimited, 2014.

Creative Library Marketing and Publicity: Best Practices. By Robert J. Lackie and M. Sandra Wood. Rowman & Littlefield, 2015.

Face2Face Using Facebook, Twitter, and Other Social Media Tools to Create Great Customer Connections. By David Lee King. Information Today, 2012.

Grassroots Library Advocacy. By Lauren Comito, Aliqae Geraci, and Christian Zabriskie. American Library Association, 2012.

The Librarian's Nitty-Gritty Guide to Content Marketing. By Laura Solomon. ALA Editions, 2016.

Marketing and Social Media: A Guide for Libraries, Archives, and Museums. By Christie Koontz and Lorri M. Mon. Rowman & Littlefield, 2014.

Say It with Data: A Concise Guide to Making Your Case and Getting Results. By Priscille Dando. ALA Editions, 2014.

School Libraries Matter. Ed. by Mirah J. Dow. Libraries Unlimited, 2013.

Start a Revolution: Stop Acting Like a Library. By Benn Bizzle and Maria Flora. ALA Editions, 2015.

Archives and Special Collections

Archives: Principles and Practices. By Laura A. Millar. Neal-Schuman, 2010.

Archives Alive: Expanding Engagement with Public Library Archives and Special Collections. By Diantha Dow Schull. ALA Editions, 2015.

Digitization and Digital Archiving: A Practical Guide for Librarians. By Elizabeth R. Leggett. Rowman & Littlefield, 2014.

Health Sciences Librarianship. Ed. by M. Sandra Wood. Rowman & Littlefield, 2014.

Rare Books and Special Collections. By Sidney E. Berger. Neal-Schuman, 2014.

Buildings and Space Planning

Building Blocks for Planning Functional Library Space. 3rd ed. By the Library Leadership and Management Association. Scarecrow Press, 2011.

Building Science 101: A Primer for Librarian. By Lynn M. Piotrowicz and Scott Osgood. American Library Association, 2010.

Checklist of Library Building Design Considerations. 6th ed. By William W. Sannwald. ALA Editions, 2016.

Planning Academic and Research Library Buildings. 3rd ed. By Philip D. Leighton and David C. Weber. American Library Association, 1999.

The Power of Play: Designing Early Learning Spaces. By Dorothy Stoltz, Marisa Conner, and James Bradberry. ALA Editions, 2015.

Cataloging and Bibliographic Control

Guide to the Library of Congress Classification. 6th ed. By Lois Mai Chan, Sheila S. Intner, and Jean Weihs. Libraries Unlimited, 2017.

Introduction to Cataloging and Classification. By Daniel N. Joudrey, Arlene G. Taylor, and David P. Miller. 11th ed. Libraries Unlimited, 2015.

Introduction to Indexing and Abstracting. 4th ed. By Donald Cleveland and Ana Cleveland. Libraries Unlimited, 2013.

Metadata. 2nd ed. By Marcia Lei Zeng and Jian Qin. ALA Editions, 2016.

RDA Essentials. By Thomas Brenndorfer. ALA Editions, 2016.

RDA Toolkit. Joint Steering Committee for Development of RDA (JSC). American Library Association. Online resource.

RDA: Resource Description and Access Print. Joint Steering Committee for Development of RDA (JSC). American Library Association, 2011. Looseleaf.

Children's and Young Adult Services and Materials

Becoming a Media Mentor: A Guide for Working with Children and Families. By Claudia Haines, Cen Campbell, and Chip Donohue. ALA Editions, 2016.

Building a Core Print Collection for Preschoolers. By Alan R. Bailey. ALA Editions, 2014.

The Coretta Scott King Awards, 1970–2014. ALA Editions, 2015.

Evaluating Teen Services and Programs. By Sarah Flowers. Neal-Schuman, 2012.

The Handbook for Storytellers. By Judy Freeman and Caroline Feller Bauer. ALA Editions, 2015.

Integrating Young Adult Literature through the Common Core Standards. By Rachel L. Wadham and Jonathan W. Ostenson. Libraries Unlimited, 2013.

Managing Children's Services in Libraries. 4th ed. By Adele M. Fasick and Leslie Edmonds Holt. Libraries Unlimited, 2013.

The Newbery and Caldecott Awards 2015: A Guide to the Medal and Honor Books. Association for Library Service to Children/ American Library Association, 2015.

Pura Belpré Awards: Celebrating Latino Authors and Illustrators. By Rose Zertuche Trevino. ALA Editions, 2006.

Young Adult Literature in Action: A Librarian's Guide. 2nd ed. By Rosemary Chance. Libraries Unlimited, 2014.

Collection Development

The Collection Program in Schools: Concepts and Practices. 6th ed. By Marcia A. Mardis and Kay Bishop. Libraries Unlimited, 2016.

Fundamentals of Collection Development and Management. 3rd ed. By Peggy Johnson. American Library Association, 2014.

Fundamentals of Electronic Resources Management. By Alana Verminski and Kelly Marie Blanchat. Neal-Schuman, 2017.

Getting Started with Demand-Driven Acquisitions for E-Books. By Theresa S. Arndt. ALA Techsource, 2015.

Rightsizing the Academic Library Collection. By Suzanne M. Ward. Association of College and Research Libraries, 2015.

Shared Collections: Collaborative Stewardship. By Dawn Hale. ALA Editions, 2016.

The Weeding Handbook: A Shelf-by-Shelf Guide. By Rebecca Vnuk. ALA Editions, 2015.

Copyright and other Legal Issues

Complete Copyright for K–12 Librarians and Educators. By Carrie Russell. American Library Association, 2012.

Copyright Law for Librarians and Educators: Creative Strategies and Practical Solutions. 3rd ed. By Kenneth D. Crews. American Library Association, 2012.

Intellectual Property for Nonprofit Organizations and Associations. By Jefferson C. Glassie, Eileen Morgan Johnson, and Dana O. Lynch. ASAE Association Management Press, 2012.

Owning and Using Scholarship: An IP Handbook for Teachers and Researchers. By Kevin L. Smith. Association of College and Research Libraries, 2014.

Privacy and Confidentiality Issues: A Guide for Libraries and their Lawyers. By Theresa Chmara. American Library Association, 2009.

History

The Book: A Global History. Ed. by Michael F. Suarez and H. R. Woudhuysen. Oxford University Press, 2013.

Historical Dictionary of Librarianship. By Mary Ellen Quinn. Rowman & Littlefield, 2014.

Libraries and the Reading Public in Twentieth-Century America. By Christine Pawley and Louise S. Robbins. University of Wisconsin Press, 2013.

The Library Beyond the Book. By Jeffrey T. Schnapp and Matthew Battles. Harvard University Press, 2014.

Part of Our Lives: A People's History of the American Public Library. By Wayne A. Wiegand. Oxford University Press, 2015.

The Untold Story of the Talking Book. By Matthew Rubery. Harvard University Press, 2016.

Human Resources and Leadership

Being Indispensable: A School Librarian's Guide to Becoming an Invaluable Leader. By Ruth Toor and Hilda K. Weisburg. American Library Association, 2011.

Fundamentals of Library Supervision. By Joan Giesecke and Beth McNeil. American Library Association, 2010.

Handbook of Academic Writing for Librarians By Christopher Vance Hollister, Rev. ed. Association of College and Research Libraries, 2014.

Library Conversations: Reclaiming Interpersonal Communications Theory for Understanding Professional Encounters. By Marie L. and Gary P. Radford. Neal-Schuman, 2017.

Mentoring A to Z. By Julie Todaro. ALA Editions, 2015.

Staff Development: A Practical Guide. 4th ed. Ed. by Andrea Wigbels Stewart, Carlette Washington-Hoagland, and Carol T. Zsulya. ALA Editions, 2013.

Success with Library Volunteers. By Leslie Edmonds Holt and Glen E. Holt. Libraries Unlimited, 2014.

Information Literacy

The Future Scholar: Researching and Teaching the Frameworks for Writing and Information Literacy. By Randall McClure and James P. Purdy. Information Today for ASIS&T, 2016.

Metaliteracy: Reinventing Information Literacy to Empower Learners. By Thomas P. Mackey and Trudi E. Jacobson. Neal-Schuman, 2014.

The One-shot Library Instruction Survival Guide. 2nd ed. By Heidi E. Buchanan and Beth A. McDonough. ALA Editions, 2017.

Online Searching: A Guide to Finding Quality Information Efficiently and Effectively. By Karen Markey. Rowman & Littlefield, 2015.

Reference and Instructional Services for Information Literacy Skills in School Libraries. 3rd ed. By Scott Lanning. Libraries Unlimited, 2014.

Web of Deceit: Misinformation and Manipulation in the Age of Social Media. Ed. by Anne P. Mintz. CyberAge Books, 2012.

Intellectual Freedom

Banned Books Resource Guide. American Library Association/Office of Intellectual Freedom, 2014.

Defending Frequently Challenged Young Adult Books: A Handbook for Librarians and Educators. By Pat Scales. Rowman & Littlefield, 2016.

Guide to Ethics in Acquisitions. By Wyoma VanDuinkerken, Wendi Arant Kaspar and Jeanne Harrell. Association for Library Collections & Technical Services, 2014.

A History of ALA Policy on Intellectual Freedom: A Supplement to The Intellectual Freedom Manual. 9th edition. By Trina J. Magi and Martin Garnar. ALA Editions, 2015.

Intellectual Freedom for Teens: A Practical Guide for Young Adult and School Librarians. By Kristin Fletcher-Speak and Kelly Tyler. ALA Editions, 2014.

Intellectual Freedom Manual. 9th ed. By Trina J. Magi, Martin Garnar, and the Office for Intellectual Freedom. ALA Editions, 2015.

Library Ethics. By Jean L. Preer. Libraries Unlimited, 2008.

Sex in the Library: A Guide to Sexual Content in Teen Literature. By Mary Jo Heller and Aarene Storms. VOYA Press, 2013.

Outreach, Programming and Services

Assistive Technologies in the Library. By Barbara T. Mates; with contrib. by William R. Reed, IV. American Library Association, 2011.

Blueprint for a Job Center at Your Library. By Bernice Kao and Megan Pittsley-Fox. Libraries Unlimited, 2014.

Community Library Programs that Work: Building Youth and Family Literacy. By Beth Maddigan and Susan Bloos. Libraries Unlimited, 2014.

Creating Inclusive Library Environments: A Planning Guide for Serving Patrons with Disabilities. By Michelle Kowalsky and John Woodruff. ALA Editions, 2017.

How to Launch an Author Awards Program at Your Library: Curating Self-Published Books, Reaching Out to the Community. By Julianne Stam and Elizabeth Clemmons. Libraries Unlimited, 2016.

Information Services to Diverse Populations: Developing Culturally Competent Library Professionals. By Nicole A. Cooke. Libraries Unlimited, 2017.

The Librarian's Guide to Book Programs and Author Events. By Brad Hooper. American Library Association, 2016.

The Library in the Life of the User: Engaging with People Where They Live and Learn. By Lynn Silipigni Connaway and OCLC Research. OCLC Research, 2015. Also online.

Library Services for Adults in the 21st Century. By Elsie A. Rogers Halliday Okobi. Libraries Unlimited, 2014.

Literacy: A Way Out for At-Risk Youth. By Jennifer Sweeney. Libraries Unlimited, 2012.

Prison Librarianship Policy and Practice. By Suzanna Conrad. McFarland, 2017.

Serving Those Who Served: Librarian's Guide to Working with Veteran and Military Communities. By Sarah LeMire and Kristen J. Mulvihill. Libraries Unlimited, 2017.

Small Business and the Public Library: Strategies for a Successful Partnership. By Luise Weiss, Sophia Serlis-McPhillips, and Elizabeth Malafi. American Library Association, 2011.

Streamlined Library Programming: How to Improve Services and Cut Costs. By Daisy Porter-Reynolds. Libraries Unlimited, 2014.

Preservation, Disaster Response, and Security

Digital Library Programs for Libraries and Archives: Developing, Managing, and Sustaining Unique Digital Collections. By Aaron D. Percell. Neal-Schuman, 2016.

Disaster Response and Planning for Libraries. 3rd ed. By Miriam B. Kahn. American Library Association, 2012.

Emergency Preparedness and Disaster Recovery in School Libraries: Creating a Safe Haven. By Christie Kaaland and William M. Lokey. Libraries Unlimited, 2015.

Library Security: Better Communication, Safer Facilities. By Steve Albrecht. ALA Editions, 2015.

Personal Archiving: Preserving Our Digital Heritage. Ed. by Donald T. Hawkins. Information Today, 2013.

The Preservation Management Handbook: a 21st-century Guide for Libraries, Archives, and Museums. Ed. by D. R. Harvey and Martha R. Mahard. Rowman & Littlefield, 2014.

Preserving Our Heritage: Perspectives from Antiquity to the Digital Age. By Michele Valerie Cloonan. Neal-Schuman, 2015.

Public Libraries

IFLA Public Library Service Guidelines. Ed. by Christie Koontz and Barbara Gubbin. De Gruyter Saur, 2010.

Public Libraries and Resilient Cities. Ed. by Michael Dudley. American Library Association, 2013.

The Public Library Policy Writer: A Guidebook with Model Policies on CD-ROM. By Jeanette C. Larson and Herman L. Totten. Neal-Schuman, 2008.

Small Public Library Management. By Jane Pearlmutter and Paul Nelson. American Library Association, 2012.

Readers' Advisory

Children's Literature in Action: A Librarian's Guide. 2nd ed. By Sylvia M. Vardell. Libraries Unlimited, 2014.

Coretta Scott King Award Books Discussion Guide: Pathways to Democracy. By Adelaide Poniatowski Phelps and Carole J. McCollough. ALA Editions, 2014.

Diversity in Youth Literature: Opening Doors Through Reading. By Jamie Campbell Naidoo and Sarah Park Dahlen. American Library Association, 2013.

The Mother of All Booklists: the 500 Most Recommended Nonfiction Reads for Ages 3 to 103. By William P. Martin. Rowman & Littlefield, 2015.

Outstanding Books for the College Bound: Titles and Programs for a New Generation. Ed. by Angela Carstensen. American Library Association, 2011.

Women's Fiction: A Guide to Popular Reading Interests. By Rebecca Vnuk and Nanette Donohue. Libraries Unlimited, 2013.

Reference Services

Conducting the Reference Interview: a How-to-do-it Manual for Librarians. 2nd ed. By Catherine Sheldrick Ross, Kristi Nilsen, and Marie L. Radford. Neal-Schuman, 2009.

Fundamentals of Government Information: Mining, Finding, Evaluating, and Using Government Resources. 2nd ed. By Eric J. Forte, Cassandra J. Hartnett, and Andrea Sevetson. Neal-Schuman, 2016.

Implementing Virtual Reference Services: A LITA Guide. Ed. by Beth C. Thomsett-Scott. ALA TechSource, 2013.

Interlibrary Loan Practices Handbook. 3rd ed. Ed. by Cherié L. Weible and Karen L. Janke. American Library Association, 2011.

Legal Reference for Librarians: How and Where to Find the Answers. By Paul D. Healey. ALA Editions, 2014.

Modern Pathfinders: Creating Better Research Guides. By Jason Puckett. Association of College and Research Libraries, 2015.

Reference and Information Services: An Introduction. 5th ed. Ed. by Linda C. Smith and Melissa A. Wong. Libraries Unlimited, 2016.

Reference Sources and Services for Youth. By Meghan Harper. Neal-Shuman, 2011.

Research and Statistics

Academic Library Trends and Statistics. Association of College and Research Libraries/ American Library Association Annual. Print and online.

ARL Annual Salary Survey. Association of Research Libraries. Annual. Print and online.

ARL Statistics. Association of Research Libraries. Annual. Print and online.

PLAmetrics: a PLDS Online Database. Public Library Association/American Library Association. Online database.

Public Libraries in the United States Survey. Institute of Museum and Library Services. Annual. Online only. Free.

Research Methods in Information. 2nd ed. By Alison Jane Pickard and Susan Childs. Neal-Schuman, 2013.

School Libraries

Empowering Learners: Guidelines for School Library Programs. American Association of School Librarians, 2009.

Enhancing Teaching and Learning: A Leadership Guide for School Librarians. By Jean Donham. Neal-Schuman, 2013.

The School Library Manager. 5th ed. By Blanche Woolls, Ann C. Weeks, and Sharon Coatney. Libraries Unlimited, 2014.

Standards for the 21st-Century Learner. American Association of School Librarians, 2007.

Standards for the 21st-Century Learner in Action. American Association of School Librarians, 2009.

21st Century Learning in School Libraries: Putting the AASL Standards to Work. Ed. by Kristin Fontichiaro. Libraries Unlimited, 2009.

Technical Services

Acquisitions: Core Concepts and Practices. By Jesse Holden. Neal-Schuman, 2017.

The Complete Guide to Acquisitions Management. 2nd ed. By Frances C. Wilkinson, Linda K. Lewis, and Rebecca L. Lubas. Libraries Unlimited, 2015.

Fundamentals of Technical Services. By John Sandstrom and Liz Miller. ALA Editions, 2015.

Integrated Library Systems: Planning, Selecting, and Implementing. By Desiree Webber and Andrew Peters. Libraries Unlimited, 2010.

Introduction to Technical Services. 8th ed. By C. Edward Evans, Sheila S. Intner, and Jean Weihs. Libraries Unlimited, 2011.

Library Automation: Core Concepts and Practical Systems Analysis. 3rd ed. By Dania Bilal. Libraries Unlimited, 2014.

Trends

BiblioTech: Why Libraries Matter More Than Ever in the Age of Google. By John G. Palfrey Basic Books, 2015.

Ecology, Economy, Equity: The Path to a Carbon-Neutral Library. By Mandy Henk. ALA Editions, 2014.

Framing Internet Safety: The Governance of Youth Online. By Nathan W. Fisk. MIT Press, 2016.

Global Mobile: Applications and Innovations for the Worldwide Mobile Ecosystem. Ed. by Peter A. Bruck and Madanmohan Rao. Information Today, 2013.

Greening Libraries. Ed. by Monika Antonelli and Mark McCullough. Library Juice, 2012.

Growing Young Minds: How Museums and Libraries Create Lifelong Learners. 2013. Institute of Museum and Library Services (U.S.). IMLS, 2013. http://purl.fdlp.gov/ GPO/gpo38726.

Library 2020: Today's Leading Visionaries Describe Tomorrow's Library. By Joseph Janes. Scarecrow Press, 2013.

Reflecting on the Future of Academic and Public Libraries. Ed. by Peter Hernon and Joseph R. Matthews. ALA Editions, 2013.

Reinventing the Library for Online Education. By Frederick J. Stielow. American Library Association, 2014

UContent: The Information Professional's Guide to User-Generated Content. By Nicholas G. Tomaiuolo. Information Today, 2012.

When We Are No More: How Digital Memory is Shaping Our Future. By Abby Smith Rumsey. Bloomsbury Press, 2016.

Periodicals

This listing of key library periodical publications includes ISSNs for print and online formats; in general, newsletters are not included. Titles have been verified against the EBSCO database as active periodicals.

Against the Grain (1043-2094)
American Archivist (Print, 0360-9081; Online, 2165-6274)
American Libraries (0002-9769)
American Libraries Direct (Online, 1559-369X)
Ariadne (1361-3200)
Archival Science (Print, 1389-0166; Online, 1573-7519)
Art Documentation (Print, 0730-7187; Online, 2161-9417)
Behavioral and Social Sciences Librarian (Print, 0163-9269; Online, 1544-4546)
Booklist (0006-7385); Booklist Online (2163-5544)
Bottom Line: Managing Library Finances (Print + Online, 0888-045X; Online, 2054-1724)
Cataloging and Classification Quarterly (Print, 0163-9374; Online, 1544-4554)
Catholic Library World (0008-820X)
Children and Libraries: The Journal of the Association for Library Service to Children (Print + Online 1542-9806)
CHOICE: Current Reviews for Academic Libraries (Print, 0009-4978; Online, 1523-8253)
Code4Lib Journal (1940-5758)
Collaborative Librarianship (Online, 1943-7528)
Collection Building (Print + Online, 0160-4953; Online 2054-5592)
Collection Management (Print, 0146-2679; Online, 1545-2549)
College & Research Libraries (Online, 2150-6701)
Computers in Libraries (1041-7915)
D-Lib Magazine (1082-9873)
DttP: A Quarterly Journal of Government Information Practice & Perspective (0091-2085)
Education for Information (0167-8329)
Electronic Library (Print + Online, 0264-0473; Online, 1758-616X)

Electronic Journal of Knowledge Management (1479-4411)
First Monday (Online, 1396-0466)
Government Information Quarterly (0740-624X)
Horn Book Magazine (0018-5078)
IFLA Journal (Print, 0340-0352; Online, 1745-2651)
In the Library with the Lead Pipe (Online, 1944-6195)
Indexer (Print, 0019-4131; Online, 1756-0632)
Information & Culture (Print + Online, 2164-8034; Online, 2166-3033)
Information Outlook (Print + Online, 1091-0808; Online, 1938-3819)
Information Research—An International Electronic Journal (1368-1613)
Information Standards Quarterly (Print + Online, 1041-0031; Online, 2161-6205)
Information Technology and Libraries (Online, 2163-5226)
Interlending & Document Supply (Print + Online, 0264-1615; Online 1758-5848)
International Journal of Geographical Information Science (Print, 1365-8816; Online, 1362-3087)
International Journal of Law and Information Technology (0967-0769)
Internet @ Schools (Print, 1546-4636; Online, 2156-843X)
Internet Reference Services Quarterly (Print, 1087-5301; Online, 1540-4749)
Issues in Science and Technology Librarianship (Online, 1092-1206)
Journal of Academic Librarianship (0099-1333)
Journal of Documentation (Print + Online, 0022-0418; Online, 1758-7379)
Journal of Education for Library and Information Science (0748-5786)
Journal of Electronic Resources Librarianship (Print, 1941-126X; Online, 1941-1278)
Journal of Information Ethics (Print, 1061-9321; Online, 1941-2894)
Journal of Information Science (Print, 0165-5515; Online, 1741-6485)
Journal of Intellectual Freedom and Privacy (Online, 2474-7459)
Journal of Interlibrary Loan, Document Delivery and Information Supply (Print + Online, 1072-303X
Journal of Librarianship & Information Science (Print, 0961-0006; Online, 1741-6477)

Journal of Library Administration (Print, 0193-0826; Online, 1540-3564)

Journal of Library Metadata (Print, 1938-6389; Online, 1937-5034)

Journal of Research on Libraries and Young Adults (2157-3980)

Journal of the American Society for Information Science and Technology (Print, 2330-1635; Online, (2330-1643)

Journal of Archival Organization (Print, 1533-2748; Online, 1533-2756)

Journal of the Medical Library Association (Print, 1536-5050; Online, 1558-9439)

Journal of Web Librarianship (Print, 1932-2909; Online, 1932-2917)

Knowledge Quest (1094-9046)

Law Library Journal (0023-9283)

Legal Reference Services Quarterly (Print, 0270-319X; Online, 1540-949X)

Library & Information Science Research (LI-BRES) (0740-8188)

Library Collections Acquisitions & Technical Services (Print, 1464-9055; Online, 1873-1821)

Library Hi-Tech Journal (0737-8831)

Library Journal (0363-0277)

Library Leadership & Management (Online, 1945-886X)

Library Management (Print + Online, 0143-5124; Online, 1758-7921)

Library of Congress Magazine (Print, 2169-0855; Online 2169-0863)

The Library Quarterly (Print, 0024-2519; Online, 1549-652X)

Library Resources & Technical Services, eLRTS (Online, 2159-9610)

Library Technology Reports (Print, 0024-2586; Online, 1945-4538)

Library Trends (Print, 0024-2594; Online, 1559-0682)

Library Worklife: HR e-news for Today's Leaders (1550-3534)

Librarysparks (1544-9092)

New Library World (Print, 0307-4803; Online, 1758-6909)

New Review of Children's Literature and Librarianship (Print, 1361-4541; Online, 1740-7885)

Notes (Music Library Association) (Print, 0027-4380; Online, 1534-150X)

Online Searcher (2324-9684)

Portal: Libraries and the Academy (Print, 1531-2542; Online, 1530-7131)

Preservation Digital Technology & Culture (Print, 2195-2957; Online, 2195-2965)

Public Libraries (0163-5506; some content online at http://publiclibrariesonline.org/)

Public Library Quarterly (Print, 0161-6846; Online, 1541-1540)

Publishing Research Quarterly (Print, 1053-8801; Online, 1936-4792)

RBM: A Journal of Rare Books, Manuscripts, and Cultural Heritage (Print, 1529-6407; Online, 2150-668X)

Reference & User Services Quarterly (Online, 1094-9054)

Reference Librarian (Print, 0276-3877; Online, 1541-1117)

Reference Services Review (Print, + Online, 0090-7324; Online, 2054-1716)

Research Library Issues (1947-4911)

School Library Journal (0362-8930)

School Library Research (2165-1019)

The Scout Report (Online, 1092-3861)

Serials Librarian (Print, 0361-526X; Online, 1541-1095)

Serials Review (Print, 0098-7913; Online, 1879-095X)

State of America's Libraries Report (Annual, Online only)

Technical Services Quarterly (Print, 0731-7131; Online, 1555-3337)

Technicalities (0272-0884)

Theological Librarianship (1937-8904)

Voice of Youth Advocates (VOYA) (0160-4201)

Young Adult Library Services (1541-4302)

Blogs (All sites checked as of March 1, 2017)

025.431: The Dewey Blog. Jonathan Furner, editor (http://ddc.typepad.com/)

ACRL Insider (http://acrl.ala.org/acrlinsider/)

ACRLog (http://acrlog.org)

American Libraries: The Scoop (http://american librariesmagazine.org/blogs/)

ALSC Blog (http://www.alsc.ala.org/blog)

Annoyed Librarian (http://lj.libraryjournal. com/blogs/annoyedlibrarian/)

AOTUS: Collector in Chief. By David Ferriero (http://blogs.archives.gov/aotus)

Archivesblogs: A syndicated collection of blogs by and for archivists (http://archives blogs.com/category/eng)

ASCLA Blog (http://ascla.ala.org/blog/)

Awful Library Books. By Holly Hibner and Mary Kelly (http://awfullibrarybooks.net)

Bibliographic Wilderness (http://bibwild. wordpress.com/)

Blue Skunk. By Doug Johnson (http://doug-johnson.squarespace.com)

The Booklist Reader (http://www.booklist reader.com/)

The Daring Librarian (http://www.thedaring librarian.com/)

David Lee King (http://www.davidleeking. com/)

Deeplinks. From Electronic Frontier Foundation (https://www.eff.org/deeplinks)

Designing Better Libraries: Exploring the Application of Design, Innovation, and New Media to Create Better Libraries and User Experiences (http://dbl.lishost.org/blog/)

The Digital Shift (http://www.thedigitalshift. com/)

Digitization 101. By Jill Hurst-Wahl (http:// hurstassociates.blogspot.com)

District Dispatch. By the ALA Washington Office (http://www.districtdispatch.org/)

Early Word. By Nora Rawlinson (http://www. earlyword.com)

5 Minute Librarian (http://www.5minlib.com/)

A Fuse #8 Production. By Elizabeth Bird (http:// blog.schoollibraryjournal.com/afuse8 production/)

Go to Hellman. By Eric Hellman (http://go-to-hellman.blogspot.com/)

Hack Library School (http://hacklibraryschool. com/)

Hangingtogether.org, from OCLC Research (http://hangingtogether.org/)

The Hub: Your Connection to Teen Reads. By the Young Adult Library Services Association (http://www.yalsa.ala.org/thehub/)

INFOdocket. By Gary Price and Shirl Kennedy (http://infodocket.com/)

Information Wants to Be Free. By Meredith Farkas (http://meredith.wolfwater.com/ wordpress)

Jenny Arch (https://jenny-arch.com/)

The Krafty Librarian (http://kraftylibrarian. com/)

Law Librarians of Congress (http://blogs.loc. gov/law/)

Leads from LLAMA (http://www.llama.ala. org/llamaleads/)

Librarian.net. By Jessamyn West (http://www. librarian.net)

LibrarianInBlack. By Sarah Houghton-Jan (http://librarianinblack.net/librarianin black/)

Library as Incubator Project. By Laura Damon-Moore, Erinn Batykefer, and Christina Endres (http://www.libraryasincubatorproject. org)

Library History Buff Blog. By Larry T. Nix (http://libraryhistorybuff.blogspot.com/)

Library Juice. By Rory Litwin (http://library juicepress.com/blog)

Library of Congress Blog (http://blogs.loc.gov/ loc/)

LibUX (http://libux.co/)

LIS News. By Blake Carver (http://lisnews. org)

LITA Blog (http://litablog.org/)

The 'M' Word—Marketing in Libraries. By Kathy Dempsey (http://themwordblog. blogspot.com)

Mr. Library Dude (https://mrlibrarydude.word press.com/)

NCAC Blog (http://ncac.org/category/blog)

NeverEndingSearch. By Joyce Valenza (http:// blogs.slj.com/neverendingsearch/)

NMRT Notes (http://www.nmrt.ala.org/notes/)

No Shelf Required. By Sue Polanka (http:// www.libraries.wright.edu/noshelfrequired)

Office for Intellectual Freedom Blog (http:// www.oif.ala.org/oif/)

Pattern Recognition. By Jason Griffey (http:// www.jasongriffey.net/wp)

Planet Cataloging (http://planetcataloging. org/) (http://prescan.wordpress.com/)

Programming Librarian (http://www.program minglibrarian.org/blogs)

RA for All http://raforall.blogspot.com/

RDA Toolkit News & Information (http:// www.rdatoolkit.org/news)

RIPS Law Librarian (http://ripslawlibrarian. wordpress.com/)

RUSA Update (http://rusa.ala.org/update/)

The Signal: Digital Preservation (http://blogs. loc.gov/digitalpreservation/)

Tame the Web: Libraries and Technology. By Michael Stephens (http://tametheweb.com)

Teen Librarian Toolbox. By Karen Jensen, Stephanie Wilkes, Christie Ross Gibrich, and Heather Booth (http://www.teenlibrarian

toolbox.com/)
Techsoup for libraries (http://www.techsoup forlibraries.org/blog)
The Unquiet Librarian (http://theunquietlibrarian.

wordpress.com/)
Walt at Random. By Walt Crawford (http://walt.lishost.org)
YALSA Blog (http://yalsa.ala.org/blog)

Ready Reference

How to Obtain an ISBN

Beat Barblan

United States ISBN/SAN Agency

The International Standard Book Numbering (ISBN) system was introduced into the United Kingdom by J. Whitaker & Sons Ltd. in 1967 and into the United States in 1968 by R. R. Bowker. The Technical Committee on Documentation of the International Organization for Standardization (ISO TC 46) is responsible for the international standard.

The purpose of this standard is to "establish the specifications for the International Standard Book Number (ISBN) as a unique international identification system for each product form or edition of a monographic publication published or produced by a specific publisher." The standard specifies the construction of an ISBN, the rules for assignment and use of an ISBN, and all metadata associated with the allocation of an ISBN.

Types of monographic publications to which an ISBN may be assigned include printed books and pamphlets (in various product formats); electronic publications (either on the Internet or on physical carriers such as CD-ROMs or diskettes); educational/instructional films, videos, and transparencies; educational/instructional software; audiobooks on cassette or CD or DVD; braille publications; and microform publications.

Serial publications, printed music, and musical sound recordings are excluded from the ISBN standard as they are covered by other identification systems.

The ISBN is used by publishers, distributors, wholesalers, bookstores, and libraries, among others, in 217 countries and territories as an ordering and inventory system. It expedites the collection of data on new and forthcoming editions of monographic publications for print and electronic directories used by the book trade. Its use also facilitates rights management and the monitoring of sales data for the publishing industry.

The "new" ISBN consists of 13 digits. As of January 1, 2007, a revision to the ISBN standard was implemented in an effort to substantially increase the numbering capacity. The 10-digit ISBN identifier (ISBN-10) is now replaced by the ISBN 13-digit identifier (ISBN-13). All facets of book publishing are now expected to use the ISBN-13, and the ISBN agencies throughout the world are now issuing only ISBN-13s to publishers. Publishers with existing ISBN-10s need to convert their ISBNs to ISBN-13s by the addition of the EAN prefix 978 and recalculation of the new check digit:

ISBN-10: 0-8352-8235-X
ISBN-13: 978-0-8352-8235-2

When the inventory of the ISBN-10s has been exhausted, the ISBN agencies will start assigning ISBN-13s with the "979" prefix instead of the "978." There is no 10-digit equivalent for 979 ISBNs.

Construction of an ISBN

An ISBN currently consists of 13 digits separated into the following parts:

1 A prefix of "978" for an ISBN-10 converted to an ISBN-13
2 Group or country identifier, which identifies a national or geographic grouping of publishers
3 Publisher identifier, which identifies a particular publisher within a group
4 Title identifier, which identifies a particular title or edition of a title
5 Check digit, the single digit at the end of the ISBN that validates the ISBN-13

For more information regarding ISBN-13 conversion services provided by the U.S. ISBN Agency at R. R. Bowker, LLC, visit the ISBN Agency Web site at http://www.isbn.org, or contact the U.S. ISBN Agency at isbn-san@bowker.com.

Publishers requiring their ISBNs to be converted from the ISBN-10 to ISBN-13 format can use the U.S. ISBN Agency's free ISBN-13 online converter at http://isbn.org/converterpub.asp. Publishers can also view their ISBNs online by accessing their personal account at http://www.myidentifiers.com.

Displaying the ISBN on a Product or Publication

When an ISBN is written or printed, it should be preceded by the letters ISBN, and each part should be separated by a space or hyphen. In the United States, the hyphen is used for separation, as in the following example: ISBN 978-0-8352-8235-2. In this example, 978 is the prefix that precedes the ISBN-13, 0 is the group identifier, 8352 is the publisher identifier, 8235 is the title identifier, and 2 is the check digit. The group of English-speaking countries, which includes the United States, Australia, Canada, New Zealand, and the United Kingdom, uses the group identifiers 0 and 1.

The ISBN Organization

The administration of the ISBN system is carried out at three levels—through the International ISBN Agency in the United Kingdom, through the national agencies, and through the publishing houses themselves. The International ISBN Agency, which is responsible for assigning country prefixes and for coordinating the worldwide implementation of the system, has an advisory panel that represents the International Organization for Standardization (ISO), publishers, and libraries. The International ISBN Agency publishes the *Publishers International ISBN Directory,* which is a listing of all national agencies' publishers with their assigned ISBN publisher prefixes. R. R. Bowker, as the publisher of *Books In Print* with its extensive and varied database of publishers' addresses, was the obvious place to initiate the ISBN system and to provide the service to the U.S. publishing industry. To date, the U.S. ISBN Agency has entered more than 180,000 publishers into the system.

ISBN Assignment Procedure

Assignment of ISBNs is a shared endeavor between the U.S. ISBN Agency and the publisher. Publishers can apply online through the ISBN Agency's website www.myidentifiers.com. Once the order is processed, an e-mail confirmation will be sent with instructions for managing the account. The publisher then has the responsibility to assign an ISBN to each title, keep an accurate record of each number assigned, and register each title in the *Books In Print* database at www. myidentifiers.com. It is the responsibility of the ISBN Agency to validate assigned ISBNs and keep a record of all ISBN publisher prefixes in circulation.

ISBN implementation is very much market-driven. Major distributors, wholesalers, retailers, and so forth recognize the necessity of the ISBN system and request that publishers register with the ISBN Agency. Also, the ISBN is a mandatory bibliographic element in the International Standard Bibliographical Description (ISBD). The Library of Congress Cataloging in Publication (CIP) Division directs publishers to the agency to obtain their ISBN prefixes.

Location and Display of the ISBN

On books, pamphlets, and other printed material, the ISBN shall be printed on the verso of the title leaf or, if this is not possible, at the foot of the title leaf itself. It should also appear on the outside back cover or on the back of the jacket if the book has one (the lower right-hand corner is recommended). The ISBN shall also appear on any accompanying promotional materials following the provisions for location according to the format of the material.

On other monographic publications, the ISBN shall appear on the title or credit frames and any labels permanently affixed to the publication. If the publication is issued in a container that is an integral part of the publication, the ISBN shall be displayed on the label. If it is not possible to place the ISBN on the item or its label, then the number should be displayed on the bottom or the back of the container, box, sleeve, or frame. It should also appear on any accompanying material, including each component of a multi-type publication.

Printing of ISBN in Machine-Readable Coding

All books should carry ISBNs in the EAN-13 bar code machine-readable format. All ISBN EAN-13 bar codes start with the EAN prefix 978 for books. As of January 1, 2007, all EAN bar codes should have the ISBN-13 appearing immediately above the bar code in eye-readable format, preceded by the acronym "ISBN." The recommended location of the EAN-13 bar code for books is in the lower right-hand corner of the back cover (see Figure 1).

Figure 1 / Printing the ISBN in Bookland/EAN Symbology

Five-Digit Add-On Code

In the United States, a five-digit add-on code is used for additional information. In the publishing industry, this code is used for price information. The lead digit of the five-digit add-on has been designated a currency identifier, when the add-on is used for price. Number 5 is the code for the U.S. dollar, 6 denotes the Canadian dollar, 1 the British pound, 3 the Australian dollar, and 4 the New Zealand dollar. Publishers that do not want to indicate price in the add-on should print the code 90000 (see Figure 2).

**Figure 2 / Printing the ISBN Bookland/EAN Number in Bar Code
with the Five-Digit Add-On Code**

978 = ISBN Bookland/EAN prefix   90000 means no information
5 = Code for U.S. $ in the add-on code
2499 = $24.99

Reporting the Title and the ISBN

After the publisher reports a title to the ISBN Agency, the number is validated and the title is listed in the many R. R. Bowker hard-copy and electronic publications, including *Books in Print; Forthcoming Books; Paperbound Books in Print; Books in Print Supplement; Books Out of Print; Books in Print Online; Books in Print Plus-CD ROM; Children's Books in Print; Subject Guide to Children's Books in Print; Books Out Loud: Bowker's Guide to AudioBooks; Bowker's Complete Video Directory; Software Encyclopedia; Software for Schools;* and other specialized publications.

For an ISBN application and information, visit the ISBN Agency website at www.myidentifiers.com, call the toll-free number 877-310-7333, fax 908-795-3515, or write to the United States ISBN Agency, 630 Central Ave., New Providence, NJ 07974.

The ISSN, and How to Obtain One

U.S. ISSN Center
Library of Congress

In the early 1970s the rapid increase in the production and dissemination of information and an intensified desire to exchange information about serials in computerized form among different systems and organizations made it increasingly clear that a means to identify serial publications at an international level was needed. The International Standard Serial Number (ISSN) was developed and became the internationally accepted code for identifying serial publications.

The ISSN is an international standard, ISO 3297: 2007, as well as a U.S. standard, ANSI/NISO Z39.9. The 2007 edition of ISO 3297 expands the scope of the ISSN to cover continuing resources (serials, as well as updating databases, looseleafs, and some websites).

The number itself has no significance other than as a brief, unique, and unambiguous identifier. The ISSN consists of eight digits in Arabic numerals 0 to 9, except for the last ("check") digit, which can be an X. The numbers appear as two groups of four digits separated by a hyphen and preceded by the letters ISSN—for example, ISSN 1234-5679.

The ISSN is not self-assigned by publishers. Administration of the ISSN is coordinated through the ISSN Network, an intergovernmental organization within the UNESCO/UNISIST program. The ISSN Network consists of national ISSN centers, coordinated by the ISSN International Centre, located in Paris. National ISSN Centers are responsible for registering serials published in their respective countries. Responsibility for the assignment of ISSN to titles from multinational publishers is allocated among the ISSN Centers in which the publisher has offices. A list of these publishers and the corresponding ISSN centers is located on the ISSN International Centre's website, http://www.issn.org.

The ISSN International Centre handles ISSN assignments for international organizations and for countries that do not have a national center. It also maintains and distributes the ISSN Register and makes it available in a variety of products, most commonly via the ISSN Portal, an online subscription database. The ISSN Register is also available via Z39.50 access, and as a data file. Selected ISSN data can also be obtained in customized files or database extracts that can be used, for example, to check the accuracy or completeness of a requestor's list of titles and ISSN. Another available ISSN service is OAI-PMH, a customizable "harvesting" protocol through which external applications can automatically and regularly gather new and updated metadata on a defined schedule. The ISSN Register contains bibliographic records corresponding to each ISSN assignment as reported by national ISSN centers. The database contains records for more than 1.7 million ISSNs.

The ISSN is used all over the world by serials publishers to identify their serials and to distinguish their titles from others that are the same or similar. It is used by subscription services and libraries to manage files for orders, claims, and back issues. It is used in automated check-in systems by libraries that wish to process receipts more quickly. Copyright centers use the ISSN as a means to collect and disseminate royalties. It is also used as an identification code by postal services and legal deposit services. The ISSN is included as a verification element in interlibrary lending activities and for union catalogs as a collocating device. In recent years, the ISSN has been incorporated into bar codes for optical recognition of serial publications and into the standards for the identification of issues and articles in serial publications. Other growing uses for the ISSN are in online systems where it can serve to connect catalog records or citations in abstracting and indexing databases with full-text journal content via OpenURL resolvers or reference linking services, and as an identifier and link in archives of electronic and print serials.

Because serials are generally known and cited by title, assignment of the ISSN is inseparably linked to the key title, a standardized form of the title derived from information in the serial issue. Only one ISSN can be assigned to a title in a particular medium. For titles issued in multiple media—e.g., print, online, CD-ROM—a separate ISSN is assigned to each medium version. If a major title change occurs or the medium changes, a new ISSN must be assigned. Centers responsible for assigning ISSNs also construct the key title and create an associated bibliographic record.

A significant new feature of the 2007 ISSN standard is the Linking ISSN (ISSN-L), a mechanism that enables collocation or linking among different media versions of a continuing resource. The Linking ISSN allows a unique designation (one of the existing ISSNs) to be applied to all media versions of a continuing resource while retaining the separate ISSN that pertains to each version. When an ISSN is functioning as a Linking ISSN, the eight digits of the base ISSN are prefixed with the designation "ISSN-L." The Linking ISSN facilitates search, retrieval, and delivery across all medium versions of a serial or other continuing resource for improved ISSN functionality in OpenURL linking, search engines, library catalogs, and knowledge bases. The 2007 standard also supports interoperability by specifying the use of ISSN and ISSN-L with other systems such as DOI, OpenURL, URN, and EAN bar codes. ISSN-L was implemented in the ISSN Register in 2008. To help ISSN users implement the ISSN-L in their databases, two free tables are available from the ISSN International Centre's home page: one lists each ISSN and its corresponding ISSN-L; the other lists each ISSN-L and its corresponding ISSNs.

In the United States, the U.S. ISSN Center at the Library of Congress is responsible for assigning and maintaining the ISSNs for all U.S. serial titles. Publishers wishing to have an ISSN assigned should download an application from the Center's website, and mail, e-mail, or fax the form to the U.S. ISSN Center. Assignment of the ISSN is free, and there is no charge for use of the ISSN.

To obtain an ISSN for a U.S. publication, or for more information about ISSN in the United States, libraries, publishers, and other ISSN users should visit the U.S. ISSN Center's website, http://www.loc.gov/issn, or contact the U.S. ISSN Center, U.S. Programs, Law, and Literature, Library of Congress, 101 Independence Ave. S.E., Washington, DC 20540-4284 (telephone 202-707-6452, fax 202-707-6333, e-mail issn@loc.gov).

For information about ISSN products and services, and for application procedures that non-U.S. parties should use to apply for an ISSN, visit the ISSN International Centre's website, http://www.issn.org, or contact the International Centre at 45 rue de Turbigo, 75003 Paris, France (telephone 33-1-44-88-22-20, fax 33-1-40-26-32-43, e-mail issnic@issn.org).

How to Obtain an SAN

Beat Barblan

United States ISBN/SAN Agency

SAN stands for Standard Address Number. The SAN system, an American National Standards Institute (ANSI) standard, assigns a unique identification number that is used to positively identify specific addresses of organizations in order to facilitate buying and selling transactions within the industry. It is recognized as the identification code for electronic communication within the industry.

For purposes of this standard, the book industry includes book publishers, book wholesalers, book distributors, book retailers, college bookstores, libraries, library binders, and serial vendors. Schools, school systems, technical institutes, and colleges and universities are not members of this industry, but are served by it and therefore included in the SAN system.

The purpose of the SAN is to ease communications among these organizations, of which there are several hundreds of thousands that engage in a large volume of separate transactions with one another. These transactions include purchases of books by book dealers, wholesalers, schools, colleges, and libraries from publishers and wholesalers; payments for all such purchases; and other communications between participants. The objective of this standard is to establish an identification code system by assigning each address within the industry a unique code to be used for positive identification for all book and serial buying and selling transactions.

Many organizations have similar names and multiple addresses, making identification of the correct contact point difficult and subject to error. In many cases, the physical movement of materials takes place between addresses that differ from the addresses to be used for the financial transactions. In such instances, there is ample opportunity for confusion and errors. Without identification by SAN, a complex record-keeping system would have to be instituted to avoid introducing errors. In addition, problems with the current numbering system—such as errors in billing, shipping, payments, and returns—are significantly reduced by using the SAN system. The SAN also eliminates one step in the order fulfillment process: the "look-up procedure" used to assign account numbers. Previously a store or library dealing with 50 different publishers was assigned a different account number by each of the suppliers. The SAN solved this problem. If a publisher prints its SAN on its stationery and ordering documents, vendors to whom it sends transactions do not have to look up the account number, but can proceed immediately to process orders by SAN.

Libraries are involved in many of the same transactions as book dealers, such as ordering and paying for books and charging and paying for various services to other libraries. Keeping records of transactions—whether these involve buying, selling, lending, or donations—entails operations suited to SAN use. SAN stationery speeds up order fulfillment and eliminate errors in shipping, billing, and crediting; this, in turn, means savings in both time and money.

History

Development of the Standard Address Number began in 1968 when Russell Reynolds, general manager of the National Association of College Stores (NACS), approached R. R. Bowker and suggested that a "Standard Account Number" system be implemented in the book industry. The first draft of a standard was prepared by an American National Standards Institute (ANSI) Committee Z39 subcommittee, which was co-chaired by Reynolds and Emery Koltay of Bowker. After Z39 members proposed changes, the current version of the standard was approved by NACS on December 17, 1979.

Format

The SAN consists of six digits plus a seventh *Modulus 11* check digit; a hyphen follows the third digit (XXX-XXXX) to facilitate transcription. The hyphen is to be used in print form, but need not be entered or retained in computer systems. Printed on documents, the Standard Address Number should be preceded by the identifier "SAN" to avoid confusion with other numerical codes (SAN XXXXXXX).

Check Digit Calculation

The check digit is based on *Modulus 11,* and can be derived as follows:

1. Write the digits of the basic number.   2 3 4 5 6 7
2. Write the constant weighting factors associated with each position by the basic number.   7 6 5 4 3 2
3. Multiply each digit by its associated weighting factor.   14 18 20 20 18 14
4. Add the products of the multiplications.   14 + 18 + 20 + 20 + 18 + 14 = 104
5. Divide the sum by Modulus 11 to find the remainder.   104 -: 11 = 9 plus a remainder of 5
6. Subtract the remainder from the Modulus 11 to generate the required check digit. If there is no remainder, generate a check digit of zero. If the check digit is 10, generate a check digit of X to represent 10, since the use of 10 would require an extra digit.   11 - 5 = 6
7. Append the check digit to create the standard seven-digit Standard Address Number.   SAN 234-5676

SAN Assignment

R. R. Bowker accepted responsibility for being the central administrative agency for SAN, and in that capacity assigns SANs to identify uniquely the addresses of organizations. No SANs can be reassigned; in the event that an organization should cease to exist, for example, its SAN would cease to be in circulation entirely. If an organization using an SAN should move or change its name with no change in ownership, its SAN would remain the same, and only the name or address would be updated to reflect the change.

The SAN should be used in all transactions; it is recommended that the SAN be imprinted on stationery, letterheads, order and invoice forms, checks, and all other documents used in executing various book transactions. The SAN should always be printed on a separate line above the name and address of the organization, preferably in the upper left-hand corner of the stationery to avoid confusion with other numerical codes pertaining to the organization, such as telephone number, zip code, and the like.

SAN Functions

The SAN is strictly a Standard Address Number, becoming functional only in applications determined by the user; these may include activities such as purchasing, billing, shipping, receiving, paying, crediting, and refunding. It is the method used by Pubnet and PubEasy systems and is required in all electronic data interchange communications using the Book Industry Systems Advisory Committee (BISAC) EDI formats. Every department that has an independent function within an organization could have a SAN for its own identification.

For additional information or to make suggestions, write to ISBN/SAN Agency, R. R. Bowker, LLC, 630 Central Ave., New Providence, NJ 07974, call 877-310-7333, or fax 908-795-3515. The e-mail address is san@bowker.com. A SAN can be ordered online through the website www.myidentifiers.com, or an application can be requested by e-mail through san@bowker.com.

Distinguished Books

Notable Books of 2016

The Notable Books Council of the Reference and User Services Association, a division of the American Library Association, selected these titles for their significant contribution to the expansion of knowledge or for the pleasure they can provide to adult readers.

Fiction

Behold the Dreamers: A Novel by Imbolo Mbue (Random House, a division of Penguin Random House).

Christodora: A Novel by Tim Murphy (Grove Press, an imprint of Grove Atlantic).

Grief Is the Thing with Feathers: A Novel by Max Porter (Graywolf Press).

Homegoing: A Novel by Yaa Gyasi (Alfred A. Knopf, a division of Penguin Random House).

I'm Thinking of Ending Things: A Novel by Iain Reid (Scout Press, an imprint of Simon & Schuster).

Missile Paradise: A Novel by Ron Tanner (Ig Publishing).

The Nix: A Novel by Nathan Hill (Borzoi Books, Alfred A. Knopf, a division of Penguin Random House).

The Sport of Kings: A Novel by C. E. Morgan (Farrar, Straus and Giroux).

To the Bright Edge of the World: A Novel by Eowyn Ivey (Little, Brown, a division of Hachette Book Group).

The Underground Railroad Colson Whitehead (Doubleday, a division of Penguin Random House).

An Unrestored Woman by Shobha Rao (Flatiron Books).

The Unseen World by Liz Moore (W.W. Norton).

Nonfiction

Are We Smart Enough to Know How Smart Animals Are? by Frans de Waal (W.W. Norton).

At the Existentialist Cafe: Freedom, Being, and Apricot Cocktails by Sarah Bakewell (Other Press).

Blood at the Root: A Racial Cleansing in America by Patrick Phillips (W.W. Norton)

The Boys in the Bunkhouse: Servitude and Salvation in the Heartland by Dan Barry (Harper, an imprint of HarperCollins Publishers).

Evicted: Poverty and Profit in the American City by Matthew Desmond (Crown Publishers, a division of Penguin Random House).

The Firebrand and the First Lady: Portrait of a Friendship Pauli Murray, Eleanor Roosevelt, and the Struggle for Social Justice by Patricia Bell-Scott (Alfred A. Knopf, a division for Penguin Random House).

The Gene: An Intimate History by Siddhartha Mukherjee (Scribner, an imprint of Simon & Schuster).

Hidden Figures: The American Dream and the Untold Story of the Black Women Mathematicians Who Helped Win the Space Race by Margot Lee Shetterly (William Morrow, an imprint of HarperCollins Publishers).

In the Darkroom by Susan Faludi (Metropolitan Books, Henry Holt).

Louisa: The Extraordinary Life of Mrs. Adams by Louisa Thomas (Penguin Press, an imprint of Penguin Random House).

Shirley Jackson: A Rather Haunted Life by Ruth Franklin (Liveright Publishing, a division of W.W. Norton).

Valiant Ambition: George Washington, Benedict Arnold, and the Fate of the American Revolution by Nathaniel Philbrick (Viking, an imprint of Penguin Random House).

Poetry

Cannibal by Safiya Sinclair (University of Nebraska Press)

The Rain in Portugal: Poems by Billy Collins (Random House, division of Penguin Random House).

Best Fiction for Young Adults

Each year a committee of the Young Adult Library Services Association (YALSA), a division of the American Library Association, compiles a list of the best fiction appropriate for young adults ages 12 to 18. Selected on the basis of each book's proven or potential appeal and value to young adults, the titles span a variety of subjects as well as a broad range of reading levels. An asterisk denotes the title was selected as a top ten.

Alexander, Kwame. *Booked.* (HMH Books for Young Readers). 320p. ISBN: 978-0544570986.

Anderson, Laurie Halse. *Ashes.* (Atheneum/Caitlyn Dlouhy Books).

Arnold, David. *Kids of Appetite.* (Viking Books for Young Readers).

*Berry, Julie. *The Passion of Dolssa.* (Viking Books for Young Readers).

Braxton-Smith, Ananda. *Merrow.* (Candlewick).

Budhos, Marina. *Watched.* (Wendy Lamb Books).

Cavallaro, Brittany. *A Study in Charlotte.* (Katherine Tegen Books).

*Chee, Traci. *The Reader.* (G. P. Putnam's Sons Books for Young Readers).

Cordova, Zoraida. *Labyrinth Lost.* (Sourcebooks Fire).

Diederich, Phillippe. *Playing for the Devil's FIre.* (Cinco Puntos Press).

Dooley, Sarah. *Free Verse.* (G. P. Putnam's Sons Books for Young Readers).

Downham, Jenny. *Unbecoming.* (David Fickling Books).

Duyvis, Corinne. *On the Edge of Gone.* (Amulet Books).

Federle, Tim. *The Great American Whatever.* (Simon & Schuster Books for Young Readers).

Friend, Natasha. *Where You'll Find Me.* (Farrar, Straus and Giroux).

Garvin, Jeff. *Symptoms of Being Human.* Jeff Garvin. (Balzer + Bray).

Gephart, Donna. *Lily and Dunkin.* (Delacorte Books for Young Readers).

Girard, M-E. *Girl Mans Up.* (HarperCollins).

Glasgow, Kathleen. *Girl in Pieces.* (Delacorte Press).

Hand, Cynthia and Ashton, Brodi and Meadows, Jodi. *My Lady Jane.* (HarperTeen).

Hapgood, Harriet Reuter. *The Square Root of Summer.* (Roaring Brook Press).

*Hardinge, Frances. *The Lie Tree.* (Amulet Books).

Hartley, A. J. *Steeplejack.* (Tor Teen).

Heilig, Heidi. *The Girl from Everywhere.* (Greenwillow Books).

Hepperman, Christine. *Ask Me How I Got Here.* (Greenwillow Books).

Hesse, Monica. *Girl in the Blue Coat.* (Little, Brown Books for Young Readers).

Hoffmeister, Peter Brown. *This Is the Part Where You Laugh.* (Knopf Books for Young Readers).

Hutchinson, Shaun David. *We Are the Ants.* (Simon Pulse).

Kiely, Brendan. *The Last True Love Story.* (Margaret K. McElderry Books).

King, A.S. *Still Life with Tornado*. (Dutton Books for Young Readers).

Lake, Nick. *Whisper to Me*. (Bloomsbury USA Children's).

Larbalestier, Justine. *My Sister Rosa*. (Soho Teen).

Lee, Stacey. *Outrun the Moon*. (G. P. Putnam's Sons Books for Young Readers). ISBN: 9780399175411.

Levithan, David and LaCour, Nina. *You Know Me Well*. (St. Martin's Griffin). 256p. ISBN: 9781250098641.

Lindstrom, Eric. *Not If I See You First*. (Poppy). 320p. ISBN: 9780316259859.

Lord, Emery. *When We Collided*. (Bloomsbury USA Children's). 352p. ISBN: 9781619638457.

Lubar, David. *Character, Driven*. (Tor Teen). 304p. ISBN: 9780765316332.

*McGinnis, Mindy. *The Female of the Species*. (Katherine Tegen Books). 352p. ISBN: 9780062320896.

McLemore, Anna-Marie. *When the Moon Was Ours*. (St. Martin's Press). 288p. ISBN: 9781250058669.

*Medina, Meg. *Burn Baby Burn*. (Candlewick). 320p. ISBN: 9780763674670.

Meyer, Marissa. *Heartless*. (Feiwel & Friends). 464p. ISBN: 9781250044655.

O'Giulin, Peadar. *The Call*. (David Fickling Books). 320p. ISBN: 9781338045611

O'Neill, Louise. *Asking for It*. (Quercus). 336p. ISBN: 9781681445373.

Patel, Sonia. *Rani Patel in Full Effect*. (Cinco Puntos Press). 224p. ISBN: 9781941026496.

Perkins, Stephanie (editor). *Summer Days and Summer Nights: Twelve Love Stories*. (St. Martin's Griffin). 400p. ISBN: 9781250079121.

Porter, Sarah. *Vassa in the Night*. (Tor Teen). 304p. ISBN: 9780765380548.

Pung, Alice. *Lucy and Linh*. (Knopf Books for Young Readers). 352p. ISBN: 9780399550485.

Quick, Matthew. *Every Exquisite Thing*. (Little, Brown Books for Young Readers). 272p. ISBN: 9780316379595.

Reeve, Philip. *Railhead*. (Switch Press). 352p. ISBN: 9781630790486.

*Reynolds, Jason. *Ghost*. (Atheneum/Caitlyn Dlouhy Books). 192p. ISBN: 9781481450157.

Russo, Meredith. *If I Was Your Girl*. (Flatiron Books). 288p. ISBN: 9781250078407.

Schmidt, Gary. *Orbiting Jupiter*. (Clarion Books). 192p. ISBN: 9780544462229.

Self, Jeffery. *Drag Teen*. Push. 261p. ISBN: 9780545829939.

*Sepetys, Ruta. *Salt to the Sea*. (Philomel Books). 400p. ISBN: 9780399160301.

*Shusterman, Neal. *Scythe*. (Simon & Schuster Books for Young Readers). 448p. ISBN: 9781442472426.

Starmer, Aaron. *Spontaneous*. (Dutton Books for Young Readers). 368p. ISBN: 9780525429746.

Stork, Francisco. *The Memory of Light*. (Arthur A. Levine Books). 336p. ISBN: 9780545474320.

Sullivan, Tara. *The Bitter Side of Sweet*. (G. P. Putnam's Sons Books for Young Readers). 320p. ISBN: 9780399173073.

Umminger, Alison. *American Girls*. (Flatiron Books). 304p. ISBN: 9781250075000.

Whaley, John Corey. *Highly Illogical Behavior*. (Dial Books). 256p. ISBN: 9780525428183.

Winters, Cat. *The Steep and Thorny Way*. (Abrams). 352p. ISBN: 9781419719158.

*Yoon, Nicola. *The Sun Is Also a Star*. (Delacorte Press). 384p. ISBN: 9780553496680.

*Zentner, Jeff. *The Serpent King*. (Crown Books for Young Readers). 384p. ISBN: 978-0553524024.

Quick Picks for Reluctant Young Adult Readers

The Young Adult Library Services Association, a division of the American Library Association, annually chooses a list of outstanding titles that will stimulate the interest of reluctant teen readers. This list is intended to attract teens who, for whatever reason, choose not to read.

The list includes fiction and nonfiction titles published from late 2014 through 2015. An asterisk denotes the title was selected as a top ten.

Nonfiction

Callery, Sean. *50 Things You Should Know About Titanic*. 2016. Illus. QEB Publishing, $15.95. 9781682970232. Facts, figures, and primary photos detail the construction of the Titanic, its passengers, and the tragedy.

Fields, Stella. *Lazy Crafternoon*. 2016. Illus. Capstone Young Readers, $15.00. 9781623707514. Enjoy an afternoon creating inexpensive and simple crafts that are sure to impress.

Freedman, Russell. *We Will Not Be Silent: The White Rose Student Resistance Movement That Defied Adolf Hitler*. 2016. Illus. Clarion/Houghton Mifflin Harcourt Publishing Company, $17.99. 9780544223790. German siblings, Hans and Sophie Scholl, risked everything to spearhead the White Rose student resistance movement against Adolf Hitler.

Harrington, Jamie. *The Unofficial Guide to Crafting the World of Harry Potter: 30 Magical Crafts for Muggles, Witches, and Wizards Alike*. 2016. Illus. Adams Media Corp, $17.99. 9781440595042. Themed crafts of varying difficulty levels for Harry Potter fans.

Harris, Samantha. *Curls, Curls, Curls! Your Go-To Guide for Rocking Curly Hair-Plus Tutorials for 60 Fabulous Looks*. 2016. Illus. Chronicle Books, $19.95. 9781452158341. Styles and products just for curly girls, including information on natural hair care.

Hidalgo, Pablo. *Star Wars: The Force Awakens Visual Dictionary*. 2015. Illus. DK Children / Dorling Kindersley Publishing, $19.99. 9781465438164. An in-depth look at characters, gear and more.

*Higgins, Nadia Abushanab. *Feminism: Reinventing the F-Word*. 2016. Illus. Twenty First Century Books/Lerner, $35.99.

9781467761475. A discussion of feminism, what it is, what it isn't, and why it is important.

Inzer, Christine Mari. *Diary of a Tokyo Teen: A Japanese-American Girl Travels to the Land of Trendy Fashion, High-tech Toilets and Maid Cafes*. 2016. Illus. Tuttle Publishing, $14.99. 9784805313961. Travel with Christine as she explores Japanese food and culture in this illustrated journal.

Keyser, Amber J. *The V-Word: True Stories about First-Time Sex*. 2016. Simon Pulse and Beyond Words/Simon & Schuster, $19.99. 9781582705903. A frank, funny, and explicit collection of essays by women about losing one's virginity across a spectrum of experiences.

Mehring, Jonathan. *Skate the World: Photographing One World of Skateboarding*. 2015. Illus. National Geographic Society, $30.00. 9781426213960. A global look at amateur and professional skateboarders.

Miller, Sarah. *The Borden Murders: Lizzie Borden and the Trial of the Century*. 2016. Illus. Schwartz & Wade Books/Penguin Random House, $17.99. 9780553498080. A modern-day investigation of one of the most infamous murders of the 20th century.

Rattini, Kristin Baird, et al. *125 Wacky Roadside Attractions: See All the Weird, Wonderful, and Downright Bizarre Landmarks from Around the World!* 2016. Illus. National Geographic Children's Books/National Geographic Society. $12.99. 9781426324079. New ideas for your next road trip.

Stebner, Beth. *Stop. Breathe. Chill: Meditations for a Less Stressful, More Awesome Life*. 2016. Adams Media Corporation, $13.99. 9781440594397. Meditate on this.

Strebe, Jenny. *100 Perfect Hair Days: Step-By-Steps for Pretty Waves, Braids, Curls, Buns, and More!* 2016. Illus. Chronicle Books. $19.95. 9781452143354. Find the best style for your hair type and occasion.

Swartz, Clay. *Who Wins?: 100 Historical Figures Go Head-to-Head and You Decide the Winner!* 2016. Illus. Workman Publishing Co., $14.95. 9780761185444. Who would survive a zombie apocalypse or slay in a rap battle—Jackie Robinson or Marie Antoinette?

Waldman, Ariel. *What's It Like in Space? : Stories from Astronauts Who've Been There.* 2016. Illus. Chronicle Books, $14.95. 9781452144764. Answers fun questions about life in space.

Winterbottom, Julie. *Frightlopedia: An Encyclopedia of Everything Scary, Creepy, and Spine-Chilling, from Arachnids to Zombies.* 2016. Illus. Workman Publishing Co., $9.95. 9780761183792. An A-Z guide to creepy, scary, and unsettling creatures and phenomena.

Fiction

Alexander, Kwame. *Booked.* 2016. HMH Books for Young Readers/Houghton Mifflin Harcourt Publishing Company, $16.99. 9780544570986. Soccer star Nick Hall is on top until his parents shatter his world. How will Nick put the pieces back together?

Andrews, Jesse. *The Haters.* 2016. Amulet/Abrams, $18.95. 9781419720789. Teens ditch jazz camp and take it on the road.

Budhos, Marina. *Watched.* 2016. Wendy Lamb / Random House Children's Books, $17.99. 9780553534184. Naeem is coerced to surveil his Muslim-American community. As he goes deeper he wonders— is he in over his head?

*Buxbaum, Julie. *Tell Me Three Things.* 2016. Delacorte Press/Random House Children's Books. $17.99. 9780553535648. A mysterious admirer helps Jessie adjust to her new life in LA.

Calame, Don. *Dan Versus Nature.* 2016. Candlewick Press, $17.99. 9780763670719. Dan tries to scare off his mom's next potential husband while on a survivalist camping adventure. What could go wrong?

Cook, Eileen. *With Malice.* 2016. Houghton Mifflin Harcourt Books, $17.99.

9780544805095. Jill has no memory of the last six weeks. Was her friend's death really an accident?

Cordova, Zoraida. *Labyrinth Lost.* 2016. Sourcebooks Fire/Sourcebooks, $17.99. 9781492620945. Alex, a teenage *bruja*, must save her family after unintentionally banishing them to the Underworld.

Friend, Natasha. *Where You'll Find Me.* 2016. Farrar, Straus & Giroux/Macmillan, $16.99. 9780374302306. Stuck living with her dad and step mom after her mother's suicide attempt, Anna discovers acceptance in the unlikeliest of places.

Garcia, Kami. *The Lovely Reckless.* 2016. Imprint, $18.99. 9781250079190. After suffering a tragedy, Frankie throws herself into the world of street racing and the arms of bad boy Marco.

*Garvin, Jeff. *Symptoms of Being Human.* 2016. Balzer + Bray/HarperCollins, $17.99. 9780062382863. Riley, the child of a Congressman, secretly blogs about being gender fluid.

Gattis, Ryan. *Air.* 2016. Adaptive Books/ Adaptive Studios, $17.99. 9780986448423. Activism and extreme sports combine on the streets of Baltimore.

Gephart, Donna. *Lily and Dunkin.* 2016. Delacorte Books for Young Readers/Penguin Random House, $16.99. 9780553536744. Lily and Dunkin struggle with gender identity, mental illness, and the eighth grade.

Grimes, Nikki. *Garvey's Choice.* 2016. Wordsong/Highlights, $16.95. 9781629797403. Garvey stands up to bullying at home and school, then finds his true talent.

Hartinger, Brent. *Three Truths and a Lie.* 2016. Simon Pulse/Simon & Schuster, $17.99. 9781481449601. Four friends spend the weekend away in an isolated cabin and things turn deadly.

Hartzler, Aaron. *What We Saw.* 2015. HarperTeen/ HarperCollins, $17.99. 9780062338747. When school athletes are accused of rape, the small community chooses sides while Kate struggles to find the truth.

Heppermann, Christine. *Ask Me How I Got Here.* 2016. Greenwillow Books/HarperCollins, $17.99. 9780062387950. Addie, a cross country star and Catholic school student, has her life turned upside down when she gets pregnant.

Hicks, Faith Erin. *The Nameless City*. 2016. Illus. First Second Books/Roaring Brook Press, $21.99. 9781626721579. A young soldier meets a street urchin and learns the secrets of the city.

*Johnston, E.K. *Exit, Pursued by a Bear*. 2016. Dutton Books/Penguin Random House, $17.99. 9781101994580. Hermione is raped at cheer camp. In the year that follows, she deals with rumors, flashbacks, and a re-centering of her life.

Johnston, Jeffry. *The Truth*. 20106. Sourcebooks Fire/Sourcebooks, $9.99. 9781492623205. Chris is being held hostage by the brother of the boy he shot eight days ago.

Kensie, Clara. *Aftermath*. 2016. Merit Press Books/F & W Media, $17.99. 9781440598708. Charlotte endured four years of captivity and abuse. Can she survive the drama of returning to a home she doesn't recognize?

Knowles, Jo. *Still a Work in Progress*. 2016. Candlewick Press, $16.99. 9780763672171. Noah and his friends are making headway getting girlfriends and figuring out middle school when the "THING THEY DON'T TALK ABOUT" returns.

Krys, Michelle. *Dead Girls Society*. 2016. Delacorte Press/Random House Children's Books, $17.99. 9780553508024. When Hope, who has Cystic Fibrosis, receives a mysterious invitation she takes the dare.

*Lemire, Jeff. *Plutona*. 2016. Illus. Image Comics, $16.99. 9781632156013. A group of teens find the body of the superhero, Plutona, and must decide how to handle the situation.

Lindstrom, Eric. *Not If I See You First*. 2015. Poppy/Little Brown and Company, $18.00. 9780316259859. Parker doesn't forgive, especially when someone takes advantage of her blindness. Is there someone worth a second chance?

Lord, Emery. *When We Collided*. 2016. Bloomsbury Childrens Books/Bloomsbury Publishing, $17.99. 9781619638457. Vivi and Jonah are both struggling with more than the average high school student, and are instantly drawn to each other. They fall in love, but is their love enough to keep the darkness at bay?

Love, Jessica. *In Real Life*. 2016. Thomas Dunne Books/St. Martin's Press, $18.99. 9781250064714. Hoping for more, Hannah takes a road trip to surprise her online friend, Nick.

*Lukavics, Amy. *Daughters Unto Devils*. 2015. Harlequin Teen/Harlequin, $17.99. 9780373211586. After a dreadful winter, Amanda and her family find a new home on the prairie. Unfortunately, the demon spirits are already waiting for them.

Mather, Adriana. *How to Hang a Witch*. 2016. Alfred A. Knopf/Random House Children's Books, $17.99. 9780553539479. Samantha Mather moves to Salem where she tangles with the descendants of the Witch Trials.

Mathieu, Jennifer. *Afterward*. 2016. Roaring Book Press, $17.99. 9781626722385. When the searchers looking for recently kidnapped Dylan find him, they also come upon Ethan, who disappeared over four years ago.

McIntosh, Will. *Burning Midnight*. 2016. Delacorte Press/Random House Children's Books, $17.99. 9780553534108. What if there were spheres hidden around the world that could enhance your sight, make you prettier, stronger, smarter? Would you jump at the opportunity, or think twice about the consequences?

Moldavsky, Goldy. *Kill the Boy Band*. 2016. Point/Scholastic, $17.99. 9780545867474. Four girls will do anything to meet the members of their favorite boy band. When the evening takes a sinister turn, "fangirl" takes on a whole new meaning.

Mukherjee, Sonya. *Gemini*. 2016. Simon and Schuster Books for Young Readers, $17.99. 9781481456777. Conjoined twins, Clara and Hailey, are queens of compromise and cooperation, but as they get older they start to dream of separate futures.

Nguyen, Jenn P. and Phuong Anh Nguyen. *The Way to Game the Walk of Shame*. 2016. Swoon Reads/Feiwel and Friends, $9.99. 9781250084071. Taylor made one little mistake, waking up next to playboy Evan.

*Nijkamp, Marieke. *This Is Where It Ends*. 2016. Sourcebooks, $17.99. 9781492622468. A violent student with a grudge and a gun holds his classmates and teachers hostage for an hour.

Parker, S. M. *The Girl Who Fell*. 2016. Simon Pulse/Simon & Schuster, $17.99.

9781481437257. Zephyr is on track to go to college and leave her small town, when she meets the intoxicating Alec. They fall head over heels, but infatuation leads to control, manipulation, and danger.

Patel, Sonia. *Rani Patel in Full Effect.* 2016. Cinco Puntos Press, $11.95. 9781941026502. Rani joins a new rap group to cope with her turbulent home life.

Phelan, Matt. *Snow White: A Graphic Novel.* 2016. Illus. Candlewick Press, $19.99. 9780763672331. A retelling of the classic tale set during the Great Depression.

Pon, Cindy. *Serpentine.* 2015. Months 9 Books. $14.99. 9781942664338. As Skybright learns more about her mysterious abilities, she becomes entangled in a battle between her origins and the people she loves.

Preller, James. *The Fall.* 2016. Feiwel and Friends/Macmillan, $16.99. 9780312643010. Sam thought it was all a game, not quite knowing the impact of words and gestures until Morgan commits suicide.

Reynolds, Jason. *Ghost.* 2016. Atheneum Books for Young Readers/Simon and Schuster, $16.99. 9781481450157. Ghost lands a spot on an exclusive track team promising to stay out of trouble, but he finds it harder than he thought.

*Reynolds, Jason and Brendan Kiely. *All American Boys.* 2015. Atheneum/Simon and Schuster, $17.99. 9781481463331. Accused of shoplifting and resisting arrest, Rashad is beaten by a police officer. Racial tension runs high as friends take sides and a community is divided.

+Riggs, Ransom. *Tales of the Peculiar.* 2016. Illus. Dutton Books/Penguin Random House, $24.99. 9780399538537. From the world of Miss Peregrine, this book tells the stories of the first Peculiars and their protector.

Rivers, Olivia. *Tone Deaf.* 2016. Sky Pony Press/Skyhorse Publishing, $17.99. 9781634507073. Ali thought she left the world of music behind her after an operation took away her hearing until she meets the chart-topping band, Tone Deaf.

Rollins, Danielle. *Burning.* 2016. Bloomsbury Children's Books/Bloomsbury USA, $17.99. 9781619637382. Angela is counting down the days until her release from Brunesfield Correctional Facility, but everything changes with the arrival of a strange, new inmate.

*Russo, Meredith. *If I Was Your Girl.* 2016. Flatiron, $17.99. 9781250078407. Amanda is facing a lot of challenges, but nothing is as big as starting over after being relentlessly bullied for her transgender identity.

Self, Jeffery. *Drag Teen.* 2016. Push/Scholastic, $17.99. 9780545829939. JT goes on a road trip with his friends in an effort to win a scholarship and be crowned Miss Drag Teen.

Skrutskie, Emily. *The Abyss Surrounds Us.* 2016. Flux/Llewellyn Worldwide Ltd, $11.99. 9780738746913. On her first mission out, Cas, a new trainer of Reckoners, bio-engineered sea monsters, is kidnapped by pirates. What will she do to survive?

Strand, Jeff. *The Greatest Zombie Movie Ever.* 2016. Sourcebooks Fire/Sourcebooks, $9.99. 9781492628149. Justin and his friends are going to make the greatest zombie movie ever- in a months' time, with no budget and no script. How hard could it be?

*Tash, Sarvenaz. *The Geek's Guide to Unrequited Love.* 2016. Simon & Schuster BFYR/Simon & Schuster, $17.99. 9781481456531. Graham has realized he is in love with his best friend and partner in comic book creation, Roxy. What better place to declare his feelings than New York Comic Con?

Watkins, Steve. *Great Falls.* 2016. Candlewick Press, $17.99. 9780763671556. After his older brother, Jeremy, returns from Afghanistan and Iraq, as a war hero, Shane notices many changes in his behavior.

+Whaley, John Corey. *Highly Illogical Behavior.* 2016. Dial Books/Penguin Random House, $17.99. 9780525428183. Solomon is afraid to leave his house, until one day Lisa barges into his life. She thinks curing Solomon will help her score a scholarship.

Wilson, G. Willow. *Ms. Marvel, Vol. 5: Super Famous.* 2016. Illus. Marvel Worldwide, Inc, $17.99. 9780785196112. Kamala Khan is dealing with high school, family commitments and being the youngest Avenger. Is Ms. Marvel up to the challenge?

Young, Suzanne. *All in Pieces.* 2016. Simon Pulse/Simon and Schuster, $17.99. 9781481418836. Savannah is solely focused on taking care of her little brother with special needs and avoiding her alcoholic father. Then she meets Cameron at her alternative high school.

Zentner, Jeff. *The Serpent King*. 2016. Crown Books for Young Readers/Random House, $17.99. 9780553524024. Dill copes with the fallout of his minister father's scandal through the help of his friends.

Series

One-Punch Man. What do you do when you've become so strong you can defeat all opposition with a single punch? You get bored.

One. *One-Punch Man*, v. 1. 2015. Illus. Viz Media, $9.99. 9781421585642.

One. *One-Punch Man*, v. 2. 2015. Illus. Viz Media, $9.99. 9781421585659.

One. *One-Punch Man*, v. 3. 2015. Illus. Viz Media, $9.99. 9780738746913.

You Choose: Spies Series. Go back in history as a spy; what happens next is up to you.

Burgan, Michael. *Spies of the Civil War: An Interactive History Adventure*. 2015. Illus. Capstone, $31.32. 9781491458594.

Burgan, Michael. *Spies of World War I: An Interactive History Adventure*. 2015. Illus. Capstone, $31.32. 9781491458600.

Raum, Elizabeth. *Stealing Nazi Secrets in World War II: An Interactive History Adventure*. 2015. Illus. Capstone, $31.32. 9781491458617.

Raum, Elizabeth. *Spies of the American Revolution: An Interactive History Adventure*. 2015. Illus. Capstone, $31.32. 9781491458587.

Amazing Audiobooks for Young Adults

Each year a committee of the Young Adult Library Services Association, a division of the American Library Association, compiles a list of the best audiobooks for young adults ages 12 to 18. The titles are selected for their teen appeal and recording quality, and because they enhance the audience's appreciation of any written work on which the recordings may be based. While the list as a whole addresses the interests and needs of young adults, individual titles need not appeal to this entire age range but rather to parts of it. An asterisk denotes the title was selected as a top ten.

Fiction

Anna and the Swallow Man by Gavriel Savit, read by Allan Corduner (Listening Library).

Beast by Brie Spangler, read by Andrew Eiden (Blackstone Audio).

Gemina by Amie Kaufman and Jay Kristoff, read by Carla Corvo, MacLeod Andrews, Steve West, and a full cast (Listening Library).

Ghost by Jason Reynolds, read by Guy Lockard (Simon & Schuster Audio).

Grimm's Fairy Tales by Jacob and Wilhelm Grimm, read by a Full Cast (Listening Library).

Half Lost by Sally Green, read by Carl Prekopp (Listening Library).

Highly Illogical Behavior by John Corey Whaley, read by Robbie Daymond and Julia Whelan (Listening Library).

Holding Up the Universe by Jennifer Niven, read by Jorjeana Marie and Robbie Daymond (Listening Library).

The Incident on the Bridge by Laura McNeal, read by Lincoln Hoppe (Listening Library).

The Inquisitor's Tale: Or, The Three Magical Children and Their Holy Dog by Adam Gidwitz, read by Vika Adam, Mark Bramhall, Jonathan Cowley, Kimberly Farr, Adam Gidwitz, Ann Marie Lee, Bruce Mann, John H Mayer, and Arthur Morey (Listening Library).

Iron Man: The Gauntlet by Eoin Colfer, read by Ari Fliakos (Listening Library).

Kill the Boy Band by Goldy Moldavsky, read by Barrett Wilbert Weed (Scholastic Audio).

A Little in Love by Susan Fletcher, read by Melody Grove (Recorded Books).

The Memory of Light by Francisco X. Stork, read by Frankie Corzo (Scholastic).

My Lady Jane by Cynthia Hand, Brodi Ashton, Jodi Meadows, read by Katherine Kellgren (HarperAudio).

My Name Is Not Friday by John Walter, read by Dion Graham (Scholastic).

Nimona by Noelle Stevenson, read by Marc Thompson, Rebecca Soler, January LaVoy, Peter Bradbury, Jonathan Davis, David Pittu, Natalie Gold (HarperAudio).

Orbiting Jupiter by Gary D. Schmidt, read by Christopher Gebauer. Recorded Books

Our Chemical Hearts by Krystal Sutherland, read by Robbie Daymond (Listening Library).

The Red Umbrella by Christina Diaz Gonzalez, read by Kyla Garcia (Ideal on Dreamscape Audio).

Salt to the Sea by Ruta Sepetys, read by Jorjeana Marie, Will Damron, Cassandra Morris, Michael Crouch (Listening Library).

The Secret Horses of Briar Hill by Megan Shepherd, read by Fiona Hardingham (Listening Library).

The Smell of Other People's Houses by Bonnie-Sue Hitchcock, read by Jorjeana Marie, Erin Tripp, Karissa Vacker, and Robbie Daymond (Listening Library).

Star Wars Ahsoka by E.K. Johnston, read by Ashley Eckstein (Listening Library).

Their Fractured Light by Amie Kaufman and Meagan Spooner, read by Kim Mai Guest, MacLeod Andrews, Abby Craden and Cynthia Holloway (Listening Library).

Thieving Weasels by Billy Taylor, read by Robbie Daymond (Listening Library).

Traffick by Ellen Hopkins, read by Kirby Heyborne, Julia Whelan, Madeleine Maby, Rebekkah Ross, Jacques Roy (Simon & Schuster).

Wink Poppy Midnight by April Genevieve Tucholke, read by Michael Crouch, Alicyn Packard, and Caitlin Davies (Listening Library).

The Reading List

Established in 2007 by the Reference and User Services Association (RUSA), a division of the American Library Association, this list highlights outstanding genre fiction that merits special attention by general adult readers and the librarians who work with them.

RUSA's Reading List Council, which consists of 12 librarians who are experts in readers' advisory and collection development, selects books in eight categories: Adrenaline (suspense, thrillers, and action adventure), Fantasy, Historical Fiction, Horror, Mystery, Romance, Science Fiction, and Women's Fiction.

Adrenaline

Orphan X by Gregg Hurwitz (Minotaur, an imprint of Macmillan).

Fantasy

Stiletto: A Novel by Daniel O'Malley (Little, Brown, a division of Hachette Book Group).

Historical Fiction

The Last Days of Night: A Novel by Graham Moore (Random House, a division of Penguin Random House).

Horror

Hex by Thomas Olde Heuvelt (Tor, a Tom Doherty Associates book).

Mystery

Darktown by Thomas Mullen (37Ink/Atria Books, an imprint of Simon & Schuster).

Romance

Forbidden by Beverly Jenkins (Avon Books, an imprint of HarperCollins Publishers).

Science Fiction

Arkwright by Allen Steele (Tor, a Tom Doherty Associates book).

The Listen List

Established in 2010 by the Reference and User Services Association (RUSA), the Listen List highlights outstanding audiobooks that merit special attention by general adult listeners and the librarians who work with them.

They are chosen by RUSA's Listen List Council, which annually selects a list of 12 titles that may include fiction, nonfiction, poetry, and plays. To be eligible, titles must be available for purchase and circulation by libraries. An annotated version of the list on the RUSA website includes more information on each choice.

Another Brooklyn: A Novel by Jacqueline Woodson. Narrated by Robin Miles (HarperAudio/Blackstone Audio).

The Bazaar of Bad Dreams: Stories by Stephen King. Narrated by Stephen King, Dylan Baker, Brooke Bloom, Hope Davis, Kathleen Chalfant, Santino Fontana, Peter Friedman, Cotter Smith, Will Patton, Edward Herrmann, Frederick Weller, Mare Winningham, Craig Wasson, Thomas Sadoski, Tim Sample (Simon & Schuster Audio).

Because of Miss Bridgerton by Julia Quinn. Narrated by Rosalyn Landor (HarperAudio/Blackstone Audio).

The Curious Charms of Arthur Pepper by Phaedra Patrick. Narrated by James Langton (Harlequin Audio/Blackstone Audio).

Evicted: Poverty and Profit in the American City by Matthew Desmond. Narrated by Dion Graham (Random House Audio/Books on Tape).

Julian Fellowes's Belgravia by Julian Fellowes. Narrated by Juliet Stevenson (Hachette Audio/Blackstone Audio).

Lily and the Octopus by Steven Rowley. Narrated by Michael Urie (Simon & Schuster Audio).

News of the World by Paulette Jiles. Narrated by Grover Gardner (Brilliance Audio).

Razor Girl: A Novel by Carl Hiaasen. Narrated by John Rubinstein (Random House Audio/Books on Tape).

Sleeping Giants by Sylvain Neuvel. Narrated by Andy Secombe, Eric Meyers, Laurel Lefkow, Charlie Anson, Liza Ross, William Hope, Christoper Ragland, Katharine Mangold, Adna Sablyich (Random House Audio/Books on Tape).

The Underground Railroad by Colson Whitehead. Narrated by Bahni Turpin (Random House Audio/Books on Tape).

A Wild Swan: And Other Tales by Michael Cunningham. Narrated by Lili Taylor, Billy Hough (Macmillan Audio).

Alex Awards

The Alex Awards are given to ten books written for adults that have special appeal to young adults ages 12 through 18. The winning titles are selected by a committee of the Young Adult Library Services Association (YALSA), a division of the American Library Association, from among the previous year's publishing. The award is sponsored by the Margaret A. Edwards Trust.

Arena by Holly Jennings, (Ace Books, an imprint of Penguin Random House).

Buffering: Unshared Tales of a Life Fully Loaded by Hannah Hart (Dey Street, an imprint of William Morrow, a division of HarperCollins Publishers).

Die Young with Me: A Memoir by Rob Rufus (Touchstone, an imprint of Simon & Schuster).

Every Heart a Doorway by Seanan McGuire, a Tor Book (Tom Doherty Associates).

In the Country We Love: My Family Divided by Diane Guerrero with Michelle Burford (Henry Holt and Co).

The Invisible Life of Ivan Isaenko by Scott Stambach (St. Martin's Press).

The Queen of Blood by Sarah Beth Durst (Harper Voyager, an imprint of HarperCollins Publishers).

The Regional Office is Under Attack! by Manuel Gonzales (Riverhead, an imprint of Penguin Random House).

Romeo and/or Juliet: A Choosable-Path Adventure by Ryan North (Riverhead Books, an imprint of Penguin Random House).

The Wasp that Brainwashed the Caterpillar by Matt Simon (Penguin Books, an imprint of Penguin Random House).

Outstanding International Books, 2016

The United States Board on Books for Young People (USBBY), the U.S. national section of the International Board on Books for Young People (IBBY), compiles an annual list of outstanding books originating outside the United States that represent the best in children's literature from around the world.

Grades Pre-K to 2

DeGennaro, Sue. *The Pros and Cons of Being a Frog.* Illus. by the author. S. & S./Paula Wiseman Bks. Australia.

Dubuc, Marianne. *The Animals' Ark.* Tr. from French. Illus. by the author. Kids Can. Canada.

Hirst, Daisy. *The Girl with the Parrot on her Head.* Illus. by the author. Candlewick. UK.

Hohn, Nadia L. *Malaika's Costume.* Illus. by Irene Luxbacher. Groundwood. Canada/set in the Caribbean.

Lanthier, Jennifer. *Hurry Up, Henry.* Illus. by Isabelle Malenfant. Puffin. Canada.

Leroy, Jean. *A Well-Mannered Young Wolf.* Tr. from French. Illus. by Matthieu Maudet. Eerdmans. France.

O'Leary, Sara. *A Family Is a Family Is a Family.* Illus. by Qin Leng. Groundwood. Canada.

Rocha, Ruth. *Lines, Squiggles, Letters, Words.* Tr. from Portuguese by Lyn Miller-Lachmann. Illus. by Madalena Matoso. Enchanted Lion. Brazil.

Sanna, Francesca. *The Journey.* Illus. by the author. Flying Eye. UK.

Stark, Ulf. *The Midsummer Tomte and the Little Rabbits.* Tr. from Swedish by Susan Beard. Illus. by Eva Eriksson. Floris. Sweden.

Viswanath, Shobha. *The Blue Jackal.* Illus. by Dileep Joshi. Eerdmans. India.

Grades 3–5

Argueta, Jorge. *Somos Como Las Nubes/We Are Like the Clouds.* Tr. by Elisa Amado. Illus. by Alfonso Ruano. Groundwood. Canada.

Cornille, Didier. *Who Built That? Bridges: An Introduction to Ten Great Bridges and Their Designers.* Tr. from French by Yolanda Stern Broad. Illus. by author. Princeton Architectural. France.

Faber, Polly. *Mango & Bambang, the Not-a-Pig.* Illus. by Clara Vulliamy. Candlewick. UK.

Fenton, Corinne. *Bob the Railway Dog: The True Story of an Adventurous Dog.* Illus. by Andrew McLean. Candlewick. Australia.

Hurst, Elise. *Imagine a City.* Illus. by the author. Doubleday. Canada.

Krishnaswami, Uma. *Book Uncle and Me.* Illus. by Julianna Swaney. Groundwood. Canada/set in India.

Kuhlmann, Torben. *Armstrong: The Adventurous Journey of a Mouse to the Moon.* Tr. from German by David Henry Wilson. Illus. by the author. NorthSouth. Germany.

Kuhn, Camilla. *Samira and the Skeletons.* Tr. from Norwegian by Don Bartlett. Illus. by author. Eerdmans. Norway.

Lagercrantz, Rose. *Life According to Dani.* Tr. from Swedish by Julia Marshall. Illus. by Eva Eriksson. Gecko. Sweden.

Martins, Isabel Minhós. *Don't Cross the Line.* Tr. from Portuguese by Daniel Hahn. Illus. by Bernardo P. Carvalho. Gecko. Portugal.

Muller, Gerda. *A Year in Our New Garden.* Tr. from German. Illus. by the author. Floris. Germany.

Parvela, Timo. *Bicycling to the Moon.* Tr. from Finnish by Ruth Urbom. Illus. by Virpi Talfitie. Gecko. Finland.

Pinfold, Levi. *Greenling.* Illus. by the author. Candlewick/Templar. Australia.

Rossell, Judith. *Withering by Sea.* Illus. by the author. S. & S./Atheneum. Australia.

Sanabria, José. *As Time Went By.* Tr. from German. Illus. by the author. NorthSouth. Switzerland.

Grades 6–8

Bogart, Jo Ellen. *The White Cat and the Monk: A Retelling of the Poem "Pangur Ban."* Illus. by Sydney Smith. Groundwood. Canada.

Davies, Linda. *Longbow Girl.* Scholastic/Chicken House. UK.

Hardstaff, Jane. *The Executioner's Daughter.* Lerner/Carolrhoda. UK.

Lea, Synne. *Night Guard.* Tr. from Norwegian by John Irons. Illus. by Stian Hole. Eerdmans. Norway.

Luurtsema, Nat. *Goldfish.* Feiwel and Friends. UK.

Stevenson, Robin. *Pride: Celebrating Diversity and Community.* Orca. Canada.

Svingen, Arne. *The Ballad of a Broken Nose.* Tr. from Norwegian by Kari Dickinson. S. & S./Margaret K. McElderry Bks. Norway.

Grades 9–12

Acioli, Socorro. *The Head of the Saint.* Tr. from Portuguese by Daniel Hahn. Delacorte. Brazil.

Downham, Jenny. *Unbecoming.* Scholastic. UK.

Hardinge, Frances. *The Lie Tree.* Abrams. UK.

Lewis, Amanda West. *The Pact.* Red Deer. Canada/set in Germany.

Williamson, Lisa. *The Art of Being Normal.* Farrar/Margaret Ferguson Bks. UK.

Woltz, Anna. *A Hundred Hours of Night.* Tr. from Dutch by Laura Watkinson. Scholastic/Arthur A. Levine Bks. Netherlands.

Wright, David & Lu Bouchard. *Away Running.* Orca. Canada/set in France.

Wung-Sung, Jesper. *The Last Execution.* Tr. from Danish by Lindy Falk van Rooyen. Atheneum/Caitlyn Dlouhy Bks. Denmark.

Notable Children's Videos

These DVD titles are selected by a committee of the Association for Library Service to Children, a division of the American Library Association. Recommendations are based on originality, creativity, and suitability for children.

Ada's Ideas: The Story of Ada Lovelace, the World's First Computer Programmer. 16 minutes. Dreamscape. 877-983-7326. Ages 3–8.

Drum Dream Girl: How One Girl's Courage Changed Music. 6 minutes. Dreamscape. 877-983-7326. Ages 3–8.

Groovy Joe: Ice Cream & Dinosaurs/José el Chévere: Helado y Dinosaurios. 6 minutes. Weston Woods. 800-243-5020. Ages 3–6.

Last Stop on Market Street. 10 minutes. Dreamscape. 877-983-7326. Ages 3–8.

The Princess and the Warrior: A Tale of Two Volcanoes. 17 minutes. Dreamscape. 877-983-7326. Ages 3–8.

Star Stuff: Carl Sagan and the Mysteries of the Cosmos. 10 minutes. Weston Woods. 800-243-5020. Ages 4–8.

Supertruck. 5 minutes. Weston Woods. 800-243-5020. Ages 2–6.

Trombone Shorty. 14 minutes. Dreamscape. 877-983-7326. Ages 3–8.

You Are (Not) Small. 5 minutes. Weston Woods. 800-243-5020. Ages 2–6.

Notable Recordings for Children

This list of notable CD recordings for children was selected by the Association for Library Service to Children, a division of the American Library Association. Recommended titles are chosen by children's librarians and educators on the basis of their originality, creativity, and suitability.

Abe's Honest Words: The Life of Abraham Lincoln. Weston Woods. 800-243-5020. Ages 7–12. Nicol Zanzarella and Trevor Murphy expertly tell the story of Lincoln's life. Special sound effects, background music, and author and illustrator notes enhance the listening experience.

Anna and the Swallow Man. Listening Library. 800-793-2665. Ages 12 and up (2017 Odyssey Award Audiobook). Allan Corduner's gentle narration guides this dark journey of a young girl and the mysterious man she befriends in the harsh environment of World War II Poland.

Arf. Weston Woods. Ages 8–12. Jim Frangione expertly personifies the confident dog Bowser, providing much levity in this murder mystery.

Arriba Abajo. Salsana. www.123andres. com All ages. 1 2 3 Andrés imparts the joy of language, music, and movement in a bilingual (English and Spanish) collection of songs that is storytime and classroom-friendly.

As Brave as You. Simon & Schuster. 800-223-2336. Ages 8 and up. Guy Lockard brings ebullience and poignancy to this funny, resonant story of two brothers and the questions, big and small, that they face over the summer at their grandparents' home.

Beetle Boy. Recorded Books. 877-732-2898. Ages 8–12. With distinct characterizations and humor, M.G. Leonard narrates her book about a boy, beetles, and the mysterious disappearance of his father.

The Cat Who Came in Off the Roof. Listening Library. Ages 6–12. A rollicking performance by Katherine Kellgren lets the listener enjoy the adventures of shy Mr. Tibble and the unusual Miss Minou.

Dream On, Amber. Recorded Books. Ages 8–12 (2017 Odyssey Honor Audiobook). Laura Kirman becomes this spirited tween in a dynamic performance that highlights Amber's humor, heart, and multicultural heritage.

Feel What U Feel. Furious Rose Records. www. lisaloeb.com All ages. Exploring various emotions, Lisa Loeb's soothing voice invites children to "Feel What U Feel."

Ghost. Simon & Schuster. Ages 10–14 (2017 Odyssey Honor Audiobook). With authentic and humorous characterizations, Guy Lockard expertly performs this story of a boy who finds his purpose on the track team.

Grayling's Song. Recorded Books. Ages 10 and up. With a flair for character vocalization and a beautiful singing voice, Katherine Kellgren takes the listener on Grayling's magical quest.

Groovy Joe: Ice Cream and Dinosaurs. Weston Woods. Ages 3–6. Mixing narrative with song, Eric Litwin presents an engaging story of a dog who loves ice cream and learns to share with his dinosaur friends.

The League of Beastly Dreadfuls: The Dastardly Deed (Book 2). Listening Library. Ages 8 and up. Rosalyn Landor deftly captures a wide range of sound effects and characters, from bats to shapeshifters, in this lively fantasy tale.

Mama's Nightingale. Recorded Books. Ages: 5–12. Robin Miles interprets this heartwarming immigration story in a simple, believable voice, that perfectly captures a tender mother-daughter relationship.

My Pen. Live Oak Media. All ages. Christopher Myers' dazzling vocalizations and masterful art come together with brilliant sound effects to create an immersive sensory experience.

The Nazi Hunters: How a Team of Spies and Survivors Captured the World's Most Notorious Nazi. Weston Woods. Ages 10–14. Jason Culp's steady narration makes vivid the story of Mossad's mission to capture notorious Nazi fugitive, Adolf Eichmann.

Nimona. HarperAudio. Ages 12 and up (2017 Odyssey Honor Audiobook). A villain, a hero, a shapeshifting teen tell a story of adventure, danger . . . and science! This full cast production brings to life the story, reminiscent of radio dramas.

The Playground Zone. School Time Music. www.alphabetrockers.com. All ages. The Alphabet Rockers' infectious hip hop songs feature empowering messages that will have everyone up and dancing.

Raymie Nightingale. Listening Library. Ages 10–14. Jenna Lamia's distinctive voices for Raymie and her friends infuse this audiobook with humor and heartbreak, making for a memorable listen.

Saddle Up: A Western Adventure Album. Okee Dokee Music. www.okeedokee.org. All ages. From jackalopes to shooting stars, The Okee Dokee Brothers take listeners on a musical adventure across the Continental Divide. Accompanying DVD visually expands upon the listening experience.

Save Me a Seat. Weston Woods. Ages 8–12. Vikas Adam and Josh Hurley's expert and authentic vocalizations humorously relay the story of the unlikely friendship between two outsiders.

Stick and Stone. Weston Woods. Ages 4–7. Maxwell Glick's concise, expressive, and clear voice beautifully narrates this sweet and humorous tale of friends lost and found. Bonus song enhances the story experience.

Storms. Live Oak Media. Ages: 6–9. Dion Graham combines excellent narration with dramatic sound effects to inform and engage early readers. Vivid photos, riddles, and quizzes enhance this read-along.

28 Days: Moments in Black History that Changed the World. Live Oak Media. Ages 7–10. A full cast of narrators performs twenty-nine poems celebrating Black History with accompanying music, sound effects, and historical recordings creating a riveting listen.

Unbound: A Novel in Verse. Weston Woods. Ages 8–14. Bahni Turpin's lyrical interpretation of righteous Grace and her cruel Missus are the heart of this poetic tale of an enslaved family who seeks freedom in the Great Dismal Swamp.

Where Are You Going, Baby Lincoln? Listening Library. Ages 6–9. In an installment of Tales from Deckawoo Drive, Lorna Raver narrates this story of Baby Lincoln's Necessary Journey, bringing Kate DiCamillo's inimitable style to life in an engaging way.

Wolf Hollow. Listening Library. Ages 10 and up. Emily Rankin's intimate narration carries the listener along on 12-year-old Annabelle's haunting journey through a web of lies in a small Pennsylvania town in the shadow of WWII.

Notable Children's Books

A list of notable children's books is selected each year by the Notable Children's Books Committee of the Association for Library Service to Children, a division of the American Library Association. Recommended titles are selected by children's librarians and educators based on originality, creativity, and suitability for children. [See "Literary Prizes, 2016" later in Part 5 for Caldecott, Newbery, and other award winners—*Ed.*]

Younger Readers

Ada Lovelace, Poet of Science: The First Computer Programmer. By Diane Stanley. Illus. by Jessie Hartland (Simon & Schuster/Paula Wiseman).

Ada Twist, Scientist. By Andrea Beaty. Illus. by David Roberts (Abrams).

Before Morning. By Joyce Sidman. Illus. by Beth Krommes (HMH).

Best Frints in the Whole Universe. By Antoinette Portis. Illus. by the author. (Roaring Brook/Neal Porter.)

Counting. By Fleur Star. illus. (DK).

Coyote Moon. By Maria Gianferrari. Illus. by Bagram Ibatoulline (Roaring Brook).

Fabulous Frogs. By Martin Jenkins. Illus. by Tim Hopgood (Candlewick).

Go, Otto, Go! By David Milgrim. Illus. by the author. (Simon & Schuster/Simon Spotlight).

Good Night Owl. By Greg Pizzoli. Illus. by the author. (Disney/Hyperion).

The Great Pet Escape. By Victoria Jamieson. Illus. by the author. (Holt).

Horrible Bear! By Ame Dyckman. Illus. by Zachariah OHora (Little, Brown).

A Hungry Lion; or, A Dwindling Assortment of Animals. By Lucy Ruth Cummins. Illus. by the author. (Atheneum).

The Infamous Ratsos. By Kara LaReau. Illus. by Matt Myers (Candlewick).

Leave Me Alone! By Vera Brosgol. Illus. by the author. (Roaring Brook).

The Night Gardener. By Terry Fan. Illus. by Eric Fan (Simon & Schuster).

Old Dog Baby Baby. By Julie Fogliano. Illus. by Chris Raschka (Roaring Brook/Neal Porter).

Oops, Pounce, Quick, Run! An Alphabet Caper. By Mike Twohy. Illus. by the author. (HarperCollins/Balzer + Bray).

Over the Ocean. By Taro Gomi. Illus. by the author. (Chronicle).

A Piece of Home. By Jeri Watts. Illus. by Hyewon Yum (Candlewick).

Puddle. By Hyewon Yum. Illus. by the author. (Farrar).

Rudas: Niño's Horrendous Hermanitas. By Yuyi Morales. Illus. by the author. (Roaring Brook/Neal Porter).

School's First Day of School. By Adam Rex. Illus. by Christian Robinson (Roaring Brook/Neal Porter).

Thunder Boy Jr. By Sherman Alexie. Illus. by Yuyi Morales (Little, Brown).

We Are Growing! A Mo Willems' Elephant and Piggie Like Reading! Book. By Laurie Keller. Illus. by the author. (Disney/Hyperion).

We Found a Hat. By Jon Klassen. Illus. by the author. (Candlewick).

Weekends with Max and His Dad. By Linda Urban. Illus. by Katie Kath (HMH).

When Andy Met Sandy. By Tomie dePaola and Jim Lewis. Illus. by Tomie dePaola (Simon & Schuster).

Where Are You Going, Baby Lincoln? By Kate DiCamillo. Illus. by Chris Van Dusen (Candlewick).

Middle Readers

The Best Man. By Richard Peck (Dial).

Dory Fantasmagory: Dory Dory Black Sheep. By Abby Hanlon (Dial).

Full of Beans. By Jennifer L. Holm (Random).

Frank and Lucky Get Schooled. By Lynne Rae Perkins. Illus. by the author. (Greenwillow).

The Girl Who Drank the Moon. By Kelly Barnhill (Algonquin).

I Am Not a Number. By Jenny Kay Dupuis and Kathy Kacer. Illus. by Gillian Newland (Second Story).

I Dissent: Ruth Bader Ginsburg Makes Her Mark. By Debbie Levy. Illus. by Elizabeth Baddeley (Simon & Schuster).

Juana & Lucas. By Juana Medina. Illus. by the author. (Candlewick).

Ms. Bixby's Last Day. By John David Anderson (HarperCollins/Walden Pond).

Pax. By Sara Pennypacker. Illus. by Jon Klassen (HarperCollins/Balzer + Bray).

A Poem for Peter: The Story of Ezra Jack Keats and the Creation of The Snowy Day. By Andrea Davis Pinkney. Illus. by Lou Fancher and Steve Johnson (Viking).

Preaching to the Chickens: The Story of Young John Lewis. By Jabari Asim. Illus. by E. B. Lewis (Penguin/Nancy Paulsen).

The Princess and the Warrior. By Duncan Tonatiuh. Illus. by the author. (Abrams).

Raymie Nightingale. By Kate DiCamillo (Candlewick).

The Secret Keepers. By Trenton Lee Stewart. Illus. by Diana Sudyka (Little, Brown/Megan Tingley).

The Sound of Silence. By Katrina Goldsaito. Illus. by Julia Kuo (Little, Brown).

Steamboat School. By Deborah Hopkinson. Illus. by Ron Husband (Disney/Jump at the Sun).

Step Right Up: How Doc and Jim Key Taught the World about Kindness. By Donna Janell Bowman. Illus. by Daniel Minter (Lee & Low).

The Storyteller. By Evan Turk. Illus. by the author (Atheneum).

The Tragic Tale of the Great Auk. By Jan Thornhill. Illus. by the author. (Groundwood).

A Voyage in the Clouds: The (Mostly) True Story of the First International Flight by Balloon in 1785. By Matthew Olshan. Illus. by Sophie Blackall (Farrar).

Wet Cement. By Bob Raczka. Roaring Brook.

When Mischief Came to Town. By Katrina Nannestad (Harcourt).

When the Sea Turned to Silver. By Grace Lin. Illus. by the author (Little, Brown).

The Wild Robot. By Peter Brown. Illus. by the author. (Little, Brown).

Older Readers

As Brave As You. By Jason Reynolds (Atheneum/Caitlyn Dlouhy).

The Ballad of a Broken Nose. By Arne Svingen. Tr. by Kari Dickson (Simon & Schuster/Margaret K. McElderry).

The Bitter Side of Sweet. By Tara Sullivan (Putnam).

Blood Brother: Jonathan Daniels and His Sacrifice for Civil Rights. By Rich Wallace and Sandra Neil Wallace. illus. (Boyds Mills/Calkins Creek).

Booked. By Kwame Alexander. HMH.

Brown v. Board of Education: A Fight for Simple Justice. By Susan Goldman Rubin. illus. (Holiday).

Cloud and Wallfish. By Anne Nesbet (Candlewick).

Cry, Heart, but Never Break. By Glenn Ringtved. Illus. by Charlotte Pardi. Tr. by Robert Moulthrop (Enchanted Lion).

Garvey's Choice. By Nikki Grimes (Boyds Mills/Wordsong).

Ghost. By Jason Reynolds (Atheneum/Caitlyn Dlouhy).

In the Shadow of Liberty: The Hidden History of Slavery, Four Presidents, and Five Black Lives. By Kenneth C. Davis. illus. (Holt).

The Inquisitor's Tale; or, The Three Magical Children and Their Holy Dog. By Adam Gidwitz. Illus. by Hatem Aly (Dutton).

The Lie Tree. By Frances Hardinge (Abrams/Amulet).

Lowriders to the Center of the Earth. By Cathy Camper. Illus. by Raul the Third (Chronicle).

March: Book Three. By John Lewis and Andrew Aydin. Illus. by Nate Powell (Top Shelf).

The Only Road. By Alexandra Diaz (Simon & Schuster/Paula Wiseman).

Presenting Buffalo Bill: The Man Who Invented the Wild West. By Candace Fleming. illus. (Roaring Brook/Neal Porter).

Sachiko: A Nagasaki Bomb Survivor's Story. By Caren Stelson. illus. (Carolrhoda).

Samurai Rising: The Epic Life of Minamoto Yoshitsune. By Pamela S. Turner. Illus. by Gareth Hinds (Charlesbridge).

To Stay Alive: Mary Ann Graves and the Tragic Journey of the Donner Party. By Skila Brown (Candlewick).

Uprooted: The Japanese American Experience during World War II. By Albert Marrin. illus (Knopf).

We Will Not Be Silent: The White Rose Student Resistance Movement That Defied Adolf Hitler.

What Elephants Know. By Eric Dinerstein (Disney/Hyperion).

Wolf Hollow. By Lauren Wolk. Dutton).

The Wolf's Boy. By Susan Williams Beckhorn (Disney/Hyperion).

You Can Fly: The Tuskegee Airmen. By Carole Boston Weatherford. Illus. by Jeffery Boston Weatherford (Atheneum).

All Ages

Animals by the Numbers: A Book of Infographics. By Steve Jenkins. Illus. by the author. (HMH).

As Time Went By. By Jose Sanabria. Illus. by the author. (North-South).

Daniel Finds a Poem. By Micha Archer. Illus. by the author. (Penguin/Nancy Paulsen).

Du Iz Tak? By Carson Ellis. Illus. by the author. (Candlewick).

Esquivel! Space-Age Sound Artist. By Susan Wood. Illus. by Duncan Tonatiuh (Charlesbridge).

Freedom in Congo Square. By Carole Boston Weatherford. Illus. by R. Gregory Christie (little bee).

Freedom over Me: Eleven Slaves, Their Lives and Dreams Brought to Life by Ashley Bry-

an. By Ashley Bryan. Illus. by the author. (Atheneum/Caitlyn Dlouhy).

Giant Squid. By Candace Fleming. Illus. by Eric Rohmann (Roaring Brook/Neal Porter).

Jazz Day: The Making of a Famous Photograph. By Roxane Orgill. Illus. by Francis Vallejo (Candlewick).

The Journey. By Francesca Sanna. Illus. by the author. (Flying Eye).

Maybe Something Beautiful: How Art Transformed a Neighborhood. By F. Isabel Campoy and Theresa Howell. Illus. by Rafael Lopez (HMH).

¡Olinguito, de la A a la Z!/Olinguito, from A to Z! Descubriendo el bosque nublado/Unveiling the Cloud Forest. By Lulu Delacre. Illus. by the author. (Lee & Low).

Radiant Child: The Story of Young Artist Jean-Michel Basquiat. By Javaka Steptoe. Illus. by the author. (Little, Brown).

Some Writer! The Story of E. B. White. By Melissa Sweet. Illus. by the author. (HMH).

Somos como las nubes/We Are Like the Clouds. By Jorge Argueta. Illus. by Alfonso Ruano. Tr. by Elisa Amado (Groundwood).

They All Saw a Cat. By Brendan Wenzel. Illus. by the author. (Chronicle).

The Water Princess. By Susan Verde and Georgie Badiel. Illus. by Peter H. Reynolds (Putnam).

When Green Becomes Tomatoes. By Julie Fogliano. Illus. by Julie Morstad (Roaring Brook/Neal Porter).

Literary Prizes, 2016

Compiled by the staff of the *Library and Book Trade Almanac*

ABC-CLIO/Greenwood Award for Best Book in Library Literature ($5,000). To recognize works that improve library management principles and practice, understanding and application of new techniques, or further the education of librarians or other information specialists. *Sponsor:* ABC-CLIO. *Administered by:* American Library Association. *Winner:* Sidney E. Berger for *Rare Books and Special Collections* (ALA Neal-Schuman).

Academy of American Poets Fellowship ($25,000). For outstanding poetic achievement. *Offered by:* Academy of American Poets. *Winner:* Natasha Trethewey.

Jane Addams Children's Book Awards. For children's books that effectively promote the cause of peace, social justice, world community, and equality. *Offered by:* Women's International League for Peace and Freedom and the Jane Addams Peace Association. *Winners:* (younger children) Susan Lynn Meyer for *New Shoes*; Lynda Blackmon Lowery for *Turning 15 on the Road to Freedom: My Story of the Selma Voting Rights March.*

Aesop Prize. For outstanding work in children's folklore, both fiction and nonfiction. *Offered by:* American Folklore Society. *Winners:* Cathy Camper and Raúl the Third. *Lowriders to the Center of the Earth*; Mordicai Gerstein. *I Am Pan!*

Agatha Awards. For mystery writing in the method exemplified by author Agatha Christie. *Offered by:* Malice Domestic Ltd. *Winners:* (contemporary novel) Ellen Byron for *Body on the Bayou* (Crooked Lane Books); (first novel) Marla Cooper for *Terror in Taffeta* (Minotaur); (historical) Jessica Estevao for *Whispers Beyond the Veil* (Berkley); (children's/YA) P. A. DeVoe for *Trapped: A Mei-hua Adventure* (Drum Tower Press); (nonfiction) Jane K. Cleland for *Mastering Suspense, Structure, and Plot: How to Write Gripping Stories that Keep Readers on the Edge of Their Seats* (Writer's Digest Books); (short story) Gretchen Archer for

Double Jinx: A Bellissimo Casino Crime Caper Short Story (Henery Press).

American Academy of Arts and Letters Award of Merit ($25,000). Given annually, in rotation, for the short story, sculpture, novel, poetry, drama, and painting. *Offered by:* American Academy of Arts and Letters. *Winner:* Henri Cole (poetry).

American Academy of Arts and Letters Awards in Literature ($10,000). To honor writers of fiction and nonfiction, poets, dramatists, and translators of exceptional accomplishment. *Offered by:* American Academy of Arts and Letters. *Winners:* Ta-Nehisi Coates, Joshua Ferris, Stephen Adly Guirgis, Terrance Hayes, Lynn Nottage, Katie Peterson, Mark Polizzotti, Spencer Reece.

American Academy of Arts and Letters Rome Fellowships. For a one-year residency at the American Academy in Rome for young writers of promise. *Offered by:* American Academy of Arts and Letters. *Winners:* Jack Livings, Matthew Neill Null.

American Book Awards. For literary achievement by people of various ethnic backgrounds. *Offered by:* Before Columbus Foundation. *Winners:* Laura Da' for Tributaries (University of Arizona); Susan Muaddi Darraj for Curious Land: Stories from Home (University of Massachusetts); Deepa Iyer for We Too Sing America: South Asian, Arab, Muslim, and Sikh Immigrants Shape Our Multiracial Future (The New Press); Mat Johnson for Loving Day (Spiegel & Grau); John Keene for Counternarratives (New Directions); William J. Maxwell for F.B. Eyes: How J. Edgar Hoover's Ghostreaders Framed African American Literature (Princeton University); Lauret Savoy Trace for Memory, History, Race, and the American Landscape (Counterpoint); Ned Sublette and Constance Sublette for The American Slave Coast: A History of the Slave-Breeding Industry (Lawrence Hill Books); Jesús Salvador Treviño for Return to Arroyo Grande (Arte Público); Nick Turse for Tomorrow's Battlefield: U.S. Proxy Wars and Secret Ops in Africa (Haymarket

Books); Ray Young Bear for Manifestation Wolverine: The Collected Poetry of Ray Young Bear (Open Road Integrated Media): (lifetime achievement) Louise Meriwether.

American Indian Youth Literature Awards. Offered biennially to recognize excellence in books by and about American Indians. *Offered by:* American Indian Library Association. *Winners:* (picture book) Richard Van Camp, author, Julie Flett, illustrator, for *Little You* (Orca); (middle school) Joseph Marshall III for *In the Footsteps of Crazy Horse* (Amulet); (young adult) Tim Tingle for *House of Purple Cedar* (Cinco Puntos).

American Poetry Review/Honickman First Book Prize in Poetry ($3,000 and publication of the book). To encourage excellence in poetry and to provide a wide readership for a deserving first book of poems. *Winner:* Tyree Daye for *River Hymns* (Copper Canyon Press).

Américas Book Award for Children's and Young Adult Literature. To recognize U.S. works of fiction, poetry, folklore, or selected nonfiction that authentically and engagingly portray Latin America, the Caribbean, or Latinos in the United States. *Sponsored by:* Consortium of Latin American Studies Programs (CLASP). *Winner:* Pam Muñoz Ryan for Echo (Scholastic Press); Ashley Hope-Pérez for Out of Darkness (Carolrhoda Lab).

Rudolfo and Patricia Anaya Lecture on the Literature of the Southwest. To honor a Chicano or Chicana fiction writer. *Offered by:* National Hispanic Cultural Center, University of New Mexico. *Winner:* Rigoberto Gonzalez.

Hans Christian Andersen Literature Award (500,000 Danish kroner, about $73,000). To a writer whose work can be compared with that of Andersen. *Offered by:* Hans Christian Andersen Literary Committee. *Winner:* Cao Wenxuan.

Anthony Awards. For superior mystery writing. *Offered by:* Boucheron World Mystery Convention. *Winners:* (novel) Chris Holm for *The Killing Kind* (Mulholland); (first novel) Glen Erik Hamilton for *Past Crimes* (Morrow); (paperback original) Lou Berney for *The Long and Faraway Gone* (Morrow); (short story) Megan Abbott for *The Little Men: A Bibliomystery* (MysteriousPress.com/Open Road); (critical or nonfiction

work) Val McDermid, for *Forensics: What Bugs, Burns, Prints, DNA, and More Tell Us About Crime* (Grove); (anthology or collection) Art Taylor, editor, for *Murder Under the Oaks: Boucheron Anthology 2015* (Down & Out).

Asian/Pacific American Awards for Literature. For books that promote Asian/Pacific American culture and heritage. *Sponsor:* Asian/Pacific American Librarians Association (APALA). *Winners:* (picture book) Jane Bahk for *Juna's Jar* (Lee & Low); (children's) Marilyn Hilton for *Full Cicada Moon* (Dial/Penguin Random House); (young adult) Jenny Han for *P.S. I Still Love You* (Simon & Schuster); (adult fiction) Viet Thanh Nguyen for *Sympathizer* (Grove Press); (adult nonfiction) Erika Lee for *The Making of Asian America: A History* (Simon & Schuster).

Audio Publishers Association Awards (Audies). To recognize excellence in audiobooks. *Winners:* (audiobook of the year, original work) *The Girl on the Train* by Paula Hawkins, read by Clare Corbett, Louise Brealey, India Fisher; (autobiography/memoir, narration by the author or authors) *Ghost Boy* by Martin Pistorius, read by Simon Bubb; (multi-voiced performance) *Illuminae* by Amie Kaufman, Jay Kristoff, read by Lincoln Hoppe, et al.; (solo narration, female) *Wild Rover No More* by L. A. Meyer, read by Katherine Kellgren; (solo narration, male) *The English Spy* by Daniel Silva, read by George Guidall (HarperCollins); (nonfiction) *Ghettoside* by Jill Leovy, read by Rebecca Lowman; (history/biography) *A Man on the Moon* by Andrew Chaikin, read by Bronson Pinchot; (inspirational/faith-based fiction) *To Win Her Favor* by Tamera Alexander, read by Melba Sibrel; (inspirational/faith-based nonfiction) *Boy Born Dead* by David Ring, et al., read by Paul Michael; (literary fiction) *Little Big Man* by David Ring, et al., read by Paul Michael; (personal development) *Wake Up Happy* by Michael Strahan, Veronica Chambers, read by Michael Strahan; (fiction) *The Nightingale* by Kristin Hannah, read by Polly Stone; (romance) *The Highwayman* by Kerrigan Byrne, read by Derek Perkins; (erotica) *Curing Doctor Vincent* by Renea Mason, read by Noah Michael Levine, Erin Deward; (science fiction)

Jurassic Park by Michael Crichton, read by Scott Brick; (paranormal) *White Trash Zombie Gone Wild* by Diana Rowland, read by Allison McLemore; (fantasy) *Nice Dragons Finish Last* by Rachel Aaron, read by Vikas Adam; (humor) *Furiously Happy* by Jenny Lawson, read by Jenny Lawson; (mystery) *Career of Evil* by Robert Galbraith, read by Robert Glenister; (thriller/suspense) *The Patriot Threat* by Steve Berry, read by Scott Brick.

Bad Sex in Fiction Award (United Kingdom). To "draw attention to the crude, badly written, often perfunctory use of redundant passages of sexual description in the modern novel, and to discourage it." *Sponsor:* Literary Review. *Winner:* Erri De Luca for *The Day Before Happiness* (Allen Lane).

Baileys Women's Prize for Fiction (United Kingdom) (formerly the Orange Prize for Fiction) (£30,000). For the best novel written by a woman and published in the United Kingdom. *Winner:* Lisa McInerney for *The Glorious Heresies* (Deckle Edge).

Bancroft Prizes ($10,000). For books of exceptional merit and distinction in American history, American diplomacy, and the international relations of the United States. *Offered by:* Columbia University. *Winners:* Andrés Reséndez *for The Other Slavery: The Uncovered Story of Indian Enslavement in America* (Houghton Mifflin Harcourt); Heather Ann Thompson for *Blood in the Water: The Attica Prison Uprising of 1971 and Its Legacy* (Pantheon); Nancy Tomes for *Remaking the American Patient: How Madison Avenue and Modern Medicine Turned Patients into Consumers* (University of North Carolina Press).

Barnes & Noble Discover Great New Writers Awards. To honor a first novel and a first work of nonfiction by American authors. *Offered by:* Barnes & Noble. *Winners:* (fiction) Abby Geni for *The Lightkeepers* (Counterpoint Press); (nonfiction) Matthew Desmond for *Evicted: Poverty and Profit in the American City* (Crown/Archetype).

Mildred L. Batchelder Award. To the American publisher of a children's book originally published in a language other than English and subsequently published in English in the United States. *Offered by:* American Library Association, Association for Library Service to Children. *Winner:* Glenn Ringtved for *Cry, Heart, But Never Break*, illustrated by Charlotte Pardi and translated by Robert Moulthrop.

BBC National Short Story Award (United Kingdom) (£15,000). *Winner:* KJ Orr for "Disappearances."

Beacon of Freedom Award. For the best title introducing American history, from colonial times through the Civil War, to young readers. *Offered by:* Williamsburg (Virginia) Regional Library and the Colonial Williamsburg Foundation. *Winner:* Nathan Hale for *One Dead Spy* (Abrams). Final award was made in 2015.

Pura Belpré Awards. To a Latino/Latina writer and illustrator whose work portrays, affirms, and celebrates the Latino cultural experience in an outstanding work of literature for children and youth. *Offered by:* American Library Association, Association for Library Service to Children. *Winners:* (writer) Juana Medina for *Juana & Lucas* (Candlewick).

Helen B. Bernstein Book Award for Excellence in Journalism ($15,000). To a journalist who has written at book length about an issue of contemporary concern. *Offered by:* New York Public Library. *Winner:* Jill Leovy for *Ghettoside: A True Story of Murder in America* (Random House).

Black Caucus of the American Library Association (BCALA) Literary Awards. *Winners:* (fiction) Jacqueline Woodson for *Another Brooklyn* (Amistad); (nonfiction) Margot Lee Shetterly for *Hidden Figures: The American Dream and the Untold Story of the Black Women Mathematicians Who Helped Win the Space Race* (William Morrow); (first novelist award, to acknowledge outstanding achievement in writing and storytelling by a first-time fiction writer) Natasha Deon for *Grace* (Counterpoint Press); (poetry) Clint Smith for *Counting Descent* (Write Bloody Publishing); (outstanding contribution to publishing citation) Tyehimba Jess for *Olio* (Wave Books).

Irma Simonton Black and James H. Black Award for Excellence in Children's Literature. To a book for young children in which the text and illustrations work together to create an outstanding whole. *Offered by:* Bank Street College of Education. *Winner:*

The Fan Brothers for *The Night Gardener* (Simon & Schuster).

James Tait Black Memorial Prize (United Kingdom) (£10,000). To recognize literary excellence in fiction and biography. *Offered by:* University of Edinburgh. *Winners:* (fiction) Benjamin Markovits for *You Don't Have to Live Like This* (HarperCollins); (biography) James Shapiro for *The Year of Lear: Shakespeare in 1606* (Simon & Schuster).

James Tait Black Prize for Drama (United Kingdom) (£10,000). *Offered by:* University of Edinburgh in partnership with the National Theatre of Scotland and in association with the Traverse Theatre. *Winner:* Gary Owen for *Iphigenia in Splott*.

Blue Peter Book of the Year (United Kingdom). To recognize excellence in children's books. Winners are chosen by a jury of viewers, ages 8–12, of the BBC television children's program "Blue Peter." *Winners:* (best story) Kieran Larwood for *Podkin One Ear* (Houghton Mifflin Harcourt); (best book with facts) David Long, for *Survivors: Extraordinary Tales From the Wild and Beyond* (Faber and Faber).

Bookseller/Diagram Prize for Oddest Title of the Year. *Sponsor: The Bookseller* magazine. *Winner:* Alan Stafford for *Too Naked for the Nazis*.

BookSense Book of the Year Awards. See Indies Choice Book Awards.

Boston Globe/Horn Book Awards. For excellence in children's literature. *Winners:* (fiction) Frances Hardinge for *The Lie Tree* (Amulet Books); (nonfiction) Steve Sheinkin for *Most Dangerous: Daniel Ellsberg and the Secret History of the Vietnam War* (Roaring Brook); (picture book) Roxane Orgill for *Jazz Day: The Making of a Famous Photograph* (Candlewick).

W. Y. Boyd Literary Award ($5,000). For a military novel that honors the service of American veterans during a time of war. *Offered by:* American Library Association. *Donor:* W. Y. Boyd II. *Winner:* Ralph Peters for *Valley of the Shadow* (Forge Books).

Branford Boase Award (United Kingdom). To the author and editor of an outstanding novel for young readers by a first-time writer. *Winners:* Horatio Clare and Penny Thomas, editor, for *Aubrey and the Terrible Yoot* (Firefly Press).

Bridport International Creative Writing Prizes (United Kingdom). For poetry and short stories. *Offered by:* Bridport Arts Centre. *Winners:* (poetry, £5,000) Mark Pajak for "Spitting Distance"; (short story, £5,000) Wendy Brandmark for "Cut Loose"; (flash fiction, 250-word maximum, £1,000) David Swann for "Drought."

British Council Award for ELT writing (£2,000). To celebrate the best writing for English language teaching. *Winner:* Philip Kerr for *Translation and Own-Language Activities* (Cambridge University Press).

British Fantasy Awards. *Offered by:* British Fantasy Society. *Winners:* (horror novel) Catriona Ward for *Rawblood* (Weidenfeld & Nicolson); (novella) Usman T. Malik for *The Pauper Prince and the Eucalyptus Jinn* (Tor.com); (short fiction) Priya Sharma for *Fabulous Beasts* (Tor.com); (anthology) Ellen Datlow, editor, for *The Doll Collection* (Tor Books); (collection) Tananarive Due for *Ghost Summer: Stories* (Prime Books); (comic/graphic novel) Kelly Sue DeConnick, Valentine De Landro, Robert Wilson IV, and Cris Peter for *Bitch Planet* (Image Comics); (artist) Julie Dillon; (nonfiction) Alexandra Pierce and Alisa Krasnostein, editors, for *Letters to Tiptree* ((Twelfth Planet Press); (magazine/periodical) Scott H. Andrews, editor, for *Beneath Ceaseless Skies* (Firkin Press); (film/television episode) for "Jonathan Strange & Mr Norrell," Peter Harness (BBC One); (newcomer) Zen Cho for *Sorcerer to the Crown* (Macmillan); (best fantasy novel, the Robert Holdstock Award) Naomi Novik for *Uprooted* (Macmillan).

Sophie Brody Medal. For the U.S. author of the most distinguished contribution to Jewish literature for adults, published in the preceding year. *Donors:* Arthur Brody and the Brodart Foundation. *Offered by:* American Library Association, Reference and User Services Association. *Winner:* Michael Chabon for *Moonglow* (Harper).

Witter Bynner Poetry Fellowships ($10,000). To encourage poets and poetry. *Sponsor:* Witter Bynner Foundation for Poetry. *Winner:* Ray Gonzalez.

Caine Prize for African Writing (£10,000). For a short story by an African writer, published in English. *Winner:* Lidudumalingani for

"Memories We Lost" in *Incredible Journey: Stories That Move You* (Burnet Media).

Randolph Caldecott Medal. For the artist of the most distinguished picture book. *Offered by:* American Library Association, Association for Library Service to Children. *Winner:* Javaka Steptoe, writer and illustrator, for *Radiant Child: The Story of Young Artist Jean-Michel Basquiat* (Little, Brown).

California Book Awards. To California residents to honor books of fiction, nonfiction, and poetry published in the previous year. *Offered by:* Commonwealth Club of California. *Winners:* (fiction) Michael Chabon for *Moonglow* (Harper); (first fiction) Melissa Yancy for *Dog Years* (University of Pittsburgh Press); (nonfiction) Andrus Resende for *The Other Slavery* (Houghton Mifflin Harcourt); (poetry) Aja Couchois Duncan for *Restless Continent* (Litmus Press); (juvenile) Anne Nosbet for *Cloud and Wallfish* (Candlewick); (young adult) Nicola Yoon for *The Sun Is Also A Star* (Delacorte); (contribution to publishing) Harold Mooney and Erika Zavaleta for *Ecosystems of California* (University of California Press); (Californiana) Benjamin Madley for *An American Genocide: The United States and the California Indian Catastrophe 1846–1873* (Yale University Press).

John W. Campbell Award. For the best new science fiction or fantasy writer whose first work of science fiction or fantasy was published in a professional publication in the previous two years. *Offered by:* Dell Magazines. *Winner:* Andy Weir for *The Martian* (Crown/Archetype).

John W. Campbell Memorial Award. For science fiction writing. *Offered by:* Center for the Study of Science Fiction. *Winners:* Eleanor Lerman for *Radiomen* (The Permanent Press).

Canadian Library Association Book of the Year for Children. *Sponsor:* Library Services Centre. *Winner:* Kenneth Oppel for *The Nest* (HarperCollins).

Canadian Library Association Amelia Frances Howard-Gibbon Illustrator's Award. *Sponsor:* Library Services Centre. *Winner:* Sydney Smith for *Sidewalk Flowers.*

Canadian Library Association Young Adult Book Award. *Winners:* Erin Bow for *The Scorpion Rules* (Simon & Schuster Canada).

Andrew Carnegie Medal for Excellence in Fiction and Nonfiction. For adult books published during the previous year in the United States. *Sponsors:* Carnegie Corporation of New York, ALA/RUSA, and *Booklist. Winners:* (fiction) Colson Whitehead for *The Underground Railroad* (Doubleday, Penguin Random House); (nonfiction) Matthew Desmond for *Evicted: Poverty and Profit in the American City* (Crown, Penguin Random House).

Carnegie Medal (United Kingdom). See CILIP Carnegie Medal.

Center for Fiction Flaherty-Dunnan First Novel Prize. See Flaherty-Dunnan First Novel Prize.

Chicago Folklore Prize. For the year's best folklore book. *Offered by:* American Folklore Society. *Winner:* Jane Beck for *Daisy Turner's Kin: An African American Family Saga* (University of Illinois Press).

Chicago Tribune Nelson Algren Short Story Award ($5,000). For unpublished short fiction. *Offered by: Chicago Tribune. Winner:* Lee Conell for "The Lock Factory."

Chicago Tribune Heartland Prize for Fiction ($7,500). *Offered by: Chicago Tribune. Winner:* Jane Smiley for *Golden Age* (Knopf).

Chicago Tribune Heartland Prize for Nonfiction ($7,500). *Offered by: Chicago Tribune. Winner:* Philip Glass for *Words Without Music* (Liveright).

Chicago Tribune Young Adult Literary Prize. To recognize a distinguished literary career. *Winner:* David Levithan.

Children's Africana Book Awards. To recognize and encourage excellence in children's books about Africa. *Offered by:* Africa Access, African Studies Association. *Winners:* (young readers) Nnedi Okorafor for *Chicken in the Kitchen* (Lantana Publishing); Franck Prévot and Aurélia Fronty for *Wangari Maathai*; (older readers) Elizabeth Wein for *Black Dove White Raven* (Disney Press); Beverley Naidoo for *Who Is King.*

Cholmondeley Awards for Poets (United Kingdom) (£1,500). For a poet's body of work and contribution to poetry. *Winners:* Maura Dooley, David Morley, Peter Sansom, Iain Sinclair.

CILIP Carnegie Medal (United Kingdom). For the outstanding children's book of the year. *Offered by:* CILIP: The Chartered Institute of Library and Information Professionals (formerly the Library Association). *Winner:* Sarah Crossan for *One* (Bloomsbury).

CILIP Kate Greenaway Medal and Colin Mears Award (United Kingdom) (£5,000 plus £500 worth of books donated to a library of the winner's choice). For children's book illustration. *Offered by:* CILIP: The Chartered Institute of Library and Information Professionals. *Winner:* William Grill for *Shackleton's Journey* (Flying Eye).

Arthur C. Clarke Award. For the best science fiction novel published in the United Kingdom. *Offered by:* British Science Fiction Association. *Winner:* Adrian Tchaikovsky for *Children of Time* (Pan Macmillan).

David Cohen Prize for Literature (United Kingdom) (£40,000). Awarded biennially to a living British writer, novelist, poet, essayist, or dramatist in recognition of an entire body of work written in the English language. *Offered by:* David Cohen Family Charitable Trust. *Winner:* Tony Harrison.

Matt Cohen Award: In Celebration of a Writing Life (C$20,000). To a Canadian author whose life has been dedicated to writing as a primary pursuit, for a body of work. *Offered by:* Writers' Trust of Canada. *Sponsors:* Marla and David Lehberg. *Winner:* Brian Brett.

Commonwealth Book Prize (United Kingdom) (£10,000). To reward and encourage new Commonwealth fiction and ensure that works of merit reach a wider audience outside their country of origin. *Offered by:* Commonwealth Institute. *Winner:* The prize, formerly known as the Commonwealth Writers' Prize, was discontinued after the 2013 competition.

Commonwealth Short Story Prize (United Kingdom) (£5,000). To reward and encourage new short fiction by Commonwealth writers. *Offered by:* Commonwealth Institute. *Winners:* (regional winner, Canada) Stephanie Seddon for "Eel"; (regional winner, Africa) Faraaz Mahomed (South Africa) for "The Pigeon"; (regional winner, Asia) Parashar Kulkarni (India) for "Cow and Company"; (regional winner, Caribbean) Lance Dowrich (Trinidad) for "Ethelbert and the Free Cheese"; (regional winner, Pacific) Tina Makereti (New Zealand) for "Black Milk."

Costa Book Awards (United Kingdom) (£5,000 plus an additional £25,000 for Book of the Year). For literature of merit that is readable on a wide scale. *Offered by:* Booksellers Association of Great Britain and Costa Coffee. *Winners:* (biography) Andrea Wulf for *The Invention of Nature* (John Murray); (novel) Kate Atkinson for *A God in Ruins* (Doubleday); (first novel) Andrew Michael Hurley for *The Loney* (John Murray); (poetry) Don Paterson for *40 Sonnets* (Faber and Faber); (children's and Book of the Year) Frances Hardinge for *The Lie Tree* (Macmillan).

Costa Short Story Award (United Kingdom). *Winners:* (first place, £3,500) Jess Kidd for "Dirty Little Fishes"; (second place, £1,500) Billy O'Callaghan for "The Boatman"; (third place, £500) Rob Ewing for "The Persistence of Memory."

Crab Orchard Review Literary Prizes ($2,000 and publication in *Crab Orchard Review*). *Winners:* (Jack Dyer Fiction Prize) Olivia Kate Cerrone for "A Member of the Tribe"; (John Guyon Literary Nonfiction Prize) Jocelyn Bartkevicius for "Mother Tongue"; (Richard Peterson Poetry Prize) T. J. McLemore for "The Bees, or Bringing Back Eurydice."

Crime Writers' Association (CWA) Dagger Awards (United Kingdom). *Winners:* (diamond dagger, for significant contribution to crime writing) Peter James; (gold dagger, for best novel) Bill Beverly for *Dodgers* (Crown/Archetype); (Ian Fleming steel dagger, for best thriller) Don Winslow for *The Cartel* (Knopf Doubleday); (John Creasey dagger, for best new crime writer) Bill Beverly for *Dodgers* (Crown/Archetype); (international dagger, for a work translated into English) Pierre Lemaitre and Frank Wynne, translator, for *The Great Swindle* (Quercus); (nonfiction dagger) Andres Hankinson for *You Could Do Something Amazing with Your Life (You Are Raoul Moat)* (ReadHowYouWant); (CWA Dagger in the Library, for a body of work) Elly Griffiths; (debut dagger, for a previously unpublished crime writer) Mark Brandi for *Wimmera*; (short story) John Connolly for "On the Anatomization of an Unknown Man (1637) by Frans Mier" in *Nocturnes 2: Night Music* (Atria/Emily Bestler Books); (CWA Endeavour historical dagger, for the best historical crime novel) David Young for *Stasi Child* (St. Martin's).

Benjamin H. Danks Award ($20,000). To a promising young writer, playwright, or composer, in alternate years. *Offered by:* American Academy of Arts and Letters. *Winner:* playwright Branden Jacobs-Jenkins.

Dartmouth Medal. For creating current reference works of outstanding quality and significance. *Donor:* Dartmouth College. *Offered by:* American Library Association, Reference and User Services Division. *Winner:* Bloomsbury Academic for *Encyclopedia of Embroidery from the Arab World.*

Derringer Awards. To recognize excellence in short crime and mystery fiction. *Sponsor:* Short Mystery Fiction Society. *Winners:* (flash story, up to 1,000 words) Herschel Cozine for "The Phone Call" in *Flash Bang Mysteries*; (short story, 1,001–4,000 words) Linda Barnes for "The Way They Do It in Boston" in *Ellery Queen's Mystery Magazine*; (long story, 4,001–8,000 words) Victoria Weisfeld for "Breadcrumbs" in *Kickass Women in Crime Fiction*, Issue 3; (novelette, 8,001–20,000 words) Terrie Farley Moran for "Inquiry and Assistance" in *Alfred Hitchcock's Mystery Magazine*; (Edward D. Hoch Memorial Golden Derringer for Lifetime Achievement) Robert Randisi.

Diagram Prize for Oddest Title of the Year. See Bookseller/Diagram Prize for Oddest Title of the Year.

Philip K. Dick Award. For a distinguished science fiction paperback published in the United States. *Sponsor:* Philadelphia Science Fiction Society and the Philip K. Dick Trust. *Winner:* Claudia Casper for *The Mercy Journals* (Arsenal Pulp Press).

Digital Book Awards. To recognize high-quality digital content available to readers as e-books and enhanced digital books. *Sponsor:* Digital Book World. *Winners:* (e-book, flowable: adult fiction) John Ashbery for *Chinese Whispers* (Open Road); (e-book, flowable: adult nonfiction) Sheila Heti, Heidi Julavits, and Leanne Shapton for *Women in Clothes* (Penguin); (e-book, flowable: children's) Laurie S. Sutton for *You Choose: Scooby-Doo! The Terror of the Bigfoot Beast* (Capstone); (e-book, fixed format/enhanced: adult fiction) Neil Gaiman for *The Truth Is a Cave in the Black Mountains* (Morrow);

(e-book, fixed format/enhanced: adult nonfiction) Shauna Miller for *Penny Chic: How to Be Stylish on a Real Girl's Budget* (Little, Brown); (e-book, fixed format/enhanced: children's) Kyo Maclear, Danielle Mulhall, and Laura Brady for *Virginia Wolf* (Kids Can).

DSC Prize for South Asian Literature ($50,000). To recognize outstanding literature from or about the South Asian region and raise awareness of South Asian culture around the world. *Sponsor:* DSC Limited. *Winner:* Anuradha Roy for *Sleeping on Jupiter* (Graywolf Press).

Dundee International Book Prize (Scotland) (£10,000 and publication by Cargo). For an unpublished novel on any theme, in any genre. *Winner:* Jessica Thummel for *The Cure for Lonely.*

Dundee Picture Book Award (Scotland) (£1,000). To recognize excellence in storytelling for children. The winner is chosen by the schoolchildren of Dundee. *Winners:* Ben Mantle for *The Best Birthday Present Ever* (Sterling Children's Books).

Educational Writers' Award (United Kingdom) (£2,000). For noteworthy educational nonfiction for children. *Offered by:* Authors' Licensing and Collecting Society and Society of Authors. *Winners:* Rachel Williams and Lucy Letherland, illustrator, for *Atlas of Adventures* (Wide Eyed Editions).

Margaret A. Edwards Award ($2,000). To an author whose book or books have provided young adults with a window through which they can view their world and which will help them to grow and to understand themselves and their role in society. *Donor:* School Library Journal. *Winner:* Sarah Dessen for *Dreamland, Keeping the Moon, Just Listen, The Truth About Forever, Along for the Ride, What Happened to Goodbye?,* and *This Lullaby* (all Penguin).

T. S. Eliot Prize for Poetry (United Kingdom) (£20,000). *Offered by:* Poetry Book Society. *Winner:* Jacob Polley for *Jackself.*

Encore Award (United Kingdom) (£10,000). Awarded biennially for the best second novel of the previous two years. *Offered by* Society of Authors. *Sponsor:* Lucy Astor. *Winner:* Sunjeev Sahota for *The Year of the Runaways* (Knopf Doubleday).

European Union Prize for Literature (€5,000). To recognize outstanding European writing. *Sponsors:* European Commission, European Booksellers Federation, European Writers' Council, Federation of European Publishers. *Winners:* (Albania) Rudi Erebara for *The Epic of the Morning Stars*; (Bulgaria) Ina Vultchanova for *The Crack-Up Is*land; (Czech Republic) Bianca Bellová for *The Lake*; (Greece) Kallia Papadaki for *Dendrites*; (Iceland) Halldóra K. Thoroddsen for *Double Glazing*; (Latvia) Osvalds Zebris for *In the Shadow of Rooster Hill*; (Malta) Walid Nabhan for *Exodus of Storks*; (Montenegro) Aleksandar Becanovic for *Arcueil*; (Netherlands) Jamal Ouariach for *A Hunger*; (Serbia) Darko Tuševljakovic for *The Chasm*; (Turkey) Sine Ergün for *Chickadee*; (United Kingdom) Sunjeev Sahota for *The Year of the Runaways*.

Fairfax Prize ($10,000). For a body of work that has "made significant contributions to American and international culture." *Sponsors:* Fairfax County (Virginia) Public Library Foundation and George Mason University. *Winner:* Sandra Cisneros.

FIELD Poetry Prize ($1,000). For a book-length poetry collection. *Offered by: FIELD: Contemporary Poetry and Poetics.* *Winner:* Jeffrey Skinner for *Chance Divine* (Oberlin).

FIL Literary Award in Romance Languages (formerly the Juan Rulfo International Latin American and Caribbean Prize (Mexico) ($150,000). For lifetime achievement in any literary genre. *Offered by:* Juan Rulfo International Latin American and Caribbean Prize Committee. *Winner:* Norman Manea.

Financial Times and McKinsey Business Book of the Year Award (£30,000). To recognize books that provide compelling and enjoyable insight into modern business issues. *Winner:* Sebastian Mallaby for *The Man Who Knew: The Life and Times of Alan Greenspan* (Penguin).

Flaherty-Dunnan First Novel Prize ($10,000). *Offered by:* Center for Fiction, Mercantile Library of New York. *Winner:* Kia Corthron for *The Castle Cross the Magnet Carter* (Seven Stories Press).

Sid Fleischman Award for Humor. See Golden Kite Awards.

ForeWord Reviews Book of the Year Awards ($1,500). For independently published books. *Offered by: ForeWord Reviews* magazine. *Winners:* (editor's choice prize, fiction) Audrey Taylor Gonzalez for *South of Everything* (She Writes Press); (editor's choice prize, nonfiction) Brian Andreas and Lorne Resnick, photographer for *Cuba*.

E. M. Forster Award ($20,000). To a young writer from England, Ireland, Scotland, or Wales, for a stay in the United States. *Offered by:* American Academy of Arts and Letters. *Winner:* Sinéad Morrissey.

Forward Prizes (United Kingdom). For poetry. *Offered by: The Forward. Winners:* (best collection, £10,000), Vahni Capildeo for *Measures of Expatriation* (Carcanet Press); (best first collection, £5,000) Tiphanie Yanique for *Wife* (Peepal Tree Press); (best single poem, £1,000) Sasha Dugdale for "Joy."

H. E. Francis Short Story Competition ($1,000). For an unpublished short story no more than 5,000 words in length. *Sponsors:* Ruth Hindman Foundation and English Department, University of Alabama, Huntsville. *Winner:* Jeremy Kamps for "The Source of Everything."

Josette Frank Award. For a work of fiction in which children or young people deal in a positive and realistic way with difficulties in their world and grow emotionally and morally. *Offered by:* Bank Street College of Education and the Florence M. Miller Memorial Fund. *Winners:* (older readers) Wendelin Van Draanen for *The Secret Life of Lincoln Jones* (Knopf).

George Freedley Memorial Award. For the best English-language work about live theater published in the United States. *Offered by:* Theatre Library Association. *Winner:* Terry Alford for *Fortune's Fool: The Life of John Wilkes Booth* (Oxford University Press).

French-American Foundation Translation Prize ($10,000). For a translation or translations from French into English of works of fiction and nonfiction. *Offered by:* French-American Foundation. *Donor:* Florence Gould Foundation. *Winners:* (fiction) Christine Donougher for her translation of *Les Misérables* by Victor Hugo (Penguin Random House); (nonfiction) Malcolm DeBevoise for his translation of *Birth of a Theorem* by Cédric Villani (Farrar, Straus and Giroux).

Frost Medal. To recognize achievement in poetry over a lifetime. *Offered by:* Poetry Society of America. *Winner:* Susan Howe.

Lewis Galantière Award. Awarded biennially for a literary translation into English from any language other than German. *Offered by:* American Translators Association. *Winner:* Katrina Dodson for literary translation of *The Complete Stories.*

Galaxy National Book Awards. See Specsavers National Book Awards.

Theodor Seuss Geisel Award. For the best book for beginning readers. *Offered by:* American Library Association, Association for Library Service to Children. *Winner:* Laurie Keller for *We Are Growing: A Mo Willems' Elephant & Piggie Like Reading! Book* (Hyperion).

David Gemmell Legend Awards for Fantasy. For novels published for the first time in English during the year of nomination. *Winners:* (best novel) Mark Lawrence for *The Liar's Key* (Penguin); (best newcomer) Peter Newman for *The Vagrant* (HarperCollins); (best cover art) Jason Chan for *The Liar's Key* (Penguin).

Giller Prize (Canada). See Scotiabank Giller Prize.

Gival Press Novel Award ($3,000 and publication by Gival Press). *Winner:* Madeleine Thien for *Do Not Say We Have Nothing* (Alfred A. Knopf Canada).

Giverny Award. For an outstanding children's science picture book. *Offered by:* 15 Degree Laboratory. *Winner:* David Mather & Stephanie Mirocha, for *Frog in the House* (Raven Productions).

Alexander Gode Medal. To an individual or institution for outstanding service to the translation and interpreting professions. *Offered by:* American Translators Association. *Winner:* Not awarded in 2016.

Golden Duck Awards for Excellence in Children's Science Fiction Literature. *Sponsored by:* Super-Con-Duck-Tivity. *Winners:* (picture book) Jeffrey Bennett for *Max Goes to the Space Station, A Science Adventure with Max the Dog* (Big Kid Science); (Eleanor Cameron Award for middle grades books) William Alexander for *Ambassador* (Margaret K. McElderry); (Hal Clement Award for young adult books) William Campbell Powell for *Expiration Day* (Tor Teen).

Golden Kite Awards. For children's books. *Offered by:* Society of Children's Book Writers and Illustrators. *Winners:* (picture book text) Lisa Wheeler for *The Christmas Boot* (Dial); (picture book illustration) Stacy Innerst for *The Music in George's Head* (Calkins Creek); (nonfiction) Russell Freedman *We Will Not Be Silent* (Clarion); (Sid Fleischman Humor Award) Chris Grabenstein for *Welcome to Wonderland: Home Sweet Motel* (Random House).

Governor General's Literary Awards (Canada) (C$25,000, plus C$3,000 to the publisher). For works, in English and French, of fiction, nonfiction, poetry, and for translation. *Offered by:* Canada Council for the Arts. *Winners:* (fiction, English) Madeleine Thien for *Do Not Say We Have Nothing* (Alfred A. Knopf Canada / Penguin Random House Canada); (nonfiction, English) Bill Waiser for *A World We Have Lost: Saskatchewan Before 1905* (Fifth House Publishers); (poetry, English) Steven Heighton for *The Waking Comes Late* (House of Anansi Press); (translation, French to English) Lazer Lederhendler for *The Party Wall*, translation of *Le mur mitoyen* by Catherine Leroux (Biblioasis).

Dolly Gray Children's Literature Awards. Presented biennially for fiction or biographical children's books with positive portrayals of individuals with developmental disabilities. *Offered by:* Council for Exceptional Children, Division on Autism and Developmental Disabilities. *Winners:* (intermediate book) Ann M. Martin for *Rain Reign* (MacMillan); (picture book) Shaila Abdullah and Aanyah Abdullah for *My Friend Suhana* (Loving Healing Press).

Kate Greenaway Medal and Colin Mears Award. See CILIP Kate Greenaway Medal.

Eric Gregory Awards (United Kingdom) (£4,000). For a published or unpublished collection by poets under the age of 30. *Winners:* Sam Buchan Watts, Dom Bury, Jen Campbell, Alex MacDonald, and Andrew McMillan.

Griffin Poetry Prizes (Canada) (C$65,000). To a living Canadian poet or translator and a living poet or translator from any country, which may include Canada. *Offered by:* Griffin Trust. *Winners:* (international) Norman Dubie for *The Quotations of Bone*

(Copper Canyon Press); (Canadian) Liz Howard for *Infinite Citizen of the Shaking Tent* (McClelland & Stewart).

Gryphon Award ($1,000). To recognize a noteworthy work of fiction or nonfiction for younger children. *Offered by:* The Center for Children's Books. *Winners:* Linda Urban, Katie Kath, illustrator, for *Weekends with Max and His Dad* (Houghton Mifflin Harcourt).

Guardian Children's Fiction Prize (United Kingdom) (£1,500). For an outstanding children's or young adult novel. *Offered by: The Guardian. Winner:* Alex Wheatle for *Crongton Knights.*

Dashiell Hammett Prize. For a work of literary excellence in the field of crime writing by a U.S. or Canadian writer. *Offered by:* North American Branch, International Association of Crime Writers. *Winner:* Lisa Sandlin for *The Do-Right* (Cinco Puntos).

R. R. Hawkins Award. For the outstanding professional/scholarly works of the year. *Offered by:* Association of American Publishers. *Winners:* (excellence in humanities) Gilbert J. Gorski and James E. Packer for *The Roman Forum: A Reconstruction and Architectural Guide* (Cambridge University Press), and Nick Sousanis for *Unflattening* (Harvard University Press); (excellence in physical sciences and mathematics) Diana Kormos Buchwald, editor, for *The Collected Papers of Albert Einstein: Digital Edition* (Princeton University Press); (excellence in social sciences) Aldon D. Morris for *The Scholar Denied: W.E.B. Du Bois and the Birth of Modern Sociology* (University of California Press); (excellence in biological and life sciences) Peter Sterling and Simon Laughlin for *Principles of Neural Design* (The MIT Press); (excellence in reference works) James D. Wright, editor, for *International Encyclopedia of the Social and Behavioral Sciences* (Elsevier/Academic Press).

Anthony Hecht Poetry Prize ($3,000 and publication by Waywiser Press). For an unpublished first or second book-length poetry collection. *Winner:* Mike White for *Addendum to a Miracle.*

Drue Heinz Literature Prize ($15,000 and publication by University of Pittsburgh Press).

For short fiction. *Winner:* William Wall for *The Islands.*

O. Henry Awards. See PEN/O. Henry Prize.

William Dean Howells Medal. In recognition of the most distinguished novel published in the preceding five years. *Offered by:* American Academy of Arts and Letters. *Winner:* William H. Gass for *Middle C* (Vintage).

Hugo Awards. For outstanding science fiction writing. *Offered by:* World Science Fiction Convention. *Winners:* (novel) N. K. Jemisin for *The Fifth Season* (Orbit); (novella) Nnendi Okorafor for *Binti* (Tom Doherty Associates); (novelette) Hao Jingfang for "Folding Beijing"; (short story) Naomi Kritzer for "Cat Pictures Please"; (related work) no award; (graphic story) Neil Gaiman for "Overture. Sandman" (DC Comics); (dramatic presentation, long form) Drew Goddard, writer, and Ridley Scott, director, "The Martian"; (dramatic presentation, short form) Melissa Rosenberg, creator, for "Jessica Jones."

IMPAC Dublin Literary Award (Ireland) (€100,000). For a book of high literary merit, written in English or translated into English; if translated, the author receives €75,000 and the translator €25,000. *Offered by:* IMPAC Corp. and the City of Dublin. *Winner:* Akhil Sharma for *Family Life* (Norton).

Independent Foreign Fiction Prize (United Kingdom) (£5,000 each for author and translator). For a work of fiction by a living author that has been translated into English from any other language and published in the United Kingdom. *Sponsor:* Arts Council England. *Winners:* Jenny Erpenbeck, author, and Susan Bernofsky, translator, for *The End of Days* (New Directions).

Indies Choice Book Awards (formerly BookSense Book of the Year Awards). Chosen by owners and staff of American Booksellers Association member bookstores. *Winners:* (adult fiction) Lauren Groff for *Fates and Furies: A Novel* (Riverhead); (adult nonfiction) Ta-Nehisi Coates for *Between the World and Me* (Spiegel & Grau); (adult debut) J. Ryan Stradal for *Kitchens of the Great Midwest: A Novel* (Pamela Dorman Books/Viking); (young adult) Gavriel Savit for *Anna and the Swallow Man* Noelle Stevenson (Knopf) and Noelle Stevenson for *Nimona* (HarperTeen).

International Prize for Arabic Fiction ($50,000 and publication in English). To reward excellence in contemporary Arabic creative writing. *Sponsors:* Booker Prize Foundation, Emirates Foundation for Philanthropy. *Winner:* Rabai al-Madhoun for *Destinies: Concerto of the Holocaust and the Nakba* (Palestine).

ILA Children's and Young Adults' Book Awards. For first or second books in any language published for children or young adults. *Offered by:* International Literacy Association. *Winners:* (primary fiction) Sangmi Ko for *A Dog Wearing Shoes* (Schwartz & Wade); (primary nonfiction) Lindsay Mattick for *Finding Winnie: The True Story of the World's Most Famous Bear* (Little, Brown); (intermediate fiction) Beth Vrabel for *A Blind Guide To Stinkville* (Sky Pony Press) and Ronald L. Smith for *Hoodoo* (Clarion); (intermediate nonfiction) Laura A. Woollett for *Big Top Burning: The True Story of an Arsonist, a Missing Girl, and The Greatest Show on Earth* (Chicago Review Press); (young adult fiction) Lance Rubin for *Denton Little's Death Date* (Knopf).

Rona Jaffe Foundation Writers' Awards ($30,000). To identify and support women writers of exceptional talent in the early stages of their careers. *Offered by:* Rona Jaffe Foundation. *Winners:* Lina María Ferreira Cabeza-Vanegas, Danielle Geller, Jamey Hatley, Ladee Hubbard, Airea D. Matthews, Asako Serizawa.

Jerusalem Prize (Israel). Awarded biennially to a writer whose works best express the theme of freedom of the individual in society. *Offered by:* Jerusalem International Book Fair. *Winner:* not awarded in 2016.

Jewish Book Council Awards. *Winners:* (Jewish Book of the Year) Daniel Gordis for *Israel: A Concise History of a Nation Reborn* (Ecco); (JBC Modern Literary Achievement) Michael Chabon for *Moonglow* (HarperCollins); (American Jewish studies) Roger Horowitz for *Kosher USA: How Coke Became Kosher and Other Tales of Modern Food* (Columbia University Press); (anthologies and collections) Jacques Picard, Jacques Revel, Michael P.

Steinberg, Idith Zertal, editors, for *Makers of Jewish Modernity: Thinkers, Artists, Leaders, and the World They Made* (Princeton University Press); (biography, autobiography, memoir) Marceline Loridan-Ivens, Sandra Smith, translator, for *But You Did Not Come Back* (Grove Atlantic); (Book Club award) Lauren Belfer for *And After the Fire* (HarperCollins); (children's literature) Debbie Levy, illustrated by Elizabeth Baddeley, for *I Dissent* (Simon and Schuster); (contemporary Jewish life and practice) David Jaffe for *Changing the World from the Inside Out: A Jewish Approach to Personal and Social Change* (Shambhala); (debut fiction) Gavriel Savit for *Anna and the Swallow Man* (Knopf); (education and Jewish identity) John Benditt for *Next Generation Judaism: How College Students and Hillel Can Help Reinvent Jewish Organizations* (Jewish Lights Publishing); (fiction) Rose Tremain for *The Gustav Sonata* (Norton); (history) Uri Bar-Joseph for *The Angel: The Egyptian Spy Who Saved Israel* (HarperCollins); (Holocaust) Michael Bazyler for *Holocaust, Genocide, and the Law: A Quest for Justice in a Post-Holocaust World* (Oxford University Press); (modern Jewish thought and experience) Miriam Udel for *Never Better! The Modern Jewish Picaresque* (University of Michigan Press); (poetry) Stanley Moss for *Almost Complete Poems* (Seven Stories Press); (scholarship) Benjamin R. Gampel for *Anti-Jewish Riots in the Crown of Aragon and the Royal Response 1391–1392* (Cambridge University Press); (Sephardic culture) Sarah Abrevaya Stein for *Extraterritorial Dreams: Europe Citizenship, Sephardi Jews, and the Ottoman Twentieth Century* (University of Chicago Press); (women's studies) Rabbi Rebecca Einstein Schorr, Rabbi Alysa Mendelson Graf, editors, for *The Sacred Calling: Four Decades of Women in the Rabbinate* (CCAR Press), (writing based on archival material) Devin E. Naar for *Jewish Salonica: Between the Ottoman Empire and Modern Greece* (Stanford University Press); (young adult literature) Rachel Mann for *On Blackberry Hill* (CreateSpace).

Sue Kaufman Prize for First Fiction ($5,000). For a first novel or collection of short stories. *Offered by:* American Academy of Arts and Letters. *Winner:* Kirstin Valdez Quade for *Night at the Fiestas* (Norton).

Ezra Jack Keats Awards. For children's picture book s. *Offered by:* New York Public Library and the Ezra Jack Keats Foundation. *Winners:* (new writer award) Jeri Watts for *A Piece of Home* (Candlewick); (new illustrator award) Micha Archer for *Daniel Finds a Poem* (Nancy Paulsen Books).

Kerlan Award. To recognize singular attainments in the creation of children's literature and in appreciation for generous donation of unique resources to the Kerlan Collection for the study of children's literature. *Offered by:* Kerlan Children's Literature Research Collections, University of Minnesota. *Winner:* John Coy.

Coretta Scott King Book Awards ($1,000). To an African American author and illustrator of outstanding books for children and young adults. *Offered by:* American Library Association, Ethnic and Multicultural Exchange Round Table (EMIERT). *Winners:* (author) Rita Williams-Garcia for *Gone Crazy in Alabama* (Amistad); (illustrator) Bryan Collier for *Trombone Shorty*, written by Troy "Trombone Shorty" Andrews and Bill Taylor (Abrams).

Coretta Scott King/John Steptoe Award for New Talent. To offer visibility to a writer or illustrator at the beginning of a career. *Sponsor:* Coretta Scott King Book Award Committee. *Winner:* Nicola Yoon for *The Sun Is Also a Star* (Delacorte Press).

Coretta Scott King/Virginia Hamilton Award for Lifetime Achievement. Given in even-numbered years to an African American author, illustrator, or author/illustrator for a body of books for children or young adults. In odd-numbered years, the award honors substantial contributions through active engagement with youth, using award-winning African American literature for children or young adults. *Winner:* no award this year.

Kirkus Prize ($50,000). For outstanding fiction, nonfiction, and young readers literature. *Offered by: Kirkus Reviews. Winners:* (fiction) C. E. Morgan for *The Sport of Kings* (Farrar, Straus and Giroux); (nonfiction) Susan Faludi for *In the Darkroom* (Henry Holt); (young readers) Jason Reynolds for *As Brave As You* (Atheneum/Caitlyn Dlouhy Books).

Lambda Literary Awards. To honor outstanding lesbian, gay, bisexual, and transgender (LGBT) literature. *Offered by:* Lambda Literary Foundation. *Winners:* (transgender fiction) Roz Kaveney for *Tiny Pieces of Skull, or a Lesson in Manners* (Team Angelica Publishing); (gay general fiction) Hasan Namir, for *God in Pink* (Arsenal Pulp Press); (lesbian general fiction) Chinelo Okparanta for *Under the Udala Trees* (Houghton Mifflin Harcourt); (LGBT debut fiction) Victor Yates for *A Love Like Blood* (Hillmont Press); (transgender nonfiction) Willy Wilkinson for *Born on the Edge of Race and Gender: A Voice for Cultural Competency* (Hapa Papa Press); (bisexual fiction) Anna North for *The Life and Death of Sophie Stark* (Penguin Random House/Blue Rider Press); (bisexual nonfiction) Emily Bingham for *Irrepressible: The Jazz Age Life of Henrietta Bingham* (Farrar, Straus and Giroux); (LGBT nonfiction) Marcia M. Gallo for *"No One Helped": Kitty Genovese, New York City, and the Myth of Urban Apathy* (Cornell University Press); (gay poetry) Carl Phillips for *Reconnaissance* (Farrar, Straus and Giroux); (lesbian poetry) Dawn Lundy Martin for *Life in a Box Is a Pretty Life* (Nightboat Books); (transgender poetry) kari edwards for succubus in my pocket (EOAGH Books); (gay mystery) Marshall Thornton for *Boystown 7: Bloodlines* (Kenmore Books); (lesbian mystery) Victoria Brownworth for *Ordinary Mayhem* (Bold Strokes Books) and Ann Aptaker for *Tarnished Gold* (Bold Strokes Books); (gay memoir/biography) Langdon Hammer for *James Merrill: Life and Art* (Knopf); (lesbian memoir/biography) Kate Carroll de Gutes, for *Objects in the Mirror Are Closer Than They Appear* (Ovenbird Books); (gay romance) Debbie McGowan for *When Skies Have Fallen* (Beaten Track); (lesbian romance) Julie Blair for *Making a Comeback* (Bold Strokes Books); (gay erotica) Miodrag Kojadinovic for *Érotiques Suprèmes* (Choose the Sword Press); (lesbian erotica) Meghan O'Brien for *The Muse* (Bold Strokes Books); (LGBT anthology) Sfé R. Monster, editor, and Taneka Stotts, assistant editor, for *Beyond: The Queer Sci-Fi and Fantasy Comic Anthology* (Beyond Press) and Damien Luxe, Heather M. Ács,

Sabina Ibarrola, editors, for *Glitter and Grit: Queer Performance from the Heels on Wheels Femme Galaxy* (Publication Studio); (LGBT children's/young adult) Tim Fed Alex Gino for *George* (Scholastic); (LGBT drama) Tanya Barfield for *Bright Half Life* (Dramatists Play Service); (LGBT graphic novel) EK Weaver for *The Less Than Epic Adventures of TJ and Amal* (Iron Circus Comics); (LGBT science fiction/fantasy/horror) Kirsty Logan for *The Gracekeepers* (Crown); (LGBT studies) Hiram Pérez, for *A Taste for Brown Bodies: Gay Modernity and Cosmopolitan Desire* (NYU Press).

Harold Morton Landon Translation Award ($1,000). For a book of verse translated into English. *Offered by:* Academy of American Poets. *Winner:* Ron Padgett for *Zone: Selected Poems by Guillaume Apollinaire* (New York Review Books).

David J. Langum, Sr. Prize in American Historical Fiction ($1,000). To honor a book of historical fiction published in the previous year. *Winner:* Michele Moore for *The Cigar Factory* (University of South Carolina Press).

David J. Langum, Sr. Prize in American Legal History or Biography ($1,000). For a university press book that is accessible to the educated general public, rooted in sound scholarship, with themes that touch upon matters of general concern. *Winner:* Risa Goluboff for *Vagrant Nation: Police Power, Constitutional Change, and the Making of the 1960s* (Oxford University Press).

Latner Writers' Trust Poetry Prize (C$25,000). To a writer with an exceptional body of work in the field of poetry. *Winner:* Gregory Scofield.

James Laughlin Award ($5,000). To commend and support a second book of poetry. *Offered by:* Academy of American Poets. *Winner:* Mary Hickman for *Rayfish* (Omnidawn Publishing).

Ruth Lilly and Dorothy Sargent Rosenberg Poetry Fellowships ($25,800). To emerging poets to support their continued study and writing of poetry. *Offered by:* The Poetry Foundation. *Winners:* Kaveh Akbar, Jos Charles, Angel Nafis, Alison C. Rollins, and Javier Zamora.

Ruth Lilly Poetry Prize ($100,000). To a U.S. poet in recognition of lifetime achievement.

Offered by: The Poetry Foundation. *Winner:* Joy Harjo.

Astrid Lindgren Memorial Award (Sweden) (5 million kroner, more than $575,000). In memory of children's author Astrid Lindgren, to honor outstanding children's literature and efforts to promote it. *Offered by:* Government of Sweden and the Swedish Arts Council. *Winner:* Meg Rosoff.

Locus Awards. For science fiction writing. *Offered by:* Locus Publications. *Winners:* (science fiction novel) Ann Leckie for *Ancillary Sword* (Orbit); (fantasy novel) Naomi Novik for *Uprooted* (Del Rey); (young adult book) Terry Pratchett for *The Shepherd's Crown* (Harper; Doubleday UK); (first novel) Ken Liu for *The Grace of Kings* (Saga); (novella) Alastair Reynolds for *Slow Bullets* (Tachyon); (novelette) Neil Gaiman for "Black Dog" (Trigger Warning); (short story) Naomi Kritzer for "Cat Pictures Please" (Clarkesworld); (collection) Neil Gaiman, for *Trigger Warning: Short Fictions and Disturbance* (Morrow); (anthology) George R. R. Martin and Gardner Dozois, editors, for *Old Venus* (Bantam); (nonfiction) Alisa Krasnostein and Alexandra Pierce, editors, for *Letters to Tiptree* (Twelfth Planet); (art book) Julie Dillon, for *Julie Dillon's Imagined Realms, Book 2: Earth and Sky* (self-published).

London Book Festival Awards. To honor books worthy of further attention from the international publishing community. *Winners:* (science fiction and grand prize) Gary Grossman for *Old Earth* (Diversion); (general fiction) Everett DeMoirer for *Thirty-Three Cecils* (Blydyn Square); (general nonfiction) Kathy Gruver for *Journey of Healing* (Infinity); (children's) Ayn Cates Sullivan for *A Story of Becoming* (Infinite Light); (young adult) Mary A. Osborne for *Alchemy's Daughter* (Lake Street); (business) Bryony Thomas for *Watertight Marketing* (Panoma); (biography/autobiography/memoir) Freya Barrington for *Known to Social Services* (Faraxa); (how to) Onyx Jones for *The Unofficial Guide to Achieving Your Goals* (iUniverse); (wild card) Ann C. Pizzorusso for *Tweeting Da Vinci* (Da Vinci); (poetry) Eric Nelson for *Some Wonder* (Gival); (spiritual) James Stroud for *Mere Christian Apologetics* (Tate); (romance) Steven H. Manchester for

Gooseberry Island (Story Plant); (photography/art) Charles Rawlings for *Living Mollusks* (The Peppertree Press); (cookbooks) Millie Snyder for *Lean and Luscious Meatless* (Headline); (history) Carl Schmitt for *Land and Sea: A World Historical Meditation* (Telos).

Elizabeth Longford Prize for Historical Biography (United Kingdom) (£5,000). *Sponsors:* Flora Fraser and Peter Soros. *Winner:* Andrew Gailey for *The Lost Imperialist—Lord Dufferin, Memory and Mythmaking in an Age of Celebrity* (Murray, John Publishers).

Los Angeles Times Book Prizes. To honor literary excellence. *Offered by: Los Angeles Times. Winners:* (biography) Volker Ullrich for *Hitler: Ascent, 1889–1939* (Knopf); (current interest) Svetlana Alexievich, author, and Bela Shayevich, translator, for *Secondhand Time: The Last of the Soviets* (Random House); (fiction) Adam Haslett for *Imagine Me* Gone (Little, Brown); (Art Seidenbaum Award for First Fiction) Nathan Hill for *The Nix* (Knopf; (graphic novel/comics) Nick Drnaso for *Beverly* (Drawn & Quarterly); (history) Benjamin Madley for *An American Genocide: The United States and the California Indian Catastrophe, 1846–1873* (Yale University Press); (mystery/thriller) Bill Beverly for *Dodgers* (Crown); (poetry) Rosmarie Waldrop for *Gap Gardening: Selected Poems* (New Directions); (science and technology) Luke Dittrich for *Patient H.M.: A Story of Memory, Madness, and Family Secrets* (Random House); (young adult literature) Frances Hardinge for *The Lie Tree* (Harry N. Abrams); (Robert Kirsch Award for lifetime achievement) Thomas McGuane; (innovator's award) Ruebén Martinez.

Amy Lowell Poetry Traveling Scholarship. For one or two U.S. poets to spend one year outside North America in a country the recipients feel will most advance their work. *Offered by:* Amy Lowell Poetry Traveling Scholarship. *Winner:* Joanna Klink.

J. Anthony Lukas Awards. For nonfiction writing that demonstrates literary grace, serious research, and concern for an important aspect of American social or political life. *Offered by:* Columbia University Graduate School of Journalism and the Nieman Foundation for Journalism at Harvard. *Winners:* (Lukas Book Prize, $10,000) Gary Younge for *Another Day In the Death of America: A Chronicle of Ten Short Lives* (Nation Books); (Mark Lynton History Prize, $10,000) Tyler Anbinder for *City of Dreams: The 400-Year Epic History of Immigrant New York* (Houghton Mifflin Harcourt); (Work-in-Progress Award, $30,000) Christopher Leonard for *Kochland* (Simon & Schuster).

Macavity Awards. For excellence in mystery writing. *Offered by:* Mystery Readers International. *Winners:* (mystery novel) Lou Berney for *The Long and Faraway Gone* (Morrow); (first mystery) Glen Erik Hamilton for *Past Crimes* (Morrow); (short story) Megan Abbott for "The Little Men" (MysteriousPress.com/Open Road); (Sue Feder Historical Mystery Award) Susanna Calkins for *The Masque of a Murderer* (Minotaur).

McKitterick Prize (United Kingdom) (£4,000). To an author over the age of 40 for a first novel, published or unpublished. *Winner:* Petina Gappah for *The Book of Memory* (Faber).

Man Booker International Prize (United Kingdom) (£60,000). Awarded biennially to a living author for a significant contribution to world literature. *Offered by:* Man Group. *Winner:* Han Kang.

Man Booker Prize for Fiction (United Kingdom) (£50,000). For the best novel written in English by a Commonwealth author. *Offered by:* Booktrust and the Man Group. *Winner:* Paul Beatty for *The Sellout* (Oneworld).

Lenore Marshall Poetry Prize ($25,000). For an outstanding book of poems published in the United States. *Offered by:* Academy of American Poets. *Winner:* Lynn Emanuel for *The Nerve of It: Poems New and Selected* (University of Pittsburgh Press).

Mason Award ($10,000). To honor authors whose body of work has made extraordinary contributions to bringing literature to a wide reading public. *Sponsors:* George Mason University and Fall for the Book. *Winner:* Emily Derbyshire, Ph.D., Livia Schiavinato Eberlin, Ph.D., Yan-Yan Hu, Ph.D., Rebekka Klausen, Ph.D., Elizabeth Sattely, Ph.D.

Somerset Maugham Awards (United Kingdom) (£2,500). For works in any genre except drama by a writer under the age of 35, to enable young writers to enrich their work by gaining experience of foreign countries. *Winners:* Jessie Greengrass for *An Account Of The Decline Of The Great Auk, According To One Who Saw It;* Daisy Hay for *Mr & Mrs Disraeli: A Strange Romance* (Farrar, Straus and Giroux); Andrew McMillan for *Physical;* Thomas Morris for *We Don't Know What We're Doing;* Jack Underwood for *Happiness.*

Addison M. Metcalf Award in Literature ($2,000). Awarded biennially in alternation with the Addison M. Metcalf Award in Art. *Winner:* Safiya Sinclair.

Vicky Metcalf Award for Literature for Young People (Canada) (C$20,000). To a Canadian writer of children's literature for a body of work. *Offered by:* Metcalf Foundation. *Winner:* Alan Cumyn.

Midwest Booksellers Choice Awards. *Offered by:* Midwest Booksellers Association. *Winners:* (fiction) J. Ryan Stradal for *Kitchens of the Great Midwest* (Pamela Dorman Books); (nonfiction) Lucie Amundsen for *Locally Laid* (Avery); (poetry) Chris Martin for *The Falling Down Dance* (Coffee House Press); (young adult) Jane St. Anthony for *Isabelle Day Refuses to Die of a Broken Heart* (University of Minnesota Press); (picture book) Aimee Bissonette for *North Woods Girl* (Minnesota Historical Society Press).

William C. Morris YA Debut Award. To honor a debut book published by a first-time author writing for teens and celebrating impressive new voices in young adult literature. *Offered by:* American Library Association, Young Adult Library Services Association. *Donor:* William C. Morris Endowment. *Winner:* Jeff Zentner for *The Serpent King* (Crown).

Mythopoeic Fantasy Awards. To recognize fantasy or mythic literature for children and adults that best exemplifies the spirit of the Inklings, a group of fantasy writers that includes J. R. R. Tolkien, C. S. Lewis, and Charles Williams. *Offered by:* Mythopoeic Society. *Winners:* (adult literature) Naomi Novik for *Uprooted* (Del Rey); (children's literature) Ursula Vernon for *Castle Hangnail* (Dial); (Mythopoeic Scholarship Award in Inklings Studies) Jamie Williamson for *The Evolution of Modern Fantasy: From Antiquarianism to the Ballantine Adult Fantasy Series* (Palgrave Macmillan US); (Mythopoeic Scholarship Award in Myth and Fantasy Studies) *Charles Williams* for *The Third Inkling* (Grevel Lindop).

National Book Awards. To celebrate the best in American literature. *Offered by:* National Book Foundation. *Winners:* (fiction) Colson Whitehead for *The Underground Railroad* (Doubleday/Penguin Random House); (nonfiction) Ibram X. Kendi for *Stamped from the Beginning: The Definitive History of Racist Ideas in America* (Nation Books); (poetry) Daniel Borzutzky for *The Performance of Becoming Human* (Brooklyn Arts Press); (young people's literature) John Lewis, Andrew Aydin and Nate Powell, artist, for *March: Book Three* (Top Shelf Productions/IDW).

National Book Awards (United Kingdom). See Specsavers National Book Awards.

National Book Critics Circle Awards. For literary excellence. *Offered by:* National Book Critics Circle. *Winners:* (fiction) Louise Erdrich for *LaRose* (Harper); (nonfiction) Matthew Desmond for *Evicted: Poverty and Profit in the American City* (Crown); (biography) Ruth Franklin for *Shirley Jackson: A Rather Haunted Life* (Liveright); (autobiography) Hope Jahren for *Lab Girl* (Knopf); (poetry) Ishion Hutchinson for *House of Lords and Commons* (Farrar, Straus and Giroux); (criticism) Carol Anderson for *White Rage: The Unspoken Truth of Our Racial Divide* (Bloomsbury); (Nona Balakian Citation for Excellence in Reviewing) Michelle Dean; (Ivan Sandrof Lifetime Achievement Award) Margaret Atwood.

National Book Foundation Literarian Award for Outstanding Service to the American Literary Community. *Offered by:* National Book Foundation. *Winner:* Cave Canem.

National Book Foundation Medal for Distinguished Contribution to American Letters ($10,000). To a person who has enriched the nation's literary heritage over a life of service or corpus of work. *Offered by:* National Book Foundation. *Winner:* Robert A. Caro.

National Translation Awards ($5,000). To honor translators whose work has made a valuable contribution to literary translation into English. *Offered by:* American Literary Translators Association. *Winners:* (prose) Eugene Ostashevsky and Matvei Yankelevich, translators from Russian, for *An Invitation for Me to Think* by Alexander Vvedensky (New York Review Books).

Nebula Awards. For science fiction writing. *Offered by:* Science Fiction and Fantasy Writers of America (SFWA). *Winners:* (novel) Naomi Novik for *Uprooted* (Del Rey); (novella) Nnedi Okorafor for *Binti* (Tor.com); (novelette) Sarah Pinsker for "Our Lady of the Open Road" in *Asimov's Science Fiction*; (short story) Alyssa Wong for "Hungry Daughters of Starving Mothers" in *Nightmare Magazine.*

John Newbery Medal. For the most distinguished contribution to literature for children. *Offered by:* American Library Association, Association for Library Service to Children. *Winner:* Kelly Barnhill for *The Girl Who Drank the Moon* (Algonquin).

Nimrod Literary Awards ($2,000 plus publication). *Offered by:* Nimrod International Journal of Prose and Poetry. *Winners:* (Pablo Neruda Prize in Poetry) Heather Altfeld for "Two Pockets" and other poems; (Katherine Anne Porter Prize in Fiction) J. Duncan Wiley for "Inclusions."

Nobel Prize in Literature (Sweden). For the total literary output of a distinguished career. *Offered by:* Swedish Academy. *Winner:* Bob Dylan.

Eli M. Oboler Memorial Award. Given biennially to an author of a published work in English or in English translation dealing with issues, events, questions, or controversies in the area of intellectual freedom. *Offered by:* Intellectual Freedom Round Table, American Library Association. *Winners:* Mark Alfino and Laura Koltutsky, editors, for *The Library Juice Press Handbook of Intellectual Freedom* (Library Juice).

Flannery O'Connor Awards for Short Fiction. For collections of short fiction. *Offered by:* University of Georgia Press. *Winners:* Lisa Graley for *The Current That Carries*; Anne Raeff for *The Jungle All Around Us* (both UGA Press).

Frank O'Connor Short Story Award (£25,000). An international award for a collection of short stories. *Offered by:* Munster Literature Centre, Cork, Ireland. *Sponsor:* Cork City Council. *Winner:* Carys Davies for *The Redemption of Galen Pike* (Salt).

Oddest Book Title of the Year Award. See Bookseller/Diagram Prize for Oddest Title of the Year.

Scott O'Dell Award for Historical Fiction ($5,000). *Offered by: Bulletin of the Center for Children's Books,* University of Chicago. *Winner:* Jennifer L. Holm for *Full of Beans* (Random House).

Odyssey Award. To the producer of the best audiobook for children and/or young adults available in English in the United States. *Sponsors:* American Library Association, ALSC/Booklist/YALSA. *Winner:* Listening Library for *The War that Saved My Life* by Kimberly Brubaker Bradley, narrated by Jayne Entwistle.

Seán Ó Faoláin Short Story Competition (€2,000 and publication in the literary journal *Southword. Offered by:* Munster Literature Centre, Cork, Ireland. *Winner:* Shauna Mackay for "The Idyllic Land of the 6's."

Dayne Ogilvie Prize (Canada) (C$4,000). To an emerging Canadian writer from the LGBT community who demonstrates promise through a body of quality work. *Offered by:* Writers' Trust of Canada. *Sponsor:* Robin Pacific. *Winner:* Leah Horlick.

Orbis Pictus Award for Outstanding Nonfiction for Children. *Offered by:* National Council of Teachers of English. *Winner:* Melissa Sweet for *Some Writer!: The Story of E.B. White* (Houghton Mifflin Harcourt).

Orion Book Awards ($3,000). To recognize books that deepen connection to the natural world, present new ideas about mankind's relationship with nature, and achieve excellence in writing. *Sponsors: Orion Magazine* and the Geraldine R. Dodge Foundation. *Winners:* (nonfiction) Sy Montgomery for *The Soul of an Octopus: A Surprising Exploration into the Wonder of Consciousness* (Atria Books).

Oxford-Weidenfeld Translation Prize. *Winners:* Paul Vincent and John Irons for their translation of *100 Dutch-Language Poems* (Holland Park Press); Philip Roughton for his translation of Jón Kalman Stefánsson's *The Heart of Man* (MacLehose Press).

PEN Award for Poetry in Translation ($3,000). For a book-length translation of poetry from any language into English, published in the United States. *Offered by:* PEN American Center. *Winner:* Sawako Nakayasu for *The*

Collected Poems of Chika Sagawa (Canarium Books).

PEN/Saul Bellow Award for Achievement in American Fiction ($25,000). Awarded biennially to a distinguished living American author of fiction. *Offered by:* PEN American Center. *Winner:* Toni Morrison.

PEN/Bellwether Prize for Socially Engaged Fiction ($25,000). Awarded biennially to the author of a previously unpublished novel that addresses issues of social justice and the impact of culture and politics on human relationships. *Founder:* Barbara Kingsolver. *Winner:* Lisa Ko for *The Leavers* (Algonquin).

PEN Beyond Margins Awards. See PEN Open Book Awards.

PEN/Robert W. Bingham Prize ($25,000). To a writer whose first novel or short story collection represents distinguished literary achievement and suggests great promise. *Offered by:* PEN American Center. *Winner:* Mia Alvar for *In the Country: Stories* (Knopf).

PEN/Diamonstein-Spielvogel Award for the Art of the Essay ($10,000). For a book of essays by a single author that best exemplifies the dignity and esteem of the essay form. *Winner:* Ta-Nehisi Coates for *Between the World and Me* (Spiegel & Grau/Random House).

PEN/ESPN Award for Literary Sports Writing ($5,000). To a living writer or writers for exceptional contributions to the field of literary sports writing. *Winner:* Scott Ellsworth for *The Secret Game: A Wartime Story of Courage, Change, and Basketball's Lost Triumph* (Little, Brown/Hachette).

PEN/ESPN Lifetime Achievement Award for Literary Sports Writing ($5,000). For a writer whose body of work represents an exceptional contribution to the field. *Winner:* John Schulian.

PEN/Faulkner Award for Fiction ($15,000). To honor the year's best work of fiction published by an American. *Winner:* James Hannaham for *Delicious Foods* (Little, Brown).

PEN/John Kenneth Galbraith Award for Nonfiction ($10,000). Given biennially for a distinguished book of general nonfiction. *Offered by:* PEN American Center. *Winner:* Matthew Desmond for *Evicted: Poverty and Profit in the American City* (Crown/Penguin Random House).

PEN/Heim Translation Fund Grants ($2,000–$4,000). To support the translation of book-length works of fiction, creative nonfiction, poetry, or drama that have not previously appeared in English or have appeared only in an egregiously flawed translation. *Winners:* Nick Admussen, Polly Barton, Elizabeth Bryer, Vital Chernetsky, Iain Galbraith, Michelle Gil-Montero, Sophie Hughes, Elisabeth Jaquette, Kira Josefsson, Adam Morris, Kaitlin Rees, Dayla Rogers, Christopher Tamigi, Manjushree Thapa, and Joyce Zonana.

PEN/Ernest Hemingway Foundation Award. For a distinguished work of first fiction by an American. *Offered by:* PEN New England. *Winner:* Yaa Gyasi for *Homegoing* (Knopf).

PEN/O. Henry Prize. For short stories of exceptional merit, in English, published in U.S. and Canadian magazines. *Winners:* Elizabeth Genovise for "Irises" in the *Cimarron Review*; Geetha Iyer for "The Mongerji Letters" in *Orion*; Elizabeth Tallent for "Narrator" in *The Threepenny Review*; Joe Donnelly for "Bonus Baby" in *ZYZZYVA*; David H. Lynn for "Divergence" in *Glimmer Train*; Shruti Swamy for "A Simple Composition" in *Agni*; Charles Haverty for "Storm Windows" in *One Story*; Asako Serizawa for "Train to Harbin" in *The Hudson Review*; Wendell Berry for "Dismemberment" in *The Threepenny Review*; Marie-Helene Bertino for "Exit Zero" in the *Epoch*; Sam Savage for "Cigarettes" in *The Paris Review;* Adrienne Celt for "Temples" in *Epoch*; Lydia Fitzpatrick for "Safety" in *One Story*; Diane Cook for "Bounty" in *Harper's*; Zebbie Watson for "A Single Deliberate Thing" in *The Threepenny Review*; Robert Coover for "The Crabapple Tree" in *The New Yorker*; Frederic Tuten for "Winter, 1965" in *Bomb*; Rebecca Evanhoe for "They Were Awake" in *Harper's;* Ottessa Moshfegh for "Slumming" in *The Paris Review;* Ron Carlson for "Happiness" in *Ecotone*.

PEN/Nora Magid Award ($2,500). Awarded biennially to honor a magazine editor who has contributed significantly to the excellence of the publication he or she edits. *Winners:* Michael Archer and *Joel Whitney* for *Guernica*.

PEN/Malamud Award. To recognize a body of work that demonstrates excellence in the art of short fiction. *Winner:* Joy Williams.

PEN/Ralph Manheim Medal for Translation. Given triennially to a translator whose career has demonstrated a commitment to excellence. *Winner:* not awarded in 2016.

PEN/Phyllis Naylor Working Writer Fellowship ($5,000). To a published author of children's or young adults' fiction to aid in completing a book-length work in progress. *Offered by:* PEN American Center. *Winner:* Ash Parsons for "A Chemical Distance" (available for publication).

PEN New England Awards. For works of fiction, nonfiction, and poetry by New England writers or with New England topics or settings. *Winners:* (nonfiction) Matthew Desmond for *Evicted: Poverty and Profit in the American City* (Crown/Penguin); (fiction) Robin MacArthur for *Half Wild* (Ecco); (poetry) David Rivard for *Standoff* (Graywolf).

PEN New England Susan P. Bloom Children's Book Discovery Award. For noteworthy unpublished children's or young adult literature. *Winner:* Michelle Cusolito for *Flying Deep.*

PEN New England Henry David Thoreau Prize for Literary Excellence in Nature Writing. *Winner:* Sy Montgomery.

PEN Open Book Award (formerly PEN Beyond Margins Award) ($5,000). For book-length writings by authors of color, published in the United States during the current calendar year. *Offered by:* PEN American Center. *Winner:* Helen Oyeyemi, for *What Is Not Yours Is Not Yours* (Riverhead/Penguin Random House).

PEN/Joyce Osterweil Award for Poetry ($5,000). A biennial award given in odd-numbered years to recognize a new and emerging American poet. *Offered by:* PEN American Center. *Winner:* Natalie Scenters-Zapico for *The Verging Cities* (Center For Literary Publishing/Colorado State University).

PEN/Laura Pels Foundation Awards for Drama. To recognize a master American dramatist, an American playwright in mid-career, and an emerging American playwright. *Offered by:* PEN American Center. *Winners:* (mid-career, $7,500) Tarell Alvin McCraney.

PEN Translation Prize ($3,000). To promote the publication and reception of translated world literature in English. *Winner:* Tess Lewis, for her translation from the German of *Angel of Oblivion* by Maja Haderlap (Archipelago Books).

PEN/Voelcker Award for Poetry. Given in even-numbered years to an American poet at the height of his or her powers. *Offered by:* PEN American Center. *Winner:* Ed Roberson.

PEN/Jacqueline Bograd Weld Award for Biography ($5,000). To the author of a distinguished biography published in the United States during the previous calendar year. *Offered by:* PEN American Center. *Winner:* Joe Jackson for *Black Elk: The Life of an American Visionary* (Farrar, Straus, & Giroux).

PEN/E. O. Wilson Literary Science Writing Award ($10,000). For a book of literary nonfiction on the subject of the physical and biological sciences. *Winner:* Luke Dittrich for *Patient H.M.: A Story of Memory, Madness, and Family Secrets* (Penguin Random House).

Maxwell E. Perkins Award. To honor an editor, publisher, or agent who has discovered, nurtured, and championed writers of fiction in the United States. *Offered by:* Center for Fiction, Mercantile Library of New York. *Winner:* Morgan Entrekin, CEO and Publisher, Grove Atlantic, Inc.

Phoenix Awards. To the authors of English-language children's books that failed to win a major award at the time of publication 20 years earlier. *Winner:* Andrew Clements for *Frindle* (Atheneum).

Edgar Allan Poe Awards. For outstanding mystery, suspense, and crime writing. *Offered by:* Mystery Writers of America. *Winners:* (novel) Noah Hawley for *Before the Fall* (Hachette/Grand Central); (first novel) Flynn Berry for *Under the Harrow* (Penguin Random House); (paperback original) Adrian McKinty for Rain Dogs ((Prometheus/Seventh Street); (fact crime) Kate Summerscale for *The Wicked Boy: The Mystery of a Victorian Child Murderer* (Penguin Random House); (critical/biographical) Ruth Franklin for *Shirley Jackson: A Rather Haunted Life* (W. W. Norton /Liveright); (short story) Lawrence Block for "Autumn at the Automat" (Pegasus Books); (juvenile) Wesley

King for *OCDaniel* (Simon & Schuster/Paula Wiseman); (young adult) Monica Hesse for *Girl in the Blue Coat* (Hachette/Little, Brown); (television episode) John Logan for "A Blade of Grass"—Penny Dreadful (Showtime); (Robert L. Fish Memorial Award) E. Gabriel Flores for "The Truth of the Neil Nyren Moment" in *Ellery Queen Mystery Magazine* (Dell Magazines); (grand master) Max Allan Collins, Ellen Hart; (Raven Awards) Dru Ann Love; (Ellery Queen Award) Neil Nyren; (Simon & Schuster Mary Higgins Clark Award) Charles Todd for *The Shattered Tree* (HarperCollins/William Morrow).

Poets Out Loud Prize ($1,000 and publication by Fordham University Press). For a book-length poetry collection. *Sponsor:* Fordham University. *Winners:* Gary Keenanfor *"Rotary Devotion"*; (editor's prize) Michael Snediker for "The New York Editions."

Katherine Anne Porter Award ($20,000). Awarded biennially to a prose writer of demonstrated achievement. *Offered by:* American Academy of Arts and Letters. *Winner:* not awarded in 2016.

Michael L. Printz Award. For excellence in literature for young adults. *Offered by:* American Library Association, Young Adult Library Services Association. *Winner:* Laura Ruby for *Bone Gap* (HarperCollins).

V. S. Pritchett Memorial Prize (United Kingdom) (£1,000). For a previously unpublished short story. *Offered by:* Royal Society of Literature. *Winner:* Fiona Marshall for "The Street of Baths."

Pritzker Military Library Literature Award ($100,000). To recognize a living author for a body of work that has profoundly enriched the public understanding of American military history. *Sponsor:* Tawani Foundation. *Winner:* Hew Strachan.

Prix Aurora Awards (Canada). For science fiction. *Winners:* (novel) A. M. Dellamonica for *A Daughter of No Nation* (Tom Doherty Associates); (young adult novel) Leah Bobet for *An Inheritance of Ashes* (Houghton Mifflin Harcourt); (short fiction) Kelly Robson for "Waters of Versailles"; (poem/song) Naru Dames Sundar for *Origami Crane/Light Defying Spaceship*; (graphic novel) Vincent Marcone for *The Lady ParaNorma*;

(related work) Michael Rimar and Hayden Trenholm, editors, for *Second Contacts*.

Prix Goncourt (France). For "the best imaginary prose work of the year." *Offered by:* Société des Gens des Lettres. *Winner:* Philippe Forest for *Aragon*.

Pulitzer Prizes in Letters ($10,000). To honor distinguished work dealing preferably with American themes. *Offered by:* Columbia University Graduate School of Journalism. *Winners:* (fiction) Colson Whitehead for *The Underground Railroad* (Knopf Doubleday); (drama) Lynn Nottage for *Sweat*; (history) Heather Ann Thompson for *Blood in the Water* (Knopf Doubleday); (biography/autobiography) Hisham Matar for *The Return* (Random House); (poetry) Tyehimba Jess for *Olio* (Wave Books); (general nonfiction) Matthew Desmond for *Evicted* (Crown/Archetype).

Raiziss/De Palchi Translation Award ($5,000 prize and a $25,000 fellowship, awarded in alternate years). For a translation into English of a significant work of modern Italian poetry by a living translator. *Offered by:* Academy of American Poets. *Winner:* Stephen Sartarelli for *The Selected Poetry of Pier Paolo Pasolini*.

RBC Bronwen Wallace Award for Emerging Writers (C$5,000) (Canada). For a writer under the age of 35 who has not yet been published in book form. *Sponsor:* RBC Foundation. *Winner:* Brendan Bowle.

Arthur Rense Poetry Prize ($20,000). Awarded triennially to an exceptional poet. *Offered by:* American Academy of Arts and Letters. *Winner:* August Kleinzahler.

Harold U. Ribalow Prize. For Jewish fiction published in English. *Sponsor:* Hadassah magazine. *Winner:* Jim Shepard, for *The Book of Aron* (Knopf).

Rita Awards. *Offered by:* Romance Writers of America. *Winners:* (first book) Pintip Dunn for *Forget Tomorrow* (Entangled Publishing); (short contemporary romance) Sarah M. Anderson for *The Nanny Plan* (Harlequin); (mid-length contemporary romance) Sarina Bowen and Elle Kennedy for *Him* (Elle Kennedy); (long contemporary romance) Maisey Yates for *Brokedown Cowboy* (Harlequin); (erotic) Alexis Hall for *For Real: A Spires Story*; (long historical) Deeanne Gist for *Tiffany Girl* (Center Point);

(short historical) Julie Anne Long for *It Started with a Scandal* (HarperCollins); (inspirational) Kristi Ann Hunter for *A Noble Masquerade* (Gale Group); (paranormal) Angela Quarles for *Must Love Chainmail* (Angela Quarles); (novella) Roni Loren for *Nice Girls Don't Ride* (Penguin); (suspense) Dana Marton for *Flash Fire* (Dana Marton); (young adult) Jenn Bennett for *The Anatomical Shape of a Heart* (Feiwel & Friends).

Rita Golden Heart Awards. For worthy unpublished romance manuscripts. *Offered by:* Romance Writers of America. *Winners:* (contemporary) Gabrielle Luthy for *Shelter Me*; (short contemporary) Carrie Nichols for *Rescuing Riley*; (historical) Elizabeth King for *The Earl and the Pussycat*; (paranormal) Tara Sheets for *Don't Call Me Cupcake*; (suspense) Tracy Brody for *In the Wrong Sight*; (young adult) Meg Kassel for *The Beekeeper.*

Rodda Book Award. To recognize a book that exhibits excellence in writing and has contributed significantly to congregational libraries through promotion of spiritual growth. The award is given to books for adults, young adults, and children on a rotational basis. *Offered by:* Church and Synagogue Library Association. *Winner:* (adult) Ron Koertge for *Coaltown Jesus* (Candlewick).

Rogers Writers' Trust Fiction Prize (Canada) (C$25,000). To a Canadian author of a novel or short story collection. *Offered by:* Rogers Communications. *Winner:* Michael Helm for *After James* (McClelland & Stewart).

Sami Rohr Prize for Jewish Literature ($100,000). For emerging writers of Jewish literature. *Offered by:* Family of Sami Rohr. *Winner:* Idra Novey for *Ways to Disappear* (Little, Brown).

Rosenthal Foundation Award ($10,000). To a young novelist of considerable literary talent. *Offered by:* American Academy of Arts and Letters. *Winner:* Sonya Shin.

Royal Society of Literature Benson Medal (United Kingdom). To recognize meritorious works in poetry, fiction, history and belles letters, honoring an entire career. The recipient may be someone who is not a writer but has done conspicuous service to literature. *Winner:* Christopher MacLehose.

Royal Society of Literature Jerwood Awards for Nonfiction (United Kingdom). For authors engaged on their first major commissioned works of nonfiction. *Offered by:* Royal Society of Literature. *Winners:* (£10,000) Violet Moller for *The Geography of Knowledge* (Pan Macmillan, 2018); (£5,000) Afua Hirsch for *BRIT(ish): Getting Under the Skin of Britain's Race Problem* (Cape, 2018); Damian Le Bas for *Stopping Places* (Chatto, 2018).

Royal Society of Literature Ondaatje Prize (United Kingdom) (£10,000). For a distinguished work of fiction, nonfiction, or poetry evoking the spirit of a place. *Offered by:* Royal Society of Literature. *Winner:* Francis Spufford for *Golden Hill* (Faber).

Juan Rulfo International Latin American and Caribbean Prize. See FIL Literary Award in Romance Languages.

Saltire Society Scotland Literary Awards. To recognize noteworthy work by writers of Scottish descent or living in Scotland, or by anyone who deals with the work or life of a Scot or with a Scottish problem, event, or situation. *Offered by:* Saltire Society. *Sponsors:* Creative Scotland, the National Library of Scotland, the Scottish Poetry Library, the Scottish Historical Review Trust, Tamdhu Speyside Sing le Malt Scotch Whisky. *Winners* (book of the year £5,000, individual categories £2,000) Isabel Buchanan *Trials* (Jonathan Cape) and Chitra Ramaswamy *Expecting* (Saraband); (fiction book of the year) Graeme Macrae Burnet for *His Bloody Project* (Contraband); (nonfiction book of the year) John Kay for *Other People's Money* (Profile Books); (research book of the year) Sebastiaan Verweij for *The Literary Culture of Early Modern Scotland: Manuscript Production and Transmission 1560–1625* (Oxford University Press); (poetry book of the year) Kathleen Jamie for *The Bonniest Companie* (Picador); (first book) Chitra Ramaswamy for *Expecting* (Saraband); (history book) James Hunter for *Set Adrift Upon the World* (Birlinn).

Carl Sandburg Literary Awards. *Sponsor:* Chicago Public Library Foundation. *Winners:* Margaret Atwood and Dave Eggers; (21st Century Award, for significant recent achievement by a Chicago-area writer) Natalie Y. Moore, author of *The South Side: A*

Portrait of Chicago and American Segregation.

Schneider Family Book Awards ($5,000). To honor authors and illustrators for books that embody artistic expressions of the disability experience of children and adolescents. *Offered by:* American Library Association. *Donor:* Katherine Schneider. *Winners:* Laurie Ann Thompson and Sean Qualls, illustrator, for *Emmanuel's Dream: The True Story of Emmanuel Ofosu Yeboah* (Random House); Lynda Mullaly Hunt for *Fish in a Tree* (Penguin); Teresa Toten for *The Unlikely Hero of Room 13B* (Random House).

Scotiabank Giller Prize (Canada) (C$100,000 first place, C$10,000 to each of the finalists). For the best Canadian novel or short story collection written in English. *Offered by:* Giller Prize Foundation and Scotiabank. *Winner:* Madeleine Thien for *Do Not Say We Have Nothing* (Alfred A. Knopf Canada); (finalists) Mona Awad for *13 Ways of Looking at a Fat Girl* (Penguin Canada); Gary Barwin for *Yiddish for Pirates* (Random House Canada); Emma Donoghue for *The Wonder* (HarperCollins); Catherine Leroux for *The Party Wall* (Biblioasis), translated by Lazer Lederhendler; Zoe Whittall for *The Best Kind of People* (House of Anansi Press).

Shamus Awards. To honor mysteries featuring independent private investigators. *Offered by:* Private Eye Writers of America. *Winners:* (hardcover novel) Ingrid Thoft for *Brutality* (Penguin Publishing Group); (first novel) Lisa Sandlin for *The Do-Right* (Cinco Puntos); (original paperback) J. L. Abramo for *Circling the Runway* (Down & Out); (Shamus Award for Lifetime Achievement) S. J. Rozan.

Shelley Memorial Award ($6,000 to $9,000). To a poet or poets living in the United States, chosen on the basis of genius and need. *Offered by:* Poetry Society of America. *Winner:* Gillian Conoley.

Robert F. Sibert Medal. For the most distinguished informational book for children. *Offered by:* American Library Association, Association for Library Service to Children. *Winner:* Duncan Tonatiuh for *Funny Bones: Posada and His Day of the Dead Calaveras* (Abrams).

Society of Authors Traveling Scholarships (United Kingdom) (£1,750). *Winners:* Jamie Bartlett, David Crane, Peter Oswald, and David Szalay.

Specsavers National Book Awards (United Kingdom) (formerly the Galaxy National Book Awards, earlier the British Book Awards). *Winners:* no awards event in 2016.

Spur Awards. *Offered by:* Western Writers of America. *Winners:* (contemporary novel C. J. Box for *Off the Grid: A Joe Pickett Novel* (G. P. Putnam's Sons); (historical novel) no award given; (traditional novel) Dusty Richards for *The Mustanger and the Lady* (Galway Press); (historical nonfiction) Paul Andrew Hutton for *The Apache Wars: The Hunt for Geronimo, The Apache Kid, and the Captive Boy Who Started the Longest War in American History* (Crown); (contemporary nonfiction) Michael Duchemin for *New Deal Cowboy: Gene Autry and Public Diplomacy* (University of Oklahoma Press); (nonfiction biography) Joe Jackson for *Black Elk: The Life of an American Visionary* (Farrar, Straus and Giroux); (original mass-market paperback novel) Johnny D. Boggs for *Return to Red River* (Pinnacle); (juvenile fiction) Nancy Oswald for *Trouble Returns: A Ruby and Maude Adventure* (Filter Press); (juvenile nonfiction) William Grill for *The Wolves of Currumpaw* (Flying Eye Books); (storyteller) Ginger Wadsworth for *Seasons of the Bear: A Yosemite Story* (Yosemite Conservancy); (short fiction) Troy D. Smith for "Odell's Bones" (Cane Hollow); (short nonfiction) Kendra Field and Daniel Lynch for "Master of Ceremonies: The World of Peter Biggs in Civil War-Era Los Angeles" (*Western Historical Quarterly*); (poem) Floyd Beard for "Ain't A Hermit" (self-published, produced by Butch Hause); (song) Jim Jones and Allan Chapman for "Halfway Down the Devil's Road" (East Mountain Music); (documentary script) Geoff O'Gara for "The Drift: An American Cattle Drive" (The Content Lab); (drama script) Taylor Sheridan for *Hell Or High Water* (Film 44/OddLot Entertainment/Sidney Kimmel Entertainment/CBS Films); (first nonfiction book) Fernanda Santos for *The Fire Line: The Story of the Granite Mountain Hotshots and One of the Deadliest Days in American Firefighting* (Flatiron Books); (first novel)

James T. Hughes for *Jasper Spring* (Dog Ear Publishing).

Wallace Stevens Award ($100,000). To recognize outstanding and proven mastery in the art of poetry. *Offered by:* Academy of American Poets. *Winner:* Sharon Olds.

Bram Stoker Awards. For superior horror writing. *Offered by:* Horror Writers Association. *Winners:* (novel) Paul Tremblay for *A Head Full of Ghosts* (Morrow); (first novel) Nicole Cushing for *Mr. Suicide* (Word Horde); (young adult novel) John Dixon for *Devil's Pocket* (Simon & Schuster); (graphic novel) Sam Weller, Mort Castle, Chris Ryall, and Carlos Guzman, editors, for *Shadow Show: Stories in Celebration of Ray Bradbury* (IDW); (long fiction) Mercedes M. Yardley for "Little Dead Red" in *Grimm Mistresses* (Ragnarok); (short fiction) John Palisano for "Happy Joe's Rest Stop" in *18 Wheels of Horror* (Big Time Books); (screenplay) David Robert Mitchell for "It Follows" (Northern Lights Films); (lifetime achievement) Alan Moore and George A. Romero.

Stonewall Book Awards. *Offered by:* Gay, Lesbian, Bisexual, and Transgender Round Table, American Library Association. *Winners:* (Barbara Gittings Literature Award) Chris McCormick for *Desert Boys* (Picador); (Israel Fishman Nonfiction Award) David France for *How to Survive a Plague: The Inside Story of How Citizens and Science Tamed AIDS* (Knopf); (Mike Morgan and Larry Romans Children's and Young Adult Literature Award) Rick Riordan for *Magnus Chase and the Gods of Asgard: The Hammer of Thor* (Disney-Hyperion), Meredith Russo for *If I Was Your Girl* (Flatiron Books).

Story Prize ($20,000). For a collection of short fiction. *Offered by:* Story magazine. *Winner:* Rick Bass for *For a Little While* (Little, Brown).

Flora Stieglitz Straus Award. For nonfiction books that serve as an inspiration to young readers. *Offered by:* Bank Street College of Education and the Florence M. Miller Memorial Fund. *Winner:* Carole Boston Weatherford for *Voice of Freedom: Fannie Lou Hamer: Spirit of the Civil Rights Movement* (Candlewick).

Theodore Sturgeon Memorial Award. For the year's best short science fiction. *Offered by:* Center for the Study of Science Fiction. *Winner:* Kelly Link for "The Game of Smash and Recovery" in *Strange Horizons.*

Sunburst Awards for Canadian Literature of the Fantastic (C$1,000). *Winners:* (adult) Gemma Files for *Experimental Film* (ChiZine Publications); (young adult) Leah Bobet for *An Inheritance of Ashes* (Scholastic Canada).

Sunday Times EFG Short Story Award (United Kingdom) (£30,000). To an author from any country for an English-language story of 6,000 words or less. *Winner:* Jonathan Tel for "The Human Phonograph."

Tanizaki Junichiro Prize (Japan) (1 million yen, approximately $8,450). For a full-length work of fiction or drama by a professional writer. *Offered by:* Chuokoron-Shinsha, Inc. *Winner:* Akiko Itoyama.

Charles Taylor Prize for Literary Nonfiction (Canada) (C$25,000). To honor a book of creative nonfiction widely available in Canada and written by a Canadian citizen or landed immigrant. *Offered by:* Charles Taylor Foundation. *Winner:* Cassi Smith.

Sydney Taylor Children's Book Awards. For a distinguished contribution to Jewish children's literature. *Offered by:* Association of Jewish Libraries. *Winners:* (younger readers) Debbie Levy, Elizabeth Baddeley, illustrator, for *I Dissent: Ruth Bader Ginsburg Makes Her Mark.* (Simon); (older readers) Adam Gidwitz, Hatem Aly, illustrator, for *The Inquisitor's Tale: Or, The Three Magical Children and Their Holy Dog* (Dutton); (teen readers) Gavriel Savit for *Anna and the Swallow Man* (Knopf).

Sydney Taylor Manuscript Competition ($1,000). For the best fiction manuscript appropriate for readers ages 8–13, both Jewish and non-Jewish, revealing positive aspects of Jewish life, and written by an unpublished author. *Winner:* Meira Drazin for *Honey and Me.*

Theatre Library Association Award. See Richard Wall Memorial Award.

Dylan Thomas Prize (United Kingdom) (£30,000). For a published or produced literary work in the English language, written by an author under 30. *Offered by:* University of Wales. *Winner:* Fiona McFarlane for *The High Places* (Farrar, Straus and Giroux).

Thriller Awards. *Offered by:* International Thriller Writers. *Winners:* (hardcover novel) Ian Caldwell for The Fifth Gospel (Simon & Schuster); (paperback original) John Gilstrap for *Against All Enemies* (Pinnacle); (first novel) Brian Panowich for *Bull Mountain* (G.P. Putnam's Sons); (e-book original) Chris Kuzneski for *The Prisoner's Gold* (Chris Kuzneski); (young adult) Michelle Painchaud for Pretending to be Erica (Viking); (short story) Joyce Carol Oates for "Gun Accident: An Investigation" in *Ellery Queen Mystery Magazine*.

Thurber Prize for American Humor ($5,000). For a humorous book of fiction or nonfiction. *Offered by:* Thurber House. *Winner:* Harrison Scott Key for *The World's Largest Man* (HarperCollins).

Tom-Gallon Trust Award (United Kingdom) (£1,000). For a short story. *Offered by:* Society of Authors. *Sponsor:* Authors' Licensing and Collecting Society. *Winner:* Claire Harmon for "Otherwise Engaged."

Betty Trask Prize and Awards (United Kingdom). To Commonwealth writers under the age of 35 for "romantic or traditional" first novels. *Offered by:* Society of Authors. *Winners:* (Betty Trask Prize, £10,000) Alex Christofi for *Glass* (Serpent's Tail); (Betty Trask Awards, £5,000) Irenosen Okojie for *The Butterfly Fish* (Jacaranda); Natasha Pulley for *The Watchmaker of Filigree Street* ((Bloomsbury); Lucy Wood for *Weathering* (Bloomsbury).

Kate Tufts Discovery Award ($10,000). For a first or very early book of poetry by an emerging poet. *Offered by:* Claremont Graduate University. *Winner:* Phillip B. Williams for *Thief in the Interior* (Alice James Books).

Kingsley Tufts Poetry Award ($100,000). For a book of poetry by a mid-career poet. *Offered by:* Claremont Graduate School. *Winner:* Vievee Francis for *Forest Primeval* (Northwestern University Press).

21st Century Award. To honor recent achievement in writing by an author with ties to Chicago. See Carl Sandburg Literary Awards.

UKLA Children's Book Awards (United Kingdom). Sponsor: United Kingdom Literacy Association. *Winners:* (ages 3–6) Alex T. Smith for *Little Red and the Very Hungry Lion* (Scholastic); (ages 7–11) A. F. Harrold and Emily Gravett for *The Imaginary* (Bloomsbury); (ages 12–16) Francis Hardinge for *The Lie Tree* (Macmillan).

Ungar German Translation Award ($1,000). Awarded biennially for a distinguished literary translation from German into English that has been published in the United States. *Offered by:* American Translators Association. *Winner:* Philip Boehm for his translation of *Anonymous: A Woman in Berlin.*

John Updike Award ($20,000). Given biennially to a writer in mid-career who has demonstrated consistent excellence. *Offered by:* American Academy of Arts and Letters. *Winner:* Zachary Lazar.

VCU/Cabell First Novelist Award ($5,000). For a first novel published in the previous year. *Offered by:* Virginia Commonwealth University. *Winner:* Angela Flournoy for *The Turner House* (Houghton Mifflin Harcourt).

Harold D. Vursell Memorial Award ($20,000). To a writer whose work merits recognition for the quality of its prose style. *Offered by:* American Academy of Arts and Letters. *Winner:* Dava Sobel.

Amelia Elizabeth Walden Award ($5,000). To honor a book relevant to adolescents that has enjoyed a wide teenage audience. *Sponsor:* Assembly on Literature for Adolescents, National Council of Teachers of English. *Winner:* Jason Reynolds and Brendan Kiely for *All American Boys* (Atheneum/Caitlyn Dlouhy Books).

Richard Wall Memorial Award (formerly the Theatre Library Association Award). To honor an English-language book of exceptional scholarship in the field of recorded performance, including motion pictures, television, and radio. *Offered by:* Theatre Library Association. *Winner:* Mark Harris for *Five Came Back* (Penguin).

George Washington Book Prize ($50,000). To recognize an important new book about America's founding era. *Offered by:* Washington College and the Gilder Lehrman Institute of American History. *Winner:* Nathaniel Philbrick for *Valiant Ambition: George Washington, Benedict Arnold, and the Fate of the American Revolution* (Viking).

Carole Weinstein Poetry Prize ($10,000). To poets with strong connections to the Commonwealth of Virginia who have made a "significant recent contribution to the art of poetry." *Winner:* Jon Pineda.

Hilary Weston Writers' Trust Prize for Nonfiction (C$60,000) (Canada). *Winner:* Deborah Campbell for *A Disappearance in Damascus: A Story of Friendship and Survival in the Shadow of War* (Knopf Canada).

Hilary Weston Writers' Trust Prize for Student Nonfiction (C$2,500 plus C$1,000 for the winner's school, and publication on Macleans.ca and Writerstrust.com) (Canada). For students in grades 9–12. *Winner:* Rosemary Sullivan for *Stalin's Daughter: The Extraordinary and Tumultuous Life of Svetlana Alliluyeva* (HarperCollins Canada).

Whitbread Book Awards. See Costa Book Awards.

E. B. White Award ($10,000). For achievement in children's literature. *Offered by:* American Academy of Arts and Letters. *Winner:* Christopher Paul Curtis.

E. B. White Read-Aloud Awards. For children's books with particular appeal as read-aloud books. *Offered by:* American Booksellers Association/Association of Booksellers for Children. *Winners:* (picture book) Ryan T. Higgins, for *Mother Bruce* (Disney-Hyperion); (middle readers) Ali Benjamin for *The Thing About Jellyfish* (Little, Brown).

Whiting Writers' Awards ($50,000). For emerging writers of exceptional talent and promise. *Offered by:* Mrs. Giles Whiting Foundation. *Winners:* (poetry) Simone White, Philip B. Willliams; (fiction) Kaitlyn Greenidge, Lisa Halliday, Tony Tulathimutte, and Jen Beagin; (nonfiction) Francisco Cantú; (drama) Clare Barron, Clarence Coo, and James Ijames

Walt Whitman Award ($5,000). To a U.S. poet who has not published a book of poems in a standard edition. *Offered by:* Academy of American Poets. *Winner:* Jenny Xie for "Eye Level."

Richard Wilbur Award ($1,000 and publication by University of Evansville Press). For a book-length poetry collection. *Winner:* Adam Tavel for "Catafalque."

Laura Ingalls Wilder Award. Awarded biennially to an author or illustrator whose books have made a substantial and lasting contribution to children's literature. *Offered by:* American Library Association, Association for Library Service to Children. *Winner:* Nikki Grimes.

Robert H. Winner Memorial Award ($2,500). To a mid-career poet over 40 who has published no more than one book of poetry. *Offered by:* Poetry Society of America. *Winner:* Heather Altfeld.

George Wittenborn Memorial Book Awards. To North American art publications that represent the highest standards of content, documentation, layout, and format. *Offered by:* Art Libraries Society of North America (ARLIS/NA). *Winner:* Stephen Little, editor, for the exhibition catalogue *17th-Century Chinese Paintings from the Tsao Family Collection.*

Thomas Wolfe Prize and Lecture. To honor writers with distinguished bodies of work. *Offered by:* Thomas Wolfe Society and University of North Carolina at Chapel Hill. *Winner:* Jill McCorkle.

Thomas Wolfe Fiction Prize ($1,000). For a short story that honors Thomas Wolfe. *Offered by:* North Carolina Writers Network. *Winner:* Alli Marshall for "Catching Out," in *The Thomas Wolfe Review.*

Helen and Kurt Wolff Translator's Prize ($10,000). For an outstanding translation from German into English, published in the United States. *Offered by:* Goethe Institut Inter Nationes, New York. *Winner:* Charlotte Collins for her translation of Robert Seethaler's *A Whole Life (Ein ganzes Leben)* (Farrar, Straus & Giroux).

World Fantasy Convention Awards. For outstanding fantasy writing. *Offered by:* World Fantasy Convention. *Winners:* (novel) Anna Smaill for *The Chimes* (Quercus); (short story) Alyssa Wong for "Hungry Daughters of Starving Mothers"; (anthology) Silvia Moreno-Garcia for *She Walks in Shadows* (Innsmouth Free Press); (collection) C. S. E. Cooney for *Bone Swans* (Mythic Delirium Books.

Writers' Trust Engel/Findley Award (C$25,000). To a Canadian writer predominantly of fiction, for a body of work. *Winner:* Eden Robinson.

Writers' Trust Poetry Prize. See Latner Writers' Trust Poetry Prize.

Writers' Trust Shaughnessy Cohen Prize for Political Writing (Canada) (C$25,000). For a nonfiction book that captures a subject of political interest. *Sponsor:* CTV. *Winner:* Kamal Al-Solaylee for *Brown: What Being Brown in the World Today Means (To Everyone)* (HarperCollins Canada).

Writers' Trust/McClelland & Stewart Journey Prize (Canada) (C$10,000). To a new, developing Canadian author for a short story or an excerpt from a novel in progress. *Offered by:* McClelland & Stewart. *Winner:* Colette Langlois for "The Emigrants" in *PRISM International.*

Writers' Trust Hilary Weston Prize for Nonfiction (Canada). See Hilary Weston Writers' Trust of Canada Prize for Nonfiction.

YALSA Award for Excellence in Nonfiction. For a work of nonfiction published for young adults (ages 12–18). *Offered by:* American Library Association, Young Adult Library Services Association. *Winner:* Steve Sheinkin for *Most Dangerous: Daniel Ellsbergand and the Secret History of the Vietnam War* (Roaring Brook Press).

Young Lions Fiction Award ($10,000). For a novel or collection of short stories by an American under the age of 35. *Offered by:* Young Lions of the New York Public Library. *Winner:* Amelia Gray for *Gutshot: Stories.* (Farrar, Straus and Giroux)

Young People's Poet Laureate ($25,000). For lifetime achievement in poetry for children. Honoree holds the title for two years. *Offered by:* The Poetry Foundation. *Winner:* Jacqueline Woodson.

Morton Dauwen Zabel Award ($10,000). Awarded biennially, in rotation, to a progressive and experimental poet, writer of fiction, or critic. *Offered by:* American Academy of Arts and Letters. *Winner:* James Hannaham.

Zoetrope Short Fiction Prizes. *Offered by:* *Zoetrope: All-Story.* *Winners:* (first, $1,000) Lindsay Zibach for "Seeing Diane Arbus"; (second, $500) Shay Azoulay for "Permaculture"; (third, $250) S. Kennedy Sobol for "We Servants."

Charlotte Zolotow Award. For outstanding writing in a picture book published in the United States in the previous year. *Offered by:* Cooperative Children's Book Center, University of Wisconsin–Madison. *Winners:* Carole Boston Weatherford for *Freedom in Congo Square* (little bee books).

Part 6
Directory of Organizations

Directory of Library and Related Organizations

Networks, Consortia, and Other Cooperative Library Organizations

This list is taken from the current edition of *American Library Directory* (Information Today, Inc.), which includes additional information on member libraries and primary functions of each organization.

United States

Alabama

Alabama Health Libraries Assn., Inc. (AL-HeLa), Lister Hill Lib., Univ. of Alabama, Birmingham 35294-0013. SAN 372-8218. Tel. 205-975-8313, fax 205-934-2230. *Pres.* Justin Robertson.

Library Management Network, Inc. (LMN), 2132 6th Ave S.E., Suite 106, Decatur 35601. SAN 322-3906. Tel. 256-308-2529, fax 256-308-2533. *Systems Coord.* Charlotte Moncrief.

Marine Environmental Sciences Consortium, Dauphin Island Sea Laboratory, Dauphin Island 36528. SAN 322-0001. Tel. 251-861-2141, fax 251-861-4646, e-mail disl@disl.org. *Coord.* John Dindo.

Network of Alabama Academic Libraries, c/o Alabama Commission on Higher Education, Montgomery 36104. SAN 322-4570. Tel. 334-242-2211, fax 334-242-0270. *Dir.* Ron P. Leonard.

Alaska

Alaska Library Network (ALN), 395 Whittier St., Anchorage 99501-2338. SAN 371-0688. Tel. 907-269-6567, e-mail info@aklib.net. *Exec. Dir.* Tracy Swaim.

Arkansas

Northeast Arkansas Hospital Library Consortium, 223 E. Jackson, Jonesboro 72401. SAN 329-529X. Tel. 870-972-1290, fax 870-931-0839. *Dir.* Karen Crosser.

California

49-99 Cooperative Library System, c/o Southern California Lib. Cooperative, Monrovia 91016. SAN 301-6218. Tel. 626-359-6111, fax 626-359-0001. *Dir.* Diane R. Satchwell.

Bay Area Library and Information Network (BayNet), 1462 Cedar St., Berkeley 94702. SAN 371-0610. Tel. 415-355-2826, e-mail infobay@baynetlibs.org. *Pres.* Debbie Abilock.

Califa, 2471 Flores St., San Mateo 94403. Tel. 650-356-2131, fax 650-349-5089, e-mail califa@califa.org. *Interim Dir.* Paula MacKinnon.

Claremont University Consortium (CUC), 150 E. 8 St., Claremont 91711. Tel. 909-621-8000; 909-621-8150, fax 909-621-8681. *CEO* Stig Lanesskog.

Consumer Health Information Program and Services (CHIPS), 12350 Imperial Hwy., Norwalk 90650. SAN 372-8110. Tel. 562-868-4003, fax 562-868-4065, e-mail referenceservices@library.lacounty.gov.

Consortium for Open Learning, 333 Sunrise Ave., No. 229, Roseville 95661-3480. SAN 329-4412. Tel. 916-788-0660, fax 916-788-0696. *Operations Mgr.* Sandra Scott-Smith.

Gold Coast Library Network, 3437 Empresa Drive, Suite C, San Luis Obispo 93401-7355. Tel. 805-543-6082, fax 805-543-9487. *Admin. Dir.* Maureen Theobald.

National Network of Libraries of Medicine– Pacific Southwest Region (NN/LM-PSR), Louise M. Darling Biomedical Lib., Los Angeles 90095-1798. SAN 372-8234. Tel. 310-825-1200, fax 310-825-5389, e-mail psr-nnlm@library.ucla.edu. *Dir.* Judy Consales.

Nevada Medical Library Group (NMLG), Barton Memorial Hospital Lib., 2170 South Ave., South Lake Tahoe 96150. SAN 370-0445. Tel. 530-543-5844, fax 530-541-4697. *Senior Exec. Coord.* Laurie Anton.

Northern and Central California Psychology Libraries (NCCPL), 2040 Gough St., San Francisco 94109. SAN 371-9006. Tel. 415-771-8055. *Pres.* Scott Hines.

Northern California Assn. of Law Libraries (NOCALL), 268 Bush St., No. 4006, San Francisco 94104. SAN 323-5777. E-mail admin@nocall.org. *Pres.* Michael Ginsborg.

Peninsula Libraries Automated Network (PLAN), 2471 Flores St., San Mateo 94403-4000. SAN 371-5035. Tel. 650-349-5538, fax 650-349-5089. *Dir., Information Technology.* Monica Schultz.

San Bernardino, Inyo, Riverside Counties United Library Services (SIRCULS), 555 W. 6th St., San Bernadino 92410. Tel. 909-381-8257, fax 909-888-3171, e-mail ils@inlandlib.org. *Exec. Dir.* Vera Skop.

San Francisco Biomedical Library Network (SFBLN), San Francisco General Hospital UCSF/Barnett-Briggs Medical Lib., 1001 Potrero Ave., Bldg. 30, First Fl., San Francisco 94110. SAN 371-2125. Tel. 415-206-6639, e-mail fishbon@ucsfmedctr.org. *Lib. Dir.* Stephen Kiyoi.

Santa Clarita Interlibrary Network (SCIL-NET), Powell Lib., Santa Clarita 91321. SAN 371-8964. Tel. 661-362-2271, fax 661-362-2719. *Libn.* John Stone.

Serra Cooperative Library System, 248 E. Foothill Blvd., Suite 101, Monrovia 91016-5522. SAN 301-3510. Tel. 626-359-6111. *Exec. Dir.* Diane R. Satchwell.

Southern California Library Cooperative (SCLC), 248 E. Foothill Blvd., Suite 101, Monrovia 91016-5522. SAN 371-3865. Tel. 626-359-6111, fax 626-359-0001, e-mail sclchq@socallibraries.org. *Dir.* Diane R. Satchwell.

Colorado

Automation System Colorado Consortium (ASCC), c/o Delta Public Lib., 211 W. Sixth St., Delta 81416. Tel. 970-874-9630, fax 970-874-8605. *Regional Mgr.* Lea Hart.

Colorado Alliance of Research Libraries, 3801 E. Florida Ave., Suite 515, Denver 80210. SAN 322-3760. Tel. 303-759-3399, fax 303-759-3363. *Exec. Dir.* George Machovec.

Colorado Assn. of Law Libraries, P.O. Box 13363, Denver 80201. SAN 322-4325. Tel. 303-492-7535, fax 303-492-2707. *Pres.* Andrea Hamilton.

Colorado Council of Medical Librarians (CCML), P.O. Box 101058, Denver 80210-1058. SAN 370-0755. Tel. 303-724-2124, fax 303-724-2154. *Pres.* Kimberly O'Neill.

Colorado Library Consortium (CLiC), 7400 E. Arapahoe Rd., Suite 75, Centennial 80112. SAN 371-3970. Tel. 303-422-1150, fax 303-431-9752. *Exec. Dir.* Jim Duncan

Connecticut

Bibliomation, 24 Wooster Ave., Waterbury 06708. Tel. 203-577-4070. *Exec. Dir.* Carl DeMilia.

Connecticut Library Consortium, 234 Court St., Middletown 06457-3304. SAN 322-0389. Tel. 860-344-8777, fax 860-344-9199, e-mail clc@ctlibrarians.org. *Exec. Dir.* Jennifer Keohane.

Council of State Library Agencies in the Northeast (COSLINE), Connecticut State Lib., 231 Capitol Ave., Hartford 06106. SAN 322-0451. Tel. 860-757-6510, fax 860-757-6503. Exec. Dir. Timothy Cherubini.

CTW Library Consortium, Olin Memorial Lib., Middletown 06459-6065. SAN 329-4587. Tel. 860-685-3887, fax 860-685-2661. *Libn. for Collaborative Projects* Lorri Huddy.

Hartford Consortium for Higher Education: 31 Pratt St., 4th fl., Hartford 06103. SAN 322-0443. Tel. 860-702-3801, fax 860-241-1130. *Exec. Dir.* Martin Estey.

Libraries Online, Inc. (LION), 100 Riverview Center, Suite 252, Middletown 06457. SAN 322-3922. Tel. 860-347-1704, fax 860-346-3707. *Exec. Dir.* Alan Hagyard.

Library Connection, Inc., 599 Matianuck Ave., Windsor 06095-3567. Tel. 860-937-8261, fax 860-298-5328. *Exec. Dir.* George Christian.

Delaware

Central Delaware Library Consortium, Dover Public Lib., Dover 19901. SAN 329-3696. Tel. 302-736-7030, fax 302-736-5087. *Dir.* Margery Kirby Cyr.

District of Columbia

Council for Christian Colleges and Universities, 321 8th St. N.E., Washington 20002. SAN 322-0524. Tel. 202-546-8713, fax 202-546-8913, e-mail council@cccu.org. *Pres.* Shirley V. Hoogstra.

District of Columbia Area Health Science Libraries (DCAHSL), P.O. Box 96920, Washington 20090. SAN 323-9918. Tel. 202-863-2518, fax 202-484-1595, e-mail mtalia ferro@aamc.org. *Pres.* Wanda Whitney.

FEDLINK/Federal Library and Information Network, c/o Federal Lib. and Info. Center Committee, 101 Independence Ave. SE, Washington 20540-4935. SAN 322-0761. Tel. 202-707-4800, fax 202-707-4818, e-mail flicc@loc.gov. *Mgr.* Joan Fitts.

Interlibrary Users Assn. (IUA), c/o Urban Institute Lib., Washington 20037. SAN 322-1628. Tel. 202-261-5534, fax 202-223-3043. *Pres.* Nancy L. Minter.

Washington Theological Consortium, 487 Michigan Ave. N.E., Washington 20017-1585. SAN 322-0842. Tel. 202-832-2675, fax 202-526-0818, e-mail wtc@washtheo con.org. *Exec. Dir.* Larry Golemon.

Florida

Florida Library Information Network, R. A. Gray Bldg., Tallahassee 32399-0250. SAN 322-0869. Tel. 850-245-6600, fax 850-245-6744, e-mail library@dos.myflorida.com. *Bureau Chief* Cathy Moloney.

Northeast Florida Library Information Network (NEFLIN), 2233 Park Ave., Suite 402, Orange Park 32073. Tel. 904-278-5620, fax 904-278-5625, e-mail office@neflin.org. *Exec. Dir.* Brad Ward.

Panhandle Library Access Network (PLAN), Five Miracle Strip Loop, Suite 8, Panama City Beach 32407-3850. SAN 370-047X. Tel. 850-233-9051, fax 850-235-2286. *Exec. Dir.* Charles Mayberry.

SEFLIN/Southeast Florida Library Information Network, Inc, Wimberly Lib., Office 452, 777 Glades Rd., Boca Raton 33431. SAN 370-0666. Tel. 561-208-0984, fax 561-208-0995. *Exec. Dir.* Jennifer Pratt.

Southwest Florida Library Network (SWFLN), 13120 Westlinks Terrace, Unit 3, Fort Myers 33913. Tel. 239-313-6338, fax 239-313-6329. *Exec. Dir.* Luly Castro.

Tampa Bay Library Consortium, Inc., 1202 Tech Blvd., Suite 202, Tampa 33619. SAN 322-371X. Tel. 813-740-3963; 813-622-8252, fax 813-628-4425. *Exec. Dir.* Charlie Parker.

Tampa Bay Medical Library Network: Medical Lib., Department 7660, 501 Sixth Ave. South, Saint Petersburg 33701. SAN 322-0885. Tel. 727-767-8557. *Chair* Joshua Brown.

Georgia

Association of Southeastern Research Libraries (ASERL), c/o Robert W. Woodruff Library, 540 Asbury Circle, Ste. 316, Atlanta 30322-1006. SAN 322-1555. Tel. 404-727-0137. *Exec. Dir.* John Burger.

Atlanta Health Science Libraries Consortium, Fran Golding Medical Lib. at Scottish Rite, 1001 Johnson Ferry Rd. NE, Atlanta 30342-1600. Tel. 404-785-2157, fax 404-785-2155. *Pres.* Kate Daniels.

Atlanta Regional Council for Higher Education (ARCHE), 133 Peachtree St., Suite 4925, Atlanta 30303. SAN 322-0990. Tel. 404-651-2668, fax 404-880-9816, e-mail arche@atlantahighered.org. *Pres.* Elizabeth Kiss.

Consortium of Southern Biomedical Libraries (CONBLS), Robert B. Greenblatt, MD Library, 1439 Laney Walker Blvd., Augusta, 30912. SAN 370-7717. Tel. 843-792-8839. *Chair* Brenda Seago.

Georgia Online Database (GOLD), c/o Georgia Public Lib. Service, 1800 Century Pl.

NE, Ste. 150, Atlanta 30345-4304. SAN 322-094X. Tel. 404-235-7200, fax 404-235-7201. *Project Mgr.* Elaine Hardy.

LYRASIS, 1438 W. Peachtree St. N.W., Suite 200, Atlanta 30309-2955. SAN 322-0974. Tel. 404-892-0943, fax 404-892-7879. *CEO* Robert Miller.

Metro Atlanta Library Assn. (MALA), P.O. Box 14948, Atlanta 30324. SAN 378-2549. https://www.facebook.com/MAtlantaLA/info/?tab=overview.

Hawaii

Hawaii Library Consortium (HLC), http://web.hawaii.edu/hlc. *Pres.* Jerome Nicholas.

Hawaii-Pacific Chapter, Medical Library Assn. (HPC-MLA), Health Sciences Lib., Honolulu 96813. SAN 371-3946. Tel. 808-692-0810, fax 808-692-1244. *Chair* Mabel Trafford.

Idaho

Canyon Owyhee Library Group (COLG), 203 E. Owyhee Ave., Homedale 83628. Tel. 208-337-4613, fax 208-337-4933. *Pres.* Pam Herman.

Cooperative Information Network (CIN), 8385 N. Government Way, Hayden 83835-9280. SAN 323-7656. Tel. 208-772-5612, fax 208-772-2498.

LYNX Consortium, c/o Boise Public Lib., 715 S. Capitol Ave., Boise 83702-7195. SAN 375-0086. Tel. 208-384-4238, fax 208-384-4025. *Dir.* Kevin Booe.

Illinois

Areawide Hospital Library Consortium of Southwestern Illinois (AHLC), c/o St. Elizabeth Hospital Health Sciences Lib., 211 S. Third St., Belleville 62222. SAN 322-1016. Tel. 618-234-2120 ext. 2011, fax 618-222-4614.

Assn. of Chicago Theological Schools (ACTS), Univ. of St. Mary of the Lake, Mundelein 60060-1174. SAN 370-0658. Tel. 847-566-6401. *Chair* Thomas Baima.

Center for Research Libraries, 6050 S. Kenwood, Chicago 60637-2804. SAN 322-1032. Tel. 773-955-4545, fax 773-955-4339. *Pres.* Bernard F. Reilly.

Chicago Area Museum Libraries (CAML), c/o Lib., Field Museum, Chicago 60605-2496. SAN 371-392X. Tel. 312-665-7970, fax 312-665-7893. *Museum Libn.* Christine Giannoni.

Committee on Institutional Cooperation, 1819 S. Neil St., Suite D, Champaign 61820-7271. Tel. 217-333-8475, fax 217-244-7127, e-mail cic@staff.cic.net. *Dir.* Barbara Mcfadden Allen.

Consortium of Academic and Research Libraries in Illinois (CARLI), 100 Trade Center Drive, Suite 303, Champaign 61820. SAN 322-3736. Tel. 217-244-4664, fax 217-244-7596, e-mail support@carli.illinois.edu. *Exec. Dir.* Susan Singleton.

Council of Directors of State University Libraries in Illinois (CODSULI), Southern Illinois Univ. School of Medicine Lib., 801 N. Rutledge, Springfield 62702-4910. SAN 322-1083. Tel. 217-545-0994, fax 217-545-0988.

East Central Illinois Consortium, Booth Lib., Eastern Illinois Univ., 600 Lincoln Ave., Charleston 61920. SAN 322-1040. Tel. 217-581-7549, fax 217-581-7534. *Mgr.* Stacey Knight-Davis.

Fox Valley Health Science Library Consortium, c/o Delnor Community Hospital Library, 300 Randall Rd., Geneva 60134. SAN 329-3831. Tel. 630-208-4299.

Heart of Illinois Library Consortium, 511 N.E. Greenleaf, Peoria 61603. SAN 322-1113. *Chair* Leslie Menz.

Illinois Library and Information Network (ILLINET), c/o Illinois State Lib., 300 S. Second St., Springfield 62701-1796. SAN 322-1148. Tel. 217-782-2994, fax 217-785-4326. *Dir.* Anne Craig.

LIBRAS, Inc., North Park Univ., 3225 W. Foster Ave., Chicago 60625-4895. SAN 322-1172. Tel. 773-244-5584, fax 773-244-4891. *Pres.* Rebecca Miller.

Metropolitan Consortium of Chicago, Chicago School of Professional Psychology, 325 N. Wells St., Chicago 60610. SAN 322-1180. Tel. 312-329-6630, fax 312-644-6075. *Coord.* Margaret White.

National Network of Libraries of Medicine–Greater Midwest Region (NN/LM-GMR), c/o Lib. of Health Sciences, Univ. of Illinois at Chicago, 1750 W. Polk St., M/C 763, Chicago 60612-4330. SAN 322-1202. Tel. 312-

996-2464, fax 312-996-2226. *Dir.* Kathryn Carpenter.

Network of Illinois Learning Resources in Community Colleges (NILRC), P.O. Box 120, Blanchardville 53516-0120. Tel. 608-523-4094, fax 608-523-4072. *Business Mgr.* Lisa Sikora.

System Wide Automated Network (SWAN), 800 Quail Ridge Dr., Westmont 60559. Tel. 844-792-6542. Exec. *Dir.* Aaron Skog.

Indiana

Central Indiana Health Science Libraries Consortium, Indiana Univ. School of Medicine Lib., Indianapolis 46202. SAN 322-1245. Tel. 317-274-8358, fax 317-274-4056. *Officer* Elaine Skopelja.

Consortium of College and University Media Centers (CCUMC), Indiana Univ., 601 E Kirkwood Ave., Bloomington 47405-1223. SAN 322-1091. Tel. 812-855-6049, fax 812-855-2103, e-mail ccumc @ccumc.org. *Exec. Dir.* Aileen Scales.

Evansville Area Library Consortium, 3700 Washington Ave., Evansville 47750. SAN 322-1261. Tel. 812-485-4151, fax 812-485-7564. *Coord.* Jane Saltzman.

Evergreen Indiana Consortium, Indiana State Lib., 315 W. Ohio St., Indianapolis 46202. Tel. 317-234-6624, fax 317-232-0002. *Coord.* Anna Goben.

Iowa

Consortium of User Libraries (CUL), Lib. for the Blind and Physically Handicapped, 524 Fourth St., Des Moines 50309-2364. SAN 305-344X. Tel. 515-281-1333, fax 515-281-1378; 515-281-1263. *Dir.* Randall E. Landgrebe.

Dubuque (Iowa) Area Library Information Consortium, c/o Burton Payne Lib., N.E. Iowa Community College, Peosta 52068. Tel. 563-556-5110 ext. 269, fax 563-557-0340. *Coord.* Deb Seiffert.

Iowa Private Academic Library Consortium (IPAL), http://www.ipalgroup.org. SAN 329-5311. Tel. 712-749-2127, 712-749-2203, fax 712-749-2059, e-mail library@ bvu.edu. *Chair* Paul Waelchli.

Polk County Biomedical Consortium, c/o Broadlawns Medical Center Lib., Des Moines 50314. SAN 322-1431. Tel. 515-

282-2394, fax 515-282-5634. *Treas.* Elaine Hughes.

Quad City Area Biomedical Consortium, Great River Medical Center Lib., West Burlington 52655. SAN 322-435X. Tel. 319-768-4075, fax 319-768-4080. *Coord.* Sarah Goff.

Sioux City Library Cooperative (SCLC), c/o Sioux City Public Lib., Sioux City 51101-1203. SAN 329-4722. Tel. 712-255-2933 ext. 255, fax 712-279-6432. *Chair* Betsy Thompson.

State of Iowa Libraries Online (SILO), State Lib. of Iowa, Des Moines 50319. SAN 322-1415. Tel. 515-281-4105, fax 515-281-6191. *State Libn.* Michael Scott.

Kansas

Associated Colleges of Central Kansas (ACCK), 210 S. Main St., McPherson 67460. SAN 322-1474. Tel. 620-241-5150, fax 620-241-5153. *Dir.* Cindy Sutton.

Dodge City Library Consortium, c/o Comanche Intermediate Center, 1601 First Ave., Dodge City 67801. SAN 322-4368. Tel. 620-227-1609, fax 620-227-4862.

State Library of Kansas/Statewide Resource Sharing Div., 300 S.W. 10 Ave., Room 343 N., Topeka 66612-1593. SAN 329-5621. Tel. 785-296-3875, fax 785-368-7291. *Dir.* Jeff Hixon.

Kentucky

Assn. of Independent Kentucky Colleges and Universities (AIKCU), 484 Chenault Rd., Frankfort 40601. SAN 322-1490. Tel. 502-695-5007, fax 502-695-5057. *Pres.* Gary S. Cox.

Eastern Kentucky Health Science Information Network (EKHSIN), c/o Camden-Carroll Lib., Morehead 40351. SAN 370-0631. Tel. 606-783-6860, fax 606-784-2178. *Lib. Dir.* Tammy Jenkins.

Kentuckiana Metroversity, Inc., 200 W. Broadway, Suite 800, Louisville 40202. SAN 322-1504. Tel. 502-897-3374, fax 502-895-1647.

Kentucky Medical Library Assn., VA Medical Center, Lib. Serices 142D, Louisville 40206-1499. SAN 370-0623. Tel. 502-287-6240, fax 502-287-6134. *Head Libn.* Gene M. Haynes.

Theological Education Assn. of Mid America (TEAM-A), Southern Baptist Theological

Seminary, Louisville 40280. SAN 377-5038. Tel. 502-897-4807, fax 502-897-4600. *Dir., Info. Resources* Ken Boyd.

Louisiana

Central Louisiana Medical Center Library Consortium (CLMLC), 2495 Shreveport Hwy., 142D, Alexandria 71306. Tel. 318-619-9102, fax 318-619-9144, e-mail clmlc 8784@yahoo.com. *Coord.* Miriam J. Brown.

Health Sciences Library Assn. of Louisiana (HSLAL), 1501 Kings Hwy., Shreveport 71103. SAN 375-0035. Tel. 318-675-5679. *Pres.* Deidra Woodson.

Loan SHARK, State Lib. of Louisiana, Baton Rouge 70802. SAN 371-6880. Tel. 225-342-4920, 342-4918, fax 225-219-4725. *Head, Access Services* Kytara A. Gaudin.

LOUIS/Louisiana Library Network, Info. Technology Services, Baton Rouge 70803. Tel. 225-578-3705, e-mail louisfb@lsu.edu. *Exec. Dir.* Sara Zimmerman.

New Orleans Educational Telecommunications Consortium, 6400 Press Dr., New Orleans 70126. SAN 329-5214. Tel. 504-524-0350, e-mail noetc@noetc.org.

Southeastern Chapter of the American Assn. of Law Libraries (SEAALL), c/o Supreme Court of Louisiana, New Orleans 70130-2104. Tel. 504-310-2405, fax 504-310-2419. *Pres.* Michelle Cosby.

Maine

Health Science Library Information Consortium (HSLIC), 211 Marginal Way, No 245, Portland 04101. SAN 322-1601. Tel. 207-795-2561, fax 207-795-2569. *Chair* Kathy Brunjes.

Maryland

Maryland Interlibrary Loan Organization (MILO), c/o Enoch Pratt Free Lib., Baltimore 21201-4484. SAN 343-8600. Tel. 410-396-5498, fax 410-396-5837, e-mail milo@prattlibrary.org. *Mgr.* Emma E. Beaven.

National Network of Libraries of Medicine (NN/LM), National Lib. of Medicine, Bethesda 20894. SAN 373-0905. Tel. 301-496-4777, fax 301-480-1467. *Dir.* Judy Consales.

National Network of Libraries of Medicine–Southeastern Atlantic Region (NN/LM-SEA), Univ. of Maryland Health Sciences and Human Services Lib., 601 W. Lombard S., Baltimore 21201-1512. SAN 322-1644. Tel. 410-706-2855, fax 410-706-0099, e-mail hshsl-nlmsea@hshsl.umaryland.edu. *Dir.* Mary Tooey.

U.S. National Library of Medicine (NLM), 8600 Rockville Pike, Bethesda 20894. SAN 322-1652. Tel. 301-594-5983, fax 301-402-1384, e-mail custserv@nlm.nih.gov. *Coord.* Martha Fishel.

Washington Research Library Consortium (WRLC), 901 Commerce Drive, Upper Marlboro 20774. SAN 373-0883. Tel. 301-390-2000, fax 301-390-2020. *Exec. Dir.* Mark Jacobs.

Massachusetts

Boston Biomedical Library Consortium (BBLC), c/o Dana Farber Cancer Trust, 44 Binney St., Boston 02115. SAN 322-1725. *Pres.* Christine Fleuried.

Boston Library Consortium, Inc., 10 Milk St., Suite 354, Boston 02108. SAN 322-1733. Tel. 617-262-0380, fax 617-262-0163, e-mail admin@blc.org. *Exec. Dir.* Susan Stearns.

Cape Libraries Automated Materials Sharing Network (CLAMS), 270 Communication Way, Unit 4E, Hyannis 02601. SAN 370-579X. Tel. 508-790-4399, fax 508-771-4533. *Exec. Dir.* Gayle Simundza.

Central and Western Massachusetts Automated Resource Sharing (C/W MARS), 67 Millbrook St., Suite 201, Worcester 01606. SAN 322-3973. Tel. 508-755-3323 ext. 30, fax 508-755-3721. *Exec. Dir.* Timothy Spindler.

Cooperating Libraries of Greater Springfield (CLGS), Springfield Technical Community College, Springfield 01102. SAN 322-1768. Tel. 413-755-4565, fax 413-755-6315, e-mail lcoakley@stcc.edu. *Coord.* Lynn Coakley.

Fenway Libraries Online, Inc. (FLO), c/o Wentworth Institute of Technology, 550 Huntington Ave., Boston 02115. SAN 373-9112. Tel. 617-442-2384, fax 617-442-1519. *Exec. Dir.* Kevin Kidd.

Massachusetts Health Sciences Libraries Network (MAHSLIN), Lamar Soutter Lib.,

Univ. of Massachusetts Medical School, Worcester 01655. SAN 372-8293. http://nahsl.libguides.com/mahslin/home. *Pres.* Dan McCloskey.

Merrimack Valley Library Consortium, 4 High St., North Andover 01845. SAN 322-4384. Tel. 978-557-1050, fax 978-557-8101, e-mail netmail@mvlc.org. *Exec. Dir.* Eric C. Graham.

Minuteman Library Network, 10 Strathmore Rd., Natick 01760-2419. SAN 322-4252. Tel. 508-655-8008, fax 508-655-1507. *Exec. Dir.* Susan McAlister.

National Network of Libraries of Medicine–New England Region (NN/LM-NER), Univ. of Massachusetts Medical School, 55 Lake Ave. N., Room S4-241, Worcester 01655. SAN 372-5448. Tel. 800-338-7657, fax 508-856-5977. *Dir.* Elaine Martin.

North Atlantic Health Sciences Libraries, Inc. (NAHSL), Hirsh Health Sciences Lib., 145 Harrison Ave., Boston 02111. SAN 371-0599. Tel. 617-636-3638, fax 617-636-3805. *Chair* Debra Berlanstein.

North of Boston Library Exchange, Inc. (NOBLE), 26 Cherry Hill Drive, Danvers 01923. SAN 322-4023. Tel. 978-777-8844, fax 978-750-8472. *Exec. Dir.* Ronald A. Gagnon.

Northeast Consortium of Colleges and Universities in Massachusetts (NECCUM), Merrimack College, 315 Turnpike St., North Andover 01845. SAN 371-0602. Tel. 978-556-3400, fax 978-556-3738. *Pres.* Richard Santagati.

Northeastern Consortium for Health Information (NECHI), Lowell General Hospital Health Science Lib., 295 Varnum Ave., Lowell 01854. SAN 322-1857. Tel. 978-937-6247, fax 978-937-6855. *Libn.* Donna Beales.

SAILS Library Network, 10 Riverside Dr., Suite 102, Lakeville 02347. SAN 378-0058. Tel. 508-946-8600, fax 508-946-8605, e-mail support@sailsinc.org. *Pres.* Melissa Campbell.

Western Massachusetts Health Information Consortium, Baystate Medical Center Health Sciences Lib., Springfield 01199. SAN 329-4579. Tel. 413-794-1865, fax 413-794-1974. *Pres.* Susan La Forter.

Michigan

Detroit Area Consortium of Catholic Colleges, c/o Wayne State University, Detroit 48202. SAN 329-482X. Tel. 313-883-8500, fax 313-883-8594. *Dir.* Chris Spilker.

Detroit Area Library Network (DALNET), 6th Floor SEL, 5048 Gullen Mall, Detroit 48202. Tel. 313-577-6789, fax 313-577-1231, info@dalnet.org. *Exec. Dir.* Steven K. Bowers.

Lakeland Library Cooperative, 4138 Three Mile Rd. N.W., Grand Rapids 49534-1134. SAN 308-132X. Tel. 616-559-5253, fax 616-559-4329. *Dir.* Sandra Wilson.

The Library Network (TLN), 41365 Vincenti Ct., Novi 48375. SAN 370-596X. Tel. 248-536-3100, fax 248-536-3099. *Dir.* James Pletz.

Michigan Health Sciences Libraries Assn. (MHSLA), 1407 Rensen St., Suite 4, Lansing 48910. SAN 323-987X. Tel. 517-394-2774, fax 517-394-2675. *Pres.* Jennifer Bowen.

Mideastern Michigan Library Cooperative, 503 S. Saginaw St., Suite 839, Flint 48502. SAN 346-5187. Tel. 810-232-7119, fax 810-232-6639. *Dir.* Denise Hooks.

Mid-Michigan Library League, 210 1/2 N Mitchell, Cadillac 49601-1835. SAN 307-9325. Tel. 231-775-3037, fax 231-775-1749. *Dir.* Sheryl L. Mase.

PALnet, 1050 W Bristol Rd., Flint 48507. Tel. 810-766-4070, fax 810-766-2041. *Dir.* Vince Molosky.

Southeastern Michigan League of Libraries (SEMLOL), Lawrence Technological Univ., 21000 W. Ten Mile Rd., Southfield 48075. SAN 322-4481. Tel. 810-766-4070, fax 248-204-3005. *Treas.* Gary Cocozzoli.

Southwest Michigan Library Cooperative, Willard Public Library, 305 Oak St., Battle Creek, 49017. SAN 308-2156. Tel. 269-657-3800, e-mail rhulsey@willard.lib.mi.us. *Dir.* John Mohney.

Suburban Library Cooperative (SLC), 44750 Delco Blvd., Sterling Heights 48313. SAN 373-9082. Tel. 586-685-5750, fax 586-685-5750. *Dir.* Tammy Turgeon.

Upper Peninsula of Michigan Health Science Library Consortium, c/o Marquette Health System Hospital, 580 W. College Ave., Marquette 49855. SAN 329-4803. Tel. 906-225-

3429, fax 906-225-3524. *Lib. Mgr.* Janis Lubenow.

Upper Peninsula Region of Library Cooperation, Inc., 1615 Presque Isle Ave., Marquette 49855. SAN 329-5540. Tel. 906-228-7697, fax 906-228-5627. *Treas.* Suzanne Dees.

Valley Library Consortium, 3210 Davenport Ave., Saginaw 48602-3495. Tel. 989-497-0925, fax 989-497-0918. *Exec. Dir.* Randall Martin.

Minnesota

Capital Area Library Consortium (CALCO), c/o Minnesota Dept. of Transportation, Lib. MS155, 395 John Ireland Blvd., Saint Paul 55155. SAN 374-6127. Tel. 651-296-5272, fax 651-297-2354. *Libn.* Shirley Sherkow.

Central Minnesota Libraries Exchange (CMLE), Miller Center, Room 130-D, Saint Cloud 56301-4498. SAN 322-3779. Tel. 320-308-2950, fax 320-654-5131, e-mail cmle@stcloudstate.edu. *Dir.* Patricia A. Post.

Cooperating Libraries in Consortium (CLIC), 1619 Dayton Ave., Suite 204, Saint Paul 55104. SAN 322-1970. Tel. 651-644-3878, fax 651-644-6258. *Exec. Dir.* Ruth Dukelow.

Metronet, 1619 Dayton Ave., Suite 314, Saint Paul 55104. SAN 322-1989. Tel. 651-646-0475, fax 651-649-3169, e-mail information @metrolibraries.net. *Exec. Dir.* Ann Walker Smalley.

Metropolitan Library Service Agency (MEL-SA), 1619 Dayton Ave., No. 314, Saint Paul 55104-6206. SAN 371-5124. Tel. 651-645-5731, fax 651-649-3169, e-mail melsa@melsa.org. *Exec. Dir.* Ken Behringer.

MINITEX Library Information Network, 15 Andersen Lib., Univ. of Minnesota–Twin Cities, 222 21st Ave. S, Minneapolis 55455-0439. SAN 322-1997. Tel. 612-624-4002, fax 612-624-4508. *Dir.* Valerie Horton.

Minnesota Library Information Network (MnLINK), Univ. of Minnesota–Twin Cities, Minneapolis 55455-0439. Tel. 800-462-5348, fax 612-624-4508. *Info. Specialist* Nick Banitt.

Minnesota Theological Library Assn. (MTLA), Luther Seminary Lib., 2375 Como Ave., Saint Paul 55108. SAN 322-1962. Tel. 651-641-3447. *Exec. Dir.* Sandra Oslund.

Northern Lights Library Network, 104 7th Ave. S., Moorhead 56563. SAN 322-2004. Tel. 218-847-2825, fax 218-847-1461, e-mail nl-office@nlln.org. *Exec. Dir.* Kathy B. Enger.

Southeastern Libraries Cooperating (SELCO), 2600 19th St. N.W., Rochester 55901-0767. SAN 308-7417. Tel. 507-288-5513, fax 507-288-8697. *Exec. Dir.* Ann Hutton.

Southwest Area Multicounty Multitype Interlibrary Exchange (SAMMIE), Southwest Minnesota State University Library, 1501 State St., Marshall 56258. SAN 322-2039. Tel. 507-532-9013, fax 507-532-2039, e-mail info@sammie.org. *Exec. Dir.* Shelly Grace.

Twin Cities Biomedical Consortium (TCBC), c/o Fairview Univ. Medical Center, 2450 Riverside Ave., Minneapolis 55455. SAN 322-2055. Tel. 612-273-6595, fax 612-273-2675. *Mgr.* Colleen Olsen.

Mississippi

Central Mississippi Library Council (CMLC), c/o Millsaps College Lib., 1701 N. State St., Jackson 39210. SAN 372-8250. Tel. 601-974-1070, fax 601-974-1082. *Chair* Stephen Parks.

Mississippi Electronic Libraries Online (MELO), Mississippi State Board for Community and Junior Colleges, Jackson 39211. Tel. 601-432-6518, fax 601-432-6363, e-mail melo@colin.edu. *Dir.* Audra Kimball.

Missouri

Greater Western Library Alliance (GWLA), 5109 Cherry St., Kansas City 64110. Tel. 816-926-8765, fax 816-926-8790. *Exec. Dir.* Joni Blake.

Health Sciences Library Network of Kansas City (HSLNKC), Univ. of Missouri–Kansas City Health Sciences Lib., 2411 Holmes St., Kansas City 64108-2792. SAN 322-2098. Tel. 816-235-1880, fax 816-235-6570. *Pres.* Cindi Kerns.

Kansas City Library Service Program (KC-LSP), 14 W. 10 St., Kansas City 64105. Tel. 816-701-3520, fax 816-701-3401, e-mail kc-lspsupport@kclibrary.org. *Library Systems and Service Program Mgr.* Melissa Carle.

Mid-America Law Library Consortium (MALLCO), 100 North Tucker Blvd., St. Louis 63101. Tel. 314-977-3449, fax 314-977-3966, e-mail mallcoexecutivedirector@gmail.com. *Exec. Dir.* Corie Dugas.

Mid-America Library Alliance/Kansas City Metropolitan Library and Information Network, 15624 E. 24 Hwy., Independence 64050. SAN 322-2101. Tel. 816-521-7257, fax 816-461-0966. *Exec. Dir.* Susan Burton.

Saint Louis Regional Library Network, 1190 Meramec Station Rd., Ballwin 63021. SAN 322-2209. Tel. 800-843-8482, fax 636-529-1396, e-mail slrln@amigos.org. *Pres.* Heidi Vix.

Nebraska

ICON Library Consortium, McGoogan Lib. of Medicine, Univ. of Nebraska, Omaha 68198-6705. Tel. 402-559-7099, fax 402-559-5498. *Exec. Secy.* Mary Helms.

Nevada

Desert States Law Library Consortium, Wiener-Rogers Law Lib., William S. Boyd School of Law, 4505 Maryland Pkwy., Las Vegas 89154-1080. Tel. 702-895-2400, fax 702-895-2416. *Collection Development Libn.* Matthew Wright.

Information Nevada, Interlibrary Loan Dept., Nevada State Lib. and Archives, 100 N. Stewart St., Carson City 89701-4285. SAN 322-2276. Tel. 775-684-3360, fax 775-684-3330. *Asst. Admin., Lib. and Development Services* Karen Starr.

New Hampshire

GMILCS, Inc., 31 Mount Saint Mary's Way, Hooksett 03106. Tel. 603-485-4286, fax 603-485-4246, e-mail helpdesk@gmilcs.org. *Systems Libn.* Kevin French.

Health Sciences Libraries of New Hampshire and Vermont, Breene Memorial Lib., 36 Clinton St., New Hampshire Hospital, Concord 03246. SAN 371-6864. Tel. 603-527-2837, fax 603-527-7197. *Admin. Coord.* Anne Conner.

Librarians of the Upper Valley Coop. (LUV Coop), c/o Hanover Town Lib., 130 Etna Rd., Etna 03750. SAN 371-6856. Tel. 603-643-3116. *Coord.* Barbara Prince.

Merri-Hill-Rock Library Cooperative, c/o Kimball Lib., Three Academy Ave., Atkinson 03811-2299. SAN 329-5338. Tel. 603-362-5234, fax 603-362-4791. *Dir.* Jon Godfrey.

New Hampshire College and University Council, 3 Barrell Court, Suite 100, Concord 03301-8543. SAN 322-2322. Tel. 603-225-4199, fax 603-225-8108. *Pres.* Thomas R. Horgan.

Nubanusit Library Cooperative, c/o Peterborough Town Lib., Two Condord St., Peterborough 03458. SAN 322-4600. Tel. 603-924-8040, fax 603-924-8041. *Exec. Dir.* Leslie MacGregor.

New Jersey

Basic Health Sciences Library Network (BHSL), Overlook Hospital Health Science Lib., 99 Beauvoir Ave., Summit 07902. SAN 371-4888. Tel. 908-522-2886, fax 908-522-2274. *Coord.* Pat Regenberg.

Bergen Passaic Health Sciences Library Consortium, c/o Health Sciences Lib., Englewood Hospital and Medical Center, 350 Engle St., Englewood 07631. SAN 371-0904. Tel. 201-894-3069, fax 201-894-9049. *Coord.* Lia Sabbagh.

Burlington Libraries Information Consortium (BLINC), 5 Pioneer Blvd., Westampton 08060. Tel. 609-267-9660, fax 609-267-4091, e-mail hq@bcls.lib.nj.us. *Dir.* Ranjna Das.

Libraries of Middlesex Automation Consortium (LMxAC), 1030 Saint Georges Ave., Suite 203, Avenel 07001. SAN 329-448X. Tel. 732-750-2525, fax 732-750-9392. *Exec. Dir.* Eileen Palmer.

LibraryLinkNJ, New Jersey Library Cooperative, 44 Stelton Rd., Suite 330, Piscataway 08854. SAN 371-5116. Tel. 732-752-7720, fax 732-752-7785. *Exec. Dir.* Kathy Schalk-Greene.

Morris Automated Information Network (MAIN), c/o Morris County Lib., 30 East Hanover Ave., Whippany 07981. SAN 322-4058. Tel. 973-631-5353, fax 973-631-5366. *Exec. Dir.* Phillip Berg.

Morris-Union Federation, 214 Main St., Chatham 07928. SAN 310-2629. Tel. 973-635-0603, fax 973-635-7827. *Exec. Dir.* Karen Brodsky.

New Jersey Health Sciences Library Network (NJHSN), Overlook Hospital Lib., 99 Beauvoir Ave., Summit 07902. SAN 371-4829. Tel. 908-522-2886, fax 908-522-2274. *Lib. Mgr.* Patricia Regenberg.

New Jersey Library Network, Lib. Development Bureau, 185 W. State St., Trenton 08608. SAN 372-8161. Tel. 609-278-2640 ext. 152, fax 609-278-2650. *Adm.* Ruth Pallante.

Virtual Academic Library Environment (VALE), William Paterson Univ. Lib., 300 Pompton Rd., Wayne 07470-2103. Tel. 973-720-3179, fax 973-720-3171. *Coord.* Judy Avrin.

New Mexico

Estacado Library Information Network (ELIN), 509 N. Shipp, Hobbs 88240. Tel. 505-397-9328, fax 505-397-1508.

New Mexico Consortium of Academic Libraries, Dean's Office, Albuquerque 87131-0001. SAN 371-6872. *Pres.* Barbara Lovato.

New Mexico Consortium of Biomedical and Hospital Libraries, c/o Presbyterian Hospital, Robert Shafer Library, 1100 Central Ave., S.E., Santa Fe 87505. SAN 322-449X. Tel. 505-820-5218, fax 505-989-6478. *Chair* Albert Robinson.

New York

Academic Libraries of Brooklyn, Long Island Univ. Lib. LLC 517, One University Plaza, Brooklyn 11201. SAN 322-2411. Tel. 718-488-1081, fax 718-780-4057. *Dir.* Ingrid Wang.

Associated Colleges of the Saint Lawrence Valley, SUNY Potsdam, 288 Van Housen Extension, Potsdam 13676-2299. SAN 322-242X. Tel. 315-267-3331, fax 315-267-2389. *Admin. Coord.* Ben Dixon.

Brooklyn-Queens-Staten Island-Manhattan-Bronx Health Sciences Librarians (BQSIMB), 150 55th St., Brooklyn 11220. Tel. 718-630-7200, fax 718-630-8918. *Pres.* Sheryl Ramer Gesoff.

Capital District Library Council (CDLC), 28 Essex St., Albany 12206. SAN 322-2446. Tel. 518-438-2500, fax 518-438-2872. *Exec. Dir.* Kathleen Gundrum.

Central New York Library Resources Council (CLRC), 6493 Ridings Rd., Syracuse 13206-1195. SAN 322-2454. Tel. 315-446-5446, fax 315-446-5590. *Exec. Dir.* Debby Emerson.

ConnectNY, Rochester Institute of Technology, Rochester 14623. Tel. 585-475-2050. *Exec. Dir.* Pamela Jones.

Library Assn. of Rockland County (LARC), P.O. Box 917, New City 10956-0917. Tel. 845-359-3877. *Pres.* Carol Connell Cannon.

Library Consortium of Health Institutions in Buffalo (LCHIB), Abbott Hall, SUNY at Buffalo, 3435 Main St., Buffalo 14214. SAN 329-367X. Tel. 716-829-3900 ext. 143, fax 716-829-2211, e-mail hubnet@buffalo.edu; ulb-lchib@buffalo.edu. *Exec. Dir.* Martin E. Mutka.

Long Island Library Resources Council (LILRC), 627 N. Sunrise Service Rd., Bellport 11713. SAN 322-2489. Tel. 631-675-1570. *Dir.* Herbert Biblo.

Medical and Scientific Libraries of Long Island (MEDLI), c/o Palmer School of Lib. and Info. Science, Brookville 11548. SAN 322-4309. Tel. 516-299-2866, fax 516-299-4168. *Pres.* Claire Joseph.

Metropolitan New York Library Council (METRO), 57 E. 11 St., 4th flr., New York 10003-4605. SAN 322-2500. Tel. 212-228-2320, fax 212-228-2598. *Exec. Dir.* Nate Hill.

New England Law Library Consortium (NELLCO), 80 New Scotland Ave., Albany 12208. SAN 322-4244. Tel. 518-694-3025, fax 518-694-3027. *Exec. Dir.* Tracy L. Thompson.

Northeast Foreign Law Libraries Cooperative Group, Columbia Univ. Lib., 435 W. 116 St., New York 10027. SAN 375-0000. Tel. 212-854-1411, fax 212-854-3295. *Coord.* Silke Sahl.

Northern New York Library Network, 6721 U.S. Hwy. 11, Potsdam 13676. SAN 322-2527. Tel. 315-265-1119, fax 315-265-1881, e-mail info@nnyln.org. *Exec. Dir.* John J. Hammond.

Rochester Regional Library Council, 390 Packetts Landing, Fairport 14450. SAN 322-2535. Tel. 585-223-7570, fax 585-223-7712, e-mail rrlc@rrlc.org. *Exec. Dir.* Kathleen M. Miller.

South Central Regional Library Council, Clinton Hall, Ithaca 14850. SAN 322-2543. Tel. 607-273-9106, fax 607-272-0740, e-mail scrlc@scrlc.org. *Exec. Dir.* Mary-Carol Lindbloom.

Southeastern New York Library Resources Council (SENYLRC), 21 S. Elting Corners Rd., Highland 12528-2805. SAN 322-2551. Tel. 845-883-9065, fax 845-883-9483. *Exec. Dir.* Tessa Killian.

SUNYConnect, Office of Lib. and Info. Services, Albany 12246. Tel. 518-443-5577, fax 518-443-5358. *Asst. Provost for Lib. and Info. Services* Carey Hatch.

United Nations System Electronic Information Acquisitions Consortium (UNSEIAC), c/o United Nations Lib., New York 10017. SAN 377-855X. Tel. 212-963-3000, fax 212-963-2608, e-mail unseiac@un.org. *Coord.* Amy Herridge.

Western New York Library Resources Council, 4950 Genesee St., Buffalo 14225. SAN 322-2578. Tel. 716-633-0705, fax 716-633-1736. *Exec. Dir.* Sheryl Knab.

North Carolina

AHEC Digital Library, http://library.ncahec.net. *Dir.* Diana McDuffee.

North Carolina Community College System, 200 W. Jones St., Raleigh 27603-1379. SAN 322-2594. Tel. 919-807-7100, fax 919-807-7175; 919-807-7164. *Assoc. V.P. for Learning Technology Systems* Bill Randall.

Triangle Research Libraries Network, Wilson Lib., Chapel Hill 27514-8890. SAN 329-5362. Tel. 919-962-8022, fax 919-962-4452. *Interim Dir.* Lisa Croucher.

Western North Carolina Library Network (WNCLN), c/o Ramsey Lib., 1 University Heights, Asheville 28804. Tel. 828-668-2368. *Network Libn.* Ben Shirley.

North Dakota

Central Dakota Library Network, Morton Mandan Public Lib., Mandan 58554-3149. SAN 373-1391. Tel. 701-667-5365, e-mail mortonmandanlibrary@cdln.info. *Dir.* Kelly Steckler.

Ohio

Assn. of Christian Librarians (ACL), P.O. Box 4, Cedarville 45314. Tel. 937-766-2255, fax 937-766-5499, e-mail info@acl.org. *Pres.* Frank Quinn.

Central Ohio Hospital Library Consortium, 127 S. Davis Ave., Columbus 43222. SAN 371-084X. Tel. 614-234-5214, fax 614-234-1257, e-mail library@mchs.com. *Dir.* Stevo Roksandic.

Christian Library Consortium (CLC), c/o ACL, Cedarville 45314. Tel. 937-766-2255, fax 937-766-5499, e-mail info@acl.org. *Coord.* Beth Purtee.

Consortium of Popular Culture Collections in the Midwest (CPCCM), c/o Popular Culture Lib., Bowling Green 43403-0600. SAN 370-5811. Tel. 419-372-2450, fax 419-372-7996. *Head Libn.* Nancy Down.

Five Colleges of Ohio, 102 Allen House, Gambier 43022. Tel. 740-427-5377, fax 740-427-5390, e-mail ohiofive@gmail.com. *Exec. Dir.* Susan Palmer.

Northeast Ohio Regional Library System (NEO-RLS), 1580 Georgetown Rd., Hudson 44236. SAN 322-2713. Tel. 330-655-0531, fax 330-655-0568. *Exec. Dir.* Catherine Hakala-Ausperk.

Northwest Regional Library System (NORWELD), 181½ S. Main St., Bowling Green 43402. SAN 322-273X. Tel. 419-352-2903, fax 419-353-8310. *Exec. Dir.* Arline V. Radden.

OCLC Online Computer Library Center, Inc., 6565 Kilgour Place, Dublin 43017-3395. SAN 322-2748. Tel. 614-764-6000, fax 614-718-1017, e-mail oclc@oclc.org. *Pres./CEO* Skip Pritchard.

Ohio Health Sciences Library Assn. (OHSLA), Medical Lib., South Pointe Hospital, Warrensville Heights 44122. Tel. 216-491-7454, fax 216-491-7650. *Pres.* Mary Pat Harnegie.

Ohio Library and Information Network (OhioLINK), 35 E. Chestnut St., 8th fl., Columbus 43215-2541. SAN 374-8014. Tel. 614-485-6722, fax 614-228-1807, email info@ohiolink.edu. *Exec. Dir.* Gwen Evans.

Ohio Network of American History Research Centers, Ohio Historical Society Archives-Lib., Columbus 43211-2497. SAN 323-9624. Tel. 614-297-2510, fax 614-297-

2546, e-mail reference@ohiohistory.org. Exec. Dir. Jackie Barton.

Ohio Public Library Information Network (OPLIN), 2323 W. 5 Ave., Suite 130, Columbus 43204. Tel. 614-728-5252, fax 614-728-5256, e-mail support@oplin.org. *Exec. Dir.* Stephen Hedges.

OHIONET, 1500 W. Lane Ave., Columbus 43221-3975. SAN 322-2764. Tel. 614-486-2966, fax 614-486-1527. *Exec. Officer* Michael P. Butler.

Southeast Regional Library System (SERLS), 252 W. 13 St., Wellston 45692. SAN 322-2756. Tel. 740-384-2103, fax 740-384-2106, e-mail dirserls@oplin.org. *Dir.* Jay Burton.

SWON Libraries Consortium, 10250 Alliance Rd., Suite 225, Blue Ash 45242. SAN 322-2675. Tel. 513-751-4422, fax 513-751-0463, e-mail info@swonlibraries.org. *Exec. Dir.* Melanie A. Blau-McDonald.

Southwestern Ohio Council for Higher Education (SOCHE), Miami Valley Research Park, Dayton 45420-4015. SAN 322-2659. Tel. 937-258-8890, fax 937-258-8899, e-mail soche@soche.org. Exec. Dir. Sean Creighton.

State Assisted Academic Library Council of Kentucky (SAALCK), 12031 Southwick Lane, Cincinnati 45241. SAN 371-2222. Tel. 800-771-1972, e-mail saalck@saalck.org. *Exec. Dir.* Anne Abate.

Theological Consortium of Greater Columbus (TCGC), Trinity Lutheran Seminary, Columbus 43209-2334. Tel. 614-384-4646, fax 614-238-0263. *Lib. Systems Mgr.* Ray Olson.

Oklahoma

Oklahoma Health Sciences Library Assn. (OHSLA), HSC Bird Health Science Lib., Univ. of Oklahoma, Oklahoma City 73190. SAN 375-0051. Tel. 405-271-2285 ext. 48755, fax 405-271-3297. Exec. Dir. Joy Summers-Ables.

Oregon

Chemeketa Cooperative Regional Library Service, c/o Chemeketa Community College, Salem 97305-1453. SAN 322-2837. Tel. 503-399-5105, fax 503-399-7316, e-mail contact@cclrs.org. *Dir.* John Goodyear.

Library Information Network of Clackamas County (LINCC), 1810 Red Soils Court, #110, Oregon City 97045. SAN 322-2845. Tel. 503-723-4888, fax 503-794-8238. *Lib. System Analyst* Greg Williams.

Orbis Cascade Alliance, 2288 Oakmont Way, Eugene 97401. SAN 377-8096. Tel. 541-246-2470. *Exec. Dir.* Dana Bostrom.

Oregon Health Sciences Libraries Assn. (OHSLA), Oregon Health and Science Univ. Lib., Portland 97239-3098. SAN 371-2176. Tel. 503-494-3462, fax 503-494-3322, e-mail library@ohsu.edu. Pres. Jackie Wirz.

Southern Oregon Library Federation, c/o Klamath County Lib., Klamath Falls 97601. SAN 322-2861. Tel. 541-882-8894, fax 541-882-6166. *Dir.* Christy Davis.

Washington County Cooperative Library Services, 111 N.E. Lincoln St., MS No. 58, Hillsboro 97124-3036. SAN 322-287X. Tel. 503-846-3222, fax 503-846-3220. *Mgr.* Eva Calcagno.

Western Council of State Libraries, Inc., 250 Winter St. NE, Salem, OR 97301-3950. Tel. 503-378-5012. *Pres.* MaryKay Dahlgreen.

Pennsylvania

Berks County Library Assn. (BCLA), Reading Public Lib., Reading 19602. SAN 371-0866. Tel. 610-478-9035; 610-655-6350. *Pres.* Christie Himmelreich.

Central Pennsylvania Consortium (CPC), Dickinson College, Carlisle 17013. SAN 322-2896. Tel. 717-245-1984, fax 717-245-1807, e-mail cpc@dickinson.edu. *Pres.* Neil Weissman.

Central Pennsylvania Health Sciences Library Assn. (CPHSLA), Office for Research Protections, Pennsylvania State Univ., University Park 16802. SAN 375-5290. Fax 814-865-1775. *Pres.* Helen Houpt.

Eastern Mennonite Associated Libraries and Archives (EMALA), 2215 Millstream Rd., Lancaster 17602. SAN 372-8226. Tel. 717-393-9745, fax 717-393-8751. *Chair* John Weber.

Greater Philadelphia Law Library Assn. (GPLLA), PO Box 335, Philadelphia 19105. SAN 373-1375. *Pres.* Lori Strickler Corso.

HSLC/Access PA (Health Science Libraries Consortium), 3600 Market St., Suite 550, Philadelphia 19104-2646. SAN 323-9780.

Tel. 215-222-1532, fax 215-222-0416, e-mail support@hslc.org. *Exec. Dir.* Maryam Phillips.

Interlibrary Delivery Service of Pennsylvania (IDS), c/o Bucks County IU, No. 22, Doylestown 18901. SAN 322-2942. Tel. 215-348-2940 ext. 1620, fax 215-348-8315, e-mail ids@bucksiu.org. *Admin. Dir.* Pamela Newman Dinan.

Keystone Library Network, Dixon Univ. Center, Harrisburg 17110-1201. Tel. 717-720-4088, fax 717-720-4453. *Coord.* Mary Lou Sowden.

Lehigh Valley Assn. of Independent Colleges, 130 W. Greenwich St., Bethlehem 18018. SAN 322-2969. Tel. 610-625-7888, fax 610-625-7891. *Exec. Dir.* Diane Dimitroff.

Montgomery County Library and Information Network Consortium (MCLINC), 301 Lafayette St., 2nd flr., Conshohocken 19428. Tel. 610-238-0580, fax 610-238-0581, e-mail webmaster@mclinc.org. *Pres.* Sharon Moreland-Sender.

National Network of Libraries of Medicine–Middle Atlantic Region (NN/LM-MAR), Univ. of Pittsburgh, Pittsburgh 15261. E-mail nnlmmar@pitt.edu. *Exec. Dir.* Renae Barger.

Northeastern Pennsylvania Library Network, c/o Marywood Univ. Lib., Scranton 18509-1598. SAN 322-2993. Tel. 570-348-6260, fax 570-961-4769. *Exec. Dir.* Catherine H. Schappert.

Northwest Interlibrary Cooperative of Pennsylvania (NICOP), Mercyhurst College Lib., Erie 16546. SAN 370-5862. Tel. 814-824-2190, fax 814-824-2219. *Archivist* Earleen Glaser.

Pennsylvania Library Assn., 220 Cumberland Pkwy, Suite 10, Mechanicsburg 17055. Tel. 717-766-7663, fax 717-766-5440. *Exec. Dir.* Christi Buker.

Philadelphia Area Consortium of Special Collections Libraries (PACSCL), P.O. Box 22642, Philadelphia 19110-2642. Tel. 215-985-1445, fax 215-985-1446, email lblanchard@pacscl.org. *Exec. Dir.* Laura Blanchard.

Southeastern Pennsylvania Theological Library Assn. (SEPTLA), c/o Biblical Seminary, Hatfield 19440. SAN 371-0793. Tel. 215-368-5000 ext. 234. *Pres.* Jenifer Gundry.

State System of Higher Education Library Cooperative (SSHELCO), c/o Bailey Lib., Slippery Rock 16057. Tel. 724-738-2630, fax 724-738-2661. *Coord.* Mary Lou Sowden.

Susquehanna Library Cooperative (SLC), Stevenson Lib., Lock Haven Univ., Lock Haven 17745. SAN 322-3051. Tel. 570-484-2310, fax 570-484-2506. *Interim Dir. of Lib. and Info. Services* Joby Topper.

Tri-State College Library Cooperative (TCLC), c/o Rosemont College Lib., Rosemont 19010-1699. SAN 322-3078. Tel. 610-525-0796, fax 610-525-1939, e-mail office@tclclibs.org. *Coord.* Ann Upton.

Rhode Island

Library of Rhode Island Network (LORI), c/o Office of Lib. and Info. Services, Providence 02908-5870. SAN 371-6821. Tel. 401-574-9300, fax 401-574-9320. *Chief of Lib. Services* Karen Mellor.

Ocean State Libraries (OSL), 300 Centerville Rd., Suite 103S, Warwick 02886-0226. SAN 329-4560. Tel. 401-738-2200, fax 401-736-8949, e-mail support@oslri.net. *Exec. Dir.* Susan Straub.

South Carolina

Charleston Academic Libraries Consortium (CALC), P.O. Box 118067, Charleston 29423-8067. SAN 371-0769. Tel. 843-574-6088, fax 843-574-6484. *Chair* Drucie Gullion.

Partnership Among South Carolina Academic Libraries (PASCAL), 1122 Lady St., Suite 300, Columbia 29201. Tel. 803-734-0900, fax 803-734-0901. *Exec. Dir.* Rick Moul.

South Carolina AHEC, c/o Medical Univ. of South Carolina, Charleston 29425. SAN 329-3998. Tel. 843-792-4431, fax 843-792-4430. *Exec. Dir.* David Garr.

South Dakota

South Dakota Library Network (SDLN), 1200 University, Unit 9672, Spearfish 57799-9672. SAN 371-2117. Tel. 605-642-6835, fax 605-642-6472. *Dir.* Warren Wilson.

Tennessee

Knoxville Area Health Sciences Library Consortium (KAHSLC), Univ. of Tennessee Preston Medical Lib., Knoxville 37920. SAN 371-0556. Tel. 865-305-9525, fax 865-305-9527. *Pres.* Cynthia Vaughn.

Tennessee Health Science Library Assn. (THeSLA), Holston Valley Medical Center Health Sciences Lib., Kingsport 37660. SAN 371-0726. Tel. 423-224-6870, fax 423-224-6014. *Pres.* Sandy Oelschlegel.

Tri-Cities Area Health Sciences Libraries Consortium (TCAHSLC), James H. Quillen College of Medicine, East Tennessee State Univ., Johnson City 37614. SAN 329-4099. Tel. 423-439-6252, fax 423-439-7025. *Dir.* Biddanda Ponnappa.

Texas

Abilene Library Consortium, 3305 N. 3 St., Suite 301, Abilene 79603. SAN 322-4694. Tel. 325-672-7081, fax 325-672-7082. *Coord.* Edward J. Smith.

Amigos Library Services, Inc., 14400 Midway Rd., Dallas 75244-3509. SAN 322-3191. Tel. 972-851-8000, fax 972-991-6061, e-mail amigos@amigos.org. *Pres./CEO* Bonnie Juergens.

Council of Research and Academic Libraries (CORAL), P.O. Box 290236, San Antonio 78280-1636. SAN 322-3213. Tel. 210-458-4885. *Pres.* Andrea Schorr.

Del Norte Biosciences Library Consortium, El Paso Community College, El Paso 79998. SAN 322-3302. Tel. 915-831-4149, fax 915-831-4639. *Coord.* Becky Perales.

Harrington Library Consortium, 413 E. 4 Ave., Amarillo 79101. SAN 329-546X. Tel. 806-378-6037, fax 806-378-6038. *Dir.* Amanda Barrera.

Health Libraries Information Network (Health LINE), 3500 Camp Bowie Blvd. LIB-222, Fort Worth 76107-2699. SAN 322-3299. E-mail dfwhealthline@gmail.com. *Chair* Peace Ossum Williamson.

Houston Area Library Automated Network (HALAN), Houston Public Lib., Houston 77002. Tel. 832-393-1411, fax 832-393-1427, e-mail website@hpl.lib.tx.us. *Chief* Judith Hiott.

Houston Area Research Library Consortium (HARLiC), c/o Univ. of Houston Libs., Houston 77204-2000. SAN 322-3329. Tel. 713-743-9807, fax 713-743-9811. *Pres.* Dana Rooks.

National Network of Libraries of Medicine–South Central Region (NN/LM-SCR), c/o HAM-TMC Library, Houston 77030-2809. SAN 322-3353. Tel. 713-799-7880, fax 713-790-7030, e-mail nnlm-scr@exch.library.tmc.edu. *Dir.* L. Maximillian Buja.

South Central Academic Medical Libraries Consortium (SCAMeL), c/o Lewis Lib.-UNTHSC, Fort Worth 76107. SAN 372-8269. Tel. 817-735-2380, fax 817-735-5158. *Dir.* Daniel Burgard.

Texas Council of Academic Libraries (TCAL), VC/UHV Lib., Victoria 77901. SAN 322-337X. Tel. 361-570-4150, fax 361-570-4155. *Chair* Karen Baen.

Texas State Library and Archives Commission (TexSHARE), P.O. Box 12927, Austin 78711. Tel. 512-463-5455, fax 512-936-2306, e-mail texshare@tsl.state.tx.us. *Dir. and State Libn.* Danielle Plumer.

Utah

National Network of Libraries of Medicine–MidContinental Region (NN/LM-MCR), Spencer S. Eccles Health Sciences Lib., Univ. of Utah, Salt Lake City 84112-5890. SAN 322-225X. Tel. 801-587-3412, fax 801-581-3632. *Dir.* Jean Shipman.

Utah Academic Library Consortium (UALC), Univ. of Utah, Salt Lake City 84112-0860. SAN 322-3418. Tel. 801-581-7701, 801-581-3852, fax 801-585-7185, e-mail UALC mail@library.utah.edu. *Fiscal Agent* Parker M. Dougherty.

Utah Health Sciences Library Consortium, c/o Spencer S. Eccles Health Sciences Lib., Univ. of Utah, Salt Lake City 84112-5890. SAN 376-2246. Tel. 801-585-5743, fax 801-581-3632. *Chair* Jean Shipman.

Vermont

Vermont Resource Sharing Network, c/o Vermont Dept. of Libs., Montpelier 05609-0601. SAN 322-3426. Tel. 802-828-3261, fax 802-828-1481. *Ref. Libn.* Gerrie Denison.

Virgin Islands

Virgin Islands Library and Information Network (VILINET), c/o Div. of Libs., Archives, and Museums, Saint Thomas 00802. SAN 322-3639. Tel. 340-773-5715, fax 340-773-3257, e-mail info@vilinet.net. *Territorial Dir. of Libs., Archives, and Museums* Ingrid Bough.

Virginia

American Indian Higher Education Consortium (AIHEC), 121 Oronoco St., Alexandria 22314. SAN 329-4056. Tel. 703-838-0400, fax 703-838-0388, e-mail info@aihec.org.

Lynchburg Area Library Cooperative, c/o Sweet Briar College Lib., Sweet Briar 24595. SAN 322-3450. Tel. 434-381-6315, fax 434-381-6173.

Lynchburg Information Online Network (LION), 2315 Memorial Ave., Lynchburg 24503. SAN 374-6097. Tel. 434-381-6311, fax 434-381-6173. *Dir.* John G. Jaffee.

NASA Libraries Information System–NASA Galaxie, NASA Langley Research Center, MS 185-Technical Lib., Hampton 23681-2199. SAN 322-0788. Tel. 757-864-2356, fax 757-864-2375. *Coord.* Phyllis Kay Costulis.

Richmond Academic Library Consortium (RALC), James Branch Cabell Lib., Virginia Commonwealth Univ., Richmond 23284. SAN 322-3469. Tel. 804-828-1110, fax 804-828-1105. *Univ. Libn.* Kevin Butterfield.

Southside Virginia Library Network (SVLN), Longwood Univ., Farmville 23909-1897. SAN 372-8242. Tel. 434-395-2431; 434-395-2433, fax 434-395-2453. *Dean of Lib.* Suzy Szasz Palmer.

Virginia Independent College and University Library Assn., c/o Mary Helen Cochran Lib., Sweet Briar 24595. SAN 374-6089. Tel. 434-381-6139, fax 434-381-6173. *Dir.* John Jaffee.

Virginia Tidewater Consortium for Higher Education (VTC), 4900 Powhatan Ave., Norfolk 23529. SAN 329-5486. Tel. 757-683-3183, fax 757-683-4515, e-mail lgdotolo@aol.com. *Pres.* Lawrence G. Dotolo.

Virtual Library of Virginia (VIVA), George Mason Univ., Fairfax 22030. Tel. 703-993-4652, fax 703-993-4662. *Dir.* Anne Osterman.

Washington

Inland NorthWest Health Sciences Libraries (INWHSL), P.O. Box 10283, Spokane 99209-0283. SAN 370-5099. Tel. 509-368-6973, fax 509-358-7928. *Dir. of Lib. Services* Anne Mackereth.

National Network of Libraries of Medicine–Pacific Northwest Region (NN/LM-PNR), T-344 Health Sciences Bldg., Univ. of Washington, Seattle 98195. SAN 322-3485. Tel. 206-543-8262, fax 206-543-2469, e-mail nnlm@u.washington.edu. *Assoc. Dir.* Catherine Burroughs.

Washington Idaho Network (WIN), Foley Center Lib., Gonzaga Univ., Spokane 99258. Tel. 509-323-6545, fax 509-324-5904, e-mail winsupport@gonzaga.edu. *Pres.* Kathleen Allen.

Wisconsin

Fox River Valley Area Library Consortium (FRVALC), c/o Polk Lib., Univ. of Wisconsin–Oshkosh, Oshkosh 54901. SAN 322-3531. Tel. 920-424-3348, 920-424-4333, fax 920-424-2175.

Fox Valley Library Council, c/o OWLS, Appleton 54911. SAN 323-9640. Tel. 920-832-6190, fax 920-832-6422. *Pres.* Paula Wright.

North East Wisconsin Intertype Libraries, Inc. (NEWIL), 515 Pine St., Green Bay 54301. SAN 322-3574. Tel. 920-448-4413, fax 920-448-4420. *Coord.* Jamie Matczak.

South Central Wisconsin Health Science Library Consortium, c/o Fort Healthcare Medical Lib., Fort Atkinson 53538. SAN 322-4686. Tel. 920-568-5194, fax 920-568-5195. *Coord.* Carrie Garity.

Southeastern Wisconsin Health Science Library Consortium, Veterans Admin. Center Medical Lib., Milwaukee 53295. SAN 322-3582. Tel. 414-384-2000 ext. 42342, fax 414-382-5334. *Coord.* Kathy Strube.

Southeastern Wisconsin Information Technology Exchange, Inc. (SWITCH), 6801 North Yates Rd., Milwaukee 53217. Tel. 414-382-6710. *Coord.* Jennifer Schmidt.

Wisconsin Library Services (WILS), 1360 Regent St., No. 121, Madison 53715-1255. Tel. 608-216-8399, e-mail information@wils.org. *Dir.* Stef Morrill.

Wisconsin Public Library Consortium (WPLC), c/o WILS, 1360 Regent St., No. 121, Madison 53715-1255. Tel. 608-216-8399, e-mail information@wils.org.

Wisconsin Valley Library Service (WVLS), 300 N. 1 St., Wausau 54403. SAN 371-3911. Tel. 715-261-7250, fax 715-261-7259. *Dir.* Marla Rae Sepnafski.

WISPALS Library Consortium, c/o Gateway Technical College, Kenosha 53144-1690. Tel. 262-564-2602, fax 262-564-2787. *Chair* Scott Vrieze.

Wyoming

WYLD Network, c/o Wyoming State Lib., Cheyenne 82002-0060. SAN 371-0661. Tel. 307-777-6339, fax 307-777-6289, e-mail wyldstaff@will.state.wy.us. *Pres.* Marci Mock.

Canada

Alberta

The Alberta Library (TAL), 6-14, 7 Sir Winston Churchill Sq., Edmonton T5J 2V5. Tel. 780-414-0805, fax 780-414-0806, e-mail admin@thealbertalibrary.ab.ca. *CEO* Grant Chaney.

Council of Prairie and Pacific University Libraries (COPPUL), LCR Admin. Suite, 6th fl. TFDL, Calgary T2N 1N4. Tel. 403-220-8133, fax 403-282-1218. *Exec. Dir.* Andrew Waller.

NEOS Library Consortium, Cameron Lib., 5th flr., Edmonton T6G 2J8. Tel. 780-492-0075, fax 780-492-8302. *Mgr.* Anne Carr-Wiggin.

British Columbia

British Columbia College and Institute Library Services, Langara College Lib., Vancouver V5Y 2Z6. SAN 329-6970. Tel. 604-323-5639, fax 604-323-5544, e-mail cils@langara.bc.ca. *Dir.* Mary Anne Epp.

British Columbia Electronic Library Network (BCELN), WAC Bennett Lib., 7th flr., Simon Fraser Univ., Burnaby V5A 1S6. Tel. 778-782-7003, fax 778-782-3023, e-mail office@eln.bc.ca. *Exec. Dir.* Anita Cocchia.

Council of Prairie and Pacific University Libraries (COPPUL), LCR Administrative Suite, 6th Floor TFDL, University of Calgary, Calgary T2N 1N4. *Exec. Dir.* Andrew Waller.

Electronic Health Library of British Columbia (e-HLbc), c/o Bennett Lib., Burnaby V5A 1S6. Tel. 778-782-5440, fax 778-782-3023, e-mail info@ehlbc.ca. *Mgr.* Leigh Anne Palmer.

Public Library InterLINK, 5489 Byrne Rd., No 158, Burnaby V5J 3J1. SAN 318-8272. Tel. 604-517-8441, fax 604-517-8410, e-mail info@interlinklibraries.ca. *Operations Mgr.* Rita Avigdor.

Manitoba

Manitoba Library Consortium, Inc. (MLCI), c/o Lib. Admin., Univ. of Winnipeg, Winnipeg R3B 2E9. SAN 372-820X. Tel. 204-786-9801, fax 204-783-8910. *Chair* Louise Ayotte-Zaretski.

Nova Scotia

Maritimes Health Libraries Assn. (MHLA-AB-SM), W. K. Kellogg Health Sciences Lib., Halifax B3H 1X5. SAN 370-0836. Tel. 902-494-2483, fax 902-494-3750. *Libn.* Shelley McKibbon.

NOVANET, 84 Chain Lake Drive, Suite 402, Halifax B3S 1A2. SAN 372-4050. Tel. 902-453-2461, fax 902-453-2369, e-mail office@novanet.ns.ca. *Mgr.* Bill Slauenwhite.

Ontario

Canadian Assn. of Research Libraries (Association des Bibliothèques de Recherche du Canada), 203-309 Cooper St., Ottawa K2P 0G5. SAN 323-9721. Tel. 613-482-9344, fax 613-562-5297, e-mail info@carl-abrc.ca. *Exec. Dir.* Susan Haigh.

Canadian Health Libraries Assn. (CHLA-AB-SC), 468 Queen St. E., LL-02, Toronto M5A 1T7. SAN 370-0720. Tel. 416-646-1600, fax 416-646-9460, e-mail info@chla-absc.ca. *Pres.* Jeanna Hough.

Canadian Research Knowledge Network (CRKN), 11 Holland Ave., Ste. 301, Ottawa

K1Y 4S1. Tel. 613-907-7040, fax 866-903-9094. *Exec. Dir.* Clare Appavoo.

Hamilton and District Health Library Network, c/o St Josephs Healthcare Hamilton, Sherman Lib., Room T2305, Hamilton L8N 4A6. SAN 370-5846. Tel. 905-522-1155 ext. 3410, fax 905-540-6504. *Coord.* Jean Maragno.

Health Science Information Consortium of Toronto, c/o Gerstein Science Info. Center, Univ. of Toronto, Toronto M5S 1A5. SAN 370-5080. Tel. 416-978-6359, fax 416-971-2637. *Exec. Dir.* Miriam Ticoll.

Ontario Council of University Libraries (OCUL), 130 Saint George St., Toronto M5S 1A5. Tel. 416-946-0578, fax 416-978-6755. *Exec. Dir.* John Barnett.

Ontario Library Consortium (OLC), c/o Georgina Public Lib., Keswick L4P 3P7. *Pres.* Gay Kozak Selby.

Perth County Information Network (PCIN), c/o Stratford Public Lib., Stratford N5A 1A2. Tel. 519-271-0220, fax 519-271-3843, e-mail webmaster@pcin.on.ca. *CEO* Sam Coglin.

Shared Library Services (SLS), Woodstock Regional Hospital Regional Library Service, Woodstock N4V 0A4. SAN 323-9500. Tel. 519-421-4233, ext. 2735, fax 519-421-4236. *Libn.* Linda Wilcox.

Southwestern Ontario Health Libraries and Information Network (SOHLIN), London Health Sciences Centre, London N6A 5W9. Tel. 519-685-8500, ext. 56038. *Pres.* Jill McTavish.

Toronto Health Libraries Assn. (THLA), 3409 Yonge St., Toronto M4N 2L0. SAN 323-9853. Tel. 416-485-0377, fax 416-485-6877, e-mail medinfoserv@rogers.com. *Pres.* Ashley Farrell.

Quebec

Assn. des Bibliothèques de la Santé Affiliées a l'Université de Montréal (ABSAUM), c/o Health Lib., Univ. of Montreal, Montreal H3C 3J7. SAN 370-5838. Tel. 514-343-6826, fax 514-343-2350. *Dir.* Monique St-Jean.

Canadian Heritage Information Network (CHIN), 15 Eddy St., 4th flr., Gatineau K1A 0M5. SAN 329-3076. Tel. 819-994-1200, fax 819-994-9555, e-mail service@chin.gc.ca. *Acting Exec. Dir.* Charlie Costain.

Réseau BIBLIO de l'Ouatouais, 2295 Saint-Louis St., Gatineau, Quebec J8T 5L8. SAN 319-6526. Tel. 819-561-6008. *Exec. Gen.* Sylvie Thibault.

National Library and Information-Industry Associations, United States and Canada

AIIM—The Association for Information and Image Management

President, Peggy Winton
1100 Wayne Ave., Suite 1100, Silver Spring, MD 20910
800-477-2446, 301-587-8202, fax 301-587-2711, e-mail aiim@aiim.org
World Wide Web http://www.aiim.org
European Office: Broomhall Business Centre, Lower Broomhall Farm, Broomhall Ln.,
Worcester WR5 2NT, UK
Tel. 44-1905-727600, fax 44-1905-727609, e-mail info@aiim.org

Object

AIIM is an international authority on enterprise content management, the tools and technologies that capture, manage, store, preserve, and deliver content in support of business processes. Founded in 1943.

Officers

Pres. and CEO Peggy Winton. E-mail pwinton@aiim.org; *V.Chair* Mark Patrick, Commander U.S. Navy (Ret.); *Treas.* Heather Newman, Content Panda; *Past Chair* Anthony Peleska, Minnesota Housing Finance Agency; *Memb.-at-Large* Ian Story, Microsoft.

Publication

The Digital Landfill (blog).

American Association of Law Libraries

Executive Director, Kate Hagan
105 W. Adams St., Suite 3300, Chicago, IL 60603
312-939-4764, fax 312-431-1097, email khagan@aall.org
World Wide Web http://www.aallnet.org

Our Mission

The American Association of Law Libraries advances the profession of law librarianship and supports the professional growth of its members through leadership and advocacy in the field of legal information and information policy.

Membership

4,000+ members. For law librarians and other legal information professionals of any professional sector. Dues (Individual) $247; (Ret.) $62; (Student) $62. Year. June–May.

Officers (2016–2017)

Pres. Ronald E. Wheeler, Jr. E-mail wheelerr@bu.edu; *V.P./Pres.-Elect* Gregory R. Lambert. E-mail glambert@jw.com; *Secy.* Katherine K. Coolidge. E-mail KCoolidge@accufile.com; *Treas.* Jean L. Willis. E-mail jwillis@saclaw.org; *Past Pres.* Keith Ann Stiverson. E-mail kstivers@kentlaw.iit.edu.

Board Members

John W. Adkins jadkins@sdlawlibrary.org; Emily R. Florio emily.florio@finnegan.com; Mary Jenkins. E-mail jenkinsmarye@gmail.

com; Meg Kribble. E-mail mkribble@law.harvard.edu; Mary E. Matuszak. E-mail matusza-km@dany.nyc.gov; Donna Nixon dnixon@email.unc.edu.

American Indian Library Association

Executive Director, Heather Devine-Hardy (Eastern Shawnee)
E-mail hhdevine@gmail.com
World Wide Web http://www.ailanet.org

Object

To improve library and information services for American Indians. Founded in 1979; affiliated with American Library Association in 1985.

Membership

Any person, library, or other organization interested in working to improve library and information services for American Indians may become a member. Dues (Inst.) $40; (Indiv.) $20; (Student) $10.

Officers (2016–2017)

Pres. Omar Poler (Mole Lake Sokaogon Chippewa Community). E-mail poler@wisc.edu; *V.P./Pres.-Elect* Naomi Bishop (Gila River Indian Community). E-mail naopoleon@gmail.com; *Secy.* Aaron LaFromboise (Blackfeet). E-mail alafromboise@bfcc.edu; *Treas.* Liana Juliano; *Past Pres.* Paulita Aguilar. E-mail paulita@umn.edu; *Memb.-at-Large* Patricia Cutright (Lakota) *(2015–2017)*, Jessica Humphries (Metis) *(2016–2018)*, Ofelia "Liz" Zepeda (Tohono O'odham) *(2016–2018)*.

Editorial Board Chairs

Newsletter Editor George Gottschalk.

Publication

AILA Newsletter (irregular). *Ed.* Danielle Geller (Navajo).

American Library Association

Executive Director, Keith Michael Fiels
50 E. Huron St., Chicago, IL 60611
800-545-2433, 312-280-1392, fax 312-440-9374. E-mail kfiels@ala.org.
World Wide Web http://www.ala.org

The mission of the American Library Association (ALA) is to provide leadership for the development, promotion, and improvement of library and information services and the profession of librarianship in order to enhance learning and ensure access to information for all. Founded 1876.

Memb. (Indiv.) 53,000; (Inst.) 4,000; (Corporate) 175; (Total) 57,175. Any person, library, or other organization interested in library service and librarians. Dues (Indiv.) 1st year, $68; 2nd year, $104; 3rd year and later, $137; (Trustee and Assoc. Memb.) $62; (Lib. Support Staff) $49; (Student) $36; (Foreign Indiv.) $82; (Non-salaried/Unemployed/Ret.) $49; (Inst.) $175 and up, depending on operating expenses of institution.

Officers

Pres. Dr. Julia B. Todaro, Austin Community College. E-mail jtodaro@austincc.edu; *Pres.-*

Elect James (Jim) Neal, Columbia Univ. E-mail jneal0@columbia.edu; *Treas.* Susan H. Hildreth, Univ. of Washington Information School. E-mail shhildreth@comcast.net; *Past Pres.* Sari Feldman, Cuyahoga County Public Lib. E-mail sfeldman@cuyahogalibrary.org;

Divisions

See the separate entries that follow: American Assn. of School Libns.; Assn. for Lib. Collections and Technical Services; Assn. for Lib. Service to Children; Assn. of College and Research Libs.; Assn. of Specialized and Cooperative Lib. Agencies; Lib. Leadership and Management Assn.; Lib. and Info. Technology Assn.; Public Lib. Assn.; Reference and User Services Assn.; United for Libraries; Young Adult Lib. Services Assn.

Board Members

John DeSantis *(2017)*; Karen Downing (2019); Loida A. Garcia-Febo *(2018)*; Peter Hepburn *(2017)*; Julius C. Jefferson, Jr. *(2018)*; Mike L. Marlin *(2018)*; Andrew K. Pace *(2019)*; Gina Persichini *(2017)*.

Endowment Trustees

Rodney M. Hersberger, Robert Randolph Newlen, Siobhan A. Reardon, Brian E. C. Schottlaender, Teri R. Switzer, Patricia A. Wand, Susan H. Hildreth, Keith D. Brown, Latasha Bryant, Keith Michael Fiels, Mark Leon.

Round Table Chairs

(ALA staff liaison in parenthesis)
Ethnic and Multicultural Information Exchange. Leslie Campbell Hime (Gwendolyn Prellwitz).
Exhibits. Kelly Coyle-Crivelli (Paul Graller).
Federal and Armed Forces Libraries. Karl Debus-Lopez (Rosalind Reynolds).
Games and Gaming. Brian Mayer (Tina Coleman).

Gay, Lesbian, Bisexual, and Transgender. Deb Sica (John Amundsen).
Government Documents. Sarah Erekson (Rosalind Reynolds).
Intellectual Freedom. Cynthia M. Robinson (James LaRue).
International Relations. Beth Cramer (Delin Guerra).
Learning. Crystan Schimpf (Lorelle R. Swader).
Library History. Ellen M. Pozzi (Kelsey Henke).
Library Instruction. Jeff Knapp (Lorelle R. Swader).
Library Research. Denise E. Agosto (Kelsey Henke).
Library Support Staff Interests. Miguel Magos (Lorelle R. Swader).
Map and Geospatial Information. Louise M. Ratliff (Danielle M. Alderson).
New Members. Kat Kosturski (Kimberly L. Redd).
Retired Members. Jean M. Doolittle (Danielle M. Alderson).
Social Responsibilities. Diedre Conkling (John Amundsen).
Staff Organizations. Leon S. Bey (Kimberly L. Redd).
Sustainability. Rene M. Tanner (John Amundsen).
Video. Michele McKenzie (Danielle M. Alderson).

Committee Chairs

(ALA staff liaison in parentheses)
Accreditation (Standing). Elizabeth S. Aversa (Kerri Price).
American Libraries Advisory (Standing). Joseph M. Eagan (Laurie Borman).
Appointments (Standing). James G. Neal (JoAnne M. Kempf).
Awards (Standing). Susan Baerg Epstein (Cheryl Malden).
Budget Analysis and Review (Standing). Ann M. Martin (Keith D. Brown).
Chapter Relations (Standing). Susan J. Schmidt (Michael Dowling).
Committee on Committees (Elected Council Committee). James G. Neal (Lois Ann Gregory-Wood).

Conference Committee (Standing). Clara Nalli Bohrer (Amy McGuigan).

Constitution and Bylaws (Standing). James R. Rettig (JoAnne M. Kempf).

Council Orientation (Standing). Joseph M. Eagan (Lois Ann Gregory-Wood).

Diversity, Literacy and Outreach Services (Standing). Lessa Kanani'opua Pelayo-Lozada (Jody Gray).

Education (Standing). Edwin M. Cortez (Kimberly L. Redd).

Election (Standing). Natalie Marie DeJonghe (Lois Ann Gregory-Wood).

Human Resource Development and Recruitment (Standing). Miranda Henry Bennett (Lorelle R. Swader).

Information Technology Policy Advisory (Standing). Marc Gartler (Alan Inouye).

Intellectual Freedom (Standing). Pamela R. Klipsch (Eleanor Diaz).

International Relations (Standing). Leslie B. Burger (Michael Dowling).

Legislation (Standing). Ann Dutton Ewbank (Rosalind Bradley).

Library Advocacy (Standing). Gina J. Millsap (Marci Merola).

Literacy (Standing). Gwendolyn N. Weaver (Kristin Lahurd).

Membership (Standing). Laurel M. Bliss (Ron Jankowski).

Membership Meetings. Holly L. Camino (Lois Ann Gregory-Wood).

Nominating (Standing). Michelle M. Jeske (JoAnne M. Kempf).

Organization (Standing). Susan Considine (LaTasha Bryant).

Policy Monitoring (Standing). Chris Corrigan (Lois Ann Gregory-Wood).

Professional Ethics (Standing). Sara Dallas (Kristin Pekoll).

Public and Cultural Programs Advisory (Standing). Cassandra G. Barnett (Sarah Ostman).

Public Awareness (Standing). Jodie L. Borgerding (Jeff Julian).

Publishing (Standing). Sandra Hirsh (Mary J. Bolduc).

Research and Statistics (Standing). Linda Hofschire (Kathy Rosa).

Resolutions. Edward L. Sanchez (Lois-Ann Gregory Wood).

Rural, Native, and Tribal Libraries of All Kinds. Susan G. Hess (Gwendolyn Prellwitz).

Scholarships and Study Grants. Sarah LeMire (Kimberly L. Redd).

Status of Women in Librarianship (Standing). Kate Kosturski (Lorelle R. Swader).

Training, Orientation, and Leadership Development. Kim Copenhaver (Lorelle R. Swader).

Website Advisory. Ron Block (Sherri L. Vanyek).

Publications

ALA Handbook of Organization (online).

American Libraries (6 a year with occasional digital supplements; memb.; organizations $70; foreign $80; single copy $11.50).

Booklist (22 a year with 4 *Book Links* print issues and access to *Booklist Online*) U.S. and Canada $165.50; foreign $184.

American Library Association
American Association of School Librarians

Executive Director, Silvia Knight Norton
50 E. Huron St., Chicago, IL 60611
312-280-4382, 800-545-2433 ext. 4382, fax 312-280-5276, e-mail aasl@ala.org
World Wide Web http://www.aasl.org

Object

The American Association of School Librarians empowers leaders to transform teaching and learning. AASL works to ensure that all members of the field collaborate to provide leadership in the total education program; participate as active partners in the teaching/learning process; connect learners with ideas and information; and prepare students for lifelong learning, informed decision making, a love of reading, and the use of information technologies.

Established in 1951 as a separate division of the American Library Association.

Membership

Memb. 7,000+. Open to all libraries, school librarians, interested individuals, and business firms, with requisite membership in ALA.

Officers (2016–2017)

Pres. Audrey Church; *Pres.-Elect* Steven Yates; *Treas.* Robbie Nickel; *Past Pres.* Leslie Preddy.

Board of Directors

Pamela Harland, Laura Hicks, Linda Weatherspoon, Wendy Stephens, Kathryn Roots Lewis, Katie Williams, Craig Seasholes, Ann Schuster, Sylvia Knight Norton (ex officio).

Section Leadership

AASL/ESLS Executive Committee. Karla Collins, Stephanie Jones, Karen Gavigan, Heather Moorefield-Lang, Jody Howard.
AASL/ISS Executive Committee. Sarah Jane Levin, Courtney Lewis, Yapha Mason, Elizabeth Nelson, Robert Hilliker.
AASL/SPVS Executive Committee. Lori Donovan, Stephanie Ham, Margaret Montgomery, Suzanna Panter, Sarah Searles.

Committee Chairs

AASL/ALSC/YALSA Joint Committee on School/Public Library Cooperation. Anna Brannin (AASL).
Affiliate Assembly. Mona Batchelor.
Alliance for Association Excellence. Robbie Nickel.
Association of American University Presses Book Selection. Annemarie Roscello.
Annual Conference. Lucy Santos Green.
Awards. Dorcas Hand.

Best Apps for Teaching and Learning. James Allen.
Best Websites for Teaching and Learning. Heather Moorefield-Lang.
Beyond Words Grant Jury. Jennisen Lucas.
Bylaws and Organization. Lynn Gordon.
CAEP Coordinating Committee. Roxanne Forgrave.
National Institute. Terri Grief.
Leadership Development. Leslie Preddy.
National Conference. Cathy Evans.
School Library Month. Suzanne Dix.
Standards and Guidelines Implementation. Mary Keeling.

Editorial Board Chairs

Knowledge Quest Editorial Board. Ann Dutton Ewbank.
School Library Research Editorial Board. Melissa Johnston, Mega Subramaniam.

Task Force Chairs

Presidential Initiative. Deb Lebitov.
65th Celebration. Carl A. Harvey.
Vision for Implementing ESSA. Eileen Kern.
Induction. Robyn Young.
Innovative Approaches to Literacy. Judi Moreillon.
K–12 Regional Accrediting Agency. Becky Johnson.
Social Media Awards. Jane Lofton.
Transform & Crisis Toolkit Revision. Elizabeth Burns.

Awards Committee Chairs

ABC-CLIO Leadership Grant. Sedley Abercrombie.
Collaborative School Library Award. Caitlin Ahearn.
Distinguished School Administrators Award. Stephanie Ham.
Distinguished Service Award. Diana Wendell.
Frances Henne Award. Stephanie Trzeciakiewicz.
Innovative Reading Grant. Nancy Keane.
Inspire Collection Development Grant. Floyd Pentlin.

Inspire Disaster Recovery Fund. Valerie Edwards.

Inspire Special Event Grant. Stacy Lickteig.

Intellectual Freedom Award. Rebecca Hunt.

National School Library Program of the Year Award. Eileen Kern.

Roald Dahl's Miss Honey Social Justice Award. Stephanie Burdic.

Ruth Toor Grant for Strong Public Schools Libraries. Lois Wine.

Student Bridge Scholarship. Judi Moreillon.

Advisory Group Staff Liaisons

Professional Development. Jennifer Habley.

Publications. Stephanie Book.

Publications

Knowledge Quest (5 a year; $50, $60 outside U.S.). *Ed.* Meg Featheringham. E-mail mfeatheringham@ala.org.

School Library Research (electronic, free, at http://www.ala.org/aasl/slr). *Eds.* Melissa Johnston. E-mail melissap@mindspring.com; Mega Subramaniam. E-mail mmsubram@umd.edu.

American Library Association
Association for Library Collections and Technical Services

Executive Director, Keri Cascio
50 E. Huron St., Chicago, IL 60611
800-545-2433 ext. 5030, fax 312-280-5033, e-mail kcascio@ala.org
World Wide Web http://www.ala.org/alcts

Object

The Association for Library Collections and Technical Services (ALCTS) envisions an environment in which traditional library roles are evolving. New technologies are making information more fluid and raising expectations. The public needs quality information anytime, anyplace. ALCTS provides frameworks to meet these information needs.

ALCTS provides leadership to the library and information communities in developing principles, standards, and best practices for creating, collecting, organizing, delivering, and preserving information resources in all forms. It provides this leadership through its members by fostering educational, research, and professional service opportunities. ALCTS is committed to quality information, universal access, collaboration, and lifelong learning.

Standards—Develop, evaluate, revise, and promote standards for creating, collecting, organizing, delivering, and preserving information resources in all forms.

Best practices—Research, develop, evaluate, and implement best practices for creating,

collecting, organizing, delivering, and preserving information resources in all forms.

Education—Assess the need for, sponsor, develop, administer, and promote educational programs and resources for lifelong learning.

Professional development—Provide opportunities for professional development through research, scholarship, publication, and professional service.

Interaction and information exchange—Create opportunities to interact and exchange information with others in the library and information communities.

Association operations—Ensure efficient use of association resources and effective delivery of member services.

Established in 1957; renamed in 1988.

Membership

Memb. 3,800. Any member of the American Library Association may elect membership in this division according to the provisions of the bylaws.

Officers (2016–2017)

Pres. Vicki L. Sipe, Albin O. Kuhn Lib. & Gallery, Univ. of Maryland, Baltimore County, 1000 Hill Top Cir., Baltimore, MD 21250. Tel. 410-455-6751, e-mail vsipeala@gmail.com; *Pres.-Elect* Mary Beth Thompson, Univ. of Kentucky, 1-85 Wm. T. Young Lib., Lexington, KY 40506-0001. Tel. 859-218-1227, e-mail mbthompson@uky.edu; *Past Pres.* Norm Madeiros, Magill Lib., Haverford College, 370 Lancaster Ave., Haverford, PA 19041. Tel. 610-896-1173, e-mail norm.medeiros@gmail.com.

Address correspondence to the executive director.

Board of Directors

Pamela Harland, Laura Hicks, Linda Weatherspoon, Wendy Stephens, Kathryn Roots Lewis, Katie Williams, Craig Seasholes, Ann Schuster, Sylvia Knight Norton (ex officio).

Section Chairs

Acquisitions. Sally Gibson
Cataloging and Metadata Management. Susan Wynne.
Collection Management. Beth R. Berhardt.
Continuing Resources. Patrick L. Carr.
Preservation & Reformatting. Mary Kristen Kern.

Committee Chairs

Advocacy and Policy. Lauren Corbett.
Affiliate Relations. Shannon Tennant.
ALCTS Outstanding Publications Award Jury. Kristin E. Martin.
Hugh C. Atkinson Memorial Award. (ALCTS/ACRL/LLAMA/LITA). Bruce Johnson. (ALCTS Representative)
Ross Atkinson Lifetime Achievement Award. Brian E. C. Schottlaender.
Budget and Finance. James J. Dooley.
Continuing Education. Alison M. Armstrong, Ginger (V. K.) Williams.
Fundraising. Harriet Wintermute.
International Relations. Nina Servizzi.
Leadership Development. Jennifer B. Bowen.

Library Materials Price Index Editorial Board. Narda Tafuri.
LRTS Editorial Board. Jennifer W. Bazeley.
Membership. Autumn Faulkner.
LITA/ALCTS Metadata Standards Committee. Jenn Riley.
Monographs Editorial Board. Susan E. Thomas.
Nominating. Mary Page.
Organization and Bylaws. Santi Allen Thompson.
Outstanding Collaboration Citation Jury. Sarah Wallbank.
Esther J. Piercy Award Jury. Susan Davis.
Planning Committee. Michele Seikel.
President's Program. Charles Wilt.
Program. Kevin Clair.
Publications. Mary E. Miller.
Standards. Sally R. Krash.
Edward Swanson Memorial Best of LRTS Award Jury. Erin S. Stalberg.
Banks-Harris Preservation Award Jury. Stephanie Lamson.
Cunha Swartzburg Preservation Award Jury. Karen E. Kiorpes.
ProQuest Coutts Award for Innovation. Erika L. Johnson.
First Step Award Jury. Debra F. Spidal.
HARRASSOWITZ Award for Leadership in Library Acquisitions Jury. Michael A. Arthur.
Margaret Mann Citation Jury. Steve Kelley.
Outstanding Publication Award. Kristin E. Martin.
Ulrich's Serials Librarianship Award. Lynnette M. Fields.

Interest Group Chairs

Acquisitions Managers and Vendors. Linda S. Geisler.
Authority Control (ALCTS/LITA). Tatyana Chubaryan.
Book and Paper. Beth Doyle, Jeanne Goodman.
Catalog Form and Function. Alayne Mundt.
Catalog Management. Kimberley A. Edwards, Andrew Sulavik.
Cataloging and Classification Research. Laura N. Evans.
Cataloging Norms. Sai Deng, Jessalyn Zoom.
Chief Collection Development Officers at Large Research Libraries. Caitlin Tillman.

Collection Development Issues for the Practitioner. Gabrielle Somnee Wiersma.

CMS Collection Development Librarians of Academic Libraries. Nancy M. Godleski.

Collection Evaluation and Assessment. Julia M. Gelfand, Caroline Muglia.

Collection Management and Electronic Resources. Sunshine Jacinda Carter.

CMS Collection Management in Public Libraries (RUSA Codes). Kristi Chadwick.

College and Research Libraries. Andrea Imre.

CaMMS Competencies and Education for a Career in Cataloging. Susan Rathbun-Grubb, Allison R. Yanos.

CaMMS Copy Cataloging. Dan Tam Thi Do, Cynthia Romanowski.

Creative Ideas in Technical Services. Amber Billey.

Digital Conversion. William Schlaak.

Digital Preservation. Chad Garrett, Marielle Veve.

Electronic Resources. George Stachokas.

Electronic Resources Management (ALCTS/LITA). Buddy D. Pennington.

CaMMS Faceted Subject Access. Magda A. El-Sherbini, Sarah Wallbank.

Heads of Cataloging Departments. Martin L. Knott, E. Jackie Shieh.

Linked Library Data (ALCTS/LITA). Jee Davis, Anne Washington.

MARC Formats Transition. Jeremy Bartczak, Debra S. Shapiro.

Metadata. Michael R. Bolam.

New Members. Carolina Delgado, Katherine P. Holder.

Newspapers. Brian Geiger.

Preservation Administrators. Kate Elena Contakos.

Preservation Metadata. Jennifer Lee Mullins.

Promoting Presservation. Eva Grizzard, Jennifer Lee Mullins.

Public Libraries Technical Services. Carey Hunt.

Publisher-Vendor-Library Relations. Eugene Holland Hayworth, Suzanne Saskia Kemperman, Lee Sochay.

Role of the Professional Librarian in Technical Services. Paul R. Burley, Mingyan Li.

Scholarly Communication. Violeta Ilik.

Technical Services Directors of Large Research Libraries. Betsy A. Friesen.

Technical Services Managers in Academic Libraries. Schott Phinney.

Technical Services Workflow Efficiency.

Publications

ALCTS News (q.; free; posted at http://www.ala.org/alcts).

Library Resources and Technical Services (LRTS) (q.; nonmemb. $100; international $100). Electronic only. *Ed.* Mary Beth Weber, Technical and Automated Services Dept., Rutgers Univ. Libs., 47 Davidson Rd., Piscataway, NJ 08854. E-mail lrseditor @lists.ala.org.

American Library Association
Association for Library Service to Children

Executive Director, Aimee Strittmatterg
50 E. Huron St., Chicago, IL 60611
312-280-2163, 800-545-2433 ext. 2163, fax 312-280-5271, e-mail alsc@ala.org
World Wide Web http://www.ala.org/alsc

Object

The core purpose of the Association for Library Service to Children (ALSC) is to create a better future for children through libraries. Its primary goal is to lead the way in forging excellent library services for all children. ALSC offers creative programming, information about best practices, continuing education, an awards and media evaluation program, and professional connections. Founded in 1901.

Membership

Memb. 4,000. Open to anyone interested in library services to children. For information on dues, see ALA entry.

Address correspondence to the executive director.

Officers

Pres. Betsy Orsburn, 4000 Gypsy Ln. Unit 519, Philadelphia, PA 19129. Tel. 215-848-3120, e-mail eco519@comcast.net; *V.P./Pres.-Elect* Nina Lindsay; *Past Pres.* Andrew Medlar, Chicago Public Lib., 400 S. State St. 10-S, Chicago, IL 60605. Tel. 312-747-4662, e-mail amedlar@chipublib.org; *Fiscal Officer* Paula Holmes. *Div. Councilor* Jenna Nemec-Loise.

Directors

Christine Caputo, Doris Gebel, Amy Koester, Karen MacPherson, Julie Roach, Vicky Smith, Mary Voors, Kay Weisman.

Committee Chairs

AASL/ALSC/YALSA Interdivisional Committee on School/Public Library Cooperation. Anna Brannin.
Advocacy and Legislation. Africa S. Hands.
ALSC/Booklist/YALSA Odyssey Award Selection 2018. Joan Schroeder Kindig.
Arbuthnot Honor Lecture 2017. Jane B. Marino.
Arbuthnot Honot Lecture 2018, Elizabeth Ramsey Bird.
Mildred L. Batchelder Award 2018. Elizabeth A. Poe.
Pura Belpré Award 2018. Alicia Karina Long.
Budget. Deanna Mae Romriell.
Randolph Caldecott Award. Letitia A. Wilson.
Children and Libraries Editorial Advisory Committee. Randall Enos.
Children and Technology. Michael P. Santangelo.
Distinguished Service Award Committee. Mary Fellows.
Early Childhood Programs and Services. Brooke E. Newberry.
Education. Danielle Eileen Hartsfield.

Every Child Ready to Read Oversight. Sue McCleaf Nespeca.
Excellence for Early Learning Digital Media. Joanna K. Fabicon
Theodor Seuss Geisel Award 2018. Sandra J. Imdieke.
Grants Administration. Jennifer Mae Smith.
Great Websites. Alia Schields, Renee Grassi.
Intellectual Freedom. Bruce Steward Farrar.
Liaison to National Organizations. Lisa Gangemi Kropp, Soraya Anne-Machel Silverman-Montano.
Library Service to Special Population Children and Their Caregivers. Lesley Mason.
Local Arrangements Committee. Brandy Dawn Morrill.
Managing Children's Services. Megan Allyn Egbert.
Membership. Amy E. Sears.
John Newbery Award Selection 2018. Cecilia P. McGowan.
Nominating. Ellen M. Riordan.
Notable Children's Books. Maeve Visser Knoth.
Notable Children's Recordings. Allison M. Knight.
Oral History. Lisa Von Drasek.
Organization and Bylaws. Ruth Anne Champion.
Preconference Planning Committee. Carla J. Kozak.
Program Coordinating. Eva Marie Volin.
Public Awareness. Celia Claudia Perez.
Quicklists Consulting. Stephanie D. Bange.
Charlmae Rollins President's Program. Christopher A. Brown, Linda L. Erns.
Scholarships. Robin J. Howe.
School-age Programs and Service. Robin Ellis Friedman.
Robert F. Sibert Award 2018. Tali Balas.
Special Collections and Bechtel Fellowship. Rachel Godwin Payne.
Website Advisory. Samantha Lumetta, Paula Willey.
Laura Ingalls Wilder Award Committee 2018. Rita Auerbach.

Publications

ALSC Matters! (q., electronic; memb. Not available by subscription.)
Children and Libraries: The Journal of the As-

sociation for Library Service to Children (q.; print and online; memb; nonmemb. $50; foreign $60).

Everyday Advocacy Matters (q., electronic; memb. Not available by subscription.)

American Library Association
Association of College and Research Libraries

Executive Director, Mary Ellen K. Davis
50 E. Huron St., Chicago, IL 60611-2795
312-280-2523, 800-545-2433 ext. 2523, fax 312-280-2520, e-mail acrl@ala.org
World Wide Web http://www.ala.org/acrl

Object

The Association of College and Research Libraries (ACRL) leads academic and research librarians and libraries in advancing learning and transforming scholarship. Founded 1940.

Membership

Memb. 11,172. For information on dues, see ALA entry.

Officers

Pres. Irene M. Herold, Univ. of Hawai'i at Manoa Lib., 2550 McCarthy Mall, Honolulu, HI 96822. Tel. 808-956-7205, e-mail heroldi@hawaii.edu; *Pres.-Elect* Cheryl A. Middleton, Oregon State Univ., 121 The Valley Library, Corvallis, OR 97331. Tel. 541-737-8527, e-mail Cheryl.Middleton@oregonstate.edu; *Past Pres.* Ann Campion Riley, 104 Ellis Lib., Univ. of Missouri, Columbia, MO 65201. Tel. 573-882-1685. e-mail kaw@umn.edu; *Budget and Finance Chair* John A. Lehner, Univ. of Houston, 4333 University Dr., Houston, TX 77204. Tel. 713-743-9801, e-mail jlehner@uh.edu; *ACRL Councilor* LeRoy Jason LeFleur, Tufts Univ., Ginn Lib., 160 Packard Avenue, Medford, MA 02155. Tel. 617-627-0854, e-mail Leroy.lafleur@tufts.edu.

Board of Directors

John P. Culshaw, Emily Daly, Mary Ellen K. Davis, Caroline Fuchs, Julia Gelfand, Irene M.H. Herold, LeRoy Jason LaFleur, John A. Lehner, Cheryl A. Middleton, Lori J. Ostapowicz-Critz, Beth McNeil, Kim Leeder Reed, Ann Campion Riley, Susan Barnes Whyte.

Section Chairs

Anthropology and Sociology Section. Helen P. Clements.
Arts. Kai A. Smith.
Asian, African, and Middle Eastern. Ruby A. Bell-Gam.
College Libraries. Patricia A. Kreitz.
Community and Junior College Libraries. Michael J. Miller.
Distance Learning. Stefanie Buck.
Educational and Behavioral Sciences. Kaya Van Beynen.
Instruction. Jennifer E. Knievel.
Literatures in English. Laura R. Braunstein.
Politics, Policy, and International Relations. David Schwieder.
Rare Books and Manuscripts. John H. Overholt.
Science and Technology. Andrew P. Stuart.
Slavic and East European. Thomas Francis Keenan.
University Libraries. Rebecca Blakiston.
Western European Studies. Katie E. Gibson.

Women and Gender Studies Section. Nina Clements.

Committee and Task Force Chairs

Academic/Research Librarian of the Year Award. Michael Courtney.

ACRL Academic Library Trends and Statistics Survey. Ted Mulvey.

ACRL 2017 Colleagues. Julia M. Gelfand, John P. Culshaw.

ACRL 2017 Contributed Papers. Theresa S. Byrd, Rhonda Kay Huisman.

ACRL 2017 Coordinating. James G. Neal.

ACRL 2017 Innovations. Ameet Doshi, Courtney Greene McDonald.

ACRL 2017 Invited Papers. Michelle Demeter, Courtney L. Young.

ACRL 2017 Keynote Speakers. Karen E. Downing, Lisa M. Stillwell.

ACRL 2017 Local Arrangements. Barbara G. Preece, Carissa Ann Tomlinson.

ACRL 2017 Panel Sessions. Adrian K. Ho, Heidi Steiner Burkhardt.

ACRL 2017 Poster Sessions. Peter D. Hepburn, Willie Miller.

ACRL 2017 Preconference. Louise S. Sherby, Krista White.

ACRL 2017 Roundtable. Athena Nicole Jackson, Janice D. Welburn.

ACRL 2017 Scholarships. Trevor A. Dawes, Kathy A. Parsons.

ACRL 2017 TechConnect Presentations. Char Booth, John Morris Jackson, II.

ACRL 2017 Virtual Conference. Heather A. Dalal, Kevin P. McDonough.

ACRL 2017 Workshops. Curtis Brundy, Cynthia K. Steinhoff.

ACRL/LLAMA Interdivisional Committee on Building Resources. Frank R. Allen, Jose O. Diaz.

Appointments. Erin L. Ellis.

Hugh C. Atkinson Memorial Award. Theresa S. Byrd.

Budget and Finance. John A. Lehner.

Choice Editorial Board. Peggy Seiden.

College & Research Libraries Editorial Board. Wendi Arant Kaspar.

College & Research Libraries News Editorial Board. Kaetrena Davis Kendrick.

Diversity. Kenny A. Garcia.

Excellence in Academic Libraries Award. Karen A. Williams.

Government Relations. Clary G. Williams.

Immersion Program. Bethany N. Herman.

Information Literacy Standards. Ted Mulvey.

Dr. E. J. Josey Spectrum Scholar Mentor Program. Michele M. Alaniz.

Leadership Recruitment and Nomination. David A. Wright.

Liaisons Assembly. Carrie Donovan.

Liaisons Coordinating. Kathy L. Magarell.

Liaisons Grants. Lori J. Phillips.

Liaisons Training and Development. Carrie Donovan.

Membership. Kate E. Gibson.

New Publications Advisory. Rebecca Kate Miller.

President's Program Planning Committee, 2017. Anne Marie Casey.

Professional Development. Carrie Forbes.

Publications Coordinating. Emily Ford.

Publications in Librarianship Editorial Board, Daniel C. Mack.

RBM Editorial Board. Jennifer Karr Sheehan.

Research Planning and Review. Wayne Bivens-Tatum.

Resources for College Libraries Editorial Board. Neal Baker.

Section Membership. Melanie Jean Meyers.

Standards. Maria E. Peppers.

Student Learning and Information Literacy Committee. Rhonda Kay Huisman.

Value of Academic Libraries. Jaime Corris Hammond.

Discussion Group Chairs

Assessment. Nancy B. Turner.

Balancing Baby and Book. Laura Bornella.

Continuing Education/Professional Development. Richard Paustenbaugh.

Copyright. Carla S. Myers.

First Year Experience. Kevin Patrick Seeber.

Heads of Public Services. (TBA)

Information Commons. Lisa K. Baker, Diane M. Fulkerson.

International Perspectives on Academic and Research Libraries. Meggan Houlihan, Raymond Pun.

Leadership. Alma Ortega.

Library and Information Science Collections. Cynthia Krolikowski, Daniel G. Tracy.

Library Support for Massive Open Online Courses (MOOCs). Kyle Kenneth Courtney.

Media Resources. Steven Dennis Milewski.

MLA International Biography. Sarah G. Wenzel.

New Members. Cara Bargaret Cadena, Samantha Minnis, Ashley Rosener.

Personnel Administrators and Staff Development. Michele Petosa. Bonnie J. Smith.

Philosophical, Religious, and Theological Studies. Desirae Zingarelli-Sweet.

Popular Cultures. Christy Goodnight.

Scholarly Communication. Nathan Frank Hall, Charlotte Roh.

Sponsored Research Administrators and Grants Managers. (TBA).

Student Retention. Quetzalli Barrientos, Matt Upson.

Undergraduate Librarians. Callie Wiygul Branstiter, Laura Sider.

Interest Group Conveners

Academic Library Services to International Students. Kendra Nan Skellen.

Access Services. Brad L. Warren.

African-American Studies Librarians. Holly A. Smith.

Contemplative Pedagogy. Samantha Schmehl Hines.

Digital Badges. Michael LaMagna.

Digital Curation. Rene M. Tanner.

Digital Humanities. Hannah Scates Kettler, Krista White.

Digital Scholarship Centers. Meris Mandernach.

Health Sciences. Sarah E. Sheehan.

Image Resources. Jasmine Burns.

Librarianship in For-Profit Educational Institutions. Erica Ann Watson.

Library and Information Science Education. Nora J. Bird.

Library Marketing and Outreach. Chris Davidson, Bonnie Cohen Lafazan.

Numeric and Geospatial Data Services in Academic Libraries. Bobray J. Bordelon, Jr.

Readers' Advisory. Meagan Lacy.

Residency. Sarah Espinosa.

Technical Services. Maurine W. McCourry.

Universal Accessibility. Teresa Slobuski.

Virtual Worlds. Norma Jean Hewlett.

Publications

Choice (12 a year; $469; Canada and Mexico $499; other international $599). *Ed.* Mark Cummings.

Choice Reviews-on-Cards (requires subscription to *Choice* or *Choice Reviews Online* $549; Canada and Mexico $589; other international $679).

Choice Reviews Online 2.0 (academic libraries [U.S.] $599; academic libraries [Non-U.S. including Mexico and Canada] $689; school libraries K–12, $375; government libraries [Including USIA, etc.], $600; public libraries [U.S.], $530; public libraries [U.S.], $579; other libraries $630; publishers/dealers $630).

College & Research Libraries (*C&RL*) (6 a year; open access online-only). *Ed.* Wendi Arant Kaspar.

College & Research Libraries News (*C&RL News*) (11 a year; memb.; nonmemb. $56; Canada and other PUAS countries $61; other international $66). *Ed.* David Free.

RBM: A Journal of Rare Books, Manuscripts, and Cultural Heritage (s. ann.; $50; Canada and other PUAS countries $56; other international $67). *Ed.* Jennifer K. Sheehan.

American Library Association
Association of Specialized and Cooperative Library Agencies

Executive Director, Susan Hornung
50 E. Huron St., Chicago, IL 60611-2795
312-280-4395, 800-545-2433 ext. 4395, fax 312-280-5273, e-mail shornung@ala.org
World Wide Web http://www.ala.org/ascla

Object

The Association for Specialized and Cooperative Library Agencies (ASCLA) enhances the effectiveness of library service by advocating for and providing high-quality networking, enrichment, and educational opportunities for its diverse members, who represent state library agencies, libraries serving special populations, library cooperatives, and library consultants. ASCLA's members are

- Librarians, library agencies, and staff serving populations with special needs, such as those with sensory, physical, health, or behavioral conditions or those who are incarcerated or detained

- Librarians and staff of state library agencies, and state library consultants—organizations created or authorized by state governments to promote library services

- Library networks and cooperatives, organizations of one or more types of libraries—academic, public, special, or school—that collaborate to maximize the funds available for provision of library services to all citizens; they may serve a community, a metropolitan area, a region, or a statewide or multistate area

- Consultants, independent or contract librarians, as well as those who work outside traditional library settings

Member activity is centered around interest groups.

Membership

Memb. 800+. For information on dues, see ALA entry.

Officers and Directors (2016–2017)

Pres. Michael A. Golrick, State Lib. of Louisiana, 701 North 4th St., Baton Rouge, LA 70802. Tel. 255-342-4917, e-mail michael. golrick@gmail.com; Pres.-Elect Jeannette P. Smithee; Secy. Wendy Jo Knapp; Past Pres. Rhonda K. Gould, Gould Lib. Consulting, 812 N. Steele St., Tacoma, WA 98406. Tel. 262-758-0234, e-mail rhondakgound@gmail.com; Div. Councilor Chris Corrigan; Dirs.-at-Large Carson Block, Janet McKenney, Susan E. Pannebaker; Dir., Cooperatives and Networks Sheryl L. Knab; Dirs., Special Populations Carrie Scott Banks, Patrice M. Johnson; Dir., Lib. Consultants/Independent Libns. Jamie Hollie; Dir. State Lib. Agencies Mary J. Soucie.

Interest Group Leaders

Alzheimers and Related Dementias. Mary Beth Riedner.
Bridging Deaf Cultures @ your library. Alec McFarlane.
Collaborative Digitization. Sandra McIntyre.
Consortial eBooks. Veronda Pitchford, Paula MacKinnon.
Consortium Management Discussion. Sheryl Knab.
Future of Libraries. Amy Paget.
Interlibrary Cooperation. To be announced.
Library Consultants. Melissa Powell.
Library Services for Youth in Custody. Camden Eadoin Tadhg.
Library Services to People with Visual or Physical Disabilities that Prevent Them from Reading Standard Print. Linda Vincent.
Library Services to the Incarcerated and Detained. To be Annnounced.
LSTA Coordinators. Raye Oldham.
Physical Delivery. Rae Cheney.
State Library Agencies. Carol Desch.

Tribal Librarians. Lillian Chavez.
Universal Access. Marti Goddard.
Youth Services Consultants. Sharon Rawlins.
For more information on ASCLA interest groups, see http://www.ala.org/ascla/interest-groups.

Committees

Accessibility Assembly, Awards Committee, Board of Directors, Conference Programming, Executive, Finance and Planning, Guidelines for Library & Information Services for the American Deaf Community, Interest Group Coordinating, Membership, Nominating, Online Learning, President's Program Planning, Publications, Web Presence.
For more information on ASCLA Committees, see http://www.ala.org/ascla/about/committees.

Board Members

Div. Councilor Christopher John Corrigan; *Dirs.-at-large* Janet McKenney, Raye L. Old-

ham, Susan E. Pannebaker; *Dir. Cooperatives and Networks* Gregory Pronevitz; *Dirs. Special Populations* Carrie Scott Banks, Lily Sacharow; *Dir. Lib. Consultants/Independent Libns.* Jamie Hollier; *Dir. State Lib. Agencies* Wendy Jo Knapp; *Ed. Ex officio* Christina Creech Way.

Committee Chairs

Accessibility Assembly: Adam S. Szczepaniak, JR; Awards: Linda S. Lyshol; Board of Directors: Rhonda K. Gould; Conference Programming: Eldon Ray James; Executive: Rhonda K. Gould; Finance & Planning: Michael A. Golrick, Kathleen Moeller-Pfeiffer; Guidelines for Lib. and Information Services for the American Deaf Community: Jolene Bertloff; Interest Group Coordinating: Michael A. Golrick; Membership: Elizabeth Marshak; Nominating: Carol Ann Desch; Online Learning: Dawn Amsberry; President's Program Planning: To be announced; Publications: To be announced; Web Presence: Nancy M. Bolt.

American Library Association
Library and Information Technology Association

Executive Director, Jenny Levine
50 E. Huron St., Chicago, IL 60611
312-280-4267, 800-545-2433, x4270, e-mail jlevine@ala.org
World Wide Web http://www.lita.org

Object

As a center of expertise about information technology, the Library and Information Technology Association (LITA) leads in exploring and enabling new technologies to empower libraries. LITA members use the promise of technology to deliver dynamic library collections and services.
LITA educates, serves, and reaches out to its members, other ALA members and divisions, and the entire library and information community through its publications, programs, and other activities designed to promote, develop,

and aid in the implementation of library and information technology.

Membership

Memb. 2,900. For information on dues, see ALA entry.

Officers (2016–2017)

Pres. Aimee Fifarek; *V.P.* Andromeda Yelton; *Past Pres.* Andromeda Yelton.

Directors

S. G. Ranti Junus, Bohyun Kim, Christopher Lawton, Susan Sharpless Smith, Jennifer Emanuel Taylor, Ken Varnum, Evviva R. Weinraub, *Div. Councillor* Aaron Dobbs.

Publication

Information Technology and Libraries (*ITAL*) (open source at http://ejournals.bc.edu/ojs/index.php/ital/issue/current). *Ed.* Robert Gerrity. For information or to send manuscripts, contact the editor.

American Library Association
Library Leadership and Management Association

Executive Director, Kerry Ward
50 E. Huron St., Chicago, IL 60611
312-280-5032, 800-545-2433 ext. 5032, fax 312-280-5033,
e-mail kward@ala.org
World Wide Web http://www.ala.org/llama

Object

The Library Leadership and Management Association (LLAMA) Strategic Plan sets out the following:

Mission: The Library Leadership and Management Association advances outstanding leadership and management practices in library and information services by encouraging and nurturing individual excellence in current and aspiring library leaders.

Vision: As the foremost organization developing present and future leaders in library and information services, LLAMA provides a welcoming community where aspiring and experienced library leaders and library supporters from all types of libraries can seek and share knowledge and skills in leadership, administration, and management in a manner that creates meaningful transformation in libraries around the world.

Core Values: LLAMA believes advancing leadership and management excellence is achieved by fostering the following values—exemplary and innovative service to and for our members, and leadership development and continuous learning opportunities for our members.

Established in 1957.

Membership

Memb. 3,900+. For information on dues, see ALA entry.

Officers (2016–2017)

Pres. John Spears, Pikes Peak Lib. Dist. Tel. 719-531-6333, ext. 2010, e-mail jspears@ppld.org; *Pres.-Elect* Pixey A. Mosley, Texas A&M Univ. Tel. 979-862-1086, e-mail pmosley@library.tamu.edu; *Treas.* Susan M. Considine, Fayetteville Free Lib.; *Past Pres.* Jeff Steely, Georgia State Univ.

Section Chairs

Assessment. Anne Cooper Moore.
Buildings and Equipment. Christopher Stewart.
Fundraising and Financial Development. Dwain Teague.
Human Resources. Scott P. Muir.
Library Organization and Management. Adriana Gonzalez.
New Professionals. Zara T. Wilkinson.
Public Relations and Marketing. Rebecca L. Metzger.
Systems and Services. Lynda L. Aldana.
Address correspondence to the executive director.

Publication

Library Leadership and Management (LL&M)
(open access at https://journals.tdl.org/llm/ index.php/llm/index). *Ed.* Gary W. White.

E-mail gww2@umd.edu.

American Library Association
Public Library Association

Executive Director, Barbara A. Macikas
50 E. Huron St., Chicago, IL 60611
312-280-5752, 800-545-2433 ext. 5752, fax 312-280-5029, e-mail pla@ala.org
World Wide Web http://www.pla.org

The Public Library Association (PLA) has specific responsibility for

1. Conducting and sponsoring research about how the public library can respond to changing social needs and technical developments

2. Developing and disseminating materials useful to public libraries in interpreting public library services and needs

3. Conducting continuing education for public librarians by programming at national and regional conferences, by publications such as the newsletter, and by other delivery means

4. Establishing, evaluating, and promoting goals, guidelines, and standards for public libraries

5. Maintaining liaison with relevant national agencies and organizations engaged in public administration and human services, such as the National Association of Counties, the Municipal League, and the Commission on Postsecondary Education

6. Maintaining liaison with other divisions and units of ALA and other library organizations, such as the Association for Library and Information Science Education and the Urban Libraries Council

7. Defining the role of the public library in service to a wide range of user and potential user groups

8. Promoting and interpreting the public library to a changing society through legislative programs and other appropriate means

9. Identifying legislation to improve and to equalize support of public libraries

PLA enhances the development and effectiveness of public librarians and public library services. This mission positions PLA to

- Focus its efforts on serving the needs of its members

- Address issues that affect public libraries

- Commit to quality public library services that benefit the general public

The goals of PLA are

- Advocacy and Awareness: PLA is an essential partner in public library advocacy.

- Leadership and Transformation: PLA is the leading source for learning opportunities to advance transformation of public libraries.

- Literate Nation: PLA will be a leader and valued partner of public libraries' initiatives to create a literate nation.

- Organizational Excellence: PLA is positioned to sustain and grow its resources to advance the work of the association.

Membership

Memb. 8,000+. Open to all ALA members interested in the improvement and expansion of public library services to all ages in various types of communities.

Officers (2016–2017)

Pres. Felton Thomas, Jr., Cleveland Public Lib., 325 Superior Ave., Cleveland, OH 44114. Tel. 216-623-2827, e-mail felton.thomas@cpl.org; *Pres.-Elect* Pam Sandlian Smith, Anythink Libs., Adams County, CO. E-mail psmith@anythinklibraries.org; *Past Pres.* Vailey Oehlke, Multnomah County Lib., 10723 SW. Capitol Hwy., Portland, OR 97219. Tel. 503-988-5403, e-mail vaileyo@multcolib.org.

Committee Chairs

Baker & Taylor Entertainment Audio Music/Video Product Award. Rebecca Harrison.
Budget and Finance. Clara Nalli Bohrer.
Gordon M. Conable Award Jury. Sally L. Miculek.
Continuing Education Advisory Group. Theresa A. Jehlik.
DEMCO New Leaders Travel Grant Jury. Trinh Jeanette Contreras.
EBSCO Excellence in Small and/or Rural Public Library Service Award. Luren E. Dickinson.
Intellectual Freedom. Stefanie Isabel Bailey.
Leadership Development. Renee Di Pilato.
Legislation and Advocacy. Nicolle Eileen Ingui Davies.
Allie Beth Martin Award Jury. Luren E. Dickinson.

Membership Advisory Group. Michael Spelman.
Nominating. Larry P. Neal.
Performance Measurement. Denise Marie Davis.
Charlie Robinson Award Jury. Susan Baerg Epstein.
PLA 2018 Local Arrangements.
PLA 2018 National Conference. Richard Kong.
PLA 2018 National Conference Program Subcommittee. Aurora Martinez.
PLA/ALSC Every Child Ready to Read Oversight Committee. Sue McCleaf
PLA Annual Conference Program Subcommittee. Michael James Bobish.
PLDS Statistical Report Advisory. Lynn Hoffman.
Polaris Innovation in Technology John Iliff Award. Brian A. Guenther.
Public Libraries Advisory. Kevin A. R. King.
Romance Writers of America Library Grant Jury. Sarah Campbell Tansley.
Technology. Robert Wayne Pasicznyuk.
Upstart Innovation Award Jury. Diana Garcia.

Publication

Public Libraries (bi-mo.; memb.; nonmemb. $65; foreign $75; single copy $10). *Ed.* Kathleen Hughes, PLA, 50 E. Huron St., Chicago, IL 60611. E-mail khughes@ala.org.

American Library Association
Reference and User Services Association

Executive Director, Susan Hornung
50 E. Huron St., Chicago, IL 60611
800-545-2433 ext. 4395, 312-280-4395, fax 312-280-5273, e-mail shornung@ala.org
World Wide Web http://www.ala.org/rusa

Object

The Reference and User Services Association (RUSA) is responsible for stimulating and supporting excellence in the delivery of general library services and materials, and the provision of reference and information services, collection development, readers' advisory, and resource sharing for all ages, in every type of library.

The specific responsibilities of RUSA are:

1. Conduct of activities and projects within the association's areas of responsibility

2. Encouragement of the development of librarians engaged in these activities, and stimulation of participation by members of appropriate type-of-library divisions

3. Synthesis of the activities of all units within the American Library Association that have a bearing on the type of activities represented by the association

4. Representation and interpretation of the association's activities in contacts outside the profession

5. Planning and development of programs of study and research in these areas for the total profession

6. Continuous study and review of the association's activities

Membership

Memb. 3,800+

Officers

Pres. Alesia M. McManus, Clark Lib. Bldg., 10901 Little Patuxent Pkwy., Columbia, MD 21044. Tel. 443-518-4634, e-mail amcmanus@howardcc.edu; *Pres.-Elect* Chris LeBeau *Secy.* Kathryn J. Oberg, Tel. 703-228- 5988; *Past Pres.* Anne M. Houston, Smith College Libs., 7 Neilson Dr., Northampton, MA 01063. Tel. 413-585-2911, e-mail ahouston@smith.edu; *Div. Councilor* Sarah Jane Hammill.

Sections

Business Reference and Services (BRASS); Collection Development and Evaluation (CODES); History (HS); Emerging Technologies (ETS); Reference Services (RSS); Sharing and Transforming Access to Resources (STARS).

Committees

Access to Information—Bryan Mark Carson.
AFL-CIO/ALA Labor Committee—Aliqae Geraci and Michael Wasser.
Andrew Carnegie Medals for Excellence in Fiction and Nonfiction—Victoria Caplinger.
Awards Coordinating Committee—Joseph Yue.
Board of Directors—Alesia M. McManus, President.
Budget and Finance Committee—Chris LeBeau.

Conference Program Coordinating Committee—Kendra Nan Skellen.
Excellence in Reference and Adult Services Award—Susan Beck.
Executive Committee—Alesia M. McManus, President.
Isadore Gilbert Mudge Award—Cheryl M. LaGuardia.
John Sessions Memorial Award—Aliqae Geraci.
Louis Shores Award—Neal Wyatt.
Margaret E. Monroe Library Adult Services Award—Barry Trott.
Membership Committee—Amber A. Prentiss.
Name Change Task Force—Nancy A. Cunningham.
Nominating Committee—Joseph A. Thompson, Jr.
Organization and Planning Committee—Elizabeth Marie German.
Planning Task Force for the LearnRT/RUSA Annual 2017 Preconference—Ryan F. Buller and Chrystal Schempf.
President's Program Planning Committee—Elizabeth A. Kocevar-Weidinger.
Professional Competencies for Reference and User Services Librarians—Nancy Huling.
Professional Development—Elizabeth A. Kocevar-Weidinger.
Publications and Communications Committee—Kirk G. MacLeod.
Reference Service Press Awards Committee—Valerie Neylon.
RUSQ Editorial Board—Barry Trott.
Standards and Guidelines Committee—Tina Baich.
Trends Subcommittee—Chair, TBA.
For section committees, and committee chairpersons, see http://www.ala.org/rusa/contact/rosters.

Publications

Reference & User Services Quarterly (online only at http://rusa.metapress.com) (memb.). *Ed.* Barry Trott, Williamsburg Regional Lib., 7770 Croaker Rd., Williamsburg, VA 23188-7064. E-mail btrott@wrl.org.
RUSA Update (q., online newsletter, at http://www.rusa.ala.org/rusaupdate).

American Library Association
United for Libraries: Association of Library Trustees, Advocates, Friends, and Foundations

Executive Director, Sally Gardner Reed
109 S. 13 St., Suite 117B, Philadelphia, PA 19107
312-280-2161, fax 215-545-3821, e-mail sreed@ala.org
World Wide Web http://www.ala.org/united

Object

United for Libraries was founded in 1890 as the American Library Trustee Association (ALTA). It was the only division of the American Library Association (ALA) dedicated to promoting and ensuring outstanding library service through educational programs that develop excellence in trusteeship and promote citizen involvement in the support of libraries. ALTA became an ALA division in 1961. In 2008 the members of ALTA voted to expand the division to more aggressively address the needs of friends of libraries and library foundations, and through a merger with Friends of Libraries USA (FOLUSA) became the Association of Library Trustees, Advocates, Friends and Foundations (ALTAFF). In 2012 members voted to add "United for Libraries" to its title.

Memb. 5,200. Open to all interested persons and organizations. For dues and membership year, see ALA entry.

Officers

Pres. Susan J. Schmidt, Montgomery County Public School, 850 Hungerford Dr., Rockville, MD 20850. Tel. 301-320-6502, e-mail Susan_J_Schmidt@mcpsmd.org; *V.P./Pres.-Elect* Steve Laird; *Past Pres.* Ed McBride, SAGE Publications Inc., 2455 Teller Rd., Thousand Oaks, CA 91320. Tel. 805-410-7198,

e-mail ed.mcbride@sagepub.com; *Councilor* Christine Lind Hage.

Committee Chairs

Annual Conference Program. Robin Hoklotubbe.
Awards. Camila Alire.
Leaders Orientation. Steve Laird.
Legislation, Advocacy, & Intellectual Freedom. Shirley Bruursema.
Newsletter & Website Advisory. Paula Beswick.
Nominating. Christine Hage.
PLA Conference Program. Marcellus Turner.

Publications

The Good, The Great, and the Unfriendly: A Librarian's Guide to Working with Friends Groups.
The Complete Library Trustee Handbook.
Even More Great Ideas for Libraries and Friends.
A Library Board's Practical Guide to Self-Evaluation.
A Library Board's Practical Guide to Hiring Outside Experts.
Getting Grants in Your Community.
Making Our Voices Heard: Citizens Speak Out for Libraries.

American Library Association
Young Adult Library Services Association

Executive Director, Beth Yoke
50 E. Huron St., Chicago, IL 60611
312-280-4390, 800-545-2433 ext. 4390, fax 312-280-5276, e-mail yalsa@ala.org
World Wide Web http://www.ala.org/yalsa
YALSA blog http://yalsa.ala.org/blog, The Hub (http://yalsa.ala.org/thehub),
Wiki (http://wikis.ala.org/yalsa), Twitter (http://twitter.com/yalsa)
Facebook (http://www.facebook.com/YALSA)

Object

In every library in the nation, high-quality library service to young adults is provided by a staff that understands and respects the unique informational, educational, and recreational needs of teenagers. Equal access to information, services, and materials is recognized as a right, not a privilege. Young adults are actively involved in the library decision making process. The library staff collaborates and cooperates with other youth-serving agencies to provide a holistic, community-wide network of activities and services that support healthy youth development. To ensure that this vision becomes a reality, the Young Adult Library Services Association (YALSA)

1. Advocates extensive and developmentally appropriate library and information services for young adults ages 12 to 18
2. Promotes reading and supports the literacy movement
3. Advocates the use of information and digital technologies to provide effective library service
4. Supports equality of access to the full range of library materials and services, including existing and emerging information and digital technologies, for young adults
5. Provides education and professional development to enable its members to serve as effective advocates for young people
6. Fosters collaboration and partnerships among its individual members with the library community and other groups involved in providing library and information services to young adults
7. Influences public policy by demonstrating the importance of providing library and information services that meet the unique needs and interests of young adults
8. Encourages research and is in the vanguard of new thinking concerning the provision of library and information services for youth

Membership

Memb. 5,100. Open to anyone interested in library services for and with young adults. For information on dues, see ALA entry.

Officers

Pres. Sarah Hill, Lake Land College, 5001 Lake Land Blvd., Mattoon, IL 61938. Tel. 217-234-5440, e-mail gsarahthelibrarian@gmail.com; *Pres.-Elect* Sandra Hughes-Hassell. E-mail smhughes@email.unc.edu; *Div. Councilor* Todd Krueger. E-mail toddbcpl@gmail.com; *Fiscal Officer* Nick Buron. E-mail nick buron.ala@gmail.com; *Secy.* Crystle Martin. E-mail crystle.martin@gmail.com; *Past Pres.* Candice Mack, Los Angeles Public Lib., 630 W. 5th St., Los Angeles, CA 90071. E-mail candice.yalsa@gmail.com.

Directors

Diane Colson, Franklin Escobedo, Kafi Kumasi, Gretchen Kolderup, Jennifer Korn, Kate McNair, Jessi Snow, Mega Subramaniam.

Publications

Journal of Research on Libraries and Young Adults (q.) (online, open source, peer-reviewed). *Ed.* Denise Agosto.

Young Adult Library Services (q.) (memb.; nonmemb. $70; foreign $80). *Ed.* Linda W. Braun.

YALSA E-News (weekly, memb.). *Ed.* Anna Lam.

American Merchant Marine Library Association (AMMLA)

Executive Director, Roger T. Korner
104 Broadway, Jersey City, NJ 07306
201-369-1100, fax 201-369-1105, e-mail ussammla@ix.netcom.com
World Wide Web http://unitedseamensservice.org/ammla

Object

Known as "the public library of the high seas," AMMLA provides ship and shore library service for American-flag merchant vessels and for the Military Sealift Command, the U.S. Coast Guard, and other waterborne operations of the U.S. government. Established in 1921.

In 2012 it distributed more than 23,000 books and magazines to American Merchant Marine, the U.S. Navy and Coast Guard, and seafarers of allied nations. A total of 240 libraries were mailed to U.S. merchant vessels transporting supplies to U.S. forces.

Officers

Pres. Edward R. Morgan; *Chair, Exec. Committee* F. Anthony Naccarato; *V.P. s* H. Marshall Ainley, Stephen Cotton, Capt. Remo Di Fiore, Paul Doell, James Given, John Halas, Capt. Don Marcus, Yasumi Morita, Dr. Conrado F. Oca, Michael Sacco, Yury Sukhorukov, Richard L. Trumka; *Secy.* Donald E. Kadlac; *Treas.* Philip W. J. Fisher; *General Counsel* John L. DeGurse, Jr.

Board of Directors

Mark H. Buzby, Joseph J. Cox, John L. DeGurse, Jr., Capt. Fred Finger, Philip W. J. Fisher, Chas, Philip H. Greene Jr., Ed Hanley, David Heindel, James Henry, Donald E. Kadlac, Edward J. Kelly, Roger T. Korner, Capt. Thomas W. Merrell, Edward R. Morgan, F. Anthony Naccarato, William Nurthen, C. James Patti, William D. Potts, Philip Shapiro, Augustin Tellez, Kenneth R. Wykle.

American Theological Library Association

Executive Director, Brenda Bailey-Hainer
300 S. Wacker Dr., Suite 2100, Chicago, IL 60606-6701
312-454-5100, fax 312-454-5505, e-mail bbailey-hainer@atla.com.
World Wide Web http://www.atla.com

Mission

The mission of the American Theological Library Association (ATLA) is to foster the study of theology and religion by enhancing the development of theological and religious libraries and librarianship.

Membership

Dues (Inst.) $100–$1,000; (Indiv. varies, based on income) $35–$181.50; (Student) $35; (Affiliates) $100.

Officers

Pres. Timothy D. Lincoln, Austin Presbyterian Theological Seminary, Stitt Lib., 100 E. 27th St., Austin, TX. Tel. 512-404-4873, fax 512-322-0901, e-mail tlincoln@austinseminary.edu; *V.P.* Matthew J. Ostercamp, North Park Univ., Brandel Lib., 5114 N. Christiana Ave., Chicago, IL 60625. Tel. 773-244-5580, e-mail mjostercamp@northpark.edu; *Secy.* Tracy Powell Iwaskow, John Creek, GA; *Past Pres.* Kelly Campbell, Columbia Theological Seminary, 701 S. Columbia Dr., Box 520, Decatur, GA 30031. E-mail campbellk@ctsnet.edu.

Board of Directors

Officers, Jennifer Bartholomew, Beth Bidlack, Kelly Campbell, Jaeyeon Lucy Chung, Ellen Frost, Brad Ost,Stephen Sweeney, Christina Torbert, Jennifer Ulrich.

Committee Chairs

Conference. Miranda Bennett.
Diversity, Equity, and Inclusion. Donna Wells.
Endowment. Sharon Taylor.
Professional Development. Megan Welsh.

Publications

Annual Reports.
ATLA Newsletter. (mo., online).
Monographs (formerly ATLA Book Series).
Theological Librarianship.
Theology Cataloging Bulletin.
ATLA *Summary of Proceedings.*

Archivists and Librarians in the History of the Health Sciences

President, Rachel Ingold
Email rachel.ingold@duke.edu
World Wide Web http://www.alhhs.org

Object

The association was established exclusively for educational purposes, to serve the professional interests of librarians, archivists, and other specialists actively engaged in the librarianship of the history of the health sciences by promoting the exchange of information and by improving the standards of service.

Membership

Memb. Approximately 150. Dues $15.

Officers

Pres. Rachel Ingold, History of Medicine Collections, Rubenstein Rare Book and Manuscript Lib., Duke Univ., 411 Chapel Dr., Durham, NC. Tel. 919-684-8549, e-mail rachel.ingold@duke.edu; *Secy.* Dawne Lucas, Health Sciences Lib., Univ. of North Carolina at Chapel Hill. E-mail dawne_lucas@unc.edu; *Treas.* Barbara J. Niss, Icahn School of Medicine at Sinai, 1428 Madison Ave., New York 10029. Tel. 212-241-7239, e-mail barbara.niss@mssm.edu; *Past Pres.* Stephen E. Novak, Archives and Special Collections, Columbia Univ. Medical Ctr., 701 W. 168th St., New York. Tel. 212-305-7931, e-mail sen13@columbia.edu; *Memb.-at-Large* Maija Anderson, Lori Curtis, Scott D. Grimwood, Polina Ilieva.

Committee Chairs

Annual Meeting 2016 Local Arrangements. Lois Hendrickson.
Annual Meeting 2016 Program: Elisabeth Brander.
Interim Archivist: Jodi Koste.
Nominating 2016. Michael North.

Publications Awards. Keith Mages. Recognition Awards 2016. Judy Chelnick. Recruiting: Jonathan Erlen. Website: Russell Johnson.

Editorial Board Chairs

The Watermark Stephen E. Novak.

Awards Committee Chairs

AlHHS Publication Award: James M. Edmonson; ALHHA Recognition of Merit: Michael Flannery; Lisabeth M. Holloway Award: Michael Flannery.

Publication

Watermark (q.; memb.). *Ed.* Stephen E. Novak. Augustus C. Long Health Sciences Lib., Columbia Univ. E-mail sen13@columbia.edu.

ARMA International

President, Tera Ladner
11880 College Blvd., Suite 450, Overland Park, KS 66210
800-422-2762, 913-341-3808, fax 913-341-3742
World Wide Web http://www.arma.org

Object

To advance the practice of records and information management as a discipline and a profession; to organize and promote programs of research, education, training, and networking within that profession; to support the enhancement of professionalism of the membership; and to promote cooperative endeavors with related professional groups.

Membership

Approximately 26,000 in more than 30 countries. Annual dues (Professional) $175; (Assoc.) $95. Chapter dues vary.

Officers

Pres. Tera Ladner, Aflac. 1932 Wynnton Rd. Columbus, GA. Tel. 706-763-2656, e-mail teraladner.arma@gmail.com; *Pres.-Elect* Ilona Koti. E-mail ilona.koti@yahoo.com; *Treas.* Michael Haley. E-mail Michaelhaley.arma@gmail.com; *Past Pres.* Peter Kurilecz. E-mail peterkurilecz.arma@gmail.com.

Directors

Mark Chardack, Margaret Hermesmeyer, Mark Levin, Peggy Syljuberget, Robin Thompson, Ryan Zilm.

Publication

Information Management (IM) (bi-mo.).

Art Libraries Society of North America

Executive Director, Robert J. Kopchinski
414-908-4954 ext. 136, email r.kopchinski@arlisna.org
World Wide Web https://www.arlisna.org

Object

The object of the Art Libraries Society of North America (ARLIS/NA) is to foster excellence in art librarianship and visual resources curatorship for the advancement of the visual arts. Established 1972.

Membership

Memb. 1,000+. Dues (Business Affiliate) $250; (Introductory) $100 (two-year limit); (Indiv.) $150; (Student) $50 (three-year limit); (Ret.) $75(Unemployed/Bridge) $50. Year. Jan. 1–Dec. 31. Membership is open to all those interested in visual librarianship, whether they be professional librarians, students, library assistants, art book publishers, art book dealers, art historians, archivists, architects, slide and photograph curators, or retired associates in these fields.

Officers

Pres. Heather Gendron, Yale Univ. 180 York St., New Haven. E-mail heather.gendron@yale.

edu; *V.P./Pres.-Elect* Eumie Imm Stroukoff, Director, Research Center, Georgia O'Keeffe Museum, Santa Fe, NM. Tel. 505-946-1011, e-mail estroukoff@okeeffemuseum.org; *Secy.* Jamie Lausch Vander Broek, Librarian for Art & Design, Univ. of Michigan, Ann Arbor. Tel. 734-764-3166, e-mail jlausch@umich. edu; *Treas.* Matthew Gengler, Head of Access Services, Cleveland Museum of Art's Ingalls Library, Cleveland. Tel. 216-707-6678, e-mail mgengler@clevelandart.org; *Past Pres.* Kristen Regina, Arcadia Dir. of the Lib. and Archives, Philadelphia Museum of Art, Philadelphia.

Address correspondence to Robert J. Kopchinski, Technical Enterprises, Inc., 7044 S. 13 St., Oak Creek, WI 53154.

Publications

ARLIS/NA Reviews (bi-mo.; memb.).
Art Documentation (2 a year; memb., subscription).
Handbook and List of Members (ann.; memb.). Occasional papers (price varies).
Miscellaneous others (request current list from headquarters).

Asian/Pacific American Librarians Association

Executive Director, Buenaventura "Ven" Basco
P.O. Box 677593 Orlando, FL 32867-7593
407-823-5048, email bbasco@mail.ucf.edu
World Wide Web http://www.apalaweb.org

Object

To provide a forum for discussing problems and concerns of Asian/Pacific American librarians; to provide a forum for the exchange of ideas by Asian/Pacific American librarians and other librarians; to support and encourage library services to Asian/Pacific American communities; to recruit and support Asian/Pacific American

librarians in the library/information science professions; to seek funding for scholarships in library/information science programs for Asian/Pacific Americans; and to provide a vehicle whereby Asian/Pacific American librarians can cooperate with other associations and organizations having similar or allied interests. Founded in 1980; incorporated 1981; affiliated with American Library Association 1982.

Membership

Approximately 300. Open to all librarians and information specialists of Asian/Pacific descent working in U.S. libraries and information centers and other related organizations, and to others who support the goals and purposes of the association. Asian/Pacific Americans are defined as people residing in North America who self-identify as Asian/Pacific American.

Officers (2016–2017)

Pres. Lessa Kanani'opua Pelayo-Lozada, Glendale Public Lib., Glendale, CA. E-mail lessalozada@gmail.com; *V.P.* Dora Ho, Los Angeles Public Lib., 630 W. 5th St., Los Angeles. E-mail dora2005@gmail.com; *Secy.* Anna Coats, Livingston Public Lib., 10 Robert Harp Dr., Livingston, NJ. Tel. 973-992-4600 ext. 255, e-mail anna.coats@livingston.bccls.org; *Treas.* Peter Spyers-Duran; *Past Pres.* Janet H. Clarke, Stony Brook Univ. Libs., 100 Nicolls Rd., Stony Brook, NY. Tel. 631-632-1217, e-mail janet.clarke@stonybrooke.edu; *Memb.-at-Large* Ariana Hussain, Brian Leaf, Alyssa Jocson Porter, Ray Pun.

Committee Chairs

Communications and Media. Alyssa Jocson Porter *(2016–2018)* (EB Liaison); Melissa Cardenas-Dow *(2016–2017)*.
Constitution and Bylaws. Young Lee.

Family Literacy Focus. Ariana Hussain, ariana.sani@gmail.com; Anna Coats, annamcoats27@gmail.com.
Finance and Fundraising. Linda Absher, absherl@pdx.edu; Heawon Paick, heawonpaick@gmail.com.
Literature Awards. Dora Ho dorah2005@gmail.com; Ven Basco ven@ucf.edu.
Membership. Monnee Tong, Brian Leaf (EB Liaison).
Mentoring. Tassanee Chitcharoen *(2015–2017)*.
Ray Pun *(2016–2018)* (EB Liaison).
Nominating. Janet Clarke.
Program Planning. Dora Ho, Alanna Aiko Moore.
Scholarships and Awards. Melanee Vicedo *(2015–2017)*, Cynthia Orozco *(2016–2018)*.

Task Force Chairs

Archives. Cat Phan.
2017 Annual ALA Diversity & Outreach Fair. Annie Pho, Jenny Yap.
2017 Midwinter Local Arrangements—Atlanta. Paolo Gujilde.
2017 Annual Local Arrangements—Chicago. Ariana Lim, Anna Coats.
Strategic Planning Task Force. Lessa Pelayo-Lozada, Janet Clarke.

Publication

APALA Newsletter (q.).

Association for Information Science and Technology

Executive Director, Richard B. Hill
8555 16th St., Ste. 850, Silver Spring, MD 20910
301-495-0900, fax 301-495-0810, email asist@asist.org
World Wide Web http://www.asist.org

Object

The Association for Information Science and Technology (ASIS&T, formerly the American Society for Information Science and Technol-

ogy) provides a forum for the discussion, publication, and critical analysis of work dealing with the design, management, and use of information, information systems, and information technology.

Membership

Regular Memb. (Indiv.) 1,100; (Student) 500. Dues (Professional) $140; (Ret.) $70; (Student) $40; (Hardship) $40; Developing Nation (varies by category); (Inst.) $650; (Corporate Patron) $800.

Officers

Pres. Lynn Silipigni Connaway, Tel. 303.246.3623. E-mail lynn_connaway@oclc.org; *Pres.-Elect* Lisa M. Given, Charles Sturt Univ., New South Wales, Australia. E-mail lgiven@csu.edu.au; *Treas.* June Abbas, Univ. of Oklahoma. E-mail jmabbas@ou.edu; *Past Pres.* Nadia Caidi, Univ. of Toronto. E-mail nadia.caidi@utoronto.ca; *Parliamentarian* Steve Hardin, Indiana State Univ. E-mail steve.hardin@indstate.edu.

Directors

Daniel Alemneh, Jamshid Beheshti, Dania Bilal, Fidelia Ibekwe-SanJuan, Kathryn La Barre, Brandi Loveday-Chesley, Heather O'Brien, Abebe Rorissa, Kayla Siddell, Kristene Unsworth.

Committee Chairs

Budget and Finance. June Abbas.
Awards and Honors. Soo Young Rieh, Ken Fleischmann.
Award Nominations. Lai Ma, Anita Komlodi.
Constitution and Bylaws. Linda C. Smith.
Education and Professional Advancement. Keren Dali, Bill Kules.
International Relations. Mega Subramaniam, Elke Greifeneder.
Leadership. Ixchel Faniel, Laura Creekmore.
Membership. Naresh Agarwal.
Nominations. Nadia Caidi.
Publications. Rong Tang, Yuelin Li.
Standards. Mark Needleman,Timothy Dickey.

Task Force Chairs

Executive Director Search. Sandra Hirsh, Clara Chu.
Knowledge Management. June Abbas, Heather Pfeiffer.
Working Group for Presidential Initiatives. Lynn Silipigni Connaway.
ASIS&T 80th Anniversary Advisory Group. Kathryn La Barre.

Publications

Periodicals

Journal of the Association for Information Science and Technology. Ed. Javed Mostafa. Available with ASIS&T membership or from Wiley Blackwell.
Bulletin of the Association for Information Science and Technology (online only).
Proceedings of the ASIS&T Annual Meeting. Available from ASIS&T.

Books and Monographs

ASIST Thesaurus of Information Science, Technology, and Librarianship, 3rd ed.
Computerization Movements and Technology Diffusion: From Mainframes to Ubiquitous Computing.
Covert and Overt.
Digital Inclusion.
Editorial Peer Review: Its Strengths and Weaknesses.
Electronic Publishing: Applications and Implications.
Evaluating Networked Information Services: Techniques, Policy and Issues.
From Print to Electronic: The Transformation of Scientific Communication.
Historical Information Science.
Historical Studies in Information Science.
The History and Heritage of Scientific and Technological Information Systems.
Information and Emotion: The Emergent Affective Paradigm in Information Behavior Research and Theory.
Information Management for the Intelligent Organization, 3rd ed.
Information Need: A Theory Connecting Information Search to Knowledge Formation.

Information Representation and Retrieval in the Digital Age, 2nd ed.

Intelligent Technologies in Library and Information Service Applications.

International Perspectives on the History of Information Science and Technology.

Introduction to Information Science and Technology.

Introductory Concepts in Information Science, 2nd ed.

Knowledge Management: The Bibliography.

Knowledge Management for the Information Professional.

Knowledge Management in Practice: Connections and Context.

Knowledge Management Lessons Learned: What Works and What Doesn't.

The New Digital Scholar.

The Next Digital Scholar.

Powering Search: The Role of Thesauri in New Information Environments.

Scholarly Metrics Under the Microscope.

Statistical Methods for the Information Professional.

Theories of Information Behavior.

The Web of Knowledge: A Festschrift in Honor of Eugene Garfield.

The above books and monographs are available from Information Today, Inc., 143 Old Marlton Pike, Medford, NJ 08055. Many are available as e-books.

Association for Library and Information Science Education

Executive Director, Andrew Estep
ALISE Headquarters, 2150 N. 107 St., Suite 205, Seattle WA 98133
206-209-5267, fax 206-367-8777, e-mail office@alise.org
World Wide Web http://www.alise.org

Object

The Association for Library and Information Science Education (ALISE) is an independent nonprofit professional association whose mission is to promote excellence in research, teaching, and service for library and information science education through leadership, collaboration, advocacy, and dissemination of research. Its enduring purpose is to promote research that informs the scholarship of teaching and learning for library and information science, enabling members to integrate research into teaching and learning. The association provides a forum in which to share ideas, discuss issues, address challenges, and shape the future of education for library and information science. Founded in 1915 as the Association of American Library Schools, it has had its present name since 1983.

Membership

700+ in four categories: Personal, Institutional, International Affiliate Institutional, and Associate Institutional. Personal membership is open to anyone with an interest in the association's objectives.

Officers

Pres. Dietmar Wolfram, Professor, Univ. of Wisconsin-Milwaukee. E-mail dwolfram@uwm.edu; *Pres.-Elect* Heidi Julien; *Secy.-Treas.* Denice Adkins, Univ. of Missouri; *Past Pres.* Louise Spiteri, Dalhousie Univ., 6100 Univ. Ave., Suite 4010, Halifax, NS B3H 4R2. Tel. 902-494-2473, e-mail louise.Spiteri@Dal.Ca.

Directors

Leanne Bowler, Cecilia Salvatore, Rong Tang.

Publication

Journal of Education for Library and Information Science (JELIS) (q.). *Ed.* Peta Wellstead, Open Polytechnic of New Zealand/Kuratini Tuwhera. E-mail jeliseditor@alise.org.

Association for Rural and Small Libraries

President, Judy Calhoun
201 E. Main St., Suite 1405, Lexington, KY 40507
859-514-9178, e-mail szach@amrms.com
World Wide Web http://www.arsl.info

Object

The Association for Rural and Small Libraries (ARSL) was established in 1978, in the Department of Library Science at Clarion University of Pennsylvania, as the Center for Study of Rural Librarianship.

ARSL is a network of people throughout the United States dedicated to the positive growth and development of libraries. ARSL believes in the value of rural and small libraries, and strives to create resources and services that address national, state, and local priorities for libraries situated in rural communities.

Its objectives are

- To organize a network of members concerned about the growth and development of useful library services in rural and small libraries
- To provide opportunities for the continuing education of members
- To provide mechanisms for members to exchange ideas and to meet on a regular basis
- To cultivate the practice of librarianship and to foster a spirit of cooperation among members of the profession, enabling them to act together for mutual goals
- To serve as a source of current information about trends, issues, and strategies
- To partner with other library and nonlibrary groups and organizations serving rural and small library communities
- To collect and disseminate information and resources that are critical to this network

- To advocate for rural and small libraries at the local, state, and national levels

Officers

Pres. Judy Calhoun, Regional Dir., Southeast Arkansas Regional Lib., 114 W. Jefferson, Monticello. Tel. 870-367-8584, e-mail director. searl@gmail.com; *V.P./Pres.-Elect* Vicki Bartz, County Libn., Ortonville/Graceville Public Lib., 412 NW 2nd St. Ortonville. E-mail vicki. bartz@pioneerland.lib.mn.us; *Secy.* Kevin Tomlinson, Lib. Consultant, Idaho Commission for Libs., 325 W. State St., Boise. E-mail kevin.tomlinson@libraries.idaho.gov; *Treas.* Susan J. Hughes. E-mail Lhsh73@hotmail. com; *Past Pres.* Jet Kofoot. E-mail jet.kofoot@ gmail.com.

Directors

Ryan Deery, Julie Elmore, Linda Green, Kieran Hixon, Jennifer Pearson, Clancy Pool, Mary J. Soucie, Jenniffer Stephenson, Meredith Wickham, Kathy Zappitello.

Committee Chairs

Marketing & Communications. Julie Elmore, Kieran Hixon.
Membership Development. Carolyn Peterson.
Partnerships. Jennifer Pearson.
Governance. Kevin Tomlinson.
Finance. Vicki Bartz, Susan Hughes.
Conference. Vicki Bartz.
Scholarship. Shirley Vonderhaar.
Nominating. Donna Brice.

Association of Academic Health Sciences Libraries

President, Neil Rambo
2150 N. 107 St., Suite 205, Seattle, WA 98133
206-209-5261, fax 206-367-8777, email office@aahsl.org
World Wide Web http://www.aahsl.org

Object

The Association of Academic Health Sciences Libraries (AAHSL) comprises the libraries serving the accredited U.S. and Canadian medical schools belonging to or affiliated with the Association of American Medical Colleges. Its goals are to promote excellence in academic health science libraries and to ensure that the next generation of health practitioners is trained in information-seeking skills that enhance the quality of health care delivery, education, and research. Founded in 1977.

Membership

Memb. 150+. Full membership is available to nonprofit educational institutions operating a school of health sciences that has full or provisional accreditation by the Association of American Medical Colleges. Full members are represented by the chief administrative officer of the member institution's health sciences library. Associate membership (and nonvoting representation) is available to organizations having an interest in the purposes and activities of the association. For dues information, contact the association.

Officers

Pres. (2015–2018) Neil Rambo, NYU Health Sciences Lib., NYU Langone Medical Center. Tel. 212-263-5394; *Pres.-Elect (2016–2019)* Jane Blumenthal, Univ. of Michigan Lib., Univ. of Michigan. Tel. 734-936-1403; *Secy. -Treas. (2016–2019)* Cynthia Henderson, Norris Medical Lib., Univ. of Southern California. Tel. 323-442-1130; *Past Pres. (2014–2017)* Ruth Riley, School of Medicine Lib., Univ. of South Carolina. Tel. 803-216-3220.

Board Members

Pamela Bradigan, Nadine Dexter, Jerry Perry.

Task Force Chairs

AAHSL Diversity, Equity, and Inclusion. Cristina A. Pope.

Association of Christian Librarians

Executive Director, Janelle Mazelin
P.O. Box 4, Cedarville, Ohio 45314
937-766-2255, fax 937-766-5499, e-mail info@acl.org
World Wide Web http://www.acl.org

Object

The mission of the Association of Christian Librarians (ACL) is to strengthen libraries through professional development of evangelical librarians, scholarship, and spiritual encouragement for service in higher education. ACL is a growing community that integrates faith, ministry, and academic librarianship through development of members, services, and scholarship.
Founded 1957.

Membership

500+ at about 150 institutions. Membership is open to those who profess the Christian faith as outlined by the association's statement of faith, and are employed at an institution of higher education. Associate memberships are available for non-librarians who both agree with ACL's statement of faith and are interested in libraries or librarianship.

Officers

Pres. (2016–2019) Denise Nelson, Point Loma Nazarene Univ.; *V.P. (2011–2017)* Rodney Birch, George Fox Univ.; *Secy. (2016–2017)*

Anita Gray, Huntington Univ.; *Treas. (2008–2019)* Sheila O. Carlblom; *Dirs.-at-Large* Nate Farley, Katie King, Linda Poston, Paul Roberts, Alice Ruleman, Jennifer Walz.

Publications

Christian Periodical Index (q.; electronic).
The Christian Librarian. (2 a year; $30).
The Librarian's Manual (English or Spanish).
ABHE Library Guidelines (memb.).

Association of Independent Information Professionals

President, Jane Langeman
8550 United Plaza Blvd., Suite 1001, Baton Rouge, LA 70809
225-408-4400, fax 225-408-4422, e-mail office@aiip.org
World Wide Web http://www.aiip.org

Object

Members of the Association of Independent Information Professionals (AIIP) are owners of firms providing such information-related services as online and manual research, document delivery, database design, library support, consulting, writing, and publishing.

The objectives of the association are

- To advance the knowledge and understanding of the information profession

- To promote and maintain high professional and ethical standards among its members

- To encourage independent information professionals to assemble to discuss common issues

- To promote the interchange of information among independent information professionals and various organizations

- To keep the public informed of the profession and of the responsibilities of the information professional

Membership

Memb. 200+. Dues (Full) $200; (Assoc.) $200; (Student) $50; (Supporting) $500; (Ret.) $75; (Emeritus) $50.

Officers

Pres. Jane Langeman, Langeman Consulting, 773 Humboldt St., Denver, CO 80218. Tel. 720-810-0165; *Pres.-Elect* Scott Attenborough, Content Capital LLC, 6501 Red Hook Plaza, Suite 201, St. Thomas. Tel. 937-344-6821; *Secy.* Shelly Azar, Insight Researchers LLC, St. Louis. Tel. 314-225-7815, e-mail infor@insightresearchers.com; *Treas.* Marydee Ojala, President, Ojala Assocs.; *Past Pres.* June M. Boyle, CeRCo Research & Consulting, 22 W. 85th St., Unit 2A, New York. Tel. 212-874-7336, e-mail info@cerco-research.com.

Board Members

Mary Ellen Bates, Jan Knight, Ken Watson.

Publications

AIIP Connections (q.).

Membership Directory (ann.).

Professional papers series.

Association of Jewish Libraries

President, Amalia Warshenbrot
P.O. Box 1118, Teaneck, NJ 07666
201-371-3255, email info@jewishlibraries.org
World Wide Web http://www.jewishlibraries.org

Object

The Association of Jewish Libraries (AJL) is an international professional organization that fosters access to information and research in all forms of media relating to all things Jewish. The association promotes Jewish literacy and scholarship and provides a community for peer support and professional development.

AJL membership is open to individuals and libraries, library workers, and library supporters. There are two divisions within AJL: RAS (Research Libraries, Archives, and Special Collections) and SSC (Schools, Synagogues, and Centers). The diverse membership includes libraries in synagogues, JCCs, day schools, yeshivot, universities, Holocaust museums, and the Library of Congress. Membership is drawn from North America and places beyond, including China, the Czech Republic, the Netherlands, Israel, Italy, South Africa, Switzerland, and the United Kingdom.

Goals

The association's goals are to

- Maintain high professional standards for Judaica librarians and recruit qualified individuals into the profession
- Facilitate communication and exchange of information on a global scale
- Encourage quality publication in the field in all formats and media, print, digital, and so forth, and to stimulate publication of high-quality children's literature
- Facilitate and encourage establishment of Judaica library collections

- Enhance information access for all through application of advanced technologies
- Publicize the organization and its activities in all relevant venues: stimulate awareness of Judaica library services among the public at large; promote recognition of Judaica librarianship within the wider library profession; and encourage recognition of Judaica library services by other organizations and related professions
- Ensure continuity of the association through sound management, financial security, effective governance and a dedicated and active membership

AJL conducts an annual convention in the United States or Canada in late June.

Membership

Memb. 600. Year: Oct.–Sept. For dues information, email membership@jewishlibraries.org.

Officers

Pres. Amalia Warshenbrot, 2411 Hamilton Mill Rd., Charlotte, NC. E-mail amaliaima@att.net; *V.P./Pres.-Elect* Dina Herbert, National Archives and Records Administration, Alexandria, VA. E-mail: dina.herbert@gmail.com; *Secy.* Nancy Sack, Univ. of Hawai'i at Manoa, 2550 McCarthy Mall, Honolulu. Tel. 808-956-2648, e-mail sack@hawaii.edu; *Treas.* Patricia Fenton, Ostrow Lib. 15600 Mulholland Dr., Los Angeles. E-mail: pfenton@aju.edu; *Past Pres.* Yaffa Weisman, Hebrew Union College, Jack H. Skirball Campus, 3077 Univ. Ave., Los

Angeles. Tel. 213-765-2170, e-mail safran-ithuc@hotmail.com; *Memb.-at-Large* Michelle Chesner, Daniel A. Scheide.

Board Members

Kathleen Bloomfield, Shulamis Hes, Fred Isaac, Rebecca J.W. Jefferson, Joy Kingsolver, Susan Kusel, Rachel Simon.

Committee Chairs

Accreditation. Rachail Kurtz.
Cataloguing. Heidi G. Lerner.
Conference, Central. James P. Rosenbloom.
Conference, Local. James P. Rosenbloom.
Conference Stipend. Lenore M. Bell.
International Liaison. Rita Saccal.
Member Relations. Heidi Rabinowitz.
News & Reviews. Uri Kolodney.
Public Relations. Aviva Adler.
Publications. Laura Schutzman.
RAS Cataloging. Geraldine Dickel.
Scholarship. Tina M. Weiss.

Editorial Board Chairs

AJL News & Reviews. Uri Kolodney.
Judaica Librarianship. Rachel Leket-Mor.

Awards Committee Chairs

Member Merit Awards. Aaron Taub. E-mail atau@loc.gov.
Reference and Bibliography Award. Rachel Simon. E-mail rsimon@princeton.edu.
Sydney Taylor Book Award. Ellen Tilman. E-mail etilman@kenesethisrael.org.
Sydney Taylor Manuscript Competition. Aileen Grossberg. E-mail library@ohebshalom.org.

Publications

AJL Conference Proceedings.
AJL News (q., digital).
AJL Reviews (q., digital).
Judaica Librarianship (annual, digital).

Association of Research Libraries

Executive Director, Elliot Shore (ex officio)
21 Dupont Circle N.W., Suite 800, Washington, D.C. 20036
202-296-2296, email elliott@arl.org
World Wide Web http://www.arl.org

Object

The Association of Research Libraries (ARL) is a nonprofit organization of 125 research libraries in the United States and Canada. ARL's mission is to influence the changing environment of scholarly communication and the public policies that affect research libraries and the diverse communities they serve. ARL pursues this mission by advancing the goals of its member research libraries, providing leadership in public and information policy to the scholarly and higher education communities, fostering the exchange of ideas and expertise, facilitating the emergence of new roles for research libraries, and shaping a future environment that leverages its interests with those of allied organizations.

Membership

Memb. 125. Membership is institutional.

Officers

Pres. Mary Case, Univ. of Illinois at Chicago, 1200 W. Harrison St., Chicago. Tel. 312-996-2716, e-mail marycase@uic.edu; *V.P./Pres.-Elect* Mary Ann Mavrinac, River Campus Libs., Univ. of Rochester. Tel. 585-275-4471; *Past Pres.* Larry Alford, Univ. of Toronto, 130

St. George St., Toronto, ON, M5S 1A5. Tel. 416-978-2292, e-mail larry.alford@utoronto.ca.

Board Members

Constantia Constantinou, Susan Gibbons, Lorraine Harricombe, Bonnie MacEwan, Steven Smith, Ann Thornton, Diane Parr Walker, Leslie Weir, John Wilkin.

Committee Chairs

Coordinating. Vivian Lewis.
Advocacy and Public Policy. Ginny Steel.
Assessment. Jennifer Paustenbaugh.
Diversity and Inclusion. Chris Bourg.
Finance. Mary Case.
Governance. Larry Alford.
Member Engagement and Outreach. Sara Lowman.
Membership. Mary Ann Mavrinac.

Advisory Groups and Working Group Chairs

ARL Academy Advisory Group. Alberta Comer.
Innovation Lab Advisory Group. Tom Wall.
Leadership Fellows Advisory Group. Xuemao Wang.

Publications

Research Library Issues: A Report from ARL, CNI, and SPARC (4 per year) digital.
ARL Academic Health Sciences Library Statistics (ann.) digital.
ARL Academic Law Library Statistics (ann.) digital.
ARL Annual Salary Survey (ann.) digital.
ARL Statistics (ann.) digital.
SPEC Kit series (4–6 a year) digital.

ARL Membership

Non-university Libraries

Boston Public Lib.; Center for Research Libs.; Lib. of Congress; National Agricultural Lib.; National Archives and Records Administration; National Lib. of Medicine; National Research Council Canada, Knowledge Management; New York Public Lib.; New York State Lib.; Smithsonian Institution Libs.

University Libraries

Alabama; Albany (SUNY); Alberta; Arizona; Arizona State; Auburn; Boston College; Boston Univ.; Brigham Young; British Columbia; Brown; Buffalo (SUNY); Calgary; California, Berkeley; California, Davis; California, Irvine; California, Los Angeles; California, Riverside; California, San Diego; California, Santa Barbara; Case Western Reserve; Chicago; Cincinnati; Colorado; Colorado State; Columbia; Connecticut; Cornell; Dartmouth; Delaware; Duke; Emory; Florida; Florida State; George Washington; Georgetown; Georgia; Georgia Inst. of Technology; Guelph; Harvard; Hawaii; Houston; Howard; Illinois, Chicago; Illinois, Urbana-Champaign; Indiana; Iowa; Iowa State; Johns Hopkins; Kansas; Kent State; Kentucky; Laval; Louisiana State; Louisville; McGill; McMaster; Manitoba; Maryland; Massachusetts; Massachusetts Inst. of Technology; Miami (Florida); Michigan; Michigan State; Minnesota; Missouri; Nebraska, Lincoln; New Mexico; New York; North Carolina; North Carolina State; Northwestern; Notre Dame; Ohio; Ohio State; Oklahoma; Oklahoma State; Oregon; Ottawa; Pennsylvania; Pennsylvania State; Pittsburgh; Princeton; Purdue; Queen's (Kingston, Ontario); Rice; Rochester; Rutgers; Saskatchewan; South Carolina; Southern California; Southern Illinois; Stony Brook (SUNY); Syracuse; Temple; Tennessee; Texas; Texas A&M; Texas Tech; Toronto; Tulane; Utah; Vanderbilt; Virginia; Virginia Tech; Washington; Washington (Saint Louis); Washington State; Waterloo; Wayne State; Western Ontario; Wisconsin; Yale; York.

Association of Vision Science Librarians

Co-Chairs D. J. Matthews, Kristin Motte
World Wide Web http://www.avsl.org

Object

To foster collective and individual acquisition and dissemination of vision science information, to improve services for all persons seeking such information, and to develop standards for libraries to which members are attached. Founded in 1968.

Harold Kohn Vision Science Lib., New York. E-mail ewells@sunyopt.edu; *Membership* Trish Duffel, Univ. of Iowa, Dept. of Ophthalmology and Visual Sciences, C.S. O'Brien Library, Iowa City. E-mail trish-duffel@uiowa. edu; *Archivist* Gale Oren, Univ. of Michigan Kellogg Eye Ctr., John W. Henderson Lib., Ann Arbor. E-mail goren@umich.edu.

Membership

Memb. (Indiv.) 150+, (Inst.) 100+.

Leadership Team

Co-Chair Leslie Holland, Southern College of Optometry, Memphis. E-mail lholland@sco. edu; *Co-Chair* Dede Rios, Rosenberg School of Optometry, Univ. of the Incarnate Word, San Antonio. E-mail dmrios1@uiwtx.edu; *Treas.* Elaine Wells, SUNY College of Optometry,

Publications

Guidelines for Vision Science Librarians.
Opening Day Book, Journal and AV Collection List–Visual Science.
Standards for Vision Science Libraries.
Union List of Vision-Related Serials (irreg.).

Meetings

Annual meeting held in the fall, mid-year mini-meeting with the Medical Library Association.

Beta Phi Mu
(International Library and Information Studies Honor Society)

Executive Director, Alison M. Lewis

P.O. Box 42139, Philadelphia, PA 19101
267-361-5018, e-mail executivedirector@betaphimu.org or headquarters@betaphimu.org
World Wide Web http://www.betaphimu.org

Object

To recognize distinguished achievement in and scholarly contributions to librarianship, information studies, or library education, and to sponsor and support appropriate professional and scholarly projects relating to these fields. Founded at the University of Illinois in 1948.

Membership

Memb. 40,000. Eligibility for membership in Beta Phi Mu is by invitation of the faculty from institutions where the American Library Association, or other recognized accrediting agency approved by the Beta Phi Mu Executive Board, has accredited or recognized a professional degree program. Candidates must be graduates of a library and information science program and fulfill the following requirements: complete the course requirements leading to a master's degree with a scholastic average of 3.75 where A equals 4 points, or complete a planned program of advanced study beyond the master's degree which require full-time study for one or more academic years with a scholastic average of 3.75 where A equals 4.0. Each chapter or approved institution is allowed to invite no more than 25 percent of the annual graduating class, and the faculty of participating library schools must attest to their initiates' professional promise.

Officers

Pres. (2015–2018) Linda C. Smith, Graduate School of Lib. and Information Science, Univ. of Illinois, 501 E. Daniel St., Champaign, IL 61820. Tel. 217-333-7742, e-mail lcsmith@illinois.edu; *V.P./Pres.-Elect (2015–2017)* Vicki Gregory, Univ. of South Florida College of Arts and Sciences, 4202 E. Fowler Ave., CIS 2036, Tampa, FL 33620. Tel. 813-974--3520, e-mail gregory@usf.edu; *Past Pres. (2014–2017)* Charles McElroy, Florida State Univ. Lib., 116 Honors Way, Tallahassee, FL 32306. Tel. 850-645-911, e-mail cnmcelroy@fsu.edu.

Directors

Charles McElroy, Krystyna Matusiak, Em Claire Knowles, Robin Canuel, Bill Davis, Vicki Gregory, Emily Knox, Laura Saunders.

Publications

Beta Phi Mu Scholar Series. Available from Rowman & Littlefield, Publishers, 4501 Forbes Blvd., Suite 200, Lanham, MD 20706. *Ed.* Andrea Falcone; *Assoc. Ed.* Jennifer Leffler.
Newsletter. *The Pipeline* (biennial; electronic only). *Ed.* Alison Lewis.

Chapters

Alpha. Univ. of Illinois at Urbana-Champaign, Grad. School of Lib. and Info. Science; *Gamma.*

Florida State Univ., College of Communication and Info.; *Epsilon.* Univ. of North Carolina at Chapel Hill, School of Info. and Lib. Science; *Theta.* Pratt Inst., Grad. School of Lib. and Info. Science; *Iota.* Catholic Univ. of America, School of Lib. and Info. Science; Univ. of Maryland, College of Info. Studies; *Lambda.* Univ. of Oklahoma, School of Lib. and Info. Studies; *Xi.* Univ. of Hawaii at Manoa, School of Lib. and Info. Studies; *Omicron.* Rutgers Univ., Grad. School of Communication, Info., and Lib. Studies; *Pi.* Univ. of Pittsburgh, School of Info. Sciences; *Sigma.* Drexel Univ., College of Computing and Informatics; *Psi.* Univ. of Missouri at Columbia, School of Lib. and Info. Science; *Omega.* San Jose State Univ., School of Lib. and Info. Science; *Beta Beta.* Simmons College, Grad. School of Lib. and Info. Science; *Beta Delta.* State Univ. of New York at Buffalo, Dept. of Lib. and Info. Studies; *Beta Epsilon.* Emporia State Univ., School of Lib. and Info. Management; *Beta Zeta.* Louisiana State Univ., School of Lib. and Info. Science; *Beta Iota.* Univ. of Rhode Island, Grad. School of Lib. and Info. Studies; *Beta Kappa.* Univ. of Alabama, School of Lib. and Info. Studies; *Beta Lambda.* Texas Woman's Univ., School of Lib. and Info. Sciences; *Beta Mu.* Long Island Univ., Palmer School of Lib. and Info. Science; *Beta Xi.* North Carolina Central Univ., School of Lib. and Info. Sciences; *Beta Pi.* Univ. of Arizona, School of Info. Resources and Lib. Science; *Beta Rho.* Univ. of Wisconsin at Milwaukee, School of Info.; *Beta Phi.* Univ. of South Florida, School of Lib. and Info. Science; *Beta Psi.* Univ. of Southern Mississippi, School of Lib. and Info. Science; *Beta Omega.* Univ. of South Carolina, College of Lib. and Info. Science; *Beta Beta Epsilon.* Univ. of Wisconsin at Madison, School of Lib. and Info. Studies; *Beta Beta Theta.* Univ. of Iowa, School of Lib. and Info. Science; *Beta Beta Kappa.* Univ. of Puerto Rico, Grad. School of Info. Sciences and Technologies; *Pi Lambda Sigma.* Syracuse Univ., School of Info. Studies; *Beta Beta Mu.* Valdosta State Univ., School of Lib. and Info. Science; *Beta Beta Nu.* Univ. of North Texas, College of Info.; *Beta Beta Omicron.* East Caroline Univ.,Lib. Science program; *Beta Beta Xi.* St. Catherine Univ., Master of Lib. and Info. Science program.

Bibliographical Society of America

Executive Director, Michèle E. Randall
P.O. Box 1537, Lenox Hill Station, New York, NY 10021
212-452-2710, email bsa@bibsocamer.org
World Wide Web http://www.bibsocamer.org

Object

To promote bibliographical research and to issue bibliographical publications. Organized in 1904.

Membership

Memb. Dues (Indiv.) $65; (Sustaining) $250; (Contributing) $100; (Student) $20; (Inst.) $100; (Lifetime) $1,250. Year. Jan.–Dec.

Officers

Pres. Martin Antonetti, Northwestern Univ.; *V.P.* Michael T. Ryan, New York Historical Society; *Secy.* Barbara Heritage, Rare Book School. E-mail barbara.heritage@virginia.edu; *Treas.* G. Scott Clemons, Brown Brothers Harriman. E-mail scott.Clemons@bbh.com. *Delegate to the ACLS* David Vander Meulen, Univ. of Virginia.

Council

(2017) Nina Musinsky, George Ong, Douglas Pfeiffer, Heather Wolfe; (2018) Jennifer Lowe, Michael Suarez, S.J., Michael Thompson, Nick Wilding; (2019) John A. Buchtel, Sonja Drimmer, Marcia Reed, Jackie Vossler.

Committee Chairs

Audit. Joan Friedman.

Fellowship. Gerald Cloud.

Finance. Michael Thompson.

Program. Marcia Reed.

Publications: George Ong.

Publication

Papers of the Bibliographical Society of America (q.; memb.).

Bibliographical Society of Canada
(La Société Bibliographique du Canada)

President, Nancy Earle
360 Bloor St. W., P.O. Box 19035 Walmer, Toronto, ON M5S 3C9
Email secretary@bsc-sbc.ca
World Wide Web http://www.bsc-sbc.ca

Object

The Bibliographical Society of Canada is a bilingual (English/French) organization that has as its goal the scholarly study of the history, description, and transmission of texts in all media and formats, with a primary emphasis on Canada, and the fulfillment of this goal through the following objectives:

- To promote the study and practice of bibliography: enumerative, historical, descriptive, analytical, and textual

- To further the study, research, and publication of book history and print culture

- To publish bibliographies and studies of book history and print culture

- To encourage the publication of bibliographies, critical editions, and studies of book history and print culture

- To promote the appropriate preservation and conservation of manuscript, archival, and published materials in various formats
- To encourage the utilization and analysis of relevant manuscript and archival sources as a foundation of bibliographical scholarship and book history
- To promote the interdisciplinary nature of bibliography, and to foster relationships with other relevant organizations nationally and internationally
- To conduct the society without purpose of financial gain for its members, and to ensure that any profits or other accretions to the society shall be used in promoting its goal and objectives

Membership

The society welcomes as members all those who share its aims and wish to support and participate in bibliographical research and publication.

Membership

Memb. Dues (Reg.) $80; (Student) $35; (Ret.) $50; (Inst.) $100; (Life) $1000.

Officers

Pres. Nancy Earle, e-mail president@bsc-sbc.ca; *1st V.P.* Ruth-Ellen St. Onge, E-mail vice_president_1@bsc-sbc.ca. *2nd V.P.* Karen Smith E-mail vice_president_2@bsc-sbc.ca; *Secy.* David Fernández. E-mail secretary@bsc-sbc.ca; *Treas.* Tom Vincent. E-mail treasurer@bsc-sbc.ca; *Past Pres.* Linda Quirk. E-mail past_president@bsc-sbc.ca.

Council

(2014–2017) Svetlana Kochkina, Annie Murray, Ruth Panofsky; *(2015–2018)* Cecily Devereux, Val K. Lem, George Parker; *(2016–2019)* Christopher Doody, Sarah Lubelski, Josée Vincent.

Board Members

Meaghan Scanlon, Marie-Claude Felton.

Committee Chairs

Awards. Christopher Young.
Communications. Karen Smith.
Fellowships. Annie Murray.

Editorial Board Chairs

Publications. Geoffrey Little.
Papers/Cahiers. Eli MacLaren.

Publications

Papers of the Bibliographical Society of Canada/Cahiers de la Société Bibliographique du Canada (s. ann).

The Bulletin/Le Bulletin (s. ann).

Black Caucus of the American Library Association

President, Denyvetta Davis
World Wide Web http://www.bcala.org

Mission

The Black Caucus of the American Library Association (BCALA) serves as an advocate for the development, promotion, and improvement of library services and resources for the nation's African American community and provides leadership for the recruitment and professional development of African American librarians. Founded in 1970.

Membership

Membership is open to any person, institution, or business interested in promoting the development of library and information services for African Americans and other people of African descent and willing to maintain good financial standing with the organization. The membership is currently composed of librarians and other information professionals, library support staff, libraries, publishers, authors, vendors, and other library-related organizations in the United States and abroad. Dues (Lifetime) $500; (Corporate) $200; (Institutional) $60; (Regular) $45; (Library Support Staff) $20; (Student) $10; (Ret.) $25.

Officers

Pres. Denyvetta Davis; *V.P./Pres.-Elect* Richard Ashby; *Secy.* Kirby McCurtis; *Treas.* Wanda K. Brown. Tel. 773-916-6970; *Past Pres.* Kelvin A. Watson, Box 5837, Chicago. E-mail kantoniow@yahoo.com.

Board Members

(2016–2018) Jason Alston, Vivian Bordeaux, Jos N. Holman, Dominique Luster, Fayrene Muhammad; *(2016–2017)* Fannie Cox; *(2015–*

2017) Elizabeth Jean Brumfield, Brian Hart, Andrew P. Jackson, Kim McNeil-Capers, Eboni Njoku; Rudolph Clay.

Committee Chairs

Affiliates. Andrew P. Jackson.
Awards. John Page.
Budget and Finance. Stanton Biddle.
Constitution and Bylaws. Jos Holman.
Fundraising. Brian Hart.
International Relations. Eboni M. Henry, Vivian Bordeaux.
Membership. Rudolph Clay Jr.
Nomination and Election. Kelvin A. Watson.
Program. Richard Ashby.
Publications. Jason Alston.
Recruitment and Professional Development. Fannie Cox, Angeline Beljour.
Technology Advisory: Ursula Jacobs-Guidry.

Awards Committee Chairs

Book Award. Gladys Smiley Bell.
E-Book Award. Gladys Smiley Bell.

Publication

BCALA News (3 a year; memb.).

Canadian Association for Information Science
(L'Association Canadienne des Sciences de l'Information)

President, Vivian Howard
World Wide Web http://www.cais-acsi.ca

Object

To promote the advancement of information science in Canada and encourage and facilitate the exchange of information relating to the use, access, retrieval, organization, management, and dissemination of information.

Membership

Institutions and individuals interested in information science and involved in the gathering, organization, and dissemination of information (such as information scientists, archivists, librarians, computer scientists, documentalists, economists, educators, journalists, and psychologists) and who support CAIS's objectives can become association members.

Officers (2016–2017)

Pres. Vivian Howard, Dalhousie Univ. E-mail vivian.howard@dal.ca; *V.P./Pres.-Elect* Dinesh Rathi, Univ. of Alberta. E-mail drathi@ualberta.ca. *Secy.-Treas.* Philippe Mongeon, Univ. of Montréal, Pavillon Lionel-Groulx, 3150 Jean-Brillant, Room C-2070, Montréal. Tel. 1-514-343-6111 ext. 1743, e-mail philippe.mongeon@umontreal.ca. *Past Pres.* Heidi Julien, Univ. at Buffalo. E-mail heidijul@buffalo.edu.

Board Members

Webmaster Sarah Polkinghorne, Univ. of Alberta. *Student Representative* Adèle Paul-Hus, Univ. de Montréal. *Ex-Officio Member* Valerie Nesset, Univ. at Buffalo.

Editorial Board Chairs

Canadian Journal of Info. and Lib. Science. Valerie M. Nesset.

Publication

Canadian Journal of Information and Library Science. (q.; memb.) *Ed.* Valerie M. Nesset, State Univ. of New York at Buffalo. E-mail vmnesset@buffalo.edu.

Canadian Association of Research Libraries
(Association des Bibliothèques de Recherche du Canada)

Executive Director, Susan Haigh
309 Cooper St., Suite 203, Ottawa, ON K2P 0G5
613-482-9344 ext. 101, e-mail info@carl-abrc.ca
World Wide Web http://www.carl-abrc.ca

Membership

The Canadian Association of Research Libraries (CARL), established in 1976, is the leadership organization for the Canadian research library community. The association's members are the 29 major academic research libraries across Canada together with Library and Archives Canada and the Canada Institute for Scientific and Technical Information (CISTI). Membership is institutional, open primarily to libraries of Canadian universities that have doctoral graduates in both the arts and the sciences. CARL is an associate member of the Association of Universities and Colleges of Canada (AUCC) and is incorporated as a not-for-profit organization under the Canada Corporations Act.

Mission

The association provides leadership on behalf of Canada's research libraries and enhances their capacity to advance research and higher education. It promotes effective and sustainable scholarly communication, and public policy that enables broad access to scholarly information.

Officers (2015–2017)

Pres. Martha Whitehead, Queen's Univ., 99 Univ. Ave., Kingston, ON. E-mail martha. whitehead@queensu.ca; *V.P.* Donna Bourne-Tyson, Dalhousie Univ., 6100 Univ. Ave., Halifax, NS. Tel. 902-494-4089, e-mail donna. bourne-tyson@dal.ca; *Secy.* Lynda Gadoury (Quebec Region Representative), Univ. of Montréal, 405 Rue Sainte-Catherine Est., Montréal. Tel. 514-987-3824, e-mail gadoury. lynda@uqam.ca; *Treas.* Lesley Balcom (Atlantic Region Representative), Univ. of New Brunswick, Harriet Irving Lib., 5 MacAulay Ln., Fredericton, NB. Tel. 506-458-7056, e-mail lbalcom@unb.ca *Past Pres.* Gerald Beasley, Univ. of Alberta, 5-07 Cameron Lib., Edmonton, Alberta. Tel. 780-492-5170, e-mail gbeasley@ualberta.ca.

Directors

Gwen Bird (Western Region Representative), Vivian Lewis (Ontario Region Representative)

Committee Chairs

Advancing Research. Joy Kirchner.
Building Capacity. Vivian Lewis.
Assessment. Colleen Cook.

Member Institutions

Univ. of Alberta, Univ. of British Columbia, Brock Univ., Univ. of Calgary, Carleton Univ., CISTI (Canada Institute for Scientific and Technical Information), Concordia Univ., Dalhousie Univ., Univ. of Guelph, Université Laval, Lib. and Archives Canada, McGill Univ., McMaster Univ., Univ. of Manitoba, Memorial Univ. of Newfoundland, Université de Montréal, Univ. of New Brunswick, Univ. of Ottawa, Université du Québec à Montréal, Queen's Univ., Univ. of Regina, Ryerson Univ., Univ. of Saskatchewan, Université de Sherbrooke, Simon Fraser Univ., Univ. of Toronto, Univ. of Victoria, Univ. of Waterloo, Western Univ., Univ. of Windsor, York Univ.

Canadian Library Association
(Association Canadienne des Bibliothèques)

Executive Director, Valoree McKay
1150 Morrison Drive, Suite 400, Ottawa, ON K2H 8S9
E-mail vmckay@cla.ca
World Wide Web http://www.cla.ca

Object

The Canadian Library Association (CLA) is the national voice for Canada's library communities. CLA champions library values and the value of libraries, influences public policy affecting libraries, inspires and supports learning, and collaborates to strengthen the library community. The association represents Canadian librarianship to the federal government and media, carries on international liaison with other library associations and cultural agencies, offers professional development programs, and supports such core library values as intellectual freedom and access to information, particularly for disadvantaged populations. Founded in 1946, CLA is a not-for-profit voluntary organization governed by an elected executive council.

Membership

Memb. (as of December 2014) (Indiv.) 957; (Inst.) 249; (Corporate) 50; (Associate) 27.

Open to individuals, institutions, library boards, and groups interested in librarianship and in library and information services.

Officers

Pres. Sandra Singh, Vancouver Public Lib., 350 W. Georgia St., Vancouver. Tel. 604-331-4007, e-mail sandra.singh@vpl.ca; *V.P./Pres.-Elect* Rosemary Bonanno, Vancouver Island Regional Lib., P.O. Box 3333, 6250 Hammond Bay Rd. Nanaimo, BC. Tel. 250-729-2310, e-mail rbonanno@virl.bc.ca; *Treas.* Mike Ridley, McLaughlin Lib., Univ. of Guelph, 50 Stone Rd., East Guelph, ON. Tel. 519-824-4120 ext. 56747, e-mail mridley@uoguelph.ca; *Past Pres.* Marie DeYoung, Saint Patrick Power Lib., Mary's Univ., 923 Robie St., Halifax, NS. Tel. 902-420-5532, e-mail marie.deyoung@smu.ca; *Councillor-at-large* Virginia Clevette, Christina Hwang, Colleen Murphy.

Committee Chairs

Copyright Advisory. Robert J. Tiessen.
Information Policy Advisory. Brent C. Roe.
Intellectual Freedom Advisory. Alvin M. Schrader.
School Libraries Advisory. Linda Shantz-Keresztes.
Elections Standing. Nancy E. Black.

Awards Committee Chairs

Amelia Frances Howard-Gibbon Illustrator's Award. Diane Guathier.
Book of the Year for Children. Reta Pyke.
Young Adult Book. Carmelita Cechetto-Shea.

Publications

CLA Digest (bi-w.; electronic newsletter).
CLA Annual Report.

Catholic Library Association

Executive Director, Bland O'Connor
8550 United Plaza Blvd., Suite 1001, Baton Rouge, LA 70809
225-408-4417, e-mail cla@cathla.org
World Wide Web http://www.cathla.org

Object

The promotion and encouragement of Catholic literature and library work through cooperation, publications, education, and information. Founded in 1921.

Membership

Memb. 1,000. Dues $25–$500. Year. July–June.

Officers

Pres. Mary Kelleher, Doherty Lib., Univ. of St. Thomas, 3800 Montrose, Houston. Tel. 713-686-4345, e-mail kellehm@stthom.edu; *V.P./ Treas.* N. Curtis LeMay, Univ. of St. Thomas, 2115 Summit Ave., Mail IRL, St. Paul, MN. Tel. 651-962-5451, e-mail nclemay@stthomas. edu. *Past Pres.* Sara R. Baron, Regent Univ. Lib., 1000 Regent Univ. Dr., Virginia Beach. Tel. 757-226-4182, e-mail sbaron@regent.edu; *Senior Association Coordinator, CLA Office* Melanie Talley. E-mail cla2@cathla.org.

Board Members

Elyse Hayes, Pat Lawton, Ann O'Hara, Kathryn Shaughnessy.

Section Chairs

Academic Libs., Archives, & Lib. Education. Open.
Children's Lib. Services. Cindy Marach.
High School and Young Adult Lib. Services. Open.
Parish and Community Lib. Services. Paul Pojman.

Publication

Catholic Library World (q.; memb.; nonmemb. $100 domestic, $125 international). *General Ed.* Sigrid Kelsey. E-mail sigridkelsey@ gmail.com.

Chief Officers of State Library Agencies

Executive Director, Timothy Cherubini
201 E. Main St., Suite 1405, Lexington, KY 40507
859-514-9150, email info@cosla.org
World Wide Web http://www.cosla.org

Object

Chief Officers of State Library Agencies (CO-SLA) is an independent organization of the chief officers of state and territorial agencies designated as the state library administrative agency and responsible for statewide library development. Its purpose is to identify and address issues of common concern and national interest; to further state library agency relationships with federal government and national organizations; and to initiate cooperative action for the improvement of library services to the people of the United States.

COSLA's membership consists solely of these top library officers, variously designated as state librarian, director, commissioner, or executive secretary. The organization provides a continuing mechanism for dealing with the problems and challenges faced by these officers. Its work is carried on through its members, a board of directors, and committees.

Officers

Pres. Sandra Treadway, Libn. of Virginia, Lib. of Virginia, 800 E. Broad St., Richmond, VA 23219. Tel. 804-692-3535, e-mail sandra.tread-way@lva.virginia.gov; *V.P./Pres.-Elect* Stacey Aldrich, State Libn., Hawaii State Public Lib. System, 44 Merchant St. Honolulu. Tel. 808-586-3704, e-mail stacey.aldrich@librarieshawaii.org; *Secy.* Kurt Kiefer, State Libn., Wisconsin Dept. of Public Instruction, P.O. Box 7841, Madison. Tel. 608-266-2205, e-mail kurt.kiefer@dpi.wi.gov; *Treas.* Karen Mellor, Chief of Lib. Svcs., State of Rhode Island Office of Lib. and Information Svcs. One Capitol Hill, Providence. Tel. 401-574-9304, e-mail karen.mellor@olis.ri.gov; *Past Pres.* Kendall Wiggin, State Libn., Connecticut State Lib., 231 Capitol Ave., Hartford, CT 06106. Tel. 860-757.6510, e-mail kendall.wiggin@ct.gov.

Directors

Charles Sherrill. E-mail chuck.sherrill@tn.gov.
Jennie Stapp. E-mail jstapp2@mt.gov.

Committee Chairs

Continuing Education. Mary Soucie.
Public Policy Committee. Julie Walker.
Networking. Jennie Stapp.
Research and Statistics. Jamie Ritter.

Chinese American Librarians Association

Executive Director, Lian Ruan
Univ. of Illinois Urbana-Champaign, 11 Gerty Dr., Champaign
217-265-6107, e-mail lruan@illinois.edu.
World Wide Web http://cala-web.org

Object

To enhance communications among Chinese American librarians as well as between Chinese American librarians and other librarians; to serve as a forum for discussion of mutual problems and professional concerns among Chinese American librarians; to promote Sino-American librarianship and library services; and to provide a vehicle whereby Chinese American librarians can cooperate with other associations and organizations having similar or allied interests.

Membership

Memb. About 600. Membership is open to anyone interested in the association's goals and activities. Dues (Regular) $30; (International/Student/Non-salaried) $15; (Inst.) $100; (Affiliated) $100; (Life) $300.

Officers (2016–2017)

Pres. Qi Chen. E-mail qi23@msn.com; *V.P./Pres.-Elect* Le Yang. E-mail le.yang@ttu.edu; *Treas.* Ying Liao. E-mail cairo_liao@hotmail.com; *Past Pres.* Lian Ruan, Univ. of Illinois Urbana-Champaign, 11 Gerty Dr., Champaign. Tel. 217-265-6107, e-mail lruan@illinois.edu.

Board Members

(2014–2017) Leping He, Weiling Liu, Zhijia Shen, Min Tong, Chengzhi Wang; *(2015–2018)* Heather Cai, Zheng Jessica Lu, Yingqi Tang, Haiwang Yuan, Andrew Lee; *(2016–2019)* Xiaojie Duan, Jianye He, Yongyi Song, Hong Wu, Fu Zhuo.

Committee Chairs

Assessment and Evaluation. Jian Anna Xiong, Yan He.
Awards. Yongyi Song, Leping He.
Best Book Award. Haiwang Yuan, Xiying Mi.
Conference Program. Le Yang.
Constitution and Bylaws. Ying Zhang, Xiaojie Duan.
Finance. Hong Miao, Mi Tong.
International Relations. Shuyong Jiang, Guoqing Li.
Membership: Le Yang, Ying Zhang.
Nominating. Lian Ruan, Le Yang.
Public Relations/Fundraising. Alison Wang, Hong Yao.
Publications. Fu Zhuo, Grace Liu.
Scholarship Committee. Ping Fu, Daniel Xiao.
Web Committee. Weiling Liu, Yanhong Wang.

Editorial Board Chairs

Cala Occasional Papers Series. Suzhen Chen.
Cala Newsletter. Sai Deng, Xiaojie Duan.

Awards Committee Chairs

Best Book Award. Yuan Li, Zhao Liu.
Conference Travel Grant. Guoying Liu, Zheng Jessica Lu.
IFLA Registration Grant. Guoying Liu, Zheng Jessica Lu.
Outstanding Library Leadership Award in Memory of Dr. Margaret Chang Fung. Wei Peng.

Publications

CALA Newsletter (2 a year; memb.; online). *Eds.* Sai Deng. E-mail sai.deng@ucf.edu;

Xiaojie Duan. E-mail xiaojie.duan@usm. edu.
Journal of Library and Information Science (JLIS) (2 a year; memb.). *Editorial Board English Co-Eds.* Huifen Chang, Oklahoma State Univ. E-mail huifen.chang@okstate.

edu; Hong Miao, Marywood Univ. hongm@maryu.marywood.edu.
Membership Directory (memb.).
Occasional Paper Series (OPS) (online). *Ed. (2012–2015)* Yunshan Ye. E-mail yye@jhu.edu.

Church and Synagogue Library Association

President, Marcia Trauernicht
10157 S.W. Barbur Blvd., No.102C, Portland, OR 97219
503-244-6919, 800-542-2752, fax 503-977-3734, e-mail csla@worldaccessnet.com
World Wide Web http://www.cslainfo.org

Object

The Church and Synagogue Library Association (CSLA) provides educational guidance in the establishment and maintenance of congregational libraries.

Its purpose is to act as a unifying core for congregational libraries; to provide the opportunity for a mutual sharing of practices and problems; to inspire and encourage a sense of purpose and mission among congregational librarians; to study and guide the development of congregational librarianship toward recognition as a formal branch of the library profession. Founded in 1967.

Membership

Memb. 1,000. Dues (Inst.) $200; (Affiliated) $100; (Congregational) $70 ($75 foreign); (Indiv.) $50 ($55 foreign); (Student) $20 ($55 foreign).

Officers

Pres. Marcia Trauernicht, 10157 SW. Barbur Blvd. #102C, Portland, OR. E-mail marciatmail@gmail.com; *1st V.P./Pres.-Elect* To be

announced. *2nd V.P./Pres.-Elect* Maria Isabel Garcia. E-mail garcia.mariaisabel1@gmail.com. *Treas.* Evelyn Pockrass. E-mail evelynp@ihcindy.org. *Past Pres.* Cheryl Cutchin. E-mail cherylcsla1@gmail.com; *Archives Coordinator* Dottie Lewis. *Chapters Coordinator* Marcia Trauernicht.

Committee Chairs

Conference. Meghan Harper, Ralph Hartsock.
Continuing Education. To be announced.
Finance. Cheryl Cutchin.
Fundraising. Carol Campbell.
Technology. Debbie Scott.
Publications. Susan Sponaas.

Awards Committee Chair

Joy Cryer.

Publications

Bibliographies (5; price varies).
Congregational Libraries Today (q.; memb.; nonmemb. $40; Canada $50).
CSLA Guides (price varies).

Coalition for Networked Information

Executive Director, Clifford A. Lynch
21 Dupont Circle, Suite 800, Washington, DC 20036
202-296-5098, fax 202-872-0884, email clifford@cni.org
World Wide Web http://www.cni.org
Facebook https://www.facebook.com/cni.org
Twitter http://twitter.com/cni_org
YouTube https://www.youtube.com/cnivideo
Vimeo http://vimeo.com/cni

Mission

The Coalition for Networked Information (CNI) promotes the transformative promise of networked information technology for the advancement of scholarly communication and the enrichment of intellectual productivity.

Membership

Memb. 240+. Membership is institutional. Dues $7,960. Year. July–June.

Staff

Associate Exec. Dir. Joan K. Lippincott, 21 Dupont Cir., Suite 800, Washington, DC 20036. Tel. 202-296-5098, e-mail joan@cni.org; *Administrative Assistant* Sharon Adams. E-mail sharon@cni.org; *Systems Coordinator* Maurice-Angelo F. Cruz. E-mail angelo@cni.org; *Office Manager* Jacqueline J. Eudell. E-mail jackie@cni.org; *Communications Coordinator* Diane Goldenberg-Hart. E-mail diane@cni.org.

Steering Committee Members

John P. Barden, Univ. of Rochester; Daniel Cohen, Digital Public Lib. of America; Joseph D. Combs, Vanderbilt Univ.; Rebecca A. Graham, Univ. of Guelph; Harriette Hemmasi, Brown Univ.; Geneva L. Henry, George Washington Univ.; Clifford A. Lynch (ex officio), Coalition for Networked Info.; John O'Brien (ex officio), EDUCAUSE; Elliott Shore (ex officio), Assoc. of Research Libs.; Oren Sreebny, Univ. of Chicago; Edward Van Gemert, Univ. of Wisconsin at Madison; Donald J. Waters, Andrew W. Mellon Foundation.

Publication

CNI-Announce (online; subscribe by online form at https://www.cni.org/resources/follow-cni/cni-announce).

Periodic reports (http://www.cni.org/resources/publications/other-publications-by-cni-staff).

Council on Library and Information Resources

President, Kathlin Fitzpatrick
1707 L St. N.W., Suite 650, Washington, DC 20036
202-939-4750, fax 202-600-9628
World Wide Web http://www.clir.org

Object

In 1997 the Council on Library Resources (CLR) and the Commission on Preservation and Access (CPA) merged and became the Council on Library and Information Resources (CLIR). CLIR is an independent, nonprofit organization that forges strategies to enhance research, teaching, and learning environments in collaboration with libraries, cultural institutions, and communities of higher learning.

CLIR promotes forward-looking collaborative solutions that transcend disciplinary, institutional, professional, and geographic boundaries in support of the public good. CLIR identifies and defines the key emerging issues relating to the welfare of libraries and the constituencies they serve, convenes the leaders who can influence change, and promotes collaboration among the institutions and organizations that can achieve change. The council's interests embrace the entire range of information resources and services from traditional library and archival materials to emerging digital formats. It assumes a particular interest in helping institutions cope with the accelerating pace of change associated with the transition into the digital environment.

While maintaining appropriate collaboration and liaison with other institutions and or-
ganizations, CLIR operates independently of any particular institutional or vested interests. Through the composition of its board, it brings the broadest possible perspective to bear upon defining and establishing the priority of the issues with which it is concerned.

Board

CLIR's Board of Directors currently has 19 members.

Officers

Chair Kathlin Fitzpatrick, Modern Language Assn.; *Pres.* Charles Henry. E-mail chenry@clir.org; *V.Chair* Max Marmor, Samuel H. Kress Foundation; *Treas.* Winston Tabb, Johns Hopkins Univ.

Address correspondence to headquarters.

Publications

Annual Report.
CLIR Issues (bi-mo.).
Technical reports.

Federal Library and Information Network

Executive Director, Meg Tulloch
Library of Congress, Washington, DC 20540-4935
202-707-4801, e-mail mtulloch@loc.gov
World Wide Web http://www.loc.gov/flicc

Object

The Federal Library and Information Network (FEDLINK) is an organization of federal agencies working together to achieve optimum use of the resources and facilities of federal libraries and information centers by promoting common services, coordinating and sharing available resources, and providing continuing professional education for federal library and information staff. FEDLINK serves as a forum

for discussion of the policies, programs, procedures, and technologies that affect federal libraries and the information services they provide to their agencies, to Congress, the federal courts, and the public.

Membership

The FEDLINK voting membership is composed of representatives of the following U.S. federal departments and agencies: Each of the national libraries (the Library of Congress, National Agricultural Library, National Library of Education, National Library of Medicine, and the National Transportation Library); each cabinet-level executive department, as defined in 5 U.S.C. § 101; additional departments and agencies (the Defense Technical Information Center; departments of the Air Force, Army, and Navy; Executive Office of the President, Government Accountability Office, General Services Administration, Government Printing Office, Institute of Museum and Library Services, National Aeronautics and Space Administration, National Archives and Records Administration, National Technical Information Service [Department of Commerce], Office of Management and Budget, Office of Personnel Management, Office of Scientific and Technical Information [Department of Energy], Office of the Director of National Intelligence, and the Smithsonian Institution); the U.S. Supreme Court and the Administrative Office of the U.S. Courts; the District of Columbia; and other federal independent agencies and government corporations.

Officers

Administrative Officer Angelina Thompson. Tel. 202-707-5351, e-mail: ahend@loc.gov.

Address correspondence to the executive director.

Medical Library Association

Executive Director, Kevin Baliozian
65 E. Wacker Place, Suite 1900, Chicago, IL 60601-7298
312-419-9094, fax 312-419-8950, e-mail websupport@mail.mlahq.org
World Wide Web http://www.mlanet.org

Object

The Medical Library Association (MLA) is a nonprofit professional education organization with nearly 4,000 health sciences information professional members and partners worldwide. MLA provides lifelong educational opportunities, supports a knowledge base of health information research, and works with a global network of partners to promote the importance of high-quality information for improved health to the health care community and the public.

Membership

Memb. (Inst.) 400+; (Indiv.) 3,200+, in more than 50 countries. Institutional members are medical and allied scientific libraries. Individual members are people who are (or were at the time membership was established) engaged in professional library or bibliographic work in medical and allied scientific libraries or people who are interested in medical or allied scientific libraries. Members can be affiliated with one or more of MLA's more than 20 special-interest sections and its regional chapters.

Officers

Pres. Teresa L. Knott, Virginia Commonwealth Univ. E-mail tlknott@vcu.edu; *Pres.-Elect* Barbara A. Epstein, Univ. of Pittsburgh; *Secy.* Lisa K. Traditi, Univ. of Colorado Anschutz Medical Campus; *Treas.* Chris Shaffer, Oregon Health & Science Univ., 3181 SW. Sam Jackson Park Rd., Portland, OR 97239. Tel. 503-494-6057, e-mail shafferc@ohsu.edu; *Past Pres.* Michelle Kraft, Senior Medical Librarian, Cleveland Clinic Alumni Lib., 9500 Euclid Ave. NA30, Cleveland, OH 44194. Tel. 216-445-7338, e-mail kraftm@ccf.org; *Section Council Liaison* Jodi L. Philbrick, Melissa Ratajeski.

Board Members

Amy Blevins, Keith W. Cogdill, Melissa De Santis, Heidi Heilemann, Melissa L Rethlefsen.

Committee Chairs

Ad Hoc Committee to Review Core Clinical Journals. Andrea M. Ketchum, Michele S. Klein-Fedyshin.
Awards. Shelly Burns.
Awards and Grants Endowment Task Force. Michelle Kraft.
Books Panel. Kristen L. Young.
Bylaws. Ellen Brassil.
Communities Strategic Goal Task Force. Rikke Sarah Ogawa.
Continuing Education. Carrie L. Iwema.
Credentialing. David Midyette.
Governmental Relations. Cristina Pope.
Joseph Leiter NLM/MLA Lectureship. Lindsay E. Blake.
Librarians Without Borders®. Gurpreet Kaur Rana.
Membership. Virginia F. Desouky.
Oral History. Andrea Wright.
Professional Recruitment and Retention. Emily Vardell.
Rising Stars. Roy Eugene Brown.
Scholarly Communications. Drew Wright.

Editorial Board Chairs

JMLA Interim Editor-in-Chief Katherine Goold Akers.
MLA News Cheryl Rowan.

Task Force Chairs

Joint MLA/AAHSL Legislative. Sandra L. Bandy
Research Imperative. Susan Lessick.

Task Force to Review MLA's Competencies for Lifelong Learning & Professional Success. Gale G. Hannigan.

Awards Committee Chairs

Grants and Scholarships. Rozalynd McConnaughy.
Virginia L. and William K. Beatty Volunteer Service. Elizabeth R. Lorbeer.
Estelle Brodman Award for the Academic Medical Librarian of the Year. Emily J. Glenn.
Lois Ann Colaianni Award for Excellence & Achievement in Hospital Librarianship. Janna C. Lawrence.
Louise Darling Medal for Distinguished Achievement in Collection Development in the Health Sciences. Kimberly Loper.
Janet Doe Lectureship. Virginia Carden.
Ida and George Eliot Prize. Kristin Hitchcock.
Fellows and Honorary Members. Beverly Murphy.
Carla J. Funk Governmental Relations. Jonathan Koffel.
T. Mark Hodges International Service. Jamie Gray.
Majors/MLA Chapter Project of the Year. Janene Batten.
Lucretia W. McClure Excellence in Education. Lisa Federer.
Erich Meyerhoff. Stephanie M. Swanberg.
Rising Stars. Shannon Demona Jones.
Rittenhouse. Carol Seiler.
Thomson Reuters/Frank Bradway Rogers Information Advancement. Linda Van Keuren.
Section Project of the Year. Ahlam Saleh.

Grants, Scholarships, and Fellowships Juries

Ysabel Bertolucci MLA Annual Meeting Grant. Eve Melton.
Naomi C. Broering Hispanic Heritage Grant. Patricia C. Higginbottom.
Continuing Education. Natalie Clairoux.
Cunningham Memorial International Fellowship. Sarah Wade.
MLA/EBSCO Annual Meeting Grant. Jeanne Sadlik.
Eugene Garfield Research Fellowship. Nancy E. Adams.

MLA/HINARI/Research4Life Grant Jury. Gurpreet Kaur Rana.

MLA/HLS Professional Development Grant. Helen-Ann Brown Epstein.

David A. Kronick Traveling Fellowship. Robert Johnson.

Donald A.B. Lindberg Research Fellowship. Nancy J. Allee.

Librarians Without Borders Ursula Poland International Scholarship. Nancy Olmos.

MLA/MIS Career Development Grant. Janis F. Brown.

MLA Research, Development, and Demonstration Project Grant. Darra R. Ballance.

MLA Scholarship. Shalu Gillum.

MLA Scholarship for Minority Students. Ricardo Andrade, Jr. MLA/Thomson Reuters Doctoral Fellowship. Maria Lopez.

Publications

Journal of the Medical Library Association (q.; electronic version, free to all through PubMed Central; print version, memb. $50; nonmemb. $190). *Ed.* Katherine G. Akers, Wayne State Univ.

MLA News (10 a year; $120). *Ed.* Cheryl Rowan.

Music Library Association

President, Michael Rogan
1600 Aspen Commons Suite 100 , Middleton, WI 53562
608-836-5825, fax 608-831-8200, e-mail mla@areditions.com
World Wide Web http://www.musiclibraryassoc.org

Object

The Music Library Association provides a professional forum for librarians, archivists, and others who support and preserve the world's musical heritage. To achieve this mission, it

- Provides leadership for the collection and preservation of music and information about music in libraries and archives

- Develops and delivers programs that promote continuing education and professional development in music librarianship

- Ensures and enhances intellectual access to music for all by contributing to the development and revision of national and international codes, formats, and other standards for the bibliographic control of music

- Ensures and enhances access to music for all by facilitating best practices for housing, preserving, and providing access to music

- Promotes legislation that strengthens music library services and universal access to music

- Fosters information literacy and lifelong learning by promoting music reference services, library instruction programs, and publications

- Collaborates with other groups in the music and technology industries, government, and librarianship, to promote its mission and values

Membership

Memb. 1,200+. Dues (Inst.) $165; (Indiv.) $130; (Ret.) $95; (Paraprofessional) $75; (Student) $65. (Foreign, add $10.) Year. July 1–June 30.

Officers

Pres. Michael Rogan, 419 Boston Ave., Medford, MA. Tel. 617-627-2846, e-mail michael.rogan@tufts.edu; *Pres.-Elect* Mark C. McKnight. E-mail mark.mcknight@unt.edu; *Secy.* Lisa Shiota, 1600 Aspen Commons, Suite 100, Middleton, WI. E-mail lshi@loc.gov; *Past Pres.* Michael Colby, 1 Shields Ave., Davis, CA. E-mail mdcolby@ucdavis.edu; *Memb.-*

at-Large (2015–2017) Andrew Justice, Laura Moody, Darwin Scott; *(2016–2018)* Suzanne Eggleston Lovejoy, Gerald A. Szymanski, Hermine Vermeij.

Board Members

Paula Hickner, Janelle West.

Committee Chairs

Archives and Special Collections. Matthew Snyder.
Career Development and Services. Ana Dubnjakovic.
Development. Susannah L. Cleveland.
Education. Lisa Hooper.
Emerging Technologies and Services. Jonathan Manton.
Finance. Andrew S. Justice.
Joint Committee: MLA, MPA, and MOLA. Elizabeth A. Davis.
Legislation. Tammy L. Ravas.
Membership. Jason Imbesi.
Nominating. Damian S. Iseminger.
Oral History. Robert S. DeLand.

Preservation. Maristella J. Feustle.
Public Libraries. Laurie A. Bailey.
Public Services. Sara J. Manus.
Publications. Bonna J. Boettcher.
Resource Sharing and Collection Development. Michael J. Duffy IV.
Web. Raymond G. Heigemeir.

Task Force Chairs

Future of Basic Music Lib.: Darwin F. Scott; MLA Services Review: Michael J. Rogan; OCLC Search & Discovery: Michael J. Duffy IV.

Publications

MLA Index and Bibliography Series (irreg.; price varies). *Ed.* Richard Griscom.
MLA Newsletter. Ed. Michelle Hahn (q.; memb.).
MLA Technical Reports (irreg.; price varies).
Music Cataloging Bulletin (mo.; online subscription only, $35).
Notes (q.; memb.; indiv. $85; inst. $100).

National Association of Government Archives and Records Administrators

President, Cathi Carmack
444 N. Capitol Street, N.W. Suite 237, Washington, DC 20001
202-508-3800, fax 202-508-3801, e-mail info@nagara.org
World Wide Web http://www.nagara.org

Object

Founded in 1984, the National Association of Government Archives and Records Administrators (NAGARA) is a nationwide association of local, state, and federal archivists and records administrators, and others interested in improved care and management of government records. NAGARA promotes public awareness of government records and archives management programs, encourages interchange of information among government archives and records management agencies, develops and implements professional standards of government records and archival administration, and encourages study and research into records management problems and issues.

Membership

Most NAGARA members are federal, state, and local archival and records management agencies.

Officers

Pres. Cathi Carmack, Archival Technical Svs. at Tennessee State Lib. and Archives, 403 7th Ave., North Nashville, TN. Tel. 615-253-3468, e-mail Cathi.Carmack@tn.gov; *Pres.-Elect* Patty Davis, U.S. Dept. of Justice, 950 Pennsylvania Ave. N.W., Washington, DC. Tel. 202-532-6559, e-mail patrice.m.davis@usdoj. gov; *V.P.* Rebekah Davis, Limestone County Archives, 102 W. Washington St., Athens, AL. Tel. 256-233-6404, e-mail rebekah.davis@ limestonecounty-al.gov; *Secy.* Jannette Goodall, City Clerk, City of Austin, 301 W. Second St., Box 1088, Austin, TX. Tel. 512-974-9045, e-mail jannette.Goodall@austintexas.gov; *Treas.* Galen Wilson, National Archives and Records Administration, 3150 Springboro Rd., Dayton, OH. Tel. 937-425-0613, e-mail galen.

Wilson@nara.gov; *Past Pres.* Pari Swift, Ohio Attorney General's Office, 30 E. Broad St., 23rd Floor, Columbus. Tel. 614-466-1356, e-mail Pari.Swift@ohioattorneygeneral.gov.

Board Members

Casey Coleman, Patricia Franks, Cherry Lawson, Anna K. Mills, Shawn Rounds, Michael Sherman, Joyce Wittenberg.

Publications

Clearinghouse (q.; memb.).
Crossroads (q.; memb.).
Local Government Records Management Technical Bulletins.

National Federation of Advanced Information Services

Executive Director, Marci Granahan
801 Compass Way, Suite 201 Annapolis, MD 21401
443-221-2980, fax 443-221-2981, email mgranahan@nfais.org
World Wide Web http://www.nfais.org

Object

The National Federation of Advanced Information Services (NFAIS) is an international nonprofit membership organization composed of leading information providers. Its membership includes government agencies, nonprofit scholarly societies, private sector businesses, and libraries. NFAIS is committed to promoting the value of credible, high-quality content. It serves all groups that create, aggregate, organize, or facilitate access to such information. In order to improve members' capabilities and to contribute to their ongoing success, NFAIS provides opportunities for education, advocacy, and a forum in which to address common interests. Founded in 1958.

Membership

Memb. 60. Full members are organizations whose main focus is any of the following activities: information creation, organization, aggregation, dissemination, access, or retrieval. Organizations are eligible for associate member status if they do not meet the qualifications for full membership.

Officers

Pres. Chris Burghardt, 1500 Spring Garden, Philadelphia; *Pres.-Elect* Peter Simon, NewsBank, Inc. 5801 Pelican Bay Blvd., Suite 600, Naples, FL; *Secy.* Lynn Willis, 750 First St. N.E., Washington, DC; *Treas.* Brenda Bailey-

Hainer, American Theological Lib. Assn.; Past Pres. Mary Sauer-Games, OCLC, 6565 Kilgour Pl., Dublin, OH 43017. Tel. 614-764-6377, e-mail sauerm@oclc.org.

Board Members

L. Suzanne BeDell, Ryan Bernier, Chris Cole, Don Hagen, Chris McCue, Deborah Ozga, Eric Swenson, Jeffrey Wilensky.

Staff

Dir. of Marketing and Communications Ken Berlack; *Dir. of Professional Development* Nancy Blair-DeLeon.

Publications

For a detailed list of NFAIS publications, go to http://www.nfais.org/publications.

National Information Standards Organization

Executive Director, Todd Carpenter
3600 Clipper Mill Rd., Suite 302, Baltimore, MD 21211-1948
301-654-2512, fax 410-685-5278, e-mail nisohq@niso.org
World Wide Web http://www.niso.org

Object

The National Information Standards Organization (NISO) fosters the development and maintenance of standards that facilitate the creation, persistent management, and effective interchange of information so that it can be trusted for use in research and learning. To fulfill this mission, NISO engages libraries, publishers, information aggregators, and other organizations that support learning, research, and scholarship through the creation, organization, management, and curation of knowledge. NISO works with intersecting communities of interest and across the entire lifecycle of an information standard. NISO standards apply both traditional and new technologies to the full range of information-related needs, including discovery, retrieval, repurposing, storage, metadata, business information, and preservation.

NISO also develops and publishes recommended practices, technical reports, white papers, and information publications. NISO holds regular educational programs on standards, technologies, and related topics where standards-based solutions can help solve problems. These programs include webinars, online virtual conferences, in-person forums, and teleconferences.

Experts from the information industry, libraries, systems vendors, and publishing participate in the development of NISO standards and recommended practices. The standards are approved by the consensus body of NISO's voting membership, representing libraries, publishers, vendors, government, associations, and private businesses and organizations. NISO is supported by its membership and grants.

NISO is a not-for-profit association accredited by the American National Standards Institute (ANSI) and serves as the U.S. Technical Advisory Group Administrator to ISO/TC 46 Information and Documentation as well as the secretariat for ISO/TC 46/SC 9, Identification and Description.

Membership

Voting Members: 80+. Open to any organization, association, government agency, or company willing to participate in and having substantial concern for the development of NISO standards. Library Standards Alliance Members: 60+. Open to any academic, public, special, or government-supported library interested in supporting the mission of NISO.

Officers

Chair B. Tommie Usdin, Mulberry Technologies, Inc., 17 W. Jefferson St., #207, Rockville,

MD. Tel. 301-315-9634, e-mail btusdin@mulberrytech.com; *V.Chair* Chris Shillum, Product Mgmt. Platform and Content, Reed Elsevier, 360 Park Ave. S., New York. Tel. 212-462-1987, e-mail c.shillum@elsevier.com; *Treas.* Keith Webster, Dean of Univ. Libs., Carnegie Mellon Univ., 5000 Forbes Ave., Pittsburgh. Tel. 412-268-2447, e-mail kwebster@andrew.cmu.edu.

Board Members

Sayeed Choudhury, Gerry Grenier, Marian Hollingsworth, Evan Owens, Oliver Pesch, Barbara Preece, Heather Reid, Chuck Thomas, Jabin White.

Committee Chairs

Architecture. Mike Teets.
Business Information Topic. Anne Campbell, Christine M. Stamison.
Content and Collection Management Topic. Marti Heyman, Jody L. DeRidder. Discovery to Delivery Topic. Pascal Calarco, Peter Murray.

Staff

Assoc. Dir. for Programs Nettie Lagace; *Member Svcs. and Engagement Mgr.* DeVonna Parks; *Educational Programs Mgr.* Henrietta (Etta) Verma.

Publications

Information Standards Quarterly (print: $130/year domestic, $165/year international, back issues $36; electronic version available in open access from the NISO website).

NISO Newsline (free e-newsletter released on the first Wednesday of each month; distributed by e-mail and posted on the NISO website).

Working Group Connection (free quarterly e-newsletter supplement to *Newsline* that provides updates on the activities of NISO's working groups; distributed by e-mail and posted on the NISO website).

For other NISO publications, see the article "National Information Standards Organization (NISO) Standards" later in Part 6 of this volume.

NISO's published standards, recommended practices, and technical reports are available free of charge as downloadable PDF files from the NISO website (http://www.niso.org). Hardcopy documents are available for sale from the website.

Patent and Trademark Resource Center Association

President, Lisha Li
World Wide Web http://www.ptrca.org

Object

The Patent and Trademark Resource Center Association (PTRCA) provides a support structure for the more than 80 patent and trademark resource centers (PTRCs) affiliated with the U.S. Patent and Trademark Office (USPTO). The association's mission is to discover the interests, needs, opinions, and goals of the PTRCs and to advise USPTO in these matters for the benefit of PTRCs and their users, and to assist USPTO in planning and implementing appropriate services. Founded in 1983 as the Patent Depository Library Advisory Council; name changed to Patent and Trademark Depository Library Association in 1988; became an American Library Association affiliate in 1996. In 2011 the association was renamed the Patent and Trademark Resource Center Association.

Membership

Open to any person employed in a patent and trademark resource center library whose responsibilities include the patent and trademark collection. Affiliate membership is also available. Dues (Reg.) $65; (Student) $10 in 2017.

Officers

Pres. Lisha Li, Atlanta, GA; *V.P./Pres.-Elect* Vacant; *Secy.* John Schlipp, W. Frank Steely Lib., Northern Kentucky Univ., Nunn Dr., Highland Heights. Tel. 859-572-5723, e-mail schlippj1@nku.edu; *Treas.* Jim Miller, McKeldin Lib., Univ. of Maryland, Lib. Ln., College Park. Tel. 301-405-9152, e-mail jmiller2@umd.edu; *Past Pres.* Karen Kitchens, Wyoming State Lib., 2800 Central Ave., Cheyenne. Tel. 307-777-7281, e-mail karen.kitchens@wyo.gov.

Board Members

Mary Kordyban, Andrew Maines, Suzanne Reinman, Siu Min Yu.

Committee Chairs (2016–2017)

Bylaws. Marian Armour-Gemman.
Conference. Spruce Fraser.
Database (Ad Hoc). Jim Miller.
Election. Leena Lalwani.
Membership and Mentoring. Lisha Li.
Program (Ad Hoc). Paulina Borrego.
Publications. Tom Rohrig.

Publication

PTRCA Journal. Electronic at http://ptrca.org/ newsletters. *Ed.* Tom Rohrig. E-mail tom. rohrig@ttu.edu.

Polish American Librarians Association

President, Leonard Kniffel
P.O. Box 7232, Prospect Heights, IL, 60070-7232
World Wide Web http://palalib.org

Object

The mission of the Polish American Librarians Association (PALA) is to positively affect services provided to library patrons of Polish descent and individuals interested in Polish culture.

The organization's vision is

- To enhance professional knowledge by developing forums for discussion and networks of communication among library staff working with Polish collections and patrons of Polish origin

- To promote understanding and respect among all cultures by expanding the means to access reliable, current information about Polish and Polish American culture

- To promote Polish American librarianship

- To provide opportunities for cooperation with other library associations

Founded in 2009.

Membership

Membership is open to librarians, students of library schools, library support staff, and others who support the vision of PALA. Dues (Regular) $25; (Support Staff, Student, Retired, Unemployed) $15.

Officers

Pres. Leonard Kniffel, PolishSon.com, 2743 N. Greenview Ave., Chicago. Tel. 773-935-3635, e-mail lkniffel@sbcglobal.net; *V.P.* Ewa Barczyk, Golda Meir Lib., Univ. of Wisconsin Milwaukee, 2311 E. Hartford Ave., Milwaukee. Tel. 414-412-5456, e-mail ewa@uwm. edu; *Secy.* Joanna Klos, Wood Dale Public Lib. District, 520 North Wood Dale Rd., Wood Dale, IL. Tel. 630-766-6762, e-mail jklos@ wooddalelibrary.org; *Treas.* Elizabeth Marszalik, Lib. Experiences and Initiatives, Oak Park Public Lib., 834 Lake St., Oak Park, IL. Tel.

708-383-8200, e-mail emarszalik@oppl.org. *Past Pres.* Patrycja Dybala, Head of Circulation Services, Warrenville Public Lib., District, 28W751, Stafford Pl., Warrenville, IL. Tel. 630-393-1171. E-mail patty@warrenville.com; *Dirs.-at-large* Paulina Poplawska, Ronald V. Stoch.

REFORMA (National Association to Promote Library and Information Services to Latinos and the Spanish-Speaking)

President, Selina Gomez-Beloz
P.O. Box 832, Anaheim, CA 92815
E-mail info@reforma.org
World Wide Web http://www.reforma.org

Object

Promoting library services to the Spanish-speaking for nearly 40 years, REFORMA, an affiliate of the American Library Association, works in a number of areas to advance the development of library collections that include Spanish-language and Latino-oriented materials; the recruitment of more bilingual and bicultural professionals and support staff; the development of library services and programs that meet the needs of the Latino community; the establishment of a national network among individuals who share its goals; the education of the U.S. Latino population in regard to the availability and types of library services; and lobbying efforts to preserve existing library resource centers serving the interest of Latinos.

Membership

Memb. 800+. Membership is open to any person who is supportive of the goals and objectives of REFORMA. Dues (Indiv.) $0–$450; (Inst.) $100–$250. Year.

Officers

Pres. Selina Gomez-Beloz, Crown Point Community Lib., 122 N. Main St., Crown Point, IN. Tel. 219-306-8071, e-mail president@ reforma.org; *V.P./Pres.-Elect* Tess Tobin, New

York City College of Technology Lib., 300 Jay St., Brooklyn. Tel. 718-260-5499, e-mail vice-president@reforma.org; *Secy.* Kenny Garcia, California State Univ.–Monterey Bay Lib., 100 Campus Ctr., Seaside, CA, Tel. 831-582-3534, e-mail secretary@reforma.org; *Treas.* Alicia M. Rodriguez, Bilingual Outreach Libn., Western Area—Westwood Branch, 1246 Glendon Ave., Los Angeles. Tel. 310-598-7007, e-mail treasurer@reforma.org; *Past Pres.* Beatriz Guevara, Scaleybark Lib., 101 Scaleybark Rd., Charlotte, NC. Tel. 704-416-6401, e-mail past-president@reforma.org; *Memb.-at-Large* Elissia Buell, San Diego Public Lib., Scripps Miramar Ranch Branch Lib., 10301 Scripps Lake Dr., San Diego. E-mail at-large-rep@reforma. org; *Chapter Reps.* Nicanor Diaz, Madeline Peña Feliz, Elizabeth Garcia.

Committee Chairs

Education. Annette Alvardo.
Finance. Isabel Espinal.
Fundraising. Cynthia Bautista.
International Relations. Ady Huertas.
Legislative. Millie Gonzalez, Angelica Fortin.
Membership. Juan Carlos Rodriguez.
Nominations. Maria Kramer.
Organizational Development and New Chapters. Martha A. Parker.
Program. Tess Tobin.
Public Relations. David Lopez.

Recruitment and Mentoring. Minerva Alaniz. REFORMA National Conferences Coordinating Committee. Jacqueline Ayala, Loanis Menendez. Scholarship. Delores Carlito. Technology. Juan Carlos Rodriguez. Translations. Nicanor Diaz. Webinar: Sujei Lugo.

Awards Committee Chairs

Pura Belpré Award. Ana E. Pavon.

Librarian of the Year. Roxana Benavides.

Publication

REFORMA (online newsletter).

Meetings

General membership and board meetings take place at the American Library Association Midwinter Meeting and Annual Conference.

Society for Scholarly Publishing

Executive Director, Melanie Dolechek
10200 W. 44th Ave., Suite 304, Wheat Ridge, CO 80033
303-422-3914, fax 720-881-6101, e-mail mdolechek@sspnet.org
World Wide Web http://www.sspnet.org

Object

To draw together individuals involved in the process of scholarly publishing. This process requires successful interaction of the many functions performed within the scholarly community. The Society for Scholarly Publishing (SSP) provides the leadership for such interaction by creating opportunities for the exchange of information and opinions among scholars, editors, publishers, librarians, printers, booksellers, and all others engaged in scholarly publishing.

Membership

Memb. 1,000+. Open to all with an interest in the scholarly publishing process and dissemination of information. Dues (New Member) $170; (Indiv. Renewal) $185; (Libn.) $85; (Early Career New) $85; (Early Career Renewal) $80; (Student) $40; (Supporting Organization) $1,850; (Sustaining Organization) $4,300; (Intl. Indiv.) $50; (Intl. Early Career) $25; (Intl. Libn.) $25; (Intl. Student); $10. Year. Jan.–Dec.

Officers

Pres. Rick Anderson, J. Willard Marriott Lib., Univ. of Utah, 295 S. 1500 E., Salt Lake City. Tel. 801-587-9989, e-mail rick.anderson@utah.edu; *Pres.-Elect* Jennifer Pesanelli, FASEB. E-mail jpesanelli@faseb.org; *Secy./ Treas.* Byron Laws, KiwiTech. E-mail byron@kiwitech.com; *Past Pres.* Ann Michael, Delta Think. Tel. 215-402-7225, e-mail ann.michael@deltathink.com; *Memb.-at-Large* Lori Carlin, David Crotty, Jocelyn Dawson, Emilie Delquié, Marian Hollingsworth, Sylvia Hunter, Alice Meadows, Greg Suprock, Bonnie Zavon.

Staff

Exec. Dir. Melanie Dolechek; *Memb. Coord.* Jan Kalne; *Web Site Coord.* Linda Pocsik; *Mtgs. Asst.* Jennifer Lanphere; *Gen. Mgr.* Amy Lydic; *Mtg. Planner* Deborah Sorgel; *Program Dir.* Helen Szigeti.

Board Members

Gen. Mgr. Amy Lydic.

Committee Chairs

Annual Meeting Program. Mary Beth Barilla, Laura Ricci, Ben Mudrak.

Audit. Lisa Hart.

Career Development. Adam Etkin, Victoria Rae.

Certification/Training. Helen Szigeti.

Communications. Michael Di Natale, Jake Zarnegar.

Community Engagement. Kerry Kroffe, Michael Mozina.

Development. Veronica Showers, Rebecca Shumbata.

Education. Peter Froehlich, Jessica Loayza.

Finance. Byron Laws.

Kitchen Cabinet. Susan Kesner.

Marketing. Patrick Franzen, Jeremy Nielsen.

Membership. Anna Jester, Tom Thrash.

Nominating and Awards. Ann Michael.

Organizational Collaboration. Lauren Kane, Judy Luther.

Task Force Chairs

Branding. Lori Carlin, Yael Fitzpatrick.

Data Access. Eileen Kiley, David Smith.

Industry Initiatives and Outreach. Bill Kasdorf, Susan Stearns.

Peer Groups. Carol Anne Meyer, Jamie Wielgus.

Publications. Sylvia Hunter, Phill Jones.

Scholarly Kitchen Renovation. Michael Clarke.

Meetings

An annual meeting is held in late May/early June. SSP also conducts a Librarian Focus Group (January) and the Fall Seminar Series (October).

Society of American Archivists

Executive Director, Nancy P. Beaumont
17 N. State St., Suite 1425, Chicago, IL 60602
866-722-7858, toll-ree 866-722-7858, fax 312-606-0728, e-mail saahq@archivists.org
World Wide Web http://www2.archivists.org

Object

Founded in 1936, the Society of American Archivists (SAA) is North America's oldest and largest national archival professional association. Representing more than 6,000 individual and institutional members, SAA promotes the value and diversity of archives and archivists and is the preeminent source of professional resources and the principal communication hub for American archivists.

Membership

Memb. 6,200+. Dues (Indiv.) $80 to $292, graduated according to salary; (Assoc. domestic) $105; (Ret.) $73; (Student or Bridge) $52; (Inst.) $320; (Sustaining Inst.) $565.

Officers

Pres. Nancy McGovern, MIT Libs. Curation and Preservation Svcs., 77 Massachusetts Ave., Cambridge. Tel. 617-253-5664, e-mail nancy mcg@mit.edu; *V.P.* Tanya Zanish-Belcher, Wake Forest Univ.; *Treas.* Cheryl Stadel-Bevans, Dept. of Housing and Urban Development, Office of the Inspector General, 451 7th St. S.W., Room 8254, Washington, DC. Tel. 202-402-8143, e-mail cstadelbevans@hudoig. gov; *Past Pres.* Dennis Meissner, Minnesota Historical Society, 345 W. Kellogg Blvd., St. Paul. Tel. 651-259-3110, e-mail dennis.meissner@mnhs.org.

SAA Council Executive Committee

Chair Nancy McGovern; Tanya Zanish-Belcher, Cheryl Stadel-Bevans, Rachel Vagts; *Ex Officio* Nancy P. Beaumont.

Board Members

Amy Cooper Cary, Courtney Chartier, Pam Hackbart-Dean, Bergis Jules, Kris Kiesling, Erin Lawrimore, Michelle Light, Bertram Lyons, Rachel Vagts.

Committee Chairs

Appointments. Jelain Chubb, William Landis.
Awards. Gerald Chaudron, Michael Doylen.
Diversity. Holly Smith.
Education. Alison Clemens.
Ethics and Professional Conduct. Tiffany Schureman, Julie Graham.
Finance. Cheryl Stadel-Bevans.
Host. Maija Anderson.
Membership. Kate Dundon.
Nominating. Holly Smith.

Program. Terry Baxter.
Public Awareness. Samantha Norling.
Public Policy. Dennis Riley.
Standards. Caitlin Caitlin, Carrie Hintz.

Editorial Board Chairs

American Archivist. Gregory Hunter.

Working Groups Chairs

Cultural Heritage. Jennifer O'Neal.
Dictionary. Rosemary Flynn.
Intellectual Property. Aprille McKay.

Publications

American Archivist (2 a year; memb.; non-memb. "premium" print and online edition $279, online only $229, print only $229). *Ed.* Gregory S. Hunter; *Reviews Ed.* Bethany Anderson.
Archival Outlook (bi-mo.; memb.). *Ed.* Teresa Brinati.
In the Loop e-newsletter (bi-wk.)

Software and Information Industry Association

President, Kenneth Wasch
1090 Vermont Ave. N.W. Sixth Floor, Washington DC 20005-4905
202-289-7442, fax 202-289-7097
World Wide Web http://www.siia.net

The Software and Information Industry Association (SIIA) was formed January 1, 1999, through the merger of the Software Publishers Association (SPA) and the Information Industry Association (IIA).

Membership

Memb. 800+ companies. Open to companies that develop software and digital information content. For details on membership and dues, see the SIIA website, http://www.siia.net.

Officers

Pres. Kenneth Wasch, 1090 Vermont Ave., N.W. Sixth Floor, Washington, DC 20005. Tel. 202-789-4440; *Senior V.P. and Managing Director, FISD* Tom Davin. Tel. 202-789-4465; *V.P., Finance and Administration* Tom Meldrum. Tel. 202-789-4451; *V.P., Public Policy* Mark MacCarthy. Tel. 202-789-4471; *Senior V.P. and Managing Dir., ETIN* Chris Lohse, *V.P., SSD* Rhianna Collier. Tel. 408-884-3834; *V.P., Membership* Eric Fredell. Tel. 202-789-4464.

Senior Staff

Kenneth Wasch, Nancy Brand, Rhianna Collier, Tom Davin, Eric Fredell, David LeDuc, Chris Lohse, Mark MacCarthy, Mike Marchesano, Tom Meldrum, Carl Schonander.

Directors

Richard Atkinson, Adobe Systems, Inc.; Mark Bohannon, Red Hat, Inc.; Denise Elliott, Kiplinger Washington Editors, Inc.; Heather Farley, Access Intelligence; David Foster, Business Valuation Resources, LLC; Kate Friedrich, Thomson Reuters; Meg Hargreaves, CQ-Roll Call Group; Randall Hopkins, Nasdaq; Stephen Laster, McGraw-Hill Education; John Lepore, RELX Group; Jason Mahler, Oracle Corp.; Doug Manoni, SourceMedia; Peter Marney, Wiley; Bernard McKay, Intuit, Inc.; Chuck Melley, Pearson; Marion Minor, EPG Media & Specialty Info.; Jessica Perry, SHRM (Society for Human Resource Mgmt.); Johanna Shelton, Google, Inc.; Ken Wasch, SIIA.

Scholarly Publishing and Academic Resources Coalition

Executive Director, Heather Joseph
21 Dupont Circle, Suite 800, Washington, DC 20036
202-296-2296, fax 202-872-0884, e-mail heather@sparcopen.org
World Wide Web http://www.sparc.arl.org

SPARC, the Scholarly Publishing and Academic Resources Coalition, is a global organization that promotes expanded sharing of scholarship in the networked digital environment. It is committed to faster and wider sharing of outputs of the research process to increase the impact of research, fuel the advancement of knowledge, and increase the return on research investments.

Developed by the Association of Research Libraries, SPARC has become a catalyst for change. Its pragmatic focus is to stimulate the emergence of new scholarly communication models that expand the dissemination of scholarly research and reduce financial pressures on libraries. Action by SPARC in collaboration with stakeholders—including authors, publishers, and libraries—builds on the unprecedented opportunities created by the networked digital environment to advance the conduct of scholarship.

SPARC's role in stimulating change focuses on

- Educating stakeholders about the problems facing scholarly communication and the opportunities for them to play a role in achieving positive change
- Advocating policy changes that advance scholarly communication and explicitly recognize that dissemination of scholarship is an essential, inseparable component of the research process
- Incubating demonstrations of new publishing and sustainability models that benefit scholarship and academe

SPARC is a visible advocate for changes in scholarly communication that benefit more than the academic community alone. Founded in 1997, it has expanded to represent more than 800 academic and research libraries in North America, the United Kingdom, Europe, and Japan.

Membership

Memb. 200+ institutions. SPARC membership is open to international academic and research institutions, organizations, and consortia that share an interest in creating a more open and diverse marketplace for scholarly communication. Dues are scaled by membership type and budget. For more information, visit SPARC's website at http://www.sparc.arl.org/membership, SPARC Europe at https://sparcopen.org/people/sparc-europe/, SPARC Japan at http://www.nii.ac.jp/sparc, or SPARC Africa at https://sparcopen.org/people/sparc-africa/.

Staff

Open Education Nicole Allen. E-mail nicole@ sparcopen.org; *Senior Consultant* Raym Crow. E-mail crow@sparcopen.org; *Dir. of Operations* Shawn Daugherty. E-mail shawn@sparc open.org; *Exec. Dir.* Heather Joseph. E-mail heather@sparcopen.org; *Programs and Operations Assoc.* Stacie Lemick. E-mail stacie@ sparcopen.org; *Asst. Dir., Right to Research Coalition* Joseph McArthur. E-mail joe@right toresearch.org; *Programs and Engagement* Nick Shockey. E-mail nick@sparcopen.org; *Consultant* Greg Tananbaum. E-mail greg@ sparcopen.org; *Asst. Dir. of Open Education* Brady Yano. E-mail brady@sparcopen.org.

Committee Chairs

Steering. Heather Joseph.

Publications

HowOpenIsIt? Open Access Spectrum (2014 revision) by Greg Tananbaum.

North American Campus-Based Open Access Funds: A Five-Year Progress Report (2014) by Greg Tananbaum.

Article-Level Metrics: A SPARC Primer (2013) by Greg Tananbaum.

The Collective Provision of Open Access Resources (2013) by Raym Crow in collaboration with Knowledge Exchange.

Implementing an Open Data Policy (2013) by Greg Tananbaum.

You've Signed the Boycott, Now What? A SPARC Guide for Campus Action (2012) (http://www.arl.org/sparc/bm~doc/sparc_ boycott_next_steps.pdf).

Open-Access Journal Publishing Resource Index (2011) by Raym Crow.

Library Publishing Services: Strategies for Success (2011) by Raym Crow, October Ivins, Allyson Mower, Daureen Nesdill, Mark Newton, Julie Speer, and Charles Watkinson.

Library Publishing Services: Strategies for Success Report, Version 1.0 (2011) by Raym Crow, October Ivins, Allyson Mower, Daureen Nesdill, Mark Newton, Julie Speer, and Charles Watkinson.

Campus-Based Open-Access Publishing Funds: A Practical Guide to Design and Implementation (2010) by Greg Tananbaum.

Campus-Based Publishing Partnerships: A Guide to Critical Issues (2009) by Raym Crow.

Income Models for Open Access: An Overview of Current Practice (2009) by Raym Crow.

The Right to Research: The Student Guide to Opening Access to Scholarship (2008), part of a campaign to engage students on the issue of research access.

Greater Reach for Research: Expanding Readership Through Digital Repositories (2008), the initiative to educate faculty on the benefits of open repositories and emerging research access policies.

Author Rights (2006), an educational initiative and introduction to the SPARC Author Addendum, a legal form that enables authors of journal articles to modify publishers' copyright transfer agreements and allow authors to keep key rights to their articles.

"Open Access News Blog," daily updates on the worldwide movement for open access to science and scholarship, written by Peter Suber and cosponsored by SPARC.

SPARC Open Access Newsletter, a monthly roundup of developments relating to open access publishing, written by Peter Suber.

SPARC e-news, SPARC's monthly newsletter featuring SPARC activities, an industry roundup, upcoming workshops and events, and articles relating to developments in scholarly communication.

Publishing Cooperatives: An Alternative for Society Publishers (2006) by Raym Crow.

Sponsorships for Nonprofit Scholarly and Scientific Journals: A Guide to Defining and Negotiating Successful Sponsorships (2005) by Raym Crow.

A more-complete list of SPARC publications, including brochures, articles, and guides, is available at https://sparcopen.org/what-we-do/ popular-resources/.

Special Libraries Association (SLA)

Executive Director, Amy Lestition Burke
7918 Jones Branch Dr., Suite 300, McLean, VA 22102
703-647-4900, fax 703-506-3266, e-mail aburke@sla.org
World Wide Web https://www.sla.org

Mission

The Special Libraries Association promotes and strengthens its members through learning, advocacy, and networking initiatives.

Strategic Vision

SLA is a global association of information and knowledge professionals who are employed in every sector of the economy. Its members thrive where data, information, and knowledge intersect, and its strategic partners support SLA because they believe in the association's mission and the future of its members. SLA's goal is to support information professionals as they contribute, in their varied and evolving roles, to the opportunities and achievements of organizations, communities, and society.

Membership

Memb. 9,000+ in 75 countries. Dues (Organizational) $750; (Indiv.) $100–$200; (Student/Intl./Salary less than $18,000 income per year) $50; (Ret.) $100.

Officers

Pres. Dee Manoni, Los Alamos National Laboratory, Box 1663, Los Alamos, NM 87545. E-mail deeslaboard@gmail.com; *Pres.-Elect* Roberto Sarmiento, Northwestern Univ., Evanston, IL. E-mail sarmiento@northwestern.edu; *Treas.* Nicholas Collison, Corporate Subscriptions, Box 648, Tel. 201-307-9900. Montvale, NJ 07645. E-mail collisonsla@gmail.com; *Past Pres.* Thomas E. Rink, Northeastern State Univ., 3100 E. New Orleans St., Broken Arrow, OK 74014. Tel. 918-449-6457, e-mail rink@nsuok.edu; *Chapter Cabinet Chair* Mary Tally. E-mail mary.talleygarcia@gmail.com; *Chapter Cabinet Chair-Elect* Emma Davidson. E-mail emmadavidson2010@gmail.com; *Past Chapter Cabinet Chair* Kim Silk. E-mail kimberly.silk@gmail.com; *Division Cabinet Chair* Tom Nielsen. E-mail escapefromnyc@gmail.com; *Division Cabinet Chair-Elect* Laura Leavitt. E-mail leavitt9@msu.edu; *Past Division Cabinet Chair* Ruth Kneale. E-mail rkneale@nso.edu.

Directors

Officers; Kevin Adams, Zena Applebaum, Barbara Kern, Catherine Lavallée-Welch.

Committee Chairs

Awards and Honors. Kate Arnold *(2015–2016)*.
Joint Governance and Bylaws. Maggie Hlava (2017–2019).
Finance. Nicholas Collison *(2016–2018)*.
Membership. Barbara Fullerton *(2016–2017)*.
Nominating. Tony Landolt.

Publication

Information Outlook (memb., nonmemb. $240/yr.)

Theatre Library Association

President, Colleen Reilly
c/o New York Public Library for the Performing Arts
40 Lincoln Center Plaza, New York, NY 10023
E-mail theatrelibraryassociation@gmail.com
World Wide Web http://www.tla-online.org/

Object

To further the interests of collecting, preserving, and using theater, cinema, and performing arts materials in libraries, museums, and private collections. Founded in 1937.

Membership

Memb. 300. Dues (Indiv.) $50; (Student/Non-salaried) $25; (Inst.) $75; (Sustaining) $150. Year. Jan.–Dec.

Officers

Pres. Colleen Reilly, Houston Community College. E-mail colleenreilly@gmail.com; *V.P.* Diana King, Univ. of California, Los Angeles. E-mail diking@library.ucla.edu; *Exec. Secy.* Laurie Murphy, New York Univ., Bobst Lib., 70 Washington Sq. S., New York. Tel. 212-998-2603, e-mail laurie.murphy@nyu.edu; *Treas.* Beth Kattelman, Ohio State Univ. E-mail kattelman.1@osu.edu; *Past Pres.* Nancy Friedland, Columbia Univ. Libs., 535 West 114th St., New York. Tel. 212-854-7402, e-mail nef4@columbia.edu.

Board of Directors

(2015–2017) John Calhoun, Doug Reside, Joseph Tally; *(2016–2018)* Diana Bertolini, Claudia Case, Matthew DiCintio, Francesca Marini; *(2017–2019)* Felicity Ann Brown, Selena Chau, Kathryn Hujda, Helice Koffler, Charlotte Price.

Committee Chairs

Conference Planning. Angela Weaver.
Membership. Laurie Murphy.
Nominating. David Nochimson.
Publications. Joseph Tally.
Strategic Planning. Angela Weaver.
Website Editorial. Eric Colleary, Angela Weaver.
Ad Hoc on Libraries. Diana King (TLA), Wade Hollingshaus (ASTR).
Ad Hoc on PAR. Joseph Tally.

Awards Committee Chairs

Book Awards. Diana Bertolini, Annemarie van Roessel.
Professional Awards. Francesca Marini.

Publications

Broadside Archive (digital backissues). *Ed.* Angela Weaver (2008–2014).
Performing Arts Resources (occasional; memb. $20/vol.; nonmemb. $30/vol.).

Urban Libraries Council

President and CEO, Susan B. Benton
1333 H St. N.W., Suite 1000 West, Washington, DC 20005
202-750-8650, e-mail info@urbanlibraries.org
World Wide Web http://www.urbanlibraries.org

Object

Since 1971 the Urban Libraries Council (ULC) has worked to strengthen public libraries as an essential part of urban life. A member organization of North America's leading public library systems, ULC serves as a forum for research widely recognized and used by public and private sector leaders. Its members are thought leaders dedicated to leadership, innovation, and the continuous transformation of libraries to meet community needs.

ULC's work focuses on helping public libraries to identify and utilize skills and strategies that match the challenges of the 21st century.

Membership

Membership is open to public libraries and to corporate partners specializing in library-related materials and services. The organization also offers associate memberships. Annual membership dues for libraries are based on the size of a library's operating budget (local + state).

Officers

Pres. and CEO Susan B. Benton. E-mail susan benton@urbanlibraries.org.

Executive Committee

Chair Michael Sherrod, Texas Christian Univ., Neely School of Business, 2900 Lubbock Ave., Fort Worth. Tel. 817-257-5735, e-mail m.s.sherrod@tcu.edu; *V.Chair/Chair-Elect* Gary Wasdin; *Immediate Past Chair* Matthew K. Poland; *Secy./Treas.* Rhea Brown Lawson.

Board Members

Jill Bourne, Vickery Bowles, Karen (Kari) E. Glover, Janet Hutchinson, John W. Laney, William (Bill) H. Meadows, Michael Meyer, C. Mary Okoye, Mary Blankenship Pointer, Richard Reyes-Gavilan, Mary J. Wardell, Allen G. Zaring.

State, Provincial, and Regional Library Associations

The associations in this section are organized under three headings: United States, Canada, and Regional. Both the United States and Canada are represented under Regional associations.

United States

Alabama

Memb. 1,200. Publication. *The Alabama Librarian* (q.).

Pres. Jeff Graveline, Univ. of Alabama at Birmingham, Mervyn H. Sterne Lib., SL 172, 1720 2nd Ave. S., Birmingham 35294. Tel. 205-934-6364, e-mail jgraveli@uab.edu; *Pres.-Elect* Sonya Jordan, Mountain Brook High School, 3650 Bethune Dr., Mountain Brook 35223. Tel. 205-414-3800 ext. 7619, e-mail jordans@student.mtnbrook.k12.al.us; *Secy.* Mandy Pinyan, Troy Univ., Rosa Parks Lib., 252 Montgomery St., Montgomery 36104. Tel. 334-241-8601, e-mail mpinyan@hmcpl.org; *Treas.* Tim Bailey, Auburn Univ. at Montgomery, Box 244023, Montgomery 36124. Tel. 334-244-3420, e-mail tbailey1@aum.edu; *Memb.-at-Large* (Central Alabama) Matt Layne, Emmet O'Neal Lib., 50 Oak St., Mountain Brook 35213, Tel. 205-908-5323, e-mail mlayne@bham.lib.al.us; (North Alabama) Craig Scott, Gadsden Public Lib., 254 College St., Gadsden 35901, Tel. 256-549-4699 ext. 120, e-mail craig@gadsdenlibrary.org; (South Alabama) Chris Shaffer, 309 Wallace Hall, Troy Univ. 36082, e-mail shafferc@troy.edu. *Past Pres.* Paula Laurita, Athens-Limeston Public Lib., 605 S. Jefferson St., Athens 35611. Tel. 256-232-1233, e-mail PaulaLaurita97@gmail.com.

Address correspondence to the association, 6030 Monticello Drive, Montgomery 36117. Tel. 334-414-0113, e-mail allibraryassoc@gmail.com.

World Wide Web http://allanet.org.

Alaska

Memb. 450+. Publication. Newspoke (q.) (online at http://akla.org/newspoke).

Pres. Sara Saxton, Wasilla Meta-Rose Public Lib., 391 N. Main St., Wasilla 99654. Tel. 907-864-9173, e-mail ssaxton@ci.wasilla. ak.us; *Pres.-Elect* Mollie Good. E-mail mgood@ci.valdez.ak.us; *Secy.* Amy Carney, Alaska State Lib., Box 110571, Juneau 99811. Tel. 907-465-1313, e-mail amy.carney@alaska.gov; *Treas.* Rebecca Moorman. E-mail rmoorman@uaa.alaska.edu; *Conference Coordinator* George Pasley. E-mail outreach@firstcitylibraries.org; *ALA Representative* Daniel Cornwall. E-mail daniel cornwall@gmail.com; *PNLA Representative* Mary Jo Joiner. E-mail mjoiner@ci.kenai. ak.us. *Past Pres.* Patty Brown, Haines Borough Public Lib., 111 3rd Ave., Haines 99827. E-mail director@haineslibrary.org.

Address correspondence to the secretary, Alaska Lib. Assn., P.O. Box 81084, Fairbanks 99708. E-mail akla@akla.org.

World Wide Web http://www.azla.org.

Arizona

Memb. 1,000. Term of Office. Nov.–Nov. Publication. *AzLA Newsletter* (6/yr.).

Pres. Sandy Edwards, AzLA, Gilbert. Tel. 480-694-9775, e-mail azlasandy@gmail.com; *Pres.-Elect* Gina Macaluso, Univ. of Arizona School of Information, 1103 E. 2nd St., Tucson. Tel. 520-621-5220, e-mail ginamacaluso@email.arizona.edu; *Secy.* Petra Pendroff, Maricopa County Lib. District; *Treas.* Kathy D. Hellman, Camp Verde Community Lib., 130 Black Bridge Rd., Camp Verde 86322. Tel. 928-554-8381, e-mail kathy.hellman@campverde.az.gov; *Exec. Secy.* Debbie J. Hanson. *Past Pres.* Amber Mathewson, County Public Lib., 101 N. Stone Ave., Tucson 85701. Tel. 520-594-5650, e-mail amber.mathewson@pima.gov.

Address correspondence to the executive secretary. Arizona Lib. Assn., 950 E. Baseline Rd. Suite 104-1025, Tempe 85283. Tel. 480-609-3999, e-mail admin@azla.org.

World Wide Web http://www.azla.org.

Arkansas

Memb. 600. Publication. *Arkansas Libraries* (4/yr.).

Pres. David Eckert, Craighead Co. Jonesboro Public Lib., 315 W. Oak Ave., Jonesboro 72401. Tel. 870-935-5133, ext. 111, e-mail david@libraryinjonesboro.org; *Pres.-Elect* Dean Covington, Univ. of Central Arkansas, 201 Donaghey Ave., Conway 72035. Tel. 501-450-5202, e-mail dcovington@uca.edu; *Secy./Treas.* Lynn Valetutti, Arkansas State Lib., 900 W. Capitol Ave., Suite 100, Little Rock 72201. Tel. 501-682-2840, e-mail lynn@library.arkansas. gov; *Exec. Admin.* Lynda Hampel, Arkansas Lib. Assn., P.O. Box 958, Benton 72018-0958. Tel. 501-860-7585, e-mail arlib2@sbcglobal. net. *Past Pres.* Judy Calhoun, SE Arkansas Regional Lib., 114 W. Jefferson Ave., Monticello 71655. Tel. 870-367-8584 ext. 222, e-mail director.searl@gmail.com.

Address correspondence to the executive administrator.

World Wide Web http://arlib.org/wp/.

California

Memb. 2,500. Publication. *CLA Chronicle* (online).

Pres. Helen McAlary, Ontario City Lib. E-mail HMcAlary@ci.ontario.ca.us; *V.P./Pres.-Elect* Dolly Goyal, Los Gatos Lib. E-mail dolly.goyal@gmail.com; *Secy.* Jennifer Baker, Napa Valley Unified School District. E-mail jenrgee@mail.com; *Treas.* Katherine R. Gould, Palos Verdes Lib. District. E-mail kgould@pvld.org; *Past Pres.* Misty Jones, San Diego Public Lib., 330 Park Blvd., San Diego 92101. E-mail mnjones@sandiego.gov.

Address correspondence to California Lib. Assn., 1055 E. Colorado Blvd., 5th Floor, Pasadena 91106. Tel. 626-204-4071, e-mail info@cla-net.org.

World Wide Web http://www.cla-net.org.

Colorado

Publication. *CAL Connections* (mo., online).

Pres. Dan Cordova, Colorado Supreme Court, Denver. E-mail daniel.cordova@judicial.state.co.us; *V.P./Pres.-Elect* Dana Abbey, National Network of Libs. of Medicine, Mid-Continental Region, Univ. of Colorado Health Sciences Lib. E-mail dana.abbey@ucdenver. edu; *Secy.* Susan Goldman,Colorado Assn. of Libs.,12011 Tejon St., Suite 700, Westminster 80234. E-mail sgoldman.lib@comcast. net; *Treas.* Mike Varnet, Pikes Peak Lib., 1175 Chapel Hills Dr., Colorado Springs 80920. Tel. 719.884.9700. E-mail mvarnet@ppld.org; *Past Pres.* Elena Rosenfeld. E-mail ERosenfeld@highplains.us.

Address correspondence to the president, Colorado Assn. of Libs., 12011 Tejon St., Suite 700, Westminster 80234. Tel. 303-463-6400, fax 303-458-0002, e-mail cal@cal-webs.org.

World Wide Web World Wide Web http://www.cal-webs.org.

Connecticut

Memb. 1,000+. Term of Office. July–June. Publication. *CLA Today* (online). E-mail editor @ctlibrarians.org.

Pres. Karen Jensen, James Blackstone Memorial Lib., 758 Main St., Branford 06405. Tel. 203-488-1441, e-mail kjensen @blackstonelibrary.org; *V.P./Pres.-Elect* Glenn Grube, Avon Free Public Lib., 281 Country Club Rd. Avon 06001. Tel. 860-673-9712, e-mail ggrube@avonctlibrary.info; *Secy.* Sunnie Scarpa, Wallingford Public Lib., 200 North Main St., Wallingford 06492. Tel. 978-869-1727, e-mail sscarpa@wallingfordlibrary. org; *Treas.* Scott R. Brill, Huntington Branch Lib., 41 Church St., Shelton 06484. Tel. 203-926-0111, fax 203-926-0181, e-mail sbrill@biblio.org; *Past Pres.* Beth A. Crowley, Scranton Memorial Lib., 801 Boston Post Rd., Madison 06443. Tel. 203-245-7365, e-mail crowley b@scrantonlibrary.org.

Address correspondence to Connecticut Lib. Assn., 234 Court St., Middletown 06457. Tel. 860-346-2444, fax 860-344-9199, e-mail cla@ctlibrarians.org.

World Wide Web http://ctlibraryassociation. org.

Delaware

Memb. 200+. Publication. *DLA Bulletin* (online).

Pres. Laurel Ferris, John Eugene Derrickson Memorial Lib., Delaware Technical Community College, 333 N. Shipley St., Wilmington 19801. Tel. 302-573-5431, e-mail lferris@dtcc.edu; *V.P.* Michelle Hughes, Dover Public Lib., 35 Loockerman Plaza, Dover 19901. Tel. 302-736-7079, fax 302-736-5087, e-mail michelle.hughes@lib.de.us; *Secy.* Adrienne Johnson, Wilmington Univ. Lib., 320 DuPont Hwy., New Castle 19720. Tel. 302-295-1177, e-mail adrienne.m.johnson@wilmu.edu; *Treas.* Ed Goyda, Lewes Public Lib., 111 Adams Ave., Lewes 19958. E-mail ed.goyda@lib.de.us; *Past Pres.* Beth Borene, Bear Public Lib., 101 Governors Pl., Bear 19701. Tel. 302-838-3300. E-mail eborene@nccde.org. *Exec. Dir.* Cathay Keough, Delaware Division of Libs., 121 Martin Luther King Jr. Blvd. N., Dover 19901. Tel. 302-983-1430, fax 302-739-6787, e-mail Cathay.Keough@lib.de.us.

Address correspondence to Delaware Lib. Assn., c/o Delaware Division of Libraries, 121 Martin Luther King Jr. Blvd. N., Dover 19901. E-mail dla@lib.de.us.

World Wide Web http://dla.lib.de.us

District of Columbia

Memb. 300+. Term of Office. July–June. Publication. *Capital Librarian* (mo., online).

Pres. Yvonne Dooley, Lib. of Congress, 101 Independence Ave. S.E., Washington 20540. E-mail dclavicepresident@gmail.com; *V.P./Pres.-Elect* Candice Townsend. E-mail dclavice president@gmail.com; *Secy.* Victor Benitez, DC Public Lib., Box 14177, Benjamin Franklin Station, Washington 20044. E-mail dcla secretary@gmail.com; *Treas.* Milea Pickett. E-mail dclatreasurer@gmail.com; *Past Pres.* Julius C. Jefferson Jr., Congressional Research Service, Lib. of Congress, 101 Independence Ave. S.E., Washington 20540. E-mail dcla president@gmail.com.

Address correspondence to District of Columbia Lib. Assn., Union Station, 50 Massachusetts Ave. S.E., P.O. Box 1653 Washington, DC 20002.

World Wide Web http://www.dcla.org.

Florida

Memb. (Indiv.) 1,000+. Publication. *Florida Libraries* (s. ann.).

Pres. Elana Karshmer, Saint Leo Univ., P.O. Box 6665, MC 2128, Saint Leo 33574. Tel. 352-588-8412, e-mail elana.karshmer@saintleo.edu; *V.P./Pres.-Elect* Robin Shader. Tel. 850-522-2109, e-mail rshader@nwrls.

com; *Secy.* Peggy Nuhn, Univ. of Central Florida, 900 Khingan Court, Apopka 32712. Tel. 407-708-2863, e-mail peggy.nuhn@ucf.edu; *Treas.* Kenny Rampersad. Tel. 561-233-2701, e-mail rampersadk@pbclibrary.org; *Past Pres.* Gene Coppola, Palm Harbor Lib., 2330 Nebraska Ave., Palm Harbor 34683. Tel. 727-784-3332 ext. 3001, e-mail gene@phlib.org; *Exec. Dir.* Dawn Pollock, Florida Lib. Assn., 541 E. Tennessee St., Suite 103, Tallahassee 32308. Tel. 850-270-9205, e-mail dawn@flalib.org.

Address correspondence to the executive director.

World Wide Web http://www.flalib.org.

Georgia

Memb. 800+. Publication. *Georgia Library Quarterly* (q., online). *Ed.* Virginia Feher, Univ. of North Georgia. Tel. 706-310-6305, e-mail virginia.feher@ung.edu.

Pres. Elizabeth McKinney, Georgia Public Lib. Service, 1800 Century Pl., Suite 150, Atlanta 30345. Tel. 404-235-7141, e-mail emckinney@georgialibraries.org; *V.P./Pres.-Elect 1st V.P./Pres.-Elect* Fred Smith, Zach S. Henderson Lib., Georgia Southern Univ., P.O. Box 8074, Statesboro 30460. Tel. 912-478-5647, e-mail fsmith@georgiasouthern.edu; *2nd V.P. Membership Committee Chair* John "Mack" Freeman, West Georgia Regional Lib., 710 Rome St., Carrollton 30117. Tel. 678-953-1646, e-mail johnmackfreeman@gmail.com; *Secy.* Geri Mullis, Marshes of Glynn Libs., 208 Gloucester St., Brunswick 31522. Tel. 912-580-4933, e-mail gmullis@glynncounty-ga.gov; *Treas.* Eli Arnold, Oglethorpe Univ., 4484 Peachtree Rd. N.E., Atlanta 30319. Tel. 404-364-8885, e-mail earnold@oglethorpe.edu; *Past Pres.* Cathy Jeffrey, Univ. of North Georgia Dahlonega Campus. E-mail Cathy.gla2016@gmail.com.

Address correspondence to the president, Georgia Lib. Assn., P.O. Box 793, Rex 30273-0793. E-mail emckinney@georgialibraries.org.

World Wide Web http://gla.georgialibraries.org.

Hawaii

Memb. 250.

Pres. Kara Plamann Wagoner, Kapi'olani Community College Lib. Email karapw@

hawaii.edu; *V.P.* D. Keali'i MacKenzie, Hawaii State Public Lib. System. E-mail david.kealii@gmail.com; *Secy.* Liz Teoli. Email teoli@hawaii.edu; *Treas.* Joy Oehlers, Kapi olani Community College Lib., 4303 Diamond Head Rd., Honolulu 96816. Tel. 808-734-9352, e-mail aichin@hawaii.edu; *Past Pres.* Brian Huffman, William S. Richardson School of Law Lib., Univ. of Hawai'i at Manoa, 2515 Dole St., Honolulu 96822. Tel. 808-956-02599, e-mail brhuffma@hawaii.edu.

Address correspondence to the Hawaii Lib. Assn. at P.O. Box 4441, Honolulu 96812-4441 or by e-mail at hawaii.library.association@gmail.com.

World Wide Web http://hawaiilibrary association.weebly.com.

Idaho

Memb. 420. Term of Office. Oct.–Oct. Publication. The Idaho Librarian Blog at http://idaho libraries.org/category/idaho-libraries-news/the-idaho-librarian/.

Pres. Amy Vecchione, Boise State Univ. Lib. E-mail amyvecchione@gmail.com; *V.P./Pres.-Elect* Erin Downey, Boise School District. E-mail erindowney.ila@gmail.com; *Secy.* Beverley Richmond, Priest Lake Public Lib. E-mail secretary@idaholibraries.org; *Treas.* Trisha Mick, Meridian Lib. District. E-mail trishamick.ila@gmail.com; *Past Pres.* Kristi Haman. E-mail khaman@adalib.org.

Address correspondence to the association, P.O. Box 8533, Moscow 83844.

World Wide Web http://idaholibraries.org.

Illinois

Memb. 3,500. Publication. *ILA Reporter* (bi-mo.).

Pres. Pattie Piotrowski, Illinois Institute of Technology, 3300 S. Federal St., Chicago 60616. Tel. 312-567-3386, e-mail piotrowski@iit.edu; *V.P./Pres.-Elect* Melissa Gardner, Palatine Public Lib. District; *Past Pres.* Betsy Adamowski, Wheaton Public Lib., 225 N. Cross St., Wheaton 60187. Tel. 630-868-7590, e-mail betsy@wheatonlibrary.org; *Exec. Dir.* Robert P. Doyle. E-mail doyle@ila.org.

Address correspondence to the executive director.

World Wide Web http://www.ila.org.

Indiana

Indiana Lib. Federation. Memb. 2,000+. Publications. *Focus on Indiana Libraries* (11 a year, memb.). *Ed.* Tisa M. Davis, 941 E. 86th Street, Suite 260, Indianapolis 46240. Tel. 317-257-2040, ext. 102, fax 317-257-1389, e-mail tdavis @ilfonline.org.

Pres. David Peter, Vincennes Univ., 1002 N. First St., Vincennes 47803. Tel. 812-888-5815, e-mail dpeter@vinu.edu; *Pres.-Elect* Edra Waterman, Hamilton East Public Lib., One Library Plaza, Noblesville 46060. Tel. 317-770-3202, e-mail ewaterman@hepl.lib.in.us; *Secy.* Diane Huerkamp, Mooresville Public Lib., 220 W. Harrison St., Mooresville 46158. Tel. 317-831-7323, e-mail dianeh@mooresville.lib. in.us; *Treas.* Stephanie Davis, Wells County Public Lib., 200 West Washington St., Bluffton 46714. Tel. 260-824-1612, e-mail sdavis@wellscolibrary.org; *Past Pres.* Robyn Young, Avon High School, 7575 E. CR 150 S., Avon 46123. Tel. 317-544-5031, e-mail rryoung@avon-schools.org; *Exec. Dir.* Lucinda Nord. Tel. 317-257-2040, ext. 101, e-mail exec@ilfonline.org.

Address correspondence to Indiana Lib. Federation, 941 E. 86 St., Suite 260, Indianapolis 46240. Tel. 317-257-2040, fax 317-257-1389.

World Wide Web http://www.ilfonline.org.

Iowa

Memb. 1,500. Publication. *Catalyst* (bi-mo., online).

Pres. Alison Ames Galstad, Coralville Public Lib., 1401 5th St., Coralville 52241. Tel. 319-248-1858, e-mail agalstad@coralville.org; *V.P./Pres.-Elect* Dan Chibnall, Drake Univ., 2507 University Ave., Des Moines 50311. Tel. 515-271-2112, e-mail dan.chibnall@drake. edu; *Secy.* Rebecca Funke, Des Moines Area Community College, 2006 S Ankeny Blvd., Ankeny 50023. Tel. 515-964-6328, e-mail rsfunke@dmacc.edu; *Treas.* Brianna Glenn, De Soto Public Lib., 405 Walnut St., De Soto 50069. Tel. 515-834-2690, e-mail desoto library@mchsi.com; *Past Pres.* Duncan Stewart, Univ. of Iowa Libs., 100 Main Lib., Iowa City 52242. Tel. 319-335-5884, e-mail duncan-stewart@uiowa.edu.

Address correspondence to the association, 6919 Vista Drive, West Des Moines 50266. Tel. 515-282-8192.

World Wide Web http://www.iowalibrary association.org.

Kansas

Kansas Lib. Assn. Memb. 1,500. Term of Office. July–June. Publication. *KLA Connects* (q.).

Pres. Gloria Creed-Dikeogu, Ottawa Univ., Myers Lib., 1001 S. Cedar St., Ottawa 66067. Tel. 785-248-2536, e-mail gloria.creed dikeogu@ottawa.edu; *First V.P.* George Seamon, Northwest Kansas Lib, System, #2 Washington Sq.; Norton 67654. Tel. 785-877-5148, e-mail director@nwkls.org; *2nd V.P.* Laura Littrell, Kansas State Univ., Lib. Planning and Assessment, 1117 Mid-Campus Dr. N., 314A Hale Lib., Manhattan 66506. Tel. 785-532-5467, e-mail laurlit@k-state.edu; *Secy.* Savannah Ball, Southwest Kansas Lib. System, 100 Military, Suite 210, Dodge City 67801. Tel. 620-225-1231 ext. 206, e-mail consultant@swkls.org; *Treas.* Diana Weaver, Basehor Community Lib., 1400 158th St., Basehor 66007. Tel. 913-724-2828, e-mail dweaver@basehorlibrary.org; *Past Pres.* Terri Summey, Professor, Emporia State Univ., Univ. Libs. and Archives, Campus Box 4051, Emporia 66801. Tel. 620-341-5058, e-mail tsummey @emporia.edu.

Address correspondence to the president, Kansas Lib. Assn., 1020 S.W. Washburn, Topeka 66604. Tel. 785-580-4518, fax 785-580-4595, e-mail kansaslibraryassociation@yahoo. com.

World Wide Web http://www.kslibassoc.org.

Kentucky

Memb. 1,600. Publication. *Kentucky Libraries* (q.).

Pres. Dave Schroeder, Kenton County Public Lib., Administration Ctr., 2171 Chamber Ctr. Dr., Ft. Mitchell 41017. Tel. 859-578-3600., e-mail dave.schroeder@kentonlibrary. org; *Pres.-Elect* Tara Griffith, Barren County Schools, 507 Trojan Trail, Glasgow 42141. Tel. 270-202-2547, e-mail tara.griffith@barren. kyschools.us; *Secy.* Michele Ruth, Georgetown College, 400 East College St., Georgetown

40324. Tel. 502-863-8412, e-mail michele_ ruth@georgetowncollege.edu; *Past Pres.* Julie Howe, Somerset Community College, Laurel North Campus, Bldg 2, 100 University Dr., Somerset 40741. Tel. 606-878-4724, e-mail julie.howe@kctcs.edu; *Exec. Dir.* John Tom Underwood, Kentucky Lib. Assn., 5932 Timber Ridge Drive, Unit 101, Prospect 40059. Tel. 502-223-5322 , fax 502-223-4937, e-mail info@kylibasn.org.

Address correspondence to the executive director.

World Wide Web http://www.klaonline.org.

Louisiana

Memb. 1,000+. Term of Office. July–June. Publication. *Louisiana Libraries* (q.). *Ed.* Celise Reech-Harper, Assoc. Dir., Beauregard Parish Lib., 205 South Washington Ave., De-Ridder 70634. Tel. 337-463-6217 ext. 22, e-mail celise@beau.org.

Pres. Mary Cosper-LeBoeuf. Tel. 985-876-5861, fax 985-876-5864, e-mail mcleboeuf@ mytpl.org; *First V.P./Pres.-Elect* Patricia Brown. Tel. 337-550-1385, e-mail pbrown@ lsue.edu; *Second V.P./Pres.-Elect* Van Viator. Tel. 985-859-7353, e-mail van.viator@ nicholls.edu; *Secy.* Laura-Ellen Ayres. Tel. 318-445-6436 ext. 227, e-mail lea@rpl.org; *Past Pres.* Paula Clemmons. Email pclemmons @episcopaldayschool.org.

Address correspondence to Louisiana Lib. Assn., 8550 United Plaza Blvd., Suite 1001, Baton Rouge 70809. Tel. 225-922-4642, 877-550-7890, fax 225-408-4422, e-mail office@ llaonline.org.

World Wide Web http://www.llaonline.org.

Maine

Maine Lib. Assn. Memb. 950. Publication. *MLA to Z* (q., online).

Pres. Bryce Cundick, Mantor Lib., Univ. of Maine at Farmington, 116 South St., Farmington 04938-1998. Tel. 207-778-7224, e-mail mla.brycecundick@gmail.com; *V.P.* Alisia Revitt, Maine InfoNet, UMaine, 5784 York Village, Suite 58, Orono 04469. Tel. 207-581-3087, e-mail mla.alisiarevitt@gmail.com; *Secy.* Lisa Shaw, Maine State Lib., 145 Harlow St., Bangor 04401. Tel. 207-947-8336 ext. 114, e-mail lisa.m.shaw@maine.gov; *Treas.*

Michael Dignan, Paris Public Lib., 37 Market Sq., Paris 04291-1509. Tel. 207-743-6994, e-mail mdignan@paris.lib.me.us; *Memb.-at-Large* Pamela Bonney, Winslow Public Lib., 136 Halifax St., Winslow 04901. Tel. 207-872-1978, e-mail pbonney@winslow-me.gov. *Past Pres.* Nissa Flanagan, Merrill Memorial Lib., 215 Main St., Yarmouth 04096. Tel. 207-846-4763, e-mail nflanagan@yarmouthlibrary.org.

Address correspondence to the Maine Lib. Assn., 93 Saco Ave., Old Orchard Beach 04064. Tel. 207-730-3028, e-mail maine library@gmail.com

World Wide Web http://mainelibraries.org.

Maryland

Maryland Lib. Assn. Memb. 1,000+. Term of Office. July–July. Publication. *The Crab* (q., online). *Ed.* Annette Haldeman. E-mail annette.haldeman@mlis.state.md.us.

Pres. Kathleen Teaze, Prince Georges County Memorial Lib., 9601 Capital Ln., Largo, MD 20774. Tel. 301-699-3500 ext. 6224, e-mail kathleen.teaze@pgcmls.info; *V.P./Pres.-Elect* Denise Davis, Cecil County Public Lib., 301 Newark Ave., Elkton 21921-5441. Tel. 410-996-1055, fax 410-996-5604, e-mail ddavis@ccplnet.org; *Secy.* Mary Anne Bowman, St. Mary's County Public Lib., 23250 Hollywood Rd., Leonardtown 20650. Tel. 301-475-2846 ext. 1015, fax 410-884-4415, e-mail ma bowman@stmalib.org; *Treas.* Patty Sundberg, Carroll County Public Lib., 705 Ridge Ave., Mount Airy 21771. Tel. 410-386-4470 ext. 4402, e-mail sundberg@carr.org; *Past Pres.* Mary Hastler, Harford County Public Lib., 1221 Brass Mill Rd., Belcamp 21017. Tel. 443-417-8531, fax 410-273-5606, e-mail hastler@hcplonline.org. *Exec. Dir.* Margaret Carty, Maryland Lib. Assn., 1401 Hollins St., Baltimore 21223. Tel. 410-947-5090, e-mail mcarty@carr.org.

Address correspondence to the association, 1401 Hollins St., Baltimore 21223. Tel. 410-947-5090, fax 410-947-5089, e-mail mla@mdlib.org.

World Wide Web http://www.mdlib.org.

Massachusetts

Massachusetts Lib. Assn. Memb. (Indiv.) 1,000; (Inst.) 100.

Pres. Nanci Milone-Hill, M.G. Parker Memorial Lib., 28 Arlington St., Dracut 01826. Tel. 978-454-5474 ext. 301, e-mail nhill@mvlc.org; *V.P.* Alexander Lent, Mills Public Lib., 961 Main St., Mills 02054. Tel. 508-376-8262, e-mail: alent@minlib.net; *Secy.* Nora Blake, Emily Williston Memorial Lib., 9 Park St., Easthampton 01027. Tel. 413-527-1031, e-mail secretary@masslib.org; *Treas.* Jennifer Pike, Worcester Public Lib., 3 Salem Sq., Worcester 01608. Tel. 508-799-1709, e-mail jpike@worcpublib.org; *Past Pres.* Eric Poulin, Westborough Public Lib., 55 West Main St., Westborough 01581. Tel. 508-871-5280, e-mail PoulinE@gcc.mass.edu.

Address correspondence to the Massachusetts Lib. Assn., P.O. Box 21, Seekonk 02771. Tel. 781-698-7764, e-mail manager@masslib. org.

World Wide Web http://www.masslib.org.

Michigan

Memb. 1,200+.

Pres. Kathleen Zaenger, Howell Carnegie District Lib., 314 W. Grand River, Howell 48843. Tel. 517-546-0720, e-mail zaenger@howelllibrary.org; *Pres.-Elect* Steven Bowers, Detroit Area Lib. Network (DALNET); *Treas.* Richard Schneider, Muskegon District Lib., 4845 Airline Rd., Unit 5, Muskegon 49444. Tel. 231-737-6248, e-mail rschneider@madl.org; *Past Pres.* Leslie Warren, Olson Lib., Northern Michigan Univ., 1401 Presque Isle Ave., Marquette 49855. Tel. 906-227-2117, e-mail lwarren@nmu.edu; *Exec. Dir.* Gail Madziar, Michigan Lib. Assn., 3410 Belle Chase Way, Suite 100, Lansing 48911. Tel. 517-394-2774 ext. 224, e-mail gmadziar@milibraries.org.

Address correspondence to the executive director.

World Wide Web http://http://www.mi libraries.org.

Minnesota

Memb. 1,100. Term of Office. (*Pres., Pres.-Elect*) Jan.–Dec.

Pres. Amy Boese, Ramsey County Lib., 2180 N. Hamline Ave., Roseville 55113. Tel. 651-724-6065, e-mail aboese@ramsey.lib. mn.us; *Pres.-Elect* Ryan McCormick, Great River Regional Lib. E-mail mcco0303@email.

arizona.edu; *Secy.* Sarah Hawkins, Great River Regional Lib. E-mail shawkins@ecrlib.org; *Treas.* Kate Anderson, School of Business, Rasmussen College. E-mail Kate.Anderson@rasmussen.edu; *Past Pres.* Margaret Stone, Dakota County Lib., 1101 W. County Rd. 42, Burnsville 55306. E-mail margaret.stone@co.dakota.mn.us.

Address correspondence to the Minnesota Lib. Assn., 400 S. 4th St., Suite 754E, Minneapolis 55415. Tel. 612-294-6549, e-mail mla@management-hq.com.

World Wide Web http://www.mnlibrary association.org.

Mississippi

Memb. 625. Term of Office. Jan.–Dec. Publication. *Mississippi Libraries* (q.). *Ed.* Tina Harry.

Pres. Jenniffer Stephenson, Greenwood-Leflore Public Lib. System, 405 W. Washington St., Greenwood 38930. Tel. 662-453-3634, e-mail jstephenson@greenwood.lib.ms.us; *V.P.* Sarah Mangrum, Univ. Libs. (USM). Tel. 601-266-4251, e-mail sarah.rials@usm.edu; *Secy.* Jennifer Wann, Bolivar County Lib. System. Tel. 662-843-2774 ext. 102, e-mail jwann@bolivar.lib.ms.us; *Treas.* Blair Booker, Holmes Community College, 412 W. Ridgeland Ave., Ridgeland 39157. Tel. 601-605-3303, e-mail bbooker@holmescc.edu; *Admin.* Barbara J. Price, P.O. Box 13687, Jackson 39236-3687. Tel. 601-981-4586, e-mail info@misslib.org. *Past Pres.* Molly McManus, U.S. Army Engineer Research and Development Ctr. Lib., 3909 Halls Ferry Rd., Vicksburg 39180. Tel. 601-634-4122, e-mail molly.S.Mcmanus@usace.army.mil.

Address correspondence to the administrator.

World Wide Web http://www.misslib.org.

Missouri

Memb. 800+. Term of Office. Jan.–Dec. Publication. *MO INFO* (bi-mo.).

Pres. Vicky Baker, Mid-Continent Public Lib., Tel. 816-521-7206, e-mail mlapresident@molib.org; *Pres.-Elect* April Roy, Kansas City Public Lib. E-mail aprilroy@kclibrary.org; *Secy. and Memb.-at-Large* Jenny Bossaller, Univ. of Missouri School of Information Science and Learning Technologies. E-mail BossallerJ@missouri.edu; *Treas. and Memb.-at-Large* Mary Beth Revels, St. Joseph Public Lib. 816-232-7729, e-mail mrevels@sjpl.lib.mo.us; *Memb.-at-Large* Anna Francesca Garcia, Kansas City Public Lib. E-mail anna.francesca.garcia@gmail.com; *Asst. Treas. and Member-at-Large* Cindy Thompson, UMKC Miller Nichols Lib. Tel. 816-235-1511, e-mail thompsoncym@umkc.edu; *Past Pres.* Jodie Borgerding, Webster Univ. Lib., 101 Edgar Rd., St. Louis 63119. Tel. 314-246-7819.

Address correspondence to the president.

World Wide Web http://www.molib.org.

Montana

Memb. 600. Term of Office. July–June. Publication. *Focus* (bi-mo.).

Pres. -Elect/Interim Pres. Lisa Mecklenberg Jackson, State Law Libn. of Montana, 215 N. Sanders, Helena 59620. Tel. 406-444-3660, e-mail lisameckjack@gmail.com; *Secy./Treas.* Mary Guthmiller, Montana State Univ. Bozeman, Bozeman 59717. Tel. 406-994-4642, e-mail guthmill@montana.edu; *Past Pres./Interim V.P.* Dawn Kingstad, Glendive Public Lib., P.O. Box 576, Glendive 59330. Tel. 406-989-1561, e-mail booksrus@midrivers.com; *Exec. Dir.* Debbi Kramer, Montana Lib. Assn., Inc., 33 Beartooth View Dr., Laurel 59044. Tel. 406-579-3121, e-mail debkmla@hotmail.com.

Address correspondence to the executive director.

World Wide Web http://www.mtlib.org.

Nebraska

Term of Office. Jan.–Dec.

Pres. Angela Kroeger, Univ. of Nebraska–Omaha. E-mail nlapres@gmail.com; *Pres.-Elect* Andrew Cano, Univ. of Nebraska–Lincoln. E-mail nlapresidentelect@gmail.com; *Secy.* Amy Wenzl, Omaha Public Lib. E-mail nlasecretary@gmail.com; *Treas.* Christa Burns Porter, Nebraska Lib. Commission. E-mail nlatreasurer@gmail.com; *Past Pres.* Julee Hector, Lincoln City Libs. E-mail nlapastpresident@gmail.com; *Exec. Dir.* Nicole Zink, Nebraska Lib. Assn., P.O. Box 21756, Lincoln 68542-1756. Tel. 402-216-0727, e-mail NLAexecutive director@gmail.com.

Address correspondence to the executive director.

World Wide Web http://nebraskalibraries. site-ym.com.

Nevada

Memb. 450. Term of Office. Jan.–Dec. Publication. *Nevada Libraries* (q.).

Pres. Amy Dodson, Douglas County Lib. District. E-mail adodson@douglas.lib.nv.us; *Pres.-Elect* Soraya Silverman-Montoya, Las Vegas–Clark County Lib. District. E-mail silvermans@lvccld.org; *Exec. Secy.* Mayra Corn, Las Vegas–Clark County Lib. District, cornm@lvccld.org; *Treas.* Gracie McDonough, Henderson Libs. E-mail gmcdonough.nla@ gmail.com; *Past Pres.* Scott Clonan, Las Vegas–Clark County Lib. District, 1401 E. Flamingo Rd., Las Vegas 89119. E-mail Clonan. NLA@gmail.com.

Address correspondence to the executive secretary.

World Wide Web http://www.nevada libraries.org.

New Hampshire

Memb. 700.

Pres. Marilyn Borgendale, GMILCS, 31 Mount Saint Mary's Way, Hooksett 03106. Tel. 603-485-4286, e-mail mborg@gmilcs.org; *V.P./Pres.-Elect* Sylvie Brikiatis, Nesmith Lib., 8 Fellows Rd, Windham 03087. Tel. 603-432-7154, e-mail SBrikiatis@NesmithLibrary.org; *Secy.* Matthew Gunby, Meredith Public Lib., 91 Main St., Meredith 03253. Tel. 603-279-4303, e-mail matthew@meredithlibrary.org; *Treas.* Cara Barlow, Derry Public Lib., 64 E. Broadway, Derry 03038. Tel. 603-432-6128, e-mail carab@derrypl.org; *Past Pres.* Jenn Hosking, Nashua Public Lib., 2 Court St., Nashua 03060. Tel. 603-589-4621, e-mail jenn.hosking@ nashualibrary.org.

Address correspondence to the association, c/o New Hampshire State Lib., Michael York, 20 Park St., Concord 03301-6314. Tel. 603-271-2397, e-mail michael.york@dcr.nh.gov.

World Wide Web http://nhlibrarians.org.

New Jersey

Memb. 1,800. Term of Office. July–June. Publication. *New Jersey Libraries NEWSletter* (q.).

Pres. Chris Carbone, South Brunswick Public Lib., 110 Kingston Ln., Monmouth Junction 08852. Tel. 732-329-4000 ext. 7287, e-mail ccarbone@sbpl.info; *1st V.P./Pres.-Elect* Michael Maziekien, Kenilworth Public Lib. E-mail maz@lmxac.org; *2nd V.P.* Keith McCoy, Somerset County Lib. System, Bridgewater Lib., 1 Vogt Dr., Bridgewater 08807. Tel. 908-526-4016 ext. 128, e-mail kmccoy@sclibnj. org; *Secy.* Maryann Ralph, Plainsboro Public Lib. E-mail maryannralph@gmail.com; *Treas.* Cynthia Lambert, Somerset County Lib. System. E-mail clambert@sclibnj.org; *Past Pres.* James Keehbler, Piscataway Public Lib., 500 Hoes Ln., Piscataway 08854. Tel. 732-463-1633, e-mail jkeehbler@piscatawaylibrary.org; *Exec. Dir.* Patricia Tumulty, New Jersey Lib. Assn., P.O. Box 1534, Trenton 08607. Tel. 609-394-8032, fax 609-394-8164, e-mail ptumulty @njla.org.

Address correspondence to the executive director.

World Wide Web http://www.njla.org.

New Mexico

Memb. 550. Term of Office. Apr.–Apr. Publication. *NMLA Newsletter* (bi-mo., online).

Pres. Lynette Schurdevin, Lomo Colorado Main Lib., 755 Lomo Colorado Blvd. N.E., Rio Rancho 87124. Tel. 505-896-8817, e-mail lschurdevin@rrnm.gov; *V.P./Pres.-Elect* Marian Royal. E-mail marianroyal13@gmail.com; *Secy.* Karla Hunt. E-mail kfort60@gmail.com; *Treas.* Lisa Pate, ABC Lib., 501 Copper Ave., N.W., Albuquerque 87102. E-mail treasurer@ nmla.org; *Memb.-at-Large* Lillian Chavez. E-mail mescalerolibrary@matisp.net; Stephanie Wilson. E-mail libsew@nmcourts.gov; Kim Baraney. E-mail kbarany@lcps.k12.nm.us; Jose Aranda. E-mail jaranda2@nmsu.edu; *ALA-APA Councilor* Jaqueline Dean, jdean@ lcps.k12.nm.us. *Past Pres.* Sharon Jenkins, David H. Townsend Lib., New Mexico State Univ.–Alamogordo, 2400 N. Scenic Dr., Alamogordo 88310. Tel. 575-439-3806, e-mail djenkins@nmsu.edu.

Address correspondence to the New Mexico Lib. Assn., Box 26074, Albuquerque 87125. Tel. 505-400-7309, fax 505-544-5740, e-mail contact@nmla.org.

World Wide Web http://nmla.org.

New York

Memb. 4,000. Term of Office. Nov.–Nov. Publication. *NYLA e-Bulletin* (6 a year, online). *Pres.* Barbara Stripling, School of Info. Studies, Syracuse Univ., 307 Hinds Hall, Syracuse 13244. Tel. 315-443-1069, e-mail bstripli@syr.edu; *Pres.-Elect* Tim Burke. Tel. 518-437-9880, e-mail tim.burke@uhls.lib.ny.us; *Treas.* Claudia Depkin, Haverstraw King's Daughters Public Lib., 10 W. Ramapo Rd., Garnerville 10923. Tel. 845-786-3800, e-mail cdepkin@rcls.org; *Treas.-Elect* Cassie Guthrie. Tel. 585-225-8951, e-mail Cassie.Guthrie@libraryweb.org; *ALA Chapter Councilor* Jennifer Ferriss. Tel. 518-584-7300 ext. 219, e-mail jferriss@sals.edu; *Past Pres.* Debby Emerson, Central New York Lib. Resources Council, 6493 Ridings Rd., Syracuse 13206. Tel. 315-446-5446, e-mail demerson@clrc.org; *Exec. Dir.* Jeremy Johannesen, New York Lib. Assn., 6021 State Farm Rd., Guilderland 12084. Tel. 518-432-6952, fax 518-427-1697, e-mail director@nyla.org.

Address correspondence to the executive director.

World Wide Web http://www.nyla.org.

North Carolina

Memb. 1,100. Term of Office. Oct.–Oct. Publication. *North Carolina Libraries* (1–2 a year, online). *Ed.* Ralph Scott. E-mail SCOTTR@ecu.edu.

Pres. Rodney Lippard, Univ. of South Carolina Aiken, 471 University Pkwy. Aiken, SC 29801. Tel. 919-923-7716, e-mail nclapresident@gmail.com; *V.P./Pres.-Elect* Michael A. Crumpton, Walter Clinton Jackson Lib., Univ. of North Carolina–Greensboro, 320 College Ave., Greensboro 27412. Tel. 336-256-1213, e-mail macrumpt@uncg.edu; *Secy.* Julie Humphrey, Educational Resource Ctr., Durham Technical Community College, 1637 E. Lawson St., Durham 27703. Tel. 919-536-7211 ext. 1602, e-mail humphreyj@durhamtech.edu; *Treas.* Lorrie Russell, High Point Public Lib., 901 Main St., High Point 27261. Tel. 336-883-3644, e-mail ncla.treasurer@gmail.com; *Treas.-Elect* Siobhan Loendorf, Catawba County Lib., 115 West C St., Newton 28658. Tel. 828-465-8292, e-mail sloendorf@catawbacountync.gov; *Past Pres.* Dale Cousins (Ret.), Wake County Public Libs., 404 Perry St., Raleigh 27608. Tel. 919-599-8801, e-mail dalenbill@gmail.com; *Exec. Asst.* Kim Parrott, North Carolina Lib. Assn., 1841 Capital Blvd. Raleigh 27604. Tel. 919-839-6252, fax 888-977-3143, e-mail nclaonline@gmail.com.

Address correspondence to the executive assistant.

World Wide Web http://www.nclaonline.org.

North Dakota

Memb. (Indiv.) 300+. Term of Office. Sept.–Sept. Publication. *The Good Stuff* (q.). *Ed.* Marlene Anderson, Bismarck State College Lib., P.O. Box 5587, Bismarck 58506-5587. Tel. 701-224-5578, e-mail marlene.anderson@bismarckstate.edu.

Pres. Wendy Wendt, Grand Forks Public Lib., 2110 Lib. Cir., Grand Forks 58201. Tel. 701-772-8116, e-mail wendy.wendt@gflibrary.com; *Pres.-Elect* Lesley Gunderson, West Fargo Public Schools. E-mail librarylesley40@gmail.com; *Secy.* Kathy Jo Cline, Beulah Public Middle and High School, 1700 Central Ave. N., Beulah 58523. Tel. 701-873-4325, e-mail kathy.cline@k12.nd.us; *Treas.* Aaron Stefanich, Grand Forks Public Lib., 2110 Lib. Cir., Grand Forks 58201. Tel. 701-772-8116, e-mail aaron.stefanich@gflibrary.com; *ALA Councilor* Laurie L. McHenry, Univ. of North Dakota–Thormodsgard Law Lib. E-mail laurie.mchenry@email.und.edu; *Past Pres.* Greta Guck, Leach Public Lib., 417 2nd Ave. N., Wahpeton 58075. Tel. 701-642-5732, e-mail greta.leachplib@midconetwork.com.

Address correspondence to the president.

World Wide Web http://www.ndla.info.

Ohio

Memb. 2,700+. Term of Office. Jan.–Dec. Publication. *OLC News* (online).

Chair Andrew Mangels, Westlake Porter Public Lib., 27333 Ctr. Ridge Rd., Westlake 44145. Tel. 440-871-2600, e-mail andrew.mangels@westlakelibrary.org; *V.Chair/Chair-Elect* Nicholas Tepe, Athens County Public Libs. Tel. 740-753-2118, e-mail cntepe@gmail.com; *Secy./Treas.* Don Yarman, Delaware County District Lib. Tel. 740-363-7277, e-mail yarmando@delawarelibrary.org; *Im-*

mediate Past Chair Alan Radnor, Vorys Sater, Seymour, & Pease, 52 E. Gay St., Columbus 43215. Tel. 614-464-6326, e-mail joalcar@aol.com; *Exec. Dir.* Douglas Evans, Ohio Lib. Council, 1105 Schrock Rd., Suite 440, Columbus, OH 43229. Tel. 614-410-8092 ext. 103, e-mail devans@olc.org.

Address correspondence to the executive director.

World Wide Web http://www.olc.org.

Oklahoma

Memb. (Indiv.) 1,000; (Inst.) 60. Term of Office. July–June. Publication. *Oklahoma Librarian* (bi-mo.). *Ed.* Jill McFall.

Pres. Melody Kellogg, Edmond Public Lib., 10 S. Blvd. St., Edmond 73034. Tel. 405-341-9282; *V.P./Pres.-Elect* Linda Pye; *Secy.* Tassey Beeson; *Treas.* Misty Long; *ALA Councilor* Nicole Sump-Crethar; *Past Pres.* Calypso Gilstrap, Norman High School Lib., 911 W. Main St., Norman 73069. E-mail cgilstrap@norman.k12.ok.us; *Exec. Dir.* Kay Boies, Oklahoma Lib. Assn., P.O. Box 6550, Edmond 73083. Tel. 405-525-5100, fax 405-525-5103, e-mail execdirector@oklibs.org.

Address correspondence to the executive director.

World Wide Web http://www.oklibs.org.

Oregon

Memb. (Indiv.) 1,000+. Publications. *OLA Hotline.* *Ed.* Berenice Prado, Emporia State Univ. E-mail olahotline@olaweb.org (bi-w.), *OLA Quarterly.* *Ed.* Charles Wood. E-mail wuchakewu@gmail.com.

Pres. Elsa Loftis, Oregon College of Arts and Crafts Lib., 8245 S.W. Barnes Rd., Portland 97229. Tel. 503-297-5544 ext. 119, e-mail olapresident@olaweb.org; *V.P./Pres.-Elect* Buzzy Nielsen, Crook County Lib. E-mail olavp@olaweb.org; *Secy.* Damon Campbell, Univ. of Oregon Lib. E-mail camp@uoregon.edu; *Treas.* Stephanie Lind, Washington County Cooperative Lib. Services, 111 N.E. Lincoln St., Suite 230-L, MS 58, Hillsboro 97124. Tel. 503-648-9809, e-mail olatreasurer@olaweb.org; *Memb.-at-Large* Jenny Pedersen, Deschutes Public Lib. E-mail jenniferp@dpls.lib.or.us; *ALA Representative* Danielle Jones, Multnomah County Lib. E-mail daniellej@multco.us; *Past Pres.* Jane Corry, Multnomah County Lib., 801 S.W. 10th Ave., Portland 97205. E-mail olapastpresident@olaweb.org.

Address correspondence to Oregon Lib. Assn., P.O. Box 3067, La Grande 97850. Tel. 541-962-5824, e-mail olaweb@olaweb.org.

World Wide Web http://www.olaweb.org.

Pennsylvania

Memb. 1,900+. Term of Office. Jan.–Dec. Publication. *PaLA Bulletin* (10 a year).

Pres. Carrie Turner, Cheltenham Township Lib. System. Tel. 215-885-0457, e-mail cturner@mclinc.org; *1st V.P.* Tina Hertel, Muhlenberg College. Tel. 484-664-3550, e-mail thertel@muhlenberg.edu; *2nd V.P.* Dana Farabaugh, Westmoreland County Federated Lib. Tel. 724-420-5638, e-mail dana.farabaugh@wlnonline.org; *3rd V.P.* Melissa Rowse, Degestein Lib. E-mail mrowse@jvbrown.edu; *Treas.* Alison Gregory, Lycoming College Lib. Tel. 570-321-4082, e-mail gregory@lycoming.edu; *ALA Councilor* Rob Lesher, Dauphin County Lib. System. Tel. 717-234-4961, e-mail rlesher@dcls.org; *Past Pres.* Jennifer Stocker, Easton Area Public Lib., Tel. 610-258-2917 ext. 310, e-mail jenns@eastonpl.org; *Exec. Dir.* Christi Buker. Pennsylvania Lib. Assn., 220 Cumberland Pkwy., Suite 10, Mechanicsburg 17055. Tel. 717-766-7663, e-mail christi@palibraries.org.

Address correspondence to the executive director.

World Wide Web http://www.palibraries.org.

Rhode Island

Memb. (Indiv.) 350+; (Inst.) 50+. Term of Office. June–June. Publication. *RILA Bulletin.* *Eds.* Brandi Fong, Andria Tieman Michney. E-mail rilabulletin@gmail.com.

Pres. Aaron Coutu, Cumberland Public Lib., 1464 Diamond Hill Rd., Cumberland 02864. Tel. 401-333-2552 ext. 128, e-mail acoutu@cumberlandlibrary.org; *V.P./Pres.-Elect* Kieran Ayton, Rhode Island College, 600 Mt. Pleasant Ave., Providence, 02908. Tel. 401-456-9604, e-mail kayton@ric.edu; *Secy.* Ryan Brennan, North Kingstown Free Lib. Tel. 401-294-3306 ext. 6113, e-mail rbrennan@nklibrary.org; *Treas.* Brigitte Hopkins, Westerly Lib. and

Wilcox Park, 44 Broad St., Westerly 02891. Tel. 401-596-2877 ext. 303, e-mail bhopkins@ westerlylibrary.org *Memb.-at-Large* Andrew Creamer, Brown Univ. Tel. 401-863-9402, e-mail Andrew_Creamer@brown.edu; Beth Ullucci, Jesse M. Smith Memorial Lib. Tel. 401-710-7800, e-mail bullucci@burrillville. org; *ALA Councilor* Jack Martin, Providence Public Lib. Tel. 401-455-8100; *Past Pres.* Jenifer Bond, Douglas and Judith Krupp Lib., Bryant Univ., 1150 Douglas Pk., Smithfield 02917 Tel. 401-232-6000 ext. 20419, e-mail jbond2@ bryant.edu.

Address correspondence to Rhode Island Lib. Assn., P.O. Box 6765, Providence 02940. Tel. 401-203-READ.

World Wide Web http://www.rilibraries.org.

South Carolina

Memb. 350+. Term of Office. Jan.–Dec. Publication. *South Carolina Libraries (bi-ann., online).* Ed. Brent Appling, Univ. of South Carolina. Tel. 803-777-0994, e-mail applingm@ mailbox.sc.edu.

Pres. Amber Conger, Kershaw County Lib., 1304 Broad St., Camden 29020; *1st V.P.* Jimmie Epling, Darlington County Lib. System, 204 N. Main St., Darlington 29532. Tel. 843-398-4940 ext. 303, e-mail jimmie.epling@darlington-lib. org; *2nd V.P.* Sarah Hood, J. Drake Edens Lib., Columbia College, 1301 Columbia College Dr., Columbia 29203. Tel. 803-786-3570, e-mail shood@columbiasc.edu; *Secy.* Melissa Poole, Clemson Univ. Libs., 116 Sigma Dr., Clemson 29634. Tel. 864-656-3358, e-mail mmpoole@ clemson.edu; *Treas.* Kevin Reynolds, Wofford College, Sandor Teszler Lib., 429 N. Church St., Spartanburg 29303. Tel. 864-597-4300, e-mail reynoldsjk@wofford.edu; *ALA Councilor* Virginia Alexander Cononie, Univ. South Carolina Upstate, 800 University Way, Spartanburg 29303. Tel. 864-503-5735, e-mail Vcononie@ uscupstate.edu; *Past Pres.* John Kennerly, Erskine College, 1 Depot St., Due West 29639. Tel. 864-379-8788, e-mail kennerly@erskine. edu; *Exec. Dir.* Donald Wood, South Carolina Lib. Assn., P.O. Box 1763, Columbia 29202. Tel. 803-252-1087, fax 803-252-0589, e-mail scla@capconsc.com.

Address correspondence to the executive secretary.

World Wide Web http://www.scla.org.

South Dakota

Memb. (Indiv.) 450+; (Inst.) 60+. Publication. *Book Marks* (q.). Ed. Kelly Henkel, McGovern Lib., Dakota Wesleyan Univ. Mitchell. E-mail bookmarkssd@gmail.com.

Pres. Danielle De Jager-Loftus, Weeks Lib., Univ. of South Dakota, 414 E. Clark St., Vermillion 57069. Tel. 605-677-5123, e-mail dloftus@usd.edu; *V.P./Pres.-Elect* Mary Fransis, Dakota State Univ., Madison. E-mail mary.francis@dsu.edu; *Recording Secy.* Craig Johnson, Augustana Univ. E-mail rcjohnson@ augie.edu; *Exec. Secy./ Treas.* Stephanie Brewer, Grace Balloch Memorial Lib., 625 N. 5th St., Spearfish 57783. E-mail sdlaest@gmail. com; *ALA Councilor* Elizabeth Fox, Briggs Lib., South Dakota State Univ., Brookings. E-mail elizabeth.fox@sdstate.edu; *Past Pres.* Kathy Wibbels, Yankton Community Lib., 515 Walnut St., Yankton 57078. E-mail KWibbels@cityofyankton.org.

Address correspondence to the executive secretary, South Dakota Lib. Assn., P.O. Box 582, Spearfish 57783. Tel. 605.641-2079, e-mail sdlaest@gmail.com.

World Wide Web http://www.sdlibrary association.org.

Tennessee

Memb. 600+. Term of Office. July–June. Publications. *Tennessee Libraries* (q.). Ed. Kristen West, Middle Tennessee State Univ. E-mail k.west@mtsu.edu; *TLA Newsletter* (q.). Ed. Sharon Holderman. E-mail sholderman@ tntech.edu. Both online at http://www.tnla.org.

Pres. Richard Groves, Williamson County Lib., 1314 Columbia Ave., Franklin 37064. E-mail richardpgroves@gmail.com; *V.P./Pres.-Elect* Jeffie Nicholson; *Secy.* Margaret Brown; *Past Pres.* Susan Jennings, Chattanooga State Community College, E. Campus, 7158 Lee Hwy., Chattanooga 37421. Tel. 423-697-2576, e-mail susan.jennings@chattanoogastate.edu; *Exec. Dir.* Annelle R. Huggins, Tennessee Lib. Assn., P.O. Box 241074, Memphis 38124-1074. Tel. 901-485-6952, e-mail arhuggins1@ comcast.net.

Address correspondence to the executive director.

World Wide Web http://tnla.org.

Texas

Memb. 6,500+. Term of Office. Apr.–Apr. Publications. *Texas Library Journal* (q.), *Ed.* Wendy Woodland. E-mail wendyw@txla.org, *TLACast* (9 a year).

Pres. Walter Betts, Mary Couts Burnett Lib., Texas Christian Univ., Box 298400, Fort Worth 76129. Tel. 817-257-6100, e-mail w.betts@ tcu.edu; *Pres.-Elect* Ling Hwey Jeng, Texas Woman's Univ. School of Lib. and Information Studies; *Treas.* Gretchen Pruett, New Braunfels Public Lib., 700 Common St., New Braunfels 78130. Tel. 830-221-4300, e-mail gpruett@ nbtexas.org; *Memb.-at-Large* Naomi Bates, Northwest HS (Justin); Kimberly Michelle Gay, Prairie View A&M Univ.; Linda Stevens, Harris County Public Lib.; Karen Vargas, Texas Medical Center Lib.; Janice Newsum, Houston ISD; *ALA Councilor* Dale McNeill, San Antonio Public Lib.; *Past Pres.* Susan Mann, Hillsboro City Lib., 118 South Waco St., Hillsboro 76645. E-mail hillsborolibrary@hillsborotx. org; *Exec. Dir.* Patricia H. Smith, Texas Lib. Assn., 3355 Bee Cave Rd., Suite 401, Austin 78746-6763. Tel. 512-328-1518, e-mail pats@ txla.org.

Address correspondence to the executive director.

World Wide Web http://www.txla.org.

Utah

Memb. 650. Publication. *Utah Libraries News* (q.) (online at http://www.ula.org/newsletter). *Ed.* Mindy Hale. E-mail mnhale@orem.org.

Pres. Jami Carter, Tooele City Lib., 128 W. Vine St., Tooele 84074. Tel. 435-882-2182, e-mail jamic@tooelecity.org; *V.P.* Dan Compton, Summit County Lib., 1885 W. Ute Blvd., Park City 84098. Tel. 435-615-3947, e-mail dcompton@summitcounty.org; *Treas.* Javaid Lal, 15 N. Temple, Salt Lake City 84150. E-mail JLal@ula.org; *Memb.-at-Large* Adriana Parker. E-mail adriana.parker@utah.edu; Peter Bromberg. E-mail pbromberg@slcolibrary. org; Erin Wimmer. E-mail erin.wimmer@ utah.edu; Joe Frazier. E-mail jfrazier@summit county.org; Shawn Bliss. E-mail snbliss@utah. gov; Michael Whitchurch. E-mail michael_ whitchurch@byu.edu; *ALA Chapter Councilor* Kent Slade. E-mail khslade@gmail.com; *Past Pres.* Dustin Fife, Western State Colorado Univ., Lib. 209, Western State Colorado Univ.,

600 N. Adams St., Gunnison, CO 81231. Tel. 970-943-2278, e-mail dfife@western.edu; *Exec. Dir.* Barbara Hopkins, Canyons School District, 9150 S. 500 W., Sandy 84070. Tel. 801-826-5095, e-mail barbaraw.hopkins@ gmail.com.

Address correspondence to the executive director, Utah Lib. Assn., P.O. Box 708155, Sandy 84070-8155.

World Wide Web http://www.ula.org.

Vermont

Memb. 400. Publication. *VLA News* (q.).

Pres. Margaret Woodruff, Charlotte Public Lib., 115 Ferry Rd., Charlotte 05445. Tel. 802-425-3864, e-mail vermontlibrariespresident@ gmail.com; *V.P./Pres.-Elect* Joy Worland, Joslin Memorial Lib., Box 359, Waitsfield 05673. E-mail vermontlibrariesvicepresident@gmail. com; *Secy.* Kelly McCagg, Burnham Memorial Lib. 898 Main St., Colchester 05446. Tel. 802-264-5661, e-mail kmccagg@colchestervt.gov; *Treas.* Angela Bernard, Dorothy Alling Memorial Lib., 21 Library Ln., Williston 05495. Tel. 802-878-4918, e-mail vermontlibraries treasurer@gmail.com; *ALA Councilor* Amy Wisehart. Hartland Public Lib., P.O. Box 137, Hartland 05048. Tel. 802-436-2473, e-mail awisehart@gmail.com; *Past Pres.* Virgil Fuller, Chelsea Public Lib., 296 VT Rte. 1110, Chelsea 05038. Tel. 802-685-2188, e-mail vermont librariespresident@gmail.com.

Address correspondence to Vermont Lib. Assn., P.O. Box 803, Burlington 05402.

World Wide Web http://www.vermont libraries.org.

Virginia

Memb. 950+. Term of Office. Oct.–Oct. Publication. *Virginia Libraries* (q.).

Pres. Keith Weimer, Univ. of Virginia Lib., P.O. Box 400113, Charlottesville 22904-4113. Tel. 434-924-7702, e-mail kweimer@virginia. edu; *Pres.-Elect* Todd D. Elliott, Portsmouth Public Lib., 601 Court St., Portsmouth 23704. Tel. 757-393-8365, e-mail elliottt@portsmouth va.gov; *2nd V.P.* M. Teresa Doherty, Virginia Commonwealth Univ. Libs., P.O. Box 842033, Richmond 23284. Tel. 804-828-8658, e-mail mtdohert@vcu.edu; *Secy.* Jennifer Resor-Whicker, MLIS, Radford Univ., McConnell

Lib., P.O. Box 6881, Radford 24142. Tel. 540-831-5691, e-mail jrwhicker@radford.edu; *Treas.* Shaunna Hunter, Walter M. Bortz III Lib., Hampden-Sydney College, P.O. Box 7, Hampden-Sydney 23943. Tel. 434-223-6193, e-mail shunter@hsc.edu; *ALA Councilor* Samantha Thomason, Central Rappahannock Regional Lib., 1201 Caroline St., Fredericksburg 22401. Tel. 540-372-1144, e-mail sthomason@crrl. org; *Past Pres.* Martha Hutzel, Central Rappahannock Regional Lib., 1201 Caroline St., Fredericksburg 22401. Tel. 540-372-1144, e-mail mhutzel@crrl.org. *Exec. Dir.* Lisa Varga, Virginia Lib. Assn., P.O. Box 56312, Virginia Beach 23456. Tel. 757-689-0594, e-mail vla. lisav@cox.net.

Address correspondence to the executive director.

World Wide Web http://www.vla.org.

Washington

Memb. (Indiv.) 742, (Inst.) 47. Publications. *Alki: The Washington Library Association Journal* (3 a year, online). *Ed.* Frank Brasile, Seattle Public Lib., 1000 Fourth Ave., Seattle 98104. E-mail alkieditor@wla.org.

Pres. Brianna Hoffman, OCLC/WebJunction. Tel. 509-380-1171, e-mail bkhoffman 1981@gmail.com; *V.P./Pres.-Elect* Craig Seasholes, Seattle Public Schools, Tel. 206-854-7956, e-mail seasholes@gmail.com; *Secy./Treas.* Irene Wickstrom, King County Lib. System, 115 E. 4th St., North Bend 98045. Tel. 425-888-0554, e-mail imwickstrom@kcls. org; *ALA Councilor* Christine Peck. Tel. 360-533-2360, e-mail cmpecks@gmail.com; *Past Pres.* Darcy Brixey, Bellevue Regional Lib., 1111 110th Ave NE., Bellevue, WA 98004. Tel. 425.450.1765. E-mail dbrixey@kcls.org; *Exec. Dir.* Kate Laughlin, Washington Lib. Assn., P.O. Box 33808, Seattle 98133. Tel. 206-823-1138, e-mail kate@wla.org.

Address correspondence to the executive director.

World Wide Web http://www.wla.org.

West Virginia

Memb. 650+. Publication. *West Virginia Libraries* (6 a year). *Ed.* Jamie Bayne, Mountwest Community and Technical College, One Mountwest Way, Huntington 25701. Tel. 304-710-3465, e-mail bayne@mctc.edu.

Pres. Gretchen Rae Beach, Morrow Lib. 205, Marshall Univ., Huntington 25755. Tel. 304-696-2312, fax 304-696-5228, e-mail beachgr @marshall.edu; *1st V.P./Pres.-Elect* Brenna Call, Vienna Public Lib., 2300 River Rd., Vienna 26105. Tel. 304-295-7771, e-mail brenna. call@mail.mln.lib.wv.us; *2nd V.P./Pres.-Elect* Steven Shackelford, Parkersburg-Wood County Public Lib., 3100 Emerson Ave., Parkersburg 26104. Tel. 304-216-2501, fax 304-420-4587, e-mail steven.shackelford@gmail.com; *Secy.* Jessica Tapia, West Virginia Univ. Libs., 1549 Univ. Ave., Morgantown 26506. Tel. 304-293-0312, e-mail jessica.tapia@mail.wvu. edu; *Treas.* Brian Raitz, Parkersburg and Wood County Public Lib., 3100 Emerson Ave., Parkersburg 26104. Tel. 304-420-4587 ext. 501, fax 304-420-4589, e-mail wvlibrarydude@gmail. com; *Past Pres.* Emilee Seese, Ritchie County Public Lib., 608 East Main St., Harrisville, WV 26362. Tel. 304-643-2717 ext. 7, fax 304-643-4019, e-mail seesee@mail.mln.lib.wv.us; *Exec. Dir.* Kelly Funkhouser, Morgantown Public Lib., West Virginia Lib. Assn., P.O. Box 1432, Morgantown 26507. Tel. 304-291-7425, e-mail wvlaexdir@gmail.com.

Address correspondence to the president.

World Wide Web http://www.wvla.org.

Wisconsin

Memb. 1,900. Term of Office. Jan.–Dec. Publication. *WLA Newsletter* (q.).

Pres. Jean Anderson; *V.P./Pres.-Elect* Marge Loch-Wouters; *Secy.* Desiree Bongers, Ripon Public Lib., Ripon. Tel. 920-748-6160, e-mail dbongers@riponlibrary.org; *Treas.* Jen Gerber; *ALA Councilor* Sherry Machones; *Past Pres.* Pamela K. Westby, Middleton Public Lib., 7425 Hubbard Ave., Middleton 53562. Tel. 608-827-7425, e-mail pamela@midlibrary.org; *Exec. Dir.* Plumer Lovelace III, Wisconsin Lib. Assn., 4610 S. Biltmore Ln., Madison 53718. Tel. 608-245-3640, e-mail lovelace@wisconsin libraries.org.

Address correspondence to the Wisconsin Lib. Assn., 4610 S. Biltmore Lane, No. 100, Madison 53718-2153. Tel. 608-245-3640, fax 608-245-3646, e-mail wla@wisconsinlibraries. org.

World Wide Web http://wla.wisconsinlibraries.org.

Wyoming

Memb. 450+. Term of Office. Oct.–Oct.
Pres. Sid Stanfill, P.O. Box 489, Pinedale 82941. Tel. 307-367-4115, e-mail vicepresident @wyla.org; *V.P.* Katrina Brown, Griffith Memorial Lib., Sheridan College, 3059 Coffeen Ave., Sheridan 82801. Tel. 307-674-6446 ext. 2506, e-mail kbrown@sheridan.edu; *Exec. Secy.* Laura Grott (ex-officio), P.O. Box 1387, Cheyenne 82003. Tel. 307-632-7622, e-mail executivesecretary@wyla.org; *ALA Representative* Brian Greene; *Past Pres.* Rebecca Schuh.
Address correspondence to the executive secretary.
World Wide Web http://www.wyla.org.

Canada

Alberta

Memb. 500. Term of Office. May–April.
Pres. Peter Bailey, St. Alberta Public Lib. E-mail president@laa.ca; *1st V.P.* Deb Cryderman, Camrose Public Lib. E-mail 1stvice president@laa.ca; *2nd V.P.* Christina Hwang, Univ. of Alberta. E-mail 2ndvicepresident@ laa.ca; *Interim Treas.* Christina Hwang, Univ. of Alberta. E-mail treasurer@laa.ca; *Past Pres.* Jason Openo, Medicine Hat College. E-mail pastpresident@laa.ca; *Exec. Dir.* Christine Sheppard, Lib. Assn. of Alberta, 80 Baker Cres. N.W., Calgary T2L 1R4. Tel. 403-284-5818, 877-522-5550, e-mail info@laa.ca.
Address correspondence to the executive director.
World Wide Web http://www.laa.ca.

British Columbia

Memb. 750+. Term of Office. April–April. Publication. *BCLA Perspectives* (q., online at https://bclaconnect.ca/perspectives). *Ed.* Timothy McMillanVancouver Public Lib. E-mail perspectives@bcla.bc.ca.
Pres. Daphne Wood, Greater Victoria Public Lib.; *V.P./Pres.-Elect* Anne Olsen, Univ. of British Columbia, Koerner Lib.; *Recording Secy.* Lilian Pintos, Vancouver Public Lib.; *Treas.* Dawn Ibey, Vancouver Public Lib.; *Asst./*

Incoming Treas. Lin Brander, BC Institute of Technology; *Past Pres.* Caroline Daniels, Kwantlen Polytechnic Univ.; *Exec. Dir.* Annette DeFaveri, British Columbia Lib. Assn., #150-900 Howe St., Vancouver V6Z 2M4. Tel. 604-683-5354 or 888-683-5354, fax 604-609-0707, e-mail execdir@bcla.bc.ca.
Address correspondence to the British Columbia Lib. Assn., 900 Howe St., Suite 150, Vancouver V6Z 2M4. Tel. 604-683-5354, e-mail exdir@bcla.bc.ca.
World Wide Web http://www.bcla.bc.ca.

Manitoba

Memb. 500+. Term of Office. May–May. Publication. *Manitoba Libraries* (mo., online, open access journal). *Ed.* Kyle Feenstra.
Pres. Alix-Rae Stefanko. E-mail president@ mla.mb.ca; *V.P./Awards* Kerry Macdonald. E-mail awards@mla.mb.ca; *Secy.* Can Li. E-mail secretary@mla.mb.ca; *Treas.* Janice Winkler. E-mail treasurer@mla.mb.ca.
Address correspondence to the Manitoba Lib. Assn., 606-100 Arthur St., Winnipeg R3B 1H3. Tel. 204-943-4567.
World Wide Web http://www.mla.mb.ca.

Ontario

Memb. 5,000+. Publications. *Open Shelf* (biwk., multi-media). *Ed.* Martha Attridge Bufton.; *Teaching Librarian* (3 a year). *Ed.* Diana Maliszewski, Agnes Macphail Public School, Toronto District School Board. E-mail TingLeditor@gmail.com.
Pres. Leslie Weir, Univ. of Ottawa. E-mail lweir@uottawa.ca; *V.P./Pres.-Elect* Kerry Badgley, North Grenville Public Lib. Board. E-mail Kerry.Badgley@inspection.gc.ca; *Treas.* Susan Kun, Oakville Public Lib. E-mail susan. kun@oakville.ca; *Past Pres.* Todd Kyle, Newmarket Public Lib. E-mail tkyle@newmarket pl.ca; *Exec. Dir.* Shelagh Paterson, Ontario Lib. Assn. E-mail spaterson@accessola.com.
Address correspondence to the Ontario Lib. Assn., 2 Toronto St., Toronto M5C 2B6. Tel. 416-363-3388 or 866-873-9867, fax 416-941-9581 or 800-387-1181, e-mail info@accessola. com.
World Wide Web http://www.accessola. com.

Quebec

Memb. (Indiv.) 100+. Term of Office. May–April. Publication. *ABQLA Bulletin* (3 a year). *Pres.* Leticia Cuenca. E-mail leticiacuenca@gmail.com; *V.P.* Julian Taylor. E-mail jtaylor qclib@gmail.com; *Exec. Secy.* Margaret Goldik, Quebec Lib. Assn., 50 boul. St-Charles, P.O. Box 26717, Beaconsfield H9W 6G7. Tel. or fax 514-697-0146, e-mail abqla@abqla. qc.ca; *Treas.* Anne Wade. E-mail wada@education.concordia.ca; *Past Pres.* Sonia Smith. E-mail sonia.smith@mcgill.ca.

Address correspondence to the executive secretary.

World Wide Web http://www.abqla.qc.ca.

Saskatchewan

Memb. 200+.

Pres. Michael Shires, Dr. John Archer Lib., Univ. of Regina, 3737 Wascana Pkwy., Regina S4S 0A2. Tel. 306-585-5418, e-mail michael. shires@uregina.ca; *V.P. Membership and Pubns.* Linda Winkler, Univ. of Regina. E-mail linda.winkler@uregina.ca; *V.P. Advocacy and Development* Nancy MacKenzie, Regina Public Lib., 2311 12th Ave., Regina S4P 0N3. Tel. 306-777-6017, e-mail nmackenzie@regina library.ca; *Treas.* Brad Doerksen, Dr. John Archer Lib., Univ. of Regina, 3737 Wascana Pkwy., Regina S4S 0A2. Tel. 306-337-2927, e-mail brad.doerksen@uregina.ca; *Memb.-at-Large* Tasha Maddison. E-mail Tasha.Maddison@Saskpolytech.ca; Alan Kilpatrick. E-mail akilpatrick@lawsociety.sk.ca; Alison Jantz. E-mail alison.jantz@usask.ca; James Hope Howard. E-mail director@pnls.lib.sk.ca; *Past Pres.* Gwen Schmidt, Saskatoon Public Lib.; *Exec. Dir.* Judy Nicholson Saskatchewan Lib. Assn., #15 – 2010 7th Ave. Regina S4R 1C2. Tel. 306-780-9413, fax 306-780-9447, e-mail slaexdir@sasktel.net.

Address correspondence to the executive director.

World Wide Web http://www.saskla.ca.

Regional

Atlantic Provinces: N.B., N.L., N.S., P.E.I.

Memb. (Indiv.) 320+; (Inst.) Publication. *APLA Bulletin* (4 a year). *Eds.* Alison Ambi, Memori-al Univ. of Newfoundland, St. John's, NL, A1B 3Y1. Tel. 709-864-7125, e-mail bulletin@apla. ca; Marc HarperBibliothèque Champlain, 18 avenue Antonine-Maillet (local 164), Moncton, NB E1A 3E9. Tel. 506-858-4154.

Pres. Suzanne van den Hoogen, Angus L. Macdonald Lib., St. Francis Xavier Univ., P.O. Box 5000, Antigonish, NS B2G 2W5. Tel. 902-867-4535, e-mail svandenh@stfx.ca; *V.P./Pres.-Elect* Kathryn Rose, Queen Elizabeth II Lib., Memorial Univ. of Newfoundland. Tel. 709-864-3139, e-mail kathrynr@mun. ca; *V.P. Membership* Carolyn DeLorey, Angus L. Macdonald Lib., St. Francis Xavier Univ., Antigonish, NS. Tel. 902-867-2343, e-mail membership@apla.ca; *Secy.* Laurinda Matheson, Angus L. Macdonald Lib., St. Francis Xavier Univ., Antigonish, NS. Tel. 902-867-4883, e-mail lmmathes@stfx.ca; *Treas.* Maggie Neilson, Acadia Univ., Vaughan Memorial Lib., Room 420, 50 Acadia St., Wolfville, NS B4P 2R6. Tel 902-585-1718, e-mail maggie jean.neilson@acadiau.ca; *Past Pres.* Lynn Somers, Nova Scotia Provincial Libr. Dept. of Communities, Culture and Heritage, 1741 Brunswick St., 2nd Fl., Halifax NS B3J 3X8. Tel. 902-424-4852, fax 902-424-0633, e-mail Lynn.somers@novascotia.ca.

Address correspondence to Atlantic Provinces Lib. Assn., c/o SIM, Kenneth C. Rowe Mgt. Bldg., Dalhousie Univ., Suite 4010, 6100 University Ave., Halifax, NS B3H 4R2. E-mail contact@apla.ca.

World Wide Web http://www.apla.ca.

Mountain Plains: Ariz., Colo., Kan., Mont., Neb., Nev., N.Dak., N.Mex., Okla., S.Dak., Utah, Wyo.

Memb. 700. Term of Office. Oct.–Oct. Publications. *MPLA Newsletter* (bi-mo., online only). *Ed.* Melanie Argo, Madison Public Lib., 209 E. Center, Madison, SD 57042. Tel. 605-256-7525, e-mail editor@mpla.us.

Pres. Mickey Coalwell, Lib. Systems and Services, LLC, 7134 McGee St., Kansas City, MO 64114. Tel. 816-804-0942, e-mail president @mpla.us; *V.P./Pres.-Elect* Melissa Clark, South Dakota State Univ., 2115 North Campus Dr., Brookings, SD 57006. E-mail vicepresident @mpla.us; *Executive Secy.* Judy Zelenski, 14293 West Center Dr., Lakewood, CO 80228. Tel. 303-985-7795, e-mail execsecretary@

mpla.us; *Recording Secy.* Kris Johnson, Montana State Univ. Lib., P.O. Box 173320, Bozeman, MT 59717-3320. Tel. 406-994-7708, e-mail secretary@mpla.us; *Past Pres.* Eric Stroshane, North Dakota State Lib., 604 E. Boulevard Ave., Dept. 250, Bismarck, ND 58505. Tel. 701-328-4661, fax 701-328-2040, e-mail pastpresident@mpla.us.

Address correspondence to the executive secretary.

World Wide Web http://www.mpla.us.

New England: Conn., Maine, Mass., N.H., R.I., Vt.

Memb. (Indiv.) 650+. Term of Office. Nov.–Oct. Publication. *NELA News* (blog).

Pres. Mary Danko, Fletcher Free Lib., Burlington, VT. E-mail president@nelib.org; *V.P.* Debbi Gadwah-Lambert, Maxfield Public Lib., Loudon, NH. E-mail vice-president@nelib. org; *Secy.* Kathrine Aydelott, Univ. of New Hampshire, Durham, NH. E-mail secretary@ nelib.org; *Treas.* Denise Van Zanten, Manchester City Lib., Manchester, NH. E-mail treasurer @nelib.org; *Senior Director* Vicki Oatis, Norwalk Public Lib., Norwalk, CT. E-mail director-sr@nelib.org; *Junior Director* Kara Reiman, Walker Memorial Lib., Westbrook, ME. E-mail director-jr@nelib.org; *Past Pres.* Deb Hoadley, Hoadley Consulting, Plaistow, NH. E-mail past-president@nelib.org.

Address correspondence to the New England Lib. Assn., 55 N. Main St., Unit 49, Belchertown, MA 01007. Tel. 413-813-5254, e-mail rscheier@nelib.org.

World Wide Web http://www.nelib.org.

Pacific Northwest: Alaska, Idaho, Mont., Ore., Wash., Alberta, B.C.

Memb. 170+. Term of Office. Aug.–Aug. Publication. *PNLA Quarterly. Eds.* Jan Zauha. Tel. 406-994-6554, fax 406-994-2851, e-mail jzauha@montana.edu; Leila Sterman. Tel. 406-994-4519, e-mail Lela.sterman@montana.edu.

Pres. Jenny Grenfell, North Mason Timberland Lib., Belfair, WA. Tel. 360-275-3232, e-mail jgrenfell@trlib.org; *First V.P./Pres.-Elect* Rick Stoddart, Univ. of Idaho Lib., Moscow, ID. Tel. 208-885-2504, e-mail rstoddart@ uidaho.edu pnla1stvp@gmail.com; *Second V.P./Membership Chair* Jay Peters, Coquitlam Public Lib., 575 Poirier St. Coquitlam BC V3J 6A9. Tel. 604-937-4148 ext. 4248, jpeters@ coqlibrary.ca; *Secy.* Candice Stenstrom, Public Lib. InterLINK / #158 - 5489 Byrne Rd., Burnaby, BC V5J 3J1. Tel. 604-437-8441, fax 604-437-8410, e-mail candice.stenstrom@ interlinklibraries.ca; *Treas.* Crystal Miller, Coeur d'Alene Public Lib., 702 E. Front, Coeur d'Alene, ID 83814. Tel. 208-769-2315 ext. 467, e-mail camiller@cdalibrary.org pnla treasurer@gmail.com; *Past Pres.* Gwendolyn Haley, Spokane County Lib. District, Spokane, WA. Tel. 509-893-8362, e-mail ghaley@scld. org pnlapastpresident@gmail.com.

Address correspondence to the president, Pacific Northwest Lib. Assn.

World Wide Web http://www.pnla.org.

Southeastern: Ala., Ark., Fla., Ga., Ky., La., Miss., N.C., S.C., Tenn., Va., W.Va.

Memb. 500. Publication. *The Southeastern Librarian (SELn)* (q.). *Ed.* Perry Bratcher, 503A Steely Lib., Northern Kentucky Univ., Highland Heights, KY 41099. Tel. 859-572-6309, fax 859-572-6181, e-mail bratcher@nku.edu.

Pres. Linda Suttle Harris, Univ. of Alabama at Birmingham. E-mail president@selaonline. org; *Pres.-Elect* Tim Dodge, Auburn Univ. Libs., Auburn, AL. E-mail president.elect@ selaonline.org; *Secy.* Melissa Dennis, Univ. of Mississippi, University, MS. E-mail secretary@ selaonline.org; *Treas.* Beverly James, Greenville County Lib. System, Greenville, SC. E-mail treasurer@selaonline.org; *Past Pres.* Camille McCutcheon, Univ. of South Carolina Upstate, Spartanburg, SC.

Address correspondence to Southeastern Lib. Assn., Admin. Services, P.O. Box 950, Rex, GA 30273-0950. Tel. 678-466-4334, fax 678-466-4349, e-mail selaadminservices@sela online.org.

World Wide Web http://selaonline.org.

State and Provincial Library Agencies

The state library administrative agency in each of the U.S. states will have the latest information on its state plan for the use of federal funds under the Library Services and Technology Act (LSTA). The directors and addresses of these state agencies are listed below.

United States

Alabama

Nancy Pack, Dir., Alabama Public Lib. Service, 6030 Monticello Dr., Montgomery 36130-6000. Tel. 334-213-3900, fax 334-213-3993, e-mail npack@apls.state.al.us. World Wide Web http://statelibrary.alabama.gov.

Alaska

Patience Frederiksen, Dir., Alaska State Lib., Historical Collections and Talking Book Center, 395 Whittier St., Juneau 99801. Tel. 907-465-2911, fax 907-465-2151, e-mail patience. frederiksen@alaska.gov. World Wide Web http://library.state.ak.us.

Arizona

Holly Henley, State Libn. and Dir. of Lib. Svcs., Arizona State Lib., Archives and Public Records, 1700 W. Washington, 7th floor, Phoenix 85007. Tel. 602-542-6181, fax 602-256-7983, World Wide Web http://www.azlibrary. gov/.

Arkansas

Carolyn Ashcroft, State Libn., Arkansas State Lib., 900 W. Capitol, Suite 100, Little Rock 72201-3108. Tel. 501-682-1526, e-mail carolyn @library.arkansas.gov. World Wide Web http:// www.library.arkansas.gov.

California

Greg Lucas, State Libn., California State Lib., P.O. Box 942837, Sacramento 94237-0001. Tel. 916-323-9759, fax 916-323-9768, e-mail greg.Lucas@library.ca.gov. World Wide Web http://www.library.ca.gov.

Colorado

Eugene Hainer, Asst. Commissioner, Colorado State Lib., 201 E. Colfax Ave., Denver 80203-1799. Tel. 303-866-6733, fax 303-866-6940, e-mail hainer_g@cde.state.co.us. World Wide Web http://www.cde.state.co.us/cdelib/.

Connecticut

Kendall F. Wiggin, State Libn., Connecticut State Lib., 231 Capitol Ave., Hartford 06106-1537. Tel. 860-757-6510, fax 860-757-6503, e-mail kendall.wiggin@ct.gov. World Wide Web http://www.ctstatelibrary.org/.

Delaware

Annie Norman, State Libn. and Dir., Delaware Division of Libs., 121 Martin Luther King Jr. Blvd. N., Dover 19901. Tel. 302-257-3001, fax 302-739-6787, e-mail annie.norman@state. de.us. World Wide Web http://libraries.delaware. gov/.

District of Columbia

Richard Reyes-Gavilan, Exec. Dir., District of Columbia Public Lib., 1990 K St. N.W., Washington, DC 20006. Tel. 202-727-1101, fax 202-727-1129, e-mail rrg@dc.gov. World Wide Web http://www.dclibrary.org.

Florida

Judith Ring, Dir., Division of Lib. and Info. Services, R.A. Gray Bldg., 500 S. Bronough St., Tallahassee 32399-0250. Tel. 850-245-6600, fax 850-245-6651, e-mail info@dos.my-florida.com. World Wide Web http://dlis.dos. state.fl.us/Library.

Georgia

Julie Walker, State Libn., Georgia Public Lib. Services, 1800 Century Pl., Suite 150, Atlanta

30345-4304. Tel. 404-235-7140, fax 404-235-7201, e-mail jwalker@georgialibraries.org. World Wide Web http://www.georgialibraries.org.

Hawaii

Stacy Aldrich, State Libn., Hawaii State Public Lib. System, Office of the State Libn., 44 Merchant St., Honolulu 96813-4311. Tel. 808-586-3704, fax 808-586-3715, e-mail stlib@librarieshawaii.org. World Wide Web http://www.librarieshawaii.org.

Idaho

Ann Joslin, State Libn., Idaho Commission for Libs., 325 W. State St., Boise 83702-6072. Tel. 208-334-2150, fax 208-334-4016, e-mail ann.joslin@libraries.idaho.gov. World Wide Web http://libraries.idaho.gov/.

Illinois

Greg McCormick, Acting Deputy Dir., Illinois State Lib., 300 S. Second St., Springfield 62701-1796. Tel. 217-782-7596, fax 217-785-4326, e-mail islinfo@ilsos.net. World Wide Web http://www.cyberdriveillinois.com/departments/library/home.html.

Indiana

Jacob Speer, State Libn., Indiana State Lib., 315 W. Ohio St., Indianapolis 46202. Tel. 317-232-3692, e-mail jspeer1@library.in.gov. World Wide Web http://www.in.gov/library.

Iowa

Michael Scott, State Libn., State Lib. of Iowa, 1112 E. Grand Ave., Des Moines 50319. Tel. 515-281-4105, e-mail Michael.Scott@iowa.gov. World Wide Web http://www.statelibraryofiowa.org/.

Kansas

Jo Budler, State Libn., Kansas State Lib., Capitol Bldg., 300 S.W. 10th Ave., Rm. 312-N, Topeka 66612-1593. Tel. 785-296-5466, fax 785-296-6650, e-mail jo.budler@ks.gov. World Wide Web http://www.kslib.info.

Kentucky

Terry Manuel, Commissioner, Kentucky Dept. for Libs. and Archives, 300 Coffee Tree Rd., P.O. Box 537, Frankfort 40602-0537. Tel. 502-564-1730, fax 502-564-5773, e-mail terry.manuel@ky.gov. World Wide Web http://www.kdla.ky.gov.

Louisiana

Rebecca Hamilton, State Libn., State Lib. of Louisiana, 701 N. 4th St., P.O. Box 131, Baton Rouge 70821-0131. Tel. 255-342-4923, fax 255-219-4804, e-mail rhamilton@crt.state.la.us. World Wide Web http://www.state.lib.la.us.

Maine

James Ritter, State Libn., Maine State Lib., 64 State House Sta., Augusta 04333-0064. Tel. 207-287-5600, fax 207-287-5624, e-mail james.ritter@maine.gov. World Wide Web http://www.maine.gov/msl/.

Maryland

Irene Padilla, Asst.State Superintendant for Libs., Maryland State Dept. of Educ., Div. of Lib. Development and Services, 200 W. Baltimore St., Baltimore 21201. Tel. 410-767-0444, fax 410-333-2507, e-mail ipadilla@msde.state.md.us. World Wide Web http://www.marylandpublicschools.org/MSDE/divisions/library/.

Massachusetts

Dianne Carty, Dir., Massachusetts Board of Lib. Commissioners, 98 N. Washington St., Suite 401, Boston 02114-1933. Tel. 617-725-1860, fax 617-725-0140, e-mail dianne.carty@state.ma.us. World Wide Web http://mblc.state.ma.us.

Michigan

Randy Riley, State Libn., Lib. of Michigan, 702 W. Kalamazoo St., P.O. Box 30007, Lansing 48909-7507. Tel. 517-373-5860, fax 517-373-5700, e-mail rileyr1@michigan.gov. World Wide Web http://www.michigan.gov/libraryofmichigan.

Minnesota

Jennifer R. Nelson, Dir. of State Lib. Services, Minnesota State Lib. Agency, Div. of State Lib. Services MN, Dept. of Educ., 1500 Hwy. 36 W., Roseville 55113-4266. Tel. 651-582-8791, e-mail jennifer.r.nelson@state.mn.us. World Wide Web http://education.state.mn.us/MDE/index.html.

Mississippi

Susan Cassagne, Exec. Dir., Mississippi Lib. Commission, 3881 Eastwood Dr., Jackson 39211. Tel. 601-432-4038, fax 601-432-4480, e-mail susan@mlc.lib.ms.us. World Wide Web http://www.mlc.lib.ms.us.

Missouri

Barbara A. Reading, State Libn., Missouri State Lib., 600 W. Main St., P.O. Box 387, Jefferson City 65101. Tel. 573-522-4036, fax 573-751-3612, e-mail barbara.reading@sos.mo.gov. World Wide Web http://www.sos.mo.gov/library.

Montana

Jennie Stapp, State Libn., Montana State Lib., 1515 E. 6th Ave., P.O. Box 201800, Helena, 59620-1800. Tel. 406-444-3116, fax 406-444-0266, e-mail jstapp2@mt.gov. World Wide Web http://msl.mt.gov/.

Nebraska

Rodney G. Wagner, Dir., Nebraska Lib. Commission, 1200 N St., Suite 120, Lincoln 68508-2023. Tel. 402-471-4001, fax 402-471-2083, e-mail rod.wagner@nebraska.gov. World Wide Web http://www.nlc.nebraska.gov.

Nevada

Jeffrey M. Kintop, Div. Admin., Nevada State Lib. and Archives, 100 N. Stewart St., Carson City 89710-4285. Tel. 775-684-3410, fax 775-684-3311, e-mail jkintop@admin.nv.gov. World Wide Web http://nsla.nv.gov/.

New Hampshire

Michael York, State Libn., New Hampshire State Lib., 20 Park St., Concord 03301-6314.

Tel. 603-271-2397, e-mail michael.York@dcr.nh.gov . World Wide Web http://www.state.nh.us/nhsl.

New Jersey

Mary Chute, State Libn., New Jersey State Lib., an affiliate of Thomas Edison State Univ., P.O.Box 520, Trenton 08625-0520. Tel. 609-278-2640 ext. 101, fax 609-278-2652, e-mail mchute@njstatelib.org. World Wide Web http://www.njstatelib.org.

New Mexico

Kathleen Moeller-Peiffer, State Libn., New Mexico State Lib., 1209 Camino Carlos Rey, Santa Fe 87507-5166. Tel. 505-476-9762, fax 505-476-9761, e-mail kathleen.peiffer@state.nm.us. World Wide Web http://www.nmstatelibrary.org/.

New York

Bernard A. Margolis, State Libn. and Asst. Commissioner for Libs., New York State Lib. Cultural Education Ctr., 222 Madison Ave., Albany 12230. Tel. 518-486-5930, fax 518-486-5786, e-mail Bernard.Margolis@nysed.gov. World Wide Web http://www.nysl.nysed.gov/.

North Carolina

Caroline "Cal" Shepard, State Libn., State Lib. of North Carolina, Administrative Section, 4640 Mail Service Ctr., 109 E. Jones St., Raleigh 27699-4600. Tel. 919-807-7410, e-mail cal.shepard@ncdcr.gov. World Wide Web http://statelibrary.ncdcr.gov.

North Dakota

Mary J. Soucie, State Libn., North Dakota State Lib., 604 E. Boulevard Ave., Dept. 250, Bismarck 58505-0800. Tel. 701-328-4654, fax 701-328-2040, e-mail msoucie@nd.gov. World Wide Web http://ndsl.lib.state.nd.us/.

Ohio

Beverly Cain, Agency Dir. and State Libn., State Lib. of Ohio, 274 E. First Ave., Suite 100, Columbus 43201. Tel. 616-644-6843, e-mail bcain@library.ohio.gov. World Wide Web http://www.library.ohio.gov/.

Oklahoma

Susan C. McVey, Dir., Oklahoma Dept. of Libs., 200 N.E. 18th St., Oklahoma City 73105-3298. Tel. 405-522-3173, fax 405-525-7804, e-mail smcvey@oltn.odl.state.ok.us. World Wide Web http://www.odl.state.ok.us.

Oregon

MaryKay Dahlgreen, State Libn., Oregon State Lib., 250 Winter St., N.E., Salem 97310-3950. Tel. 503-378-4367, fax 503-585-8059, e-mail marykay.dahlgreen@state.or.us. World Wide Web http://oregon.gov/OSL/.

Pennsylvania

Glenn Miller, Deputy Secy. of Educ., Commissioner of Libs., and State Libn., State Lib. of Pennsylvania, Forum Bldg., 607 South Dr., Harrisburg, PA 17120-0600. Tel. 717-787-2646, fax 717-772-3265, e-mail glennmille@pa.gov. World Wide Web http://www.statelibrary.pa.gov.

Rhode Island

Karen Mellor, Chief of Lib. Services, Rhode Island Office of Lib. and Information Services, One Capitol Hill, Providence 02908-5803. Tel. 401-574-9304, fax 401-574-9320, e-mail karen.Mellor@olis.ri.gov. World Wide Web http://www.olis.ri.gov.

South Carolina

Leesa M. Aiken, Acting Agency Dir., South Carolina State Lib., 1500 Senate St., Columbia 29201. Tel. 803-734-8668, fax 803-734-8676, e-mail laiken@statelibrary.sc.gov. World Wide Web http://www.statelibrary.sc.gov.

South Dakota

Daria Bossman, State Libn., South Dakota State Lib., MacKay Bldg., 800 Governors Dr., Pierre 57501-2294. Tel. 605-773-3131 option 6, fax 605-773-6962, e-mail daria.bossman@state.sd.us. World Wide Web http://library.sd.gov/.

Tennessee

Charles A. Sherrill, State Libn. and Archivist, Tennessee State Lib. and Archives, 403 7th Ave. N., Nashville 37243-0312. Tel. 615-741-7996, e-mail chuck.sherrill@tn.gov. World Wide Web http://www.tennessee.gov/tsla/.

Texas

Mark Smith, Dir. and Libn., Texas State Lib. and Archives Commission, 1201 Brazos St., P.O. Box 12927, Austin 78711-2927. Tel. 512-463-5460, fax 512-463-5436, e-mail director.librarian@tsl.texas.gov. World Wide Web http://www.tsl.state.tx.us.

Utah

Donna Jones Morris, State Libn. and Dir., Utah State Lib. Div., 250 N. 1950 W., Suite A, Salt Lake City 84116-7901. Tel. 801-715-6770, fax 801-715-6767, e-mail dmorris@utah.gov. World Wide Web http://library.utah.gov/.

Vermont

Scott Murphy, State Libn., Vermont Dept. of Libs., 109 State St., Montpelier 05609-0601. Tel. 802-828-3265, fax 802-828-2199, e-mail scott.murphy@vermont.gov. World Wide Web http://libraries.vermont.gov.

Virginia

Sandra Gioia Treadway, Libn., Lib. of Virginia, 800 E. Broad St., Richmond 23219-8000. Tel. 804-692-3500, e-mail sandra.treadway@lva.virginia.gov. World Wide Web http://www.lva.virginia.gov/.

Washington

Cindy Aden, State Libn., Washington State Lib., Office of the Secretary of State, P.O. Box 42460, Olympia 98504-2460. Tel. 360-704-5276, e-mail cindy.aden@sos.wa.gov. World Wide Web http://www.sos.wa.gov/library.

West Virginia

Karen Goff, Exec. Secy., West Virginia Lib. Commission Cultural Ctr., Bldg. 9, 1900 Kanawha Blvd. E., Charleston 25305. Tel. 304-558-2041 ext. 2084, fax 304-558-2044, e-mail karen.e.goff@wv.gov. World Wide Web http://www.librarycommission.wv.gov/.

Wisconsin

Kurt Kiefer, Asst. State Superintendent, Wisconsin Dept. of Public Instruction, Div. for Libs. and Tech., 125 S. Webster St., Madison 53703. Tel. 608-266-2205, fax 608-266-8770, e-mail kurt.kiefer@dpi.wi.gov. World Wide Web http://dpi.wi.gov.

Wyoming

Jamie Markus, Interim State Libn., Wyoming State Lib., 2800 Central Ave., Cheyenne 82002. Tel. 307-777-5914, e-mail jamie.markus@wyo.gov. World Wide Web http://library.wyo.gov/.

American Samoa

Justin H. Maga, Acting Territorial Libn., Feleti Barstow Public Lib., Box 997687, Pago Pago 96799. Tel. 684-633-5816, fax 684-633-5823, e-mail justinmaga@gmail.com. World Wide Web http://feletibarstow.org.

Federated States of Micronesia

Rufino Mauricio, Dir., Office of National Archives, Culture, and Historic Preservations, PS173, Palikir, Pohnpei State 96941. Tel. 691-320-2343-6922, fax 691-320-5632, e-mail hpo@mail.fm. World Wide Web http://www.fsmgov.org.

Guam

Krishnan Seerengan, Chair, Guam Public Lib. System, 254 Martyr St., Hagatna 96910-5141. Tel. 671-475-4765, fax 671-477-9777, e-mail gpls@gpls.guam.gov. World Wide Web http://gpls.guam.gov/.

Northern Mariana Islands

Erlinda Naputi, Acting Dir., CNMI Joeten-Ki-yu Public Lib., Insatto St., Beach Road Susupe, P.O. Box 501092, Saipan 96950. Tel. 670-235-7322, e-mail cnmistatelibrary@gmail.com. World Wide Web http://cnmilib.org.

Palau

Sinton Soalalai, Chief of School Mgt., Palau Ministry of Educ., P.O. Box 7080, Koror 96940. Tel. 680-488-2570, fax 680-488-2380, e-mail ssoalablai@palaumoe.net. World Wide Web http://palaugov.org/division-of-chool-management/.

Puerto Rico

Miguel A Hernández, Dir., Lib. and Info. Services Program, Puerto Rico Dept. of Educ., Box 190759, San Juan 00919-0759. Tel. 787-773-3564, fax 787-753-6945, e-mail hernandez_mi@de.gobierno.pr. World Wide Web http://www.de.gobierno.pr/conoce-al-de.

Republic of the Marshall Islands

Amenta Matthew, Exec. Dir., Alele Museum, Lib., and National Archives, P.O. Box 629, Majuro 96960. Tel. 011-692-625-3372, fax 011-692-625-3226, e-mail alele@ntamar.com. World Wide Web http://alelemuseum.tripod.com/Index.html.

U.S. Virgin Islands

Ingrid Bough, Territorial Dir. of Libs., Archives, and Museums, The Division of Libraries, Archives and Museums, 1122 King St. Christiansted, St. Croix 00820. Tel. 340-773-3715, fax 340-773-5327, e-mail ingrid.bough@dpnr.vi.gov. World Wide Web http://www.virginislandspubliclibraries.org/usvi/.

Canada

Alberta

Diana Davidson, Dir., Public Lib. Services Branch, Alberta Municipal Affairs, 803 Standard Life Centre, 10405 Jasper Ave., Edmonton T5J 4R7. Tel. 780-415-0284, fax 780-415-8594, e-mail diana.davidson@gov.ab.ca or libraries@gov.ab.ca. World Wide Web http://www.municipalaffairs.alberta.ca/alberta_libraries.cfm.

British Columbia

Beverley Shaw, Dir., Public Lib. Services Branch, Ministry of Educ., P.O. Box 9161, Stn.

Prov. Govt., Victoria V8W 9H3. Tel. 250-415-1662, fax 250 953-4985, e-mail bev.shaw@gov.bc.ca. World Wide Web http://www.bced.gov.bc.ca/pls.

Manitoba

Dir., Public Lib. Services, Manitoba Dept. of Tourism, Culture, Heritage, Sport and Consumer Protection, 300-1011 Rosser Ave., Brandon R7A OL5. Tel. 204-726-6590, fax 204-726-6868, e-mail pls@gov.mb.ca. World Wide Web http://www.gov.mb.ca/chc/pls/index.html.

New Brunswick

Sylvie Nadeau, Exec. Dir., New Brunswick Public Lib. Service, Place 2000, 250 King St., P.O. Box 6000, Fredericton E3B 5H1. Tel. 506-453-2354, fax 506-444-4064, e-mail Sylvie.NADEAU@gnb.ca. World Wide Web http://www.gnb.ca/0003/index-e.asp.

Newfoundland and Labrador

Andrew Hunt, Exec. Dir., Provincial Info. and Lib. Resources Board, 48 St. George's Ave., Stephenville A2N 1K9. Tel. 709-643-0900, fax 709-643-0925, e-mail ahunt@nlpl.ca. World Wide Web http://www.nlpl.ca.

Northwest Territories

Alison Hopkins, Territorial Libn., NWT Lib. Services, 75 Woodland Dr., Hay River X0E 1G1. Tel. 867-874-6531, fax 867-874-3321, e-mail alison_hopkins@gov.nt.ca. World Wide Web http://www.nwtpls.gov.nt.ca.

Nova Scotia

Nova Scotia Provincial Lib., 6016 University Ave., 5th Fl., Halifax B3H 1W4. Tel. 902-424-2457, fax 902-424-0633, e-mail nspl@nova scotia.ca. World Wide Web http://www.library.ns.ca.

Nunavut

Ron Knowling, Mgr., Nunavut Public Lib. Services, P.O. Box 270, Baker Lake X0C 0A0.

Tel. 867-793-3353, fax 867-793-3360, e-mail rknowling@gov.nu.ca. World Wide Web http://www.publiclibraries.nu.ca.

Ontario

Rod Sawyer, Ontario Government Ministry of Tourism, Culture, and Sport, 401 Bay St., Suite 1700, Toronto M7A 0A7. Tel. 416-314-7627, fax 416-212-1802, e-mail rod.sawyer@ontario.ca. World Wide Web http://www.mtc.gov.on.ca/en/libraries/contact.shtml.

Prince Edward Island

Public Lib. Service of Prince Edward Island, P.O. Box 7500, Morell C0A 1S0. Tel. 902-961-7320, fax 902-961-7322, e-mail plshq@gov.pe.ca. World Wide Web http://www.library.pe.ca.

Quebec

Christiane Barbe, Chair and CEO, Bibliothèque et Archives Nationales du Québec (BAnQ), 2275 rue Holt, Montreal H2G 3H1. Tel. 800-363-9028 or 514-873-1100, fax 514-873-9312, e-mail pdg@banq.qc.ca. World Wide Web http://www.banq.qc.ca/portal/dt/accueil.jsp.

Saskatchewan

Provincial Lib. and Literacy Office, Ministry of Educ., 409A Park St., Regina S4N 5B2. Tel. 306-787-2976, fax 306-787-2029, e-mail barb.griffiths@gov.sk.ca. World Wide Web http://www.education.gov.sk.ca/provincial-library/public-library-system.

Yukon Territory

Julie Ourom, Dir., Public Libs., Community Development Div., Dept. of Community Services, Government of Yukon, P.O. Box 2703, Whitehorse Y1A 2C6. Tel. 867-667-5447, fax 867-393-6333, e-mail julie.ourom@gov.yk.ca. World Wide Web http://www.ypl.gov.yk.ca.

State School Library Media Associations

Alabama

Children's and School Libns. Div., Alabama Lib. Assn. Memb. 600+.

Pres. Jeff Graveline, Univ. of Alabama at Birmingham, Mervyn H. Sterne Lib., SL 172, 1720 2nd Ave. S., Birmingham 35294-0014. Tel. 205-934-6364, e-mail jgraveli@uab.edu; *Pres.-Elect* Sonya Jordan, Mountain Brook High School, 3650 Bethune Dr., Mountain Brook 35223. Tel. 205-414-3800 ext. 7619, e-mail jordans@student.mtnbrook.k12.al.us; *Secy.* Mandy Pinyan, Troy Univ., Rosa Parks Lib., 252 Montgomery St., Montgomery 36104. Tel. 334-241-8601, e-mail mpinyan@hmcpl.org; *Treas.* Tim Bailey, Auburn Univ. at Montgomery, P.O. Box 244023, Montgomery 36124-4023. Tel. 334-244-3420, e-mail tbailey1@aum.edu; *Memb.-at-Large* Central Alabama: Matt Layne, Emmet O'Neal Lib., 50 Oak St., Mountain Brook 35213. Tel. 205-908-5323, e-mail mlayne@bham.lib.al.us; South Alabama: Chris Shaffer, 309 Wallace Hall, Troy Univ. 36082. E-mail shafferc@troy.edu; *Past Pres.* Paula Laurita, Athens-Limestone Public Lib., 605 S. Jefferson St., Athens 35611. Tel. 256-232-1233, e-mail PaulaLaurita97@gmail.com.

Address correspondence to the association administrator, Alabama Lib. Assn., 6030 Monticello Drive, Montgomery 36117. Tel. 334-414-0113, e-mail allibraryassoc@gmail.com.

World Wide Web http://allanet.org.

Alaska

Alaska Assn. of School Libns. Memb. 100+. Publication. *The Puffin* continuing basis online at http://akasl.org/puffin-newsletter. Submissions e-mail akasl.puffin@gmail.com.

Pres. Karla Barkman, Kenai Peninsula Borough School District (KPBSD). E-mail akasl. president@gmail.com; *Pres.-Elect* Jill Gann, Kenai Central High School and Kenai Middle School, KPBSD. E-mail akasl.presidentelect@gmail.com; *Secy.* Deborah Rinio, Hutchison High School, Fairbanks. E-mail akasl.secretary@gmail.com; *Treas.* Laura Guest, Turnagain Elementary School, 3500 W. Northern Lights Blvd., Anchorage 99517. Tel. 907-742-7200, e-mail akasl.treasurer@gmail.com; *Past Pres.* Sheryl Wittig, Auke Bay Lib., Auke Bay Elementary School, 10014 Crazy Horse Dr., Juneau 99801. Tel. 907-796-5275, e-mail akasl. pastpresident@gmail.com.

World Wide Web http://www.akasl.org.

Arizona

Teacher-Libn. Div., Arizona Lib. Assn. Memb. 1,000. Term of Office. Jan.–Dec. Publication. *AZLA Newsletter.*

Chair Jean Kilker, Maryvale High School, 3415 N. 59th Ave., Phoenix 85033. Tel. 602-764-2134, e-mail jkilker@phoenixunion.org.

Address correspondence to the chairperson.

World Wide Web http://www.azla.org/?page=TLD.

Arkansas

Arkansas Assn. of School Libns., div. of Arkansas Lib. Assn.

Chair Sloan Powell, Raymond and Phyllis Simon Middle School, 1601 Siebenmorgan Dr., Conway 72032. E-mail powells@conway schools.net; *Chair-Elect* Ashley Cooksey, West Magnet Elementary, 850 North Hill St., Batesville, AR 72501. E-mail acooksey@batesville schools.org. *Past Chair* Lori Bush.

Address correspondence to E-mail arasl. chair@gmail.com.

World Wide Web https://arlib.org/wp/.

California

California School Lib. Assn. Memb. 1,200+. Publications. *CSLA Journal* (2 a year). *Ed.* Mary Ann Harlan, San Jose State Univ. E-mail maryann.harlan@sjsu.edu; *CSLA Newsletter* (10 a year, memb., via e-mail).

(State Board) *Pres.* Terry Lai, P. Giannini Middle School, 3151 Ortega St., San Francisco 94122. Tel. 415-759-2770, e-mail cslaofficer@gmail.com; *Pres.-Elect* Renée Ousley-Swank, Curriculum Frameworks and Instructional Resources Div., California Dept. of Educ., 1430 N St., Sacramento 95814-5901. Tel. 916-319-

0449, e-mail ROusleySwank@cde.ca.gov; *Secy.* Nina Jackson, Franklin Classical Middle School, 540 Cerritos Ave., Long Beach 90802. E-mail njcatsandbooks@gmail.com; *Treas.* Yvonne Weinstein, Frank Augustus Miller Middle School, 17925 Krameria Ave., Riverside 92504. Tel. 951-789-8181 ext. 57115. E-mail mrsweinstein@fastmail.fm; *Past Pres.* Sue Heraper, Newbury Park High School, 456 N Reino Rd., Newbury Park 91320. Tel. 805 498-3676, e-mail sueheraper@gmail.com; (Northern Region) *Pres.* Nancy Lucero, San Francisco Unified School District, 555 Franklin St., San Francisco 94102; *Pres.-Elect* Cathy Pope, 6844 Alexandria Pl., Stockton 95207. Tel. 209-953-8984, e-mail cpope@lusd.net; (Southern Region) *Pres.* Erin Southam, Hilltop Middle School, 44 East J St., Chula Vista 91910. Tel. 619-498-2730, e-mail elsoutham@gmail.com; *Pres.-Elect* Heather Gruenthal, Lindsey International Studies, 5075 Daisy Ave., Long Beach 90805. Tel. 562-423-6451, e-mail hgruenthal@lbschools.net.

Address correspondence to the association at 6444 E. Spring St., No. 237, Long Beach 90815-1553. Tel./fax 888-655-8480, e-mail info@csla.net.

World Wide Web http://www.csla.net.

Colorado

Colorado Assn. of School Libns. Memb. 250+.

Co-Pres. Becky Russell, Colorado Dept. of Educ. E-mail russell_b@cde.state.co.us.; *Co-Pres.* Molly Gibney, Mountain View Elementary. E-mail mgibney@comcast.net.

World Wide Web http://www.cal-webs. org/?page=casl.

Connecticut

Connecticut Assn. of School Libns. (formerly Connecticut Educ. Media Assn.). Memb. 500+. Term of Office. July–June.

Pres. Shelley Stedman, E-mail president@ctcasl.org; *V.P.* Jane Martellino, E-mail vice-president@ctcasl.org; *Secy.* Chris Barlow, E-mail secretary@ctcasl.org; *Treas.* Jody Pillar, E-mail treasurer@ctcasl.org.

Address correspondence to the president.

World Wide Web https://casl.wildapricot. org.

Delaware

Delaware Assn. of School Libns., div. of Delaware Lib. Assn. Memb. 100+. Publications. *DASL Newsletter* (online; irreg.); column in *DLA Bulletin* (2 a year).

Pres. Rachel West, Salesianum School, 1801 N. Broom St., Wilmington 19802. Tel. 302-356-2636, e-mail rwest@salesianum. org; *Secy.* Jennifer O'Neill, Heritage Elementary School, 2815 Highlands Ln., Wilmington 19808. Tel. 302-454-3424 ext. 131, e-mail jennifer.o'neill@redclay.k12.de.us; *Treas.* Tamara Carr, MLIS AHIP, Lake Forest High School, 5407 Killens Pond Rd., Felton 19943. Tel. 302-284-9291 ext. 201; *Past Pres.* Jen Delgado, Henry B. du Pont Middle School, 735 Meeting House Rd., Hockessin 19707. Tel. 302-239-3420, e-mail jennifer.delgado@redclay.k12.de.us.

Address correspondence to the president.

World Wide Web http://dla.lib.de.us/divisions/dasl/.

District of Columbia

District of Columbia Assn. of School Libns. Memb. 8. Publication. *Newsletter* (4 a year).

Address correspondence to André Maria Taylor, 330 10th St. N.E., Washington, DC 20002. Tel. 301-502-4203, e-mail contactdcasl@gmail.com.

World Wide Web http://dcasl.weebly.com.

Florida

Florida Assn. for Media in Educ. Memb. 1,400+. Term of Office. Nov.–Oct. Publication. *Florida Media Quarterly. Ed.* Nancy G. Mijangos. E-mail MijangosN@santarosa.k12.fl.us.

Pres. Elizabeth Zdrodowski, Glades Central Community High School, 1001 SW. Ave. M., Belle Glade 33430. Tel. 561-993-4425, e-mail elizabeth.zdrodowski@palmbeachschools. org; *Pres.-Elect* Andrea Parisi. E-mail andrea. parisi@ocps.net; *Secy.* Ashlee Cornett. E-mail cornetta@osceola.k12.fl.us; *Treas.* Lorraine Stinson. E-mail lorraine.stinson@stjohns.k12. fl.us; *Parliamentarian* Sandra McMichael. E-mail sandymc@bellsouth.net; *Past Pres.* Lucretia Miller, St. Johns Country Day School, 3100 Doctors Lake Dr., Orange Park 32073. E-mail lmiller@sjcds.net.

Address correspondence to FAME, P.O. Box 941169, Maitland FL 32794-1169. Tel. 863-585-6802, e-mail FAME@floridamediaed.org. World Wide Web http://www.floridamedia ed.org.

Georgia

Georgia Lib. Media Assn. Memb. 700+.
Pres. Michelle Easley; *Pres.-Elect* Jennifer Helfrich; *Secy.* Theresa Quilici; *Treas.* Lora Taft; *Past Pres.* Beth Miller.
Address correspondence to GLMA Executive Office, 2700 Cumberland Pkwy., Suite 570, Atlanta 30339. Tel. 404-299-7700, fax 404-299-7029, e-mail sally@associationstrategy group.us.
World Wide Web http://www.glma-inc.org.

Hawaii

Hawaii Assn. of School Libns. Memb. 145. Term of Office. June–May. Publication. *HASL Newsletter* (3 a year). *Newsletter Chair* Eileen Uchima. E-mail myhaslnews@gmail.com.
Co-Pres. MB Ogawa and *Co-Pres.* Sandy Yamamoto, Kapolei High School; *V.P. Programming* Patty Louis, Aliamanu Elementary School, 3265 Salt Lake Blvd., Honolulu 96818. Tel. 808-421-4280; *V.P. Membership* Betty Arai, Mililani High School, 95-1200 Meheula Pkwy., Mililani 96789. E-mail bettya@ aloha.com; *Secy.* Deb Peterson, Punahou High School; *Corresponding Secretary* Debbie Anderson, Waiakea Intermediate School; *Treas.* Johanna Akina, Aiea Elementary School; *Past Pres.* Sherry Rose, Wallace Rider Farrington High School, 1564 N. King St., Honolulu 96817. Tel. 808-832-3600, e-mail roses@hawaii antel.net.
Address correspondence to the association, P.O. Box 235284, Honolulu 96823.
World Wide Web https://sites.google.com/ site/haslsite/.

Idaho

School Libs. Div., Idaho Lib. Assn. Memb. 40+.
Chair Julie Hatcher, Sawtooth Middle School, West Ada School District. E-mail hatcher.julie@westada.org; *Chair-Elect* Kiersten Kerr, Coeur d'Alene High School. E-mail kkerr@cdaschools.org.

Address correspondence to the chairperson. World Wide Web http://www.idaholibraries. org/about-us/officersdivisionscommittees/edu-cational-media-division.

Illinois

Illinois School Lib. Media Assn. Memb. 1,000. Term of Office. July–June. Publications. *ISLMA News* (4 a year). *Ed* David P. Little.
Pres. Patti Fleser, Deer Path Middle School, 95 W. Deerpath Rd., Lake Forest 60045. E-mail president@islma.org; *Pres.-Elect* Jacob Roskovensky, Charleston High School, Charleston. E-mail pres-elect@islma.org; *Secy.* Carrie Light, South Park Elementary School, 1421 Hacklberry Rd., Deerfield 60015. E-mail secretary@islma.org; *Treas.* Katherine Femal, Woodstock High School, Woodstock. E-mail treasurer@islma.org; *Past Pres.* Angie Green, Trewyn K–8 School, Peoria. E-mail pastpres@ islma.org.
Address correspondence to the Illinois School Library Media Association. P.O. Box 1326, Galesburg 61402-1326. Tel. 309-341-1099, fax 309-341-2070, e-mail execsecretary @islma.org.
World Wide Web http://www.islma.org.

Indiana

Assn. of Indiana School Library Educators (AISLE). Publications. *Focus on Indiana Libraries* (mo.). *Ed.* Tisa M. Davis. Tel. 317-257-2040, ext. 102, fax 317-257-1389, e-mail tdavis@ilfonline.org.
Pres. David Peter, Vincennes Univ., 1002 N. First St., Vincennes 47803. Tel. 812-888-5815, e-mail dpeter@vinu.edu; *Pres.-Elect* Edra Waterman, Hamilton East Public Lib., One Library Plaza, Noblesville 46060. Tel. 317-770-3202, e-mail ewaterman@hepl.lib.in.us; *Secy.* Diane Huerkamp, Mooresville Public Lib., 220 W. Harrison St., Mooresville 46158. Tel. 317-831-7323, e-mail dianeh@mooresville.lib. in.us; *Treas.* Stephanie Davis, Wells County Public Lib., 200 W. Washington St., Bluffton 46714. Tel. 260-824-1612, e-mail sdavis@ wellscolibrary.org; *Past Pres.* Robyn Young, Avon High School, 7575 E CR 150 S., Avon 46123. Tel. 317-544-5031, e-mail rryoung@ avon-schools.org.

Address correspondence to the association, c/o Indiana Lib. Federation, 941 E. 86 St., Suite 260, Indianapolis 46240. Tel. 317-257-2040, fax 317-257-1389, e-mail ilf@indy.net. World Wide Web http://www.ilfonline. org/?AISLE.

Iowa

Iowa Assn. of School Libns., div. of the Iowa Lib. Assn. Memb. 180+. Term of Office. Jan.–Jan.

Pres. Sara Staudt. E-mail slstaudt@gmail. com; *V.P.* Val Ehlers. E-mail valehlers1@ gmail.com; *Secy./ Treas.* Jen Keltner. E-mail kaseyjenkeltner@gmail.com; *Memb.-at-Large* Jill Hofmockel.

Address correspondence to the president.
World Wide Web http://www.iasl-ia.org.

Kansas

Kansas Assn. of School Libns. Memb. 600.

Pres. Marla Wigton. E-mail kaslpresident@ gmail.com; *Pres.-Elect* Martha House. E-mail mhouse@cgrove417.org; *Secy.* Rachel Yoder. E-mail kaslsecretary@gmail.com; *Treas.* Brenda Lemon. E-mail blemon@473mail.net; *Past Pres.* Nancy McFarlin. E-mail kaslpastpresident@gmail.com; *Exec. Secy.* Barb Bahm. E-mail kaslexecsecretary@gmail.com.

Address correspondence to the executive secretary.

World Wide Web http://www.ksschool librarians.org.

Kentucky

Kentucky Assn. of School Libns. (KASL), section of Kentucky Lib. Assn. Memb. 600+. Publication. *KASL News.* (blog) http://kaslblog. edublogs.org.

Pres. Renee Hale, Henry F. Moss Middle School, 2565 Russellville Rd., Bowling Green 42101. Tel. 270-843-0166, e-mail renee.hale@ warren.kyschools.us; *Pres.-Elect* Amanda Hurley. E-mail amanda.hurley@fayette.kyschools. us; *Secy.* Lori Hancock. E-mail lhancock@ thelexingtonschool.org; *Treas.* Fred Tilsley. E-mail ftilsley@windstream.net; *Past Pres.* James Allen, Eminence Independent School, 254 W. Broadway St., Eminence 40019. E-mail james.allen@eminence.kyschools.us.

Address correspondence to the president.

World Wide Web http://www.kasl.us.

Louisiana

Louisiana Assn. of School Libns., section of Louisiana Lib. Assn. Memb. 230. Term of Office. July–June.

Pres. Cathy Seal. Tel. 225-405-9899, e-mail cseal2@gmail.com; *1st V.P./Pres.-Elect* Susan Gauthier. Tel. 225-226-7610, e-mail sgauthier1@ebrschools.org; *2nd V.P.* Leslie Carloss. Tel. 337-942-5404 ext.104, e-mail carlossl@ ocsvikings.com; *Secy.* Janet Gary. Tel. 337-364-3927, e-mail jgary@iberia.k12.la.us; *Past Pres.* Jade Calais. E-mail jrcampbell@lpssonline.com; *Parliamentarian* Jan McGee. E-mail janmcgee55@gmail.com.

Address correspondence to the association, c/o Louisiana Lib. Assn., 8550 United Plaza Blvd., Suite 1001, Baton Rouge 70809. Tel. 225-922-4642, fax 225-408-4422, e-mail office @llaonline.org.

World Wide Web http://laslonline.weebly. com.

Maine

Maine Assn. of School Libs. Memb. 200+.

Pres. Tina Taggart, Foxcroft Academy, 975 W. Main St., Dover-Foxcroft 04426. E-mail tina.taggart@staff.foxcroftacademy.org; *Pres.-Elect* Amanda Kozaka, Cape Elizabeth Middle School; *Secy.* Janet Patterson, Belgrade Public Lib., 124 Depot Rd., Belgrade 04917. E-mail janet.patterson.mls@gmail.com; *Treas.* Dorothy Hall-Middle, Greely Middle School, 351 Tuttle Rd., Cumberland Ctr. 04021. E-mail dorothyhallriddle@gmail.com; *Past Pres.* Joyce Lucas (Ret.). Tel. 207-859-2442, e-mail jolukeme@gmail.com.

Address correspondence to the president.

World Wide Web http://www.maslibraries. org.

Maryland

Maryland Assn. of School Libns. (formerly Maryland Educ. Media Organization).

Pres. Melissa Grabill, Howard County Public School System, 10910 Clarksville Pike, Elliott City 21042. Tel. 410-313-7179, e-mail Melissa_Grabill@hcpss.org; *Pres.-Elect* Emmanuel Faulkner, The Historic Samuel Coleridge-Taylor Elementary School,

Baltimore County Public Schools. E-mail EFaulkner@bcps.k12.md.us; *Secy.* Laura Hicks, Frederick High School, 650 Carroll Pkwy., Frederick 21701. E-mail laura.hicks@fcps.org; *Treas.* Catherine Francoeur, Professional Lib., Prince George's County Public Schools. E-mail maslmaryland@gmail.com. *Memb.-at-Large* Brittany Tignor, Snow Hill Middle School, Worcester County Public Schools. E-mail BDHulme-Tignor@mail.worcester.k12.md.us; Jessie Simmons-Taylor, Largo High School, Prince George's County Public Schools. E-mail jessie.simmonstaylor@pgcps.org; *Past Pres.* Laura Hicks.

Address correspondence to the association, Box 21127, Baltimore 21228.

World Wide Web http://maslmd.org.

Massachusetts

Massachusetts School Lib. Assn. Memb. 800. Publication. *MSLA Forum* (3 a year). *Eds.* Jennifer Dimmick, Katherine Steiger.

Pres. Anita Cellucci, Westborough High School, 90 W. Main St., Westborough 01581. E-mail acellucci@maschoolibraries.org; *Pres.-Elect* Carrie Tucker, E. Bridgewater Jr./Sr. High School. E-mail ctucker@maschoolibraries.org; *Secy.* Robyn York, Bishop Feehan High School, 70 Holcott Dr., Attleboro 02703. E-mail ryork@maschoolibraries.org; *Treas.* Jennifer Varney, MLKing, Jr. School, Cambridge. E-mail jvarney@maschoolibraries.org; *Exec. Dir.* Kathy Lowe, Massachusetts School Lib, Assn., Box 658, Lunenburg 01462. E-mail klowe@maschoolibraries.org.

Address correspondence to the executive director.

World Wide Web http://www.maschoolibraries.org.

Michigan

Michigan Assn. for Media in Educ. Memb. 1,200. Publications. *Media Spectrum* (2 a year); *MAME Newsletter* (6 a year).

Pres. Lisa Kelley, Rochester Community Schools, University Hills, 600 Croydon, Rochester Hills 48309. Tel. 248-726-4404, e-mail lkelley@mimame.org; *Pres.-Elect* Klaudia Janek; *Secy.* Rachel Markel, Portage Public Schools, 12th Street/Haverhill Elementaries, 6501 South 12th St., Portage 49024. Tel. 269-

323-6985, e-mail rmarkel@portageps.org; *Treas.* Bruce Popejoy. E-mail bpopejoy@mimame.org; *Past Pres.* Lisa Brakel, Airport Community Schools, 11200 Grafton Rd., Carleton. Tel. 734-654-6205, e-mail lbrakels@mimame.org.

Address correspondence to MAME, 1407 Rensen, Suite 3, Lansing 48910. Tel. 517-394-2808, fax 517-492-3878, e-mail mame@mimame.org.

World Wide Web http://www.mimame.org.

Minnesota

Info. and Technology Educators of Minnesota (ITEM) (formerly Minnesota Educ. Media Organization). Memb. 400+. Term of Office. July–June.

Co-Pres. Dawn French, Saint Paul Public Schools. E-mail dawnief@gmail.com; *Co-Pres.* Paula Hansen, Lakeville Public Schools, 8670 210th St., W., Lakeville 55044. E-mail pjhansen55044@gmail.com; *Co-Pres.-Elect* Lisa Gearman, Chaska High School. E-mail gearmanl@district112.org; *Co-Pres.-Elect* Sara Swenson, Edina High School. E-mail sara.swenson@edinaschools.org; *Secy.* Kristi Wobbema, Bloomington Public Schools, 1350 W. 106th St., Minneapolis 55431. E-mail kwobbema@isd271.org; *Treas.* Robin Weber, Horace Mann School, Saint Paul Public Schools, 2001 Eleanor Ave., Saint Paul 55116. Tel. 651-293-8965, e-mail rwfurahi@gmail.com; *Past Co-Pres.* Andi Bodeau, Osseo Public Schools, 11200 93rd Ave., N. Maple Grove 55369. E-mail bodeaua@gmail.com; *Past Co-Pres.* Jen Legatt, Hopkins Public Schools, E-mail Jen.M.Legatt@gmail.com.

Address correspondence to Info. and Technology Educators of Minnesota (ITEM), P.O. Box 130555, Roseville 55113. Tel. 651-771-8672, e-mail admin@mnitem.org.

World Wide Web http://mnitem.org.

Mississippi

School Lib. Section, Mississippi Lib. Assn. Memb. 1,300.

Chair Holly Gray, Tupelo High Schools, 4125 Golden Wave Dr., Tupelo 38801. Tel. 662-841-8979, e-mail ehgray@gmail.com.

Address correspondence to School Section, Mississippi Lib. Assn., P.O. Box 13687, Jackson 39236-3687. Tel. 601-981-4586, e-mail info@misslib.org.

World Wide Web http://www.misslib.org.

Missouri

Missouri Assn. of School Libns. Memb. 1,000. Term of Office. July–June.

Pres. Amy Taylor, Lee's Summit West High School, 2600 S.W. Ward Rd., Lee's Summit 64082. E-mail amy.taylor@lsr7.net; *1st V.P.* Mernie Maestas, Boone Trail Elementary, Wentzville R-IV School District. E-mail merniemaestas@wsdr4.org; *2nd V.P.* Jennifer Millikan, St. Joseph's Academy. E-mail jmillikan@stjosephacademy.org; *Secy.* Rene Burress, Univ. of Central Missouri, 108 W. South St., Warrensburg 64093. E-mail burress@ucmo.edu; *Treas.* Diana Gehrt, Congress Middle School, Park Hill School District. E-mail gehrtd@parkhill.k12.mo.us; *Past Pres.* Margaret Sullivan, Rockwood Summit High and Marquette High Schools, Rockwood School District, 111 East N. St., Eureka 63025. E-mail sullivanmargaret@rsdmo.org.

Address correspondence to the association, P.O. Box 2107, Jefferson City 65102. Tel. 573-893-4155, fax 573-635-2858, e-mail info@maslonline.org.

World Wide Web http://www.maslonline.org.

Montana

School Lib. Div., Montana Lib. Assn. Memb. 200+. Publication. *FOCUS* (published by Montana Lib. Assn.) *Eds.* Caroline Campbell. E-mail mlaFOCUSeditor@gmail.com; Kendra Mullison. E-mail mlaFOCUSeditor@gmail.com (q.).

Co-Chair Dianne Mattila, Newman Elementary Lib.; 605 S. Billings Blvd., Billings 59101. Tel. 406-281-6215, e-mail mattilad@billingsschools.org. *Exec. Dir.* Debbi Kramer, 33 Beartooth View Dr., Laurel 59044. Tel. 406-579-3121, e-mail debkmla@hotmail.com.

Address correspondence to the Montana Lib. Assn. executive director.

World Wide Web http://www.mtlib.org.

Nebraska

Nebraska School Libns. Assn. Memb. 300+. Term of Office. July–June. Publication. *NSLA News* (q.).

Pres. Paula McClung, Lincoln High School, 2229 J St., Lincoln 68510. Tel. 402-436-1301, e-mail pmcclung@lps.org; *Pres.-Elect* Angie Richeson. E-mail richesonac@unk.edu; *Secy.* Carole Matthews. E-mail carole.matthews1@gmail.com; *Treas.* Cynthia Stogdill. E-mail cynthia.stogdill@fpsmail.org; *Past Pres.* Laura Pietsch, Omaha Public Schools, 3215 Cuming St., Omaha 68131. Tel. 402-557-2520, e-mail laura.pietsch@ops.org. *Exec. Secy.* Kim Gangwish. E-mail contactnsla@gmail.com.

Address correspondence to the executive secretary.

World Wide Web http://www.neschoollibrarians.org.

Nevada

Nevada School and Children Libns. Section, Nevada Lib. Assn. Memb. 120.

Chair Larry Johnson, Las Vegas-Clark County Lib. District. E-mail johnsonl@lvccld.org; Susan Thurnbeck, Las Vegas-Clark County Lib. District. E-mail thurnbecks@lvccld.org; *Exec. Secy.* Kristy Islal. E-mail ardainia@yahoo.com; *Past Chair* Shar Murphy, The Honors Academy of Literature, 195 N. Arlington Ave., Reno 89501. E-mail ms.shar@academyoflit.org.

Address correspondence to the executive secretary.

World Wide Web http://www.nevadalibraries.org/handbook/nscls.html.

New Hampshire

New Hampshire School Lib. Media Assn. Memb. 250+. Term of Office. July–June. Publication. *NHSLMA Newsletter* (irreg.; online).

Pres. Donna Zecha, Hopkinton Middle/High School Lib., 297 Park Ave., Contoocook 03229. E-mail hophslibrary@hopkintonschools.org *V.P.* Rachel Hopkins, Salem High School, Salem. E-mail rachel.hopkins@sau57.org; *Recording Secy.* Caitlin Bennett, Londonderry Middle School, Londonderry. E-mail cbennett@londonderry.org; *Treas.* Helen Burnham, Lincoln Street School, Exeter. E-mail hburnham@sau16.org; *Past Pres.* Carol Sweny, Henniker Community School, 51 Western Ave., Henniker 03242. E-mail cdsweny@comcast.net.

Address correspondence to the president, NHSLMA, P.O. Box 418, Concord 03302-0418.

World Wide Web http://nhslma.org.

New Jersey

New Jersey Assn. of School Libns. (NJASL). Memb. 1,000+. Term of Office. Aug. 1–July 31. Publication. *Bookmark Newsletter* (mo.).

Pres. Bruce DeBoff, Pennsauken Intermediate School, 8125 Park Ave., Pensauken 08109. E-mail president@njasl.org; *Pres.-Elect* Lisa Bakanas, Cherokee High School, 120 Tomlinson Mill Rd., Marlton 08053. Tel. 856-983-5140 ext. 2357, e-mail lbakanas@lrhsd.org; *V.P.*Christina Cucci; *Recording Secy.* Michelle McGrievey, Hoboken Junior Senior High School, 800 Clinton St., Hoboken 07030. Tel. 201-356-3700 ext. 7228, e-mail secretary@njasl.org; *Treas.* Jean Stock, Parchment Elementary School, 301 Larchmont Blvd., Mt. Laurel 08054. Tel. 856-273-3700 ext.17508; *Memb.-at-Large* Elizabeth Ullrich, Beth Thomas; *Past Pres.* Janet Clark, Cleveland St. School, 355 Cleveland St., City of Orange, NJ 07050. E-mail president@njasl.org.

Address correspondence to recording secretary, New Jersey Assn. of School Libns., P.O. Box 1460, Springfield 07081.

World Wide Web http://www.njasl.org.

New York

Section of School Libns., New York Lib. Assn. Memb. 800+. Term of Office. Nov.–Oct. Publications. *School Library Update* (3 a year).

Pres. Michele Miller, Gorham Intermediate Lib., Marcus Whitman, 2705 Rte. 245, Stanley 14561. Tel. 585-526-6351 ext. 4005, e-mail mmiller@mwcsd.org; *Pres.-Elect* Penny Sweeney. E-mail psweeney@liverpool.k12.ny.us; *Secy.* Gail Brisson. E-mail Gail.brisson@gmail.com; *Treas.* Anne Paulson. E-mail paulsonap@yahoo.com; *Past Pres.* Susan Polos, Mount Kisco Elementary School, 47 W. Hyatt Ave., Mt. Kisco 10549. Tel. 914-266-2677, e-mail spolos0882@bcsdny.org.

Address correspondence to New York Lib. Assn., 6021 State Farm Rd., Guilderland, NY 12084. Tel. 518-432-6952, fax 518-427-1697, e-mail info@nyla.org.

World Wide Web https://www.nyla.org/max/4DCGI/cms/review.html?Action=CMS_Document&DocID=221&MenuKey=ssl.

North Carolina

North Carolina School Lib. Media Assn. Memb. 1,000+. Term of Office. Nov.–Oct.

Pres. Sedley Abercrombie, Davidson County Schools, 2065 E. Holly Grove Rd., Lexington 27292. Tel. 336-242-5639, e-mail ncslmapresident@gmail.com; *Pres.-Elect* Brene Duggins, East Davidson High School, 1408 Lake Rd., Thomasville 27360. Tel. 336-476-4814, e-mail ncslmapresidentelect@gmail.com; *Secy.* Allison Long, Mooresville Middle School, 305 N. Main St., Mooresville 28115. Tel. 704-658-2530, e-mail ncslmasecretary@gmail.com; *Treas.* Jennifer Abel, North Henderson High School, 35 Fruitland Rd., Hendersonville 28792. Tel. 828-697-4500, e-mail ncslmatreasurer@gmail.com; *Past Pres.* Walter Carmichael, Cook Literacy Model School, 920 11th St. N.W., Winston-Salem 27106. Tel. 336-703-4201, e-mail pastpresident@gmail.com.

Address correspondence to the president.

World Wide Web http://www.ncslma.org.

North Dakota

School Lib. and Youth Services Section, North Dakota Lib. Assn. Memb. 100. Publication. *The Good Stuff* (q.) *Ed.* Marlene Anderson, Bismarck State College Lib. E-mail: marlene.anderson@bismarckstate.edu.

Chair Amy Soma, Fargo Public Schools. E-mail: somaa@fargo.k12.nd.us;

Address correspondence to the North Dakota Lib. Assn. P.O. Box 1595, Bismarck 58502-1595.

World Wide Web http://ndlaonline.org.

Ohio

Ohio Educ. Lib. Media Assn. Memb. 1,000.

Pres. Kelly Silwani, Olentangy Local Schools. E-mail krs1614@gmail.com; *V.P.* Deb Logan, Mount Gilead Schools. E-mail deb.jd3logan@gmail.com; *Secy.* Christina Van Dyke, Tolles Career and Technical Ctr. E-mail cvandyke@tollestech.com; *Treas.* Lisa Barnes Prince, Akron Public Schools. E-mail lbarnesprince@att.net; *Dir. of Services* Lisa Kirr; *Past Pres.* Liz Deskins, Hilliard City Schools. Tel. 614-870-1641, e-mail?liz.library@gmail. com.

Address correspondence to the association, 17 South High St., Suite 200, Columbus 43215. Tel. 614-228-4733, fax 614-221-1989, e-mail OELMA@assnoffices.com.

World Wide Web http://www.oelma.org.

Oklahoma

Oklahoma School Libns. Div., Oklahoma Lib. Assn. Memb. 200+. Publication. *Oklahoma Librarian* (bi-mo.). *Ed.* Jil McFall. E-mail editor @oklibs.org.

Chair Kelsey Gourd, Lakeview Elementary School, 3310 108th Ave. N.E., Norman 73026. E-mail kgourd@norman.k12.ok.us; *V.Chair/Chair-Elect* TBD; *Secy.* TBD; *Treas.* TBD; *Past Chair* Tara Hixon, Piedmont Public Schools, 713 Piedmont Rd. N., Piedmont 73078. E-mail taradhixon@sbcglobal.net.

Address correspondence to the chairperson, School Libs. Div., Oklahoma Lib. Assn., P.O. Box 6550, Edmond 73083. Tel. 405-348-0506.

World Wide Web http://www.oklibs.org/ ?page=OKSL.

Oregon

Oregon Assn. of School Libs. Memb. 600. Publication. *Interchange* (3 a year).

Pres. Peggy Christensen. E-mail president@ oasl.olaweb.org; *Pres.-Elect* Paige Battle. E-mail presidentelect@oasl.olaweb.org; *Secy.* Jenny Takeda. E-mail secretary@oasl.olaweb. org; *Treas.* Stuart Levy. E-mail treasurer@ oasl.olaweb.org; *Memb.-at-Large* Kate Weber, Laurie Nordahl; *Past Pres.* Robin Rolfe, E-mail pastpresident@oasl.olaweb.org.

Address correspondence to the association, P.O. Box 3067, La Grande 97850. Tel. 541-962-5824, e-mail ola@olaweb.org.

World Wide Web http://ola.memberclicks. net/oasl-home.

Pennsylvania

Pennsylvania School Libns. Assn. Memb. 800+. Publication *PSLA Newsletter* (online).

Pres. Allison Burrell. E-mail aburrell@psla. org; *Pres.-Elect* Jennifer Bates. E-mail jbates@ psla.org; *V.P.* Allison Mackley. E-mail amackley @psla.org; *Secy.* Patricia McNeill. E-mail pslaboard@psla.org; *Treas.* Natalie Hawley; *Past Pres.* Michael Nailor. E-mail mnailor@ psla.org.

Address correspondence to the president.

World Wide Web http://www.psla.org.

Rhode Island

School Libns. of Rhode Island (formerly Rhode Island Educ. Media Assn.). Memb. 350+.

Pres. Sarah Hunicke. E-mail SLRI.prez@ gmail.com; *V.P.* Lisa Girard. E-mail SLRI.viceprez@gmail.com; *Secy.* Lisa Casey. E-mail SLRI.secretary@gmail.com; *Treas.* Jillian Waugh. E-mail SLRI.treasurer@gmail.com; *Past Pres.* Jane Perry.

Address correspondence to the president.

World Wide Web http://www.slri.info.

South Carolina

South Carolina Assn. of School Libns. Memb. 900. Term of Office. July–June.

Pres. Cindy Symonds. E-mail president@ scasl.net; *Pres.-Elect* Cathy Nelson. E-mail president.elect@scasl.net; *Secy.* Heather Thore. E-mail secretary@scasl.net; *Treas.* Gloria Coleman. E-mail glorysee@hotmail. com; *Past Pres.* Jennifer?Tazerouti. E-mail tazerouti@gmail.com.

Address correspondence to the association, P.O. Box 2442, Columbia 29202. Tel./fax 803-492-3025.

World Wide Web http://www.scasl.net.

South Dakota

South Dakota School Lib. Media Section, South Dakota Lib. Assn., P.O. Box 582, Spearfish 57783. Tel. 605-641-2079. Memb. 140+. Term of Office. Oct.–Sept.

Chair Laura Allard, Memorial Middle School, 1401 S. Sertoma Ave., Sioux Falls 57106. E-mail laura.allard@k12.sd.us; *Past Chair* Sharlene Lien, Discovery Elementary School, 1506 South Discovery Ave., Sioux Falls 57106. E-mail sharlene.lien@k12.sd.us.

Address correspondence to the chairperson.

World Wide Web http://www.sdlibraryassociation.org/page/Sections.

Tennessee

Tennessee Assn. of School Libns. Memb. 450. Term of Office. Jan.–Dec. Publication. *TASL Talks.*

Pres. Misti Jenkins, Blackman High School, 3956 Blaze Dr., Murfreesboro 37128. E-mail misti.jenkins.tasl@gmail.com; *Pres.-Elect* Blake Hopper, Powell Valley Elementary, 323 Hopper Circle, Speedwell 37870. E-mail blake.hopper.tasl@gmail.com; *Secy.* Vicki Winstead, Vance Middle School, 815 Edgemont Ave., Bristol 37664. E-mail vcwinstead.tasl@gmail.com; *Treas.* Lynn Lilley, McGavock High School, 3150 McGavock Pike, Nashville 37214. E-mail lynn.lilley.tasl@gmail.com; *Past Pres.* Mindy Nichols, Crockett County High School, 402 Hwy. 88, Alamo 38001. E-mail mindy.nichols.tasl@gmail.com.

Address correspondence to the president.

World Wide Web http://www.tasltn.org.

Texas

Texas Assn. of School Libns., div. of Texas Lib. Assn. Memb. 4,000+. Term of Office. Apr.–Mar.

Chair Becky Calzada, Leander Independent School District, 204 W. South St., Leander 78646. Tel. 512-570-0273, e-mail becky.Calzada@leanderisd.org *Chair-Elect* Kate DiPronio. E-mail Kate_DiPronio@roundrockisd.org; *Secy.* Lucy Podmore. E-mail Lucy.Podmore@nisd.net; *Past Chair* Renee Dyer, Weslaco East High School, 810 S. Pleasantview Dr., Weslaco 78596. E-mail rdyer@wisd.us.

Address correspondence to Texas Lib. Assn., 3355 Bee Cave Rd., Suite 401, Austin 78746. Tel. 512-328-1518, fax 512-328-8852, e-mail tla@txla.org.

World Wide Web http://www.txla.org/groups/tasl.

Utah

Utah Educ. Lib. Media Assn. Memb. 500+. Publication. *UELMA Works* (q.).

Pres. Selena Campbell, Northridge High School, 2430 N Hill Field Rd., Layton 84041. Tel. 801-402-8588, e-mail secampbell@dsdmail.net; *Pres.-Elect* Lorraine Wyness, Taylorsville High School, 5225 S Redwood Rd., Taylorsville 84123. Tel. 385-646-6929, e-mail lwyness@graniteschools.org; *Past Pres.* Sarah Herron, East High School, 870 S. 1300 E., Salt Lake City 84102. Tel. 801-583-1661, e-mail sarah.herron@slcschools.org; *Exec. Dir.* Larry Jeppesen. Tel. 435-512-6809, e-mail larry.jeppesen@comcast.net.

Address correspondence to the executive director.

World Wide Web http://www.uelma.org.

Vermont

Vermont School Lib. Assn. (formerly Vermont Educ. Media Assn.). Memb. 220+. Term of Office. May–May.

Pres. Cheryl Kissel, Emily Dean Morse Memorial Lib., 37 Cross St., Northfield 05663. Tel. 802-485-9000 ext. 2121, e-mail KisselC@wssu.org; *Pres.-Elect* Donna Sullivan-Macdonald. E-mail dmacdonald@sbschools.net; *Secy.* Susan Monmaney. E-mail susanm@mpsvt.org; *Treas.* Megan Sutton, Weybridge Elementary School Lib., 210 Quaker Village Rd., Weybridge 05753. Tel. 802-545-2113, e-mail msutton@addisoncentralsu.org; *Past Pres.* Kathy Lawrence, Hiawatha Elementary School, 30 Hiawatha Ave., Essex Junction 05452. Tel. 802-857-7000, ext. 4208, e-mail klawrence@ccsuvt.org.

Address correspondence to the president.

World Wide Web https://vsla.wildapricot.org.

Virginia

Virginia Assn. of School Libns. (VAASL) (formerly Virginia Educ. Media Assn. [VEMA]). Memb. 1,200. Term of Office. Nov.–Nov. Publication. *VAASL Voice* (q.; memb.) *Eds.* Jennie Cooper, Hattie Garrow. E-mail VOICE@VAASL.org.

Pres. Kelly Miller. E-mail kelly.miller@vaasl.org; *Pres.-Elect* Laurie Bolt. E-mail laurie.bolt@vaasl.org; *Secy.* Kendel Lively. E-mail kendel.lively@vaasl.org; *Treas.* Kathryn Schweers. E-mail Treasurer@vaasl.org; *Past Pres.* Carolyn Vibbert. E-mail carolyn.vibbert@vaasl.org; *Exec. Dir.* Margaret Baker. E-mail executive@vaasl.org.

Address correspondence to the association, P.O. Box 2015, Staunton 24402-2015. Tel. 540-416-6109, e-mail Executive@VAASL.org.

World Wide Web http://vaasl.org.

Washington

School Lib. Div., Washington Lib. Assn. (formerly Washington Lib. Media Assn.). Memb. 700+. Term of Office. Apr.–Apr.

Chair Craig Seasholes. E-mail seasholes@ gmail.com; *Chair-Elect* Marianne Costello. E-mail costellom1@mac.com; *Secy.* Ann Hayes-Bell. E-mail ann.hayes.bell@k12.shoreline schools.org; *Past Chair* Sharyn Merrigan. E-mail smerrigan28@gmail.com.

Address correspondence to the Washington Lib. Assn. P.O. Box 33808, Seattle 98133. Tel. 206-823-1138, e-mail info@wla.org.

World Wide Web http://www.wla.org/ school-libraries.

West Virginia

School Lib. Div., West Virginia Lib. Assn. Memb. 50. Term of Office. Nov.–Nov. Publication. *WVLA School Library News* (5 a year).

Chair Lynda Suzie Martin, Brookhaven Elementary, 147 Estate Dr., Morgantown, WV 26508. Tel. 304-282-0147. E-mail library nbct@gmail.com; *Past Chair* Cathy Davis, East Fairmont Junior High School, 1 Orion Ln., Fairmont, WV 26554. Tel. 304-367-2123. E-mail davisc57@hotmail.com.

Address correspondence to the chairperson.

World Wide Web http://www.wvla.org.

Wisconsin

Wisconsin Educ. Media and Technology Assn. Memb. 1,100+. Publication. *The Digital Dispatch* (q.; memb.).

Pres. Heidi Catlin, School District of Rhinelander, 665 Coolidge Ave., Ste. B, Rhinelander 54501. Tel. 715-365-9747, e-mail rhinelander. k12.wi.us/technology.cfm; *V.P.* Michele Green, New London; *Pres.-Elect* Amy Pugh, Pewaukee; *Secy.* Peg Billing, Tomahawk; *Treas.* Renee Deschard, Monona Grove High School, 4400 Monona Dr., Monona 53716. E-mail treasurer@wemta.org; *Past Pres.* Kim Bannigan, DeForest Area School District, Administrative Ctr., 520 East Holum St., DeForest 53532. Tel. 608-842-6536, e-mail kbannigan@ deforestschools.org.

Address correspondence to WEMTA, P.O. Box 44578, Madison 53744-4578. Tel. 608-848-1232, fax 608-848-9266, e-mail wemta@ wiscow.com.

World Wide Web http://www.wemta.org.

Wyoming

School Lib. Interest Group (formerly Teacher-Libn. Interest Group), Wyoming Lib. Assn. Memb. 100+.

Group Leader Kathy Bjornestad. E-mail bjornestadk@gmail.com.

Address correspondence to the group leader.

World Wide Web http://www.wyla.org/ interest-groups.

International Library Associations

International Association of Agricultural Information Specialists

Federico Sancho Guevara, President
IAALD, P.O. Box 63, Lexington, KY 40588-0063
Fax 859-257-8379, e-mail info@iaald.org
World Wide Web http://www.iaald.org

Object

The International Association of Agricultural Information Specialists (IAALD) facilitates professional development of and communication among members of the agricultural information community worldwide. Its goal is to enhance access to and use of agriculture-related information resources. To further this mission, IAALD will promote the agricultural information profession, support professional development activities, foster collaboration, and provide a platform for information exchange. Founded 1955.

Membership

Memb. 400+ in more than 75 countries. Dues (Inst.) US$130; (Indiv.) US$60.

Publication

Agricultural Information Worldwide (q.) (memb.).

International Association of Law Libraries

Jeroen Vervliet, President
P.O. Box 5709, Washington, DC 20016
E-mail j.vervliet@ppl.nl
World Wide Web http://www.iall.org

Object

The International Association of Law Libraries (IALL) is a worldwide organization of librarians, libraries, and other persons or institutions concerned with the acquisition and use of legal information emanating from sources other than their jurisdictions and from multinational and international organizations.

IALL's purpose is to facilitate the work of librarians who acquire, process, organize, and provide access to foreign legal materials. IALL has no local chapters but maintains liaison with national law library associations in many countries and regions of the world.

Membership

More than 800 members in more than 50 countries on five continents.

Officers

Pres. Jeroen Vervliet, Peace Palace Lib., Carnegieplein 2, 2517 KJ The Hague, Netherlands. Tel. 31-70-302-4242, e-mail j.vervliet@ppl. nl; *V.P.* Barbara Garavaglia, Univ. of Michigan Law Lib., Ann Arbor 48109-1210. Tel. 734 764-9338, fax 734 764-5863, e-mail bvaccaro@umich.edu; *Secy.* David Gee, Institute of Advanced Legal Studies, Univ. of London,

17 Russell Sq., London WC1B 5DR, United Kingdom. Tel. +44 (0)20 7862 5822, fax +44 (0)20 7862 5770, e-mail David.Gee@sas. ac.uk; *Treas.* Kurt Carroll, Lib. of Congress, Washington, DC 20540. Tel. +1 202-707-1494, e-mail kcarr@loc.gov.

Board of Directors

Daniel Boyer, Nahum Gelber Law Lib., McGill Univ.; Lily Echiverri, Univ. of the Philippines, Quezon City; Mark D. Engsberg (ex-officio), MacMillan Law Lib., Emory School of Law, Atlanta; Michel Fraysse, Université Toulouse 1 Capitole Libs.; Ryan Harrington, UNCITRAL Law Lib., Vienna International Centre; Kerem Kahvecioglu, Istanbul Bilgi Univ., Sisli, Istanbul; Petal Kinder, High Court of Australia, Canberra; Gloria Orrego-Hoyos, Law School, Univ. de San Andrés, Buenos Aires.

Publication

International Journal of Legal Information (IJLI) (3 a year; memb.).

IALL Newsletter (3 a year; memb.).

International Association of Music Libraries, Archives, and Documentation Centres

Pia Shekhter, Secretary-General
Gothenburg University Library, P.O. Box 210, SE 405 30 Gothenburg, Sweden
Tel. 46-31-786-4057, cell 46-703-226-092, fax 46-31-786-40-59, e-mail secretary@iaml.info.
World Wide Web http://www.iaml.info.

Object

The object of the International Association of Music Libraries, Archives, and Documentation Centres (IAML) is to promote the activities of music libraries, archives, and documentation centers and to strengthen the cooperation among them; to promote the availability of all publications and documents relating to music and further their bibliographical control; to encourage the development of standards in all areas that concern the association; and to support the protection and preservation of musical documents of the past and the present.

Membership

Memb. 1,700.

Officers

Pres. Barbara Dobbs Mackenzie, *Répertoire International de Littérature Musicale* (*RILM*), New York. E-mail president@iaml.info; *Pres.-* *Elect* Stanis aw Hrabia, Uniwersytet Jagiello ski, Kraków. E-mail presidentelect@iaml. info; *Secy.-Gen.* Pia Shekhter, Gothenburg Univ. Lib., Box 210, SE 405 30 Gothenburg. Tel. 46-31-786-40-57, e-mail secretary@iaml. info; *Treas.* Thomas Kalk, Stadtbüchereien Düsseldorf. E-mail treasurer@iaml.info; *V.P.s* Jane Gottlieb, The Juilliard School, New York; Joseph Hafner, McGill Univ., Montréal; Balázs Mikusi, National Széchényi Lib., Budapest; Rupert Ridgewell, British Lib., London.

Publication

Fontes Artis Musicae (q.; memb.). *Ed.* James P. Cassaro, Univ. of Pittsburgh, B-30 Music Bldg., Pittsburgh, PA 15260. Tel. 412-624-4131, e-mail fontes@iaml.info.

Professional Branches

Archives and Music Documentation Centres. *Chair* Marie Cornaz, Bibliothèque Royale de Belgique, Brussels. E-mail archives@ iaml.info.

Broadcasting and Orchestra Libraries. *Chair* Nienke de Boer, Het Balletorkest, Amsterdam. E-mail broadcasting-orchestra@iaml. info.

Libraries in Music Teaching Institutions. *Chair* Johan Eeckeloo, Koninklijk Conservatorium, Brussels. E-mail teaching@iaml.info.

Public Libraries. *Chair* Carolyn Dow, Polley Music Lib., Lincoln City Libs., Lincoln, Neb. E-mail public-libraries@iaml.info.

Research Libraries. *Chair* Thomas Leibnitz. Musiksammlung der Österreichischen Nationalbibliothek, Vienna. E-mail research-libraries@iaml.info.

Subject Commissions

Audio-Visual Materials. *Chair* Andrew Justice. Univ. of Southern California, Los Angeles. E-mail ajustice@usc.edu.

Bibliography. *Chair* Rupert Ridgewell, British Lib., London. E-mail bibliography@iaml. info.

Cataloguing. *Chair* Joseph Hafner. McGill Univ., Montreal. E-mail cataloguing@iaml. info.

Service and Training. *Chair* Jane Gottlieb. Juilliard School, New York. E-mail service@ iaml.info.

Sub-commission on Unimarc. *Chair* Isabelle Gauchet Doris. Centre de Documentation de la Musique Contemporaine, Paris. E-mail isabelle.gauchet.doris@cdmc.asso.fr.

International Association of School Librarianship

Kathleen Combs, Executive Director
65 E. Wacker Place, Suite 1900, Chicago, IL 60601
e-mail iasl@mlahq.org
World Wide Web http://www.iasl-online.org

Mission and Objectives

The mission of the International Association of School Librarianship (IASL) is to provide an international forum for those interested in promoting effective school library programs as viable instruments in the education process. IASL also provides guidance and advice for the development of school library programs and the school library profession. IASL works in cooperation with other professional associations and agencies.

Membership is worldwide and includes school librarians, teachers, librarians, library advisers, consultants, education administrators, and others who are responsible for library and information services in schools. The membership also includes professors and instructors in universities and colleges where there are programs for school librarians, and students who are undertaking such programs.

The objectives of IASL are to advocate the development of school libraries throughout all countries; to encourage the integration of school library programs into the instruction and curriculum of the school; to promote the professional preparation and continuing education of school library personnel; to foster a sense of community among school librarians in all parts of the world; to foster and extend relationships between school librarians and other professionals in connection with children and youth; to foster research in the field of school librarianship and the integration of its findings with pertinent knowledge from related fields; to promote the publication and dissemination of information about successful advocacy and program initiatives in school librarianship; to share information about programs and materials for children and youth throughout the international community; and to initiate and coordinate activities, conferences, and other projects in the field of school librarianship and information services.

Founded 1971.

Membership

Approximately 600.

Officers

Pres. Katy Manck, Independent Book Reviewer, Gilmer, Tex. Email: katyroo@gmail.com or Katy.Manck@gmail.com; *V.P. Assn. Operations* Mihaela Banek Zorica, Univ. of Zagreb, Faculty of Humanities and Social Sciences, Dept. of Information Sciences, Zagreb, Croatia. E-mail mbanek@ffzg.hr; *V.P. Assn. Relations* Albert Boekhorst, Brasil, Netherlands. E-mail albertkb@gmail.com; *V.P. Advocacy and Promotion* Patricia Carmichael, Queensland, Australia. E-mail isabell.rina@gmail.com or iasl.giggle.it@gmail.com; *Treas.* Suzanne Johnson, George F. Johnson Memorial Lib., Endicott, N.Y. E-mail impedogs@yahoo.com.

Regional Board of Directors

Jerry Mathema, Africa; Hanna Chaterina George, Asia; Dianne Oberg, Canada; Paulette Stewart, Latin America/Caribbean; Annie Tam, East Asia; Vanja Jurilj, Europe; Ayse Yuksel-Durukan, North Africa/Middle East; Susan La Marca, Oceania; Tom Adamich, USA; Madhu Bhargava, International Schools.

Publications

School Libraries Worldwide (http://www.iasl-online.org/publications/slw/index.html), the association's refereed research and professional journal (2 a year; memb.).

IASL Newsletter (http://www.iasl-online.org/publications/newsletter.html) (3 a year; memb.).

International Association of Scientific and Technological University Libraries (IATUL)

Reiner Kallenborn, President
World Wide Web http://www.iatul.org

Object

The main object of the International Association of Scientific and Technological University Libraries (IATUL) is to provide a forum where library directors and senior managers can meet to exchange views on matters of current significance and to provide an opportunity for them to develop a collaborative approach to solving problems. IATUL also welcomes into membership organizations that supply services to university libraries, if they wish to be identified with the association's activities.

Membership

250+ in 60 countries.

Officers

Pres. Reiner Kallenborn, Technische Universität München, Munich, Germany. E-mail kallenborn@ub.tum.de; *V.P.* Gwendolyn Ebbett, Univ. of Windsor, Ontario, Canada. E-mail gebbett@uwindsor.ca; *Secy.* Elisha R. T. Chiware, Cape Peninsula Univ. of Technology, South Africa. E-mail ChiwareE@cput.ac.za; *Treas.* Sharon Bostick, Illinois Institute of Technology, Chicago. E-mail sbostick@iit.edu.

Board Members

Officers; Shirley C. W. Wong, The Hong Kong Polytechnic Univ.; Howard Amos, Univ. of Otago, Dunedin, New Zealand; Anne Horn, Univ. of Sheffield, Sheffield, UK; Jill Benn, Univ. of Western Australia, Perth.

Publication

IATUL Conference Proceedings (at http://iatul.org/conferences/pastconferences/) (ann.).

International Council on Archives

David A. Leitch, Secretary-General
60 rue des Francs-Bourgeois, 75003 Paris, France
Tel. 33-1-40-27-63-06, fax 33-1-42-72-20-65, e-mail ica@ica.org
World Wide Web http://www.ica.org

Object

The mission of the International Council on Archives (ICA) is to establish, maintain, and strengthen relations among archivists of all lands, and among all professional and other agencies or institutions concerned with the custody, organization, or administration of archives, public or private, wherever located. Established 1948.

Membership

Memb. Approximately 1,400 (representing nearly 200 countries and territories).

Officers

Pres. David Fricker, Australia; *V.P.s* M. Normand Charbonneau, Canada; Henri Zuber, France; *Secy.-Gen.* David Leitch, France; *Deputy Secy.-Gen.* Margaret Crockett.

Board Members

Officers; Hamad Bin Mohammed Al-Dhawyani, Oman; Opeta Alefaio, Fiji; Alexander Lukas Bieri, Switzerland; Paola Caroli, Italy; Eric Chin Sze Choong, Singapore; Mercedes De Vega, Mexico; Abdulla A. Kareem El Reyes, United Arab Emirates; Emilie Gagnet Leumas, Usa; Mustari Irawan, Indonesia; Takeo Katoh, Japan; Kelvin L. White, Usa; Hervé Lemoine, France; Antoine Lumenganeso Kiobe, Congo; Milovan Misic, Switzerland; Ivan Munhamo Murambiwa, Zimbabwe; Vilde Ronge, Norway; Günther Schefbeck, Austria; Fina Sola I Gasset, Spain; David Sutton, United Kingdom; Rita Tjien-Fooh, Suriname; Karel Velle, Belgium; Amatuni Virabyan, Armenia; Saroja Wettasinghe, Sri Lanka; Lara Wilson, Canada; Atakilty Assefa Asgedom (ex-officio), Ethiopia.

Publications

Comma (memb.) (2 a year, memb.).
Flash (2 a year; memb.).
ICA Newsletter (mo.).
Conference Papers and Proceedings.

International Federation of Film Archives
(Fédération Internationale des Archives du Film)

Secretariat, 42 rue Blanche, B-1060 Brussels, Belgium
Tel. 32-2-538-30-65, fax 32-2-534-47-74, e-mail info@fiafnet.org
World Wide Web http://www.fiafnet.org

Object

Founded in 1938, the International Federation of Film Archives (FIAF) brings together not-for-profit institutions dedicated to rescuing films and any other moving-image elements considered both as cultural heritage and as historical documents.

FIAF is a collaborative association of the world's leading film archives whose purpose has always been to ensure the proper preservation and showing of motion pictures. More than 150 archives in more than 75 countries collect, restore, and exhibit films and cinema documentation spanning the entire history of film.

FIAF seeks to promote film culture and facilitate historical research, to help create new archives around the world, to foster training and expertise in film preservation, to encourage the collection and preservation of documents and other cinema-related materials, to develop cooperation between archives, and to ensure the international availability of films and cinema documents.

Officers

V.P./Pres.-Elect Eric Le Roy; *Secy.-Gen.* Michael Loebensten; *Treas.* Jon Wengström.

Address correspondence to Christophe Dupin, Senior Administrator, c/o FIAF Secretariat. E-mail c.dupin@fiafnet.org.

Publications

Journal of Film Preservation. Ed. Elaine Burrows. E-mail jfp.editor@fiafnet.org.
International Index to Film Periodicals. (OVID).
FIAF International Index to Film Periodicals. (ProQuest).
International Index to Television Periodicals database.
Treasures from the Film Archives database.

For additional FIAF publications, see http://www.fiafnet.org.

International Federation of Library Associations and Institutions

Gerald Leitner, Secretary-General
P.O. Box 95312, 2509 CH The Hague, Netherlands
Tel. 31-70-314-0884, fax 31-70-383-4827, e-mail ifla@ifla.org
World Wide Web http://www.ifla.org

Object

The object of the International Federation of Library Associations and Institutions (IFLA) is to promote international understanding, cooperation, discussion, research, and development in all fields of library activity, including bibliography, information services, and the education of library personnel, and to provide a body through which librarianship can be represented in matters of international interest. IFLA is the leading international body representing the interests of library and information services and their users. It is the global voice of the library and information profession. Founded 1927.

Officers

Pres. Donna Scheeder, Lib. Strategies International, Washington, DC; *Pres.-Elect* Glòria Pérez-Salmerón, Federación Española de Sociedades de Archivística, Biblioteconomía, Documentación y Museística, Spain; *Treas.* Christine Mackenzie, Public Libraries Victoria Network, Australia; *Past Pres.* Sinikka Sipilä, Finnish Lib. Assn.

IFLA Journal (4 a year).

IFLA Professional Reports.

IFLA Publications Series.

IFLA Series on Bibliographic Control.

Governing Board

Margaret Allen (Australia), Kirsten Boelt (Denmark), Loida Garcia-Febo (USA), Ágnes Hajdu Barát (Hungary), Ngian Lek Choh (Singapore), Andrew McDonald (United Kingdom), Ellen Ndeshi Namhila (Namibia), Victoria Owen (Canada), Christine Wellems (Germany), plus the chairs of the IFLA Professional Committee and divisions.

Publications

IFLA Annual Report.

Global Studies in Libraries and Information (irreg.).

American Membership

Associations

American Lib. Assn., Assn. for Lib. and Info. Science Educ., Assn. of Research Libs., Chief Officers of State Lib. Agencies, Medical Lib. Assn., Special Libs. Assn., Urban Libs. Council, Chinese American Libns. Assn., Polish American Lib. Assn.

Institutional Members

More than 100 libraries and related institutions are institutional members or consultative bodies and sponsors of IFLA in the United States (out of a total of more than 1,000 globally), and more than 100 are individual affiliates (out of a total of more than 300 affiliates globally).

International Organization for Standardization

Kevin McKinley, Secretary-General
ISO Central Secretariat, Chemin de Blandonnet 8, CP 401
1214 Vernier, Geneva, Switzerland
Tel. 41-22-749-01-11, fax 41-22-733-34-30, e-mail central@iso.org
World Wide Web http://www.iso.org

Object

The International Organization for Standardization (ISO) is a worldwide federation of national standards bodies, founded in 1947, at present comprising 163 members, one in each country. The object of ISO is to promote the development of standardization and related activities in the world with a view to facilitating international exchange of goods and services, and to developing cooperation in the spheres of intellectual, scientific, technological, and economic activity. The scope of ISO covers international standardization in all fields except electrical and electronic engineering standardization, which is the responsibility of the International Electrotechnical Commission (IEC). The results of ISO technical work are published as international standards.

Officers

Pres. Zhang Xiaogang, China; *Pres.-Elect* John Walter, Canada; *V.P. (Policy)* Scott Steedman, United Kingdom; *V.P. (Technical Management)* Piet-Hein Daverveldt, Netherlands; *V.P. (Finance)* Bronwyn Evans, Australia; *Treas.* Dominique Christin, Switzerland; *Acting Secy.-Gen.* Kevin McKinley, Canada.

Technical Work

The technical work of ISO is carried out by more than 200 technical committees. These include:

ISO/TC 46—Information and documentation (Secretariat, Association Française de Normalization, 11 ave. Francis de Pressensé, 93571 La Plaine Saint-Denis, Cedex, France). Scope: Standardization of practices relating to libraries, documentation and information centers, indexing and abstracting services, archives, information science, and publishing.

ISO/TC 37—Terminology and language and content resources (Secretariat, INFOTERM, Aichholzgasse 6/12, 1120 Vienna, Austria, on behalf of Österreichisches Normungsinstitut). Scope: Standardization of principles, methods, and applications relating to terminology and other language and content resources in the contexts of multilingual communication and cultural diversity.

ISO/IEC JTC 1—Information technology (Secretariat, American National Standards Institute, 25 W. 43 St., 4th fl., New York, NY 10036). Scope: Standardization in the field of information technology.

Publications

ISO Annual Report.

ISOfocus (6 a year).

ISO International Standards.

ISO Online information service on World Wide Web (http://www.iso.org).

Foreign Library Associations

The following is a list of regional and national library associations around the world. A more complete list can be found in *International Literary Market Place* (Information Today, Inc.).

Regional

Africa

Standing Conference of Eastern, Central, and Southern African Lib. and Info. Assns. (SCECSAL), c/o Swaziland Lib. Assn., P.O. Box 2309, Mbabane H100, Swaziland. Tel. 268-404-2633, fax 268-404-3863, e-mail fmkhonta@uniswacc.uniswa.sz, World Wide Web http://www.swala.sz.

The Americas

Assn. of Caribbean Univ., Research, and Institutional Libs. (ACURIL), P.O. Box 21609, San Juan, Puerto Rico 00931-1906. Tel. 787-763-6199, e-mail executivesecretariat@acuril.org. *Pres.* Dorcas R. Bowler; *Exec. Secy.* Luisa Vigo-Cepeda.

Seminar on the Acquisition of Latin American Lib. Materials (SALALM), c/o *Exec. Secy.* Hortensia Calvo, SALALM Secretariat, Latin American Lib., 422 Howard Tilton Memorial Lib., Tulane Univ., 7001 Freret St., New Orleans, LA 70118-5549. Tel. 504-247-1366, fax 504-247-1367, e-mail salalm@tulane.edu, World Wide Web http://www.salalm.org. *Pres.* Luis Gonzales. E-mail luisgonz@indiana.edu.

Asia

Congress of Southeast Asian Libns. (CON-SAL), c/o Jl Salemba Raya 28A, Jakarta 10430, Indonesia. Tel. 21-310-3554, World Wide Web http://www.consal.org. *Secy.-Gen.* Aristianto Hakim.

The Commonwealth

Commonwealth Lib. Assn. (COMLA), P.O. Box 144, Mona, Kingston 7, Jamaica. Tel. 876-978-2274, fax 876-927-1926, e-mail comla72@yahoo.com. *Interim Pres.* Elizabeth Watson.

National and State Libs. Australasia, c/o State Lib. of Victoria, 328 Swanston St., Melbourne, Vic. 3000, Australia. Tel. 3-8664-7512, fax 3-9639-4737, e-mail nsla@slv.vic.gov.au, World Wide Web http://www.nsla.org.au. *Chair* Alan Smith.

U.K. Library and Archives Group on Africa (SCOLMA, formerly the Standing Conference on Lib. Materials on Africa), c/o Marion Wallace, Social Science Collections and Research, British Lib., St. Pancras, 96 Euston Rd., London NW1 2DB, England. Tel. 20-7412-7829, World Wide Web http://scolma.org.

Europe

Ligue des Bibliothèques Européennes de Recherche (LIBER) (Assn. of European Research Libs.), Postbus 90407, 2509 LK The Hague, Netherlands. Tel. 070-314-07-67, fax 070-314-01-97, e-mail liber@kb.nl, World Wide Web http://www.libereurope.eu. *Pres.* Kristiina Hormia-Poutanen. E-mail kristiina.hormia@helsinki.fi; *V.P.* Jeannette Frey. E-mail jeannette.frey@bcu.unil.ch; *Secy.-Gen.* Ann Matheson. E-mail a.matheson@tinyworld.co.uk.

National

Argentina

Asociación de Bibliotecarios Graduados de la República Argentina (ABGRA) (Assn. of Graduate Libns. of Argentina), Parana 918, 2do Piso, C1017AAT Buenos Aires. Tel. 11-4811-0043, fax 11-4816-3422, e-mail info@abgra.org.ar, World Wide Web http://www.abgra.org.ar. *Pres.* Antonio Bellofatto; *V.P.* Tatiana María Carsen; *Secy.-Gen.* Mirta Estela Villalba.

Australia

Australian Lib. and Info. Assn., Box 6335, Kingston, ACT 2604. Tel. 2-6215-8222, fax 2-6282-2249, e-mail enquiry@alia.org.au, World Wide Web http://www.alia.org.au. *Pres.* Damian Lodge; *CEO* Sue McKerracher. E-mail sue.mckerracher@alia.org.au.

Australian Society of Archivists, P.O. Box A623, Sydney South, NSW 1235. Tel. 618-8411-5550, e-mail office@archivists.org.au, World Wide Web http://www.archivists.org.au. *Pres.* Kylie Percival; *V.P.* Adelaide Parr.

Austria

Österreichische Gesellschaft für Dokumentation und Information (Austrian Society for Documentation and Info.), c/o OGDI, Wollzeile 1-3, P.O. Box 43, 1022 Vienna. E-mail office@oegdi.at, World Wide Web http://www.oegdi.at. *Secy.-Gen.* Hermann Huemer. E-mail hermann.huemer@oegdi.at.

Vereinigung Österreichischer Bibliothekarinnen und Bibliothekare (VOEB) (Assn. of Austrian Libns.), Vorarlberg State Lib., Fluherstr. 4, 6900 Bregenz. E-mail voeb@ub.tuwein.ac.at, World Wide Web http://www.univie.ac.at/voeb/php. *Pres.* Werner Schlacher, Universitätsbibliothek Graz, Universitätsplatz 3, 8010 Graz. E-mail werner.schlacher@uni-graz.at.

Bangladesh

Bangladesh Assn. of Libns., Info. Scientists and Documentalists (BALID), 67/B, Rd. 9/A, Dhanmondi, Dhaka 1209. *Chair* Mirza Mohd Rezaul Islam. E-mail balidbd@gmail.com.

Barbados

Lib. Assn. of Barbados, P.O. Box 827E, Bridgetown, Barbados. E-mail milton@uwichill.edu.bb. *Pres.* Junior Browne.

Belgium

Archief- en Bibliotheekwezen in België (Belgian Assn. of Archivists and Libns.), Keizerslaan 4, 1000 Brussels. Tel. 2-519-53-93, fax 2-519-56-10.

Association Belge de Documentation/Belgische Vereniging voor Documentatie (Belgian Assn. for Documentation), Chaussée de Wavre 1683, B-1160 Brussels. Tel. 2-675-58-62, fax 2-672-74-46, e-mail abdbvd@abd-bvd.be, World Wide Web http://www.abd-bvd.be. *Pres.* Guy Delsaut. E-mail guy.delsaut@skynet.be; *Secy.-Gen.* Marc Van Den Bergh. E-mail mvdbergh@serv.be.

Association Professionnelle des Bibliothécaires et Documentalistes (Assn. of Libns. and Documentation Specialists), Chaussée de Charleroi 85, 5000 Namur, Belgique. Tel. 71-52-31-93, fax 71-52-23-07, World Wide Web http://www.apbd.be. *Pres.* Françoise Dury.

Vlaamse Vereniging voor Bibliotheek-, Archief-, en Documentatiewezen (Flemish Assn. of Libns., Archivists, and Documentalists), Statiestraat 179, B-2600 Berchem, Antwerp. Tel. 3-281-44-57, e-mail vvbad@vvbad.be, World Wide Web http://www.vvbad.be. *Coord.* Bruno Vermeeren.

Belize

Belize National Lib. Service and Info. System (BNLSIS), P.O. Box 287, Belize City. Tel. 223-4248, fax 223-4246, e-mail nls@btl.net, World Wide Web http://www.nlsbze.bz. *Chief Libn.* Joy Ysaguirre.

Bolivia

Centro Nacional de Documentación Cientifica y Tecnológica (National Scientific and Technological Documentation Center), Av. Mariscal Santa Cruz 1175, Esquina c Ayacucho, La Paz. Tel. 02-359-583, fax 02-359-586, e-mail iiicndct@huayna.umsa.edu.bo, World Wide Web http://www.bolivian.com/industrial/cndct.

Bosnia and Herzegovina

Drustvo Bibliotekara Bosne i Hercegovine (Libns. Society of Bosnia and Herzegovina), Zmaja od Bosne 8B, 71000 Sarajevo. Tel. 33-275-5325, fax 33-212-435, e-mail nubbih@nub.ba, World Wide Web http://www.nub.ba. *Pres.* Nevenka Hajdarovic. E-mail nevenka@nub.ba.

Botswana

Botswana Lib. Assn., Box 1310, Gaborone. Tel. 371-750, fax 371-748, World Wide Web http://www.bla.org.bw. *Pres.* Kgomotso Radijeing. E-mail president@bla.org.bw.

Brazil

Associação dos Arquivistas Brasileiros (Assn. of Brazilian Archivists), Av. Presidente Vargas 1733, Sala 903, 20210-030 Rio de Janiero RJ. Tel. 21-2507-2239, fax 21-3852-2541, e-mail aab@aab.org.br, World Wide Web http://www.aab.org.br. *Pres.* Margareth da Silva.

Brunei Darussalam

Persatuan Perpustakaan Negara Brunei Darussalam (National Lib. Assn. of Brunei), c/o Class 64 Lib., SOASC, Jalan Tengah, Bandar Seri Begawan BS8411. Fax 2-222-330, e-mail pobox.bla@gmail.com, World Wide Web http://bruneilibraryassociation.word press.com. *Hon. Secy.* Hjh Rosnani. E-mail rosnaniy@hotmail.com.

Cameroon

Assn. des Bibliothécaires, Archivistes, Documentalistes et Muséographes du Cameroun (Assn. of Libns., Archivists, Documentalists, and Museum Curators of Cameroon), BP 14077, Yaoundé. World Wide Web http://www.abadcam.sitew.com. *Pres.* Jérôme Ndjock.

Chile

Colegio de Bibliotecarios de Chile (Chilean Lib. Assn.), Avda. Diagonal Paraguay 383, Torre 11, Oficina 122, 6510017 Santiago. Tel. 2-222-5652, e-mail cbc@bibliotecarios.cl, World Wide Web http://www.bibliotecarios. cl. *Pres.* Gabriela Pradenas Bobadilla; *Secy.-Gen.* Victor Candia Arancibia.

China

Lib. Society of China, 33 Zhongguancun S, Beijing 100081. Tel. 10-8854-5283, fax 10-6841-7815, e-mail ztxhmsc@nlc.gov. cn, World Wide Web http://www.nlc.gov.cn. *Dir.* Zhou Heping.

Colombia

Asociación Colombiana de Bibliotecólogos y Documentalistas (Colombian Assn. of Libns. and Documentalists), Calle 21, No. 6-58, Oficina 404, Bogotá D.C. Tel. 1-282-3620, fax 1-282-5487, e-mail secretaria@ ascolbi.org, World Wide Web http://www. ascolbi.org. *Pres.* Marisol Goyeneche Reina.

Congo (Republic of)

Assn. des Bibliothécaires, Archivistes, Documentalistes et Muséologues du Congo (ABADOM) (Assn. of Librarians, Archivists, Documentalists, and Museologists of Congo), BP 3148, Kinshasa-Gombe. *Pres.* Desire Didier Tengeneza. E-mail didier teng@yahoo.fr.

Côte d'Ivoire

Direction des Archives Nationales et de la Documentation, BP V 126, Abidjan. Tel. 20-21-75-78. *Dir.* Venance Bahi Gouro.

Croatia

Hrvatsko Knjiznicarsko Drustvo (Croatian Lib. Assn.), c/o National and Univ. Lib., Hrvatske bratske zajednice 4, 10 000 Zagreb. Tel./fax 1-615-93-20, e-mail hkd@nsk.hr, World Wide Web http://www.hkdrustvo.hr. *Pres.* Marijana Misetic. E-mail mmisetic@ffzg.hr.

Cuba

Asociación Cubana de Bibliotecarios (ASCUBI) (Lib. Assn. of Cuba), P.O. Box 6670, Havana. Tel. 7-555-442, fax 7-816-224, e-mail ascubi@bnjm.cu, World Wide Web http://www.bnjm.cu/ascubi. *Chair* Margarita Bellas Vilariño. E-mail ascubi@bnjm.cu.

Cyprus

Kypriakos Synthesmos Vivliothicarion (Lib. Assn. of Cyprus), c/o Pedagogical Academy, P.O. Box 1039, Nicosia.

Czech Republic

Svaz Knihovniku a Informacnich Pracovniku Ceske Republiky (SKIP) (Assn. of Lib. and Info. Professionals of the Czech Republic),

National Lib., Klementinum 190, 110 00 Prague 1. Tel. 221-663-379, fax 221-663-175, e-mail skip@nkp.cz, World Wide Web http://skipcr.cz. *Pres.* Roman Giebisch. E-mail roman.giebisch@nkp.cz.

Denmark

Arkivforeningen (Archives Society), c/o Rigsarkivet, Rigsdagsgarden 9, 1218 Copenhagen. Tel. 3392-3310, fax 3315-3239, World Wide Web http://www.arkivarforeningen. no. *Chair* Lars Schreiber Pedersen. E-mail lape02@frederiksberg.dk.

Danmarks Biblioteksforening (Danish Lib. Assn.), Vartov, Farvergade 27D, 1463 Copenhagen K. Tel. 3325-0935, fax 3325-7900, e-mail db@db.dk, World Wide Web http://www.db.dk. *Pres.* Steen Bording Andersen. E-mail sba@byr.aarhus.dk.

Danmarks Forskningsbiblioteksforening (Danish Research Lib. Assn.), c/o Statsbiblioteket, Tangen 2, 8200 Arhus N. Tel. 89-46-22-07, e-mail df@statsbiblioteket.dk, World Wide Web http://www.dfdf.dk. *Pres.* Michael Cotta-Schønberg. E-mail mcs@kb.dk; *Secy.* Hanne Dahl.

Dansk Musikbiblioteks Forening (Assn. of Danish Music Libs.), c/o Koge Lib., Kirkestr. 18, 4600 Koge. E-mail sekretariat @dmbf.nu, World Wide Web http://www.dmbf.nu. *Pres.* Emilie Wieth-Knudsen. E-mail emwk@ltk.dk.

Kommunernes Skolebiblioteksforening (Assn. of Danish School Libs.), Farvergade 27 D, 2 sal, 1463 Copenhagen K. Tel. 33-11-13-91, e-mail ksbf@ksbf.dk, World Wide Web http://www.ksbf.dk. *Dir.* Gitte Frausing. E-mail gf@ksbf.dk.

Ecuador

Asociación Ecuatoriana de Bibliotecarios (Ecuadoran Lib. Assn.), c/o Casa de la Cultura Ecuatoriana, Casillas 87, Quito. E-mail asoecubiblio@gmail.com. *Pres.* Eduardo Puente. E-mail epuente@flacso.edu.ec.

El Salvador

Asociación de Bibliotecarios de El Salvador (ABES) (Assn. of Salvadorian Libns.), Jardines de la Hacienda Block D pje, 19 No. 158, Ciudad Merliot, Antiguo Cuscatlan,

La Libertad. Tel. 503-2534-8924, fax 523-2228-2956, e-mail abeselsalvador@gmail. com. *Co-Chairs* Ernesto Jonathan Menjivar, Ana Yensi Vides.

Finland

Suomen Kirjastoseura (Finnish Lib. Assn.), Runeberginkatu 15 A 23, 00100 Helsinki. Tel. 44-522-2941, e-mail info@fla.fi, World Wide Web http://www.fla.fi. *Exec. Dir.* Sinikka Sipilä.

France

Association des Archivistes Français (Assn. of French Archivists), 8 rue Jean-Marie Jego, 75013 Paris. Tel. 1-46-06-39-44, fax 1-46-06-39-52, e-mail secretariat@ archivistes.org, World Wide Web http:// www.archivistes.org. *Pres.* Katell Auguié; *Secy.* Marie-Edith Enderlé-Naud.

Association des Bibliothécaires Français (Assn. of French Libns.), 31 rue de Chabrol, F-75010 Paris. Tel. 1-55-33-10-30, fax 1-55-30-10-31, e-mail info@abf.asso.fr, World Wide Web http://www.abf.asso.fr. *Pres.* Anne Verneuil; *Gen. Secy.* Sophie Rat.

Association. des Professionnels de l'Information et de la Documentation (Assn. of Info. and Documentation Professionals), 25 rue Claude Tillier, F-75012 Paris. Tel. 1-43-72-25-25, fax 1-43-72-30-41, e-mail adbs@ adbs.fr, World Wide Web http://www.adbs. fr. *Co-Pres.* Anne-Marie Libmann, Véronique Mesguich; *CEO* Karine Cuney.

Germany

Arbeitsgemeinschaft der Spezialbibliotheken (Assn. of Special Libs.), c/o Herder-Institute eV, Bibliothek, Gisonenweg 5-7, 35037 Marburg. Tel. 6421-184-151, fax 6421-184-139, e-mail geschaeftsstelle@aspb.de, World Wide Web http://aspb.de. *Chair* Henning Frankenberger. E-mail frankenberger@ mpisoc.mpg.de.

Berufsverband Information Bibliothek (Assn. of Info. and Lib. Professionals), Gartenstr. 18, 72764 Reutlingen. Tel. 7121-3491-0, fax 7121-3004-33, e-mail mail@bib-info. de, World Wide Web http://www.bib-info. de. *Deputy Chairs* Tom Becker. E-mail tom. becker@fh-koeln.de; Petra Kille. E-mail

kille@ub.uni-kl.de; *Acting Managing Dir.* Bernd Raja. E-mail schleh@bib-info.de.
Deutsche Gesellschaft für Informationswissenschaft und Informationspraxis eV (German Society for Information Science and Practice eV), Windmühlstr. 3, 603294 Frankfurt-am-Main. Tel. 69-43-03-13, fax 69-490-90-96, e-mail mail@dgi-info.de, World Wide Web http://www.dgi-info.de. *Pres.* Reinhard Karger, German Research Center for Artificial Intelligence.

Deutscher Bibliotheksverband eV (German Lib. Assn.), Fritschestr. 27–28, 10585 Berlin. Tel. 30-644-98-99-10, fax 30-644-98-99-29, e-mail dbv@bibliotheksverband.de, World Wide Web http://www.bibliotheksverband. de. *Pres.* Gudrun Heute-Bluhm.

VdA—Verband Deutscher Archivarinnen und Archivare (Assn. of German Archivists), Woerthstr. 3, 36037 Fulda. Tel. 661-29-109-72, fax 661-29-109-74, e-mail info@vda.archiv. net, World Wide Web http://www.vda.archiv. net. *Chair* Irmgard Christa Becker.

Verein Deutscher Bibliothekare eV (Society of German Libns.), Universitaetsbibliothek München, Geschwister-Scholl-Platz 1, 80539 Munich. Tel. 89-2180-2420, e-mail geschaeftsstelle@vdb-online.org, World Wide Web http://www.vdb-online.org. *Chair* Klaus-Rainer Brintzinger, Munich Univ. Lib., Geschwister-Scholl-Platz 1, 80539 Munich. E-mail vorsitzender@vdb-online.org.

Ghana

Ghana Lib. Assn., Box GP 4105, Accra. Tel. 244-17-4930, e-mail ghanalibassoc@gmail. com, World Wide Web http://gla-net.org. *Pres.* Perpetua S. Dadzie; *V.P.* Samuel B. Aggrey.

Greece

Enosis Hellinon Bibliotekarion (Assn. of Greek Libns.), Skoufa 52, P.O. Box 10672, Athens. Tel./fax 210-330-2128, e-mail info@eebep.gr, World Wide Web http:// www.eebep.gr. *Pres.* George Glossa. E-mail glossiotis@gmail.com; *Gen. Secy.* Rena Choremi-Thomopoulou. E-mail rhoremi@ hotmail.com.

Guyana

Guyana Lib. Assn., c/o National Lib., P.O. Box 10240, Georgetown.

Hong Kong

Hong Kong Lib. Assn., GPO Box 10095, Hong Kong, China. E-mail hkla@hkla.org, World Wide Web http://www.hkla.org. *Pres.* Bryant McEntyre. E-mail mbmcentire@yahoo. com.

Hungary

Magyar Könyvtárosok Egyesülete (Assn. of Hungarian Libns.), H-1054, Hold u 6, Budapest. Tel./fax 1-311-8634, e-mail mke@ oszk.hu, World Wide Web http://www.mke. oszk.hu. *Pres.* Klara Bakos; *Secy. Gen.* Miklós Fehér.

Iceland

Upplysing—Felag bokasafns-og upplysingafraeoa (Information—The Icelandic Lib. and Info. Science Assn.), Lyngas 18, 210 Gardabaer. Tel. 354-864-6220, e-mail upplysing@upplysing.is, World Wide Web http://www.upplysing.is.

India

Indian Assn. of Special Libs. and Info. Centres, P-291, CIT Scheme 6M, Kankurgachi, Kolkata 700-054. Tel. 33-2362-9651, e-mail iaslic@vsnl.net, World Wide Web http://www.iaslic1955.org.in. *Pres.* Barun Mukherjee. *Gen. Secy.* Pijushkanti Panigrahi. E-mail panigrahipk@yahoo.com.

Indian Lib. Assn., A/40-41, Flat 201, Ansal Bldg., Mukerjee Nagar, New Delhi 110009. Tel./fax 11-2765-1743, e-mail dvs-srcc@ rediffmail.com, World Wide Web http:// www.ilaindia.net. *Pres.* Ashu Shokeen. E-mail shokeen_ashu@rediffmail.com; *Gen. Secy.* Pardeep Rai. E-mail raipardeep@ gmail.com.

Indonesia

Ikatan Pustakawan Indonesia (Indonesian Lib. Assn.), 11 Jalan Medan Merdeka Selatan, Jakarta 10110. Tel./fax 21-385-5729, e-mail pi2012_2015@yahoo.com, World Wide Web http://ipi.pnri.go.id.

Ireland

Cumann Leabharlann na hEireann (Lib. Assn. of Ireland), c/o 138–144 Pearce St., Dublin 2. E-mail president@libraryassociation.ie, World Wide Web http://www.libraryassociation. ie. *Pres.* Jane Cantwell. E-mail president@ libraryassociation.ie.

Israel

Israeli Center for Libs., 22 Baruch Hirsch St., P.O. Box 801, 51108 Bnei Brak. Tel. 03-6180151, fax 03-5798048, e-mail meida@ gmail.com or icl@icl.org.il; World Wide Web http://www.icl.org.il.

Italy

Associazione Italiana Biblioteche (Italian Lib. Assn.), Biblioteca Nazionale Centrale, Viale Castro Pretorio 105, 00185 Rome RM. Tel. 6-446-3532, fax 6-444-1139, e-mail aib@legalmail.it, World Wide Web http:// www.aib.it. *CEO* Enrica Manenti. E-mail manenti@aib.it.

Jamaica

Lib. and Info. Assn. of Jamaica, P.O. Box 125, Kingston 5. Tel./fax 876-927-1614, e-mail liajapresident@yahoo.com, World Wide Web http://www.liaja.org.jm. *Pres.* Viviene Kerr-Williams. E-mail vskwilliams@gmail. com.

Japan

Info. Science and Technology Assn., Sasaki Bldg., 2-5-7 Koisikawa, Bunkyo-ku, Tokyo 112-0002. Tel. 3-3813-3791, fax 3-3813-3793, e-mail infosta@infosta.or.jp, World Wide Web http://www.infosta.or.jp.

Nihon Toshokan Kyokai (Japan Lib. Assn.), 1-11-14 Shinkawa, Chuo-ku, Tokyo 104 0033. Tel. 3-3523-0811, fax 3-3523-0841, e-mail info@jla.or.jp, World Wide Web http://www.jla.or.jp. *Pres.* Shiomi Noboru.

Senmon Toshokan Kyogikai (Japan Special Libs. Assn.), c/o Japan Lib. Assn., Bldg. F6, 1-11-14 Shinkawa Chuo-ku, Tokyo 104-

0033. Tel. 3-3537-8335, fax 3-3537-8336, e-mail jsla@jsla.or.jp, World Wide Web http://www.jsla.or.jp.

Jordan

Jordan Lib. and Info. Assn., P.O. Box 6289, Amman 11118. Tel./fax 6-462-9412, e-mail jorla_1963@yahoo.com, World Wide Web http://www.jorla.org. *Pres.* Omar Mohammad Jaradat.

Kenya

Kenya Assn. of Lib. and Info. Professionals (formerly Kenya Lib. Assn.), Buruburu, P.O. Box 49468, 00100 Nairobi. Tel. 20-733-732-799, e-mail gitachur@yahoo.com, World Wide Web http://www.kenyalibrary association.or.ke. *Chair* Rosemary Gitachu.

Korea (Democratic People's Republic of)

Lib. Assn. of the Democratic People's Republic of Korea, c/o Grand People's Study House, P.O. Box 200, Pyongyang. E-mail korea@ korea-dpr.com.

Korea (Republic of)

Korean Lib. Assn., San 60-1, Banpo-dong, Seocho-gu, Seoul 137-702. Tel. 2-535-4868, fax 2-535-5616, e-mail license@kla. kr, World Wide Web http://www.kla.kr.

Laos

Association des Bibliothécaires Laotiens (Lao Lib. Assn.), c/o Direction de la Bibliothèque Nationale, Ministry of Educ., BP 704, Vientiane. Tel. 21-21-2452, fax 21-21-2408, e-mail bailane@laotel.com.

Latvia

Latvian Libns. Assn., Terbatas iela 75, Riga LV-1001. Tel./fax 6731-2791, e-mail lbb@ lbi.lnb.lv, World Wide Web http://www.lnb. lv.

Lebanon

Lebanese Lib. Assn., P.O. Box 13-5053, Beirut 1102 2801. Tel. 1-786-456, e-mail kjaroudy@lau.edu.lb, World Wide Web http://www.llaweb.org. *Pres.* Randa Chidiac. E-mail randachidiac@usek.edu.lb.

Lesotho

Lesotho Lib. Assn., Private Bag A26, Maseru 100. Tel. 213-420, fax 340-000, e-mail s.mohai@nul.ls. *Contact* Makemang Ntsasa.

Lithuania

Lietuvos Bibliotekininku Draugija (Lithuanian Libns. Assn.), S Dariaus ir S Gireno g 12, LT-59212 Birstonas. Tel./fax 8-319-65760, e-mail lbd.sekretore@gmail.com, World Wide Web http://www.lbd.lt. *Pres.* Irma Kleiziene. E-mail bmb@is.lt.

Luxembourg

Association Luxembourgeoise des Bibliothécaires, Archivistes, et Documentalistes (ALBAD) (Luxembourg Assn. of Libns., Archivists, and Documentalists), c/o National Lib. of Luxembourg, BP 295, L-2012 Luxembourg. Tel. 352-22-97-55-1, fax 352-47-56-72, World Wide Web http://www.albad.lu. *Pres.* Jean-Marie Reding; *Secy. Gen.* Bernard Linster. E-mail bernard.linster@hotmail.com.

Malawi

Malawi Lib. Assn., c/o Univ. Libn., P.O. Box 429, Zomba. Tel. 524-265, fax 525-255, World Wide Web http://www.mala.mw. *Pres.* Fiskani Ngwire; *Secy. Gen.* Robin Mwanga.

Malaysia

Persatuan Pustakawan Malaysia (Libns. Assn. of Malaysia), P.O. Box 12545, 50782 Kuala Lumpur. Tel./fax 3-2694-7390, e-mail ppm55@po.jaring.my, World Wide Web http://ppm55.org.

Mali

Association Malienne des Bibliothécaires, Archivistes et Documentalistes (Mali Assn. of Libns., Archivists, and Documentalists) (AMBAD), BP E4473, Bamako. Tel. 20-

29-94-23, fax 20-29-93-76, e-mail dnbd@afribone.net.ml.

Malta

Malta Lib. and Info. Assn. (MaLIA), c/o Univ. of Malta Lib., Msida MSD 2080. E-mail info@malia-malta.org, World Wide Web http://www.malia-malta.org. *Chair* Mark Camilleri.

Mauritania

Association Mauritanienne des Bibliothécaires, Archivistes, et Documentalistes (Mauritanian Assn. of Libns., Archivists, and Documentalists), c/o Bibliothèque Nationale, BP 20, Nouakchott. Tel. 525-18-62, fax 525-18-68, e-mail bibliothequenationale@yahoo.fr.

Mauritius

Mauritius Lib. Assn., Ministry of Educ. Public Lib., Moka Rd., Rose Hill. Tel. 403-0200, fax 454-9553. *Pres.* Abdool Fareed Soogali.

Mexico

Asociación Mexicana de Bibliotecarios (Mexican Assn. of Libns.), Angel Urraza 817-A, Colonia Del Valle, Benito Juárez, Mexico DF, CP 03100. Tel. 55-55-75-33-96, e-mail correo@ambac.org.mx, World Wide Web http://www.ambac.org.mx. *Pres.* María Asunción Mendoza Becerra; *V.P.* Armendáriz Saúl Sánchez.

Myanmar

Myanmar Lib. Assn., c/o National Lib. of Myanmar, 85 Thirimingalar Yeiktha Lane, Kabar Aye Pagoda Rd., Yankin Township, Yangon. Tel. 1-662-470, e-mail myanmarlibraryassociation.mla@gmail.com, World Wide Web https://www.facebook.com/pages/Myanmar-Library-Association/759155320812626.

Nepal

Nepal Lib. Assn., GPO 2773, Kathmandu. Tel. 977-1-441-1318, e-mail info@nla.org.np, World Wide Web http://www.nla.org.np. *Pres.* Prakash Kumar Thapa. E-mail kyammuntar@yahoo.com.

The Netherlands

KNVI—Koninklijke Nederlandse Vereniging van Informatieprofessionals (Royal Dutch Association of Information Professionals) (formerly Nederlandse Vereniging voor Beroepsbeoefenaren in de Bibliotheek-Informatie-en Kennissector or Netherlands Assn. of Libns., Documentalists, and Info. Specialists), Mariaplaats 3, 3511 LH Utrecht. Tel. 30-233-0050, e-mail info@ knvi.net, World Wide Web http://http:// knvi.net. *Chair* Michel Wesseling. E-mail m.g.wesseling@gmail.com.

New Zealand

New Zealand Lib. Assn. (LIANZA), P.O. Box 12212, Thorndon, Wellington 6144. Tel. 4-801-5542, fax 4-801-5543, e-mail officeadmin@lianza.org.nz, World Wide Web http://www.lianza.org.nz. *Pres.* Corin Haines. E-mail librarianboy@gmail.com; *Pres.-Elect* Kris Wehipeihana. E-mail kris. wehipeihana@toiwhakaari.ac.nz; *Exec. Dir.* Joanna Matthew. E-mail joanna@lianza.org. nz.

Nicaragua

Asociación Nicaraguense de Bibliotecarios y Profesionales Afines (ANIBIPA) (Nicaraguan Assn. of Libns.), Bello Horizonte, Tope Sur de la Rotonda 1/2 cuadra abajo, J-11-57, Managua. Tel. 277-4159, e-mail anibipa@hotmail.com. *Pres.* Yadira Roque. E-mail r-yadira@hotmail.com.

Nigeria

National Lib. of Nigeria, Sanusi Dantata House, Central Business District, PMB 1, Abuja GPO 900001. Tel. 805-536-5245, fax 9-234-6773, e-mail info@nla-ng.org, World Wide Web http://www.nla-ng.org. *Pres.* Alhaji Rilwanu Abdulsala.

Norway

Arkivarforeningen (Assn. of Archivists), Fredrik Glads gate 1, 0482 Oslo. Tel. 913-16-895, e-mail imb@steria.no, World Wide Webhttp://www.arkivarforeningen.no.*Chair* Inge Manfred Bjorlin. E-mail inge.bjorlin@ gmail.com.

Norsk Bibliotekforening (Norwegian Lib. Assn.), Postboks 6540, 0606 Etterstad, Oslo. Tel. 23-24-34-30, fax 22-67-23-68, e-mail nbf@norskbibliotekforening. no, World Wide Web http://www. norskbibliotekforening.no. *Gen. Secy.* Hege Newth Nouri. E-mail hege.newth.nouri@ norskbibliotekforening.no.

Pakistan

Library Promotion Bureau, Karachi Univ. Campus, P.O. Box 8421, Karachi 75270. Tel./fax 21-3587-6301. *Pres.* Ghaniul Akram Sabzwari, 4213 Heritage Way Drive, Fort Worth, TX 76137. E-mail gsabzwari@ hotmail.com, World Wide Web http://www. lpb-pak.com,.

Panama

Asociación Panameña de Bibliotecarios (Lib. Assn. of Panama), c/o Biblioteca Interamericana Simón Bolivar, Estafeta Universitaria, Panama City. E-mail biblis2@arcon.up.ac. pa, World Wide Web https://www.facebook. com/asociacionpanamenabibliotecarios/ info.

Paraguay

Asociación de Bibliotecarios Graduados del Paraguay (Assn. of Paraguayan Graduate Libns.), Facultad Politecnica, Universidad Nacional de Asunción, 2160 San Lorenzo. Tel. 21-585-588, e-mail abigrap@pol.una. py, World Wide Web http://www.pol.una.py/ abigrap. *Chair* Emilce Sena Correa. E-mail esena@pol.una.py.

Peru

Asociación de Archiveros del Perú (Peruvian Assn. of Archivists), Av. Manco Capac No. 1180,Dpto 201,La Victoria,Lima.Tel.1-472-8729, fax 1-472-7408, e-mail contactos @adapperu.com. *Pres.* Juan Manuel Serrano Valencia.

Philippines

Assn. of Special Libs. of the Philippines, c/o Goethe-Institut Philippinen, G/4-5/F Adamson Centre, 121 Leviste St., Salcedo Village,

1227 Makati City. Tel. 2-840-5723, e-mail aslpboard@yahoo.com.ph, World Wide Web http://aslpwiki.wikispaces.com. *Pres.* Brinerdine G. Alejandrino. Philippine Libns. Assn., Room 301, National Lib. Bldg., T. M. Kalaw St., 1000 Ermita, Manila. Tel. 525-9401. World Wide Web http://plai.org.ph. *Pres.* Elizabeth R. Peralejo.

Poland

Stowarzyszenie Bibliotekarzy Polskich (Polish Libns. Assn.), al Niepodleglosci 213, 02-086 Warsaw. Tel. 22-825-83-74, fax 22-825-53-49, e-mail biuro@sbp.pl, World Wide Web http://www.sbp.pl. *Chair* Elizabeth Stefanczyk. E-mail e.stefanczyk@bn.org.pl; *Secy. Gen.* Marzena Przybysz.

Portugal

Associação Portuguesa de Bibliotecários, Arquivistas e Documentalistas (Portuguese Assn. of Libns., Archivists, and Documentalists), Rua Morais Soares, 43C, 1 Dto e Frte, 1900-341 Lisbon. Tel. 21-816-19-80, fax 21-815-45-08, e-mail apbad@apbad.pt, World Wide Web http://www.apbad.pt.

Puerto Rico

Sociedad de Bibliotecarios de Puerto Rico (Society of Libns. of Puerto Rico), Apdo 22898, San Juan 00931-2898. Tel./fax 787-764-0000, World Wide Web http://www.sociedadbibliotecarios.org. *Pres.* Juan Vargas. E-mail juan.vargas3@upr.edu.

Russia

Rossiiskaya Bibliotechnaya Assotsiatsiya (Russian Lib. Assn.), 18 Sadovaya St., St. Petersburg 191069. Tel./fax 812-110-5861, e-mail rba@nlr.ru, World Wide Web http://www.rba.ru. *Exec. Secy.* Elena Tikhonova.

Senegal

Association Sénégalaise des Bibliothécaires, Archivistes et Documentalistes (Senegalese Assn. of Libns., Archivists, and Documentalists), BP 2006, Dakar RP, Université Cheikh Anta Diop, Dakar. Tel. 77-651-00-

33, fax 33-824-23-79, e-mail asbad200@hotmail.com, World Wide Web http://www.asbad.org. *Pres.* Lawrence Gomis Baaya; *Secy. Gen.* Alassane Ndiath.

Serbia and Montenegro

Jugoslovenski Bibliografsko Informacijski Institut, Terazije 26, 11000 Belgrade. Tel. 11-2687-836, fax 11-2687-760.

Sierra Leone

Sierra Leone Assn. of Archivists, Libns., and Info. Scientists, c/o Sierra Leone Lib. Board, Rokel St., P.O. Box 326, Freetown. Tel. 022-220-758.

Singapore

Lib. Assn. of Singapore, National Lib. Board, 100 Victoria St., No. 14-01, Singapore 188064. Tel. 6332-3255, fax 6332-3248, e-mail lassec@las.org.sg, World Wide Web http://www.las.org.sg. *Pres.* Lee Cheng Ean. E-mail president@las.org.sg.

Slovenia

Zveza Bibliotekarskih Druötev Slovenije (Union of Assns. of Slovene Libns.), Turjaöka 1, 1000 Ljubljana. Tel. 1-2001-176, fax 1-4257-293, e-mail info@zbds-zveza.si, World Wide Web http://www.zbds-zveza.si. *Pres.* Sabina Fras Popovic. E-mail sabina.fras-popovic@mb.sik.si.

South Africa

Lib. and Info. Assn. of South Africa, P.O. Box 1598, Pretoria 0001. Tel. 12-328-2010, fax 12-323-4912, e-mail liasa@liasa.org.za, World Wide Web http://www.liasa.org.za. *Pres.* Ujala Satgoor. E-mail president@liasa.org.za.

Spain

Federación Española de Archiveros, Bibliotecarios, Muséologos y Documentalistas (ANABAD) (Spanish Federation of Assns. of Archivists, Libns., Archaeologists, Museum Curators, and Documentalists), de las Huertas, 37, 28014 Madrid. Tel. 91-575-1727, fax 91-578-1615, e-mail anabad@

anabad.org, World Wide Web http://www.
anabad.org. *Pres.* Miguel Ángel Gacho San-
tamaría.

Sri Lanka

Sri Lanka Lib. Assn., Sri Lanka Professional Centre 275/75, Stanley Wijesundara
Mawatha, Colombo 7. Tel./fax 11-258-
9103, e-mail slla@slltnet.lk, World Wide
Web http://www.slla.org.lk. *Pres.* Shivanthi
Weerasinghe; *Gen. Secy.* Lilamani Amer-
asekera.

Swaziland

Swaziland Lib. Assn. (SWALA), P.O. Box
2309, Mbabane H100. Tel. 404-2633, fax
404-3863.

Sweden

Svensk Biblioteksförening Kansli (Swedish
Lib. Assn.), World Trade Center, D5, Box
70380, 107 24 Stockholm. Tel. 8-545-
132-30, fax 8-545-132-31, e-mail info@
biblioteksforeningen.org, World Wide Web
http://www.biblioteksforeningen.org. *Chair*
Calle Nathanson; *Secy. Gen.* Niclas Lindberg. E-mail nl@biblioteksforeningen.org.
Svensk Förening för Informationsspecialister
(Swedish Assn. for Info. Specialists), Box
2001, 135 02 Tyresö. E-mail kansliet@sfis.
nu, World Wide Web http://www.sfis.nu/om.
Chair Ann-Christin Karlén Gramming. E-
mail ann-christin.karlen@vinge.se.
Svenska Arkivsamfundet (Swedish Archival Society), Association Hall, Virkesvä-
gen 26, 120 30 Stockholm. E-mail info@
arkivsamfundet.se, World Wide Web http://
www.arkivsamfundet.se.

Switzerland

Bibliothek Information Schweiz/Bibliothèque
Information Suisse/Biblioteca Informazione
Swizzera/Library Information Switzerland
(BIS), Bleichemattstrasse 42, 5000 Aarau.
Tel. 41-62-823-19-38, fax 41-62-823-19-39,
e-mail info@bis.ch. *Managing Dir.* Hans
Ulrich Locher. E-mail halo.locher@bis.info.
Verein Schweizer Archivarinnen und Archivare
(Assn. of Swiss Archivists), Schweizeri-
sches Bundesarchiv, Büro Pontri GmbH,

Solohurnstr. 13, Postfach CH-3322, Urte-
nen Schönbühl. Tel. 41-31-312-26-66, fax
41-31-312-26-68, e-mail info@vsa-aas.ch,
World Wide Web http://www.vsa-aas.org.
Pres. Claudia Engler.

Taiwan

Lib. Assn. of the Republic of China (LAROC),
20 Zhongshan South Rd., Taipei 10001. Tel.
2-2361-9132, fax 2-2370-0899, e-mail lac@
msg.ncl.edu.tw, World Wide Web http://
www.lac.org.tw.

Tanzania

Tanzania Lib. Assn., P.O. Box 33433, Dar es
Salaam. Tel./fax 255-744-296-134, e-mail
tla_tanzania@yahoo.com, World Wide Web
http://www.tla.or.tz.

Thailand

Thai Lib. Assn., 1346 Akarnsongkhro 5 Rd.,
Klongchan, Bangkapi, Bangkok 10240.
Tel. 02-734-9022, fax 02-734-9021, e-mail
tla2497@yahoo.com, World Wide Web
http://tla.or.th.

Trinidad and Tobago

Lib. Assn. of Trinidad and Tobago, P.O. Box
1275, Port of Spain. Tel. 868-687-0194,
e-mail info@latt.org.tt, World Wide Web
http://www.latt.org.tt. *Pres.* Selwyn Rod-
ulfo.

Tunisia

Association Tunisienne des Documentalistes,
Bibliothécaires et Archivistes (Tunisian
Assn. of Documentalists, Libns., and Archi-
vists), BP 380, 1000 Tunis RP. Tel. 895-450.

Turkey

Türk Kütüphaneciler Dernegi (Turkish Libns.
Assn.), Necatibey Cad Elgun Sok 8/8,
06440 Kizilay, Ankara. Tel. 312-230-13-
25, fax 312-232-04-53, e-mail tkd.dernek@
gmail.com, World Wide Web http://www.
kutuphaneci.org.tr. *Pres.* Ali Fuat Kartal.

Uganda

Uganda Lib. and Info. Assn., P.O. Box 8147, Kampala. Tel. 772-488-937, e-mail info@ ulia.or.ug. *Pres.* Constant Okello-Obura; *Gen. Secy.* Simon Engitu.

Ukraine

Ukrainian Lib. Assn., Vasylkovska 12, Office 5, Code 5, 01004, Kyiv. Tel. 380-44-239-74-87, fax 380-44-35-45-47, e-mail u_b_a@ ukr.net, World Wide Web http://www.uba. org.ua.

United Kingdom

Archives and Records Assn., UK and Ireland (formerly the Society of Archivists), Prioryfield House, 20 Canon St., Taunton TA1 1SW, England. Tel. 1823-327-077, fax 1823-271-719, e-mail societyofarchivists@ archives.org.uk, World Wide Web http:// www.archives.org.uk. *Chief Exec.* John Chambers; *Chair* David Mander.

ASLIB, the Assn. for Info. Management, Howard House, Wagon Lane, Bingley BD16 1WA, England. Tel. 01274-777-700, fax 01274-785-201, e-mail support@aslib.com, World Wide Web http://www.aslib.com.

Bibliographical Society, Institute of English Studies, Senate House, Malet St., London WC1E 7HU, England. E-mail admin@ bibsoc.org.uk, World Wide Web http://www. bibsoc.org.uk. *Pres.* Henry Woudhuysen. E-mail president@bibsoc.org.uk.

Chartered Institute of Lib. and Info. Professionals (CILIP) (formerly the Lib. Assn.), 7 Ridgmount St., London WC1E 7AE, England. Tel. 20-7255-0500, fax 20-7255-0501, e-mail info@cilip.org.uk, World Wide Web http://www.cilip.org.uk. *Pres.* Jan Parry. E-mail jan.parry@cilip.org.uk; *Chief Exec.* Annie Mauger. E-mail annie.mauger@cilip. org.uk.

School Lib. Assn., 1 Pine Court, Kembrey Park, Swindon SN2 8AD, England. Tel. 1793-530-166, fax 1793-481-182, e-mail info@ sla.org.uk, World Wide Web http://www.

sla.org.uk. *Pres.* Kevin Crossley-Holland; *Chair* Karen Horsfield; *Dir.* Tricia Adams.

Scottish Lib. and Info. Council, 151 W. George St., Glasgow G2 2JJ, Scotland. Tel. 141-228-4790, e-mail info@scottishlibraries. org, World Wide Web http://www. scottishlibraries.org. *CEO* Amina Shah. E-mail a.shah@scottishlibraries.org.

Society of College, National, and Univ. Libs (SCONUL) (formerly Standing Conference of National and Univ. Libs.), 94 Euston St., London NW1 2HA, England. Tel. 20-7387-0317, fax 20-7383-3197, e-mail info@ sconul.ac.uk, World Wide Web http://www. sconul.ac.uk. *Chair* Liz Jolly; *Exec. Dir.* Ann Rossiter.

Uruguay

Agrupación Bibliotecológica del Uruguay (Uruguayan Lib. and Archive Science Assn.) and Asociación de Bibliotecólogos del Uruguay (Uruguayan Libns. Assn.), Eduardo V. Haedo 2255, CP 11200, Montevideo. Tel. 2409-9989, e-mail abu@adinet.com.uy. *Pres.* Alicia Ocaso.

Vietnam

Hôi Thu-Vien Viet Nam (Vietnam Lib. Assn.), National Lib. of Vietnam, 31 Trang Thi, Hoan Kiem, 10000 Hanoi. Tel. 4-3825-5397, fax 4-3825-3357, e-mail info@nlv. gov.vn, World Wide Web http://www.nlv. gov.vn.

Zambia

Zambia Lib. Assn., P.O. Box 38636, 10101 Lusaka. *Chair* Benson Njobvu. E-mail benson njobvu@hotmail.com.

Zimbabwe

Zimbabwe Lib. Assn., Harare City Lib., Civic Centre, Rotten Row, P.O. Box 1987, Harare. Tel. 263-773-060-307, e-mail info@zimla. co.za, World Wide Web http://zimbabwe reads.org/zimla. *Chair* T. G. Bohwa.

Directory of Book Trade and Related Organizations

Book Trade Associations, United States and Canada

For more extensive information on the associations listed in this section, see the annual edition of *Literary Market Place* (Information Today, Inc.).

AIGA—The Professional Assn. for Design (formerly American Institute of Graphic Arts), 233 Broadway, 17th floor New York, NY 10279. Tel. 212-807-1990, fax 212-807-1799, e-mail aiga@aiga.org, World Wide Web http://www.aiga.org. *Pres.* Su Mathews Hale, AIGA San Francisco. E-mail su.mathews@lippincott.com; *Treas.* Andrew Twigg, AIGA Pittsburgh. E-mail andrewtwigg@gmail.com; *Exec. Dir.* Julie Anixter, AIGA. Tel. 212 710 3100.

American Book Producers Assn. (ABPA), 151 W. 19 St., third fl., New York, NY 10011. Tel. 212-675-1363, fax 212-675-1364, e-mail office@ABPAonline.org, World Wide Web http://www.abpaonline.org. *Pres.* Richard Rothschild; *V.P.* Nancy Hall; *Treas.* Valerie Tomaselli; *Admin.* Michael Centore.

American Booksellers Assn., 333 Westchester Ave. Suite S202, White Plains, NY 10604. Tel. 800-637-0037, fax 914-417-4013, e-mail info@bookweb.org, World Wide Web http://www.bookweb.org. *Pres.* Betsy Burton, The King's English Bookshop, Salt Lake City. Tel. 801-484-9100, e-mail btke@comcast.net; *V.P./Secy.* Robert Sindelar, Third Place Books, 17171 Bothell Way NE, Lake Forest Park, WA 98155-4204. Tel. 206-366-3309, e-mail rsindelar@thirdplacebooks.com; *CEO* Oren Teicher. E-mail oren@bookweb.org.

American Literary Translators Assn. (ALTA), Univ. of Texas at Dallas, 800 W. Campbell Rd., Mail Sta. JO51, Richardson, TX 75080. Tel. 972-883-2092, fax 972-883-6303, World Wide Web http://www.utdallas.edu/alta. *Managing Dir.* Erica Mena. E-mail altacentral2014@gmail.com.

American Printing History Assn., Box 4519, Grand Central Sta., New York, NY 10163-4519. World Wide Web http://www.printinghistory.org. *Pres.* Nina Schneider; *Treas.* David Goodrich; *Secy.* Erin Schreiner; *Exec. Secy.* Lyndsi Barnes. E-mail secretary@printinghistory.org.

American Society for Indexing, 1628 E. Southern Ave., No. 9-223, Tempe, AZ 85282. Tel. 480-245-6750, e-mail info@asindexing.org, World Wide Web http://www.asindexing.org. *Pres.* Diana Witt. E-mail president@asindexing.org; *V.P./Pres.-Elect* Kendra Millis. E-mail presidentelect@asindexing.org; *Exec. Dir.* Gwen Henson. E-mail gwen@asindexing.org.

American Society of Journalists and Authors, 355 Lexington Avenue, 15th Floor, New York, NY 10017-6603. Tel. 212-997-0947, fax 212-937-2315, e-mail asjaoffice@asja.org, World Wide Web http://www.asja.org. *Pres.* Sherry Beck Paprocki. E-mail president@asja.org; *V.P.* Milt Toby. E-mail vicepresident@asja.org; *Exec. Dir.* Holly Koenig.

American Society of Media Photographers, 150 N. 2 St., Philadelphia, PA 19106. Tel. 877-771-2767, e-mail asmp@vpconnections.com, World Wide Web http://www.asmp.org. *Chair* Jenna Close. E-mail close@asmp.org; *V. Chair* Luke Copping.

E-mail copping@asmp.org; *Exec. Dir.* Tom Kennedy. E-mail kennedy@asmp.org.

American Society of Picture Professionals, 201 E. 25 St., No. 11C, New York, NY 10010. Tel. 516-500-3686, e-mail director@aspp.com, World Wide Web http://www.aspp.com. *Pres.* Cecilia de Querol. E-mail president@aspp.com; *Exec. Dir.* Darrell Perry. E-mail director@aspp.com.

American Translators Assn., 225 Reinekers Lane, Suite 590, Alexandria, VA 22314. Tel. 703-683-6100, fax 703-683-6122, e-mail ata@atanet.org, World Wide Web http://www.atanet.org. *Pres.* David C. Rumsey; *Pres.-Elect* Corinne L. McKay; *Secy.* Jane E. Maier; *Treas.* Ted R. Wozniak; *Exec. Dir.* Walter W. Bacak, Jr. E-mail walter@atanet.org.

Antiquarian Booksellers Assn. of America, 20 W. 44 St., No. 507, New York, NY 10036-6604. Tel. 212-944-8291, fax 212-944-8293, World Wide Web http://www.abaa.org. *Pres.* Mary Gilliam; *V.P./Secy.* Vic Zoschak; *Treas.* Charles Kutcher; *Exec. Dir.* Susan Benne. E-mail sbenne@abaa.org.

Assn. Media and Publishing, National Press Bldg., 529 14th Street, N.W., Suite 750, Washington, DC 20045. Tel. 202-591-2457, e-mail info@associationmediaandpublishing.org, World Wide Web http://www.associationmediaandpublishing.org. *Pres.* John Falcioni; *V.P.* Joe Vallina; *Exec. Dir.* Meredith Taylor. Tel. 703-234-4107, e-mail ExecutiveDirector@associationmediaandpublishing.org.

Assn. of American Publishers, 71 Fifth Ave., New York, NY 10003. Tel. 212-255-0200, fax 212-255-7007. Washington Office 455 Massachusetts Ave. N.W., Suite 700, Washington, DC 20001. Tel. 202-347-3375, fax 202-347-3690, World Wide Web http://www.publishers.org. *Chair* Y.S. Chi; *Vice Chair* Markus Dohle; *Treas.* W. Drake McFeely.

Assn. of American University Presses, 1412 Broadway, Suite 2135, New York, NY 10018. Tel. 212-989-1010, fax 212-989-0275, e-mail info@aaupnet.org, World Wide Web http://aaupnet.org. *Pres.* Darrin Pratt, Univ. Press of Colorado; *Pres.-Elect* Nicole Mitchell, Univ. of Washington Press; *Past Pres.* Meredith Babb, Univ. Press of Florida; *Treas.* Donna Shear, Univ. of Nebraska

Press; *Exec. Dir.* Peter Berkery. Tel. 917-288-5594, e-mail pberkery@aaupnet.org.

Assn. of Canadian Publishers, 174 Spadina Ave., Suite 306, Toronto, ON M5T 2C2. Tel. 416-487-6116, fax 416-487-8815, e-mail admin@canbook.org, World Wide Web http://www.publishers.ca. *Pres.* Matt Williams, House of Anansi Press, 110 Spadina Ave., Suite 801, Toronto, ON M5V 2M5. Tel. 416-363-4343, fax 416-363-1017, e-mail matt@anansi.ca; *V.P.* Glenn Rollans, Brush Publishing, 6531-111 St., Edmonton AB T6H 4R5. Tel. 780-989-0910, fax 780-989-0930, e-mail glenn.rollans@me.com; *Treas.* Semareh Al-Hillal, Kids Can Press, 25 Dockside Dr., Toronto, ON M5A 0B5. Tel. 416-479-6482, fax 416-960-5437, e-mail sal-hillal@kidscan.com; *Exec. Dir.* Kate Edwards. Tel. 416-487-6116 ext. 2340, e-mail kate_edwards@canbook.org.

Assn. of Educational Publishers (AEP). Merged in 2013 with the School Division of the Assn. of American Publishers (AAP).

Audio Publishers Assn., 333 Hudson Street Suite 503, New York, NY 10013. Tel. 646-688-3044, e-mail info@audiopub.org; World Wide Web http://www.audiopub.org. *Pres.* Linda Lee; *V.P.* Anthony Goff; *V.P., Member Communications* Suzanne Galvez; *Secy.* Janet Benson; *Treas.* Sean McManus; *Exec. Dir.* Michele Cobb. E-mail mcobb@audiopub.org.

Authors Guild, 31 E. 32 St., seventh fl., New York, NY 10016. Tel. 212-563-5904, fax 212-564-5363, e-mail staff@authorsguild.org, World Wide Web http://www.authorsguild.org. *Pres.* James Gleick; *V.P.* Richard Russo; *Secy.* Daniel Okrent; *Treas.* Peter Petre.

Book Industry Study Group, 1412 Broadway, 21st Floor, Office 19, New York, NY 10018. Tel. 646-336-7141, e-mail info@bisg.org, World Wide Web http://bisg.org. *Chair* Maureen McMahon, Kaplan Publishing; *V. Chair* Peter Balis, John Wiley & Sons; *Secy.* Kempton Mooney, Nielsen Book; *Treas.* Fran Toolan, Firebrand Technologies; *Exec. Dir.* Brian O'Leary. Tel. 646-336-7141 ext. 12. e-mail brian@bisg.org.

Book Manufacturers' Institute (BMI), P.O. Box 731388, Ormand Beach, FL 32173. Tel. 386-986-4552, fax 386-986-4553, World Wide Web http://www.bmibook.org. *Pres.*

Kent H. Larson, Bridgeport National Bindery; *Exec. V.P./Secy.* Daniel N. Bach; *V.P./ Pres.-Elect* James H. Fetherston, Worzalla Publishing Company; *Treas.* Paul Genovese, Lake Book Manufacturing.

Bookbuilders of Boston, 115 Webster Woods Lane, North Andover, MA 01845. Tel. 781-378-1361, fax 419-821-2171, e-mail office@bbboston.org, World Wide Web http://www.bbboston.org. *Pres.* Iris Febres. E-mail iris.febres@bbboston.org; *1st V.P.* Jackie Shepherd. E-mail jackie.shepherd@bbboston.org; *2nd V.P.* David Stirling. E-mail david.stirling@bbboston.org; *Treas.* James Taylor. E-mail james.taylor@bbboston.org; *Clerk* Kate Elwell. E-mail kate.elwell@bbboston.org.

Bookbuilders West. See Publishing Professionals Network.

Canadian Booksellers Assn. Now part of Retail Council of Canada. Toronto office: 1881 Yonge St., Suite 800. Toronto, ON M4S 3C4.

Canadian International Standard Numbers (ISNs) Agency, c/o Lib. and Archives Canada, 395 Wellington St., Ottawa, ON K1A 0N4. Tel. 866-578-7777 (toll-free) or 613-996-5115, World Wide Web http://www.collectionscanada.ca/isn/index-e.html.

Canadian Printing Industries Assn., 2-2026 Lanhier Dr., Suite 407, Orleans, ON K1A 0N6. Tel. 416-285-3219, World Wide Web http://www.cpia-aci.ca. *Chair* Sandy Stephens. E-mail sstephens@informco.com; *Secy.-Treas.* Jamie Barbieri. Tel. 866-244-3311. e-mail james.barbieri@groupepdi.com.

CBA: The Assn. for Christian Retail (formerly Christian Booksellers Association), 9240 Explorer Drive, Suite 200, Colorado Springs, CO 80920. Tel. 719-265-9895, fax 719-272-3510, e-mail info@cbaonline.org, World Wide Web http://www.cbaonline.org. *Chair* Sue Smith, Baker Book House; *V. Chair* Robin Hogan, Christian Cultural Center Bookstore.

Children's Book Council, 54 W. 39 St., 14th fl., New York, NY 10018. Tel. 212-966-1990, e-mail cbc.info@cbcbooks.org, World Wide Web http://www.cbcbooks.org. *Chair* Jon Anderson, Simon & Schuster; *V. Chair* Lauri Hornik, Dial; *Exec. Dir.* Carl Lennertz.

Christian Booksellers Association. See CBA: The Assn. for Christian Retail.

Copyright Society of the USA, 1 E. 53 St., eighth fl., New York, NY 10022. Tel. 212-354-6401, World Wide Web http://www.csusa.org. *Pres.* Nancy E. Wolff; *V.P./Pres.-Elect* Glenn Pudelka; *Secy.* Craig S. Mende; *Treas.* Naomi Jan Gray; *Exec. Dir.* Kaitland E. Kubat.

Community of Literary Magazines and Presses, 154 Christopher St., Suite 3C, New York, NY 10014. Tel. 212-741-9110, e-mail info@clmp.org, World Wide Web http://www.clmp.org. *Co-chairs* Nicole Dewey, Gerald Howard; *Exec. Dir.* Jeffrey Lependorf. E-mail jlependorf@clmp.org.

Educational Book and Media Assn. (formerly Educational Paperback Assn.), P.O. Box 3363, Warrenton, VA 20188. Tel. 540-318-7770, e-mail info@edupaperback.org, World Wide Web http://www.edupaperback.org. *Pres.* Jill Faherty; *V.P.* Joyce Skokut; *Treas.* Nancy Stetzinger; *Past Pres.* Jennifer Allen.

Evangelical Christian Publishers Assn., 9633 S. 48 St., Suite 140, Phoenix, AZ 85044. Tel. 480-966-3998, fax 480-966-1944, e-mail info@ecpa.org, World Wide Web http://www.ecpa.org. *Chair* Byron Williamson; *V. Chair* David Moberg; *Secy.* Cory Verner; *Treas.* Tammy Gaines; *Exec. Dir.* Stan Jantz.

Graphic Artists Guild, 31 West 34th St., eighth Floor, New York, NY 10001. Tel. 212-791-3400, e-mail admin@graphicartistsguild.org, World Wide Web http://www.graphicartistsguild.org. *Pres.* Lara Kisielewska. E-mail president@graphicartistsguild.org; *Admin. Dir.* Paula Hinkle. E-mail membership@graphicartistsguild.org.

Great Lakes Independent Booksellers Assn., c/o Exec. Dir. Deb Leonard, 2113 Roosevelt, Ypsilanti, MI 48197. Tel. 734-340-6397, fax 734-879-1129, e-mail deb@gliba.org, World Wide Web http://www.gliba.org. *Pres.* Kate Schlademan, The Learned Owl, 204 N Main St., Hudson, OH 44236. Tel. 330-653-2252, e-mail Kates@learnedowl.com.

Guild of Book Workers, 521 Fifth Ave., New York, NY 10175. Tel. 212-292-4444, e-mail communications@guildofbookworkers.org, World Wide Web http://www.guildofbookworkers.org. *Pres.* Bexx Caswell. E-mail president@guildofbookworkers.org; *V.P.*

Brien Beidler. E-mail vicepresident@guildofbookworkers.org; *Secy.* Katy Baum. E-mail secretary@guildofbookworkers.org.; *Treas.* Laura Bedford. E-mail treasurer@guildofbookworkers.org.

Horror Writers Assn., P.O. Box 56687, Sherman Oaks, CA 91413. E-mail hwa@horror.org, World Wide Web http://www.horror.org. *Pres.* Lisa Morton. E-mail president@horror.org; *V.P.* John Palisano . E-mail vp@horror.org; *Secy.* Joe McKinney. E-mail secretary@horror.org; *Treas.* Leslie Klinger. E-mail treasurer@horror.org.

Independent Book Publishers Assn. (formerly PMA), 1020 Manhattan Beach Blvd., Suite 204, Manhattan Beach, CA 90266. Tel. 310-546-1818, fax 310-546-3939, e-mail info@ibpa-online.org, World Wide Web http://www.ibpa-online.org. *Chair* Peter Goodman, Stone Bridge Press; *Treas.* Robert Price, Price World Publishing; *Secy.* Elizabeth Turnbull, Light Messages; *CEO* Angela Bole. E-mail angela@ibpa-online.org; *COO* Terry Nathan. E-mail terry@ibpa-online.org.

International Standard Book Numbering U.S. Agency, 630 Central Ave., New Providence, NJ 07974. Tel. 877-310-7333, fax 908-219-0188, e-mail isbn-san@bowker.com, World Wide Web http://www.isbn.org. *Dir., Identifier Services* Beat Barblan.

Jewish Book Council, 520 Eighth Ave., fourth fl., New York, NY 10018. Tel. 212-201-2920, fax 212-532-4952, e-mail jbc@jewishbooks.org, World Wide Web http://www.jewishbookcouncil.org. *Pres.* Jane Weitzman; *V.P.s* Joy Greenberg, Carol Levin, Lenore J. Weitzman; *Secy.* Elisa Spungen Bildner; *Treas.* William Daroff; *Exec. Dir.* Naomi Firestone-Teeter.

Library Binding Institute/Hardcover Binders International, see Book Manufacturers' Institute (BMI).

Midwest Independent Publishers Assn. (MIPA), P.O. Box 7132, St. Paul, MN 55107-0132. Tel. 651-917-0021, World Wide Web http://www.mipa.org. *Pres.* Pat Morris, Book Architects, Tel. 651-797-3801, e-mail pat@bookarchitects.net; *V.P.* Jerry Mevissen, Jackpine Writer's Bloc, Inc. Tel. 218-472-3400, e-mail rivermanjm@gmail.com; *Secy.* Patrick Ledray, Romanian Dragons LLC. Tel. 612.991.0564, e-mail romaniandragons@aol.com; *Treas.* Dorie McClelland, Spring Book Design. Tel. 651-457-0258, e-mail dorie@springbookdesign.com.

Miniature Book Society. Tel. 619-226-4441, e-mail member@mbs.org, World Wide Web http://www.mbs.org. *Pres.* Stephen Byrne. E-mail sb@finalscore.demon.co.uk; *V.P.* Jim Brogan; *Secy.* Gail Faulkner; *Treas.* Cathie Abney.

Minnesota Book Publishers' Roundtable. E-mail information@publishersroundtable.org, World Wide Web http://www.publishersroundtable.org. *Pres.* Jennie Goloboy, Red Sofa Literary. P.O. Box 40482, St. Paul, MN 55104. E-mail jennie@redsofaliterary.com; *V.P.* Laura Zats, Wise Ink Creative Publishing, 837 Glenwood Ave., Minneapolis, MN 55405. E-mail laura@wiseinkpub.com; *Secy.* Elizabeth Dingmann Schneider. E-mail e.schneider@redlineeditorial.com; *Treas.* Carla Valadez. E-mail carla@coffeehousepress.org.

Mountains and Plains Independent Booksellers Assn., 3278 Big Spruce Way, Park City, UT 84098. Tel. 435-649-6079, fax 435-649-6105, e-mail laura@mountainsplains.org, World Wide Web http://www.mountainsplains.org. *Pres.* Anne Holman, The King's English Bookshop, 1511 South 1500 E., Salt Lake City, UT 84105. Tel. 801-484-9100, fax 801-484-1595, e-mail books@kingsenglish.com; *V.P.* Heather Duncan. E-mail heather.duncan@tatteredcover.com; *Treas.* Danielle Foster. E-mail danielle@bkwrks.com; *Secy.* Nicole Sullivan. E-mail info@bookbardenver.com *Exec. Dir.* Laura Ayrey Burnett.

MPA—The Assn. of Magazine Media (formerly Magazine Publishers of America), 757 Third Ave., 11th fl., New York, NY 10017. Tel. 212-872-3700, e-mail mpa@magazine.org, World Wide Web http://www.magazine.org. *Chair* Stephen M. Lacy.

National Assn. of College Stores, 500 E. Lorain St., Oberlin, OH 44074-1294. Tel. 800-622-7498, 440-775-7777, fax 440-775-4769, e-mail info@nacs.org, World Wide Web http://www.nacs.org. *Pres.* Loreen J. Maxfield; *Pres.-Elect* Steve Alb; *CEO* Robert A. Walton. E-mail rwalton@nacs.org.

National Book Foundation, 90 Broad St., Suite 604, New York, NY 10004. Tel. 212-685-

0261, fax 212-213-6570, e-mail national book@nationalbook.org, World Wide Web http://www.nationalbook.org. *Chair* David Steinberger, Perseus Books Group; *Vice Chair* Morgan Entrekin, Grove/Atlantic; *Secy.* Calvin Sims; *Treas.* W. Drake McFeely; *Exec. Dir.* Lisa Lucas. E-mail llucas@nationalbook.org.

National Coalition Against Censorship (NCAC), 19 Fulton St., Suite 407, New York, NY 10038. Tel. 212-807-6222, fax 212-807-6245, e-mail ncac@ncac.org, World Wide Web http://www.ncac.org. *Dirs.* Jon Anderson, Michael Bamberger, Joan E. Bertin, Judy Blume, Susan Clare, Tim Federle, Chris Finan, Eric M. Freedman, Martha Gershun, Robie Harris, Phil Harvey, Michael Jacobs, Emily Knox Chris Peterson, Larry Siems, Emily Whitfield; *Exec. Dir.* Joan E. Bertin.

New Atlantic Independent Booksellers Assn. (NAIBA), 2667 Hyacinth St., Westbury, NY 11590. Tel. 516-333-0681, fax 516-333-0689, e-mail naibabooksellers@gmail.com, World Wide Web http://www.newatlanticbooks.com. *Pres.* Mark LaFramboise, Politics and Prose; *V.P.* Todd Dickinson, Aaron's Books; *Secy-Treas.* Bill Reilly, The River's End Bookstore; *Exec. Dir.* Eileen Dengler. E-mail NAIBAeileen@gmail.com.

New England Independent Booksellers Assn. (NEIBA), 1955 Massachusetts Ave., Cambridge, MA 02140-1405. Tel. 617-547-3642, fax 617-547-3759, e-mail steve@neba.org, World Wide Web http://www.newenglandbooks.org. *Pres.* Gillian Kohli, Wellesley Books, Wellesley, MA; *V.P.* Courtney Flynn, Trident Booksellers and Cafe, Boston, MA; *Treas.* Suzanna Hermans, Oblong Books & Music, Rhinebeck, NY; *Exec. Dir.* Steve Fischer.

New York Center for Independent Publishing (formerly the Small Press Center), c/o General Society of Mechanics and Tradesmen Lib., 20 W. 44 St., New York, NY 10036. Tel. 212-764-7021, e-mail info@nycip.org, World Wide Web http://nycip.wordpress.com.

Northern California Independent Booksellers Assn., 651 Broadway, second Floor, Sonoma, CA 95476. Tel. 415-561-7686, fax 415-561-7685, e-mail info@nciba.com, World Wide Web http://www.nciba.com.

Pres. Amy Thomas; *V.P.* Jeff Battis; *Treas.* Melinda Powers; *Exec. Dir.* Calvin Crosby. E-mail calvin@nciba.com.

PEN American Center, Div. of International PEN, 588 Broadway, Suite 303, New York, NY 10012. Tel. 212-334-1660, fax 212-334-2181, e-mail pen@pen.org, World Wide Web http://www.pen.org. *Pres.* Andrew Solomon; *Exec. V.P.* Markus Dohle; *V.P.s* Masha Gessen, Tracy Higgins; *Secy.* Theresa Rebeck; *Treas.* Yvonne Marsh; *Exec. Dir.* Susanne Nossel. E-mail snossel@pen.org.

Publishers Marketing Assn. (PMA). See Independent Book Publishers Assn.

Publishing Professionals Network (formerly Bookbuilders West), 9328 Elk Grove Blvd., Suite 105, Elk Grove, CA 95624. Tel. 415-670-9564, e-mail operations@bookbuilders.org, World Wide Web http://pubpronetwork.org. *Pres.* Scott Norton. E-mail snorton@ucpress.edu; *Secy.* Brenda Ginty. E-mail brenda.ginty@cengage.com.

Romance Writers of America, 14615 Benfer Rd., Houston, TX 77069. Tel. 832-717-5200, e-mail info@rwa.org, World Wide Web http://www.rwa.org. *Pres.* Leslie Kelly. E-mail president@rwa.org; *Pres.-Elect* Dee Davis. E-mail deedavisnyc@gmail.com; *Exec. Dir.* Allison Kelley. E-mail allison.kelley@rwa.org.

Science Fiction and Fantasy Writers of America, P.O. Box 3238, Enfield, CT 06083-3238. World Wide Web http://www.sfwa.org. *Pres.* Cat Rambo. E-mail president@sfwa.org; *V.P.* Erin M. Hartshorn. E-mail erin.hartshorn@sfwa.org; *Secy.* Susan Forest. E-mail secretary@sfwa.org; *CFO* Bud Sparhawk. E-mail cfo@sfwa.org; *Exec. Dir.* Kate Baker. E-mail office@sfwa.org.

Society of Children's Book Writers and Illustrators (SCBWI), 4727 Wilshire Blvd., Suite 301, Los Angeles, CA 90010. Tel. 323-782-1010, e-mail scbwi@scbwi.org, World Wide Web http://www.scbwi.org. *Pres.* Stephen Mooser. E-mail stephenmooser@scbwi.org; *Exec. Dir.* Lin Oliver. E-mail linoliver@scbwi.org.

Society of Illustrators (SI), 128 E. 63 St., New York, NY 10065. Tel. 212-838-2560, fax 212-838-2561, e-mail info@societyillustrators.org, World Wide Web http://www.societyillustrators.org. *Pres.* Tim O'Brien; *Exec. V.P.* Victor Juhasz; *V.P.* Karen Green; *Secy.* Leslie Cober-Gentry; *Exec. Dir.* Anelle Miller. E-mail anelle@society illustrators.org.

Southern Independent Booksellers Alliance (SIBA), 3806 Yale Ave., Columbia, SC 29205. Tel. 803-994-9530, fax 309-410-0211, e-mail info@sibaweb.com, World Wide Web http://www.sibaweb.com. *Pres.* Doug Robinson. E-mail doug@eagleeye-books.com; *Exec. Dir.* Wanda Jewell. E-mail wanda@sibaweb.com.

Western Writers of America, c/o Candy Moulton, 271 CR 219, Encampment, WY 82325 Tel. 307-329-8942, e-mail wwa.moulton@gmail.com, World Wide Web http://www.westernwriters.org. *Pres.* Kirk Ellis; *V.P.* Nancy Plain; *Past Pres.* Sherry Monahan; *Exec. Dir./Secy.-Treas.* Candy Moulton.

Women's National Book Assn., P.O. Box 237, FDR Sta., New York, NY 10150. Tel. 866-610-WNBA (9622), e-mail info@wnba-books.org, World Wide Web http://www.wnba-books.org. *Pres.* Jane Kinney-Denning, e-mail nationalpresidentWNBA@gmail.com; *V.P.s/Pres.-Elects* Rachelle Yousuf, Bebe (Sarah) Brechner; *Secy.* Celine Keating; *Treas.* Nicole Pilo; *Past Pres.* Carin Siegfried.

International and Foreign Book Trade Associations

For Canadian book trade associations, see the preceding section, "Book Trade Associations, United States and Canada." For a more extensive list of book trade organizations outside the United States and Canada, with more detailed information, consult *International Literary Market Place* (Information Today, Inc.), which also provides extensive lists of major bookstores and publishers in each country.

International

African Publishers' Network, c/o Ghana Book Publishers Assn. (GBPA), P.O. Box LT 471, Lartebiokorshie, Accra, Ghana. Tel. 233-21-912765, e-mail ghanabookpubs@yahoo.com.

Afro-Asian Book Council, 4835/24 Ansari Rd., New Delhi 110002, India. Tel. 11-2325-8865, fax 11-2326-7437, e-mail afro@aabcouncil.org, World Wide Web http://www.aabcouncil.org. *Secy.-Gen.* Sukumar Das. E-mail sukumar4das21@gmail.com; *Dir.* Saumya Gupta. E-mail sgupta@aabcouncil.org.

Centro Régional para el Fomento del Libro en América Latina y el Caribe (CERLALC) (Regional Center for Book Promotion in Latin America and the Caribbean), Calle 70, No. 9-52, Bogotá, Colombia. Tel. 1-540-2071, fax 1-541-6398, e-mail libro@cerlalc.com, World Wide Web http://www.cerlalc.org. *Dir.* Fernando Zapata López.

Federation of European Publishers, rue Montoyer 31, Boîte 8, 1000 Brussels, Belgium. Tel. 2-770-11-10, fax 2-771-20-71, e-mail info@fep-fee.eu, World Wide Web http://www.fep-fee.eu. *Pres.* Pierre Dutilleul; *Dir.-Gen.* Anne Bergman-Tahon.

International Board on Books for Young People (IBBY), Nonnenweg 12, 4003 Basel, Switzerland. Tel. 61-272-29-17, fax 61-272-27-57, e-mail ibby@ibby.org, World Wide Web http://www.ibby.org. *Exec. Dir.* Elizabeth Page.

International League of Antiquarian Booksellers (ILAB), c/o Rue Toepffer 5, Case postale 499, 1211 Geneva 12, Switzerland. E-mail secretary@ilab.org, World Wide Web http://www.ilab.org. *Pres.* Norbert Donhofer; *Gen. Secy.* Ulrich Hobbeling.

International Publishers Assn. (Union Internationale des Editeurs), 23 ave. de France, CH-1202 Geneva, Switzerland. Tel. 22-704-1820, e-mail secretariat@internationalpublishers.org, World Wide Web http://www.internationalpublishers.org. *Pres.* Youngsuk Chi; *Secy.-Gen.* Jens Bammel.

STM: The International Assn. of Scientific, Technical, and Medical Publishers, 267 Banbury Rd., Oxford OX2 7HT, England. Tel. 44-1865-339-321, fax 44-1865-339-325, e-mail info@stm-assoc.org, World Wide Web http://www.stm-assoc.org. *CEO* Michael Mabe.

National

Argentina

Cámara Argentina del Libro (Argentine Book Assn.), Av. Belgrano 1580, 4 piso, C1093AAQ Buenos Aires. Tel. 11-4381-8383, fax 11-4381-9253, e-mail cal@editores.org.ar, World Wide Web http://www.editores.org.ar. *Pres.* Isaac Rubizal.

Fundación El Libro (Book Foundation), Yrigoyen 1628, 5 piso, C1089AAF Buenos Aires. Tel. 11-4370-0600, fax 11-4370-0607, e-mail fundacion@el-libro.com.ar, World Wide Web http://www.el-libro.org.ar. *Admin. Mgr.* Daniel Monzo; *Chair* Martin Gremmelspacher.

Australia

Australian and New Zealand Assn. of Antiquarian Booksellers (ANZAAB), Apartment 1, 122 Raglan St., Mosman, NSW 2088. E-mail admin@anzaab.com, World Wide Web http://www.anzaab.com. *Pres.* Jörn Harbeck; *Secy.* Rachel Robarts.

Australian Booksellers Assn., 828 High St., Unit 9, Kew East, Vic. 3102. Tel. 3-9859-7322, fax 3-9859-7344, e-mail mail@aba.org.au, World Wide Web http://www.aba.

org.au. *Pres.* Patricia Genat; *CEO* Joel Becker.

Australian Publishers Assn., 60/89 Jones St., Ultimo, NSW 2007. Tel. 2-9281-9788, e-mail apa@publishers.asn.au, World Wide Web http://www.publishers.asn.au. *Pres.* Louise Adler; *CEO* Maree McCaskill. E-mail maree.mccaskill@publishers.asn.au.

Austria

Hauptverband des Österreichischen Buchhandels (Austrian Publishers and Booksellers Assn.), Grünangergasse 4, A-1010 Vienna. Tel. 1-512-15-35-26, fax 1-512-84-82, e-mail sekretariat@hvb.at, World Wide Web http://www.buecher.at. *Mgr.* Inge Kralupper. E-mail kralupper@hvb.at.

Verband der Antiquare Österreichs (Austrian Antiquarian Booksellers Assn.), Grünangergasse 4, A-1010 Vienna. Tel. 1-512-1535-14, e-mail sekretariat@hvb.at, World Wide Web http://www.antiquare.at.

Belarus

National Book Chamber of Belarus, 31a V Khoruzhei Str., Rm. 707, 220002 Minsk. Tel. 17-289-33-96, fax 17-334-78-47, World Wide Web http://natbook.org.by. *Dir.* Elena V. Ivanova. E-mail elvit@natbook.org.by.

Belgium

Boek.be (formerly Vlaamse Boekverkopersbond, Flemish Booksellers Assn.), Te Buelaerlei 37, 2140 Borgerhout. Tel. 03-230-89-23, fax 3-281-22-40, World Wide Web http://www.boek.be. *CEO* Geert Joris; *Communication Mgr.* Patricia De Laet. E-mail patricia.delaet@boek.be.

Vlaamse Uitgevers Vereniging (Flemish Publishers Assn.). See Boek.be.

Bolivia

Cámara Boliviana del Libro (Bolivian Book Chamber), Calle Capitan Ravelo No. 2116, 682 La Paz. Tel. 2-211-3264, e-mail cabolib@entelnet.bo, World Wide Web http://www.cabolib.org.bo. *Gen. Mgr.* Ana Patricia Navarro.

Brazil

Cámara Brasileira do Livro (Brazilian Book Assn.), Rua Cristiano Viana 91, Jardim Paulista, 05411-000 Sao Paulo-SP. Tel./fax 11-3069-1300, e-mail cbl@cbl.org.br, World Wide Web http://www.cbl.org.br. *Pres.* Karine Goncalves Pansa.

Sindicato Nacional dos Editores de Livros (Brazilian Publishers Assn.), Rue da Ajuda 35-18 andar, 20040-000 Rio de Janeiro-RJ. Tel. 21-2533-0399, fax 21-2533-0422, e-mail snel@snel.org.br, World Wide Web http://www.snel.org.br. *Pres.* Sonia Machado Jardim.

Chile

Cámara Chilena del Libro AG (Chilean Assn. of Publishers, Distributors, and Booksellers), Av. Libertador Bernardo O'Higgins 1370, Oficina 501, Santiago. Tel. 2-672-0348, fax 2-687-4271, e-mail prolibro@tie.cl, World Wide Web http://www.camlibro.cl. *Pres.* Arturo Infante.

Colombia

Cámara Colombiana del Libro (Colombian Book Assn.), Calle 35, No. 5A 05, Bogotá. Tel. 57-1-323-01-11, fax 57-1-285-10-82, e-mail camlibro@camlibro.com.co, World Wide Web http://www.camlibro.com.co. *Exec. Chair* Enrique González Villa; *Secy.-Gen.* José Manuel Ramirez Sarmiento.

Czech Republic

Svaz ceských knihkupcu a nakladatelu (Czech Publishers and Booksellers Assn.), P.O. Box 177, 110 01 Prague. Tel. 224-219-944, fax 224-219-942, e-mail sckn@sckn.cz, World Wide Web http://www.sckn.cz. *Chair* Martin Vopěnka.

Denmark

Danske Boghandlerforening (Danish Booksellers Assn.), Slotsholmsgade 1 B, 1216 Copenhagen K. Tel. 3254-2255, fax 3254-0041, e-mail ddb@bogpost.dk, World Wide Web http://www.boghandlerforeningen.dk. *Chair* Mogens Eliasson.

Danske Forlæggerforening (Danish Publishers Assn.), Børsen DK-1217 Copenhagen K. Tel. 45-33-15-66-88, e-mail danishpublishers@danishpublishers.dk, World Wide Web http://www.danskeforlag.dk.

Ecuador

Cámara Ecuatoriana del Libro, Avda. Eloy Alfaro, N29-61 e Inglaterra, Edf. Eloy Alfaro, 9 no. piso, Quito. Tel. 2-5533-11, fax 2-222-150, e-mail celnp@uio.satnet.net, World Wide Web http://celibro.org.ec. *Pres.* Fabian Luzuriaga.

Egypt

General Egyptian Book Organization (GEBO), P.O. Box 235, Cairo 11511. Tel. 2-257-7531, fax 2-257-54213, e-mail info@gebo.gov.eg, World Wide Web http://www.gebo.gov.eg. *Chair* Nasser Al-Ansary.

Estonia

Estonian Publishers Assn., Roosikrantsi 6-207,10119 Tallinn. Tel. 372-644-9866, fax 372-617-7550, e-mail kirjastusteliit@eki.ee, World Wide Web http://www.estbook.com. *Managing Dir.* Kaidi Urmet.

Finland

Kirjakauppaliitto Ry (Booksellers Assn. of Finland), Urho Kekkosen Katu 8 C 34b, 00100 Helsinki. Tel. 9-6899 112, e-mail toimisto@kirjakauppaliitto.fi, World Wide Web http://www.kirjakauppaliitto.fi. *CEO* Katriina Jaakkola.
Suomen Kustannusyhdistys (Finnish Book Publishers Assn.), P.O. Box 177, Lönnrotinkatu 11 A, FIN-00121, Helsinki. Tel. 358-9-228-77-250, fax 358-9-612-1226, World Wide Web http://www.kustantajat.fi/en. *Chair* Pasi Vainio; *Dir.* Sakari Laiho.

France

Bureau International de l'Edition Française (BIEF) (International Bureau of French Publishing), 115 blvd. Saint-Germain, F-75006 Paris. Tel. 01-44-41-13-13, fax 01-46-34-63-83, e-mail info@bief.org, World Wide Web http://www.bief.org. *Pres.* Vera

Michalski-Hoffmann; *CEO.* Jean-Guy Boin.
New York Branch French Publishers Agency, 853 Broadway, Suite 1509, New York, NY 10003-4703. Tel./fax 212-254-4540, World Wide Web http://frenchpubagency.com.
Cercle de la Librairie (Circle of Professionals of the Book Trade), 35 rue Grégoire-de-Tours, F-75006 Paris. Tel. 01-44-41-28-00, fax 01-44-41-28-65, e-mail commercial@electre.com, World Wide Web http://www.electre.com.
Syndicat de la Librairie Française, Hotel Massa, 38 rue du Faubourg Saint-Jacques, F-75014 Paris. Tel. 01-53-62-23-10, fax 01-53-62-10-45, e-mail contact@union-librarie.fr, World Wide Web http://www.syndicat-librairie.fr. *Mgr.* Guillaume Husson.
Syndicat National de la Librairie Ancienne et Moderne (SLAM) (National Assn. of Antiquarian and Modern Booksellers), 4 rue Gît-le-Coeur, F-75006 Paris. Tel. 01-43-29-46-38, fax 01-43-25-41-63, e-mail slam-livre@wanadoo.fr, World Wide Web http://www.slam-livre.fr. *Pres.* Frederic Castaing.
Syndicat National de l'Edition (SNE) (National Union of Publishers), 115 blvd. Saint-Germain, F-75006 Paris. Tel. 01-44-41-40-50, fax 01-44-41-40-77, World Wide Web http://www.sne.fr. *Pres.* Vincent Mountain.

Germany

Börsenverein des Deutschen Buchhandels e.V. (Stock Exchange of German Booksellers), Braubachstr. 16, 60311 Frankfurt-am-Main. Tel. 49-69-1306-0, fax 49-69-1306-201, e-mail info@boev.de, World Wide Web http://www.boersenverein.de. *CEO* Alexander Skipis.
Verband Deutscher Antiquare e.V. (German Antiquarian Booksellers Assn.), Geschäftsstelle, Seeblick 1, 56459 Elbingen. Tel. 6435-90-91-47, fax 6435-90-91-48, e-mail buch@antiquare.de, World Wide Web http://www.antiquare.de. *Chair* Christian Hesse.

Greece

Hellenic Federation of Publishers and Booksellers, 73 Themistocleous St., 106 83 Athens. Tel. 2103-300-924, fax 2133-301-617, e-mail secretary@poev.gr, World Wide Web http://www.poev.gr. *Pres.* Annie Ragia; *Secy.-Gen.* Nicholas Stathatos.

Hungary

Magyar Könyvkiadók és Könyvterjesztök Egyesülése (Assn. of Hungarian Publishers and Booksellers), Postfach 130, 1367 Budapest. Tel. 1-343-2540, fax 1-343-2541, e-mail mkke@mkke.hu, World Wide Web http://www.mkke.hu. *Managing Dir.* Péter László Zentai.

Iceland

Félag Islenskra Bókaútgefenda (Icelandic Publishers Assn.), Baronsstig 5, 101 Reykjavik. Tel. 511-8020, fax 511-5020, e-mail fibut@fibut.is, World Wide Web http://www.bokautgafa.is. *Chair* Egill Örn Jóhannsson.

India

Federation of Indian Publishers, Federation House, 18/1C Institutional Area, Aruna Asaf Ali Marg, New Delhi 110067. Tel. 11-2696-4847, fax 11-2686-4054, e-mail fip1@sify.com, World Wide Web http://www.fipindia.org. *Exec. Dir.* P. K. Arora.

Indonesia

Ikatan Penerbit Indonesia (Assn. of Indonesian Book Publishers), Jl. Kalipasir 32, Cikini Jakarta Pusat 10330. Tel. 21-3190-2532, fax 21-3192-6124, e-mail sekretariat@ikapi.org, World Wide Web http://www.ikapi.org.

Ireland

Publishing Ireland/Foilsiu Eireann (formerly CLÉ: The Irish Book Publishers' Assn.), 25 Denzille Lane, Dublin 2. Tel. 639-4868, e-mail info@publishingireland.com, World Wide Web http://www.publishingireland.com. *Pres.* Michael McLouglin. E-mail president@publishingireland.com.

Israel

Book Publishers' Assn. of Israel, 29 Carlebach St., 67132 Tel Aviv. Tel. 3-561-4121, fax 3-561-1996, e-mail info@tbpai.co.il, World Wide Web http://www.tbpai.co.il. *Chair* Rachel Edelman.

Italy

Associazione Italiana Editori (Italian Publishers Assn.), Corso di Porta Romana 108, 20122 Milan. Tel. 2-89-28-0800, fax 2-89-28-0860, e-mail aie@aie.it, World Wide Web http://www.aie.it. *Dir.* Alfieri Lorenzon.

Associazione Librai Antiquari d'Italia (Antiquarian Booksellers Assn. of Italy), Via dei Bononcini 24, 41121 Modena. Tel. 347 646-9147, fax 06 9293-3756, e-mail alai@alai.it, World Wide Web http://www.alai.it. *Pres.* Fabrizio Govi.

Japan

Antiquarian Booksellers Assn. of Japan, 27 Sakamachi, Shinjuku-ku, Tokyo 160-0002. Tel. 3-3357-1417, fax 3-3356-8730, e-mail abaj@abaj.gr.jp, World Wide Web http://www.abaj.gr.jp. *Pres.* Masaji Yagi.

Japan Assn. of International Publications (formerly Japan Book Importers Assn.), c/o UPS, 1-32-5 Higashi-shinagawa, Shinagawa-ku, Toyko 140-0002. Tel. 3-5479-7269, fax 3-5479-7307, e-mail office@jaip.jp, World Wide Web http://www.jaip.jp. *Exec. Dir.* Takashi Yamakawa.

Japan Book Publishers Assn., 6 Fukuro-machi, Shinjuku-ku, Tokyo 162-0828. Tel. 3-3268-1302, fax 3-3268-1196, e-mail research@jbpa.or.jp, World Wide Web http://www.jbpa.or.jp. *Pres.* Masahiro Oga.

Kenya

Kenya Publishers Assn., P.O. Box 42767, Nairobi 00100. Tel. 20-375-2344, e-mail info@kenyapublishers.org, World Wide Web http://www.kenyapublishers.org. *Chair* Lawrence Njagi.

Korea (Republic of)

Korean Publishers Assn., 105-2 Sagan-dong, Jongro-gu, Seoul 110-190. Tel. 735-2701-4, fax 2-738-5414, e-mail webmaster@kpa21.or.kr, World Wide Web http://eng.kpa21.or.kr. *Pres.* Sok-Ghee Baek.

Latvia

Latvian Publishers' Assn., Baznicas iela 37-3, LV-1010 Riga. Tel./fax 67-217-730, e-mail lga@gramatizdeveji.lv, World Wide Web http://www.gramatizdeveji.lv. *Pres.* Renāte Punka.

Lithuania

Lithuanian Publishers Assn., The Capitol, 5-317, LT-01108 Vilnius. Tel./fax 5-261-77-40, e-mail info@lla.lt, World Wide Web http://www.lla.lt. *Pres.* Remigijus Jokubauskas; *Exec. Dir.* Aida Dobkevičiūtė.

Malaysia

Malaysian Book Publishers' Assn., No. 7-6, Block E2, Jl PJU 1/42A, Dataran Prima, 47301 Petaling Jaya, Selangor. Tel. 3-7880-5840, fax 3-7880-5841, e-mail info@mabopa.com.my, World Wide Web http://www.mabopa.com.my. *Pres.* Husammuddin Haji Yaacub.

Mexico

Cámara Nacional de la Industria Editorial Mexicana (Mexican Publishers' Assn.), Holanda No. 13, Col. San Diego Churubusco, Deleg. Coyoacan, 04120 Mexico DF. Tel. 155-56-88-20-11, fax 155-56-04-31-47, e-mail contacto@caniem.com, World Wide Web http://www.caniem.com. *Pres.* José Ignacio Echeverría.

The Netherlands

KVB—Koninklijke Vereeniging van het Boekenvak (Royal Society for the Book Trade), P.O. Box 12040, AA Amsterdam-Zuidoost. Tel. 20-624-02-12, fax 20-620-88-71, e-mail info@kvb.nl, World Wide Web http://www.kvb.nl. *Dir.* Marty Langeler.

Nederlands Uitgeversverbond (Royal Dutch Publishers Assn.), Postbus 12040, 1100 AA Amsterdam. Tel. 20-430-9150, fax 20-430-9199, e-mail info@nuv.nl, World Wide Web http://www.nuv.nl. *Pres.* Loek Hermans.

Nederlandsche Vereeniging van Antiquaren (Netherlands Assn. of Antiquarian Booksellers), Singel 319, 1012 WJ Amsterdam. Tel. 70-364-98-40, fax 70-364-33-40, e-mail info@nvva.nl, World Wide Web http://www.nvva.nl. *Pres.* Frank Rutten.

Nederlandse Boekverkopersbond (Dutch Booksellers Assn.), Postbus 32, 3720 AA Bilthoven. Tel. 30-228-79 56, fax 30-228-45-66, e-mail info@boekbond.nl, World Wide Web http://www.boekbond.nl. *Pres.* Dick Anbeek.

New Zealand

Booksellers New Zealand, Featherstone St., P.O. Box 25033, Wellington 6011. Tel. 4-472-1908, fax 4-472-1912, e-mail info@booksellers.co.nz, World Wide Web http://www.booksellers.co.nz. *Chair* Mary Sangster; *CEO* Lincoln Gould.

Nigeria

Nigerian Publishers Assn., GPO Box 2541, Dugbe, Ibadan. Tel. 2-751-5352, e-mail info@nigerianpublishers.org, World Wide Web http://www.nigerianpublishers.org. *Pres.* N. O. Okereke.

Norway

Norske Bokhandlerforening (Norwegian Booksellers Assn.), Øvre Vollgate 15, 0158 Oslo. Tel. 22-40-45-40, fax 22-41-12-89, e-mail post@bokogsamfunn.no, World Wide Web http://www.bokogsamfunn.no. *Editor* Dag H. Nestegard.

Norske Forleggerforening (Norwegian Publishers Assn.), Øvre Vollgate 15, 0158 Oslo. Tel. 22-00-75-80, fax 22-33-38-30, e-mail dnf@forleggerforeningen.no, World Wide Web http://www.forleggerforeningen.no. *Chair* Tom Harald Jenssen; *CEO* Kristenn Einarsson.

Peru

Cámara Peruana del Libro (Peruvian Publishers Assn.), Av. Cuba 427, Jesús María, Apdo. 10253, Lima 11. Tel. 1-472-9516, fax 1-265-0735, e-mail cp-libro@cpl.org.pe, World Wide Web http://www.cpl.org.pe. *Pres.* Coronado Germán Vallenas.

Philippines

Philippine Educational Publishers Assn., c/o St. Mary's Publishing Corporation, 1308 P. Guevarra St., Sta. Cruz, Manila. Tel. 2-734-7790, fax 2-735-0955.

Poland

Polish Society of Book Editors, Holy Cross 30, lok 156, 00-116 Warsaw. Tel. 22-407-77-30, e-mail ptwk@ptwk.pl, World Wide Web http://www.wydawca.com.pl. *Dir.* Maria Kuisz.

Władze Stowarzyszenia Księgarzy Polskich (Assn. of Polish Booksellers), ul. Mazowiecka 6.8 def. 414, 00-048 Warsaw. Tel./fax 0-22-827-93-81, e-mail skp@ksiegarze.org.pl, World Wide Web http://www.ksiegarze.org.pl. *Chair* Waldemar Janaszkiewicz.

Portugal

Associação Portuguesa de Editores e Livreiros (Portuguese Assn. of Publishers and Booksellers), Av. dos Estados Unidas da America 97, 6 Esq., 1700-167 Lisbon. Tel. 21-843-51-80, e-mail geral@apel.pt, World Wide Web http://www.apel.pt. *Pres.* João Alvim.

Russia

Assn. of Book Publishers of Russia, ul. B. Nikitskaya 44, 121069 Moscow. Tel. 495-202-1174, fax 495-202-3989, e-mail askibook@gmail.com, World Wide Web http://www.aski.ru. *Pres.* Konstantin V. Chechenev.

Rossiiskaya Knizhnaya Palata (Russian Book Chamber), Kremlin Embankment, 1.09, Bldg. 8, 19019 Moscow. Tel. 495-688-96-89, fax 495-688-99-91, e-mail info@bookchamber.ru, World Wide Web http://www.bookchamber.ru. *Dir. Gen.* Elena Nogina.

Serbia and Montenegro

Assn. of Yugoslav Publishers and Booksellers, Kneza Milosa 25/I, 11000 Belgrade. Tel. 11-642-533, fax 11-646-339.

Singapore

Singapore Book Publishers Assn., 86 Marine Parade Central No. 03-213, Singapore 440086. Tel. 6344-7801, fax 6344-0897, e-mail info@singaporebookpublishers.sg, World Wide Web http://www.singaporebookpublishers.sg. *Pres.* Triena Noeline Ong.

Slovenia

Zdruzenie Zaloznikov in Knjigotrzcev Slovenije Gospodarska Zbornica Slovenije (Assn. of Publishers and Booksellers of Slovenia), Dimieva ulica 13, SI 1000 Ljubljana. Tel. 1-5898-000, fax 1-5898-100, e-mail info@gzs.si, World Wide Web http://www.gzs.si/slo.

South Africa

Publishers Assn. of South Africa (PASA), P.O. Box 18223, Wynberg 7824. Tel. 21-762-9083, fax 21-762-2763, e-mail pasa@publishsa.co.za, World Wide Web http://www.publishsa.co.za. *Chair* Mandla Balisa; *Exec. Dir.* Brian Wafawarowa.

South African Booksellers Assn. (formerly Associated Booksellers of Southern Africa), P.O. Box 870, Bellville 7535. Tel. 21-945-1572, fax 21-945-2169, e-mail saba@sabooksellers.com, World Wide Web http://sabooksellers.com. *Chair and Pres.* Sydwell Molosi.

Spain

Federación de Gremios de Editores de España (Federation of Spanish Publishers Assns.), Cea Bermúdez 44-2, 28003 Madrid. Tel. 91-534-51-95, fax 91-535-26-25, e-mail fgee@fge.es, World Wide Web http://www.federacioneditores.org. *Pres.* Xavier Mallafré; *Exec. Dir.* Antonio María Ávila.

Sri Lanka

Sri Lanka Book Publishers Assn., 53 Maligakanda Rd., Colombo 10. Tel./fax 0094-112-696-821, fax, e-mail bookpub@sltnet.lk, World Wide Web http://www.bookpublishers.lk. *Pres.* Vijitha Yapa.

Sudan

Sudanese Publishers' Assn., c/o Institute of African and Asian Studies, Khartoum Univ., P.O. Box 321, Khartoum 11115. Tel. 11-77-0022. *Dir.* Al-Amin Abu Manga Mohamed.

Sweden

Svenska Förläggareföreningen (Swedish Publishers Assn.), Queen St. 97, S-11360 Stockholm. Tel. 8-736-19-40, e-mail info@forlaggare.se, World Wide Web http://www.forlaggare.se. *Pres. and Dir.* Kristina Ahlinder.

Switzerland

Swiss Booksellers and Publishers Association (SBVV), Alder Strasse 40, P.O. Box 8034, Zurich. Tel. 44-421-36-00, fax 44-421-36-18, e-mail info@sbvv.ch, World Wide Web https://www.sbvv.ch. *CEO* Dani Landolf.

Thailand

Publishers and Booksellers Assn. of Thailand, 83/159 Moo Chinnakhet 2, Ngam Wong Wan Rd., Tungsonghong Lak Si, Bangkok 10210. Tel. 2-954-9560-4, fax 2-954-9566, e-mail info@pubat.or.th, World Wide Web http://www.pubat.or.th. *Pres.* Charun Homtientong.

Uganda

Uganda Publishers Assn., P.O. Box 7732, Kampala. Tel. 414-286-093, fax 414-286-397. *Chair* David Kibuuka; *Gen. Secy.* Martin Okia.

United Kingdom

Antiquarian Booksellers Assn., Sackville House, 40 Piccadilly, London W1J 0DR, England. Tel. 20-7439-3118, fax 20-7439-3119, e-mail admin@aba.org.uk, World Wide Web http://www.aba.org.uk. *Admin.* Clare Pedder; *Secy.* Tony Russ.

Assn. of Learned and Professional Society Publishers, 1-3 Ship St., Shoreham-by-Sea, West Sussex BN43 5DH, England. Tel. 1275-858-837, World Wide Web http://www.alpsp.org. *Chief Exec.* Audrey McCulloch.

Booktrust, Book House, 45 East Hill, Wandsworth, London SW18 2QZ, England. Tel. 20-8516-2977, fax 20-8516-2978, e-mail query@booktrust.org.uk, World Wide Web http://www.booktrust.org.uk. *Pres.* Michael Morpurgo; *Chair* Karen Brown.

Publishers Assn., 29B Montague St., London WC1B 5BW, England. Tel. 20-7691-9191, fax 20-7691-9199, e-mail mail@publishers.org.uk, World Wide Web http://www.publishers.org.uk. *Pres.* Dominic Knight; *Chief Exec.* Richard Mollet.

Scottish Book Trust, Sandeman House, Trunk's Close, 55 High St., Edinburgh EH1 1SR, Scotland. Tel. 131-524-0160, e-mail info@scottishbooktrust.com, World Wide Web http://www.scottishbooktrust.com. *CEO* Marc Lambert.

Welsh Books Council (Cyngor Llyfrau Cymru), Castell Brychan, Aberystwyth, Ceredigion SY23 2JB, Wales. Tel. 1970-624-151, fax 1970-625-385, e-mail info@wbc.org.uk, World Wide Web http://www.cllc.org.uk. *Chief Exec.* Elwyn Jones.

Uruguay

Cámara Uruguaya del Libro (Uruguayan Publishers Assn.), Colon 1476, Apdo. 102, 11000 Montevideo. Tel. 2-916-93-74, fax 2-916-76-28, e-mail gerencia@camaradellibro.com.uy, World Wide Web http://www.camaradellibro.com.uy. *Pres.* Alicia Guglielmo.

Venezuela

Cámara Venezolana del Libro (Venezuelan Publishers Assn.), Av. Andrés Bello, Centro Andrés Bello, Torre Oeste 11, piso 11, of. 112-0, Caracas 1050. Tel. 212-793-1347, fax 212-793-1368, e-mail cavelibrocgeneral@gmail.com, World Wide Web http://www.cavelibro.org. *Pres.* Ivan Dieguez Vazquez; *Exec. Dir.* Dalila Da Silva.

Zambia

Booksellers Assn. of Zambia, P.O. Box 51109, 10101 Lusaka. E-mail bpaz@zamtel.zm.

Zimbabwe

Zimbabwe Book Publishers Assn., P.O. Box 3041, Harare. Tel. 4-773-236, fax 4-754-256.

National Information Standards Organization (NISO)

Content and Collection Management

ANSI/NISO Z39.2-1994 (R2009)   Information Interchange Format
ISBN 978-1-937522-23-0

ANSI/NISO Z39.14-1997 (R2015)   Guidelines for Abstracts
ISBN 978-1-937522-44-5

ANSI/NISO Z39.18-2005 (R2010)   Scientific and Technical Reports—
Preparation, Presentation, and Preservation
ISBN 978-1-937522-21-6

ANSI/NISO Z39.19-2005 (R2010)   Guidelines for the Construction, Format,
and Management of Monolingual
Controlled Vocabularies
ISBN 978-1-937522-22-3

ANSI/NISO Z39.23-1997 (S2015)   Standard Technical Report Number Format
and Creation
ISBN 978-1-937522-45-2

ANSI/NISO Z39.29-2005 (R2010)   Bibliographic References
ISBN 978-1-937522-26-1

ANSI/NISO Z39.32-1996 (R2012)   Information on Microfiche Headers
ISBN 978-1-937522-29-2

ANSI/NISO Z39.41-1997 (S2015)   Placement Guidelines for Information on
Spines
ISBN 978-1-937522-46-9

ANSI/NISO Z39.43-1993 (R2011)   Standard Address Number (SAN) for the
Publishing Industry
ISBN 978-1-937522-28-5

ANSI/NISO Z39.48-1992 (R2009)   Permanence of Paper for Publications and
Documents in Libraries and Archives
ISBN 978-1-937522-30-8

ANSI/NISO Z39.71-2006 (R2011)   Holdings Statements for Bibliographic
Items
ISBN 978-1-937522-31-5

ANSI/NISO Z39.73-1994 (R2012)   Single-Tier Steel Bracket Library Shelving
ISBN 978-1-937522-32-2

ANSI/NISO Z39.74-1996 (R2012)   Guides to Accompany Microform Sets
ISBN 978-1-937522-40-7

ANSI/NISO Z39.78-2000 (R2010)	Library Binding ISBN 978-1-937522-33-9
ANSI/NISO Z39.84-2005 (R2010)	Syntax for the Digital Object Identifier ISBN 978-1-937522-34-6
ANSI/NISO Z39.85-2012	The Dublin Core Metadata Element Set ISBN 978-1-937522-14-8
ANSI/NISO Z39.86-2005 (R2012)	Specifications for the Digital Talking Book ISBN 978-1-937522-35-3
ANSI/NISO Z39.96-2012	JATS: Journal Article Tag Suite ISBN 978-1-937522-10-0
ANSI/NISO Z39.98-2012	Authoring and Interchange Framework for Adaptive XML Publishing Specification ISBN 978-1-937522-07-0
ANSI/NISO/ISO 12083-1995 (R2009)	Electronic Manuscript Preparation and Markup ISBN 978-1-880124-20-8

Standards for Discovery to Delivery

ANSI/NISO Z39.19-2005 (R2010)	Guidelines for the Construction, Format, and Management of Monolingual Controlled Vocabularies ISBN 978-1-937522-22-3
ANSI/NISO Z39.50-2003 (S2014)	Information Retrieval (Z39.50) Application Service Definition and Protocol Specification ISBN 978-1-937522-42-1
ANSI/NISO Z39.83-1-2012	NISO Circulation Interchange Part 1: Protocol (NCIP) version 2.02 ISBN 978-1-937522-03-2
ANSI/NISO Z39.83-2-2012	NISO Circulation Interchange Protocol (NCIP) Part 2: Implementation Profile 1, version 2.02 ISBN 978-1-937522-04-9
ANSI/NISO Z39.85-2012	The Dublin Core Metadata Element Set ISBN 978-1-937522-14-8
ANSI/NISO Z39.87-2006 (R2011)	Data Dictionary—Technical Metadata for Digital Still Images ISBN 978-1-937522-37-7
ANSI/NISO Z39.88-2004 (R2010)	The OpenURL Framework for Context- Sensitive Services ISBN 978-1-937522-38-4
ANSI/NISO Z39.89-2003 (S2014)	The U.S. National Z39.50 Profile for Library Applications ISBN 978-1-937522-43-8

| ANSI/NISO Z39.99-2014 | ResourceSync Framework Specification
ISBN 978-1-937522-19-3 |

Business Information

| ANSI/NISO Z39.7-2013 | Information Services and Use: Metrics and Statistics for Libraries and Information Providers—Data Dictionary
ISBN 978-1-937522-15-5 |
| ANSI/NISO Z39.93-2014 | The Standardized Usage Statistics Harvesting Initiative (SUSHI) Protocol
ISBN 978-1-937522-47-6 |

Preservation and Storage

ANSI/NISO Z39.32-1996 (R2012)	Information on Microfiche Headers ISBN 978-1-937522-29-2
ANSI/NISO Z39.48-1992 (R2009)	Permanence of Paper for Publications and Documents in Libraries and Archives ISBN 978-1-937522-30-8
ANSI/NISO Z39.73-1994 (R2012)	Single-Tier Steel Bracket Library Shelving ISBN 978-1-937522-32-2
ANSI/NISO Z39.78-2000 (R2010)	Library Binding ISBN 978-1-937522-33-9

In Development/NISO Initiatives

NISO develops new standards, reports, and best practices on a continuing basis to support its ongoing standards development program. NISO working groups are currently developing or exploring the following:

- Alternative Metrics Recommended Practices
- Bibliographic Vocabulary Use and Reuse; Vocabulary Documentation; and Vocabulary Preservation
- Journal Article Versions (JAV) Addendum (NISO RP-8-201x)
- Protocol for Exchanging Serial Content (NISO RP-23-201x)
- Standard Interchange Protocol (SIP) (NISO Z39.100-201x)
- Permanence of Paper for Publications and Documents in Libraries and Archives (revision to Z39.48)
- SUSHI Lite (NISO TR-06-201x)

NISO Recommended Practices

A Framework of Guidance for Building Good Digital Collections, 3rd ed., 2007
ISBN 978-1-880124-74-1

NISO RP-2005-01	Ranking of Authentication and Access Methods Available to the Metasearch Environment ISBN 978-1-880124-89-5
NISO RP-2005-02	Search and Retrieval Results Set Metadata ISBN 978-1-880124-88-8
NISO RP-2005-03	Search and Retrieval Citation Level Data Elements ISBN 978-1-880124-87-1
NISO RP-2006-01	Best Practices for Designing Web Services in the Library Context ISBN 978-1-880124-86-4
NISO RP-2006-02	NISO Metasearch XML Gateway Implementers Guide ISBN 978-1-880124-85-7
NISO RP-6-2012	RFID in U.S. Libraries ISBN 978-1-937522-02-5
NISO RP-7-2012	SERU: A Shared Electronic Resource Understanding ISBN 978-1-937522-08-7
NISO RP-8-2008	Journal Article Versions (JAV) ISBN 978-1-880124-79-6
NISO RP-9-2014	KBART: Knowledge Bases and Related Tools ISBN 978-1-937522-41-4
NISO RP-10-2010	Cost of Resource Exchange (CORE) Protocol ISBN 978-1-880124-84-0
NISO RP-11-2011	ESPReSSO: Establishing Suggested Practices Regarding Single Sign-On ISBN 978-1-880124-98-7
NISO RP-12-2012	Physical Delivery of Library Resources ISBN 978-1-937522-01-8
NISO RP-14-2014	NISO SUSHI Protocol: COUNTER-SUSHI Implementation Profile ISBN 978-1-937522-45-2
NISO RP-15-2013	Recommended Practices for Online Supplemental Journal Article Materials ISBN 978-1-937522-12-4
NISO RP-16-2013	PIE-J: The Presentation and Identification of E-Journals ISBN 978-1-937522-05-6
NISO RP-17-2013	Institutional Identification: Identifying Organizations in the Information Supply Chain ISBN 978-1-937522-11-7
NISO RP-20-2014	Open Discovery Initiative: Promoting Transparency in Discovery ISBN 978-1-937522-42-1

NISO RP-21-2013   Improving OpenURLs Through Analytics (IOTA):
                   Recommendations for Link Resolver Providers
                   ISBN 978-1-937522-18-6

NISO RP-22-2015   Access License and Indicators
                   ISBN 978-1-937522-49-0

NISO RP-24-2015   Transfer Code of Practice, version 3.0
                   ISBN 978-1-937522-40-7

NISO Technical Reports

NISO TR01-1995   Environmental Guidelines for the Storage of Paper Records
                   by William K. Wilson
                   ISBN 978-1-800124-21-5

NISO TR02-1997   Guidelines for Indexes and Related Information Retrieval
                   Devices
                   by James D. Anderson
                   ISBN 978-1-880124-36-9

NISO TR03-1999   Guidelines for Alphabetical Arrangement of Letters and
                   Sorting of Numerals and Other Symbols
                   by Hans H. Wellisch
                   ISBN 978-1-880124-41-3

NISO TR04-2006   Networked Reference Services: Question/Answer
                   Transaction Protocol
                   ISBN 978-1-880124-71-0

NISO TR-05-2013   IOTA Working Group Summary of Activities and
                   Outcomes
                   ISBN 978-1-937522-17-9

Other NISO Publications

The Case for New Economic Models to Support Standardization
    by Clifford Lynch
    ISBN 978-1-880124-90-1

The Exchange of Serials Subscription Information
    by Ed Jones
    ISBN 978-1-880124-91-8

The Future of Library Resource Discovery
    by Marshall Breeding
    ISBN 978-1-937522-41-4

Information Standards Quarterly (*ISQ*) [NISO quarterly open access magazine]
    ISSN 1041-0031

Internet, Interoperability and Standards—Filling the Gaps
    by Janifer Gatenby
    ISBN 978-1-880124-92-5

Issues in Crosswalking Content Metadata Standards
by Margaret St. Pierre and William P. LaPlant
ISBN 978-1-880124-93-2

Making Good on the Promise of ERM: A Standards and Best Practices Discussion Paper
by the ERM Data Standards and Best Practices Review Steering Committee
ISBN 978-1-9357522-00-1

Metadata Demystified: A Guide for Publishers
by Amy Brand, Frank Daly, and Barbara Meyers
ISBN 978-1-880124-59-8

The Myth of Free Standards: Giving Away the Farm
by Andrew N. Bank
ISBN 978-1-880124-94-9

NISO Newsline [free monthly e-newsletter]
ISSN 1559-2774

NISO Working Group Connection (free quarterly supplement to Newsline)
Patents and Open Standards
by Priscilla Caplan
ISBN 978-1-880124-95-6

The RFP Writer's Guide to Standards for Library Systems
by Cynthia Hodgson
ISBN 978-1-880124-57-4

Streamlining Book Metadata Workflow
by Judy Luther
ISBN 978-1-880124-82-6

Understanding Metadata
ISBN 978-1-880124-62-8

Up and Running: Implementing Z39.50: Proceedings of a Symposium Sponsored by the State Library of Iowa
edited by Sara L. Randall
ISBN 978-1-880124-33-8

Z39.50: A Primer on the Protocol
ISBN 978-1-880124-35-2

Z39.50 Implementation Experiences
ISBN 978-1-880124-51-2

NISO standards are available online at http://www.niso.org/standards. Recommended Practices, Technical Reports, White Papers, and other publications are available on the NISO website at http://www.niso.org/publications.

For more information, contact NISO, 3600 Clipper Mill Rd., Suite 302, Baltimore, MD 21211. Tel. 301-654-2512, fax 410-685-5278, e-mail nisohq@niso.org, World Wide Web http://www.niso.org.

Calendar, 2017–2025

The list below contains information on association meetings or promotional events that are, for the most part, national or international in scope. State and regional library association meetings are also included. To confirm the starting or ending date of a meeting, which may change after the *Library and Book Trade Almanac* has gone to press, contact the association directly. Addresses of library and book trade associations are listed in Part 6 of this volume. For information on additional book trade and promotional events, see *Literary Market Place* and *International Literary Market Place,* published by Information Today, Inc., and other library and book trade publications such as *Library Journal, School Library Journal,* and *Publishers Weekly.* The American Library Association (ALA) keeps an online calendar at http://www.ala.org/conferencesevents/planning-calendar. An Information Today events calendar can be found at http://www.infotoday.com/calendar.shtml.

2017

June

4–8	Assn. of Caribbean University, Research and Institutional Libraries (AURIL)	San Juan, Puerto Rico
5–7	Assn. of Canadian Publishers Annual Meeting	Toronto, ON
5–7	Specialized Information Publishers Assn.	Washington, DC
11–13	Assn. of American University Presses	Austin, TX
12–15	Assn. of Christian Librarians	Grand Rapids, MI
14–18	Seoul International Book Fair	Seoul, South Korea
18–20	Special Libraries Assn.	Phoenix, AZ
19–21	Assn. of Jewish Libraries	New York, NY
22–27	American Library Assn. Annual Conference	Chicago, IL
22–27	American Assn. of School Librarians @ ALA	Chicago, IL

July

2–4	Assn. of European Research Libraries (LIBER)	Patras, Greece
12–15	National Assn. of Government Archives and Records Administrators (NAGARA)	Boise, ID
14–18	Church and Synagogue Library Assn.	Rochester, NY
15–17	International Literacy Assn.	Orlando, FL

July 2017 *(cont.)*

15–18	American Assn. of Law Libraries (AALL)	Austin, TX
18–20	IEEE Technically Sponsored SAI Computing Conference (formerly Science and Information Conference)	London, UK
19–25	Hong Kong Book Fair	Hong Kong
23–29	Society of American Archivists	Portland, OR

August

2–4	Pacific Northwest Library Assn.	Post Falls, ID
4–8	International Assn. of School Librarianship (IASL)	Long Beach, CA
12–28	Edinburgh International Book Festival	Edinburgh, UK
19–25	83rd IFLA General Conf. and Assembly	Wrocław, Poland
23–27	Beijing International Book Fair	Beijing, China

September

4–6	International Symposium on Information Management and Big Data	Lima, Peru
6–10	Moscow International Book Fair	Moscow, Russia
10–11	Wyoming Library Assn.	Sheridan, WY
20–23	Kentucky Library Assn./Kentucky Assn. of School Librarians Annual Conference	Louisville, KY
24–26	Arkansas Library Assn.	Rogers, AR
27–29	South Dakota Library Assn.	Oacoma, SD
28–Oct. 1	Goteborg Book Fair	Gothenburg, Sweden

October

4–6	Idaho Library Assn.	Boise, ID
4–6	Missouri Library Assn.	Saint Louis, MO
4–6	North Dakota Library Assn.	Grand Forks, ND
4–6	Ohio Library Council	Dayton, OH
5–6	Minnesota Library Assn.	Rochester, MN
5–7	Georgia Library Assn./Georgia Council of Media Organizations	Columbus, GA
9–12	International Conference of Indigenous Archives, Libraries, and Museums	Santa Ana Pueblo, AZ
10–12	Illinois Library Assn.	Tinley Park, IL
11–13	Nebraska Library Assn.	Kearney, NE
11–13	South Carolina Library Assn.	Columbia, SC
11–13	Virginia Library Assn.	Norfolk, VA

11–15	Frankfurt Book Fair	Frankfurt, Germany
14–16	Colorado Assn. of Libraries	Loveland, CO
15–18	Pennsylvania Library Assn.	Pittsburgh, PA
15–18	Nevada Library Assn./Mountain Plains Library Assn.	Stateline, NV
17–18	Internet Librarian international	London, UK
17–20	Mississippi Library Assn.	Hattiesburg, MS
17–20	North Carolina Library Assn.	Winston-Salem, NC
17–20	Wisconsin Library Assn.	Wisconsin Dells, WI
18–20	Iowa Library Assn.	Coralville, IA
22–24	New England Library Assn./Vermont Library Assn. Joint Conference	South Burlington, VT
22–29	Belgrade International Book Fair	Belgrade, Serbia
23–25	Internet Librarian	Monterey, CA
24–27	Kansas Library Assn.	Wichita, KS
25–27	Arizona Library Assn.	Mesa, AZ
26–29	Helsinki Book Fair	Helsinki, Finland
27–28	Hawai'i Library Assn./Hawai'i Assn. of School Librarians Joint Conference	Manoa, HI
27–Nov. 1	Assn. for Information Science and Technology (ASIS&T)	Washington, DC

November

1–3	New Mexico Library Assn.	Albuquerque, NM
2–3	Streaming Media West	Huntington Beach, CA
2–4	California Library Assn.	Riverside, CA
3	New Hampshire Library Assn.	Hooksett, NH
4–12	Istanbul International Book Fair	Istanbul, Turkey
6–10	International Conference on Information and Knowledge Management (CIKM)	Singapore
7–9	KM World	Washington, DC
8–10	West Virginia Library Assn.	White Sulphur Springs, WV
8–11	New York Library Assn.	Saratoga Springs, NY
8–12	Buch Wien International Book Fair	Vienna, Austria
9–11	American Assn. of School Librarians	Phoenix, AZ
13–15	Indiana Library Federation	Indianapolis, IN
15–20	Salon du Livre de Montréal	Montreal, QC
22–24	Bibliographical Society of Australia and New Zealand	Hobart, Tasmania, Australia
27–29	Guadalajara International Book Fair	Guadalajara, Mexico

December 2017

10–13	International Conference on Information Systems (ICIS)	Seoul, South Korea

2018

February

9–13	American Library Assn. Midwinter Meeting	Denver, CO

March

20–24	Public Libraries Assn.	Philadelphia, PA

April

4–6	Tennessee Library Assn.	Memphis, TN
10–13	Texas Library Assn.	Dallas, TX
17–19	Computers in Libraries	Arlington, VA

May

30–June 1	Book Expo America (BEA)	New York, NY

June

21–26	American Library Assn. Annual Conference	New Orleans, LA
21–26	American Assn. of School Librarians @ ALA	New Orleans, LA

July

14–17	American Assn. of Law Libraries (AALL)	Baltimore, MD

September

21–23	Kentucky Library Assn.	Louisville, KY
26–28	South Dakota Library Assn.	Sioux Falls, SD

October

4–6	Nebraska Library Assn./Nebraska School Library Assn.	Lincoln, NE
7–11	California Library Assn.	Santa Clara, CA
14–17	Pennsylvania Library Assn.	Harrisburg, PA
16–20	North Carolina Library Assn.	Winston-Salem, NC
23–26	Kansas Library Assn.	Wichita, KS
23–26	Wisconsin Library Assn.	Wisconsin Dells, WI

November

6–8   KM World   Washington, DC

2019
January

8–11   Hawaii International Conference on System
           Sciences   Maui, HI
25–29   American Library Assn. Midwinter Meeting   Seattle, WA

April

7–10   Pennsylvania Library Assn.   Erie, PA
15–18   Texas Library Assn.   Austin, TX

June

11–13   Special Libraries Assn.   Baltimore, MD
20–25   American Library Assn. Annual Conference   Washington, DC
20–25   American Assn. of School Librarians   Washington, DC

July

13–16   American Assn. of Law Libraries (AALL)   Washington, DC

September

 25–27   South Dakotal Library Assn.   Spearfish, SD

October

8–11   Wisconsin Library Assn.   Wisconsin Dells, WI

November

5–7   KM World   Washington, DC
14–17   American Assn. of School Librarians   Louisville, KY

2020
January

24–28   American Library Assn. Midwinter Meeting   Philadelphia, PA

March

24–27   Texas Library Assn.   Houston, TX

June 2020

23–28	American Library Assn. Annual Conference	Washington, DC
23–28	American Assn. of School Librarians @ ALA	Washington, DC

July

11–14	American Assn. of Law Libraries (AALL)	New Orleans, LA

2021

January

22–26	American Library Assn. Midwinter Meeting	Indianapolis, IN

April

20–23	Texas Library Assn.	San Antonio, TX

June

24–29	American Library Assn. Annual Conference	Chicago, IL
24–29	American Assn. of School Librarians @ ALA	Chicago, IL

October

21–24	American Assn. of School Librarians	Salt Lake City, UT

2022

January

21–25	American Library Assn. Midwinter Meeting	San Antonio, TX

April

5–8	Texas Library Assn.	Fort Worth, TX

June

23–28	American Library Assn. Annual Conference	Washington, DC
23–28	American Assn. of School Librarians @ ALA	Washington, DC

2023

January

27–31	American Library Assn. Midwinter Meeting	New Orleans, LA

April

18–21   Texas Library Assn.   Austin, TX

June

22–27   American Library Assn. Annual Conference   Chicago, IL
22–27   American Assn. of School Librarians @ ALA Chicago, IL

2024
February

9–13   American Library Assn. Midwinter Meeting   Denver, CO

April

18–21   Texas Library Assn.   Dallas, TX

June

27–July 2   American Library Assn. Annual Conference   San Diego, CA
27–July 2   American Assn. of School Librarians @ ALA San Diego, CA

2025
June

26–July 1   American Library Assn. Annual Conference   Philadelphia, PA
26–July 1   American Assn. of School Librarians @ ALA Philadelphia, PA

Acronyms

A

AALL. American Association of Law
    Libraries
AASL. American Association of School
    Librarians
ABA. American Booksellers Association
ABOS. Association of Bookmobile and
    Outreach Services
AC. Access Copyright
ACRL. Association of College and Research
    Libraries
AIIP. Association of Independent
    Information Professionals
AILA. American Indian Library Association
AJL. Association of Jewish Libraries
ALA. American Library Association
ALCTS. Association for Library Collections
    and Technical Services
ALIC. Archives Library Information Center
ALISE. Association for Library and
    Information Science Education
ALS. Academic Libraries Survey
ALSC. Association for Library Service to
    Children
ALTAFF. Association of Library Trustees,
    Advocates, Friends, and Foundations
AMMLA. American Merchant Marine
    Library Association
APALA. Asian/Pacific American Librarians
    Association
ARL. Association of Research Libraries
ARLIS/NA. Art Libraries Society of North
    America
ARSL. Association for Rural and Small
    Libraries
ASCLA. Association of Specialized and
    Cooperative Library Agencies
ASIS&T. American Association for
    Information Science and Technology
ATLA. American Theological Library
    Association
ATN. Access Text Network

B

BARD. Braille and Audio Reading
    Download
BCALA. Black Caucus of the American
    Library Association
BEA. BookExpo America
BLC. Brody Learning Commons
BSA. Bibliographical Society of America

C

CACUL. Canadian Association of College
    and University Libraries
CAIS. Canadian Association for Information
    Science
CALA. Chinese-American Librarians
    Association
CAPL. Canadian Association of Public
    Libraries
CARL. Canadian Association of Research
    Libraries
CASLIS. Canadian Association of Special
    Libraries and Information Services
CGP. Catalog of U.S. Government
    Publications
CLA. Canadian Library Association
CLIR. Council on Library and Information
    Resources
CLTA. Canadian Library Trustees
    Association
CNI. Coalition for Networked Information
COSLA. Chief Officers of State Library
    Agencies
CSLA. Church and Synagogue Library
    Association

CWA. Crime Writers' Association

D

DLF. Digital Library Federation
DPLA. Digital Public Library of America
DRM. Digital rights management
DTIC. Defense Technical Information
    Center

E

EAR. Export Administration Regulations
EDB. Energy Science and Technology
    Database
EMIERT. Ethnic and Multicultural
    Information and Exchange Round
    Table
ESEA. Elementary and Secondary Education
    Act

F

FAA. Foreign Intelligence Surveillance Act
FAFLRT. Federal and Armed Forces
    Librarians Round Table
FAIFE. Freedom of Access to Information
    and Freedom of Expression
FBI. Federal Bureau of Investigation
FDLP. Federal Depository Library Program
FDsys. Federal Digital System
FEDRIP. Federal Research in Progress
    Database
FIAF. International Federation of Film
    Archives
FRPAA. Federal Research Public Access Act

G

GLBTRT. Gay, Lesbian, Bisexual, and
    Transgendered Round Table
GLIN. Global Legal Information Network
GODORT. Government Documents Round
    Table
GPO. Government Printing Office
GSU. Georgia State University

I

IAALD. International Association of
    Agricultural Information Specialists
IACs. Information Analysis Centers
IALL. International Association of Law
    Libraries
IAML. International Association of
    Music Libraries, Archives and
    Documentation Centres
IASL. International Association of School
    Librarians
ICA. International Council on Archives
ICBS. International Committee of the Blue
    Shield
IDPF. International Digital Publishing
    Forum
IFLA. International Federation of Library
    Associations and Institutions
ILS. Integrated Library System
IMLS. Institute of Museum and Library
    Services
ISBN. International Standard Book Number
ISO. International Organization for
    Standardization
ISOO. Information Security Oversight
    Office
ISSN. International Standard Serial Number

L

LAC. Library and Archives Canada
LC. Library of Congress
LCA. Library Copyright Alliance
LCI. Leading Change Institute
LEED. Leadership in Energy and
    Environmental Design
LHHS. Labor, Health, and Human Services
    Appropriations Bill
LHRT. Library History Round Table
LIS. Library/information science
LITA. Library and Information Technology
    Association
LJ. Library Journal
LLAMA. Library Leadership and
    Management Association
LRRT. Library Research Round Table
LSCM. Library Services and Content
    Management
LSTA. Library Services and Technology Act

M

MLA. Medical Library Association; Music Library Association
MOOCs. massively open online courses

N

NAGARA. National Association of Government Archives and Records Administrators
NAL. National Agricultural Library
NARA. National Archives and Records Administration
NCBI. National Center for Biotechnology Information
NCES. National Center for Education Statistics
NDC. National Declassification Center
NDIIPP. National Digital Information Infrastructure and Preservation Program
NEH. National Endowment for the Humanities
NFAIS. National Federation of Advanced Information Services
NIH. National Institutes of Health
NISO. National Information Standards Organization
NLE. National Library of Education
NLM. National Library of Medicine
NMRT. New Members Round Table
NTIS. National Technical Information Service
NTRL. National Technical Reports Library

O

ORI. Owners' Rights Initiative
OWF. Operation Warfighter

P

PLA. Public Library Association
PTDLA. Patent and Trademark Depository Library Association
PW. Publishers Weekly

R

RDA. Resource Description and Access
RUSA. Reference and User Services Association

S

SAA. Society of American Archivists
SAN. Standard Address Number
SIIA. Software and Information Industry Association
SLA. Special Libraries Association
SPARC. Scholarly Publishing & Academic Resources Coalition
SRRT. Social Responsibilities Round Table
SRS. Selected Research Service
SSP. Society for Scholarly Publishing
STEM. science, technology, engineering, and mathematics
StLA. state libraries and library agencies

T

TLA. Theatre Library Association

U

ULC. Urban Libraries Council
USCIS. United States Citizenship and Immigration Service

W

WDL. World Digital Library
WIPO. World Intellectual Property Organization
WISE. Web-based Information Science Education Consortium
WNC. World News Connection
WRP. Workforce Recruitment Program

Y

YALSA. Young Adult Library Services Association

Index of Organizations

Please note that many cross-references refer to entries in the Subject Index.

Subject Index

Please note that many cross-references refer to entries in the Index of Organizations.